The Behavioral Sciences and Health Care

Praise for This Edition

"At a time when every major report on the future of health care calls for a broad perspective and greater teamwork, it is refreshing to see a major textbook propose, as well as extensively document, an 'integrated sciences model' for uniting the contributions of the biomedical and the behavioral sciences in teaching and practice. This text should be **required reading for all health sciences students and their faculties**, as we move toward a system of truly collaborative, interprofessional health care delivery."

DeWitt C. Baldwin, Jr., MD, Professor emeritus of Psychiatry and Behavioral Sciences, University of Nevada School of Medicine, Reno, NV

"The person, the patient, must be the focus of health care, not the system or the profession. This outstanding book by O.J. Sahler, MD, and Jack Carr, PhD, and its integrated sciences model go a long way towards making this a reality. **It is more than a standard text for medical students – it should also be required reading for students of pharmacy, nursing, social work, psychology, and sociology and their attendings** – as well as for health care administrators and politicians."

Albert H. Eaton, Ph.D., MDiv, President of the Association for the Behavioral Sciences and Medical Education (ABSAME)

"An **outstanding integration of the most up-to-date scientific knowledge** gathered across disciplines, targeted for clinicians. Understandable, timely; straightforward yet pleasantly sophisticated. A wonderful desk reference for primary care providers."

Pat DeLeon, PhD, MPH, JD, former President of the American Psychological Association

"This is **a wonderful volume** incorporating information normally found in separate textbooks for psychiatry residents, graduate students in clinical psychology, health psychology, social work and public health. Rarely would this information be gathered into one volume and integrated into a model that seriously considers biology and psychology. The book is especially timely as efforts at health care reform have emphasized an integrated model of medicine that takes into account genes, environment and their interactive processes. The book provides a reasoned rationale for these efforts. As advances in health and illness are made, it becomes obvious to clinicians and researchers that the boundaries between biology and psychology are less clear and more fluid. The book is comprehensive, dealing with historical topics such as Freud's psychoanalytic theory as well as contemporary topics such as the brain networks discussed by Michael Posner, a leading neuroscientist. Traditional psychopathology is presented as well as current concerns about social and cultural effects on health/illness. The book will do much to initiate the life -long education of health professionals about these issues or as a primer for these who are new or less familiar with the interplay of behavior and health."

Barry A. Hong, PHD, ABPP, Professor of Psychiatry and Medicine at the Washington University, St. Louis, MO

"The publication of the new edition of *The Behavioral Sciences and Health Care* could not come at a better time. Its editors, Drs. Olle Jane Z. Sahler and John E. Carr, are two superb senior scholars who have updated their volume just as the American Association of Medical Colleges has declared that physicians must be better prepared in the behavioral sciences if they are to understand a myriad of health problems they now must treat. The talented group of chapter authors and the breadth covered in this volume make it necessary reading for all medical students. Its readability and currency also make it a fine preparation for students about to take the Medical College Admissions Test, which has added a new emphasis on the behavioral sciences. **This volume has no peer in educating aspiring physicians** in how a biopsychosocial understanding of medicine's challenges is the only approach a thoroughly prepared medical practitioner can take."

Edward P. Sheridan, PhD, LHD, ABPP, former Chief of Psychiatry Outpatient Services and Professor and Chairman of the Division of Psychology at Northwestern University Medical School. Currently, he is University Professor and Senior Vice President and Provost Emeritus at the University of Houston.

"This textbook provides a comprehensive overview of health care that can be **a valuable resource for any clinician working in a medical setting**. It offers a well-rounded view of the various aspects of the biopsychosocial model that helps to integrate theory into practice. As a music therapist, it gives insight into how the medical field works from a behavioral approach, which is very much in line with the Medical Music Therapy perspective. I plan to use it with all interns as part of their orientation process for working in the medical setting."

Rosemary Oliva Obi, MS, LCAT, MT-BC, Music Therapist at the University of Rochester Medical Center Golisano Children's Hospital, Rochester, NY

The Behavioral Sciences and Health Care

3rd Edition

Editors

Olle Jane Z. Sahler, MD

Professor of Pediatrics, Psychiatry, Medical Humanities, and Oncology at the
University of Rochester School of Medicine and Dentistry, Rochester, NY

John E. Carr, PhD

Professor emeritus of Psychiatry & Behavioral Sciences and Psychology at the
University of Washington School of Medicine, Seattle, WA

Associate Editors

Julia B. Frank, MD

Associate Professor of Psychiatry and Behavioral Sciences at the George Washington
University School of Medicine and Health Sciences, Washington, DC

João Vieira Nunes, MD

Associate Medical Professor of Physiology and Pharmacology at the Sophie Davis
School of Biomedical Education at The City College of New York, NY

Library of Congress Cataloging-in-Publication Data

is available via the Library of Congress Marc Database under the
Library of Congress Control Number: 2012931374

Library and Archives Canada Cataloguing in Publication

The behavioral sciences and health care / editors, Olle Jane Z. Sahler, John E. Carr ;
associate editors, Julia B. Frank, João Vieira Nunes. -- 3rd ed.

Includes bibliographical references and index.
ISBN 978-0-88937-433-1

1. Medicine and psychology--Textbooks. 2. Social medicine--Textbooks. 3. Psychology,
Pathological--Textbooks. I. Sahler, Olle Jane Z., 1944- II. Carr, John E III. Frank, Julia (Julia B.)
IV. Nunes, João Vieira

R726.5.B452 2012   616.001'9   C2012-900649-1

© 2012 by Hogrefe Publishing

PUBLISHING OFFICES
USA: Hogrefe Publishing, 875 Massachusetts Avenue, 7th Floor, Cambridge, MA 02139
              Phone (866) 823-4726, Fax (617) 354-6875; E-mail customerservice@hogrefe-publishing.com
EUROPE: Hogrefe Publishing, Merkelstr. 3, 37085 Göttingen, Germany
              Phone +49 551 99950-0, Fax +49 551 99950-425, E-mail publishing@hogrefe.com

SALES & DISTRIBUTION
USA: Hogrefe Publishing, Customer Services Department,
              30 Amberwood Parkway, Ashland, OH 44805
              Phone (800) 228-3749, Fax (419) 281-6883, E-mail customerservice@hogrefe.com
EUROPE: Hogrefe Publishing, Merkelstr. 3, 37085 Göttingen, Germany
              Phone +49 551 99950-0, Fax +49 551 99950-425, E-mail publishing@hogrefe.com

OTHER OFFICES
CANADA: Hogrefe Publishing, 660 Eglinton Ave. East, Suite 119-514, Toronto, Ontario, M4G 2K2
SWITZERLAND: Hogrefe Publishing, Länggass-Strasse 76, CH-3000 Bern 9

Hogrefe Publishing
Incorporated and registered in the Commonwealth of Massachusetts, USA, and in Göttingen, Lower Saxony,
Germany

Printed and bound in the USA
ISBN 978-0-88937-433-1

About the Editors

Olle Jane Z. Sahler, MD, Co-Editor, is Professor of Pediatrics, Psychiatry, Medical Humanities, and Oncology at the University of Rochester School of Medicine and Dentistry. She is a behavioral pediatrician with a special interest in the care of chronically and terminally ill children and their families, and in the treatment of children and adolescents with chronic pain syndromes using an integrative medicine approach. She has written widely on medical student, resident, and practitioner education in the areas of child development, management of behavioral problems at home and school, and palliative care, end-of-life care, and bereavement counseling. Her foundation and National Cancer Institute funded multi-institutional research over 25 years has focused on siblings and mothers of children with cancer. She has also been funded by the National Center for Complementary and Alternative Medicine of the National Institutes of Health to study the effects of using music therapy on symptom control and immune reconstitution in the management of patients undergoing stem cell transplantation.

As an educator, she was the Director of the Pediatric Clerkship at the University of Rochester School of Medicine for 17 years and the Director of the Department of Education at the American Academy of Pediatrics in 1995–1996. She was the founding chairperson of the Medical Student Education Special Interest Group of the Academic Pediatric Association (formerly, the Ambulatory Pediatric Association) and founding president of the Council on Medical Student Education in Pediatrics (COMSEP). As President of the Association for the Behavioral Sciences and Medical Education (ABSAME) in 1992–1993, she began a project to develop a comprehensive curriculum guide for medical student and resident education in the behavioral sciences that was published in 1995. An updated version of this curriculum guide, reflecting the many advances in the behavioral sciences that occurred around the turn of the century, forms the foundation for this book, now in this third edition. The authors and editors who contributed to this text represent the diverse experience and expertise of ABSAME's membership, working in conjunction with other expert professionals dedicated to excellence in education.

A graduate of Radcliffe College/Harvard University, Dr. Sahler received her MD degree with distinction in research at the University of Rochester, was a resident in Pediatrics at the Duke University Medical Center, and completed a fellowship in Behavioral and Developmental Pediatrics/Child and Adolescent Psychiatry at the University of Rochester. She served as a Captain in the U.S. Army Medical Corps and received a Special Commendation Award for her work in child abuse in the military.

John E. Carr, PhD, Co-Editor, is Professor emeritus of Psychiatry & Behavioral Sciences and Psychology at the University of Washington where he served a four year term as Acting Chair of the Department of Psychiatry & Behavioral Sciences, was Director of Undergraduate Medical Education, and played a principal role in developing behavioral science curricula for the School of Medicine. He has written extensively about the need for an "Integrated Sciences Model" for the behavioral and biological sciences in medical education and clinical psychology graduate training. He has served as a consultant to the World Health Organization on Behavioral Sciences in Health Care Training, and co-coordinated a cooperative venture between the Association for the Behavioral Sciences and Medical Education, the Association of Medical School Psychologists, and the International Union of Psychological Societies in developing behavioral science training modules for WHO.

Dr. Carr received an MA in Industrial Psychology and a PhD in Clinical Psychology from Syracuse University. He is a Diplomate in Health Psychology of the American Board of Professional Psychology. He is a Fellow of the American Psychological Association, Association of Psychological Science, Society of Behavioral Medicine, and the Academy of Behavioral Medicine Research. He has served on the National Board of Medical Examiners Behavioral Sciences Test Committee, and is a founding member and was twice elected to the Presidency of the Association of Psychologists in Academic Health Centers. His promotion of an integrated sciences model in medical education and graduate psychology training reflects his bio-behavioral orientation and a career-long research program focused upon identifying the mechanisms of bio-behavioral interaction in stress, anxiety, and depression.

He is the recipient of a Distinguished Educator Award from the Association of Psychologists in Academic Health Centers, the Gary Tucker Award for Lifetime Achievement in Teaching and Dedication to Education from the Department of Psychiatry of the University of Washington, and Distinguished Psychologist Awards for Contribution in Scholarship and for Contribution to the Field of Psychology from the Washington State Psychological Association.

Julia B. Frank, MD, Associate Editor, is Associate Professor of Psychiatry and Behavioral Sciences and is the Director of Medical Student Education in Psychiatry and Director of the Psychiatry Clerkship at the George Washington University School of Medicine and Health Sciences. Her responsibilities include organizing the pre-clinical behavioral sciences curriculum and integrating it with the psychiatry clerkship. As a graduate of the GWU Master Teachers Program, she has developed an interest in multiple modes of student learning, including team based learned, problem based learning, medical readers theater, medical humanities, and self-directed learning. She co-authored a question/review book for NBME Step One, which became the foundation of many of the review questions in the second and third editions of *The Behavioral Sciences and Health Care*. She became co-editor of the third edition specifically to help align it with current thinking about the role of evolutionary processes in pathology in general and psychopathology in particular.

Dr. Frank is a member of the Society of Distinguished Teachers, a former board member of the Association for Behavioral Sciences and Medical Education, a Diplomate of the American Board of Psychiatry and Neurology, and a Distinguished Fellow of the American Psychiatric Association. She was named Psychiatrist of the Year by the Washington Psychiatric Society in 2005, based on organizing colleagues to work with survivors of Hurricane Katrina. Her other scholarly writing includes co-authorship with her father,

Jerome D. Frank, MD, PhD, of *Persuasion and Healing: A Comparative Study of Psychotherapy* (1991), a classic work explaining the universal processes and effects of psychotherapy, written especially for medical students and trainees in other mental health disciplines. More recently, she co-edited, with Renato Alarcón, *The Psychotherapy of Hope: The Legacy of Persuasion and Healing* (Baltimore: Johns Hopkins Press; 2012). Other scholarly interests include research into the pharmacological treatment of post-traumatic stress disorder and writing about women's mental health, victims of violence, and various topics in the history of medicine. She has also published medical comic poetry in the *New England Journal of Medicine*.

A graduate of Yale University School of Medicine, the internal medicine internship of the Michael Reese Hospital in Chicago, and the psychiatry residency of the Yale Department of Psychiatry, Dr. Frank has provided clinical psychiatric care to chronically mentally ill veterans, medically ill patients, university students, and refugees seeking asylum. Her current practice serves outpatients with anxiety, mood disorders, perinatal psychiatric syndromes, and a wide range of other adaptive disorders.

João Vieira Nunes, MD, Associate Editor, is Associate Medical Professor of Physiology and Pharmacology at the Sophie Davis School of Biomedical Education at The City College of New York, City University of New York. He has been instrumental in developing behavioral science, neuropsychiatry, and doctoring curricula at Sophie Davis. He is a Diplomate of the American Board of Psychiatry and Neurology, a psychiatrist and child and adolescent psychiatrist with a special interest in brain and behavior, childhood development and psychopathology, health disparities related to sleep disorders and chronobiology, and personal narratives for the understanding of food-related behaviors. He has written widely on medical student education, on sleep disorders and chronobiology, and health disparities. He has dedicated much of his career to providing medical care in underserved areas of The Bronx and Harlem in New York City (where he still practices), to the cause of facilitating access of under-represented minorities to medical education, and to undergraduate and graduate medical education as course director currently, and, in the past, as psychiatry clerkship and residency program director. He directs or co-directs three required courses in undergraduate medical education.

As a member and former board member of the Association for the Behavioral Sciences and Medical Education, he played an important role in the development of the Behavioral Science Curriculum Guide published in 1995 to provide an educational template in the behavioral sciences for medical students and residents and their teachers.

Beyond the medical field, he composes and performs music and writes poetry, having recently published, with two other poets, a bilingual (English/Portuguese) anthology titled *True Word*.

A graduate of the Faculty of Medicine of Espirito Santo Federal University, Brazil, he completed residencies in Pediatrics, Psychiatry, and Child Psychiatry at the Rio de Janeiro Federal University. After moving to New York, he completed residency and fellowship training in Psychiatry and Child and Adolescent Psychiatry at Albert Einstein College of Medicine, and has attended the Harvard-Macy Institute for Physician Educators.

Preface to the Third Edition

In prior editions, we stressed the critical importance of combining the principles of the behavioral sciences with those of the biological sciences to develop a comprehensive understanding of health and illness. This concept of an integrated sciences model of research, clinical training, and health care delivery anticipated an explosion of interdisciplinary studies focused on the mechanisms by which biological and behavioral factors interact to influence health outcomes. Simultaneously, there has been increasing recognition that transdisciplinary collaboration among health care professionals is essential if we are to create unified, efficacious, and cost effective delivery systems.

Our objectives in this new edition are twofold: (1) to amplify our understanding of the mechanisms and processes contributing to bio-behavioral interactions by reviewing recent research advances from behavioral genomics, cognitive and social neurosciences, psychoneuroendocrinology, and other interdisciplinary research fields relevant to health care; and (2) to examine how transdisciplinary practice can promote the broader application of knowledge gained from integrating the biological and behavioral sciences in the training of all health care professionals.

The Association for the Behavioral Sciences and *Medical* Education (ABSAME) gave rise to this textbook through the development of a set of educational guidelines for the behavioral sciences, and has supported its evolution over the past decade. This year, ABSAME is in the process of changing its name to the Association for the Behavioral Sciences and *Health Professions* Education. This shift in focus and membership reflects a growing understanding that it is only through transdisciplinary efforts that we can keep the world's population as free of disease as possible and maximize the sense of self-efficacy and well-being that is essential to living a full and productive life.

There are limits to the resources that professionals can rely on to improve and maintain the health of society. It is clear that the expertise of many different disciplines and the accountability of all members of the team are crucial elements of an efficient, effective health care system. Thus, it is incumbent on all of us to integrate scientific knowledge and apply our respective skills cooperatively toward achieving our mutual goals.

In keeping with these objectives, this text is designed to provide an understanding of how the behavioral and biological sciences interact to influence health care. It is also designed to provide information and insight from the behavioral sciences that can be applied to the clinical practice of any health care provider regardless of discipline. In the section on the Clinical Encounter, we use the physician-patient relationship as an example of the broader clinician-client relationship that is the backbone of health care. However, the professional responsibility to provide information, teach, advise, guide decision making, and advocate for the best interests of the person seeking our counsel, all with the utmost integrity, is inherent in the standards of all provider groups. We hope that the universal role the behavioral sciences play in optimizing well-being will be self-evident and that you will find these principles applicable in every health care encounter.

The Editors

Acknowledgments

A project as large as revising a textbook takes the efforts of many people who give freely of their time, energy, and expertise. When we decided that the time had come to revise and update *The Behavioral Sciences and Health Care,* our first step was to ask colleagues, trainees, and students to review the second edition critically and give us their recommendations about how to make the text even more useful and user friendly. Among all the people who answered the call, we must highlight the enthusiasm that J. LeBron McBride, PhD, MPH, Director of Behavioral Medicine at the Floyd Medical Center Family Medicine Residency in Rome, Georgia brought to the task. Dr. McBride, as a family therapist and pastoral counselor as well as an educator, has been the primary author of the chapter on the family for all editions of this textbook. He enlisted the aid of Adriana Pratt, MD, who was then a second- year resident, and Thomas L. Garcia, DO, who was then a third-year resident and chief resident at the Floyd Medical Center program, to provide comprehensive critiques of the book. It was not possible to include all of their suggestions, but their attention to detail as well as the overall *gestalt* of the book was extremely helpful in our thinking about changes in approach that we needed to consider and implement where possible.

We would also like to acknowledge the work of Barbara Schuman who has been the administrative assistant for both Editions 2 and 3. She has provided more than due diligence in keeping us organized and on schedule. We also want to acknowledge the editorial efforts of Stephanie M. Kawzenuk, BM, who undertook the task of reading and proofing the entire final copy, and the major word processing and editing tasks completed not only by Stephanie but also by Rosemary Oliva Obi, MS, LCAT, MT-BC, and Tiffany Robison, MS, all of whose expertise in human development and the therapeutic process was a critical asset in completing this project. And, our thanks to Karen Rothenburgh, who graciously stepped in to assume a major role in manuscript preparation. Finally, our thanks to Lisa Bennett of Hogrefe Publishing whose very capable editing brought the text to life.

Table of Contents

About the Editors v

Preface ix

Acknowledgments x

Table of Contents xi

Section I	**The Behavioral Sciences and Health** 1	
	Introduction and How to Use this Book 3	
	1	Evolving Models of Health Care 5
Section II	**Brain Systems** 13	
	2	Predisposition 15
	3	The Nervous System 22
	4	Brain Networks in Health and Illness 31
Section III	**Homeostatic Systems and Disorders** 37	
	5	Nutrition, Metabolism, and Feeding Disorders 39
	6	Chronobiology and Sleep Disorders 44
	7	Stress, Adaptation, and Stress Disorders 52
Section IV	**Individual-Environment Interaction** 63	
	8	Emotion and Learning 65
	9	Cognition and Social Interaction 74
Section V	**Development Through the Life Cycle** 83	
	10	Selected Theories of Development 85
	11	The Fetus, Newborn, and Infant 92
	12	Toddlerhood and the Preschool Years 98
	13	The School Years 104
	14	The Adult Years 112
	15	The Family 121
Section VI	**Social and Cultural Issues** 131	
	16	Social Behavior and Groups 133
	17	Theories of Social Relations 139
	18	Culture and Ethnicity 146
	19	Health Care in Minority and Majority Populations 155
	20	Sexuality and Sexual Disorders 162
	21	Health Care Issues Facing Gay, Lesbian, Bisexual, and Transgender Individuals . . 173
	22	Geriatric Health and Successful Aging 181

Section VII **Societal and Behavioral Health Challenges** 191
   23 Obesity 193
   24 Eating Disorders 199
   25 Substance Abuse 206
   26 Interpersonal Violence 212
   27 Poverty and Homelessness 220
   28 Suicide 227
   29 Health Literacy 235

Section VIII **The Health Care System, Policy, and Economics** 241
   30 The U.S. Health Care System 243
   31 Complementary and Integrative Medicine 254
   32 Palliative Care 264
   33 Ethical and Legal Issues in Patient Care 274

Section IX **The Clinical Relationship** 283
   34 The Physician-Patient Relationship 285
   35 The Medical Encounter and Clinical Decision Making 292
   36 Motivating Healthy Behavior 301
   37 Physician Health, Impairment, and Misconduct 308

Section X **Psychopathology** 315
   38 Introduction to Psychopathology 317
   39 The Psychiatric Evaluation 322
   40 Principles of Psychotherapy 329
   41 Pharmacological Interventions for Psychiatric Disorders 335
   42 Somatization and Somatoform Disorders 343
   43 Adjustment Disorders, Bereavement, and Demoralization 348
   44 Dementia 352
   45 Delirium and Secondary Syndromes 359
   46 Anxiety and Dissociative Disorders 365
   47 Major Mood Disorders 373
   48 Schizophrenia and Other Psychotic Disorders 381
   49 Personality and Impulse Control Disorders 388
   50 Disorders of Infancy, Childhood, and Adolescence 396

Appendices
Appendix A Epidemiology 409
Appendix B Biostatistics 416

Review Questions – Answer Key 407

Practice Exam
Questions 425
Answers 475

Contributors 525

Subject Index 531

Section I

The Behavioral Sciences and Health

Introduction and How to Use this Book

In the course of human experience, people are born, mature, feel emotion, develop relationships, produce and reproduce, and struggle to cope with a myriad challenges to their survival and well-being. This book is about the diverse ways in which health can be compromised; the many factors that contribute to an individual's predisposition, vulnerability, and resilience; the wide range of precipitating events that can trigger a disease, injury, or malfunction; and the complex array of individual differences that determine each patient's unique response to a disease as well as its treatment.

When health and well-being are challenged, humans have, for millennia, sought the aid of healers, individuals who are purported to possess special knowledge about the etiology and treatment of various disorders. History has witnessed the evolution of health care from a spiritually based healing art to a scientifically based technical profession, reflecting advances in our knowledge of the biological functioning of the human body. After World War II, there was a gradual shift away from medicine's exclusive focus on linear causal relationships between a disease and its biological etiology. Physicians began to refer to a "biopsychosocial model," which proposed that psychosocial variables were as important as biological variables in determining health status.

Although a major step forward in understanding that complex interactions exist, the biopsychosocial model failed to explain *how* psychosocial variables actually interact with biological variables. That is, what are the specific connections that exist among the biological (e.g., neurotransmitter systems), psychological (e.g., emotional reactions to stress or memory), and social (cultural prescriptions and proscriptions about appropriate physical and interpersonal responses) factors that define health and illness, and by what mechanisms are they established and maintained? In the final decades of the 20th century, medical researchers began to explore the knowledge and methodology of psychology, sociology, anthropology, and other social and behavioral sciences as they apply specifically to medicine. Focusing on bio-behavioral connections, their studies have given rise to new fields such as behavioral genetics, behavioral neuroscience, psychoneuroendocrinology, behavioral pharmacology, social biology, and behavioral medicine.

The model presented in this book calls attention to the clinical significance of the *interaction* among biopsychosocial variables, and focuses in greater detail on identifying the mechanisms that interconnect these variables. We call this extension of the biopsychosocial model the "integrated sciences model" (ISM) because it focuses on demonstrating the interdependence of the contributions made by *all of the sciences* basic to medicine.

In *Section I*, we briefly trace the evolution of health care practices and models, the development of contemporary health provider practice, and the integrated sciences model. In *Section II*, we present a brief review of the human nervous system and how its evolution has contributed to the unique survival capabilities of *Homo sapiens*. In *Section III*, we discuss the basic homeostatic systems and the critically important role that the stress response plays in human adaptation. In *Section IV*, we review basic psychological principles and the bio-behavioral mechanisms involved in sensation, learning, cognition, emotion, and social interaction and cooperation. In *Section V*, we review human development through the life cycle and important aspects of major developmental theories as they apply to the individual and to the family. In *Section VI*, we examine social behavior and groups, and the influence of culture, ethnicity, and other social factors on health and health care. In *Section VII,* we explore several contemporary social issues that contribute to, complicate, or are major problems in health care.

In *Section VIII*, we examine the organization and functioning of the health care system, the role that certain areas of special focus such as palliative care play, the rise of complementary and alternative medicine (now integrative medicine), and some of the ethical and legal implications for patients as well as health care providers. In *Section IX,* we discuss the clinical encounter and examine the relevance of basic, clinical, and social science to understanding the patient's complaints, eliciting and interpreting findings, making a diagnosis, negotiating a treatment plan, and motivating patient behavior. We also explore the importance of patients' health literacy and provider impairment in effecting health outcomes. In *Section X,* we summarize the field of psychopathology, present brief descriptions of the more common psychiatric disorders, and show how basic behavioral science principles help us to understand this complex area of health care.

Each chapter in this volume begins with a set of bulleted questions designed to focus your attention on key learning points. Each chapter also concludes with a short set of review questions based on information in the text. We have chosen to emphasize ideas, principles, and established research findings, and to minimize references in favor of providing selected recommended readings. Finally, significant scientific observations from the behavioral sciences as well as clinical applications and examples have been included to make the theoretical practical.

In the Appendices, we have presented the elements of epidemiology and biostatistics that are essential to understanding and interpreting both medical and behavioral science data. Lastly, we have included more than 350 multiple-choice questions with explanations of the correct answer and why the incorrect choices are, in fact, incorrect. Some of the questions in this section provide additional review of material in the text. However, many questions are focused on new material to make the contents of the book even more comprehensive through the use of brief, directed discussions. The construction of these questions is designed to give you a sense of the kind of material and question format you may encounter later in training.

Good medicine is science artfully applied. The laws of probability should be interpreted in the light of experience and intuition, and common sense appreciated as a useful guide to decision making. Respect for the autonomy and self-efficacy of the patient will usually lead to the best outcome – although not everyone may agree with what the patient wants as the outcome.

We have tried to be explicit in defining the mechanisms of bio-behavioral interaction where they are known and to incorporate typical patient experiences where relevant. Some of the material will seem self-evident, some will seem counterintuitive, but all derives from the amalgam of research findings from the biological, behavioral, cognitive, sociocultural, and environmental sciences that contribute to our knowledge of the determinants of health and illness important for you as well as your patients.

Olle Jane Z. Sahler, MD
John E. Carr, PhD
Julia B. Frank, MD
Joao V. Nunes, MD

1 Evolving Models of Health Care

John E. Carr, PhD, Olle Jane Z. Sahler, MD, Julia B. Frank, MD, and João V. Nunes, MD

- How does the World Health Organization define health?
- How do disease, sickness, and illness differ?
- What is the difference between direct and indirect health risks?
- What shared concepts underlie traditional and modern health care systems?
- Why is the biomedical model discipline specific?
- What is the biopsychosocial model?
- What is an integrated sciences model?

Health, Disease, Sickness, and Illness

How does the World Health Organization define health?

The **World Health Organization** (WHO) defines **health** as "a state of physical, social, and mental well-being," measured by the patient's ability to cope with everyday activities, and fully function physically, socially, and emotionally. At its optimal level, good health provides for a life marked by spiritual serenity, zestful activity, a sense of competence, and psychological well-being.

How do disease, sickness, and illness differ?

Disease is the manifestation of impaired bodily functions. Disease is recognized and classified by the type of organ damage (e.g., cirrhosis of the liver, myocardial infarction), by functional impairment (e.g., diabetes), or by an underlying etiological process (e.g., infectious disease). **Sickness** refers to those behaviors manifested by an individual who feels ill or believes that he or she is ill. An individual can feel sick, yet have no identifiable disease. Conversely, someone may have a disease but not feel or act sick. Being perceived as sick or feeling sick leads to adopting the **sick role** relative to the rest of the community. This frees a person

from the obligation to perform the tasks of everyday living without blame ("I feel too sick to go to work"). However, the sick person has obligations: (1) to pursue and accept help and (2) to adhere to culturally or professionally prescribed regimens that facilitate return to health.

Illness represents the totality of the patient's experience, how the patient feels, behaves, and perceives his or her condition, and how others respond to the patient. Responses vary according to the person's place within the family or community, as shaped by cultural beliefs and expectations. Beliefs about how or why the illness occurred (**explanatory models**) and the course the illness takes determine how the patient behaves and how the larger community responds.

Risk and Prevention

What is the difference between direct and indirect health risks?

Direct risks to health include dangerous practices (e.g., reckless driving, smoking) and various pathogenic conditions (e.g., environmental toxins, contaminated water). *Indirect risks* to health are lower risk practices or prevention failures (e.g., high fat diet, not exercising). While some risk factors (e.g., age, race, gender, genetic makeup) are not modifiable, many risk factors are related to a person's **lifestyle** and are, therefore, modifiable. Other risk factors, such as occupation, social class, religious practices, and cultural traditions, affect health status in complex ways that may or may not be modifiable.

The concept of health care extends from the treatment of disease to the *prevention* of disease, injury, sickness, and illness, and the *promotion* of health. To achieve these goals, health care professionals not only apply medical treatments, but also seek to *change patient behaviors*, *beliefs*, *social and cultural practices*, and *environmental conditions*. Such work requires knowledge of the ways these factors interact, how they affect patient health, and the methods by which they can be effectively modified.

Primary prevention involves practices to protect, promote, and maintain health. These include the concerns of specialized public health professionals, whose role is to promote sanitation and occupational safety, and to monitor environmental conditions. Primary prevention in medical settings involves advising patients about personal habits like exercising regularly, maintaining normal weight, eating nutritional foods, and avoiding smoking, substance use, or other activities that jeopardize health. **Secondary prevention**, for which many types of health professionals may assume responsibility, involves practices such as immunization, medical surveillance, **harm reduction**, and health screening to enhance resistance to or buffer the impact of risk factors.

Evolving Approaches to Health Care

Archeological evidence suggests that humans have practiced some form of health care for at least the past 30,000 years. Early human beliefs about sickness encompassed observable *natural causes* such as climatic events, *personal behaviors*, and unobservable, incomprehensible, or *supernatural causes* such as sorcery. Naturalistic treatments presumably involved simply accepting fate, or the use of herbs, tonics, and oils whose healing or curative properties would have been discerned empirically over time. Since healing and religion have been so intertwined in human history, treatment of supernaturally caused conditions involved rituals that were interpreted and administered by priests or Shamans knowledgeable about the relationships between the mystical and natural realms.

Recorded information about the human body and theories of health care appeared roughly 6,000 years ago in the time of the Babylonians. The **Code of Hammurabi** defined surgical operations to be performed, a scale of fees, and penalties for malpractice. Egyptian records from 5,000 years ago describe symptoms of abdominal, eye, and heart disorders, treatment of wounds, fractures and dislocations, and an understanding that brain lesions may be associated with paralysis of the opposite side of the body.

What shared concepts underlie traditional and modern health care systems?

Major systems of traditional Chinese, Ayurvedic, and Greek medicine began to evolve between 1,500 and 500 B.C/B.C.E. and constitute the basis for many current health care practices. Despite cultural and geographic differences, there was vigorous exchange of knowledge throughout the ancient world, likely through trade and conquest, resulting in common doctrines fundamental to all of these systems:

1. The universe is an integrated whole that is subject to laws governing all phenomena including human behavior and health;
2. The individual is an integrated system of physical, mental, cultural, and spiritual qualities;
3. Health is a state of balance (homeostasis) between the individual and the outside world, and among the elements, humors, and forces within the individual;
4. All living things are endowed with a life force composed of vital energies that must be kept in balance (e.g., male/female, yin/yang) in order to maintain optimal health;
5. Disease results from disruption or imbalance within the life force, an imbalance between the life forces and external events (stress), or an imbalance among humors and bodily functions;
6. Symptoms represent the body's efforts to restore balance and health; and
7. Healers supplement or strengthen the body's efforts to restore balance by applying treatments based on universal principles.

These conceptualizations of disease and health, rooted in indigenous cultural beliefs, constitute the subject matter of **ethnomedicine** (see Chapter 18, Culture and Ethnicity) and reflect an awareness of certain concepts found in both traditional and modern health care systems. Common or universal principles include the interaction and interdependence of *etiological factors*, the principle of "balance" or **homeostasis**, the influence of **stress**, and an appreciation of the *role of the healer*.

Modern concepts of health care have their roots in the writings of **Hippocrates** (b. 460 B.C.), credited with establishing the first school dedicated to the scientific study of medicine. Hippocratic medicine was the definitive standard for medical knowledge and professional ethics until **Galen**, a Roman practitioner in the 2nd century A.D./C.E., who compiled the medical knowledge of his time and began anatomical and physiological investigations. Because of religious constraints, Galen could carry out dissections only on animals. As a result, many of his anatomical findings proved to be in error, although he made significant contributions to understanding the functioning of the respiratory, circulatory, digestive, and neural systems.

Galen laid the scientific foundations for **allopathic medicine** by asserting that lesions in specific body organs led to dysfunctions, establishing the principle that persons schooled in the study of pathology (physicians) should be the definitive healers in society. Galenic *treatments,* only loosely grounded in his scientific work, were based on the *law of opposites*, i.e., diseases were treated with medicines or interventions that created an effect opposite to the symptom.

Despite its limitations, Galenic medicine dominated medicine for 1,400 years. His work was rediscovered in Europe through the preservation and translation of Roman, Greek, and Arabic texts and its worldwide dispersal influenced most major medical systems but, paradoxically, stifled scientific advancement. While the applied law of opposites presumably benefitted some cases (e.g., applying cooling remedies in cases of fever), it often justified inappropriate and dangerous "treatments" such as the indiscriminate use of enemas, bloodletting, purging, and other toxic and invasive procedures.

The resurgence of rationality, critical discourse, and experimental investigation that marked the *Renaissance* and the later *Age of Enlightenment* led to important advances in the development of medicine. Seventeenth century developments in the natural sciences led to important discoveries of the physical, mechanical, and chemical functions of the human body. Subsequent challenges to Galenism re-affirmed the *physician's role* in mobilizing and assisting the body's own healing efforts. This led to the development of *homeopathic*, *osteopathic*, *naturopathic*, and *chiropractic* approaches to medicine (see Chapter 31, Complementary and Integrative Medicine).

Biomedical Model – Discipline Specific

Why is the biomedical model discipline specific?

By the end of the 19th century, the scientific foundation of medicine included systematic observation, objective measurement, and experimental tests of theories. These activities were developed and taught within specific disciplines such as pathology, microbiology, physiology, and pharmacology. Corresponding clinical techniques gradually became more sophisticated and disease specific. Advances in *microbiology*, for example, showed that microorganisms contributed to disease and could be controlled by sterilization, antiseptics, and immunization.

Medicine's increased scientific sophistication led to intense scrutiny of the quality of North American medical training. The ***Flexner Report***, issued by the Carnegie Foundation in 1910, critically evaluated the scientific curricula of all the medical schools in the US and Canada. The report called for the establishment of higher standards for medical education, grounded in the *biological sciences* and *the scientific method*. These recommendations became the defining criteria for the **biomedical model**, making medicine *discipline specific*. Flexner downplayed, even discounted, the contributions of the behavioral and social sciences to medicine. In consequence, post-Flexnerian medical education and practice became heavily biomedical and partly lost sight of the broader human and social context of disease and health care.

The limitations of **biomedicine** became glaringly evident during the two world wars, when the treatment of large numbers of soldiers suffering "shell shock" or "battle fatigue" (now posttraumatic stress disorder) raised awareness of the influence of *psychosocial factors* on a patient's illness and treatment outcome. This awareness led to the development of **psychosomatic medicine** and *psychosocial models* of health care as alternatives to biomedicine. Though helpful, these psychosocial models were closely tied to the specific behavioral science disciplines of psychology, sociology, and anthropology. Their disciplinary base led them to emphasize the importance of their specific contributions, but failed to take into account how psychosocial factors interacted with biological and other etiological variables. By the mid 1970s, society recognized that a more comprehensive *multidisciplinary* approach to health care was needed.

Biopsychosocial Model – Multidisciplinary

What is the biopsychosocial model?

In 1977, **George Engel** published an article in *Science* entitled "The Need for a New Medical Model: A Challenge for Biomedicine." Engel asserted that in contrast to the biomedical model, the **biopsychosocial model** recognized (1) *multiple determinants* in the development of disease and the resultant illness process and (2) a *hierarchical organization* of biological and social systems that contribute to the disease and illness experience (See Figure 1.1). Each system was seen as a component of a higher, more abstract system. Therefore, change in one system would change other systems, especially those most closely linked to it. Psychological and social sciences were as important as the biological sciences in understanding the determinants of illness, and researchers began to identify specific psychosocial factors associated with specific diseases/illnesses.

Determinants of health are not simply a collection of individual psychosocial and biological variables, each linearly related to some specific health outcome, nor are they discipline-specific systems only hierarchically related to one another. Rather, health is determined *by multiple etiological variables, continuously interacting via complex mechanisms, and interdependent processes*

(see Figure 1.2). Identifying the determinants of disease/illness requires identifying not only the biological processes involved in the etiology of the condition and the psychosocial factors that influ-

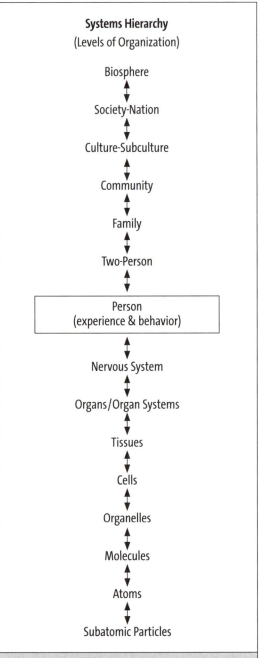

Systems Hierarchy
(Levels of Organization)

Biosphere

Society-Nation

Culture-Subculture

Community

Family

Two-Person

Person
(experience & behavior)

Nervous System

Organs/Organ Systems

Tissues

Cells

Organelles

Molecules

Atoms

Subatomic Particles

Figure 1.1. Biopsychosocial model. Reprinted with permission from Engel GL. The clinical application of the biopsychosocial model. *American Journal of Psychiatry* **1980; 137: 535–544. © 1980 by American Psychiatric Association**

Table 1.1. Interdisciplinary research fields in health care include:

Genomic sciences, which seek to identify the genetic processes associated with normal and abnormal development and functioning, and the mechanisms by which these processes influence and are influenced by human behaviors, social and biological functioning, and environmental interaction.

Cognitive neurosciences, which seek to determine the brain structures and neuroendocrine mechanisms that contribute to and are influenced by specific cognitive processes (perception, learning, memory, problem solving).

Social neurosciences, which seek to determine the specific biological systems and mechanisms that implement social processes and behaviors, and the mechanisms by which those social processes modify and influence organ-based, neural, neuroendocrine, and immunological functions.

Psychoneuroimmunology, which seeks to define the mechanisms by which stressful events and emotional responses influence neurological and immune system functioning.

---

ence these processes, but also the mechanisms by which psychosocial and biological factors *interact* to determine behavioral outcomes. Efforts to identify these mechanisms of bio-behavioral interaction have prompted the growth of a number of interdisciplinary fields (see Table 1.1), in which behavioral and biological scientists collaborate by combining theoretical and methodological efforts.

Clinical Application of the Biopsychosocial Model

Since people can function normally physiologically with only one kidney, a kidney donor will continue to have normal renal functioning. In the biomedical model, once recovered from surgery, a donor returns to full health. By contrast, the biopsychosocial model directs attention to the psychosocial parameters of the donor's and recipient's conditions, not merely their biological functioning. This model recognizes that a donor's recovery and sense of self-worth may be facilitated, even enhanced, if he or she knows the recipient was helped by the donation, the community applauds the donor for the gift, and the donor believes the recipient will make a full recovery. On the other hand, the knowledge of having only one kidney may leave the donor feeling damaged or otherwise impaired. The donor may feel diminished if insufficient gratitude was expressed. These latter perceptions may impair full functional recovery.

While no *biomedical* intervention beyond appropriate postoperative care for a donor is required, the *biopsychosocial* model implies that education is essential to reassure a donor of his or her biological integrity, that information about the benefits to the recipient will reinforce a donor's sense of self worth, and that the support of family and community are essential to recovery and return to a state of full health.

These research collaborations reflect the evolution of the biopsychosocial model from a *multidisciplinary* view of behavioral and biological sciences as distinct but equal to a more complex *interdisciplinary* view that focuses upon (1) the interdependence of biological and behavioral processes, (2) the mechanisms of their interaction, and (3) the integration of biological and behavioral scientific principles, concepts, and theories into an integrated sciences model.

Integrated Sciences Model – Interdisciplinary

What is an integrated sciences model?

The survival of the human species is largely attributable to the evolution of the human brain. In response to some random but beneficial genetic anomalies and epigenetic events, the brain and the associated neuroendocrine subsystem developed an array of remarkable abilities that enable Homo sapiens to respond to threat both reflexively and by planning to avoid dangers. Over eons, these abilities evolved into a highly complex, integrated system of **executive functions**, which enable humans to record and learn from experience, to adapt to, anticipate, plan for, and modify those experiences, and to relate to, cooperate with, care for, and communicate with other humans. Such functions provide our species with extraordinary tools for mastering the environment and insuring survival.

All information relevant to the interaction of the organism with the environment is processed,

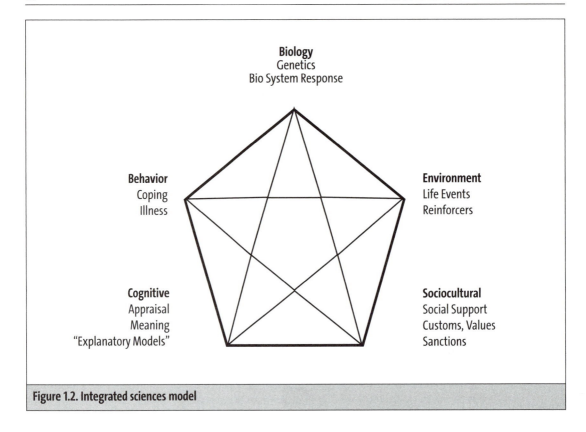

Figure 1.2. Integrated sciences model

coordinated, and integrated through the executive functions of the brain and its associated subsystems, in accord with basic biological and behavioral principles. In recent decades, scientists have further clarified how experience modifies the expression of genes and the structure and function of all biological systems, including the nervous system. These findings underlie the concepts of **neuronal plasticity** and **gene-environment interaction.**

In an **integrated sciences model** (ISM), all psychosocial and biological phenomena are viewed as *interdependent* and functionally *interactive*. The principles of interaction involve discipline specific as well as common principles and processes, such as homeostasis, stress, adaptation, learning, development, and genetic modification. The individual can be viewed as a complex *integrated system* of many interacting variables organized under five disciplinary domains: *biological*, *behavioral*, *cognitive*, *sociocultural*, and *environmental* (see Figure 1.2). Elements within each domain contribute to the individual's condition, while constantly interacting with variables in all the other domains. As in the original biopsychosocial model, change in any domain effects a

change in all the others, as the organism constantly strives to maintain *optimal balance* within and among domains. Thus, the concept of **homeostasis** applies to both psychosocial and biological phenomena.

Stress – The Engine of Adaptation

Any challenge to homeostasis is defined as **stress**. This term connotes not the commonly described situational stress, but rather the interdisciplinary principle of a *"system under strain"* (i.e., the systemic effects of any change, in any variable, in any domain). Challenges to homeostasis, which range from genetically regulated processes of growth to varying social and environmental conditions, initiate an *adaptive response* in other domains, whereby the organism attempts to resolve, cope with, and learn from the stressful condition. Stress is the engine that drives adaptation, the *raison d'être* for the evolution of the brain's remarkable capabilities.

Stress, or challenge, itself is not necessarily destructive. Indeed, various stress responses allow

Integrated Sciences Model

1. The individual is a complex integrated system of many interacting variables organized under five disciplinary domains: biological, behavioral, cognitive, sociocultural, and environmental.
2. Any challenge to homeostasis within and between these domains constitutes "stress."
3. Variables within each domain interact with those in other domains via diverse mechanisms. Hence, stress in one domain initiates responses in all domains.
4. Challenges to the organism are ongoing and this interactive system is constantly evolving as the system is continuously adapting.
5. Disease is a byproduct of the failure of the stress response system. Therefore, accurately assessing the differential role of stress conditions and other risk factors in each domain is essential to determining the best intervention strategy.
6. Treatment or intervention itself may have additional biological, behavioral, and cognitive effects on the patient (side effects), as well as cultural and environmental impact.
7. Identifying the mechanisms and processes by which variables within the multiple domains interact is the focus of ongoing interdisciplinary biobehavioral research.
8. Interdisciplinary research is guided by an *integration* of the concepts and methodologies of the sciences and disciplines that contribute to health care.

the organism to learn from its adaptive efforts. The nature, intensity, and outcome of the stress response are determined, in part, by the *degree of stress*. Every college student is familiar with the "inverted U" shaped curve describing the relationship between stress and productivity. Too little challenge (stress) undermines motivation and may result in poor performance. Too much challenge (stress) may discourage effort and impair performance. Optimal challenge (stress) motivates and inspires, but does not overwhelm.

The adaptive success of the **stress response** defines individual health; its breakdown or dysfunction contributes to disease or disorder. Ironically, an over-functioning stress response may itself contribute to disease and disorder, as in *autoimmune diseases* where the immune system that normally protects against external pathogens attacks the host body. The bio-behavioral mechanisms of the stress response involved in adaptation and illness are discussed in greater detail in Chapter 7, Stress, Adaptation, and Stress Disorders.

Integrated Assessment

Assessment should involve a detailed exploration of the differential and *interactive* contributions of biological, behavioral, cognitive, cultural, and environmental risk factors. This information informs the health care professional about the bio-behavioral mechanisms and processes that contribute to a particular disorder and, therefore, may be appropriate targets for treatment.

In the vignette below, an integrated sciences model illustrates the complexity of factors contributing to smoking addiction, and why treatments that focus only on one domain (e.g., changing a smoker's cognitions) or one variable (e.g., stopping cigarette advertisements) are likely to fail.

Clinical Application of an Integrated Sciences Model

A patient has been advised by his doctor to give up smoking because of chronic obstructive pulmonary disease (COPD). With reduced smoking behavior as the treatment goal, we review the domains in Figure 1.2 and the variables that influence smoking using (–) after a variable if it discourages smoking and (+) if it encourages smoking:

Biological:	COPD (–), nicotine dependence (+), genetic vulnerabilities (+/–)
Behavioral:	peer smoking (+), social gatherings (+), social censure (–), stress reduction (+), "cool" image (+)
Cognitive:	knowledge of smoking risks (–), belief "I'm invulnerable, and can quit anytime" (+)
Cultural:	value systems (+/–), gender models (+), social sanctions (+), roles in interaction (+/–)
Environmental:	tobacco accessible (+), relatively inexpensive (+), reinforcing advertisements (+)

The probability of changing complexly determined health behaviors is maximized only if treatments address as many of the contributing factors as possible. In the example, a *multimodal approach* would involve the following strategies:

- *Biological*: nicotine patches to counter nicotine dependence
- *Behavioral*: alternative work breaks such as exercise; social gatherings in nonsmoking venues; stress management training; meditation
- *Cognitive*: requiring the patient to explain to others (e.g., young people) how smoking is harmful; exposure to high-profile, high-status nonsmokers as models
- *Cultural*: encouraging family to reinforce no smoking; limiting smoking to inconvenient and uncomfortable places; encouraging the patient to join a "smokers anonymous" group
- *Environmental*: making smoking materials less accessible (e.g., raising taxes, restricting access; promoting nonsmoking social and recreational areas)

As can be seen, a multimodal treatment plan should have a significantly better outcome than a treatment plan that focuses only on a single domain. Though certain interventions may not always be practical or worthwhile, multimodal perspectives foster greater flexibility in treatment strategizing. Also, even though a specific factor may be important in the etiology of a condition, it may not be an effective target in treatment (e.g., while new drugs improve survival rates in HIV/AIDS patients, behavioral management of the social and psychological aspects of the disease is still a major focus of disease management.

In the chapters that follow, we explore the biological, behavioral, cognitive, sociocultural, and environmental domains that influence human functioning and the bio-behavioral mechanisms and processes by which factors in these domains interact and contribute to human health and illness.

Recommended Readings

Berntson GG, Cacioppo JT. *Handbook of Neurosciences for the Behavioral Sciences.* Hoboken, NJ: Wiley & Sons; 2009.

Carr JE. Proposal for an integrated sciences curriculum in medical education. *Teaching and Learning in Medicine* 1999; 10:3–7.

Cuff PA, Vanselow NA (Eds.). *Improving Medical Education: Enhancing the Behavioral and Social Science Content of Medical School Curricula.* Washington, DC: National Academies Press; 2004.

Engel GL. The need for a new medical model: A challenge for biomedicine. *Science* 1977; 196:129–136.

Gazzaniga, MS. (Ed.). *The Cognitive Neurosciences,* 4th ed. Cambridge, MA: The MIT Press; 2010.

Review Questions

1. _____ refers to the behaviors manifested by an individual who believes that she is in need of medical care.
   A. Disease
   B. Explanatory model
   C. Illness
   D. Lifestyle
   E. Sickness

2. Which of the following theoretical models would be described as multidisciplinary?
   A. Biomedical
   B. Biopsychosocial
   C. Integrated Sciences
   D. Psychoanalytic
   E. Psychological

3. The first school dedicated to the scientific study of medicine was attributed to
   A. Engel.
   B. Flexner.
   C. Galen.
   D. Hammurabi.
   E. Hippocrates.

Key to review questions: p. 407

Section II

Brain Systems

2 Predisposition

João V. Nunes, MD, and John E. Carr, PhD

- What distinguishes genotype from phenotype?
- What do genes do and how does the environment influence genetic functioning?
- What information is provided by a pedigree study?
- How does gene-environment interaction differ from gene-environment correlation?
- What does diathesis-stress interaction mean?
- How does personality contribute to illness vulnerability?

Genetic Predisposition

What distinguishes genotype from phenotype?

Eons of evolutionary development have provided the central nervous system (CNS) with the mechanisms that enable humans to interact with the environment, learn from experience, and adapt to ever changing environmental demands. Because the CNS of the newborn has not yet accumulated experience, it must rely on the collective evolutionary experience, adaptations, and mutations of prior generations made available through the parental genetic programs (genotype) that determine the anatomical, biochemical, physiological, behavioral, and personal characteristics (phenotype) of the individual.

The **genotype** is the genetic constitution (genome) of a cell. The **phenotype** results from the interaction of the genotype with the environment and refers to the composite of biological and behavioral characteristics manifested by the individual under certain environmental circumstances. Each personal characteristic is called a **trait**, and virtually all traits are the product of gene-environment interaction. Indeed, the activation of an individual's genetic predisposition (**gene expression**) is dependent upon the influence of environmental events, beginning with prenatal, then postnatal, then early childhood challenges, which activate selective genes. This prompts genetic changes, setting the stage for subsequent behaviors, traits, resiliencies, and vulnerabilities.

What do genes do and how does the environment influence genetic functioning?

Each gene carries the **DNA code** for the production of a protein. Gene expression, the translation of a DNA sequence into a protein, is largely dependent upon accessibility to **transcription** processes of the **gene promoter region** (which controls gene expression). DNA is stored as heterochromatin, a form of chromatin that, being tightly wound, limits transcriptional activity. Environmental events and other **epigenetic** (in addition to genetic) factors alter the structure of the heterochromatin without changing the DNA sequence (see Figure 2.1). This permits the enzyme RNA polymerase to "read" the DNA code to produce a messenger RNA (mRNA). Gene expression is accomplished when mRNA transcription of the DNA sequence is translated into a protein.

Two epigenetic mechanisms initiate transcriptional activity: **histone modification** and **DNA methylation**. Heterochromatin owes its tight presentation to the relationship between DNA and histone proteins: DNA envelopes histone proteins, the "tails" of which protrude and wrap around the DNA. Enzymatically mediated acetylation modifies histones, making DNA more accessible. Acetylation diminishes the interac-

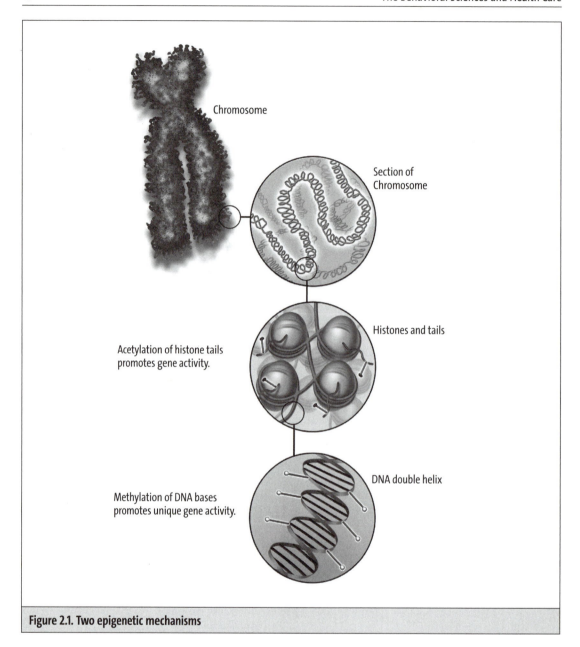

Figure 2.1. Two epigenetic mechanisms

tion between histones and DNA, relaxing the structure of heterochromatin. This relaxed state, called **euchromatin**, promotes gene transcription. Enzymatically-mediated de-acetylation reverses chromatin to a re-condensed state.

Through DNA methylation, a methyl group is added to DNA sequences of the promoter region. This affects gene transcription by "turning off," or silencing, the gene. The patterns of methylation are heritable and influence cell differentiation during development by enabling the cell to produce unique patterns of gene activity creating differ-

ent cell types. Such gene activity determines the chemical organizers that mediate cell migration in embryonic brain cortex formation, and the enzymatic synthesis of neurotransmitters.

Since environmental and epigenetic factors influence the structure and functioning of the nervous system, even minor variations or alterations can have significant behavioral and biological consequences on individual functioning. These may be adaptive or maladaptive, contributing to resilience or vulnerability. Individuals inherit susceptibilities to certain environmental factors that can then precipitate disease or play a role in its etiology. Examples are diseases that result from genetic susceptibilities triggered or amplified by modifiable environmental (e.g., infectious, chemical, physical, nutritional, social, and behavioral) factors.

Research Approaches to Defining Heritable Diseases

Family Risk Studies

Family risk studies determine the rate of occurrence of a condition or trait in **first-degree relatives** (parents, siblings, children, i.e., those who share 50% of their genetic material) and more distant relatives of an affected person (**proband**). These rates are then compared with rates for the general population. A genetic component is suggested if the rates for probands and their first-degree relatives have the highest *concordance rates*, followed by other relatives' rates, followed by lowest concordance rates in the general population.

Twin Studies

The concept of **heritability** is derived from comparisons of concordance rates between monozygotic twins and dizygotic twins. Higher concordance rates between monozygotic twins have been interpreted as evidence of the primacy of genetic factors in determining the condition.

Adoption Studies

Adoption studies are used in determining the risk of having a trait/disorder for adopted children by comparing risk in biological versus adoptive relatives. If the risk is higher among biological relatives, a genetic factor is likely. If the risk is higher among adopted relatives, environmental factors are suspected.

In **cross-fostering studies**, the risk of having the trait/disorder can also be determined by comparing the risk in adoptees whose adoptive parents are normal, but who have a biological parent who has the trait/disorder, with the risk for adoptees whose biological parents are normal, but who are raised by an affected adoptive parent. Such comparisons help identify both genetic and environmental influences.

What information is provided by a pedigree study?

Pedigree Studies

Pedigree (ancestral lineage) **studies** rely on the construction of a family tree, beginning with an individual who manifests the trait or disorder (proband), and then tracing evidence of the trait or disorder in relatives spanning many generations. **Linkage mapping** in pedigree studies involves identifying markers along the human genome (single nucleotide polymorphisms) as points of reference to determine what strands of DNA are linked to a certain trait or disease. These studies seek to associate the trait/disease with another gene (the "marker"), which has a *Mendelian* mode of inheritance and whose chromosomal position (locus) is known. If the trait under study and the marker are neighbors on the same chromosome, they are likely to be inherited together, or linked. Traditional markers include human leukocyte antigens (HLA), blood groups, and color blindness. To be conclusive, linkage studies depend on a large pedigree (a large number of relatives) whose condition is known or who are willing to be studied, usually through blood or tissue testing. Linkage studies are less successful with low heritability traits or small family trees, and are highly influenced by environmental factors.

The study of genetic traits and disease often relies on plant and animal models. For example, Mendel established the laws of monogenic inheritance using pea plants. Other scientists use fruit

---

DNA Markers

DNA markers can be used to identify the chromosomal locations of genes responsible for several disorders, such as:

- some forms of Alzheimer disease that are linked to polymorphisms on genes on chromosomes 14, 19, and 21
- Huntington disorder, which is linked to DNA repeats on a gene on chromosome 4

fly models in linkage and recombination studies for gene mapping. Because of their genetic and physiological similarities to humans, rats, mice, rhesus macaques, and other mammals are used to investigate genetic principles applicable to humans. To develop such models, human disease must be induced by altering the genomes of non-human animals, since they typically do not have the genetic diseases common to people. Although helpful in aiding our understanding of human disease, animal models have been less helpful in developing therapy, since the reciprocity between animal models and humans is not perfect.

With recent advances in sequencing and analytic technology, it has become possible to compare the entire genome sequences of a proband to those of unaffected individuals. Any differences become potential foci for identifying candidate trait-specifying genes. This advanced methodology has enabled researchers to discover complex arrays of genes associated with **multigenic disorders**, such as asthma and diabetes. As the complexities of genetic predisposition in disease and illness are unraveled, the impact of environmental factors upon genetic processes has become an important focus of research.

Genetic-Environment Interactions

How does gene-environment interaction differ from gene-environment correlation?

Genetic characteristics predispose the individual to react to or be influenced by certain environmental conditions. In the early stages of development, some genetic expression is activated only by interactions with specific environmental conditions during specific **critical periods**. **Imprinting**, **bonding**, and language development are examples of time-specific gene-environment-development interactions. As the organism develops, these reciprocal interactions become more complex:

1. *Gene-Environment Interaction*
    Individuals react differently to the same environmental conditions. This differential reactivity may be genetically influenced or modified by the environment and the effects of experience.

2. *Genetic-Environmental Correlation*
    How individuals tend to experience or interact with the environment is correlated with their genetic predisposition.
    a. *Passive* – refers to the correlation between the genotype a child inherits from parents and the environment in which the child is raised, which is also influenced by the parents' heritable characteristics.
    b. *Evocative* – refers to the correlation between an individual's heritable behavior and the environmental response such behavior evokes (e.g., hostile, aggressive behavior elicits hostile, aggressive responses).
    c. *Active* – refers to the correlation between an individual's heritable characteristics and the environmental conditions the individual seeks out (e.g., extroverted individuals seek out highly social situations).

3. *Genetic-Environmental-Developmental Interactions*
    Developmental changes in the nature of learning reflect a temporal transaction process. At birth, in response to a survival imperative, genetic influences are manifested in reflexive responses to environmental stimuli. As development progresses, genetic predisposition requires specific environmental stimuli during critical periods to activate certain survival responses (e.g., imprinting, bonding). With further development, the organism begins to respond to experience, albeit still reflexively (one-trial learning). Increasingly, experience plays a more important role in learning (e.g., classical conditioning, operant conditioning, modeling, social learning) (see Chapter 8, Emotion and Learning).

Temperament

The human newborn has observable genetically determined patterns of personal attributes and behavioral tendencies that are stable and develop into distinctive personality and behavioral characteristics. Differences in these tendencies contribute to differences in infant reaction patterns. **Temperament** is perceived as positive or negative and leads to parental perceptions that a child is "easy," "slow-to-warm-up," or "difficult." Such

Table 2.1. Elements of temperament

1. Activity level
2. Rhythmicity
3. Approach
4. Adaptability
5. Intensity of reaction
6. Threshold of responsiveness
7. Mood
8. Distractibility
9. Attention span/persistence

Diathesis-Stress Interaction and Depression

Individuals who possess a certain familial serotonin transporter genotype and are exposed to high levels of stressful life events are at high risk for depression. They are especially vulnerable to loss (e.g., of a valued person, role, self-esteem), to perceive events negatively, and to persistently engage in maladaptive behavior that further increases their vulnerability to stressors. This combination of diatheses increases the risk of behaviors and cognitions (e.g., reduced initiative, avoidant behavior, learned helplessness, self-criticism, anticipated bad outcomes) that contribute to depression.

perceptions are based on how the child responds to various environmental stimuli, and the ease with which the child achieves contentment (see Table 2.1).

Contemporary concepts of temperament emphasize psycho-physiological reactivity and self-regulation of emotion. Inhibited children have higher sustained heart rates and more widely dilated pupils than uninhibited children. These physiological differences are readily seen when children are stressed, but also may be present when no stress is discernible. Differences in temperament may be modified by environmental experiences that foster or inhibit certain behaviors, e.g., parental intervention (acclimating the inhibited child to peer interactions by inviting a friend to a sleepover) or age-related expectation ("I'm too old to be afraid of the dark"). Physiological responses can be moderated through judicious use of biofeedback or pharmacological interventions.

Diathesis-Stress Interactions

What does diathesis-stress interaction mean?

With increasing recognition of the importance of genetic-environmental interaction, researchers have broadened the concept of predisposition. For example, behavioral genetics focuses on the role that genes and post-conception biological, developmental, social, and environmental events play in determining individual differences in predispositions. These, in turn, determine an individual's **diathesis** or vulnerability to particular stressors and subsequently define temperament, personality, and coping.

Personality

Personality is the distinctive and consistent set of characteristics that predict how an adult individual will respond in various situations (response patterns). It is the developmentally advanced version of temperament but, unlike childhood temperament, which is fairly stable regardless of context, personality reflects a correlation between the predisposition to respond (personality trait) and a specific situation.

Personality traits show a pattern of normative change across the life span. *Social vitality* and *openness* increase during adolescence, but decrease during old age. There is an increase in *social dominance, conscientiousness,* and *emotional stability,* especially in early adulthood. Personality assessment is, in part, a function of the observer's implicit personality theory, i.e., while a personality characteristic may be observable, how it gets labeled is in the eye of the beholder. A personality characteristic is typically labeled a *trait* if it is unique, distinctive, and enduring, in contrast to a *state*, which is a more situation-specific response.

Personality and Illness Vulnerability

How does personality contribute to illness vulnerability?

Resilience

As a result of genetic predisposition, early socialization, and life experiences, some people are more resistant to stress, disease, and illness (**resilience**), while others are more vulnerable. The development of resilient persons has predictable aspects. Resilient children come from households with stable value systems and from communities that provide counsel and emotional support. Resilient children are active, affectionate, and good-natured. They demonstrate the ability to be autonomous, to cope effectively, and to ask for needed help. They bond closely with competent role models attuned to the child's needs, and possess social qualities that elicit positive responses from a range of caregivers.

In elementary school, they become impressive problem solvers and communicators. By adolescence, they have an identified talent, are confident, and are emotionally sensitive. Across gender and ethnic lines and at major life transition points (e.g., adolescence, early adulthood), resilient individuals are able to adapt to and rebound from obstacles, negative experiences, and setbacks.

In adults, resilience, or hardiness, is characterized by commitment, challenge, and control. Commitment refers to the tendency to see the world as meaningful. Challenge involves seeing stresses or new experiences as opportunities to learn. Control refers to confidence in one's ability to influence life events, sometimes referred to as self-efficacy.

Locus of Control

Control has been further studied with regard to the **locus of control**, i.e., whether the individual perceives life events as being under one's personal control (*internal* locus of control) or the control of others (*external* locus of control).

Positive Reappraisal

Resilient persons have the ability to re-evaluate a situation, adapt, and find new solutions and, thus, cope more effectively by having influenced the emotional impact of the situation. This process, referred to as **positive reappraisal**, is linked to the functioning of the limbic system, prefrontal cortex, and the reward system (see Chapter 3, The Nervous System and Chapter 7, Stress, Adaptation, and Stress Disorders).

Type A Response Style

Lack of resilience, being incapable of positive reappraisal, and an external locus of control are psychological risk factors, or vulnerabilities that affect health status. These vulnerabilities are comparable to other health risks, such as hypertension or hypercholesterolemia. For example, there is evidence that **Type A personality** – a **response style** – puts the individual at risk for cardiovascular disease. Type A individuals respond to stress with hard driving, time-urgent, and hostile behaviors. Type B individuals, in contrast, are easygoing, patient, soft-spoken, and more resilient. Type A personality was initially associated with a high risk for angina, silent and overt heart attacks, and coronary death. Today, it refers to a behavioral style composed of cynicism, hostility, anger, and suspiciousness that is more clearly identified as a predictor of heart disease. Not surprisingly, such traits correlate with a lack of resilience, incapacity for positive reappraisal, and external locus of control. A plausible pathophysiological hypothesis suggests that, faced with persistent stressors, Type A individuals experience an excessive and sustained rise of catecholamines, which increases plaque development in the circulatory system.

Personality and Brain Functioning

There is considerable evidence to suggest that the multiple personality traits researchers have identified can be subsumed under five general personality factors (the "Big Five"): extraversion, neuroticism, agreeableness, conscientiousness, and openness/intellect (see Table 2.2). Efforts have been made to associate these personality factors with the functioning of specific brain regions, and significant correlations between trait functioning and the volume of specific brain regions have been reported for four of the five factors (see Chapter 3, The Nervous System).

Table 2.2. The "Big Five" personality traits and associated brain regions		
Trait	**Function**	**Brain Regions**
Extraversion	Reward systems	Nucleus accumbens, amygdala, orbito frontal cortex
Neuroticism	Sensitivity to threat/punishment	Dorsomedial prefrontal cortex, hippocampus, mid cingulate gyrus
Agreeableness	Social information processing	Superior temporal sulcus, posterior cingulate cortex
Conscientiousness	Self regulation	Middle frontal gyrus in left lateral prefrontal cortex
Openness/intellect	Working memory, attention	Parietal cortex

Recommended Readings

Champagne FA. Early adversity and developmental outcomes: Interaction between genetics, epigenetics, and social experience across the life span. *Perspectives on Psychological Science* 2011; 5:564–574.

DeYoung CG, Hirsh JB, Shane MS, Papademetris X, Rajeevan N, Gray JR. Testing predictions from personality. Neuroscience: brain structure and the big five. *Psychological Science* 2010; 21:820–828.

Qui J. Unfinished symphony. *Nature* 2006; 441:143–145.

Roberts WR, Walton KE, Viechtbauer W. Patterns of mean-level change in personality traits across the life course: A meta-analysis of longitudinal studies. *Psychological Bulletin* 2006; 132:1–15.

Rutter M. *Genes and Behavior: Nature-Nurture Interplay Explained.* Oxford, UK: Blackwell; 2006.

Review Questions

1. The genome or genetic composition of a cell or an individual is called a(n)
   A. epigenetic effect.
   B. genotype.
   C. phenotype.
   D. state.
   E. trait.

2. The association between the genotype a child inherits from her parents and the environment provided by the parents for the child's development is an example of
   A. active gene-environment correlation.
   B. diathesis-stress interaction.
   C. epigenetic-environment interaction.
   D. evocative gene-environment correlation.
   E. passive gene-environment correlation.

3. The ability to evaluate new situations, take into account new contextual information, adapt, and derive new solutions to problems refers to which of the following personality concepts?
   A. Hardiness
   B. Locus of control
   C. Positive reappraisal
   D. Resilience
   E. Type A personality

Directions: The items below consist of lettered headings followed by numbered descriptions. For each numbered description choose the one lettered heading to which it is *most* closely associated. Each lettered heading may be used *once, more than once,* or *not at all.*

Match the study design with the numbered description.
   A. Adoption
   B. Family risk
   C. Linkage
   D. Pedigree
   E. Twin

4. Look for trait and disease within families by connecting trait and marker.
5. Use a family tree as a major tool.
6. Investigate how often a disease occurs in family members of a proband compared with the general population.

Key to review questions: p. 407

3 The Nervous System

João V. Nunes, MD, Ian M. Kodish, MD, PhD, and Julia B. Frank, MD

- What is neuronal plasticity?
- What role does synaptic pruning play in the development of executive functions?
- How does experience-dependent plasticity differ from experience-expectant plasticity?
- How do neurotransmitters work?
- How does the limbic system contribute to learning, memory, and emotional responsivity?
- What are mirror neurons and what do they do?

The Nervous System and Environmental Adaptation

In all animals, the nervous system promotes survival by maintaining homeostasis and organizing adaptive responses to diverse, ever-changing environmental challenges. Species differ in the size, shape, and organization of their brain. While basic elements – like the structure of neurons and the processes of neuronal transmission – appear in both simple and complex organisms, the anatomical differences between species are determined by the complexity of demands placed upon a nervous system and reflect the functions that have evolved in order to meet those demands.

> The human brain is complex, comprising many specialized areas and multiple parallel, elaborate networks that contribute to the unique qualities of perception, thought, complex behavior, and social interaction that have allowed our species to adapt to an extraordinary range of existential demands.

Evolutionary-Experiential Interaction

What is neuronal plasticity?

Species also differ in the degree to which **evolution** influenced the development of one brain structure over another. Rats have elaborate olfactory systems that encompass a large portion of their brain, contributing to extraordinary olfactory sensitivity. Humans have an elaborate cortex that encompasses a large portion of the brain and overlies more primitive brain structures. It folds in upon itself, maximizing the number of neurons and neuronal connections possible, enabling humans to engage in highly sophisticated cognitive functions, such as understanding the context of behavioral demands and appreciating the impact of one's behavior on another person.

All mammalian nervous systems have specialized cells and discreet areas for registering touch, vision, odors, tastes, and sounds, but the sensitivity of these functions varies across species. The sensitivity of a particular area often correlates with the local density or "**arborization**" of neurons. In humans, for example, the volume of the brain area devoted to processing sensation from the fingertips or lips is far larger than that from the lower back.

> Nervous system structures are shaped by experience, as well as evolving genetic programs, as they continually adapt to meet environmental demands. This process, termed **neuronal plasticity**, is continuous throughout the life span, although more robust in certain species and during certain developmental periods than others.

Similarly, the elaborate neuronal arborization, extending into multiple columnar circuits within the human prefrontal cortex, permits greater integrative functioning than the simpler networks that encode basic sensory information.

In early (embryonic and early post-natal) development, neurons have limited synaptic connections and exhibit spontaneous activity. In response to experience, neurons begin to form more specialized connections (**synapses**) with other neurons. Neurons not stimulated atrophy or die, while others proliferate in response to programmed neurotropic expression patterns. In rats, for example, if one eye is closed at birth, the brain regions that process visual information from that eye atrophy, while those that process visual information from the other eye proliferate. Synaptic density also increases in response to the complexity of the demands it has evolved to meet. For example, rats exercising on a treadmill show increased density of cortical blood vessels, but those exposed to more complex acrobatic training develop increased synaptic connectivity in motor areas.

Evolutionary Refinement

Over time, evolution has equipped the nervous system to more effectively respond to environmental demands, building refinement and complexity on adaptive successes achieved over broad time periods. Humans and sea slugs share similar reflex arcs. The neuronal interpretation of a signal (in humans, tapping on the patellar tendon) rapidly results in a behavioral effect (the extension of the leg). Reflexes are simple (peripheral, without synapsing in the brain) and typically unconscious. Thus, much of the nervous system's responsiveness in humans

occurs outside the individual's awareness, e.g., breathing more rapidly in higher altitudes.

The human brain processes, integrates, and interprets information relayed by the five common senses, but has other conscious and unconscious means of obtaining information as well. For instance, the brain is able to perceive balance, orientation, temperature, hunger, pain, etc., and impairments in these areas can have profound effects on a person's ability to function.

The brain structures and functions required to process complex information have become increasingly specialized through evolution. When someone looks at something, the retinas perceive the object and, through the optic nerve, convey signals to thalamic centers, which send the signals to various parts of the brain specialized to respond to the information. While the bulk of the information goes to occipital regions that code information (e.g., shape and color) from each eye, some information is directed to emotionally-attuned regions of the brain, which rapidly appraise the salient features of an object (threat? harmless? novel?).

The information that generates visual details in the occipital regions also undergoes processing in complex integrative parallel networks, creating various streams of additional information, e.g., form, depth, and motion. The streams converge to form an integrated perception of a coherent object. Eventually, meaning and context are assigned to the information, which can now guide behavioral responses. This use of **parallel processing** and **regional specialization** within the brain enables humans to adapt to the environment in increasingly complex and detailed ways.

Developmental Fine Tuning

> While human brains have regions that resemble the brains of lower animals, human neuronal networks became more specialized and elaborate to suit human needs. The autonomic nervous system, which controls visceral functions, is often viewed as a "lower" aspect of the nervous system, regulated by "primitive" brain regions. Yet the autonomic nervous system also has evolved to respond to the demands of the environment, exhibiting neuronal arrangements similar to those in higher cortical regions.

> What role does synaptic pruning play in the development of executive functions?

With development there is "fine tuning" of neuronal networks on many levels. The volume of the human brain at age three years is close to that of an adult, yet a three year old is not as capable of responding to environmental cues as an adult. As development unfolds, synaptic connections undergo a cycle of increased density through vast overproduction, followed by a reduction in syn-

> Following extensive pruning in adolescence, overall synaptic density diminishes gradually throughout adulthood. Conversely, myelin (the insulating lipid that comprises white matter and supports neuronal function) increases, resulting in gradually less dense but increasingly efficient neuronal networks.

aptic connections. The process, called **synaptic pruning**, results in the formation of more stable and functional networks. Pruning is most pronounced in prefrontal regions during adolescence. This reorganization results in the development of refined networks that facilitate the acquisition of complex behaviors and abstract thinking, collectively named **executive functions**. This permits adolescents to develop strategies to handle tasks requiring an appreciation of goals and contexts, and to shift behaviors in response to changing demands and circumstances. Primary sensory regions undergo "developmental tuning" earlier than more integrative regions. Network refinements build on one another over the normal course of development as networks become more elaborate in response to environmental stimuli.

Experiential-Developmental Interaction and Brain Development

> How does experience-dependent plasticity differ from experience-expectant plasticity?

Brain networks vary in their sensitivity and readiness to respond to stimulus cues over the lifespan. This pattern of variability in the readiness to respond reflects developmental changes in experiential learning. There are two recognized processes by which brain network development can be influenced by experience: unanticipated experiences that are not affected by developmental sensitivity (experience-*dependent* plasticity), and common, expected experiences that have evolutionarily driven a programmed developmental sensitivity timed to that specific experience (experience-*expectant* plasticity).

In **experience-dependent plasticity**, behavior is altered as a result of learning from experience

and occurs throughout the lifespan. **Experience-expectant plasticity**, however, involves specific experiences occurring during time-limited sensitive periods of development (**critical periods**). For example, the coordinated use of two eyes leads to the experience of a single three-dimensional image rather than the two-dimensional images created by light in each eye. This effect depends on visual experiences during the second half of the first year of life, occurring during a critical period when the neural system is ready to respond to these inputs. Experience-expectant plasticity works to fine-tune aspects of development that cannot proceed to optimum outcomes as a result of environmental or genetic factors working alone.

Neuronal Structures and Functions

Neurons are the defining cellular units of the central and peripheral nervous systems. They gather and transmit information from the environment and other neurons via *synapses* to specific neural networks which, in turn, process, appraise, plan, and elicit appropriate responses for survival.

Glial cells, derived from neuronal progenitor cells, are uniquely specialized to physically and chemically support neuronal functioning. They comprise *myelin sheaths* that protect the quality and strength of neuronal signals, participate in synaptic transmission by inactivating certain neurotransmitters and maintaining chemical homeostasis, elaborate to form scar tissue after CNS injury, line the fluid-filled brain ventricles, and function as immune defenses by removing cellular debris and monitoring the synaptic milieu to defend against infection.

Neuronal Development

Genes and experience-dependent plasticity are the primary guides to neuronal development and the modification of brain functioning throughout life. Neuronal development is guided by morphogenic processes such as differential cell proliferation; migration; cell growth (*neurogenesis*); neural connectivity balanced between synaptogenesis, dendritic branching and pruning; myelination; and programmed cell death (*apoptosis*).

Brain structures and circuitry are grossly established by birth, guided by physical cell-to-cell communication and chemical signals. This is followed by maturation, at first furious, then slower, then picking up speed at certain points during the life cycle. Throughout this developmental process, dendritic branching and pruning and refinement of synaptic connections and neurotransmitter systems lead to the establishment and maturation of increasingly interconnected and parallel neuronal networks.

Action Potentials and Neurotransmission

The impetus for the propagation of information in the nervous system is an electrical current that travels along the neuronal membrane. The semi-permeable nature of this membrane permits and sustains different concentrations of positively and negatively charged ions on the cytosol side of the membrane compared to the extracellular fluid. The net electrical charge of the cytosol side is negatively polarized, relative to that of the extracellular fluid, with a *resultant resting potential* of -65 millivolts.

Activation of **membrane ion channels**, such as (a) *ligand-gated channels*, responsive to chemical signals; (b) *voltage-gated channels*, responsive to changes in the membrane potential; and (c) *channels sensitive to heat or mechanical distortion of the membrane* cause changes to the membrane potential. Excitation elicits the opening of membrane sodium ion (Na^+) channels to allow an influx of Na^+ into the cell, turning the cytosol side of the membrane progressively less negative. If this depolarization proceeds beyond a threshold, an **action potential** is generated, i.e., an "all-or-nothing" electrical event that propagates along the neuronal membrane of the axon toward the synaptic junction.

Neurotransmission

How do neurotransmitters work?

In the axon terminal, action potentials promote the release of **neurotransmitters** from synaptic vesi-

cles into the synaptic cleft and onto postsynaptic receptors, permitting neurons and their projections to transmit to networks in distant brain regions, interconnected via multiple circuits. These circuits can be examined anatomically (histology and imaging), chemically (radioactive labeling), functionally (blood flow changes during cognitive tasks), and electrically (electroenecephalography) to promote understanding of specific brain functions and malfunctions.

Neurotransmitters bind to specific receptors in the postsynaptic cell membrane, which triggers opening or closing of ion channels in the postsynaptic neuronal membrane, and consequent depolarization (excitation) or hyperpolarization (inhibition) of postsynaptic cells. The complexity of neuronal activity owes in part to mechanisms that control electrical activation of cellular regions.

Receptors can be classified into transmitter-gated ion channels (ionotopic) and G-protein-coupled (metabotropic) receptors. *Ionotopic receptors* have an ion channel core that responds directly to neurotransmitter action, opening or closing ion channels, producing the fastest and briefest responses. *Metabotropic receptors* are indirectly connected to ion channel activity by activating intracellular mechanisms such as *second messenger* enzymatic cascades. Prominent second messengers include cyclic nucleotides, Ca^{++}, and inositol triphosphate (IP_3). Activation of **second messenger systems** typically leads to *phosphorylation of ion channels*, changing their functional state to induce slower but longer-lasting postsynaptic responses.

Neurotransmitter activity is terminated through (1) **diffusion** away from the synaptic cleft; (2) **enzymatic degradation**; and (3) **reuptake** (active transport) into the presynaptic terminal. After reuptake, neurotransmitters may be reloaded into synaptic vesicles for future use or degraded enzymatically. Both neuronal and glial cell membranes possess active transport mechanisms that assist in neurotransmitter removal from the synaptic cleft.

The major neurotransmitters in the brain include glutamate, gamma-amino-butyric acid (GABA), acetylcholine (ACh), norepinephrine (NE), dopamine (DA), serotonin (5-HT), and histamine. Molecules such as neuropeptides and hormones play modulatory roles that modify neurotransmission over longer time periods.

For specific examples relating neurotransmitter activity to clinical syndromes, see Section X on Psychopathology.

Brain Structures and Functions

The **central nervous system** (CNS) is comprised of the brain and spinal cord. The brain consists of three major parts, **hindbrain**, **midbrain** and **forebrain** (cerebrum), each with anatomical and functional subdivisions. The diencephalon, the hindbrain includes the cerebellum. The midbrain and hindbrain constitute the brainstem. The forebrain consists of the two cerebral hemispheres. (To visualize these and other neuronal structures, see www.radnet.ucla.edu/sections/DINR/index.htm).

Brainstem

The **brainstem** integrates and regulates vital functions, such as respiration, cardiovascular activity, and consciousness. Sensory information from the spinal cord ascends through brainstem tracts to specific cerebral and cerebellar sites. After incoming information is processed, a motor response is elicited via the brainstem back to the spinal cord, then to motor systems for bodily action.

Forebrain

The **diencephalon** includes the thalamus and hypothalamus. The **thalamus** is the gateway to the cerebral cortex for all sensory information except olfaction, which synapses directly into the cerebrum (entorhinal cortex) and the amygdala. Thalamic nuclei reciprocally connect with most of the cerebral cortex through thalamic radiations, fiber bundles that constitute a large portion of the **internal capsule**. The thalamus relays information from the basal ganglia and cerebellum to the cerebral cortex which then formulates plans for the execution of smooth and coordinated motor responses. The thalamus also plays a role in regulating emotional expression, memory, and cognition by relaying information to the limbic system and integrative cortical regions. These reciprocal thalamocortical radiations are thought to be involved in the abnormalities of emotion pro-

In response to stress, the hypothalamus releases corticotropin-releasing hormone (CRH), which stimulates the anterior pituitary to release adrenocorticotropic hormone (ACTH) into the bloodstream, where it affects adrenal cortices to release cortisol (glucocorticoid), the stress hormone. Cortisol, in turn, triggers epinephrine and norepinephrine release from the adrenal medulla, and then feeds back to the HPA axis to down-regulate further secretions. This neuroendocrine feedback loop is common to all mammals and most vertebrates, and there is evidence that dysregulation contributes to clinical impairments in mood and anxiety disorders.

cessing and regulation found in disorders such as schizophrenia.

The **hypothalamus** is central to the functioning of the **autonomic nervous system**. Anterior and medial hypothalamic areas control *parasympathetic* activity while the lateral and posterior hypothalamic areas control *sympathetic* activity. The hypothalamus integrates input for appropriate autonomic and somatic responses that maintain homeostatic balance. It mediates neuroendocrine-induced physiological changes related to feeding, drinking, pleasure, displeasure, aversion, emotional functioning, and behavioral inhibition (see Chapter 5, Nutrition, Metabolism, and Feeding Disorders).

Anatomically, hypothalamic nuclei project neuroendocrine fibers to the anterior pituitary gland to regulate systemic stress responses in the adrenal cortex. This circuit is termed the **hypothalamic-pituitary-adrenal axis** (HPA) or the hypothalamic-pituitary-endocrine axis, and utilizes the neuroendocrine system to up- or down-regulate other hormonal responses in a coordinated effort to respond to stress appropriately.

The Limbic System

How does the limbic system contribute to learning, memory, and emotional responsivity?

The **limbic system** consists of structures that initiate affective evaluative responses to incoming information, thereby contributing to learning, memory, and emotional responses to experience. The components of the limbic circuits have been redefined over time, but generally include pathways between the amygdala, the septal nucleus, and the hippocampus, with anterior thalamic nuclei, cingulate gyrus, parahippocampal gyrus, and several regions of prefrontal cortex. Emotional responsivity is coordinated in parallel by the limbic system and neocortical regions, and modulated via reciprocal connections to and from subcortical regions.

The **amygdala** receives information from every sensory modality. Information is rapidly integrated via interconnections within the amygdala, and then passed on to the hypothalamus and brainstem centers, which regulate autonomic function. The amygdala also connects with areas associated with the interpretation of the meaning of stimuli (frontal and cingulate cortices), and with episodic memory (hippocampus). Thus, the amygdala shapes the interpretation of a sensory stimulus drawing on cortical processes and memories to initiate an adaptive response and emotional expression.

The **hippocampus** is located in the lower medial wall of the temporal lobe, behind the amygdala, and interacts with the hypothalamus, the amygdala, and the neocortex to promote learning and memory.

> Hippocampal input provides temporal and spatial context to incoming information and, together with the amygdala, refines the interpretation of sensory stimuli. It is thought to contribute images, words, and ideas to dreaming, and is generally considered a gatekeeper for consolidation of working memory.

The **septal nucleus**, located anterior to the third ventricle near the hypothalamus, generally inhibits extreme arousal in order to preserve quiescence and readiness for action. Connections with the hippocampus and hypothalamus modulate the autonomic and neuroendocrine reactivity of the amygdala and hypothalamus, primarily through inhibition.

Cerebro-spinal-cerebellar-peripheral connections

Ascending and descending tracts relay information between the cerebrum, peripheral nervous system, and other bodily systems via the brainstem and the spinal cord. The dorsal column-medial lemniscal pathway and the anterior-lateral pathway are long ascending tracts that start from the spinal cord and carry sensory information originating in the body. The **dorsal column-medial lemniscal pathway** transmits tactile and vibratory senses, whereas the **anterior-lateral pathway** conveys pain and temperature.

At the brainstem, pathways for hearing, taste, and general sensory modalities from the face, merge with the spinal sensory pathways to form the **lemniscal system**. The lemniscal system carries information to the cerebral cortex via the thalamus for the perception of pain, temperature, touch, taste, hearing, discriminative touch, and the appreciation of form, weight, and texture. The conscious experience of these sensations is mediated by the **reticular system**, which originates in the spinal cord, courses through the brain stem, hypothalamus, and thalamus, and terminates in the frontal lobes. The reticular system also organizes patterns of visceromotor activity (e.g., gastric motility and respiratory and cardiovascular activities), and is essential for consciousness, arousal, sleep, and attention.

Incoming sensory information that demands action (e.g., muscle activity) triggers commands from the motor cortex. These travel through the corticospinal tract to reach the cranial nerve nuclei, pons, and medulla, and continue on to comprise the lateral and ventromedial pathways (descending tracts within the spinal cord that synapse to form peripheral connections to the skeletal muscles). The lateral pathways control voluntary movement of the distal musculatures while the ventromedial pathways control the trunk musculature for posture and locomotion.

The **cerebellum** receives information from the cerebral cortex, spinal cord, and vestibular system. It transforms the information into cerebellum-modulated motor commands and directs them back to the motor cortex and brainstem motor centers. The cerebellum-modulated motor commands are then sent to the lower motor neurons, which turn them into precise, smooth, and coordinated motor activity.

The Cerebral Hemispheres

Each **cerebral hemisphere** contains basal ganglia and cerebral cortex. The **cerebral cortex** on either side is divided into four lobes: frontal, parietal, temporal, and occipital. Each lobe has a primary sensory or motor region surrounded by larger association cortices. Though serving some specific functions, cortical regions are highly interconnected anatomically and functionally by association and commissure fibers, within and between hemispheres. The **corpus callosum** is a large midline structure underlying the cortex, comprised of white matter fibers, which transmits information between cortical hemispheres. The **limbic lobe**, a cortical strip encircling the corpus callosum and part of the medial surface of the temporal lobe, is occasionally considered the fifth lobe as its anatomical organization resembles other cortical regions.

The **basal ganglia** include four nuclei deeply situated within each cerebral hemisphere: *caudate*, *putamen*, *globus pallidus*, and *subthalamic nucleus*, and one midbrain structure, the *substantia nigra*. The basal ganglia connect to the cerebral cortex via the thalamus and also receive direct cortical projections. The structures of the basal ganglia are organized in three functional loops. The **motor loop**, which facilitates the initiation of willed movement, is formed as the putamen receives projections from the sensorimotor cortex and sends projections to the motor and premotor cortices. The **executive loop**, which facilitates cognitive functions, involves the caudate, which receives projections from cortical association areas and sends projections to the prefrontal cortex. The **limbic loop**, which regulates emotional behaviors, involves reciprocal projections between the limbic lobe and the nucleus accumbens, located where the head of the caudate meets the putamen.

Frontal Lobe

The **frontal lobe** makes up about half the area and volume of the cerebral cortex and has three functional regions: (1) the primary motor cortex, (2) the premotor cortex, and (3) the prefrontal cortex.

The **primary motor cortex** is located in the precentral gyrus. Its neuronal projections comprise about 40% of the volume of the corticospinal tract and make monosynaptic and polysynaptic connections with motor neurons in the spinal cord. The monosynaptic connections primarily move individual fingers during skillful tasks while the polysynaptic connections move the limbs during complex behaviors, like walking and reaching for objects.

The **premotor cortex**, which lies anterior to the primary motor cortex and contributes about 30% to the volume of the corticospinal tract, plans and selects movements.

The **prefrontal cortex** comprises the rest of the frontal cortex, and has three main regions: (1) the dorsal prefrontal association area, (2) the ventral orbito-frontal cortex, and (3) the medial prefrontal cortex.

The **dorsal prefrontal association area** integrates motor information with multimodal sensory information coming from the parietal and temporal lobes. After processing, the information contributes to cognitive judgments and more complex motor planning. Connections to the premotor and motor cortices allow for subsequent implementation via other bodily systems, e.g., the voluntary muscles. **Broca's speech area** and the **frontal eye field** exemplify this sensory-motor integration. Broca's speech area receives and integrates information from sensorimotor and visual cortices, and from **Wernike's area** (verbal understanding) before initiating the motor responses that produce speech. Through its connections with cortical and brainstem structures, the frontal eye field integrates information to initiate saccades, moving the eyes toward objects of interest, and coordinating eye-head movements.

The **ventromedial prefrontal cortex** (VMPFC) plays a role in emotional appraisal during decision making, preference judgment, and risk taking to influence reward responses, including those related to social appraisal, and is thought to be involved in the development of empathy. The **orbito-frontal cortex**, which is also associated with social functions, is often included as part of the VMPFC since the areas work in unison. They have direct connections with the limbic system, and studies of patients with *post traumatic stress disorder* (PTSD) indicate that these are the important connections that link events with their emo-

According to the somatic marker hypothesis, the VMPFC enables individuals to use emotional reactions (somatic markers) to decide between positive or negative alternatives in social situations, and that damage or dysfunction of the VMPFC impairs this ability, resulting in maladaptive social behavior.

tional associations. The influence of the VMPFC may be unconscious, mediated by the brainstem and ventral striatum, or conscious, through cortical involvement.

What are mirror neurons and what do they do?

Some neurons have been found to fire not only when a person performs an action, but also when that person observes another person performing a similar action. These neurons "mirror" the actions of another person's neurons as though they were engaged in the action being observed. This suggests that **mirror neurons** are important for social interactions (e.g., affiliation, imitation, empathy, social cognition, and language acquisition) and may play a role in the etiology of autism. Mirror neurons have been found in the premotor cortex, supplementary motor area, primary somatosensory cortex, and inferior parietal cortex. In the human brain, these areas overlap with Broca's area, highlighting the important social function of language.

Parietal Lobe

The **parietal lobe** processes and integrates somatosensory and visuospatial information for localizing the body and surrounding objects, and for learning tasks requiring coordination of the body in space. The parietal lobe has three functional regions: (1) the primary somatosensory cortex, (2) the somatosensory unimodal association area, and (3) the multimodal sensory association area.

The **primary somatosensory cortex** (PSC) is located in the postcentral gyrus and receives and interprets somesthetic information from the contralateral part of the body.

The **somatosensory unimodal association area** (SUAA), located immediately posterior to the PSC, further processes somesthetic information to facilitate improved recognition, e.g., identify an object based solely on tactile information (size, shape, texture, and weight).

The **multimodal sensory association area** (MSAA) receives and integrates somesthetic, visual, auditory, and movement-related information from several association cortices. It enables a person to discern (a) the three-dimensional position of objects in space; (b) body image and the

space in which the body moves; (c) direction of movement; and (d) location of sound. The *left inferior parietal lobule* is thought to integrate sensorimotor information for performance of skilled, temporally sequential motor acts, perception and production of written language, and arithmetic calculations.

Occipital Lobe

The **occipital lobe** has two functional regions: (1) the *primary visual cortex*, located along the calcarine fissure, processes visual information relayed by the thalamus, and (2) the *visual unimodal association area* further processes the visual information coming from the primary visual cortex. These regions extend beyond the anatomical boundaries of the occipital lobe to occupy the inferior-lateral surfaces of the occipital and temporal lobes, and contribute to parallel processing of visual information, which later converges into an integrated perception.

Temporal Lobe

The **temporal lobe** processes auditory, gustatory, visceral, and olfactory stimuli, while the inferior temporal cortex allows facial recognition. The temporal lobe has several functional regions: (1) the primary auditory cortex, (2) the auditory unimodal association cortex, (3) the visual unimodal association cortex, (4) the multimodal sensory association area, and several limbic system structures, such as (5) the limbic association area, (6) the amygdala, and (7) the hippocampus.

Hemispheric Dominance

At birth, the left and right cerebral hemispheres are functionally disconnected because the **corpus callosum** and anterior and posterior **commissures** are not yet myelinated. Therefore, until age 5, when myelination becomes complete, each brain hemisphere primarily develops independently. **Hemispheric dominance** is defined in terms of the *laterality of functions* or functional specialization of one hemisphere over the other. The left hemisphere is dominant for language in up to 99% of right-handed people, and in up to 70% of left-handed

> Lateralization, though more pronounced in the neo-cortex, is also observed in limbic structures. The right amygdala-hippocampus complex processes nonverbal, emotional memory, while the left amygdala-hippocampus complex processes verbal memory.

people. The right hemisphere is dominant for spatial location and orientation, but not to the same degree the left hemisphere is dominant for language.

Left hemisphere functions include verbal comprehension and differentiation, identification, and linguistic labeling of visual, auditory, and somesthetic information. *Right hemisphere functions* include visual-spatial perception, facial recognition, body image, voice tone, melody and rhythm perception, and various aspects of emotionality.

Recommended Readings

Andreasen N, Black DW. *Introductory Textbook of Psychiatry*, 4th ed. Arlington, VA: American Psychiatric Publishing; 2006.

Bavelier D, Levi DM, Li RW, Dan Y, Hensch TK. Removing brakes on adult brain plasticity: From molecular to behavioral interventions. *Journal of Neuroscience* 2010; 30:14964–14971.

Eroglu C, Barres BA. Regulation of synaptic connectivity by glia. *Nature* 2010; 468:223–231.

Gogtay N, Thompson PM. Mapping gray matter development: Implications for typical development and vulnerability to psychopathology. *Brain and Cognition* 2010; 72:6–15.

Holtmaat A, Svoboda K. Experience-dependent structural synaptic plasticity in the mammalian brain. *Nature Reviews Neuroscience* 2009; 10:647–658.

Online Resource

Bank W, Bergrall U, Byrd S, et al (2010). Salamon's Neuroanatomy and Neurovascular Web Atlas Resource. Available at www.radnet.ucla.edu/sections/DNR/index.htm

Review Questions

1. A 7-year-old boy is diagnosed with ADHD based on his restlessness, difficulty focusing attention, and tendency to blurt out things without thinking. Failure to regulate impulsive behavior suggests dysfunction at which of the following areas of the brain as a site affected by his disorder?
   A. Brainstem
   B. Hypothalamus
   C. Limbic system
   D. Occipital lobe
   E. Prefrontal cortex

2. Strategies for developing drugs that would increase and stabilize the activity of a particular neurotransmitter in the synapses of the brain might usefully include
   A. adding compounds that block ligand-gated receptors.
   B. altering cell DNA to increase production of neurotransmitters.
   C. blocking enzymes that degrade the transmitters after they are released.
   D. changing the pH of cerebrospinal fluid to inhibit diffusion.
   E. enhancing reuptake into the releasing neuron.

3. Closing one eye of a rat pup for three weeks after birth, then opening it, will result in an adult rat with
   A. exaggerated stress responses.
   B. neural atrophy in the area receiving input from the closed eye.
   C. no perception of the side of the body of the closed eye.
   D. normal vision.
   E. reduced total brain volume.

4. During adolescence, sex steroids change the architecture of the brain leading to acceleration in cell death and increase in the density of the cell connections that remain. This process results in
   A. increased ability to acquire and process language.
   B. increased brain size and head circumference.
   C. increased experience-expected learning.
   D. more appreciation of the context of perceived information.
   E. new critical periods for skill acquisition.

Key to review questions: p. 407

4 Brain Networks in Health and Illness

Michael I. Posner, PhD, and Mary K. Rothbart, PhD

- What is a functional brain network?
- What is the significance of connectivity in defining a functional brain network?
- How is brain network efficiency measured?
- How do genes influence brain network development?
- How do brain networks contribute to health and illness?

Functional Brain Networks

The ability to image the human brain at rest and during task performance has transformed our understanding of normal and atypical brain function. When cells in a particular region of the brain become more active, blood flow to the region increases. Changes in blood flow can be examined using radionuclides that emit particles that can be sensed by detectors outside of the head. Similarly, changes in hemoglobin can be examined using *functional magnetic resonance imaging* (fMRI). These methods provide: (1) structural images of the brain; (2) maps of brain activity; and (3) measures of connectivity between brain areas.

In the late 1980s, *positron emission tomography* (PET) was used to examine blood flow in subjects as they heard or read individual words. A major development in the 1990s was the use of fMRI to measure localized changes in blood oxygen as a means of mapping brain activity noninvasively. fMRI was not only able to show well-defined localized activity, but because it did not rely on radioactivity, a given person could safely be scanned repeatedly. This made it possible to present different types of trials in a random order and then average the outcomes of the trials, preventing participants from developing special strategies for each trial type.

What is a functional brain network?

In some areas of cognition, such as attention, memory, and language, extensive work in the 1970s and 1980s in cognitive science and artificial intelligence led to the development of computerized laboratory tasks and experimental methods that could be associated with specific mental operations. These methods often involved subtracting reaction times found in simpler conditions from those in more complex conditions to isolate the mental operations added by the more complex tasks. Using these methods, it was possible to delineate the **cognitive functions** involved in the task and, via the scanner, to map the areas of the brain found to be active during the performance of the task. For example, the reading of individual words could be divided into visual, phonological, and semantic operations, which could be isolated by tasks like visual matching, reading aloud, and classifying word meanings. Use of these tasks indicated that one posterior brain area seems to be involved in grouping the letters of a word into a single unit (left fusiform gyrus), while another area is involved in assigning a sound for the word (left temporal parietal cortex). These two areas are connected to brain areas involved in temporary storage (left ventral frontal), word meaning (Wernicke's area), and attention (anterior cingulate). Thus, what seems like a simple act of reading a word is actually a complex set of functions made possible by a network of widely separated brain areas working together. Imaging with fMRI has been applied extensively to many areas of cognition and emotion such as arithmetic, autobiographical memory, fear, object perception, self reference, and spatial navigation. In all of these studies, a set of widely scattered but orchestrated neural areas were activated by a specific task. These brain areas are called **functional brain networks** and, as research progresses, the component mental operations performed by each individual area are gradually being identified.

> Both behavioral and imaging methods show that it is possible to measure not only the connectivity, but also the efficiency of brain networks involved in carrying out high level tasks. These measurements show that connectivity and efficiency differ among normal individuals, change with experience and development, and can be influenced by training.

Network Connectivity and Efficiency

> What is the significance of connectivity in defining a functional brain network?

Correlations in the fMRI signal between remote neural areas have been used to study their **connectivity** within a specific functional brain network. These correlations indicate which areas are working together during the performance of a functional task. Connectivity can also be determined by the use of *diffusion tensor imaging* (DTI), a non-invasive method that shows the location, orientation, and directionality of white matter connections between the brain areas of a functional network by measuring the diffusion of water molecules. These white matter bundles of axons connect large groups of neurons over long distances via highly connected focal brain areas. This extensive connectivity makes communication possible between anatomically separate areas both within and between functional brain networks, even when the brain is at rest (i.e., not engaged in any specific cognitive activity.) It has been suggested that this resting connectivity facilitates the passive development of new associations, insights, intuitions, and adaptations even though the brain is not otherwise involved in any goal-oriented tasks. For example, there is evidence that when solving the simple multiplication problem 4 x 3 = 12, the response "7" is activated, indicating a linkage between addition and multiplication functions involving the numbers 3 and 4.

phy (EEG) scalp electrodes or magnetic detectors (MEG) can be used to follow the flow of information over time between brain areas. The speed of information processing along a pathway provides a measure of the **network efficiency** of the connection. Measuring the speed of performing laboratory tasks provides a behavioral method for measuring the *efficiency* of brain networks. For example, an important brain network is involved in monitoring and resolving conflict induced by presenting stimuli that lead to conflicting responses. In the laboratory, a participant is instructed to respond to a central arrow by pressing one key when it points to the right and another key when it points to the left. Conflict is induced by presenting flanking arrows that point in the same or opposite direction to the central arrow. Reaction times for responding when the flanking arrows point in the same direction (congruent condition) are subtracted from reaction times when the flanking arrows point in the opposite direction (conflict condition). The difference in reaction times provides a measure of the *efficiency* of a high level attention network involved in monitoring conflict among response tendencies. Brain images taken during the performance of this conflict task show increased activity in the dorsal anterior cingulate. In addition, the *efficiency* of transmission along white matter pathways leading from the cingulate to frontal and parietal areas is correlated with the speed of resolving the conflict, further indicating that these three areas are important components of an attention network involved in dealing with conflict among response tendencies.

> How is brain network efficiency measured?

Since vascular changes measured by fMRI are slow, recordings from electroencephalogra-

> How do genes influence brain network development?

Genetic-Environmental Interaction in Network Development

The degree of **genetic influence** in the development of brain networks is reflected in the differences between identical twins, who share the same genes, and fraternal twins, whose genes are only as similar as those of siblings. The difference between the two twin types provides a rough index of how much of the differences between individuals is due to genetic causes (heritability). Results from twin studies indicate that the efficiency of brain networks, as measured by processing speed, is about 50% heritable.

There are no specific genes that determine functional brain networks. Rather, an array of genes code for different proteins that provide the instructions for neuronal development. These instructions specify the various neuro-modulators that contribute to the connectivity and efficiency of brain networks. Although, in general, all humans have the same genes, many of the genes are *polymorphic*, that is, they may be expressed in different forms. Among genes having a great deal of variability are those associated with *dopamine d4 receptor (DRD4), dopamine transporter (DAT1), monoamine oxidase a (MAOA), catechol-o-methyl transferase (COMT)*, and *serotonin neurotransmitter* systems. This variability helps to explain individual differences in behavior. For example, the DRD4 gene has a 48-base pair sequence that may be repeated a different number of times, and these differences change the sensitivity of the receptor to dopamine. One version of this gene (in which the 48 base pairs are repeated seven times) has been associated with attention deficit/hyperactivity disorder, and with the tendency to take risks among individuals in the normal population.

There is evidence that the seven repeat allele is increasing in human evolution. A possible explanation is suggested by studies of child behavior in which children with the seven repeat allele are found to be more susceptible to social and cultural influences provided by, for example, caregivers and peers. This greater susceptibility to social and environmental influence could increase reproductive success and thus influence natural selection. This explanation would be consistent with the view that individual differences in the efficiency

Methylation/demethylation and other similar transcription factors (e.g., acetylation) can be rapidly altered by environmental stimuli, and are utilized by the hippocampus in the consolidation of memory, turning "off" memory suppressor genes, and turning "on" memory promoter genes.

of brain networks are dependent upon *genetic* variation, *epigenetic* or environmental influences, and *development*. One particular epigenetic mechanism that is receiving considerable attention is *DNA methylation*. Gene expression can be changed when a methyl chemical group attaches to the promoter region of the cell and essentially silences the gene.

In addition to network connections that are activated during the performance of tasks (e.g., attention, alerting, object perception), there are network connections that are in evidence even when the person is at rest. For example, a **default mode network** (DMN) links the posterior cingulate cortex with the medial prefrontal, medial temporal, and bilateral inferior parietal regions. Two large **attention networks** have also been shown to be connected and active at rest: a set of fronto-parietal brain areas related to orienting to sensory stimuli regardless of modality; and a cingulo-opercular network related to the resolution of conflict. The fronto-parietal network in adults is involved in short-term control operations common when orienting to sensory signals. The cingulo-parietal network is involved in longer, more strategic control, which is an important property of executive system functions like conflict resolution.

Because the analysis of resting connectivity does not require performance of a task, it can be readily studied in infancy. During the first year of life, the anterior cingulate shows little or no connectivity to other areas, but after the first year, infants begin the slow process of developing the long range connectivity typical of adults. The functional organization of the brain also becomes increasingly differentiated. Thus, children at age 9 show evidence of many shorter local connections, while adults have longer network connections. In addition, adults have separate networks related to orienting and executive attention, but these networks are less well defined in children.

New Learning and Network Development

Since fMRI is noninvasive, it is possible to use multiple scans to examine the network changes that occur with learning and development. The connectivity of brain networks can be enhanced by practicing the tasks with which they are associated. In addition, goal-directed learning experiences, or training, contribute to a progressive change from the primarily local network connections dominant in children to the longer network connections prominent in adults. These changes reflect how learning from adaptive life experiences interacts with maturation and genetic predisposition (**genetic-environmental-developmental interaction**) to enhance development of brain network organization, connectivity, and efficiency.

Two types of **training** influence brain network functioning. The first type of training involves *task generalization*, i.e., practice on a task specific to a particular network that subsequently generalizes to other tasks using that network. For example, training in working memory has been shown to affect not only the many tasks that involve working memory but also general intelligence, and, in addition, has been shown to improve functions that underlie the symptoms of attention deficit disorder. The second type of training involves *network generalization*, i.e., training in one network that subsequently influences other networks, even though those networks are not involved in the same task or function. For example, aerobic exercise has been shown to affect aspects of an individual's physical condition, such as respiration and muscle tone, as well as cognitive functions related to memory and attention. Cognitive training with a form of *mindfulness meditation* also has been shown to improve attention and mood, reduce stress, and enhance immune function.

Network Disorder and Health

How do brain networks contribute to health and illness?

There is evidence that impaired brain network activity contributes to several specific disorders, such as *multiple sclerosis* and *callosal agenesis*, due to degradation of the myelination of axonal tracts and decreased structural integrity of the fibers at the corpus callosum. Disruption of brain organization is also believed to be involved in conditions like *autism spectrum disorders* and *attention-deficit/hyperactivity disorder*. Decreased levels of cognitive performance in *aging* also have been related to reduced resting state activity, decreased functional connectivity, degeneration of the microstructural organization of white matter tracts, and altered microstructural organization of the cingulum tract.

Imaging studies have provided a perspective on brain network functioning associated with other disorders. Patients with *schizophrenia* have been found to have alterations in both resting state activity and organization of white matter tracts. A brain network that includes cortical and subcortical areas has been found to have reduced activation in persons suffering from depression. Treatment with anti-depressant medications, shown to be effective in some patients, influenced primarily subcortical areas, while equally effective behavioral therapy influenced primarily cortical areas.

The structure and organization of brain systems, like all human organ systems, have evolved in the service of the survival of the species, and determine the ability of individuals to adapt to and cope with conditions that challenge homeostasis and normal functioning. As the executive coordinator and regulator of multiple organ and life support systems, the brain plays a critical role in managing the survival of each person. Its success in that endeavor appears to be directly related to the particular structural integrity, interconnectedness, and efficiency of its functional brain networks.

Recommended Readings

Fair DA, Cohen AL, Power JD, Dosenbach NUF, Church JA, Meizin FM, Schlager BL, Petersen SE. Functional brain networks developed from a "local to distributed" organization. *PLoS Computational Biology* 2009; 5:e1000381.

Goldapple K, Segal Z, Garson C, Lau M, Bieling P, Kennedy S, Mayberg H. Modulation of cortical-limbic pathways in major depression: Treatment specific effects of cognitive behavior therapy. *Archives of General Psychiatry* 2004; 61(1):34–41.

Greicius MD, Kaustubh S, Vinod M, Dougherty R. Resting-state functional connectivity in the default mode network. *Cerebral Cortex* 2009; 19:72–78.

Raichle ME. A paradigm shift in functional imaging. *Journal of Neuroscience* 2009; 29:12729–12734.

Rothbart MK. *Becoming Who We Are: Temperament and Personality in Development.* New York: Guilford; 2011.

Review Questions

1. Positron emission tomography (PET) and functional magnetic resonance imaging (fMRI) provide researchers and clinicians with brain images that
   A. allow localization of abnormalities.
   B. determine the efficiency of white matter pathways.
   C. identify active brain areas.
   D. identify connections between brain areas.
   E. all of the above.

2. A set of widely scattered but orchestrated neural areas activated by a specific task is called
   A. a bilateral insular region.
   B. a cortical hub.
   C. a DNA methylation.
   D. a functional brain network.
   E. none of the above.

3. There is evidence that impaired functional brain network activity is involved in which of the following disorders?
   A. Autism spectrum disorders and attention-deficit/hyperactivity disorder
   B. Multiple sclerosis and callosal agenesis
   C. Schizophrenia and depression
   D. A and C
   E. All of the above

Key to review questions: p. 407

Section III

Homeostatic Systems and Disorders

5 Nutrition, Metabolism, and Feeding Disorders

Rachel E. Zigler, MD, and Barbara J. Davis, PhD

- What are the major functions of the hypothalamus?
- What is energy homeostasis?
- Why do patients with anorexia nervosa have dysfunctions in other organ systems?

The human organism is the unique product of eons of evolutionary change, designed to enable Homo sapiens to survive by adapting to hostile, ever-changing conditions. Essential to this capacity for adaptation was the development of a series of life support systems (e.g., respiration, circulation, digestion, metabolism, elimination) that made it possible for the organism to survive independently.

Each system was capable of meeting challenges to homeostasis. However, an "executive" system was required to communicate with and regulate these basic life support systems. In order to carry out this regulatory function effectively, the nervous system evolved to interact with the environment, learn from experience, and innovate.

The **hypothalamus** serves as a master regulatory center, controlling basic homeostatic functions by regulating rhythms of glandular (especially pituitary) secretions. It receives input from many areas of the CNS and acts on three major systems: (1) the *autonomic nervous system* (both *parasympathetic* and *sympathetic* components), (2) the *endocrine system*, and (3) a less well defined system involved with *motivation*. Thus, almost every major subdivision of the CNS communicates with the hypothalamus, and is subject to its influence. It is through these multiple complex connections that the hypothalamus integrates autonomic and neuroendocrine functions as well as behavioral responses such as feeding to ensure body homeostasis.

Hypothalamic Functions

What are the major functions of the hypothalamus?

Hypothalamic functions include:
- *Control of energy metabolism* by regulation of food intake, including meal size and frequency, regulation of metabolic rate through the hypothalamic-pituitary-thyroid axis, and regulation of blood glucose levels and digestive functions through parasympathetic and sympathetic input to the pancreas, liver, and digestive tract. Hypothalamic circuits also control body temperature by activating heat conservation or dissipation mechanisms.
- *Control of body fluid balance* by regulation of fluid and salt appetite through circumventricular organs (described below), and control of plasma osmolality by hypothalamic osmoreceptors that cue the kidneys to promote water reabsorption.
- *Regulation of circadian rhythms and sleep-wake cycles* by direct neural inputs from the retina to the *circadian rhythm generator* in the hypothalamus, and to neural circuitry interconnecting hypothalamic sleep centers with the brainstem reticular activating system (see Chapter 6, Chronobiology and Sleep Disorders).
- *Regulation of reproduction* through hormonal control of the menstrual cycle, mating, pregnancy, and lactation. Sexual behavior and orientation are strongly influenced by the hormonal environment of the hypothalamus during embryonic and fetal development.

- *Regulation of emergency responses to stress* mediated through the autonomic and immune systems, including regulation of blood flow to muscles, secretion of adrenal stress hormones, activation of the cardiovascular and respiratory systems (see Chapter 7, Stress, Adaptation, and Stress Disorders).

The hypothalamus regulates these basic processes by receiving afferent information from olfactory, gustatory, visual, auditory, tactile and nocioceptive sensors, and neurons in the hypothalamus that are sensitive to osmolality and plasma levels of glucose, sodium, and other blood or cerebrospinal fluid (CSF) borne substances (e.g., hormones, cytokines). This sensory information is integrated and compared with information about **biological set points** for, among others, body adiposity, osmolality, and blood glucose, sodium, and hormone levels. The efferent output of the hypothalamus is activated when deviations from set points are detected. This output involves autonomic, neuroendocrine and behavioral responses to restore homeostasis. A specific example of how this circuitry works is the regulation of feeding behavior and body weight.

Hypothalamic Regulation of Feeding and Energy Balance

What is energy homeostasis?

Energy homeostasis involves adjustment of food intake over time to promote stability in the amount of body fuel stored as fat. The hypothalamus responds to hormonal and nutrient signals that provide information about fuel status and energy stores. This information is integrated with cognitive and sensory signals to regulate food intake and, ultimately, *body adiposity*.

Leptin is an *adipokine* (peptide hormone secreted by adipocytes) that has a profound effect on feeding and energy metabolism. Circulating levels of leptin are proportional to body fat content. Binding of leptin to specific receptors in the hypothalamus triggers a series of cellular events that trigger changes in food intake and energy metabolism.

Leptin carries the message that fat reserves are sufficient. It promotes a reduction in fuel intake and an increase in energy expenditure to maintain fat stores at a constant level.

Weight loss with a reduction of fat stores results in decreased levels of leptin and, thus, decreased leptin input to the hypothalamus. Lower levels of leptin signal the hypothalamus that increased food intake and decreased energy metabolism are needed to replenish fat stores. **Gut hormones** also play an important role in regulation of food intake and energy balance. When food is consumed, hormones are released from the viscera, and sensory pathways innervating the alimentary tract are stimulated. These hormones and sensory pathways regulate neurons in the nucleus of the *tractus solitarius* of the brainstem, as well as other brainstem areas that are reciprocally connected with the hypothalamus. The gut hormones that have received the most attention are *cholecystokinin* and *peptide YY*, intestinal hormones that act as satiety signals, and *ghrelin*, a gastric hormone that has powerful orexigenic (appetite stimulation) action. These hormones interact with leptin-sensitive neurons in the hypothalamus to alter food intake and energy metabolism.

The *arcuate nucleus* of the hypothalamus is the main target of leptin and gut hormone action in controlling food intake and energy metabolism. The arcuate nucleus contains two populations of leptin-sensitive neurons. One population, *orexigenic* neurons, project to other brain areas to stimulate feeding and decrease energy metabolism. The second population of neurons are *anorexigenic,* and project to other brain areas to reduce food intake and stimulate energy metabolism. Thus, when *adipocyte* (fat cell) stores are abundant, leptin inhibits feeding and increases metabolism by stimulating anorexigenic neurons of the arcuate nucleus. When weight loss occurs and adipocyte stores decline, leptin levels fall, which activates orexigenic neurons of the arcuate nucleus, resulting in feeding and decreased metabolism to replenish adipocyte stores.

Physiologically, the drive to eat is a response to hunger, the sensation experienced to maintain homeostasis. But, eating behavior is not just a motor response to this internal drive. There are strong motivational components, both appetitive

An 18-year-old female college freshman was recently diagnosed with anorexia nervosa. She is 5'5" and weighs 90 lbs (BMI =15 kg/m²). Two years ago, her weight was 130 lbs (BMI = 21.6 kg/m²). On physical exam, her resting heart rate is 50 bpm. Her BP is 95/65 seated and drops when she stands. Her temperature is 36°C and her fingers are cool to touch. Her fingers and toes are slightly cyanotic and she has lanugo (soft, fine hair) covering her arms and legs. Her skin is dry and the hair on her head is thin. She has not had a period in about a year, which coincides with her weight loss. Her food diary shows she eats only fruit totaling less than 500 calories/day and drinks 2–3 quarts of water. She exercises multiple times a day between classes. She has difficulty sleeping for more than a few hours or remembering things she just learned in class. When asked what she thinks when she looks in the mirror, she states that she sees an overweight girl.

and aversive, related to the sensory qualities of a food, such as appearance, aroma, texture, and taste that are acquired through experience. These, in turn, are influenced by cultural, familial, and social influences which, as they interact with homeostatic processes, contribute to the complexity of the bio-behavioral mechanisms that determine eating behavior and make eating disorders difficult to treat. These complex interactions are especially evident, for example, in anorexia nervosa (see Chapter 24, Eating Disorders).

> Why do patients with anorexia nervosa have dysfunctions in other organ systems?

Pathogenesis of Anorexia Nervosa

A combination of genetic, biological, psychological, cultural, and environmental risk factors contribute to the etiology of **anorexia nervosa** (AN). Eating behavior is significantly influenced by psychosocial variables, which are discussed in Chapter 23, Obesity and Chapter 24, Eating Disorders. At the same time, AN involves alterations in CNS neural transmitters and dysregulated neural circuitry in key brain areas, including the hypothalamus and limbic system, that are associat-

ed with feeding and regulation of energy balance. Because of the interconnectedness of all homeostatic systems, patients with AN will also have dysfunctions in other systems subject to regulation by the hypothalamus, including sleep-wake cycles and stress responsivity.

Evidence of a familial pattern of AN has prompted research focusing on the genetic basis of the disorder. Research is also exploring the potential roles of neurotransmitters, neuropeptides, adipokines, and other signaling molecules in AN.

Serotonin

Serotonin (5-hydroxytryptamine or 5-HT) is a monoamine neurotransmitter derived from tryptophan. While much of the body's serotonin is synthesized in the gut, a portion is synthesized in serotonergic neurons in the brainstem *raphe nuclei*. Serotonin has multiple functions within the CNS, including regulation of mood, sleep, learning, and memory. Individuals with AN may have genetically influenced heightened responsivity to serotonin leading to increased anxiety that prompts the individual to engage in behaviors that return serotonin levels to baseline. It is known that lowering food intake decreases tryptophan intake, thereby decreasing serotonin synthesis. Thus, decreasing food intake may relieve anxiety in a person with hyperreactivity to serotonin; this feeling of relief reinforces fasting. However, although reducing serotonin relieves anxiety, it may also induce other symptoms such as difficulty sleeping, decreased memory, and depression as seen in the case example.

Dopamine and Norepinephrine

Dopamine is a catecholamine neurotransmitter produced in multiple areas of the brain, including the arcuate nucleus. There are multiple dopaminergic pathways within the brain, including the *nigrostriatal pathway,* important in motor control, the *hypothalamic-pituitary pathway*, which regulates pituitary function, and the *mesolimbic pathway*, which activates the reward system and influences motivation.

Norepinephrine is a catecholamine that is synthesized from dopamine. It is released from chromaffin cells in the *adrenal medulla* and from sympathetic nerve endings in the peripheral nervous system. Norepinephrine has been found to be at low basal levels in patients with AN, which may account for the decreased sympathetic response, including bradycardia and hypotension (leading to cyanosis and cold skin), seen in the case study.

Evolutionary processes may account for the symptoms of starvation and increased exercise in AN. Historically, when food was not plentiful and early humans became hungrier, they increased their activity levels in desperate efforts to find food and stay alive. This hyperactivity, termed *food anticipatory activity,* led some AN researchers to coin the phrase, "activity-based anorexia." When individuals with AN starve themselves, they subsequently become hyperactive (note the excessive exercising in the case example). When exercise is increased, levels of dopamine and norepinephrine rise. Increasing levels of norepinephrine relieve depressed mood and irritability as well as symptoms that may be associated with hypotension, such as headache. Additionally, an increase in dopamine after exercise can cause feelings of reward, pleasure, euphoria, and compulsion, all of which are reinforcing and contribute to the addictive qualities of exercise and fasting behavior in AN patients.

Leptin and Ghrelin

In AN, low fat stores (as seen in the case example who had a BMI of only 15 kg/m²) should normally lead to feeding as a result of low leptin levels. Instead, it leads to starvation-induced hyperactivity. Thus, low levels of **leptin** can signal hunger, but the hyperactivity produces reward (i.e., through increased dopamine), which replaces in many cases – and apparently exceeds – the reward feeling that food can provide.

Ghrelin levels increase before meals (hunger) and decrease after meals (satiety). However, in AN, the ghrelin mechanism, like the leptin mechanism, does not function normally, perhaps due to the same hyperactivity-induced dopaminergic reward system effect described above.

Recommended Readings

Kaye W. Neurobiology of anorexia and bulimia nervosa. *Physiology and Behavior* 2008; 94:121–135.

Klein D, Walsh BT. Eating disorders: Clinical features and pathophysiology. *Physiology and Behavior* 2004; 81:359–374.

Lingford-Hughes A, et al. Neuropharmacology of addiction and how it informs treatment. *British Medical Bulletin* 2010; 96:93–110.

Morton CJ, et al. Central nervous system control of food intake and body weight. *Nature* 2006; 443:289–295.

Scheurink A, et al. Neurobiology of hyperactivity and reward: Agreeable restlessness in Anorexia Nervosa. *Physiology and Behavior* 2010; 100:490–495.

Review Questions

1. Recent studies suggest that excessive use of artificial sweeteners such as aspartame may actually promote weight gain by damaging neurons in the hypothalamus that respond to satiety signals such as leptin. Which of the following hypothalamic nuclei would be most likely to show aspartame-related damage?
   A. Anterior
   B. Arcuate
   C. Dorsomedial
   D. Preoptic
   E. Supraoptic

2. A 14-year-old girl presents to the office with recent extreme weight loss. Her fingers are slightly cyanotic, her bones are protruding, and she is bradycardic. She reports that along with being upset about her body, she is having difficulty sleeping. Her difficulty sleeping may be due to a decrease in a neurotransmitter that is formed in what area of the brain?
   A. Basal Nucleus of Meynert
   B. Hypothalamus
   C. Locus Ceruleus
   D. Raphe Nuclei
   E. Subthalamic Nuclei

3. A severely underweight 16-year-old girl exercises at the gym for 4 hours each day. Her mother asks the physician how her daughter is able to starve herself with such an intense

workout regimen. The physician explains this question is still being researched, but might be due to

A. absence of dopamine.
B. decreased dopamine.
C. decreased leptin.
D. increased dopamine.
E. increased leptin.

Key to review questions: p. 407

6 Chronobiology and Sleep Disorders

João V. Nunes, MD, Girardin Jean-Louis, PhD, Hans J. von Gizycki, PhD, and Ferdinand Zizi, MBA

- What is circadian rhythm?
- How does circadian rhythm affect organ system functioning?
- What is the difference between REM and non-REM sleep?
- How do the sleep patterns of infants, mid-age adults, and the elderly differ?
- Why is it easier to accommodate to a flight from London to New York than from New York to London?
- What are the potential outcomes of severe obstructive sleep apnea?
- What are the differences between nightmares and night terrors?

Biological Rhythms

Homeostatic control and coordination of basic life support functions are achieved through hypothalamic regulation of rhythms of hormonal secretion and autonomic nervous system activity. These biological rhythms provide the individual with a unique adaptive capability – to vary the timing and duration of biological/behavioral activity in each system – in response to environmental change. **Chronobiology** is the discipline that studies the effect of these biological rhythms on essential processes from eating and sleeping to cellular regeneration and susceptibility to infection.

What is circadian rhythm?

The most important biological rhythm is the **circadian rhythm**. It affects fluctuations in the release of critical hormones that cause fluctuations in phenomena such as core body temperature, metabolic activity, and serum cortisol level in 24-hour cycles. Physiological and behavioral processes that have these predictable temporal fluctuations in sensitivity to environmental factors can be categorized according to the specific time of day they routinely occur, e.g., *diurnal*, *nocturnal*, and *crepuscular* (twilight) *cycles*.

Other rhythms important to human functioning are **ultradian rhythms** ($\leq$ 24 hours; e.g., the 180-minute growth hormone production cycle and the 90-minute REM sleep cycle) and **infradian rhythms** ($\geq$24 hours, e.g., menstrual and reproduction cycles). **Gene oscillation** describes a pattern of differential gene expression at different times during the day.

The timing of biological rhythms is governed by endogenous biological mechanisms in concert with exogenous cues or **zeitgebers**, German for "time giver" or "synchronizer." The strongest zeitgeber for animals is daylight. The earth's approximate 24-hour light/dark cycle synchronizes the endogenous time-keeping system, or clock, a process called **entrainment**. Zeitgebers promote changes in the molecular components of the clock to match what is appropriate according to the specific phase of the 24-hour period. Humans, like other organisms, have been entrained to synchronize activity and rest to specific times of the earth's light/dark cycle. For example, changes in ambient light may induce or inhibit sleep.

Control of the Sleep-Wake Cycle

The earth's light/dark cycle also cues other environmental rhythms responsive to non-photic zeitgebers such as ambient temperature, eating/drinking patterns, pharmacological responsivity, and exercise. For example, the menstrual cycles of women who

> The endogenous biological clock that controls the sleep-wake cycle is composed of cells located in the suprachiasmatic nucleus (SCN) of the hypothalamus. The SCN induces pineal gland secretion of *melatonin* when environmental light decreases (sunset) and inhibits secretion when environmental light increases (sunrise).

stay in close proximity for long periods become synchronous. The zeitgeber responsible for this synchronization may be a female pheromone.

The complex **neuroendocrine network**, which connects the *hypothalamus* and HPA axis to all homeostatic systems, enables the organism to selectively activate or deactivate functions, depending upon conditions affecting the organism. However, because of this interlinking, hormonal fluctuations can affect multiple systems. For example, *orexin* or *hypocretin*, a hypothalamic neuropeptide, plays a role in maintaining sleep/wakefulness states. Orexin neurons, which are regulated by monoamines and acetylcholine, respond to metabolic cues such as leptin, glucose, and ghrelin (involved in feeding and energy metabolism), and are linked to the dopaminergic reward system. Thus, fluctuations in any of these hormones can influence sleep, eating behavior, reward processes, emotional regulation, and vigilance to potential stressors. As a result, all homeostatic systems are vulnerable to dysfunction in any one system, such that disorders in eating, for example, can generate associated disorders in sleep, sexual behavior, immune system functioning, and, subsequently, every organ system.

Circadian Rhythm and Organ System Functioning

> How does circadian rhythm affect organ system functioning?

Cardiac contractility shows daytime activity peaks, nighttime inactivity troughs, and graded changes over 24 hours. Generally, there is a trough in the early morning before typical wake-up time, a rising phase just prior to wake-up time, a peak in the early afternoon or evening, a fall before bed-

time, and a steep decline at sleep onset continuing into the sleep period. The incidence of cerebral vascular accidents, myocardial infarction, and sudden death increases between 6 a.m. and noon. The association of typical chronophysiological patterns of cardiac contractility with adverse cardiac events suggests that imbalance between cardiac demand and myocardial oxygen supply is most likely to occur in the morning, along with other physiological changes, e.g., increased arterial blood pressure, increased platelet aggregability, and decreased fibrinolytic activity, that may contribute to adverse vascular events.

Respiratory changes occur during sleep. Changes in the CO_2 chemoreceptor increase the CO_2 threshold (the concentration of CO_2 that triggers breathing), which decreases the ventilatory drive. This produces a decrease in minute ventilation (the volume of air breathed per minute) during sleep. In addition, there is decreased respiratory accessory muscle tone and increased bronchoconstriction.

> Chemical and mechanical challenges to breathing during sleep contribute to low nocturnal oxygen levels (hypoxemia) and high carbon dioxide levels (hypercapnia).

Gastrointestinal motor activity, such as gastric emptying rate, slows during the evening and overnight. Many drugs taken by mouth in the evening are absorbed more slowly, possibly delaying their onset of action. Although gastric acid secretion is normally lower during sleep compared to the waking state, it is increased in duodenal ulcer patients, consistent with the observation that gastrointestinal symptoms often worsen around midnight.

> Evening administration of antacids or proton pump inhibitors provides protection during the period of greatest vulnerability of the gastrointestinal system.

Musculoskeletal system activity also changes with the time of day. Morning joint swelling and stiffness, diagnostic hallmarks of rheumatoid arthritis, appear to be associated with the rhythmic nocturnal fall in circulating endogenous corticosteroids.

In the *immune system*, allergen skin testing shows a greater response if done in late evening compared to the morning. Results from tests done in the morning should be viewed cautiously to avoid false-negatives. In contrast to skin reactivity, hay fever symptoms are more pronounced upon awakening. Total T-lymphocyte and CD4 T-lymphocyte concentrations peak around 4 a.m., about the same time that kidney transplant rejection is most likely to occur. The efficacy and rate of adverse effects of platinum and other agents used to treat ovarian cancer are influenced by time of day. Similarly, maintenance chemotherapy for acute lymphoblastic leukemia administered in the evening appears to be more effective.

> Immunosuppressant treatment to avoid tissue rejection is most beneficial when administered at night.

Sleep

> What is the difference between REM and non-REM sleep?

Sleep is divided into **rapid-eye-movement (REM) sleep** and four levels of **non-REM sleep** (stage 1, or light sleep, to stage 4, or deep sleep). During REM sleep, the brain is highly active and is driven by spontaneous neural discharges originating primarily in the *pontine reticular formation*. However, the neural pathways associated with sensory input and motor output are inhibited. Thus, vivid dreaming and decreased perception of and reaction to the environment are characteristic of REM sleep.

In contrast, during non-REM sleep, the brain is less activated and there is less cognitive activity. Stages 3 and 4, the deep sleep stages, are called **slow-wave sleep (SWS)**. Throughout the night, non-REM sleep and REM sleep alternate in approximately 90-minute cycles. SWS typically occurs during the earlier portion of the night, and REM sleep predominates in the last third of the night.

> During REM sleep, the brain may activate cortical areas normally involved in visual perception and motor movements, leading the individual to perceive seeing objects and making movements, but actually doing neither.

Sleep Patterns and Architecture

> How do the sleep patterns of infants, mid-age adults, and the elderly differ?

Sleep patterns vary across age groups. Average daily total sleep time decreases from up to 18 hours during infancy, to about 10 hours in early childhood, to about 8 hours in adulthood. Among the elderly, nighttime sleep is diminished but daytime napping is increased; as a result, total sleep time is similar to that of mid-age adults.

Sleep architecture changes with age. Newborn infants spend about 50% of their sleep time in REM sleep and 50% in non-REM sleep with predominantly slow-wave activity. Infant sleep is polyphasic and occurs in 3- to 4-hour cycles. During the second year of life, children develop a diurnal pattern of sleep that includes a long episode of nocturnal sleep and a brief nap during the afternoon. As children mature, the percentages of REM sleep and SWS decrease. For example, the time spent in REM sleep decreases to about 20 to 25% by late adolescence and remains stable until older age. The percentage of SWS, however, diminishes gradually throughout life. Complaints of difficulty maintaining sleep are more common among older people. These sleep difficulties may be due to an underlying health condition, medication, or types of sleep disorder that are more prevalent among the elderly (e.g., breathing disturbances, periodic limb movements).

Sleep Hygiene

> A set of simple measures collectively called **sleep hygiene** help persons who have sleep difficulties regain consistent sleep.
> 1. Use the bed for sleep and sex only (e.g., not for eating, reading, or watching TV).
> 2. Go to bed only when sleepy.
> 3. If not asleep after 20 minutes, do some boring activity in another room. Return to bed when sleepy.
> 4. Sleep only the amount to feel refreshed, and sleep the same amount every night (no sleeping in).
> 5. Maintain sleep conditions close to ideal and avoid excessive ambient warmth or coldness.

6. Go to bed and wake up around the same time each day.
7. Exercise regularly but not close to bedtime.
8. Avoid napping.
9. Avoid substances such as alcohol, tobacco, and caffeine near bedtime.
10. Limit use of sedatives.
11. If eating near bedtime, eat lightly.
12. Practice relaxation.
13. A body temperature-raising 20-minute hot bath near bedtime may be helpful.

Assessment

The assessment of sleep disorders requires a thorough clinical history, including the sleep-related history, a mental status exam, a review of systems, and a physical exam and indicated laboratory studies. Thorough assessment is warranted since sleep disorders may be primary or secondary to other medical disorders, including psychiatric conditions. The subjective and objective behavioral aspects of sleep must be carefully assessed and accurately recorded. Patients should be referred to a sleep disorder center for polysomnography if the diagnosis is not clear or they need special help (e.g., specific diagnosis, sleep staging, determination of severity of the disorder, precise determination of daytime sleepiness or fitting a mask for continuous positive airway pressure therapy).

Sleep-Wake Schedule Disorders

Sleep disorders can arise either from a defect in the **circadian oscillator** (the *suprachiasmatic nucleus*, which serves as the endogenous timing system) or from the limited capacity of the internal timing system to adjust to changes in external clock time. The shifting capacity of the human circadian rhythm is 2 hours per day or less. Therefore, sleep difficulties can occur whenever the sleep-wake schedule is shifted outside an individual's range of entrainment.

Disorders of the sleep-wake schedule, also known as **circadian rhythm disorders,** result from disturbances in the timing of actual sleep-wake behavior relative to the person's circadian sleep-wake rhythm. Such disturbances can be transient (e.g., jet lag or work shift changes) or more persistent (e.g., delayed sleep phase syndrome, advanced sleep phase syndrome, permanent rotating shift work). Affected individuals cannot stay awake or stay asleep when it is necessary or desired to do so.

Jet Lag

Why is it easier to accommodate to a flight from London to New York than from New York to London?

Jet lag results from rapid changes in time zone due to transmeridian travel. Symptoms include insomnia, fatigue, and gastrointestinal complaints. Westbound travel is generally less disruptive than east-bound travel because delaying the sleep-wake cycle (to adjust to the prevailing clock time after westbound travel) is easier to accomplish than advancing the sleep-wake cycle. Sleep disruptions can persist for up to 8 days after travel but jet lag usually requires no treatment. Jet lag during brief trips is minimized by adhering to the clock time of the original time zone.

Shift Work

Shift work, or any acute change in work schedule, can desynchronize sleep within the circadian cycle. The problem is transient if the worker remains on the new work schedule; however, it can become a persistent disorder if the worker is required to rotate shifts continually. Insomnia, mood changes, and gastrointestinal symptoms are common side effects. The shift worker who is required to work at night and sleep during the day also must contend with lower levels of arousal at night, which can cause performance deficits, as well as with higher levels of arousal during the day, which can impair the ability to sleep. Unacceptable error rates associated with erratic and prolonged shift work have led to efforts to attune work patterns to normal.

Delayed Sleep Phase Syndrome

Delayed sleep phase syndrome (DSPS) is a chronic sleep disorder in which the individual's timing of sleep, peak alertness, hormonal and core temperature fluctuations, and other circadian rhythms are delayed relative to societal norms. The syndrome typically develops during childhood or adolescence. Affected individuals will have essentially normal sleep if allowed to go to sleep and wake up late. However, they often suffer from *sleep-onset insomnia* if they attempt to fall asleep earlier to obtain an adequate amount of sleep before arising at the time required for school or work. Allowing themselves to sleep on a delayed schedule on weekends or vacations reinforces DSPS. Symptoms include grogginess in the morning and irritability.

Advanced Sleep Phase Syndrome

Advanced sleep phase syndrome (ASPS) is an uncommon, strongly genetically linked syndrome characterized by the inability to stay awake in the evening and stay asleep in the early morning. Because their circadian rhythms cycle hours earlier than those of the average person, affected individuals have normal sleep if it occurs from the early evening to the early morning. Most people with this syndrome do not seek medical treatment unless symptoms interfere with their family or work life. They may report *sleep-maintenance insomnia* when they come to medical attention for becoming sleep deprived from chemically postponing their bedtime without being able to sleep later in the morning.

Treatment of Sleep Phase Disorders

Transient sleep disorders (e.g., jet lag) usually require no treatment if the dyssynchrony is isolated. However, short-acting hypnotics and melatonin can improve alertness and promote sleep following abrupt changes in the sleep-wake schedule.

ASPS has been treated successfully using chronotherapy, a technique intended to reset the internal clock through manipulating bedtime. To be rested, a useful step before starting chronotherapy, the individual is allowed to keep his/her habitual sleep pattern for at least one week. Two types of chronotherapy can then be used. Most often, the individual is instructed to delay bedtime by about 2 hours daily until the desired bedtime is attained. This maneuver is designed to shift the individual's sleep period so that it lasts until later in the morning in order to preserve the duration of sleep. To maintain this change in sleep pattern, the process should be repeated every few months. Alternatively, the individual is instructed to stay awake one whole night and day. At that point, he or she goes to bed three hours earlier than the usual bedtime and maintains this new bedtime for a week. The steps are repeated weekly until the desired pattern is achieved.

Chronotherapy can be used to manage DSPS, but the response to treatment is often poor.

The use of bright light (phototherapy) to promote a phase shift has been helpful in the treatment of sleep-wake cycle or circadian rhythm disorders. Bright light, usually of 10,000 lux, is administered for 30–90 minutes at the individual's habitual waking time.

Narcolepsy

Narcolepsy has been conceptualized as an abnormal intrusion of components of REM sleep into wakefulness. It is a chronic neurological disorder characterized by four major symptoms:

1) *Excessive daytime sleepiness* may be relatively continuous or episodic. Severity varies from a mild desire to sleep to an irresistible "sleep attack." Daytime sleep bouts vary from seconds of nodding to short naps of 20 minutes. Patients with narcolepsy usually awaken feeling refreshed.

2) *Cataplexy* is a sudden loss of muscle tone triggered by strong emotions. The patient is awake during the weakness, which typically lasts seconds to minutes. The muscle weakness may be localized or affect all postural muscles. The loss of muscle tone during cataplexy is the result of the same neural mechanisms that produce the active inhibition of the musculature typical of REM sleep.

3) *Sleep paralysis* is the inability to move at sleep onset or upon awakening. It is a manifestation of REM sleep muscle inhibition.

4) *Hypnagogic hallucination*, or dreaming while still awake, is the result of a normal component of REM sleep occurring during wakefulness.

The diagnosis of narcolepsy is confirmed using the *Multiple Sleep Latency Test* (MSLT), which consists of four or five naps spaced 2 hours apart. The patient is placed in a quiet, dark bedroom and monitored by polysomnography. The time from lights out to sleep onset (sleep latency) is measured for each nap, and the appearance of REM sleep within 15 minutes, called a sleep-onset REM period, is noted. Findings consistent with narcolepsy include an average sleep latency of 6 minutes or less, which documents pathological sleepiness, and the appearance of at least two sleep-onset REM periods. Treatment consists of stimulant medications, good nocturnal sleep, and prophylactic naps. Cataplexy, sleep paralysis, and hypnagogic hallucinations are responsive to tricyclic and some selective serotonin reuptake inhibitor antidepressants.

Mechanical/Structural Sleep Disorders

Sleep-disordered breathing results when respiratory control is adversely affected by chemical information (chemoreceptor changes in PaO_2, $PaCO_2$, and pH), behavioral information derived from cortical activity, and mechanical feedback via stretch receptors in the chest wall, upper airway, and lung. Arousal from sleep is produced by low oxygen levels (hypoxemic response), high levels of carbon dioxide (hypercapnic response), or occlusion or obstruction to airflow. The arousal threshold to these stimuli is state related; awakening is more difficult from REM sleep than from non-REM sleep.

> Benzodiazepines, barbiturates, sedating antidepressants, antihistamines, antipsychotics, narcotics, and alcohol can all suppress ventilation. A careful drug history is essential when screening for sleep-disordered breathing.

Obstructive Sleep Apnea

> What are the potential outcomes of severe obstructive sleep apnea?

Obstructive sleep apnea syndrome affects 2% to 4% of the general population overall, but is especially prominent in middle-aged men and postmenopausal women. The condition consists of temporary but recurrent obstruction of the upper airway during sleep that produces apnea (cessation of airflow for ≥ 10 seconds). The most common sites of occlusion are the soft palate and the base of the tongue.

During an episode of obstructive apnea, chest and abdominal movements are ineffective in moving air. A brief period of electrocortical arousal follows the episode and is accompanied by deep gasping resuscitative breathing and loud snoring. In severe cases, up to 500 episodes of apnea can occur each night producing abnormal hemodynamics, blood gas changes, cognitive deficits, disrupted sleep, and daytime sleepiness. Some cases are fatal.

> In addition to age and gender, risk factors for sleep apnea include obesity, diastolic hypertension, large neck circumference, and structural abnormalities of the upper airway.

Treatment options include mechanical devices, behavioral interventions, and surgery. The most common treatment for moderate and severe cases is *continuous positive airway pressure* (CPAP) via the nose. In milder cases, an oral appliance that advances the mandible and frees up space in the oropharynx is worn during sleep. Behavioral therapy includes weight loss and avoiding the supine sleeping position, alcohol, and sedating medications. Surgical options include uvulopalatopharyngoplasty, tonsillectomy-adenoidectomy, and a variety of mandibulomaxillary advancement procedures. Tracheostomy may be necessary in extreme cases associated with life-threatening cardiopulmonary complications.

Central sleep apnea syndrome is an uncommon sleep disorder manifested by insomnia, gasping for air, arousals from sleep, and either mild or absent snoring. In this form of apnea, the absence of ventilatory effort results in the cessation of airflow.

Cardiac, neurological, and cerebrovascular disease play a role in the pathophysiology of this disorder.

Cheyne-Stokes respiration with central sleep apnea is a form of periodic breathing characterized by recurrent cessation of breathing alternating with increased airflow (hyperpnea) in a crescendo-decrescendo pattern. The condition is seen most commonly in patients with congestive heart failure and CNS disease. The reduced circulatory time from alveolar unit to chemoreceptor and the length of the crescendo-decrescendo cycle have been implicated in the etiology of this breathing pattern. Treatment can be difficult. Nasal CPAP, oxygen, respiratory stimulants, such as acetazolamide or theophylline, and mechanical ventilation all have specific risks and benefits.

Insomnia

Insomnia, the most common sleep disorder, has a significant negative effect on quality of life, mood, cognitive functioning, performance capacity, and alertness. In addition to psychiatric disorders that interfere with adequate sleep, the etiology of insomnia includes sleep-related breathing dysfunction, periodic limb movements, circadian rhythm dysregulation, worry about sleeplessness, late night exercise, caffeine ingestion, daytime napping, and medical conditions. General treatments include better sleep hygiene, such as setting a regular wake-up time; eliminating napping, alcohol, and caffeine; and relaxing before bedtime with a ritual to reduce physiological hyperarousal. In addition, patients should be instructed to get out of bed if they do not fall asleep in 20 minutes. Cognitive approaches target arousing, worrisome, and self-defeating thoughts that can sustain insomnia. A variety of rapid-acting hypnotic drugs are safe when taken alone and can help induce and maintain sleep

Nightmares and Night Terrors

What are the differences between nightmares and night terrors?

A **nightmare** is a terrifying dream that awakens the dreamer from REM sleep. Nightmares tend to occur during the early morning when REM periods are naturally more intense. They are common in children and decrease with age. Nightmares may be induced by stressful conditions or events. Nightmares can be caused by certain medications such as L-dopa and beta blockers. Alcohol and other drugs have a REM-suppressing effect. When these drugs are discontinued, an increase in the amount and intensity of REM sleep (rebound) can cause especially emotional and frightening dreams.

Night terrors, unlike nightmares, occur during slow-wave sleep, in the first half of the night. They are characterized by a confused arousal in which the person appears to be terrified, often crying out. Attempts to rouse or calm the person are futile. Unlike the person who has nightmares, the person who has night terrors cannot recall details about what was going through his or her mind. In fact, in the morning, the person usually has forgotten the event altogether. Night terrors are common in children less than 10 and uncommon in adults.

Recommended Readings

España RA, Scammell TE. Sleep neurobiology from a clinical perspective. *SLEEP* 2011; 34(7): 845–858.

Palmer JD. *The Living Clock.* Oxford, UK: Oxford University Press; 2002.

Stern TA, Fricchione GL, Cassem NH, Jellineck MS, Rosenbaum JF (Eds.). *Massachusetts General Hospital Handbook of General Hospital Psychiatry,* 5th ed. St. Louis, MO: Mosby; 2004.

Smallwood P, Quinn, DK, Stern TA. Patients with disordered sleep. In Stern TA, Fricchione GL, Cassem NH, Jellineck MS, Rosenbaum JF (Eds.), *Massachusetts General Hospital Handbook of General Hospital Psychiatry,* 6th ed. Philadelphia, PA: Saunders; 2010, pp. 289–302

Wright K. Times of our lives. *Sci Am* 2006; 16:26–33.

Online Resources

Healthy Sleep from the Division of Sleep Medicine at Harvard Medical School and WGBH. Available at HealthySleep.med.harvard.edu

Review Questions

1. For the past 2 years, Mark, a 20-year-old college student, has had an undiagnosed illness that has seriously disrupted his previously excellent academic performance. His most recent physician's report mentioned, among other symptoms and signs, cataplexy, sleep paralysis, and hypnagogic hallucinations, all of which responded to treatment with a tricyclic antidepressant. Among the following, the most likely diagnosis is
   A. advanced sleep phase syndrome.
   B. central sleep apnea.
   C. narcolepsy.
   D. night terrors.
   E. transient sleep disorder.

2. Over time, most organisms have come to restrict rest and activity to specific times of the day in synchrony with environmental day-night cycles. This process has resulted in circadian rhythms that are adjusted to environmental rhythms and has been beneficial to survival. This process is called
   A. biological clock activity.
   B. circadian rhythmicity.
   C. entrainment.
   D. light-dark cycling.
   E. zeitgebers.

3. Mrs. M., who is 55 years old and 5 years post-menopause, comes to see you because her husband is concerned about her loud snoring and gasping. She also reports disrupted sleep, daytime sleepiness, and forgetfulness. Vital signs include a blood pressure of 175/106 and her BMI is 35. Physical exam reveals poor air flow into the lungs. Among the following, her most likely diagnosis is
   A. delayed sleep phase syndrome.
   B. insomnia.
   C. narcolepsy.
   D. obstructive sleep apnea.
   E. sleep-wake schedule disorder.

4. The brain may activate visual perception and motor cortical areas in such a way that an individual perceives that he or she is seeing objects and making movements, while actually doing neither. This phenomenon is most characteristic of

   A. circadian oscillator activity.
   B. polyphasic sleep.
   C. REM sleep.
   D. sleep-wake schedules.
   E. slow wave sleep.

Key to review questions: p. 407

7 Stress, Adaptation, and Stress Disorders

John E. Carr, PhD, and Peter P. Vitaliano, PhD

- What are the components of the stress response?
- How does the acute stress response differ from the chronic stress response?
- What role do the glucocorticoids play in the regulation of the stress response?
- Most illnesses seen in primary care are a by-product of what evolutionary objective?
- By what bio-behavioral mechanisms does stress contribute to immune system disorders?
- By what bio-behavioral mechanisms does stress contribute to cardiovascular disorders?

Stress, Adaptation, and Evolution

Derived from physics, the concept of stress originally referred to external forces causing internal structural or *systemic strain*. Applied to medicine, **stress** refers to any challenge to the integrity or survival of the organism, and includes the complex *interaction of biological, behavioral, cognitive, sociocultural, and environmental changes that can disrupt genetically predisposed homeostasis.* Any such challenge will trigger "strains" within the body's systems and activate a **stress response**, setting into motion an array of defensive and adaptive mechanisms designed to restore **homeostasis** within each of these systems. This process of restoring stable functioning is referred to as **allostasis**. Disease and dysfunction typically occur in response to the failure of allostasis, but can also occur as the result of **allostasis overload**, i.e., sustained adaptive responses that begin to wear down the body. Thus, many of the illnesses that physicians treat can be best understood as by-products of the body's **stress response,** the mechanisms involved in its function, and the consequences of their actions.

The **stress response** involves a complex *gene-environment interaction* in which the individual is genetically predisposed to certain precipitating stressor conditions that, over time, effect changes in gene expression through a variety of epigenetic alterations. This gene-environment-stress interaction results in a medley of physiological, cognitive, emotional, and behavioral reactions that vary with the intensity and duration of the stressor. In his **General Adaptation Syndrome (GAS)** model, **Selye** referred to the initial stage of the stress response as the *alarm stage* in which the body's adaptive defenses are mobilized**.** This is followed by a *resistance stage*, during which the organism attempts to cope and adapt utilizing available resources. During this stage, the individual is susceptible to *diseases of adaptation* that are by-products of the body's stress response. The final *exhaustion stage* occurs when demand exceeds available resources, defensive efforts fail, and the individual is increasingly susceptible. Thus, stress effects depend not only on the nature and intensity of the stressor, but also on its duration.

The Stress Response

What are the components of the stress response?

Chronic vs. Acute Stress

How does the acute stress response differ from the chronic stress response?

Whereas the **acute stress response** evolved to protect and "heal" the body, under conditions of sustained or chronic stress, the body's adaptive mechanisms can be overwhelmed, resulting in disease and dysfunction. Adaptation to chronic as well as acute stress requires two types of stress response. First, there is an *immediate nervous system response*. After receiving sensory input indicating a stressor condition, the response focuses upon *emergency functions* in keeping with the organism's survival imperative. Energy is mobilized from storage sites while further storage is temporarily halted; muscles are fueled with glucose, simple fats, proteins, and oxygen for *fight or flight*. Sympathetic nervous system (SNS) activation increases heart rate, blood pressure, and respiration providing rapid delivery of oxygen and fuel to muscle cells. Simultaneously, noncritical functions such as digestion, growth, and reproduction are put on hold. The SNS also activates the immune system, which releases T-cells, B-cells, and pro-inflammatory cytokines to fight infection.

Stress, Performance, and Learning

Selye distinguished between *eustress*, meaning healthy stress, and *distress* or unhealthy stress. Eustress, typically evoked in response to mod-

erate challenge, represents the optimal degree of arousal required to perform well or learn. Distress, typically evoked in response to high stress, occurs when arousal impedes performance. The **Yerkes-Dodson Law** (see Figure 7.1) states that performance and adaptive learning are optimal under moderate rather than either high or low stress (arousal) conditions. High stress may interfere with performance, as evidenced by overly anxious students who cannot concentrate on an exam. Low stress (arousal) may lead to low motivation and, thus, a lackluster performance. Two important corollaries to the Yerkes-Dodson Law apply to specific learning situations. (1) *Learning* new or difficult tasks is optimal under low/moderate stress conditions (recall how difficult it is to learn new material when anxious). (2) *Performance* of well-learned tasks is optimal under high stress conditions (e.g., the track star runs fastest when "pumped").

Although little or no stress may be insufficient to stimulate a response, moderate stress conditions activate the limbic system, facilitating the coordinated ability of the amygdala, hippocampus, and prefrontal cortex to analyze, respond to, and learn from the challenge. Chronic stress results in persistently increased activation of the amygdala, increased release of glucocorticoid and other stress hormones, and decreased modulation of the hippocampus, resulting in impaired learning and performance (see Chapter 8, Emotion and Learning).

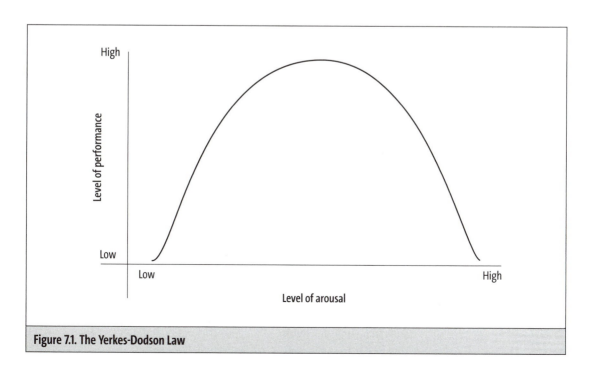

Figure 7.1. The Yerkes-Dodson Law

Bio-behavioral Mechanisms of the Stress Response

Emotional, cognitive, and physiological reactions mutually influence each other. For example, in response to stressors, incoming sensory information is collected by the thalamus and forwarded simultaneously to the amygdala, hippocampus, and cortical association areas (see Figure 7.2.). Analogous to an "emergency response team," the **amygdala** coordinates an emergent reaction (fight or flight), arousing and mobilizing the organism via the **sympatho-adrenomedullary (SAM) axis**, which triggers the release of catecholamines and glucocorticoids through activation of the **hypothalamus-pituitary-adrenal axis (HPA)**. The amygdala's response is modulated by the **hippocampus** and **prefrontal cortex** (PFC), analogous to an "intelligence agency," that references cortical memories relevant to the incoming information to determine its importance and meaning and an appropriate response. If the incoming information is judged to be important, the emergent response continues. If it is judged to be of limited or no importance, the response may be altered or terminated. Thus, the function of the hippocampus is to inform and modulate the amygdala's fine tuning and activation of the acute stress response.

With activation of the HPA axis, sympathetic neural pathways originating in the hypothalamus trigger release of *epinephrine* from these synapses and the adrenal medulla. Concurrently, *norepi-nephrine* is released at all other sympathetic syn-

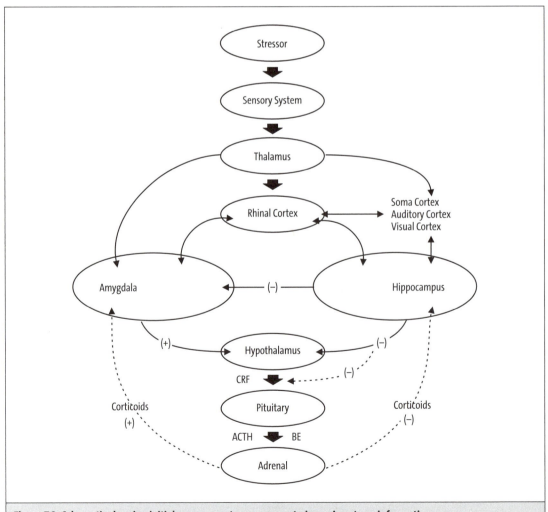

Figure 7.2. Schematic showing initial nervous system response to incoming stress information

apses in the body to act on the postsynaptic receptors of end organs. These two catecholamines promote generalized sympathetic arousal. Once the acute stress ceases, parasympathetic pathways originating in the hypothalamus activate *glucocorticoid, cholinergic, and other inhibitory system* receptor neurons that feed back this information to the hypothalamus, which then "turns off" the arousal. Thus, the body's initial reaction to stress is an immediate but relatively brief **autonomic nervous system**-initiated response.

> What role do the glucocorticoids play in the regulation of the stress response?

Glucocorticoids are steroid hormones that regulate and influence biological functions in indi-viduals, including growth, development, and homeostatic adaptation. In response to stress, the hypothalamus secretes *corticotropin-releasing hormone (CRH)*, which is transported to the pituitary via hypothalamic-pituitary-portal circulation. The anterior pituitary secretes *adrenocorticotropic hormone (ACTH), beta endorphin (BE), and other hormones* into the blood stream. ACTH is transported to the adrenal cortex and stimulates *glucocorticoid* secretion into the circulatory system, which, via glucocorticoid receptors in various brain structures (e.g., hippocampus), signals the stress response to shut down. In some individuals, as time passes and stress is sustained, HPA activity may subside and glucocorticoid secretion returns to normal. Thus, in certain instances, the body appears to be able to utilize mechanisms to adapt to even chronic stressors. However, in gen-

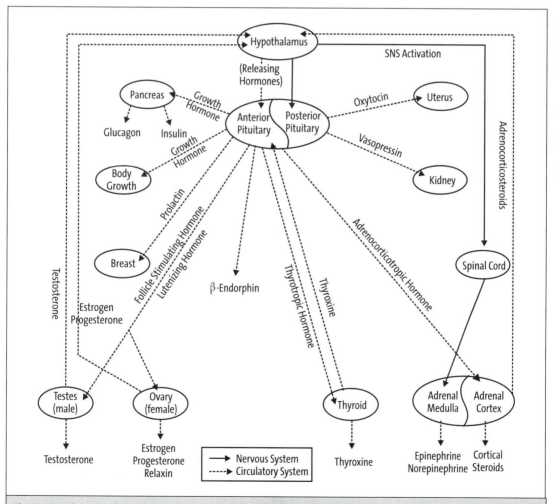

Figure 7.3. Schematic showing initial nervous system response to incoming stress information

eral, as stress becomes chronic, *glucocorticoid receptor response* can become impaired. As a result, glucocorticoid secretion does not return to normal, resulting in a glucocorticoid "flood" that can inhibit protein synthesis and accelerate protein catabolism, increase lipolysis, and decrease peripheral glucose utilization. This results in bone loss, muscle wasting, metabolic syndrome, immune system suppression, and impaired neurogenesis in the hippocampus, limiting its ability to modulate the amygdala and the HPA-activated stress response.

When Homeostatic Systems Fail

> Most illnesses seen in primary care are a by-product of what evolutionary objective?

Homeostatic systems have evolved to optimally serve two primary objectives: the survival of the organism and the survival of the species. We have seen that the diverse homeostatic systems that carry out these objectives are coordinated via interlinked pathways and a common neuroendocrine system. The failure of any of these adaptive homeostatic functions increases the risk of disorder or disease, not only in the failed systems, but in all systems due to the highly integrated network that connects them. Thus, failure of the nutritional/metabolic system, the chronobiological system, the stress response system, or any homeostatic system can result not only in eating, sleep, or stress disorders, but also in an array of disturbances in all areas of human functioning. Since a threat to homeostasis constitutes stress, the stress response system plays a central role in the organism's coordinated efforts to maintain homeostasis. It follows that the majority of illnesses seen by primary care physicians are the results of the body's evolving efforts to adapt to these challenges and restore homeostasis.

Stress and Metabolic Processes

Acute stress triggers an emergency response that includes shunting of stored nutrients to muscle and organ sites, and the shutting down of digestion and other non-emergent functions. Chronic stress causes this process to turn on and off repeatedly. As a result, nutrient stores are depleted faster than they are replaced and the body begins to catabolize muscle tissue to make up for the loss. The stressors driving this process can be serendipitous or purposeful (e.g., exercise or weight management programs) and, if not well managed, can lead to eating disorders (see Chapter 24, Eating Disorders).

In some individuals, the excess glucocorticoids resulting from chronic stress can impair the cell's ability to respond to insulin, leading to increased glucose and fat in the blood stream and impeding oxygen flow and organ efficiency. In fact, hyperinsulinemia in response to chronic stress and subsequent poor health habits (e.g., poor diet, sedentary life style) predict Type 2 diabetes and coronary artery disease, and is a major process in the development of **metabolic syndrome**.

Metabolic syndrome is increasingly common in the US, and while it is associated with many conditions and risk factors, the two most important risk factors are:
- extra weight around the middle of the body (central obesity), and
- insulin resistance, in which the body cannot use insulin effectively to control the amount of sugar in the body.

With insulin resistance, the body does not respond to insulin, and blood sugar (glucose) cannot get into cells. As a result, the body produces more insulin. Both insulin and blood sugar levels rise, which affects kidney function and raises the level of blood fats, such as triglycerides. Metabolic syndrome is especially prevalent in older obese individuals where *diabetes mellitus, type 2* is a major health problem (see Chapter 23, Obesity, and Chapter 22, Geriatric Health and Successful Aging). Some individuals may suffer from *diabetes mellitus, type 1* due to a genetically influenced shortage of insulin. The onset of this disease may be triggered by a viral infection of the pancreas that initiates an autoimmune response in which the insulin-producing cells of the pancreas are attacked. Studies of older adults have shown that chronic stress is more highly associated with elevated insulin levels than with any other physiological measure.

Stress and Growth Processes

Like other aspects of human functioning, growth is determined by the interaction of genetic predisposition and environmental events. Moderate stress has a facilitative effect on growth processes, optimizing pituitary secretion of *growth hormone*, bone growth, cell division, and distribution of nutrients for tissue growth. However, chronic stress also impairs normal growth and development via (1) sympathetic nervous system arousal (where growth functions are put on hold and digestion and metabolism disrupted), (2) inhibited growth hormone release (due in part to excess levels of glucocorticoids that reduce target cell sensitivity and impair synthesis of new proteins and DNA in cell division), and (3) the shortening of *telomeres* (the DNA sequences that program the number of cell divisions).

Stress and Reproductive Processes

Because of the interconnectedness of homeostatic systems, biological and behavioral processes combine to contribute to obesity, resulting in the release of adipose derived hormones (e.g., leptin, adiponectin, kisspeptins, ghrelin), which, in turn, influence reproductive functions, puberty, and fertility. High levels of chronic stress can result in glucocorticoid inhibition of hypothalamic release of *luteinizing hormone* (LH) and *follicle stimulating hormone* (FSH). The effect is to inhibit *testosterone* release and *sperm production* in males, and *estrogen* release and *egg production* in females. Stress can also impede the parasympathetic activation required for male penile erections resulting in *impotence* or *premature ejaculation*. Stress-induced fat cell consumption in females can impede *estrogen* production, resulting in a relative buildup of male hormone that contributes to *amenorrhea*. The lowering of *progesterone* levels combined with glucocorticoid blockade of bone re-calcification can lead to *osteoporosis*. Other consequences may include *atherosclerosis* and impaired uterine wall nutrition, increasing the risk of miscarriage and preterm labor.

Stress and the Immune System

> By what bio-behavioral mechanisms does stress contribute to immune system disorders?

Immune system disorders further illustrate gene-environment interactions in the etiology of disease. Although acute/moderate stress generally activates the genetically programmed *immune system*, chronic stress and the resultant excess levels of glucocorticoids in the blood may impair the production of B cells and T cells, and induce premature migration of T cells from the thymus, leading to thymus shrinkage. Moreover, chronic stress impairs natural killer cell activity, undermining a major defense against tumors and viruses. Thus, individuals under chronic stress are more susceptible to diseases associated with immune system suppression. Ironically, chronic stress can also heighten immune system responses where organs or tissues in the host body are attacked. Such *autoimmune disorders* include multiple sclerosis, pernicious anemia, rheumatoid arthritis, juvenile diabetes, and various allergies. Autoimmune diseases can be organ specific, where the antigenic response focuses on a specific tissue or organ, like Hashimoto's thyroiditis (thyroid) or multiple sclerosis (nerve cell myelin sheaths). Autoimmune diseases can also be non-organ specific, where the antigen is universal, attacking parts of every cell, as in systemic lupus erythematosus (onset believed to be precipitated by viral infection) or forms of rheumatoid arthritis (onset believed to be precipitated by bacterial infection). Supporting this mechanism of action, meta-analyses have shown that chronic stress is associated with reduced ability to produce antibodies, a critically important immunological response.

Stress and Cancer

Because chronic stress can impair normal cell processes, such as **apoptosis** (cell death and recycling), cells can become "immortal" resulting in rapid, seemingly endless cell division. In addition, *regulatory genes* can be mutated by carcinogens, such as UV rays or toxic chemicals, impairing cell growth processes. Chronic stress can also impair the ability of the immune system to mobilize defenses against invading tumor cells, inadvertently enhance tumor cell growth, and facilitate *angiogenesis* (increased capillary growth) and nutrient feeding of tumor cells. Thus, especially with tumors that are viral in origin, stress may not only directly enhance the growth of the tumor, but also – even if indirectly – contribute to its origin by suppressing the immune response.

Stress and Cardiovascular Disorders

> By what bio-behavioral mechanisms does stress contribute to cardiovascular disorders?

Cardiovascular disorders are the product of a complex **gene-environment interaction** where individuals who are genetically predisposed (have a family history) and behaviorally vulnerable (eat a poor diet and get little exercise) to cardiovascular disease are especially susceptible to precipitating stressor conditions (sudden shock or unexpected major loss).

> Individuals who regularly smoke, consume excessive amounts of alcohol, are overweight, have a sedentary life style, get little regular physical exercise, and consume an unhealthy diet are at increased risk for diabetes, hypertension, hypercholesterolemia, and hyperlipidemia, each of which significantly increases their vulnerability, when stressed, to cardiovascular disease.

Acute stress alters the normally functioning cardiovascular system by diminishing arterial flow; increasing blood pressure and heart rate; diverting blood flow from the digestive tract, kidneys, and skin to brain and muscles; decreasing urine to conserve water and blood volume; and emptying the bladder to reduce weight. Conditions of high or chronic stress significantly amplify the severity of these same responses, raising the risk of organ system dysfunction and damage. Otherwise unexplained, or *essential hypertension* (BP 140/90 mm Hg), is the cardiovascular sign in 90% of cases. Stress-induced chronic arterial constriction, combined with high cholesterol levels, can result in clogging (*atherosclerosis*) and impeded blood oxygen flow (*myocardial ischemia*). This, in

Table 7.1. Other disorders associated with chronic stress-induced system failures	
Gastrointestinal:	irritable bowel syndrome, esophageal reflux
Respiratory:	hyperventilation, asthma
Dermatologic:	eczema, acne, alopecia universalis
Musculoskeletal:	muscle strain, low back pain
Cognitive:	low self-esteem and self-efficacy, pessimistic expectancy, learned helplessness
Emotional:	affective and adjustment disorders, posttraumatic stress disorder, transient psychosis, substance abuse

turn, can lead to chest pain (*angina*), or, in more severe cases, to cell death (*infarct*). Chronic stress can also result in the heart muscle lapsing into an asynchronous or disorganized rhythm (*arrhythmia* or *fibrillation*). In addition, persons who are exposed to chronic stress, and who already have coronary artery disease, have significantly higher insulin levels than do persons who have coronary artery disease but without chronic stress.

Migraine headache results from a spasm of the arterial vasculature in response to stressor-induced sympathetic nervous system activity, and can be precipitated by an array of biological, environmental, cognitive, or sociocultural stressors. *Raynaud's phenomenon*, another vasospastic disorder, involves vasoconstriction of the fingers and toes in response to cold temperature. Table 7.1 lists other common stress disorders that are consequences of chronic stress-induced system breakdowns.

Psychological Consequences

Chronic stress that induces continued emotional arousal can have serious psychological consequences. Conditions leading to an excessive fight or flight response can result in chronic **anticipatory anxiety**, a dread that pending situations will trigger a fear response, especially the physiological components (see Chapter 8, Emotion and Learning, and Chapter 46, Anxiety and Dissociative Disorders, for a more detailed discussion of conditioned fear responses). Similarly, exposure to repeated loss, failure, or interpersonal disappointment can lead to **depression** and a sense of **learned helplessness** (see Chapter 47, Major Mood Disorders). In addition, emotional responses and physical symptoms can become conditioned to specific thoughts, memories, self-statements, or acts so that whenever these cognitions or events recur they activate these same emotional states and physical symptoms (e.g., "every time I fail, I get depressed and get a headache").

Sudden, life-threatening, *traumatic events* can generate intense feelings of *helplessness* and *powerlessness* leading to the development of *post traumatic stress disorder* (PTSD). The precipitating event, although necessary, is not responsible for PTSD; rather PTSD is the result of a stress response so severe that the emergency function of the amygdala overwhelms the ability of the hippocampus to act as modulator (to analyze past relevant contextual experience, learn, and offer an appropriate adaptive response). The emotional consequences of the stressor event cannot be anchored in any identifiable contextual memory (cognition), resulting in nightmares and "flashbacks" (re-experiencing the emotional memory as if the original event is actually happening), as well as insomnia, heightened physiological arousal, and emotional hypervigilance.

Moderating the Stress Response

A stressor is any agent (including pathogens), event, or condition that challenges the homeostatic integrity of the human organism or any of its component systems. Stressors can originate under

Table 7.2. Life events and their respective stress units		
Death of spouse 100	Divorce 73	Marital separation 65
Jail term 63	Death of close family member 63	Personal injury or illness 53
Marriage 50	Being fired 47	Marital reconciliation 45
Retirement 45	Health change of family member 44	Pregnancy 40
Sexual difficulties 39	Having a baby 39	Change in finances 38
Death of close friend 37	New line of work 36	Increased fighting with spouse 35
Large mortgage 31	Foreclosure 31	Son or daughter leaving home 30
In-law troubles 29	Spouse starts or stops work 26	Begin or end school 26
Trouble with boss 23	Moving into new home 20	Change in sleeping habits 16
Change in eating habits 16	Vacation 13	Total:____

The total number of "life change units" accumulated in the past year of an individual's life provides an estimate of the impact of stress on health. If the total score is 300+, there is an 80% risk of illness. If the total score is 150–299+, there is a 50% risk of illness. If the total score is ≤ 150, there is a slight risk of illness.

Adapted from Holmes T, Rahe R. The Social Reajustment Rating Scale. *Journal of Psychosomatic Research*, 2: 213–218, 1967. © 1967. Reprinted with permission from Elsevier.

an array of genetic, biological, behavioral, cognitive, sociocultural, or environmental conditions. However, the term "stressor" is most commonly applied within the context of daily life events (i.e., changes in health, sleep habits, finances, or social interactions).The relationship between life events and physical or psychological well-being has long been an object of research. In the 1960s and 70s, **Holmes and Rahe** attempted to quantify the relative importance of life changes in terms of distress or "morbidity load" on the individual. They investigated the relationship between stress and illness, and developed a life stress scale composed of 43 **life events**, each weighted for the severity of the stressor. By correlating life events with illnesses that occurred in the following 6–12 months, they found that the total number of "life change units" accumulated in a year's time provided an estimate of the impact of life stress on the individual's health (see Table 7.2). While negative events such as the death of a family member, breakup of a relationship, or economic hardship were obviously stressful, positive events, such as a wedding or holiday, could also be stressful.

Subsequent research has shown that predictive validity of such a life events scale may be improved by taking into account the degree to which an event or condition is stressful "in the eye of the beholder." As such, one person's severe "stressor" may be only another person's moderate challenge. Thus, the impact of a stressor is determined in part by the individual's **appraisal**, or judgment of significance and meaning.

The stress response is also influenced by an individual's **vulnerabilities**. For example, a patient can be genetically vulnerable (Down syndrome), cognitively vulnerable (depressive, defeatist beliefs), behaviorally vulnerable (a smoker or drinker), or socioculturally vulnerable (poor, undernourished, denied health care or economic opportunities). Among the individual's *resources* are **coping skills**, which reflect one's adaptive abilities in the form of behavioral skills, cognitive strategies, sense of self-efficacy or confidence, and motivation. Another resource, **social support**, refers to the validation, support, and assistance that the individual can count on from others. Additional resources may be material, financial, educational, intellectual, cognitive, health, creative, and social skills and include benefits such as access to health care the individual can marshal or call upon.

While individuals may seek to limit exposure, learning to effectively manage stress is a more realistic and appropriate goal than trying to eliminate stress. Thus, a person's stress response can best be moderated and regulated by interventions that reduce predisposing vulnerabilities, enhance stress appraisal abilities (cognitive) and coping skills, and increase skills for recruiting social support and identifying and utilizing other resources.

Recommended Readings

McEwen BS. Stress and Coping. In Berntson GB, Cacioppo JT (Eds.), *Handbook of Neurosciences for the Behavioral Sciences.* Hoboken, NJ: John Wiley & Sons; 2009, pp. 1220–1235.

Miller G, Chen E, Cole SW. Health psychology: Developing biologically plausible models linking the social world and physical health. *Annual Review of Psychology* 2009; 60:501–524.

Sapolsky RM. Stress and Cognition. In Gazzaniga MS (Ed.), *Cognitive Neurocience*, 3rd ed. Cambridge, MA: MIT Press; 2004, pp. 1031–1042.

Review Questions

1. The concept of stress refers to any system under strain, such as a challenge to the homeostasis or integrity of the organism. Thus, stress disorders can have their origins in which of the following systems?
   A. Biological
   B. Cognitive behavioral
   C. Environmental
   D. Sociocultural
   E. All of the above

2. The _____ plays a key role in the organism's initial emergent response to stress, while the _____ modulates the stress response based upon memories of relevant past experience.
   A. amygdala, hippocampus
   B. amygdala, hypothalamus
   C. hippocampus, prefrontal cortex
   D. pituitary, thalamus
   E. thalamus, hypothalamus

3. Which of the following is a true statement about the effect of chronic stress on the immune system?
   A. Chronic stress can suppress but not heighten immune system responses.
   B. Chronic stress contributes to non-organ-specific but not organ-specific autoimmune disorders.
   C. Chronic stress induces migration of T cells into the thymus resulting in thymic swelling.
   D. Excess levels of circulating glucocorticoids damages or impairs T cells.
   E. Immune system stress responses occur primarily in the setting of genetic vulnerability.

4. Medical disorders are generally caused by the breaking down or overwhelming of the body's defensive efforts. However, the body's defenses can sometimes be too effective, resulting in
   A. autoimmune diseases.
   B. cardiovascular diseases.
   C. hematopoietic diseases.
   D. neuroendocrine diseases.
   E. sensory diseases.

Key to review questions: p. 407

Section IV

Individual–Environment Interaction

8 Emotion and Learning

John E. Carr, PhD

- What role does emotion play in adaptation?
- What role does learning play in evolution?
- What bio-behavioral mechanisms are involved in implicit vs. explicit learning?
- What is the developmental significance of different kinds of learning?
- What bio-behavioral mechanism makes reinforcement possible?
- What is exposure therapy and how does it work?

Emotion

What role does emotion play in adaptation?

States of physiological arousal are experienced as an **emotion**, feeling, or affect that alerts the organism to the significance of incoming sensory information. How the information and the physiological arousal are interpreted depends upon the situational context in which it occurs and the cognitive interpretation, or meaning, assigned to that context, based on the individual's past experience.

The earliest emotions in the newborn are genetically programmed reflexive expressions of distress, designed to generate caregiving behaviors in parents. The *most basic emotion* is pleasure-displeasure, which differentiates into other *primary emotions* (e.g., joy, sadness, fear, anger, interest, surprise, disgust) as the infant develops. These early emotional expressions are universal, suggesting they are genetically determined for their survival value. As the individual develops, emotional expression becomes increasingly complex, influenced by physiological, cognitive, sociocultural, and environmental stimuli. As emotion is increasingly influenced by culture (See Chapter 18, Culture and Ethnicity), expression is governed by *display rules* that define when, where, and how specific emotions are expressed. While primary emotions are predominately individual and reflexive, *social emotions* (e.g., guilt, shame, embarrassment, empathy, compassion, admiration, respect) develop in response to interactions with others (e.g., family, community).

Gender and Emotion

Males and females generally use similar emotional experiences and similar emotional language to describe their experiences, but may differ in the manner in which emotions are behaviorally expressed. Both genders tend to accept the stereotype that men conceal their feelings more than women, although women can be as inhibited as men, and men can be as emotional as women. When challenged, men are more likely to express anger-aggression, associated with the release of *testosterone*, during the male stress response. Women are more likely to express nurturing feelings, fear, and sadness, especially within the context of family and friends. These gender-specific emotional expressions originate in the differential responses of male and female brains to the actions of *adrenal steroids, gonadal hormones*, and other *excitatory neuromodulators*.

Emotional expressions and associated social roles are common to many cultures, which suggests an evolutionary bio-behavioral interaction between heredity and sociocultural sanctions.

Bio-Behavioral Mechanisms of Emotion

The amount of *glucocorticoid* released from the adrenal cortex and *catecholamine* released from the adrenal medulla and sympathetic nerve endings defines the intensity of a stress response and, therefore, the perceived importance of the stress event. These actions, and the associated emotional state, are thereby *conditioned* to the stimulus event. This composite memory converges in the basolateral *amygdala* and is forwarded to the *hippocampus, caudate nucleus,* and *cortex,* where it is consolidated, stored, and readily accessed, automatically or unconsciously, in similar future situations. The strength of a memory is proportional to the intensity of the emotional response and serves to alert the individual in the future to potentially threatening, benign, or pleasurable situations.

> While generally adaptive, the conditioning of emotional responses can have unintended consequences, as in anxiety or phobic disorders. For example, fear associated with an injection can be conditioned to the nurse administering the shot, resulting in a conditioned fear response whenever the patient sees a nurse. Elements of incoming sensory information from the thalamus (sight of the nurse) and prefrontal cortex (fear memory of the injection) converge simultaneously in the lateral nucleus of the amygdala. This connects to the central nucleus of the amygdala which, in response to the incoming information, activates the HPA axis-mediated stress response, now influenced by the emotional memory (fear). As a result, the sight of any nurse may trigger a (fear) response.

Bio-Behavioral Mechanisms of Emotion Regulation

Any emotional response that can be conditioned can be "un-conditioned" or *extinguished.* However, this does not mean that the response is eliminated. Rather, it means the response becomes less relevant in light of new information or a change in circumstances. The ability to alter a response as circumstances change is essential to successful adaptation and survival. The situation to which fear (or any emotion) is conditioned defines the *context* of the fear. Thus, situations previously perceived as threatening may be re-appraised in a new context and found to be benign.

In addition to contextual change, fear can be replaced with more adaptive emotional responses through emotion regulation strategies involving specific bio-behavioral mechanisms. When the circumstances of an emotional response are altered, the prefrontal cortex and hippocampus exercise inhibitory control over the amygdala and introduce new contextual information. A new response is learned and takes priority over the old response. Learning to cope with an emotional response establishes a new context and appears to involve activation of the striatum. All of these strategies are especially effective immediately following the activation of the emotional response before memory can be reconsolidated and is, therefore, still "vulnerable." These mechanisms underlie the effectiveness of behavioral interventions.

Learning

> What role does learning play in evolution?

Human adaptation is possible because the brain can associate and store sequences and patterns of events in time and space. This capability contributes to the development of behaviors, traits, and characteristics that are most successful in overcoming environmental challenges. These successful adaptations are then genetically passed on to offspring through **natural selection**. Thus, the current human genome is the result of an accumulation of *gene-development-environment interactions* that promote survival. However, the genetic contribution to this evolutionary process is not *what was learned* but rather the development of the brain systems that facilitated the *ability to learn.* As a result, learning enables the organism to adapt and modify behavior, incentives, and future goals. **Behavior modification** involves altering behavior associated with events contiguous in time and space. **Incentive modification** involves anticipating outcomes and altering future goals based on "lessons learned" from past experience. Incentive modification may also involve learning how to delay gratification or inhibit certain responses in order to achieve, at a later date, desired outcomes that cannot be fully achieved immediately.

Principle of Association

The **principle of association** refers to the ability of organisms to "record" relationships between environmental events, biological responses, cognitions, or behaviors and their consequences. Associations range from simple sequential connections *(if* I push the button, *then* the horn will honk) to more complex associations incorporating temporal, spatial, and causal relationships, contextual cues, and consequences (if I honk the horn late at night in a residential area, I may get an angry response). Thus, *contextual cues* play an important role in guiding attention, emotional response, learning, and memory retrieval, thereby influencing subsequent behavior.

> Time is an especially important contextual cue because the passage of time constantly changes the context.

Bio-Behavioral Mechanisms of Learning

Stimulus characteristics are stored in memory in the form of individual nerve cell responses and are associated via **synaptic transmission** between nerve cells. The extensive dendritic tree of a single vertebrate neuron can form 100,000–200,000 receptive synaptic contacts with other neurons, thus providing an extraordinary array of potential associative networks. There are two types of learning based on the level and complexity of the neuronal mechanisms involved:

1. **Implicit learning** is the association of immediately sequential sensory and motor system responses via lower levels of cortical mediation. The information stored is limited to predictive relationships between events. Implicit learning can be immediate (reflexive) or cumulative over time, but tends to be automatic, often without the conscious participation of the individual.

2. **Explicit learning** involves more abstract associations between diverse stimuli and events that vary across time and space. Explicit learning tends to be intentional, and typically requires more active conscious participation by the individual. Explicit learning outcomes may be immediate (e.g., instantaneous "insight") or delayed (e.g., extended "reflection").

> What bio-behavioral mechanisms are involved in implicit vs. explicit learning?

Implicit Learning

During implicit learning, excitation of a sensory neuron stimulates release of the neurotransmitter, **serotonin**. Serotonin initiates a series of biochemical changes, including activation of a protein kinase that prolongs the action potential, allowing more neurotransmitters to be released at the synaptic junction. Sequential stimulation of two adjacent neurons results in the convergence of two signals at the synaptic junction. The first signal sensitizes the synapse, which potentiates or amplifies the effect of the second signal and enhances the associative link between the two neurons. Through this mechanism, the organism records information in the form of *sensory memories* derived from environmental interactions. These sensory memories are short lived due to the limited time span of synaptic firing. However, the process can be enhanced and made more durable by repeated associations with other sensory or motor signals occurring in connection with the same stimulus event. *Procedural memory* involves the acquisition and retrieval of motor sequences (tying shoe laces) and cognitive sequences (organizing a schedule). Information of low interest or infrequent utility may be retained for a few minutes in *short-term memory* areas such as the prefrontal cortex, but will erode if not consolidated.

Explicit Learning

Explicit learning requires activation and coordination of structures in the cortex, especially the temporal lobe and other mediating brain networks, for the longer-term processing, coding, and storing of complex information. The **limbic system** (hippocampus, amygdala, basal forebrain, and thalamus) receives and integrates incoming sensory information. The diverse sensory inputs of an event (e.g., time, space, contextual cues) are collated by the thalamus and then referred on to the amygdala, which records its "emotional" significance, and to the hippocampus, which assigns it a temporal and spatial context. These contextual cues facilitate learning by enabling the limbic system to reference the new incoming information to related memories in the cortex.

The hippocampus and its associated structures in the limbic system serve as a central switchboard, connecting the various storage sites distributed throughout the cortex to form combined memories. When new learning occurs, these connections constitute temporary or short-term memory and are easily lost or reorganized as additional information is received. However, over time, as some memories are repeatedly activated and continue to have predictive value, they are eventually forwarded by the hippocampus to the prefrontal cortex to become part of long-term memory.

Major neural pathways of the hippocampus use the excitatory amino acid **glutamate** as a neurotransmitter. After neuronal excitation, glutamate binds with two types of protein receptors on the cell membrane of the postsynaptic neuron: (1) **NMDA receptors** (N-methyl D-aspartate), and (2) all other or **non-NMDA receptors**. The NMDA receptor response is blocked by magnesium ions until the cell is unblocked by depolarization due to the stimulation of non-NMDA receptors. The intensity of the stimulus determines the magnitude of the depolarization and, therefore, the intensity of the cell response. The convergence of NMDA and non-NMDA receptor activation produces a slow, long-lasting synaptic response. In complex learning situations requiring multiple stimulus associations, the repeated convergence of these excitatory changes on two or more neurons serves to potentiate and prolong the sensitivity of the synaptic link. This **long-term potentiation (LTP) effect**, however, requires that the two signals – glutamate binding to the receptor and depolarization of the postsynaptic cell – take place simultaneously, thus providing the associative linkage.

Neurogenesis

The human capacity for learning is facilitated by **neurogenesis**, the ability of the nervous system to generate new neurons and neuronal connections. The process involves the proliferation, survival, migration, differentiation, and integration of neuronal cells essential to learning. The new cells are generated from stem cells and, although there is evidence of neurogenesis in several areas of the brain, its occurrence in the dentate gyrus of the hippocampus is especially important as it explains the significant role the hippocampus plays in the mediation and processing of new information.

Learning and Developmental Demands

What is the developmental significance of different kinds of learning?

From birth to maturity, humans must adapt to increasingly demanding interactions with the environment, especially the social environment, requiring the development of progressively more complex and sophisticated learning processes.

Reflexive behavior represents the cumulative result of ancestral learning genetically programmed into the organism. Reflexes (e.g., distress cries, sucking) require minimal interaction with the environment and promote survival during early life, before the individual can learn from experience.

Critical period learning is also the result of genetic programming but involves an increasing interaction with the environment. **Imprinting** and **bonding** occur in response to specific stimulus cues in the environment (e.g., nurturing or "maternal" figures) essential to continued survival. Critical period learning, however, is time limited, e.g., the organism is responsive to the stimulus for only a brief time.

One-trial learning behaviors are reflexive in their survival value, but involve even more interaction with the environment. The strength or durability of learning depends upon the intensity of the stimulus, the intensity of the subsequent biological/emotional response, and the relevance to the organism's survival. Examples include touching a hot stove or ingesting an intensely nauseating substance.

Classical conditioning reflects the ability of the organism to learn from increasingly complex interactions with the environment. It involves the association of two sequential events (A and B) such that one event (B) acquires the ability to elicit responses (R) formerly associated with the other event (A).

> After repeated trips to the hospital for chemotherapy (unconditioned stimulus, US), the side effects of which include nausea (unconditioned response, UR), a patient may begin to experience nausea (conditioned response, CR) as soon as the hospital (conditioned stimulus, CS) comes into view. Thus, through associative learning, the hospital acquires the ability to induce nausea.

Operant conditioning is an advanced form of learning that makes it possible for the individual to learn from the positive or negative consequences of interactions with the environment, thus becoming more effective in assessing and adapting to stressful challenges. **Social learning**, an advanced form of operant conditioning, is a further adaptation of human learning to environmental demands, especially the complexities of interpersonal relationships (see Chapter 9, Cognition and Social Interaction).

Reinforcement

A fundamental principle of operant conditioning, the **Law of Effect**, states that if a behavior is followed by positive consequences (reinforcement), that behavior will increase in frequency over time. Conversely, if a certain behavior is followed by negative consequences (punishment), that behavior will decrease over time. A *reinforcer* is any biological, behavioral, cognitive, sociocultural, or environmental event that reduces stress and restores homeostasis. Since stress reduction and the restoration of homeostasis are positive con-

sequences, any behavior that contributes to them will be rewarded and, thereby, increase in frequency over time.

The Premack Principle

If an individual engages repeatedly in an activity, it implies that the activity is rewarding. Based on this observation, psychologist David Premack proposed that a frequently performed behavior can be used as a reinforcer for a preferred target behavior. A mother invokes this principle when she tells her 6-year-old, "If you pick up your toys, you can watch your favorite TV show."

Having a rewarding experience is positively reinforcing, while avoiding an unpleasant or punishing experience is negatively reinforcing. In both cases, the behavior is reinforced and, therefore, will continue or increase over time. **Negative reinforcement** explains several aspects of human behavior, such as studying to *avoid* failing or obeying the speed limit to *avoid* getting a traffic ticket. It also explains why many patients *avoid* going to the doctor to *avoid* experiencing pain (e.g., injections, blood draws), unpleasant examinations (e.g., prostate/pelvic examinations), hearing bad news (e.g., diagnosis of cancer), or unpleasant treatments (e.g., dietary changes, abstinence from alcohol).

Stimulus generalization is a process by which a response can be elicited by other stimuli in a common context. Stimulus generalization explains why a long-time smoker finds it difficult to stop smoking behavior that has been conditioned to an array of contextual cues, all of which can trigger the smoking response (e.g., coffee breaks, social events, specific times or locations).

Bio-Behavioral Interaction in Reinforcement

What bio-behavioral mechanism makes reinforcement possible?

The **endogenous reward system** is the mechanism that drives adaptive learning in enabling the individual to identify and reinforce those cognitions and behaviors that have adaptive and survival value. The core of this endogenous system is a neuronal conduit, the **median forebrain bundle**, which includes the *nucleus accumbens*, the *ventral tegmental area*, the *ventromedial* and *lateral nuclei of the hypothalamus*, and the *amygdala*. This conduit connects to all the structures within the limbic system, including the hippocampus, septal nuclei, and anterior cingulate gyrus, as well as the hypothalamus and amygdala. Recall that the limbic system regulates homeostasis, emotion, learning, and memory, and coordinates the neuroendocrine response to stress. Since it regulates almost every endocrine, visceral, and autonomic function, it is in a position to assess all incoming information, determine what functions, behaviors, substances, or strategies constitute an optimal response, and provide a rewarding inducement for the retention of that response. The inducement comes primarily in the form of increased dopaminergic neurotransmitter release at the neuronal synapses within the endogenous reward system.

As incoming sensory information is processed by the brain (new learning), the amygdala assesses the emotional impact of the information, and the hippocampus and prefrontal cortex assess the adaptive value of the information, contrasting it with already stored memories. If the new experience is judged less adaptive than comparable past experience, then the new information or behavior is not rewarded and is unlikely to be retained. If the new information is more valued, the association is strengthened by the rewarding impact of the dopaminergic neurotransmitter system and the memories/behaviors are reinforced and retained.

The HPA axis also plays a role in the endogenous reward system. Recall that stress-induced activation of the HPA axis releases a cascade of hormones that includes *endogenous opioids* (e.g., endorphins, enkephalins) whose anti-pain, anti-anxiety properties can also have significant reinforcing effects.

Clinical Applications

Since many illness behaviors, symptoms, emotional responses, and health-related beliefs are learned, clinical strategies using learning principles have been developed to assist patients to modify maladaptive responses and learn more adaptive and healthy behaviors.

Conditioning therapy is based on classical conditioning principles. This technique has been applied in the treatment of cancer where chemotherapies to suppress immune functioning may have severely noxious side effects. By repeatedly pairing the treatment with a pleasant odor, the odor acquires the ability to elicit the treatment effect (immunosuppression) but with fewer of the noxious side effects of the chemotherapy.

Aversive conditioning involves conditioning a noxious stimulus to an undesired response, leading to the extinction of the undesired response. This approach has been used in alcohol treatment programs by conditioning noxious substances (e.g., disulfiram) to drinking behavior.

Contingency management involves selectively manipulating the consequences of a behavior to (1) increase desired behaviors via positive reinforcement; (2) extinguish undesirable behaviors; and (3) avoid undesirable consequences via negative reinforcement. Contingency management is effective in the treatment of chronic pain (see above). Reinforcers of pain-related complaining behavior (e.g., attention) are identified, eliminated, or gradually reduced *(fading)* leading to the extinction of this undesirable behavior. The approach is also used to develop desirable health behaviors through *shaping* (i.e., reinforcing progressive steps in a diet program such as cutting intake of carbonated beverages by 25% each week for a month to attain abstinence).

Stimulus control involves the use of anticipatory cues to guide behavior toward more rewarding consequences. If a child sees reminders to brush her teeth when entering the bathroom, brushing is more likely to occur and can be reinforced by

A patient receiving pain medication PRN (as needed) and attentive care complains of pain. Over time, the patient complains more frequently of increased pain. The pain reduction associated with taking medication and the attention received from nursing staff actually reinforces the pain complaints, so that they become more frequent and the perceived intensity of the pain increases. The attending physician orders pain medication administered every four hours and limited nursing attention to pain complaints. Gradually, the patient's pain complaints and pain intensity decrease. Why?

the parent ("What sparkling teeth you have!"). In addition to rewarding desirable behavior, undesirable behavior can be extinguished by removing the opportunity for reinforcement (time out), or forfeiture of positive reinforcers (response cost). Reinforcement is the basis of **token economy** programs where patients accumulate "tokens" or points for successful completion of treatment sequences (e.g., rehab), which they can use to obtain rewards or privileges.

Feedback, based on the principle that information is reinforcing, involves communicating to the patient information that promotes self-monitoring and adaptive change. **Biofeedback**, utilizing electronic or other external physiological monitors, provides the patient with information about otherwise unperceived autonomic, neuroendocrine, and other biological system responses to stress. Feedback on progress can reinforce relevant skills, and thus increase the likelihood that these skills will be utilized in the future. Maintaining behavioral records of stimulus events, symptom frequency, associated cognitions and behaviors, and outcomes is the most useful and fundamental feedback technique.

Cognitive restructuring refers to the modification of the patient's perceived significance of bodily sensations, self-esteem, self-efficacy (coping effectiveness), nature and severity of illness, effectiveness of treatments, competence of health professionals, prognosis, and other perceptions that influence health and health care.

A 35-year-old man with no history of cardiac risk factors visits the ER several times with complaints of "pain in my chest." He presents with elevated heart rate, sweating, dizziness, and shortness of breath, yet cardiac function tests are normal and the symptoms disappear within an hour. A careful history reveals that the patient is interpreting a twinge in his chest as a sign of an impending heart attack. This "catastrophic" belief then apparently initiates the stress response, which, in turn, produces even more sympathetic nervous system activation. A cognitive restructuring intervention would involve teaching the patient to challenge his "catastrophic" belief by considering the evidence (e.g., no personal or familial risk factors; cardiac testing normal), explaining the nature of the stress response, and considering alternative explanations, e.g., current life stress, heartburn, or muscle strain.

Relaxation and breathing training teaches patients how to modulate physical symptoms of the stress response (e.g., muscle tension, hyperventilation) that contribute to or complicate illnesses. Relaxation training is often used in conjunction with biofeedback techniques. Through self-monitoring, the patient in the example might learn that once he notices atypical chest sensations and interprets them as dangerous, he immediately starts hyperventilating. The patient could then learn to regulate his breathing under these circumstances and abort the cycle of sympathetic nervous system arousal.

What is exposure therapy and how does it work?

Exposure therapy invokes a number of "re-learning" and context-changing strategies to reduce fear reactions and avoidant responses. The patient is exposed to stimuli that trigger undesirable symptoms (e.g., anxiety), but under conditions that minimize reinforcement (e.g., sympathy) or maladaptive responses (e.g., avoidance). To control the intensity of the response, exposure therapies can be applied via imagery (i.e., imagining a stressful situation), virtual reality situations (e.g., computer generated), or *in vivo* (i.e., real life/real time). The patient can be exposed gradually from minimal to more intense stimuli (*systematic desensitization*) or in a single "flooded" exposure *(immersion)*. Systematic desensitization usually has more positive and longer-lasting treatment outcomes than immersion techniques.

Interoceptive exposure refers to exercises that encourage the patient to experience the bodily sensations of the stress response, but under controlled conditions. The primary goal is to assist the patient in better understanding, tolerating, and controlling the stress response. The patient may be instructed to hyperventilate, climb stairs, and spin on a chair to induce feared sensations, then notice how they dissipate homeostatically without having to seek medical attention or reassurance.

Imaginal exposure refers to exercises that encourage the patient to recall stressful events or conditions, thereby cognitively inducing conditioned stress response symptoms. The goal, as in all exposure exercises, is to enable patients to better understand the stress response mechanisms that produce their symptoms and thereby increase their tolerance and control over the symptoms. Gradual and repeated exposures to these memories will eventually lead to associated reductions in the fear response when thinking about or actually participating in a feared behavior (e.g., flying in a plane, riding a horse, speaking in public).

In vivo **exposure** refers to exercises carried out in real time/life with the same goals of assisting patients to better understand the stress response mechanism so they can increase tolerance and control. For example, a patient avoids driving his car on busy streets for fear of losing control of the vehicle. *In vivo* exposure exercises involve having him drive in progressively more dense traffic and busier roadways. Teaching individuals to approach previously avoided situations is an important learning experience that provides them with new contextual information (i.e., the event is not as fearful as anticipated). Recent technological advances make exposure possible through **virtual reality** simulations. This approach is effective as an intermediary treatment step between imaginal and *in vivo* approaches.

How Does Exposure Therapy Work?

Exposure, imaginal or real, triggers the stress response, which includes the simultaneous release of **adrenocorticotropic hormone** (ACTH), which has excitatory effects, and **beta endorphin** (BE), which has analgesic and anxiolytic effects. The ACTH contributes to the "fight or flight" response, and, because it is antagonistic to BE, momentarily blocks BE receptors. Within minutes, however, the ACTH decays biochemically; the BE, which has a longer half-life, moves into the receptors, producing an anxiolytic effect. This mechanism appears to coincide with the patient's report of initial heightened arousal (stress hormones, including ACTH), followed, in minutes, by a reduction in anxiety (due to the BE). Confronting the stress situation, tolerating the stress, and being rewarded by biologically mediated stress reduction (new context) reinforces coping behavior and increases a sense of self control.

Problem-Solving Therapy (PST) involves developing skills for resolving stressful situations and enhancing self-esteem. The five major steps of problem solving include (1) identifying the problem, (2) generating possible solutions, (3) choos-

ing the most plausible solution, (4) implementing the solution, and (5) evaluating the outcome.

Cognitive Behavioral Therapy (CBT). Stress response symptoms can be conditioned to the patient's cognitions as well as his/her behavior, and can be maladaptive, contributing to the disease-illness process. CBT strategies modify patients' maladaptive beliefs by restructuring cognitions, teaching more effective coping skills, explaining the nature of the stress response, and increasing the patient's ability to effectively problem solve and adapt to stressor conditions. Evidence of the effectiveness of CBT for medical and psychiatric disorders is well established. The application of these treatments has given rise to the fields of health psychology and behavioral medicine, and recognition of the value of combined biomedical and behavioral treatments to ensure effective intervention, follow-up, and prevention.

Motivational Interviewing (MI) is a guided intervention designed to help patients resolve ambivalence about behavior change. Developed as a strategy for motivating behavioral change in problem drinkers, it is based on five psychotherapeutic principles: (1) *accurate empathy* (understanding the patient's viewpoint and communicating that to the patient); (2) *expressing respect* for and affirmation of the patient; (3) *eliciting and selectively reinforcing* the patient's problem recognition, desire to change, and self-efficacy; (4) monitoring the patient's resistance to change until ready to change; and (5) *affirming the patient's control* over decisions and behavior change.

Recommended Readings

Cuff PA, Vanselow NA (Eds.). *Improving Medical Education: Enhancing the Behavioral and Social Sciences in Medical School Curricula.* Washington, DC: National Academies Press; 2004.

Eichenbaum H. Memory. In Berntson GG, Cacioppo JT (Eds.), *Handbook of Neurosciences for the Behavioral Sciences.* Hoboken, NJ: Wiley and Sons; 2009.

Hartley CA, Phelps EA. Changing fear: The neurocircuitry of emotion regulation. *Neuropsychopharmacology* 2010; 35:136–146.

Steinmetz JE, Lindquist DH. Neuronal Basis of Learning. In Bertson GG, Cacioppo JT (Eds.), *Handbook of Neurosciences for the Behavioral Sciences.* Hoboken, NJ: Wiley and Sons; 2009.

Review Questions

1. Which of the following statements about gender and emotion are true?
   A. Males and females are equal in their expression of happiness/sadness.
   B. Males and females use similar emotional language to describe experiences.
   C. Males and females use the same emotional expressions.
   D. Males are more likely to show anger toward others when challenged.
   E. All of the above.

2. Five-year-old Eloise has a temper tantrum if mother does not buy her candy at the grocery store. Mother tries to persuade her otherwise, but often relents to avoid making a scene. Eloise's behavior is most likely the result of which of the following reinforcement schedules?
   A. Continuous
   B. Intermittent
   C. Negative
   D. Positive
   E. Primary

3. In learning situations, the neurotransmitter that appears to be most involved in the reinforcement of new adaptive experiences is
   A. dopamine.
   B. epinephrine.
   C. glutamate.
   D. norepinephrine.
   E. serotonin.

4. Encouraging patients to gradually experience, tolerate, and focus on the bodily sensations associated with their stress response describes which of the following CBT methodologies?
   A. Imaginal exposure
   B. Interoceptive exposure
   C. *In vivo* exposure
   D. Virtual reality exposure
   E. All of the above

5. Mrs. Schwartz experiences nausea as a side effect of the chemotherapy she receives for her cancer. On days of her scheduled treatments, she begins to feel nauseated even before the infusion begins. Which of the following likely explains her nausea?
   A. Imprinting
   B. Reflux
   C. Response generalization
   D. Social reinforcement
   E. Stimulus generalization

Key to review questions: p. 407

9 Cognition and Social Interaction

John E. Carr, PhD

- What is declarative memory?
- What is cognitive style?
- What purpose does attachment serve?
- What is empathy?
- What neuronal development most likely made human speech possible?
- How do culture and cognition influence one another?

Cognition

Cognition refers to those bio-behavioral processes by which the information acquired through sensation and learning is analyzed, forwarded to appropriate cortical centers, organized and stored in memory for future retrieval, and used in problem solving and communication.

Cognitive Processes

Consciousness: state of arousal. Activation of the CNS results in awareness of self and the environment.

Alertness: level of response to the environment. Maximal alertness occurs at times of stress or challenge.

Attention: ability to focus. Characterized by intensity, selectivity, voluntary control, and concentration.

Memory: ability to receive, retain, store, and retrieve information.

Concept formation: ability to identify, record, and label commonalities and distinctions among stimuli.

Perception: analysis and interpretation of incoming information based on past experience.

Thought: application of stored concepts, schemas and strategies to appraise, cope, and problem solve.

Intelligence: ability to learn from and adapt to new experiences.

Communication/Language: ability to communicate one's own and comprehend another's cognitions and intentions.

Memory

What is declarative memory?

Memory refers to the ability of the brain to acquire, store, retain, and retrieve information. The brain is especially "tuned" to retain information that has adaptive value or is critical to the survival of the individual. Research delineates three types of memory functions:

1. **Sensory memory** is the acquisition of incoming information from each of the sensory systems and includes *evaluative memory*, which records the emotional significance of stimuli, and *procedural memory*, which includes the encoding of basic motor sequences (tying shoe laces) and, later, with maturation, the encoding of cognitive sequences (organizing a schedule). Sensory memory is prioritized and forwarded to short-term memory.

2. *Short-term* or **working memory** serves as a temporary "inbox" for information necessary for day-to-day tasks such as language comprehension, learning, and problem solving. Working memory has three sub-components: an attention controlling system, a visual imagery "sketch pad" system, and a phonological system for speech-based information. As the term implies, short-term or working memory decays rapidly. Information in working memory is temporarily retained in the prefrontal

cortex, and then, if replicated and validated, is consolidated and transmitted via the amygdala, hippocampus, and prefrontal cortex to cortical areas for storage as long-term memory. The *consolidation* phase of long-term memory is the time required for memory to become sufficiently permanent that it cannot be erased or altered by pharmacological or electrical interventions. In humans, achieving consolidation that is resistant to pharmacological erasure may take only a few hours. Electroconvulsive therapy (ECT) may produce temporary loss of both *anterograde* (immediately before an event) and *retrograde* (immediately after an event) memory, but memory loss is usually restricted to hours or days.

3. *Long-term memory* is comprised of **declarative memory**, which includes *semantic memory,* the retention and retrieval of structured information (e.g., facts, events, dates, concepts, theories), and contextual or *episodic memory*, the retention and retrieval of sequential events and recollections of personal experiences that become the basis for the concept of self.

> In general, episodic memory does not develop until around age 2 due to the delayed maturation of the hippocampus, which is essential to the processing of contextual information like personal experiences.

The bio-behavioral mechanisms of memory retrieval involve information from the cortical association areas being transmitted to *prefrontal cortical areas* that surround the *hippocampus*. The perirhinal cortex receives input from prefrontal cortical areas that process information about specific objects ("what" and "who"), while the parahippocampal cortex receives input from areas that process contextual or temporal and spatial information ("where" and "when"). The perirhinal and *parahippocampal cortices* project to the *entorhinal cortex*, which then feeds the information to the *hippocampus* where object and context are integrated. Thus, through its circuitry and neurogenic properties, the hippocampus is able to represent complex sequences of events and links between them in relational networks that make inferential problem solving possible under moderately challenging conditions. However, under conditions of severe, traumatic, or chronic stress, the ability of the hippocampus to encode or retrieve declarative information is impaired. This impairment is largely due to the impact of excessive *glucocorticoid* release, reduced glucocorticoid receptor response, and the resulting reduction in neuronal plasticity that jeopardizes the individual's adaptive or problem-solving capability (see Chapter 46, Anxiety and Dissociative Disorders).

> **Memory, Stress, and Coping**
>
> Neurogenesis, learning, and memory acquisition are promoted by moderate levels of stress or challenge, but are impaired by chronic/severe stress that increases glucocorticoid and other stress hormone levels. This, in turn:
> – stimulates amygdala functions and
> – impairs hippocampus functions, which
> – impairs explicit learning/memory and thereby
> – impairs adaptive response to stress, which
> – can result in futility, learned helplessness, and depression.

Concept Formation

In **concept formation**, the brain identifies and records commonalties among classes of stimuli (e.g., objects, places, events), sorts them into categories (*concepts*) that share the same features, and stores this information in semantic memory. Conceptualizations of operations (e.g., how to bake a cake, repair a motor, conduct a war) are called *schemas,* and are stored in procedural memory. Concepts and schemas are learned as the individual attempts to adapt to life challenges. As new challenges are experienced, these new events are compared to the memories of past experiences through hypothesis testing. If the hypothesis is confirmed, it is rewarded and retained. If disconfirmed, it is not rewarded and either changed or extinguished.

Intelligence

Intelligence refers to the quality and power of the individual's ability to learn from and adapt to new experiences and is determined by both heredity and experience. It is scientifically defined in terms of *verbal ability* and *spatial problem-solving skills*, but cultural definitions vary. In Western cultures, speed of processing information is valued. In other cultures, cautious introspection may be more highly valued. All cultures regard social judgment as a measure of intelligence but differ widely with regard to specific behaviors.

It is generally agreed that there are no significant differences in intelligence across populations distinguished by race, ethnicity, or culture. Studies that claim to identify such differences have been faulted on the basis of linguistic, ethnic, or cultural bias of the measuring instruments.

Intelligence usually reflects *convergent thinking* (the individual responds with typical solutions to a problem) and *divergent thinking* (the individual responds with alternative solutions to a problem). Divergent thinking is more creative (events are perceived in unusual ways that generate novel solutions) and reflects unique associative links in the brain applied to particular learning experiences.

Perceptual Development

Perception refers to the process of interpreting and assigning meaning to incoming sensory information based upon concepts and schemas learned from past experience. As experiences accumulate, perception develops throughout childhood. Early learning prompts **neurogenesis** in the hippocampus and prefrontal cortex, and increases in grey matter in the frontal lobes up to around age 11–12 years. With continuing experience and trial and error learning, the brain begins to "prune" incorrect or maladaptive neuronal connections. Adaptive information is reinforced and progressively insulated within a myelin sheath. Thus, a complex integrated cognitive structure, capable of mature perception and judgment, becomes available only in late adolescence or early adulthood.

Cognitive Style

What is cognitive style?

Cognitive style is the individual's unique manner in which a new experience is perceived, interpreted, and organized, ultimately producing a predictable *coping response*. One cognitive style is *locus of control* (generalized expectations about whether rewards are brought about through one's own efforts [internal], or are due to factors outside one's control [external]). Individuals with an internal locus of control believe they exert significant self-control over themselves and their environment, whereas individuals with an external locus of control believe they are at the mercy of forces beyond their control. Other cognitive styles include *learned helplessness* (a self-defeating cognitive style), *hardiness* or *resiliency* (a sense of "toughness" in which stress is viewed as a challenge rather than as a threat), *self-efficacy* (the individual's level of confidence about successfully coping with a challenging situation), and the *Type A personality*, characterized by excessive competitiveness, impatience, time urgency, and hostility that have been linked to high rates of coronary artery disease (see Chapter 2, Predisposition).

High levels of external locus of control and learned helplessness are found in patients with chronic depression.

Individuals with a Type A personality are at high risk for coronary artery disease. Low levels of hardiness or resiliency are associated with poor immune system response.

Defense Mechanisms

The concept of **defense mechanisms** is derived from psychoanalytic theory and refers to cognitive processes that influence the ways individuals perceive, interpret, and respond to situations that challenge cognitive, psychological, or biological homeostasis. Table 9.1 describes the more common defense mechanisms, redefined in terms of the cognitive processes involved rather than as used in psychoanalytic theory.

Table 9.1. Common defense mechanisms
Denial: incoming information that is threatening or contradictory to stored memory is refuted.
Repression: perceptions of events that are threatening or contradictory to past experiences are neither recognized nor retrievable from memory.
Intellectualization: an event or memory is re-conceptualized in sufficiently abstract terms to "distance" it from its original referent and associated conditioned emotional responses.
Projection: an idea, feeling, or behavior inconsistent with one's self-concept is attributed to another person.
Regression: stress is responded to using cognitive processes from earlier developmental stages associated with periods of less stressful coping.

Other cognitive processes that may buffer or exacerbate stress include *cognitive distortions*. These include *catastrophizing* (magnifying consequences into disastrous proportions), *over generalizing* (sweeping conclusions based on a single example), *personalization* (applying general information to oneself), *mind reading* (making assumptions about others' motives without evidence), and *unsubstantiated expectations* (of others' behaviors and motives).

Social Processes

An especially important contribution to the successful evolution of *Homo sapiens* has been the brain's facilitation of **social processes** that make collaborative efforts for adaptation and survival possible. While many species developed social processes to facilitate reproduction, care of offspring, and limited collaboration among immediate clan/pack members, humans are capable of contributing to significantly more complex social perceptions, functions, and organizations.

Attachment and Separation

What purpose does attachment serve?

The earliest social relationship is the **attachment** (see also Chapter 11) that develops between par-

ent and offspring Designed to provide safety and nurturance during the offspring's most vulnerable maturational phase, the bond facilitates the development of social processes necessary for survival. Early attachment is manifested by smiling and the infant's preference for sensations associated with the primary caregiver (e.g., the mother's voice).

> The attachment bond is an adaptive social process that has evolved to provide the human offspring with the degree of nurturance, safety, and social guidance appropriate to their changing developmental needs as they mature.

Gradually, the child develops into an increasingly self-sufficient social being. However, during the early childhood years, any disruption in the attachment bond (separation, abandonment, abuse) can have serious *developmental* as well as *epigenetic* consequences (see Chapters 47, Major Mood Disorders and 46, Anxiety and Dissociative Disorders). Separation from familiar caregivers (usually the mother) results in the withdrawal of the infant's primary source of nutrition, body heat, sensorimotor contact, and general comfort. As a consequence, the infant experiences a traumatic emotional reaction, the **biphasic protest-despair response**, in which the child first cries out to and seeks to locate mother (protest), followed by a period of decreased responsiveness (despair). Thus, important regulatory processes, critical to the infant's physical as well as social development, are dependent upon stable relationships with primary caregivers.

As the child develops, caregivers form a safe base from which to explore the world. Through the attachment bond, the caregiver also provides training in more complex social interactions such as *affiliation, imitation, reciprocity, play, empathy*, and *communication*, progressively developing the social perception and relational skills that will be required for successful survival and social adaptation in adulthood.

Affiliation

The attachment bond may be the evolutionary foundation for the development of the **affilia-**

tion response, the tendency to come together to provide and receive joint protection in response to threat or other stressors. The caring for offspring and affiliating with others has been called the *"tend and befriend" response*, and describes basic relational survival skills that are universal to all cultures and ethnic groups. There is evidence that the release of *oxytocin* from the hypothalamus during autonomic nervous system activation in response to social stressors is a key component of the bio-behavioral mechanism of this response. The release of oxytocin appears to be facilitated by estrogens and, together with dopaminergic and opioid systems, prompts affiliative behavior in females. Androgens, such as testosterone, inhibit oxytocin release while promoting the release of vasopressin, another hormone related to oxytocin. Thus, androgens, such as testosterone, are more likely to facilitate relationships for mutual defense rather than "tend and befriend" purposes.

Social learning in childhood is largely *vicarious* or *observational*. Through *imitation* of parents and significant others who model behavior, and through reciprocity and play, the child acquires social and coping skills that may, or may not, be appropriate and adaptive. Social learning can be positively reinforced through attention, praise, and affection, or negatively reinforced through efforts to avoid punishment, physical or verbal abuse, or abandonment. Since information is reinforcing, an important element of social learning is *evaluative feedback*, provided by parents, significant others, and the community, or by the consequences of the social activity itself. The degree of success the individual experiences not only reinforces the social behavior, but also helps to define a sense of self-efficacy or confidence in one's ability to cope and function well in social relationships.

Empathy

What is empathy?

An evolutionary development in affiliation is **empathy**, or the ability to intuitively share and comprehend another's cognitive perceptions and emotional experiences. Empathy is a complex phenomenon that involves both cognitive and emotional components, and is not to be confused with **sympathy**, which reflects an emotional response to the situation of others, without necessarily understanding how the other perceives the situation.

Accurate empathy requires the ability of an individual to (1) *comprehend* the perception as well as emotional expression of another person, (2) *communicate* that understanding to the other person, in the other person's conceptual terms, and (3) have that understanding *confirmed* by the other person.

Helping and comforting behavior has been observed in children as young as 1 year, although it more commonly appears between the ages of 2 and 3 as children become more prosocial. The bio-behavioral mechanisms contributing to empathy appear to include (1) a bottom-up processing of affective arousal involving the amygdala, hypothalamus, and orbitofrontal cortex; (2) emotional understanding and self/other awareness that involve the frontomedial and ventromedial cortices; and (3) a top-down process of emotion regulation involving the executive functions served by the network of connections within the prefrontal areas linked to the limbic system.

Recent research indicates that *mirror neurons* may play a central role in the development of empathic responses. That is, mirror neurons appear to be able to respond to the intention of the behavior observed, a defining characteristic of empathy (see Chapter 3, The Nervous System).

Research suggests that individuals with lower socioeconomic status (SES) are more empathic than individuals with higher SES. It may be that, because lower SES individuals have less influence or control over the social and economic environment in which they must function, they must constantly be sensitive to and able to "read" the actions and intentions of others who do have influence.

Communication and Language

Given the evolutionary trajectory of *attachment, affiliation*, and *empathy*, the ability to *communicate* interpersonally was a logical next step in the unfolding of social processes that facilitate mutual support, social collaboration, and survival of the species. The ability to comprehend one another's cognitions and intentions in social interactions is critical to achieving mutually beneficial social goals. Early in the evolutionary process, prior to the development of language, **communication** was based largely upon *interactive behavior*, i.e., gestures or imitative and demonstrative actions and sounds that later would convey semantic information. Thus, from the beginning, the *ability to communicate* behaviorally preceded and was separate from the process of coding and de-coding *linguistic information*. In fact, the ability to conceive and design a communicative message requires cortical systems different from those required for activating and carrying out linguistic tasks. The intention to communicate with another activates the medial prefrontal cortex, left temporal-parietal junction, and portions of the temporal lobes, which together constitute what has been called the *mentalizing network*. In contrast, linguistic coding/decoding activates the left inferior frontal cortex and the left inferior parietal cortex.

> The ability of humans to communicate was advanced by an important evolutionary change in brain structure that appears to have occurred over 100,000 years ago. A mutation of the **FoxP2 gene** enabled the brain to learn, remember, and conceptualize auditory representations of experience (i.e., transfer the meaning of a gesture into the meaning of an abstract sound). Since the genetic change leading to the development of spoken language is presumed to have occurred at about the same time as the "out of Africa" migration of *Homo erectus*, it has been suggested that the increased ability to communicate was influential in enabling proto humans to plan and coordinate group actions like migrations.

> What neuronal development most likely made human speech possible?

While the first human communications were behavioral responses to visual events, in time these behaviors and events became associated with specific sounds that acquired specific situational or object meanings. This association between observed events, behaviors, and vocal expression suggests that the biological basis for language occurred when neural connections between visual association areas, auditory association areas, hand/arm and facial motor areas, and speech production areas were established. However, the key to this transition from gesture to speech appears to have been the advent of the **mirror neuron** system, which provided a direct visual and auditory link between sender and receiver (i.e., a neuronal "wifi system"). The gestural behavior of the sender involves motor acts or action sounds that, via the premotor cortex, initiate similar motor responses in the receiver, allowing the receiver to understand the sender's message. Evidence suggests that components of human language, such as phonology and syntax, are linked to the motor system thus providing a foundation for more linguistic communication.

Genetic-Environmental Interaction in Language Development

> All human languages are composed of the same basic structural elements:
> **Phonemes:** basic *sound units*
> **Morphemes:** basic *meaning units* (the smallest number of sounds that will produce a meaning)
> **Syntax:** rules for combining words into phrases and sentences *(grammar)*
> **Semantics:** *meaning* associated with words and sentences
> **Prosody:** *vocal intonation* that modifies the meaning of words and sentences

The universality of language structure suggests that *language is genetically determined by the structure and function of the brain*. Indeed, by 3–6 months of age, there is evidence of a biological readiness to develop language that includes an inherent mechanism for imposing structure on whatever language the child learns. However, language structure is also influenced by the *ecology* in which a specific language develops that, in turn, influences the speaker's perception of the environment. For example, the multiple specific words used by Alaska Natives to describe ice and snow would be incomprehensible to Bedouins. In contrast, because trade languages evolve to facilitate communication and understanding among peoples from widely varying cultures, they tend to be more general and have less ecological specificity.

While language structure is universal, the semantic meaning inherent in language is more a function of learning, experience, culture, and interaction with the environment. As a result, the concepts, memories, and perceptions that underlie language are highly idiosyncratic in meaning, with the result that the same words or phrases may have significantly different meanings to different individuals. Thus, communication requires ongoing clarification and accommodation as each person strives to assure that what is being communicated is being accurately comprehended.

> A physician cannot assume that because a patient uses a term familiar to the physician to describe a symptom that the patient's meaning is the same as the physician's. Failure to clarify and agree on that meaning can result in the misdiagnosis and improper treatment of the patient's disorder.

Culture-Cognition Interaction

> How do culture and cognition influence one another?

The continued evolution of social collaboration in the service of human survival inevitably led to social groupings based upon similarities in beliefs and behavioral practices. Research on **cultural mapping**, which seeks to identify the ways that cognitions and behaviors converge within groups, suggests that there are three bio-behavioral mechanisms that contribute to culturally specific cognitions and behaviors.

The first mechanism is *gene-culture interaction*. European and Japanese populations differ with regard to the nature of the 5-HTT serotonin transporter gene. Japanese tend to carry more short vs. long alleles of the 5-HTT serotonin transporter gene, while Europeans tend to carry more long vs. short alleles. The difference has significant cultural implications, since individuals carrying the short allele are prone to higher levels of anxiety, depression, and impulsive aggression than carriers of the long allele.

The second mechanism is a *neurogenesis-culture interaction*. Cultural learning in the form of bilingual education and culturally specific display rules for emotional expression show unique patterns of activation in the left inferior frontal cortex and the amygdala, respectively. Both reflect the important role of neurogenesis in new cultural learning.

The third bio-behavioral mechanism is a *brain function-environmental structure interaction*. There is evidence of culture- and language-specific patterns of activation in response to environmental stimuli and patterns. For example, Chinese and Japanese writing require greater activation of visual areas in the brain than does Western writing.

Recommended Readings

Decety J. The neurodevelopment of empathy in humans. *Developmental Neuroscience* 2010; 32:1–11.

Eichenbaum H. An Information Processing Framework for Memory Representation by the Hippocampus. In Gazzaniga M. (Ed.), *The Cognitive Neurosciences*. Cambridge, MA: MIT Press; 2004, 679–690.

Rizzolatti G, Fabbri-Destro M. The Mirror Neuron System. In Berstson GG, Cacioppo JT (Eds.), *Handbook of Neurosciences for the Behavioral Sciences*. Hoboken, NJ: Wiley & Sons; 2009, pp. 337–360.

Taylor SE. Tend and befriend: Biobehavioral bases of affiliation under stress. *Current Directions in Psychological Science* 2006; 15(6):273–277.

Willems RM, Varley R. Neural insights into the relation between language and communication. *Frontiers in Human Neuroscience* 2010; 4:1–8.

Review Questions

1. The retention and retrieval of abstract information involves what kind of memory?
   A. Declarative
   B. Episodic
   C. Procedural
   D. Semantic
   E. Sensory

2. People with amnesia acquire and retrieve information regarding motor and cognitive sequences but do not know they have such information because of impaired

     A. consolidated memory.
     B. declarative memory.
     C. procedural memory.
     D. sensory memory.
     E. short-term memory.

3. The labeling of an emotion requires which of the following combinations?
     A. Arousal, situational context, cognitive interpretation
     B. Situational context, concept formation, operational schema
     C. Situational context, cultural norms, social sanctions
     D. Stimulus, response, reinforcement
     E. Stress, arousal, stress response

Key to review questions: p. 407

Section V

Development Through the Life Cycle

10 Selected Theories of Development

Emily F. Myers, MD, Forrest C. Bennett, MD, and Hans. O. Doerr, PhD

- How does conservation relate to compensation in cognitive development?
- What are the basic concepts of psychoanalytic theory?
- How is libidinal energy expressed during psychosexual development?
- How do Erikson's "ages" compare to Freud's developmental stages?
- According to social learning theory, how does a person "unlearn" maladaptive behaviors?
- How do Kohlberg's moral stages relate to Piaget's cognitive stages?

Many theories have been proposed to explain the cognitive, social, and emotional developmental processes that transform the simple reflexive behaviors of the infant into the complex informed behaviors of the adult. In this chapter, several of the more foundational theories are presented as background for the chapters on development through the life cycle.

Piaget's Theory of Cognitive Development

According to **Jean Piaget**, children are born with two cognitive functions: *organizational ability* and *adaptive ability*. Children construct their understanding of the world by organizing their experiences into *concepts*, and concepts into more complex structures called *schemas*. In effect, children are theory builders who use concepts and schemas to make sense of the environment, employing two strategies: assimilation and accommodation.

In **assimilation**, experiences are interpreted and acted upon within the framework of an existing cognitive schema: "all objects that can be fitted into the mouth provide nutrition." In **accommodation**, schemas are altered to fit disconfirming experiences that cause disequilibrium between cognitive understanding and external reality: "a thumb [put] into the mouth does not, in fact, pro-

vide food." As development progresses, schemas are modified further to fit ongoing experiences with reality. An integral part of Piaget's theory is that children play an active role in their own growth and development.

Four Major Stages of Cognitive Development (see Table 10.1)

Sensorimotor Stage (Birth to 2 Years)
During the first year of life, cognitive schemas progress from performing inborn reflexive activity to repeating interesting acts and finally to combining acts to solve simple problems. The concept of **object permanence** is established during this stage. That is, the infant learns that objects that have moved out of sight or been concealed continue to exist and can be searched for and found.

Preoperational Stage (2 to 7 Years)

How does conservation relate to compensation in cognitive development?

During this stage, children learn to use language and other symbols. Problem solving is intuitive rather than logical or rational, and analytic thinking is poorly developed. For example, intuitive reasoning, common in children this age, is illustrated by a child's failure to appreciate the law of

Table 10.1. Piaget: Stages of cognitive development		
Age (Approximate Years)	**Stage**	**Distinguishing Characteristics**
0 to 2	**Sensorimotor**	*Preverbal* Development of object permanence and rudimentary thought Reflexive activity leading to purposeful activity
2 to 7	**Preoperational**	*Prelogical* Development of semiotic functioning (use of symbols, representational language) Inability to deal with several aspects of a problem simultaneously
7 to 12	**Concrete Operational**	Logical Problem solving initially restricted to physically present objects/imagery Development of logical operations (e.g., classification, conservation)
12+	**Formal Operational**	*Abstract* Comprehension of purely abstract or symbolic content Development of advanced logical operations (e.g., complex analogy, deduction)

conservation (recognition that a given property of a substance remains the same despite irrelevant changes such as physical rearrangement). This is illustrated in Piaget's classical conservation experiment in which children in the preoperational stage were not able to appreciate that two identical portions of liquid, transferred from identical containers to two differently shaped containers (one taller and thinner than the other), are still equal in volume although unequal in height.

Piaget suggests that the inability to conserve is due to the preoperational child's inability to carry out a cognitive function called **compensation** (considering multiple dimensions of a problem simultaneously and appreciating the interaction between them). In the case presented, the child is unable to consider both height and width simultaneously.

Concrete Operational Stage (7 to 12 Years)

In this stage, the child is able to conceptualize the world from an external point of view; thinking becomes dynamic, decentralized, reversible, and relational. Relational thinking is characterized by **transitivity** (mental arrangement of dimensions of objects) and **seriation** (appreciation of relationships among objects in a serial order). During the early concrete operational stage, children can only solve a problem if the elements of the problem are physically present (*concrete*); often they must actually manipulate the elements for full understanding. Later in this stage, they can solve problems of time and space; *conserve* substance, quantity, weight, and volume; and *classify* objects into hierarchical systems based on past experiences with similar issues or objects, often without any actual experience with the specific issues or objects being considered.

Formal Operational Stage (12 Years through Adulthood)

Formal operational thinking is characterized by the ability to use *abstraction*. Both tangible and intangible problems can be solved through flexible, complex reasoning and **hypothesis formation**. Being able to conceive an ideal situation forms a backdrop for evaluating specific life circumstances and participating in social action and civil disobedience.

Piagetian Stages and Health-Related Behaviors

Piaget's cognitive developmental stages clarify how children and adolescents view illness causation and death. *Stress* can impair an individual's ability to use higher order cognitive skills and regressed cognition is common. *Magical thinking* (my wish equals action) or *egocentrism* (my action caused some externally determined and unrelated event), which are common among preschoolers, can occur even in adults who are in crisis. The inability to think futuristically, characteristic of children's thinking prior to late adolescence, hinders their ability to understand the long-term consequences of current actions (e.g., lung cancer as a result of smoking; becoming a parent as a result of sexual intercourse without contraception).

Freud's Theory of Psychosexual Development

> What are the basic concepts of psychoanalytic theory?

The major concepts of psychoanalytic theory are:
1. behavior is motivated by unconscious biological urges, instincts, or drives;
2. behavior is influenced by unconscious memories that are kept from awareness by defense mechanisms; and
3. psychic energy is channeled through three parts of the personality: id, ego, and superego.

The **id** is the original reservoir for all psychic energy. It expresses drives and impulses based on biological needs, such as food, sleep, and procreation. The **ego** serves as the id's intermediary with the external world. It operates on the reality principle and energizes learning and logical thinking. The **superego**, or conscience, assures that the ego's actions are socially and morally correct.

Five Stages of Psychosexual Development

> How is libidinal energy expressed during psychosexual development?

Sigmund Freud proposed five stages of psychosexual development. These stages reflect the developmental sequence of body areas invested with *libidinal energy* (sexual or life force).

Fixation, or impaired resolution of certain psychological conflicts that arise at the oral, anal, and phallic stages, is presumed to result in specific adult behaviors.

Oral Stage (Birth to 1 Year)
Libidinal energy is concentrated in the mouth, lips, and tongue. It serves the basic need of the infant to take nutrition. Fixation in the oral stage may manifest itself in adults as excessive smoking, eating, or craving social contact.

Anal Stage (1 to 3 Years)
Libidinal energy is invested in the anal sphincter and bladder. Toilet training demands that urges be inhibited or delayed. Fixation in the anal stage may show itself as excessive orderliness or obstinate, retentive behaviors.

Phallic Stage (3 to 6 Years)
Children become aware of male-female differences and derive pleasure from self-stimulation or masturbation. They develop sexual longing for the parent of the opposite gender and jealousy toward the parent of the same gender (*Oedipal conflict*). Fixation in the phallic stage may manifest as difficulties with sexual relationships.

Latency Stage (6 Years to Puberty)
During this period, sexual strivings are largely suppressed by the superego. Libidinal energy is channeled into socially acceptable behaviors, such as study or sports.

Genital Stage (Puberty to Adulthood)
The onset of this stage coincides with physiological maturation and reinvestment of libidinal energy in the sex organs. The underlying goal is reproduction through a sexual relationship.

Erikson's Theory of Psychosocial Development

Erik Erikson agreed with Freud that people are born with biological drives, but he focused on *society* rather than the family as the setting in which these drives are expressed. Erikson is considered an *ego psychologist* because he emphasized visible, rational, and adaptive aspects of personality.

Erikson's emphasis on relevant, adaptive behavior and the integration of social and cultural factors into classical psychoanalytic theory highlights the interplay between internal and external reality. Psychotherapy based on Erikson's theory is directed at working through unresolved conflicts, starting at the stage where the person is *"developmentally arrested."* Erikson's psychosocial theory was among the first to formulate personality development as a lifelong, sequential process.

Eight "Ages" of Psychosocial Development

How do Erikson's "ages" compare to Freud's developmental stages?

For each of his eight developmental stages or *"ages of man,"* Erikson defined the major psychosocial conflict and its possible resolutions in active, behavioral terms.

Basic Trust vs. Basic Mistrust (Birth to 1 Year)

This age corresponds to the Freudian Oral Stage. The task is to learn to trust a caregiver. If care is not given or only inconsistently given, infants come to see human relationships as too disappointing or dangerous to rely upon.

Autonomy vs. Shame and Doubt (1 to 3 Years)

This age corresponds to the Freudian Anal Stage. The challenge is to become independent in rudimentary aspects of living: feeding, making choices, keeping, and letting go. Failure to pass through this stage successfully will lead to self-doubt.

Initiative vs. Guilt (3 to 6 Years)

This age corresponds to the Freudian Phallic Stage. The need to have mastery over the environment can lead to conflicts with others (e.g., parents) producing guilt. The child must learn to set internal limits and to achieve balance between his or her own and another's desires.

Industry vs. Inferiority (6 to 12 Years)

This age corresponds to the Freudian Latency Stage. Primary challenges are learning to meet school and social demands and acquiring academic and athletic skills. Output is measured and graded, and competition with peers increases. Failure leads to feelings of inequality, inferiority, and worthlessness.

Identity vs. Role Confusion (12 to 20 Years)

This age corresponds to the beginning of the Freudian Genital Stage and marks the transition from childhood to young adulthood. Experiences with role models outside the family (e.g., teachers) broaden the individual's value system. The primary challenge is to establish a sense of self as a physical, sexual, and vocational being. Failure leads to indecision, vacillation, and a sense of purposelessness.

Intimacy vs. Isolation (20 to 40 Years)

In this age, the individual moves from a self-centered focus to affiliation and partnership with others. Love and companionship transcend interpersonal boundaries and permit commitment to another. Lack of friendships and intimate relationships lead to loneliness, emptiness, and isolation.

Generativity vs. Stagnation (40 to 65 Years)

During this age, individuals become teachers of the next generation. They repay society for having nurtured them by sharing their work and creativity and assisting younger people. They develop a sense of responsibility for society. Failure leads to stagnation and boredom.

Ego Integrity vs. Despair (65 Years to Death)

This age involves the acceptance of one's life, with its successes and failures. Reflection leads to an integration of experiences and sense of order and meaning. Without self-acceptance, a person experiences cynicism and hopelessness.

Gesell's Maturational Theory of Development

Contrasting with both Freud's and Erikson's interactional theories of human development, the *maturational theory* of **Arnold Gesell** postulates that human development progresses in a regimented and mostly predetermined biologic manner. Gesell's biological theory states that cognitive development and motor development occur in parallel and in regular sequence according to a *genetic blueprint* through a process called maturation. According to Gesell, teaching or outside environmental influences cannot override the natural biological progression of human development; children develop when they are ready. Innate neurophysiological differences underlie human diversity and brain-based neurological processes control the sequence and timing.

As a result of his research, Gesell identified many of the developmental milestones seen in the early years of life, and described their progression throughout childhood. These milestones are still used regularly today to assess development.

Social Learning Theory

> According to social learning theory, how does a person "unlearn" maladaptive behaviors?

In contrast to Gesell's maturational theory, **social learning theory** postulates that the broad constellation of behaviors that comprise "personality" is the result of the individual's social learning history. Learning occurs through *observation* and *imitation* of the behavior of others. Learning is a cognitive activity during which internal representations of modeled behavior are constructed. Subsequently, these representations are used to *imitate* (reproduce behaviorally what was observed). Behaviors that are *reinforced* (praised, rewarded, gain attention) are repeated. Both adaptive and maladaptive behaviors are acquired or extinguished through social learning.

Extinction of maladaptive behaviors requires the elimination of the reinforcers of those behaviors by pairing those behaviors with noxious consequences; then, by imitating others, the person learns more adaptive responses. Thus, observing adaptive role models can modify nonfunctional behavior patterns.

In social learning theory, development is the result of an ongoing *interaction between the individual and the environment*. Although genetic and biological factors influence individual predispositions early in life, developmental changes are increasingly influenced by social factors as the individual matures. Critics of social learning theory argue that this view of development is too simplistic and de-emphasizes biological influences on behavior. Proponents counter that this view of behavior reflects the increasing influence of social factors with age and provides a theoretical framework for society-based clinical interventions.

Kohlberg's Theory of Moral Development

> How do Kohlberg's moral stages relate to Piaget's cognitive stages?

Stages of Moral Development

The development of *morality* (i.e., the sense of right and wrong) has been postulated to follow an orderly sequence. **Lawrence Kohlberg** proposed three basic levels of morality encompassing six stages of development (see Table 10.2).

(1) **Preconventional morality** is characteristic of children in the sensorimotor and preoperational stages of cognitive development. Judgments about right and wrong are based on external consequences (rewards and punishments) and external higher authority (parent). Personal benefit is a highly motivating factor.

(2) **Conventional morality** is characteristic of children in the concrete operational stage of cognitive functioning. Moral judgments are based on fulfilling the expectations of others and following the rules. Thus, an action is morally good if others say it is, and maintaining law and order is essential. In decision making, intent is emerging as a more important factor than outcome.

(3) **Postconventional morality** is characteristic of individuals who are in the formal operational stage of cognitive functioning. Judgments are based on personal adherence to principles that are perceived as valid by the individual, apart from any external authority or convention.

According to postconventional morality, laws are judged with regard to their conformity with obligations and contracts and their congruence with basic standards of human rights. Under certain circumstances it may be morally right to disobey a law in the service of broader social principles (*civil disobedience*).

Self-chosen *ethical principles* of justice, reciprocity, respect, and equality inform morality. The moral person who has attained this stage of development can transcend his/her own person and see issues and dilemmas from the perspective of all others involved. This blend of regard for universal justice and compassion and respect for all individu-

Age (years)	Level	Basis of Moral Judgment	Developmental Stage	Characteristics
0–2	I. Preconventional (premoral)	Consequences (reward or punishment) Conformity to imposed rules	1. Punishment-obedience	Egocentric, no moral concepts
2–6	II. Conventional (moral)	Good and right roles	2. Instrumental-relativistic 3. "Good Boy"–"Nice Girl"	Satisfaction of own needs Desire to please others
6–12		Principles, rights, values	4. "Law and order"	Obligation to duty Respect for authority
12+	III. Postconventional (principled)		5. Social contract-legalistic	Relativism of personal values and opinions
			6. Universal-ethical-principled	Conscience dictates action in accord with self-chosen principles

Table 10.2. Kohlberg: Development of moral judgment

als is considered to lead to optimal moral decision making.

Clinical and Research Considerations

The basic moral developmental milestones elaborated by Kohlberg are useful as markers of individual development. They are also helpful in providing guidelines for effective parenting. That is, successfully rearing children requires an understanding of what motivates behavior at certain ages so that parental responses to both desirable and undesirable behavior will be appropriate.

Research, including cross-cultural studies, has verified a strong positive correlation between cognitive developmental stage and sophistication of moral thinking, supporting Kohlberg's contention that the stages are sequential. However, moral development does not progress automatically; *social experience* appears to be essential for the child to advance through subsequent stages.

Questions have been raised about whether moral reasoning predicts moral behavior. In gen-

eral, the correlation is limited. In addition, the theory has been challenged with regard to its relevance to women. For example, it has been suggested that girls and women, faced with solving a moral dilemma, are more likely than boys and men (the subjects of Kohlberg's studies) to use *relational thinking* ("how will my actions affect others?") rather than strictly following the rules. The relevance of Kohlberg's theory to non-Western cultures has also been challenged. That is, the emphasis Kohlberg places on *individual moral reasoning*, especially in the postconventional stages, may not represent the cultural norms present in tribal and hierarchical societies.

Recommended Readings

Bandura A. *Social Learning Theory*. Englewood Cliffs, NJ: Prentice-Hall; 1977.

Crain W. *Theories of Development: Concepts and Applications*, 4th ed. Upper Saddle River, NJ: Prentice Hall; 2000.

Erickson E. *Childhood and Society*, 2nd ed. New York: W.W. Norton & Co.; 1963.

Freud S. *New Introductory Lectures in Psychoanalysis*, 2nd ed. London: Hogarth Press; 1937.

Geiger, TC, Sahler OJZ. Psychological Social Development of Children. In McInerny TK, Adam HM, Campbell DE, Kamat, DM, Kelleher, KJ (Eds.), *American Academy of Pediatrics' Textbook of Pediatric Care.* Elk Grove Village, IL: American Academy of Pediatrics; 2009, pp. 997–1014.

Kohlberg L. *The Meaning and Measurement of Moral Development.* Worcester, MA: Clark University Press; 1980.

Piaget J, Inhelder B. *The Psychology of the Child.* New York: Basic Books; 1969.

Review Questions

Directions: The items below consist of lettered headings followed by numbered scenarios. For each numbered scenario, choose the one lettered heading to which it is *most* closely associated. Each lettered heading may be used *once, more than once, or not at all.*

Match the Piagetian concept illustrated by the scenario.
A. Accommodation
B. Assimilation
C. Concrete operational thinking
D. Conservation
E. Magical thinking

1. Timmy, who is 5 years old, worries that hitting his 8-year-old sister in the leg with a Frisbee caused her osteosarcoma of the femur.
2. Maryellen and Sally both get 4 oz of apple juice for snack but Maryellen gets hers in a 6 oz cup and Sally gets hers in an 8 oz cup. Sally is upset because she thinks that Maryellen is getting more juice.

Match the Eriksonian age with the scenario that fits it best.
A. Ego integrity vs. despair
B. Generativity vs. stagnation
C. Industry vs. inferiority
D. Initiative vs. guilt
E. Trust vs. mistrust

3. John Phillips just retired at age 70. After about 2 weeks at home, he went to the community literacy center and volunteered to become a reading tutor.

4. Marian Morton has been living at the retirement center for 10 years. The walls of her room are covered with pictures of her 6 children, 15 grandchildren, and 23 great grandchildren ("and one on the way!").

Match the Kohlberg stage of moral development with the moral action in the scenario.
A. Good boy – nice girl
B. Instrumental – relativistic
C. Law and order
D. Punishment – obedience
E. Universal – ethical – principled

5. A driver slows to the speed limit when she sees a police car ahead.
6. A college student marches against gender discrimination.

Key to review questions: p. 407

11 The Fetus, Newborn, and Infant

Emily F. Myers, MD, and Forrest C. Bennett, MD

- What effects do maternal health and lifestyle have on the developing fetus?
- What does the Apgar score assess?
- How do growth parameters change during infancy?
- What changes in motor skill and response to stimuli occur during infancy?
- What is object permanence?
- What is attachment?

Developmental change takes place throughout the entire life cycle and is punctuated by stages and intervening transition periods. Milestones serve as guidelines for assessing a person's developmental stage. Genetics, environment, culture, and the development of physical and mental abilities influence not only when but which behaviors and skills are learned, constituting a biopsychosocial model of development.

The Fetus

Prenatal Growth and Challenges to Development

The growth of the human fetus can vary based on family history and ethnicity. Generally, the mature human fetus is delivered at 37–42 weeks after conception and is called a **full-term infant**. Full-term infants have a mean birthweight of 3,500 gm. Other growth parameters that are measured at birth include head circumference and total body length, with means of 50 cm and 35 cm, respectively.

Alterations in growth during fetal life can have significant effects on an infant's future developmental capacity. Weight is one such growth factor. *Low birthweight* refers to infants weighing < 2,500 gm; *very low birthweight* refers to weight < 1,500 gm; and *extremely low birthweight* is defined as being born weighing < 1,000 gm.

Adequate and appropriate weight gain during the fetal period is vital for long-term neurodevelopment. Infants who are growing too little or too much for their gestational age are at increased risk of having negative developmental and medical consequences.

Head size can be too large (**macrocephaly**) or too small (**microcephaly**). Macrocephaly is head size greater than two standard deviations (SDs) above the mean, or > 37cm for a term infant. Microcephaly is < 33 cm for a term neonate. Both these growth abnormalities carry increased risk of negative developmental consequences.

Genetic/Chromosomal Abnormalities

Genetic or chromosomal differences result in alterations in the CNS and other organ development, and account for more chronic childhood disability than all of the acquired extrinsic brain insults combined. While Down syndrome (trisomy 21) is the best known and most common chromosomal syndrome, trisomy 13 and trisomy 18 are also well known, but, unlike Down Syndrome, are typically fatal in early life. Unlike these well described chromosomal abnormalities, a condition like optic fibrosis can result from a mutation in any of several genes, only some of which have been identified. Thus, a positive result is quite reliable but a negative result is not definitive. New techniques of examining the human genome are revealing hundreds of genetic/chromosomal aberrations each year, many of which have been correlated with clinical findings.

Maternal-Fetal Infections/Maternal Disease

Maternal-fetal infections during pregnancy can have significant effects on the neurodevelopmental outcome of an infant. Although there are many infections that significantly affect the fetus, cytomegalovirus, herpes simplex virus, and human immunodeficiency virus (HIV) are among the most common and well studied. *Cytomegalovirus* (CMV) affects approximately 30,000–40,000 infants in the US per year. Up to 20% of congenitally infected neonates are left with adverse major and minor outcomes, including severe sensorineural hearing loss, visual deficits, hydrocephalus, cerebral palsy, intellectual disability, and learning disabilities.

Neonatal herpes simplex virus causes an infection that can be passed to the neonate traveling through the birth canal at delivery. Its incidence is 1 in 3,500 births. Organ systems commonly involved in infected neonates include the CNS, skin, liver, and lung. Infants can have seizures, microcephaly, brain atrophy, and visual deficits, all of which can have significant effects on long-term neurodevelopment.

Maternal HIV infection can be transmitted to the fetus either through the placenta during birth or through breast feeding, especially if the mother is not being treated with antiretrovirals. In developed countries, HIV positive mothers should be counseled against breast feeding; but this may be a matter of debate in developing countries because of the uncertainty of obtaining clean water for formula preparation. If the mother is untreated during pregnancy, 25% of infants develop an infectious or neurological complication within the first year of life. The virus itself can enter the nervous system causing progressive motor impairment, loss of developmental milestones, and poor brain growth. Congenital HIV can lead to early infant death. Fortunately, in the US and increasingly elsewhere, vigorous drug treatment during pregnancy has reduced the congenital infection rate to approximately 1%.

Maternal Health Problems

> What effects do maternal health and lifestyle have on the developing fetus?

Certain maternal medical conditions may have significant effects on neonatal development and beyond. For example *maternal diabetes mellitus* (particularly insulin-dependent disease) increases the likelihood of major congenital malformations (e.g., spina bifida, congenital heart disease, cleft lip/palate), and impaired neurodevelopmental performance (e.g., poorer physiological control and interactive capacities, immature motor processes, reduced cognition). This is of particular concern because of the increasing incidence of obesity in the US, leading to rising rates of gestational diabetes. *Persistent maternal hypertension* can produce uteroplacental insufficiency, leading to intrauterine growth retardation and asphyxia, often resulting in premature birth or neurodevelopmental impairment.

Intrauterine Exposures

Maternal use of *prescribed medications*, such as anticonvulsants used to treat seizures (e.g., valproic acid, carbamazepine, hydantoins) have been linked to physical birth defects, malformation syndromes, and long-term neurodevelopmental abnormalities. Other commonly used medications for a variety of different medical problems can cause birth defects as well. Examples include retinoic acid, methotrexate, and lithium, used to treat acne, cancer, and bipolar disorder, respectively.

Several *recreational drugs* can have a variety of both physical and developmental effects on the fetus. Fetal alcohol syndrome (FAS) is the most common preventable non-genetic cause of mental retardation. Approximately 4 million infants born each year are exposed to alcohol during gestation. The diagnosis is made through the identification of facial features, growth retardation, and CNS anomalies. Fetal alcohol syndrome is one diagnosis among a spectrum of disorders associated with fetal alcohol exposure that affect all aspects of development and behavior, causing language delays, attention-deficit disorder, and learning disabilities.

Maternal *tobacco consumption* can result in fetal growth retardation from decreased uterine blood flow during pregnancy; birthweight decreases in a dose-response manner to tobacco exposure. Fetal brain growth has been shown to be adversely affected by heavy maternal smoking with sub-optimal language and social and cognitive outcomes.

Certain *recreational substances* including cocaine, methamphetamines, and marijuana produce varying combinations of neonatal symptomatology and long-term developmental-behavioral dysfunction. Opiates such as *heroin* can cause neonatal addiction, as well as withdrawal (*neonatal abstinence syndrome*) after the infant is born. Maternal use of cocaine usually does not produce an acute withdrawal syndrome in the newborn. However, the children of cocaine-abusing mothers do frequently suffer from neurobehavioral problems as well as academic and social difficulties that have been linked to low birthweight, interruptions in maternal care due to addiction, rehabilitation, or incarceration, and low socioeconomic status.

The Newborn

The Premature Neonate

Preterm birth, birth at < 37 weeks gestation, is a major cause of neurodevelopmental complications. About 11–12% of births in the US are preterm, and account for 64–75% of infant deaths. The incidence of preterm births is rising, as is the survival rate. Survival at 23–25 weeks gestational age is becoming more common (approximately 50% at 24 weeks).

The complications associated with preterm birth are caused by the immaturity of fetal organ systems, delivery complications, and medical interventions that are required to sustain life. *Fetal hypoxia, ischemia, intracranial hemorrhage, hydrocephalus, hypoglycemia,* and *infection* are all risks for neurodevelopmental and behavioral disorders, and are common in infants born prematurely.

Major adverse outcomes associated with prematurity include cerebral palsy, intellectual disability, and hearing and visual impairments. *Minor adverse outcomes* include mild gross motor impairments and coordination problems, difficulties with fine motor tasks, attention-deficit/hyperactivity disorder, executive dysfunction, language delays, learning disabilities, and behavior problems.

Birth Complications

Fetal distress from intrapartum asphyxia can result from uteroplacental insufficiency, umbilical cord compression, or placental abruption. The *asphyxia syndrome* includes components of hypoxia, ischemia, hypotension, and impaired perfusion of multiple organs, particularly the brain. If brain damage occurs before the infant is delivered and adequately resuscitated, any of a wide range of neurodevelopmental disabilities such as cerebral palsy, intellectual disability, seizures, and learning and behavior problems can occur.

Birth trauma can adversely affect the development of the infant. Malpresentation (e.g., breech, transverse lie), an exceptionally large fetus, or a delivery requiring instrumentation with forceps or vacuum extraction can lead to intracranial contusions or hemorrhages, fractures, spinal cord injuries, and other nerve damage.

Jaundice, or *hyperbilirubinemia*, is a common newborn condition, and, if severe, can lead to significant adverse developmental outcomes. Jaundice, the yellow discoloration in the skin of neonates, is caused by a build-up of bilirubin, which can be deposited not only in the skin but in other organs including the brain. It can be treated effectively in most cases with phototherapy. However, if inadequately treated and the bilirubin reaches critical levels, a neurological condition known as kernicterus can occur.

Kernicterus (bilirubin encephalopathy) affects areas of the brain responsible for balance, motor coordination, and hearing (the basal ganglia and brainstem). This damage is permanent and can lead to severe motor and sensory disabilities.

Developmental Assessment of the Newborn

What does the Apgar score assess?

The **Apgar score** is a numerical rating of the adequacy of the neurophysiological transition to extrauterine life in the newborn infant and is the standard method of post-delivery assessment. Its principal utility is assessment of current status and it serves as an indicator of the potential need for neonatal resuscitation. The score is assigned and recorded at one and five minutes of life, but can be extended to 10, 15, and 20 minutes. Scores of

7–10 indicate no CNS depression; 4–6 indicate some depression; and 0–3 indicate severe depression that requires resuscitation. These early scores, particularly if very low, may presage long-term neurodevelopmental abnormalities.

Another neonatal assessment tool is the **Ballard Neonatal Examination** and is used to estimate gestational age and determine the adequacy of intrauterine growth. This examination is particularly useful when the length of the pregnancy is uncertain and can be used in conjunction with birthweight in anticipating potential problems.

The **Brazelton Neonatal Behavioral Assessment Scale** provides a neurobehavioral assessment of such characteristics as visual attention, alertness, auditory responsivity, and habituation. The scale can be administered serially to provide an objective measure of change over time. Although these scores do not necessarily have predictive value for future developmental capabilities, they can be used to promote more sensitive interactions between at-risk newborns and mothers.

The Infant (Birth to 12 Months)

How do growth parameters change during infancy?

Infancy is marked by rapid growth and development. Whereas the average newborn infant weighs 3.5 kg and spends virtually the entire day sleeping, crying, eating, and eliminating waste, the average 12-month-old infant weighs approximately 10 kg, has a distinct personality, can crawl or walk, feeds him- or herself, and communicates with gestures and a few words. Infant development is influenced by both biologic and environmental factors in an endless series of dynamic transactions. Biological factors include genetic makeup, temperament, and state of health. The most significant environmental factors affecting infants are parents, extended family, and the skills, attitudes, culture, and socioeconomic status of the family.

Infant Physical Growth

Birthweight is doubled by 4–5 months of age and tripled by 12 months. Length increases by 50% in the first year of life. Head growth is very rapid early on, increasing by approximately 6 cm during the first three months and an additional 6 cm over the next 9 months. The volume of the infant's brain at birth is about 25% of adult volume; by 12 months it is more than 50% of adult volume. Physiological changes that occur during infancy include improvement in respiratory pattern, coordination of sucking and swallowing, and temperature control. Changes in respiratory pattern include a gradual decline in respiratory rate from 30–50 breaths per minute at birth to 25–35 breaths per minute at 12 months. By 12 months of age, the infant has progressed from taking only liquid food to being able to personally put solid food into his or her mouth and then chew and swallow without difficulty. Temperature regulation is established during the first few days of life making the infant capable of maintaining a core temperature of 37° C under normal ambient conditions.

Motor Development

What changes in motor skill and response to stimuli occur during infancy?

Development of the infant's motor capabilities facilitates learning about the social and inanimate world. During the first year, infant movement progresses in an orderly cephalo-caudal sequence from a mainly supine or prone position to sitting, crawling, and even walking independently. In order to create volitional movement, primitive reflexes gradually recede during the first few months of life and are replaced by planned *gross motor movements* such as rolling over (4–5 mo), sitting independently (8–9 mo), and walking (10–15 mo). Wide variation exists in the exact timing of gross motor milestones.

Fine motor movements progress in a stepwise proximal-distal fashion, as the sensory system becomes more refined. Grasping and reaching for objects emerges and solidifies between 3–6 months of age. By 9 months of age, infants can orient their hands to pick up an object. A pincer grasp (securing an object between thumb and forefinger) is mastered by approximately 10–11 months. Less variability is seen in the normal acquisition of fine motor milestones than of gross motor milestones.

Language Development

At birth, although infants do not have the motor control to form words, they *communicate* through other sensory modalities (e.g., gestures, cry, gaze). Infants acquire **language** through reciprocal interactions with caregivers and others. With early vocalizations and nonverbal cues, caregivers and infants learn to respond to one another or to take turns communicating. By 1 month of age, an infant has developed a range of cries to signify different needs that parents can recognize. At 4–6 months of age, infants can produce consonant sounds; by 10–12 months of age, they can speak their first words.

Cognitive Development

What is object permanence?

An infant's developing sensory systems (tactile, visual, and auditory) have vital roles that allow observation and interaction with the social and inanimate environment. By 1 month of age, infants are able to visually track an object to midline and by two months, can track an object past midline. At 3–6 months of age, an infant is able to coordinate extraocular muscles, permitting binocular vision; at 6–8 months, there is evidence of depth perception. Infants just after birth will be alert to sounds and can turn to a sound by 3 months. At 4 months of age, an infant not only turns to sound but can look toward the origin of the sound as well. The ability to localize sound approaches that of an adult by 12 months.

Early cognitive development is characterized by sensory-motor exploratory behaviors and interactions with the environment. During the first several months, major change occurs as the infant's behaviors develop from reflexive responses to learned intentional activities, such as reaching.

One of the core milestones of infant cognition is **object permanence**, which is the concept of knowing an object's existence even if it is not in the field of vision. During the first month of life, images cease to exist when they are no longer perceived. By 7–9 months of age, the infant learns that objects exist even when they are not visible, and will search for objects that are not in view.

Social-Emotional Development

What is attachment?

Bonding and **attachment** (see also Chapter 9) describe the affectional relationships that develop between primary caregivers (usually parents) and infants. Bonding begins before and immediately after birth and reflects the feeling of the parents toward the newborn. Attachment refers to the reciprocal feelings between parent and infant that gradually develop over the first years. Thus, the infant is an active participant in the development of attachment.

By 10 days of age, infants can distinguish the smell of their own mother's breast milk from that of other women. At about 5–6 weeks of life, the infant becomes able to recognize individuals and smiles responsively. By 3–5 months of life, the infant will show preference for a primary caregiver by smiling and vocalizing. Parents respond to the infant's "social smile" with mutual gaze, friendly facial expressions, "parentese" (high-pitched, vowel-rich verbal messages), and touching. The infant follows the parents intently, first with the eyes and later by crawling after them. Although the mother is usually the primary attachment figure if she is the person most constantly present, infants will form an attachment to whomever is consistently responsive to them. Most infants form multiple attachments, which helps protect them in the event of the absence or loss of their primary caregiver.

Stranger anxiety develops at about 8–9 months of life when the infant becomes fretful at the sight of a stranger and seeks parental comfort and reassurance. Such behaviors reinforce the parent's protectiveness in response to the infant's signaling of potential danger. Stranger anxiety often peaks again at 12–15 months, and then diminishes.

Separation anxiety becomes apparent at 6–9 months. The infant begins to understand simple cause-and-effect relationships and anticipates separations (e.g., seeing mother putting on her coat). When the mother actually leaves the infant's presence, the infant will cry and actively look for her. This behavior persists to about 2½ to 3 years of age, when, through experience, the child learns the mother will return and no longer fears her going. However, if the primary caregiver(s) never leave the infant with others (to practice going and then returning), the child may have difficulty passing through this stage, particularly if he or she is shy, fearful, or anxious in temperament.

Temperament refers to the patterns of personal attributes and behavioral tendencies of a person. It has a distinct role in social-emotional development and it has been classically categorized as difficult, slow to warm up, and easy. *Difficult infants* are described as having traits such as largely negative mood, high intensity, and poor adaptability. The *slow to warm up infant* can have a negative mood initially, but gradually becomes more positive as the encounter evolves. An *easy infant* has a positive mood and adapts well to change. The behavioral makeup of a given individual can include traits from all temperament categories. Temperament can have a significant effect on bonding, attachment, and, in fact, all interactions between infants and caregivers. Temperament persists, in modified form, into adulthood.

Bonding, attachment, stranger anxiety, and separation anxiety are tasks that are typically mastered by the end of infancy. Mastery is dependent on an infant's recognition that its caregivers are responsive to his or her physical and emotional needs. Further, a knowledge that individuals who are not caregivers do exist and should be regarded with caution is vital not only for an infant's social-emotional development but also for survival.

Gender identity, the sense of being male or female, begins to be established as soon as the parents discover the sex of their infant. Thus, biological, genetic, and environmental factors play a significant role in the development of gender identity as the infant is given a sex assignment and is named, dressed, and played with (typically more aggressive play with boy infants and more gentle, soothing play with girl infants).

Recommended Readings

American Academy of Pediatrics. *Your Baby's First Year*, 3rd ed. Elk Grove Village, IL: American Academy of Pediatrics; 2010.

Bennett FC. Developmental Outcome. In MacDonald MG, Mullett MD, Seisha MMK (Eds.), *Avery's Neonatology: Pathology and Management of the Newborn*, 6th ed. Philadelphia, PA: Lippincott Williams & Wilkins; 2005.

Brazelton TB. *Infants and Mothers: Differences in Development*, rev. ed. New York: Dell Publishing; 1983.

Gopnick A, Metlzoff AN, Kuhl PK. *The Scientist in the Crib*. New York: Harper Collins; 1999.

Neonatology. In Marino BS, Fine KS, McMillan JA (Eds.). *Blueprints Pediatrics*, 3rd ed. Malden, MA: Blackwell Publishing; 2004.

Olsen IE, Groveman SA, Lawson ML, Reese HC, Zemel BS. New intrauterine growth curves on United States data. *Pediatrics* 2010; 125:214–220.

Review Questions

1. The rate of congenital HIV infection in the US is currently
   A. 0.1%.
   B. 1%.
   C. 3%.
   D. 5%.
   E. 10%.

2. The children of cocaine-abusing mothers frequently suffer from neurobehavioral dysfunction as well as academic and social difficulties. These problems have been linked to each of the following etiological factors EXCEPT
   A. low birthweight.
   B. low socioeconomic status.
   C. maternal drug addiction.
   D. maternal incarceration.
   E. postnatal drug withdrawal.

3. A pregnant woman's use of which of the following substances is responsible for the greatest number of cases of neurodevelopmental dysfunction in childhood?
   A. Alcohol
   B. Cocaine
   C. Heroin
   D. LSD
   E. Tobacco

4. Stranger anxiety is a protective mechanism that makes the child wary of unfamiliar people. The initial onset of stranger anxiety usually occurs at about
   A. 1–3 months
   B. 4–6 months
   C. 7–9 months
   D. 10–12 months
   E. 13–15 months

Key to review questions: p. 407

12 Toddlerhood and the Preschool Years

Emily F. Myers, MD, and Forrest C. Bennett, MD

- When is a child ready for toilet training?
- How does language evolve between 12 and 16 months?
- How does a child's play change between 12 and 36 months?

Toddlerhood (Ages 1 to 3 Years)

As children move through infancy and enter the toddler and preschool years, their activities mature and become more nuanced. A child's mobility dramatically changes, moving from crawling to walking, running, and jumping. Increasing receptive and expressive language capacity allows children to use words and gestures to communicate. Social-emotional relationships become more rich and complex as they begin to include greater interaction and experience with people outside the family.

Physical Development

When is a child ready for toilet training?

Toilet training is one of the most important examples of the physiological maturation process of toddlerhood. Before voluntary bladder and bowel control can occur, the sensory pathways from the bladder and bowel must be mature enough to transmit signals to the cerebral cortex indicating bladder and bowel fullness. Toddlers must also demonstrate an interest in control of elimination, as well as an ability to follow adult instruction. These abilities together demonstrate a *developmental readiness* for toilet training. Toddlers must then learn to associate these signals with the need to (1) eliminate, followed by the need to (2) tighten the sphincter to prevent immediate elimination, and finally, after tightening, the need to (3) loosen the sphincter to permit elimination at

the proper moment. The child must have the fine motor skill to remove clothing quickly and reliably before urinating and defecating. Toddlers are not able to voluntarily postpone elimination until they are at least 15–18 months of age. By 2 years of age some toddlers are able to remain dry during the day although many children wear diapers until age 3. Most children are not fully bowel trained until they are 4 years old. Environmental/cultural expectations and demands influence the exact timing of these events. As we shall see, a relatively predictable sequence of events lays the foundation for successful toilet training.

Motor Development

Early in the second year of life, children complete the transition from crawling to walking. Multiple factors are involved in this process, including the development of an upright posture and the ability to shift weight, alternate leg movements, and process sensory information while moving. Most 1-year-olds initially walk with a wide-based gait and short, waddling steps that have given rise to the term "toddler."

The average age of taking first independent steps is 12 months, although some infants will not begin walking until 16–18 months. By 24 months, toddlers are beginning to jump and some can walk up and down stairs by themselves. By age 36 months, most toddlers have an adult-like *heel-to-toe* gait; they are able to run and change direction with agility; they like to try new types of movements such as galloping; and they are fully able to jump with both feet. Many toddlers can pedal a tricycle at 36 months of age. Because there is such a wide range of normal variation in the development of most gross motor milestones, no single motor skill can or should be used to describe overall neuromotor development.

Two-year-olds can toss or roll a ball. They progress from finger feeding to self-feeding with a spoon and fork, and can build a tower of 4–6 blocks. This progression parallels the toddler's ability to recognize objects and associate them with their functions. Thus, the toddler begins to use objects appropriately rather than just mouthing and banging them. Three-year-olds can dress with help and can hold a glass with one hand. These fine motor milestones are necessary for mastering activities that occur in preschool settings, and are important precursors to the development of handwriting skills.

Language Development

> **How does language evolve between 12 and 36 months?**

At 12 months, use of specific words is often limited to "mama" and "dada" for their parents, and two or three other words. "*Jargoning*," utterances that sound like statements but contain no real words, is common. During the second year, their repertoire of words accumulates slowly and then increases dramatically. By 18 months, they will express 10–20 words, and by 2 years, 50–100. At 2 years, toddlers begin to combine words. The earliest word pairings before true noun-verb combinations are actually phrases ("go bye-bye") or labels ("baby baby") that the child perceives and uses as a single entity.

Because **receptive language** (what a child is able to understand) generally precedes the development of **expressive language** (what a child is able to produce), toddlers can point to pictures and understand body parts before they can name them. Similarly, they can follow one- or two-part commands before they are able to express such commands themselves.

By the end of the third year, utterances are typically three to four words long. Grammar becomes more correct, and plural nouns are used occasionally. The speech of most 3-year-olds is 50–75%

intelligible to a stranger, although imperfect diction is still common. Problems with the rhythm and pacing of speech (*developmental dysfluencies*) frequently occur. These dysfluencies usually resolve without specific intervention. Factors associated with slower acquisition of language milestones include male gender, prematurity, multiple gestation (twins, triplets), bilingualism, and disadvantaged socioeconomic status.

Cognitive Development

> **How does a child's play change between 12 and 36 months?**

Beginning at about 7–9 months and extending into the second year of life, the toddler learns that an object exists even when it is not present by developing a mental image (**object permanence**, see also Chapter 10). During the second year, toddlers will quickly look for an object that they observed being moved through a series of displacements. By 18–24 months, toddlers begin to search for a hidden object even if it was moved while they were not watching; furthermore, they will check several possible locations in an attempt to find it.

In the second year of life, toddlers begin to understand that their actions can cause novel reactions and they become experimenters within their environment. They learn that seemingly unrelated behaviors can have certain consequences. For example, by age 2, a toddler will know to wind a toy to make it move.

Long-term memory develops in the second year of life allowing toddlers to make associations such as matching a place at the table with one person. In fact, they may get upset if someone else sits in that place. They also "memorize" stories, making it close to impossible to skip a few pages of bedtime reading.

Play is an important aspect of development, and reflects increasing mental abilities. At 12 months, toddlers begin to use objects in play (e.g., banging a spoon). After this stage, they begin to use the object functionally (e.g., pretending to eat with the spoon). In the next stage, typically about 18–24 months, the toddler uses a toy to represent a real action (e.g., using a toy telephone to "call Daddy"). These activities are known as *symbolic play* (one object [toy] stands for another object

Selected Developmental Milestones from 12 Months to 36 Months			
Age (months)	Gross Motor	Fine Motor	Language
12	Wide-based independent walking	Pincer grasps	"mama" "dada" + 2–3 other words
15	Runs	Imitates scribbling	3–6 words
18	Walks upstairs while holding on	Brushes teeth with help	10–20 words
24	Jumps with two feet	Builds tower 4–6 blocks	50–100 words Combines two words 25–50% intelligibility
36	Heel-toe gait Pedals tricycle	Copies a circle	3–4 word sentences 50–75% intelligibility

[telephone]). Toddlers at this stage also engage in *parallel play* (despite being situated near one another, they play independently with little interaction or joint play).

Toddlers in the third year of life continue to develop the ability to represent reality to themselves through the use of words and symbols, including gestures. Their thinking is **preoperational** (they can solve simple problems, understand ordination [one book, two books] and classification [a dog is an animal], and sort by color and shape).

Egocentrism, the belief that they are the center and initiator of all activity and the inability to put themselves in the place of others, are prominent features of children's thinking at age 2–3 years. As toddlers enter their fourth year, egocentrism begins to recede, and they begin to understand that others may have a different perspective from their own.

Social-Emotional Development

Toddlers become increasingly adept at reading the primary caregiver's cues regarding the safety of novel social interactions. For example, a toddler is more easily calmed if the caregiver smiles and is reassuring while in a new situation like a doctor's office. This behavior is called **social referencing** and is typically mastered during this time and continues to be a useful skill throughout life.

By 18 months of age, toddlers can guide the attention of one person to share in their experiences of other objects. This is called **joint attention**, and shows the emergence of understanding that other people have their own interests and behaviors. This leads toddlers to having the ability to respond to others' distress. For example, when confronted with the distress of someone else, they are capable of understanding that the distress is affecting another person and not themselves. They may even try to comfort the other person.

Walking and using language promote new forms of social relations as toddlers learn that they can share experiences and compare reactions. The process of developing a *sense of self* leads to a new awareness of their own ability to create plans or do things independently. This increasing competence is the basis for the emerging autonomy characteristic of this time.

A toddler's sense of **autonomy** is also accompanied by a strong desire to see personal wishes fulfilled. Given that they lack the ability to think rationally and logically, they cannot understand rational and logical arguments for or against specific behaviors provided by their parents. They are also unable to understand postponement of their immediate desires and so are in frequent conflict with others. Because they lack sufficient language skills to express their disappointment or frustration, they demonstrate these feelings behaviorally through *tantrums*, the hallmark of the "terrible two's." Particular features of toddlerhood include *negativism* (this is the age of the mandatory "no"), rigidity, and emotional lability. All of these make calm, controlled parenting a challenge.

Between 12 and 24 months of age, toddlers begin to experience learned *secondary emotions* of embarrassment, jealousy, pride, shame, guilt, and envy. These secondary emotions do not appear until toddlers are able to think about and evaluate themselves in terms of some social standard, rule, or desired goal. Thus, secondary emotions can be considered social emotions because they involve either challenge to or enhancement of the toddler's sense of self.

Increasing autonomy and sense of self enhance the development of **gender identity**. By 2 years of age, toddlers are able to discriminate whether a playmate is male or female. Identification of gender is based on anatomical inspection as well as an understanding of core gender identity. By 3 years of age, toddlers know their own identity as male or female. Although in their fantasy life there may be mixtures of male and female elements in how they see themselves, toddlers will nonetheless be protective of their gender identity.

Health Risks

Although toddlers eat a variety of foods, it is common for them to go through periods when they will eat only certain foods (e.g., peanut butter and jelly sandwiches every day). Despite their idiosyncrasies, toddlers virtually always take in what they need to grow appropriately. In fact, research has shown that children are responsive to the energy content of their diets. Routine monitoring of growth is mandatory, however, and each year children should have growth parameters entered onto an appropriate height and weight growth chart to verify adequate progress over time. In addition to the standard curves developed for the average child In the US, the World Health Organization has developed dozens of charts representing average growth in height and weight for children in a number of countries.

The significant risk of injury during toddlerhood is a function of the child's increasing motor ability and desire to explore. During this period, accidental injury, poisoning, and drowning are major concerns because an energetic 2 year old can get into trouble quickly. The strong sense of autonomy that is characteristic of toddlers puts them at high risk of child maltreatment from excessive physical and emotional punishment in response to their negative and egocentric behaviors. Health care at this age should include parental guidance in accident prevention and management of temper tantrums.

Preschool Years (Ages 3 to 5 Years)

Motor Development

Between the ages of 3 and 5 years, preschool children begin to master more complex gross and fine motor tasks. By 4 years of age, children are learning to skip, climb stairs independently, catch bouncing balls, and swing. By 5 years of age, most children are able to ride a bicycle with training wheels. Children at this age also draw circles, crosses, and squares, draw faces with bodies, cut with scissors, and use the toilet independently. At 4–5 years, the typical child will be able to print his or her first name.

Preschool Language Development

Preschool children can carry on a conversation reflecting their ability to describe several activities that occurred during the day. Three-year-old children are also full of "why" questions. Their grammar and syntax is becoming increasingly correct. Mean length of utterance should equal chronologic age in the first 5 years of life; thus, the typical 5-year-old speaks in sentences that average five words. Articulation continues to mature with most 5-year-old children being at least 90% intelligible. The rhythm and pacing of speech is improving rapidly and developmental dysfluencies are disappearing.

Preschool Cognitive Development

As children progress beyond 3 years of age, their play matures from *symbolic* to *imaginary.* For example, the child may have a "mother" doll feed a "baby" doll. *Joint* or *associative play* emerges, during which groups of children cooperate and take turns with one another, laying the foundation for group activities. *Learning to share* is a major milestone that requires understanding ownership and delaying gratification.

At this age, the preschool setting facilitates learning through *imitation.* Sociocultural rules are integrated into learning at this time, and children are assessed for their readiness to attend school based, in part, on many of these pre-academic skills. In fact, most experts agree that school readiness decisions should consider all developmental and behavioral domains as well as factors such as gender, birth date, and physical size.

Preschool Social-Emotional Development

Gender role identification is solidified in the preschool years. As children's concept of gender identity forms, they become adept at labeling themselves as boys or girls. Soon, they develop a gender role schema for "boy" and "girl" and are able to identify objects and behaviors that are associated with each gender role. Social reinforcement of gender specific behaviors leads to children placing value on those things associated with their gender role and they imitate them.

Sexual play among preschool children is a natural consequence of their cognitive, social, and emotional development. Children are interested in "private parts" and what distinguishes "boys" from "girls." They are fascinated with toileting activities. Preschool children may participate in games of "mommy and daddy" or "doctor" in order to further explore gender differences. Sexual play is common and does not predict fixation on these behaviors as an adult. However, preschool children should be educated about the differences between "good touching" and "bad touching."

An important part of social-emotional development at this time is the development of a **social conscience** or **morality**. Preschool children apply the concepts of morality independently of what is right or wrong; their primary motivation for good behavior is to avoid punishment. Preschool children obey adult rules even though they do not understand why the rules exist. They have little understanding of intent or motive behind a particular behavior because (1) they still have difficulty understanding another person's perspective, and (2) they cannot focus on more than one characteristic of an object or event at a time (amount of damage done vs. intent). As a result, the degree of guilt or blame a child typically ascribes is associated with the degree of damage. As children move through the later preschool years (≥ 4), they are better able to understand reasons for rules, particularly in group settings.

In combination with the development of a moral sense of self, preschool children develop greater **autonomy** and are interested in trying new tasks and experiences on their own. At the same time, they are becoming more aware of others' emotions and agendas, and they want to share their experiences with others. "Terrific three's" describes an age of relative emotional calm and equilibrium. However, this respite is often followed by the "out of bounds four's" with its high energy, boisterousness, and general dysequilibrium.

Preschool Health Risks

Trauma is the greatest health risk during the preschool years, likely related in part to children's facile complex motor abilities. In addition, caregivers often have difficulty containing the child's willfulness and limit testing. Because children of this age often attend childcare or preschool, exposure to *communicable diseases* is another common health concern.

Recommended Readings

Augustyn M, Frank DA, Zuckerman BS. Infancy and Toddler Years. In Carey WB, Crocker AC, Coleman WL, Elias ER, Feldman HM (Eds.), *Developmental-Behavioral Pediatrics*, 4th ed. New York: Saunders Elsevier; 2009.

Goswami U (Ed.). *Blackwell Handbook of Childhood Cognitive Development*. Oxford, UK: Blackwell Publishing; 2002.

Hamel SC, Pelphrey A. Preschool Years. In Carey WB, Crocker AC, Coleman WL, Elias ER, Feldman HM (Eds.), *Developmental-Behavioral Pediatrics*, 4th ed. New York: Saunders Elsevier; 2009.

Siegel DJ. *The Developing Mind*. New York: Guilford Press; 2002.

Smith P, Hart C (Eds.). *Blackwell Handbook of Childhood Social Development*. Oxford, UK: Blackwell Publishing; 2002.

Review Questions

1. The most common age for children to become bowel and bladder trained is
   A. 18 months.
   B. 24 months.
   C. 3 years.
   D. 4 years.
   E. 6 years.

2. The manner in which toddlers play with one another is often described as
   A. imaginary.
   B. magical.
   C. obstinate.
   D. parallel.
   E. reciprocal.

3. Which of the gross motor milestones below is typically associated with a 3-year-old child?
   A. Jumps with two feet
   B. Pedals a tricycle
   C. Pincer grasp
   D. Pushes a toy while walking
   E. Snips with scissors

4. The stable conceptualization of being either male or female despite superficial features such as dress or mannerism is
   A. gender identity.
   B. sex role schema.
   C. sex role stereotype.
   D. sexual orientation.
   E. sexual preference.

Key to review questions: p. 407

13 The School Years

Elizabeth McCauley, PhD

- Why is thinking during middle childhood called "concrete operational?"
- What are the characteristics of peer groups during middle childhood?
- What motivates a 10-year-old child to "do the right thing?"
- What are the major health concerns of middle childhood?
- How does timing of pubertal development influence self-concept?
- How do "developmental trajectories" manifest themselves during adolescence?

Middle Childhood (6 to 12 Years)

Although **middle childhood** is a period of significant physical, cognitive, social, and emotional development, changes are more gradual and subtle than the dramatic growth surges found during the infancy/preschool and adolescent years.

Physical Development

From the age of 6 years until the adolescent growth spurt, children grow about 6 cm and gain approximately 3 kg each year. As early as age 7, **hormonal changes** occur, including the increased production of *adrenal steroids* in both boys and girls, followed by increases in *estrogen* and then *androgen* production. As a result, fat is deposited in subcutaneous tissues beginning at approximately age 8 in girls and age 10 in boys. In many girls, the first pubertal changes of breast budding, followed by pubic and axillary hair growth, occur during middle childhood. *Menarche* (onset of menses) occurs after the growth spurt. In girls, the growth rate begins to accelerate as early as 10 years of age, with most girls experiencing their major growth spurt between 11 and 13 years. Boys typically develop later than girls but can have signs of puberty, such as testicular enlargement, as young as 10 years of age. Most of the major growth spurt in boys occurs during adolescence (13–15 years of age).

Bone and muscle growth during middle childhood results in enhanced physical coordination and more complex motor skills. Whereas the 5-year-old can run, ride a tricycle, print his or her name, and throw a ball, most 10-year-olds have mastered a two-wheel bike, can run and dribble a ball simultaneously, and write in cursive.

Permanent teeth begin erupting during the early elementary school period. Loss of the primary or deciduous (baby) teeth occurs at a rate of about four teeth per year, from age 6 to 14.

Neurological changes promote important cognitive developments. Continued *myelinization of the cortex* is accompanied by increased numbers and density of dendrites and synaptic connections. Brain cell genesis, nerve myelinization, and dendritic pruning, particularly in the frontal cortex, increase during late childhood and early adolescence and continue into young adult life. During childhood, the thickness of the cerebral cortex varies with periods of thickening and thinning, and cortical fissures become more prominent. Electroencephalographic (EEG) activity transitions from primarily delta wave (frequency: 3–5/sec) to predominantly alpha wave (frequency: 8–13/sec) activity after age 6. EEG activity also becomes increasingly stable, localized, and function specific, depending on the task the child is doing.

Cognitive Development

Why is thinking during middle childhood called "concrete operational?"

By the age of 7, most children can consider more than one characteristic of an object or issue simultaneously, and understand that an object does not change merely because its appearance varies. For example, the child recognizes that the amount of liquid remains the same even if poured from a tall container into a shorter but wider container. Piaget termed this phenomenon **conservation**.

Other important skills learned at this time include **seriation**, the ability to conceptualize quantifiable differences (e.g., Jane is taller than Sue), and **transivity**, the ability to infer relations among elements in a serial order (e.g., if I am taller than Jane, and Jane is taller than Sue, then I am taller than Sue). These new mental skills allow children to perform simple mathematical functions, and enhance the child's conception of time so that waiting for a turn, anticipating a holiday, and planning for a future event become possible.

Memory improves as children learn to use rehearsal or categorizing to help organize daily tasks. However, these skills are still connected to the physical world (things the child can see, feel, or manipulate). Thus, this stage is termed the **concrete operational stage** of thinking. It is not until adolescence that the cognitive ability to manipulate ideas, possibilities, and abstract concepts emerges.

Cognitive structures and early problem-solving skills evolve during middle childhood through complex *fantasy play* and following *rules*. The elementary school-aged child typically enjoys board games and team sports. A major developmental step is the transition from the need to interpret rules strictly to the ability to negotiate changes in rules, and the ability to apply rules from one situation to another similar situation (generalization). These skills are typically learned by trial and error and repetition.

Social Cognition

Social cognition refers to skills that reflect a person's sense of self and relations to others. At ages 6–7, children compare their personal qualities with those of others, but are bound to observable physical attributes, such as who runs the fastest or counts the highest. At age 8-10, children begin to recognize *psychological attributes* such as fairness or generosity. Late middle childhood children can evaluate traits like shyness or reliability. Despite this progress, they remain tied to concrete (observable) representations of behaviors, and cannot yet understand that different social or emotional situations may elicit different behaviors without changing the basic characteristics of a person.

As children develop a more complex sense of self and others, they demonstrate increased ability to *take another person's perspective*. Most 10-year-old children are able to consider another person's point of view but cannot easily consider two points of view (theirs and the other person's) simultaneously. By age 12, however, almost all children can consider multiple perspectives simultaneously as long as the issue is tied to the concrete world (e.g., discussion of how a parent, teacher, and child might react differently to a rule-breaking situation). As children move into early adolescence, they begin to understand that ability is a stable trait and to infer that repeated failures may represent a lack of ability rather than a chance occurrence.

What are the characteristics of peer groups during middle childhood?

During elementary school, children belong primarily to same-sex **peer groups**. These groups are more formalized than previously, and selection of friends is based on common interests or personality traits rather than merely living close by or being in the same classroom. Members of a peer group interact on a regular basis, have a shared set of *norms*, and a sense of belonging to the group. Gradually, roles emerge with particular members becoming leaders or followers. As the child matures, peers become less interchangeable and lasting friendships are established. The importance of peers and the time spent with them increases steadily throughout middle childhood.

Personal and Social Competence

According to **Erikson**, the major task of middle childhood is developing a sense of *personal com-*

petence by mastering new physical, cognitive, and social skills introduced by school and community activities. School work, athletics, and hobby groups all focus on practice, motivation, and *accomplishment.* Children who do not find areas of success and accomplishment, even in doing such activities as chores around the house or self-care, develop a sense of inferiority and failure that can lead to decreased self-esteem and reluctance to take on new challenges and responsibilities.

Children who have poor *social skills* (e.g., inaccurate sense of personal space, inadequate hygiene, clinging or demanding behavior) have difficulty maintaining social relationships despite a strong desire for companionship. They are usually bewildered by their lack of acceptance because their behaviors result from not perceiving the subtle intricacies of relationship rather than any conscious rudeness or disrespect. "She just doesn't get it" is a perfect description. Children with *learning and attention problems* are vulnerable to social rejection as they may, because of their learning difficulties or impulsivity, have problems reading and responding to social cues. For some children, intentional buffoonery or antisocial behavior becomes the only means of peer "acceptance."

Moral Development

> What motivates a 10-year-old child to "do the right thing?"

Early research on **moral development** suggested that children move through an invariant sequence of stages of moral judgment, transitioning from an early childhood focus on rules, expectations of authority figures, and avoiding punishment to, in middle childhood, a more internalized set of rules that culminates in late adolescence into an individualized set of moral values based on personal principles. Using this early paradigm, for the 6- to 7-year-old child, goodness or badness is determined by the *consequences* of an act. By age 9, children become fascinated with *rules*. Most children of this age have a strong sense of right and wrong with difficulty appreciating and accommodating to changing circumstances. By about age 10, children begin to consider *intent* in under-

standing their own and others' behavior, and the cognitive process underlying moral judgments shifts to a desire to behave in ways that gain *social approval.*

More recent developmental research has provided a richer understanding of the process and suggests that moral judgments are influenced by the child's social interactions. This research suggests that moral decisions are shaped by emotional responses and social judgments, and that development does not follow an invariant sequence. Even toddlers are capable of sympathetic and empathetic reactions to others. Further, children in early and middle childhood appear to be able to make distinctions between moral, social, and personal judgments, allowing them to decide whether or not something is right or fair, based on the circumstances of the situation rather than merely following a rule or doing what is most socially acceptable.

Gender Identity and Sex Role Development

By middle childhood, *gender-related behavioral patterns* are well-established and children are clear about "boy" versus "girl" behaviors. Open curiosity about other children's bodies and bodily functions is less common during middle childhood than it was at earlier ages. Many children are modest about their body and want privacy while bathing or toileting. Bedwetting may still occur among 6- to 8-year-olds and may interfere with social activities that involve an overnight stay away from home. Jokes about embarrassing bodily functions are common, but given the strong taboos against sexual play in western culture, most sexual interactions become covert during middle childhood. Many children engage in some same-sex sexual play, consisting primarily of comparing genitalia and some touching.

> Practicing boy-girl social relationship roles is common during middle childhood. In the primary grades, boys and girls engage in chasing and teasing games; later, many children experience their first real crush. Many gay and lesbian adults report knowing they had "different" romantic interests as early as middle childhood, even before having a clear cognitive understanding of sexual orientation.

Health Risks

What are the major health concerns of middle childhood?

The major health concerns arising during middle childhood fall into three categories: (1) *chronic medical conditions* such as diabetes or asthma; (2) *injuries* associated with increasing involvement in physical activities including "I dare you" games; and (3) *learning or attention disorders*. In addition to attention difficulties, which affect school and social success, anxiety-related problems commonly present during middle childhood. In general, the anxieties of middle childhood are responsive to brief behavioral interventions and most resolve as children mature.

It is critical that children who have a chronic medical condition be treated within the context of their developmental needs. This means encouraging the child and family to normalize the child's life as much as possible by encouraging appropriate school and peer activities. Because children of this age are forming their sense of self, it is essential that they, and their families, not define themselves in terms of the child's medical or behavioral condition. The physician can assess and reinforce this sense of balance by including questions about participation in school, athletic, and social activities as part of every health care visit.

Adolescence (12 to 19 Years)

Adolescence is defined as extending from the appearance of secondary sex characteristics to the cessation of somatic growth. After the neonatal period, it is the time of most dramatic physical, cognitive, social, and emotional change.

Physical Development

How does timing of pubertal development influence self-concept?

Physical changes associated with **pubertal development** are a primary concern for most adolescents. The onset and course of pubertal events are organized around a feedback mechanism that involves the integration of protein peptide hormones released by the hypothalamus and pituitary with steroid hormones secreted by the gonads. **Gonadotropin-releasing hormone (GnRH)** is synthesized and stored in the hypothalamus. When released, this small peptide regulates the production and release of two anterior pituitary hormones, or gonadotropins, **luteinizing hormone (LH)**, and **follicle-stimulating hormone (FSH).** The two primary sex steroids produced by the gonads, **estradiol** and **testosterone**, act on peripheral target organs and tissues and within a negative feedback loop to suppress hypothalamic release of GnRH. The notable exception to this negative feedback loop is the regulation of **ovulation** where positive feedback of ovarian steroid ultimately produces an LH surge and ovulation.

The *hypothalamus* acts as a central common pathway for impulses from the cortex, limbic system, and pineal gland and is sensitive to *catecholamine* and *indolamine* stimulation. Neuroendocrine response to stress and nutritional status influence pubertal manifestations like linear growth and menstruation.

As these feedback systems are activated, the individual moves through a series of physical changes that have a dramatic effect on appearance. These changes begin gradually during middle childhood and culminate with completed pubertal development and linear growth during adolescence, when the final 25% of adult height and 50% of adult weight are attained. Significant visible changes focus the teenager's attention on the *self* and heighten concern about **body image**.

The pubertal **growth spurt** occurs earlier in females than in males. On average, 12-year-old girls are taller than 12-year-old boys although there is marked variability. When boys begin to grow, their spurt is longer and of greater magnitude than that of girls. Given the considerable variation in the timing of pubertal change, most young people need reassurance that they are normal. Concerns related to body changes should be taken seriously and explained to allay unnecessary anxiety. Youth who experience their development as "out of synch" with their peers are at increased risk for behavioral and emotional problems. Early maturation was long considered to have positive effects on boys' self-confidence and social status, but more recent research suggests that both early and late maturation confer increased risk for depression and anxiety in boys.

Phases of Adolescence		
	Age	Sexual Maturity Rating
Early	12–13	1–2
Middle	14–16	3–5
Late	17+	5

Early-maturing girls, especially those with obvious physical changes such as early breast development, are the group at most risk for increased behavioral problems. Early-developing girls may seek out peers who are like them physically (although a year or more older) and find themselves in demanding social and emotional situations without the necessary coping skills. Early development is most problematic when friendships with more deviant peers develop in the context of lax parental supervision. Parents should be encouraged to help their child cope with the physical changes of puberty by promoting healthy activities that are in keeping with the youth's skills and developmental status.

Recent research has shown that adolescence involves a period of marked *brain development* with increased cell genesis, myelinization, and dendritic pruning, particularly in the frontal/prefrontal cortex. These are brain areas believed to control self-regulation skills such as inhibitory control and the perception and evaluation of risks and rewards. Brain development in early and middle adolescence lays the foundation for the development of more sophisticated problem-solving skills in late adolescence and early adulthood. Some neurodevelopmental changes occurring in adolescence are triggered by pubertal hormones. These hormones are thought to stimulate the brain systems that regulate arousal and appetite, contributing to moodiness, changes in the sleep-wake cycle, increases in romantic interests, risk taking, and novelty seeking behavior observed in many adolescents.

Adolescent **sleep patterns** are marked by a physiological alteration or phase delay that leads to a natural shift toward later bedtimes. Changes in adolescent sleep architecture result in less deep, slow wave sleep. Insufficient sleep negatively affects mood and ability to perform in school. Therefore, it is important to educate adolescents and their parents about normative shifts in sleep patterns, while stressing the importance of getting adequate sleep, including increasing opportunities for sleep by turning off computers and cell phones.

> In a recent survey, 45% of adolescents reported not getting enough sleep on school nights and feeling irritable and sleepy during the school day.

Cognitive Development

The ability to use abstract thought, consider theoretical notions, devise hypotheses, examine cause-and-effect relationships, and make judgments based on future considerations emerges during adolescence. This stage of **formal operations** typically does not begin to develop until late adolescence with only 35% of 16- to 17-years-olds exhibiting this skill. Many adolescents can think more abstractly when considering topics such as political issues, but are less flexible in their thinking about personal, social, or emotional issues. Further, not all individuals fully develop these abilities, and many reach adulthood with only a limited ability to deal with abstract concepts like religion, morality, philosophy, and ethics. During this period, **regression** in cognitive processing to a more concrete stage of thinking is common in the face of physical or emotional stress.

Moral Development

Past research suggested that children in middle childhood and early adolescence made moral judgments based on *conventional moral reasoning,* i.e., internalization of societal rules and decision making that reflects what is best for the community, not just what is best for the individual. Recent research finds that delayed or immature moral reasoning is strongly associated with juvenile delinquency, regardless of socioeconomic status, gender, age, or intelligence, and that mature moral development acts as a barrier to engaging in antisocial acts. Research further suggests that adolescents' moral motivation is positively associated with the quality of the parent-child relationship and the adolescent's own rating of the importance of social justice.

Emotional Development

Emotional regulation, the ability to identify, process, and express feelings appropriately, is an important milestone in adolescent development. Both brain maturation and experience help youth to gradually master the skills needed to make sound decisions, even in the face of intense emotions. As cognitive coping skills mature, adolescents become better able to resist emotional impulses and make decisions based on longer-term goals. Problem solving and planning are intellectual functions still under active reorganization during the adolescent years.

> How do different "developmental trajectories" manifest themselves during adolescence?

Recent studies of both normal healthy adolescents and those with a variety of chronic illnesses describe three **developmental trajectories**: continuous, surgent, and tumultuous. Long-term follow-up of youths in each of these categories has shown that no group experiences significantly more psychopathology than any other group, and overall adjustment in young adulthood is comparable across groups. It is normal for teenagers to experience transient disturbances in self-esteem, anxiety and depression, and oversensitivity to shame and humiliation in response to stressful situations. Less than a third of all teenagers experience severe turmoil.

Types of Developmental Trajectories

1. *Continuous:* No major crises, high self-esteem, stable environment
2. *Surgent:* Prone to depression, less socially active
3. *Tumultuous:* Anxious, dependent on peers, less secure self concept, family problems

Social Development

Learning the responsibilities and nuances of **peer friendships** is a prerequisite to healthy adult friendships. Being "popular" is not as important as having at least a small group of accepting friends. Social isolation during adolescence increases risks for academic difficulty, delinquency, and feelings of inadequacy. Purely social, rather than athletic or task-oriented activities, become increasingly common during this period. This is also a time when adolescents experiment with more **intimate relationships**, and social learning becomes based less on peer group influences and more on the influence of a boy- or girlfriend. Social development also plays an important role in the process of **identity formation** as youth try out different roles and interests.

Establishing a sense of identity is an ongoing process that extends into early adulthood. The process takes shape in adolescence as youth search for **personal identity** or that sense of self that combines the person's diverse and often conflicting social roles (e.g., child, friend, student, athlete), talents (artistic, musical, analytic), values, and attitudes.

Early adolescents are preoccupied with the *physical changes* associated with puberty. Although early adolescents engage in role experimentation and seek independence via close relationships with peers, family relationships and parental approval remain important. Younger adolescents focus on "being like" their friends in terms of dress, hairstyles, and interests.

Middle adolescents are preoccupied with their *social role* and are intensely aware of how they appear to and are judged by their peers. They begin experimenting with risk-taking behaviors and asserting their independence from family. By the end of middle adolescence, many teens feel more confident and begin to express more nonconformity.

Older adolescents are preoccupied with decisions about *work and career*. Family influences become less important as *intimate relationships* are established. Some older adolescents postpone physical and financial independence from the family because of their need for resources to complete their education. This period of continued family reliance, termed the **psychosocial moratorium**, extends into the mid 20s and even early 30s for some.

Gender Identity and Sexual Development

During puberty, **sexual functioning** matures and takes on new meaning. **Menarche** represents the culmination of puberty in the adolescent female and the beginning of the reproductive years for the mature female. Although relative infertility without regular ovulatory cycles is common during the first 3–24 months following menarche, **contraception** is indicated for any sexually active adolescent female. Most hormonal forms of contraception can be used safely beginning immediately after menarche.

Virtually all adolescent boys and many adolescent girls engage in **masturbation**. About 50% of 16-year-old boys and 50% of 17-year-old girls from all social classes have had **sexual intercourse**. One third of sexually active adolescents become pregnant and 40% of these obtain abortions. **Sexually transmitted diseases**, especially chlamydial and human papillomavirus infections, are common. Recent trends suggest declining rates of adolescent sexual activity, pregnancy, and childbirth.

Homosexual fantasies occur among both male and female heterosexual teenagers. Some young adolescents have exploratory homosexual experiences. These experiences do not necessarily predict future **sexual orientation**. The percentage of the overall population who identify themselves as exclusively homosexual is difficult to determine, but appears to be 4–10%. Although many gay and lesbian adults report having had feelings of marginality or of being different during childhood, homosexual identity formation (personally acknowledging, exploring, and accepting) generally occurs during mid-adolescence. The "coming out" process typically occurs during late adolescence or early adulthood.

Health Issues

Approximately 20% of presumably healthy 12- to 19-year-olds have previously unrecognized health problems, mostly related to the rapid growth and maturation of puberty. These problems include structural (e.g., idiopathic scoliosis) and functional (e.g., "shin splints" disorders of the skeletal system) problems; failure to achieve puberty at the appropriate time (e.g., pituitary insufficiency); sexually transmitted disease; pregnancy; violence; and substance abuse. Mental health concerns, particularly depression, also become more prevalent during adolescence.

Health care providers must be alert to signs of **depression**, especially in accident-prone adolescents, because accidents can represent "masked" **suicide** attempts. Adolescents often have difficulty verbalizing their feelings, allowing depression

and suicidal thoughts to go unrecognized. When the risk of suicide is present, precautions must be taken to ensure the adolescent's safety, including informing guardians or other responsible adults.

> A sense of self-competence is the most important predictor of adherence to a medical regimen. The teenager who has a positive self-image is likely to follow the physician's advice. Other factors that promote adherence include a treatment schedule tailored to the teenager's personal lifestyle (few side effects; simple, easy-to-follow; requires minimal time and effort) and satisfaction (feels fully informed; feels privacy and confidentiality will be respected).

The three leading causes of death among adolescents are *accidents*, *homicide*, and *suicide*. Many accidental deaths are preventable, including motor vehicle collisions and drowning. In deaths due to homicide, the perpetrator is often an acquaintance or family member.

The first use of **illicit drugs** can occur in some elementary school children but is most common among adolescents. Youth who are rebellious, place a low value on achievement, are alienated from their parents and community, and live in a chaotic environment are most likely to be substance abusers.

Tobacco use remains a major public health problem among adolescents. Approximately 30% of teenage females in the US smoke on a regular basis; the percentage is somewhat lower among males.

The prevalence of **violence** increased dramatically over the last two decades of the 20th century. Active school and community anti-violence programs led to small but promising declines just before the turn of the century. However, the percentage of high school students who have carried a gun, knife, or other weapon at least once during the preceding month still exceeds 75% in some urban areas.

Recommended Readings

Adams G, Berzonsky M. *Blackwell Handbook of Adolescence*. Oxford, UK: Blackwell Publishing; 2002.

Bee H, Boyd D. *The Developing Child*, 12th ed. Boston: Allyn & Bacon; 2009.

Craig W. *Childhood Social Development.* Oxford, UK: Blackwell Publishing; 2000.

Dahl, RE, Spear, LP (Eds.). *Adolescent Brain Development: Vulnerabilities and Opportunities.* New York: New York Academy of Sciences; 2004.

Fisher MM, Alderman EA, Kreipe RE, Rosenfeld WA (Eds.). *Textbook of Adolescent Health Care.* Elk Grove Village, IL: American Academy of Pediatrics; 2011.

Steinberg, Laurence. Cognitive and affective development in adolescence. *Trends in Cognitive Sciences* 2005; 9:69–74.

C. Boys' growth spurts are shorter and of lesser magnitude than girls'.

D. Contraception is unnecessary until regular ovulation is established.

E. The growth spurt occurs earlier in males than females.

Key to review questions: p. 407

Review Questions

1. Hormonal changes that lead to puberty are
   A. evident as early as age 7 with increases in adrenal steroids.
   B. marked by estrogen increases in girls only.
   C. seldom observed during the middle childhood years.
   D. undetectable until after pubic hair develops.
   E. unrelated to increases in subcutaneous fat during middle childhood.

2. Neurological development during middle childhood is characterized by a significant increase in
   A. delta wave EEG activity.
   B. glial cell proliferation.
   C. head circumference.
   D. number of neurons.
   E. synaptic connections.

3. During middle childhood, most children prefer
   A. being with older adults.
   B. peer groups with common interests.
   C. playing with mixed groups of boys and girls.
   D. simple fantasy games.
   E. structured games and sports.

4. Which of the following statements concerning adolescence is true?
   A. Adolescents are quite flexible in thinking about personal, social, and emotional issues.
   B. Adolescents' moral motivation is associated with the quality of parent-child relationships.

14 The Adult Years

James A.H. Farrow, MD

- What is the major task of young adulthood?
- How do relationships with parents change during young adulthood?
- What is the correlation between divorce rate and age at marriage?
- What are some of the risks and benefits of becoming a parent?
- How does sexual functioning in middle-aged men and women differ?
- Why do some people have a "mid-life crisis?"
- Why do some "empty" nests become "elastic" nests?
- What kinds of organ system changes occur with increasing age?
- What are the common causes of despair in older adults?

Young Adulthood (20 to 40 Years)

The human body reaches peak strength, flexibility, functioning, and efficiency between the ages of 20 and 30. The combination of strong musculature, exceptional stamina, high resistance to disease, and rapid repair of tissue damage allows the young adult to develop specialized motor skills and maximal athletic and physical prowess. Poor health during this time is usually related to lifestyle choices and behaviors such as alcohol and substance abuse, poor exercise and nutritional habits, obesity, and mental health problems such as depression and stress-related conditions.

Cognitive Development

Brain cell development peaks during the 20s. However, *new synaptic pathways* are formed throughout adulthood, permitting the individual to learn new information and skills at any age. Young adults are informed, knowledgeable, and able to make complex decisions using cognitive abilities termed **formal operations**. They can organize, plan, and consider the short- and long-term consequences of actions.

Intellectual functioning continues to evolve throughout adulthood into an advanced phase of problem solving. This level of cognitive functioning is influenced by education, tolerance of diverse viewpoints, and *dialectical thinking* (i.e., ability to re-examine ideas as a result of critique). Cognitive and learning impairments identified during childhood and adolescence (e.g., attention-deficit/ hyperactivity disorder – ADHD) may continue well into adulthood. These disorders may be manifested by difficulty with the more challenging academic work in college or graduate studies or in organizing activities of daily living (*executive functioning*).

Moral Development

By adulthood, most individuals have developed a personal standard of behavior and adhere to *universal ethical principles*, including abiding by a *social contract* and respecting individual rights. When an individual's principles do not conform to existing law, conscience directs behavior. Accepting responsibility for one's actions and empathizing with others are part of that development. Key features of sociocultural development during this time are increasing prosocial behavior, civic engagement, and a sense of purpose within society's standards of morality.

Gender and Sexuality

The **reproductive system** of both males and females is fully mature by the age of 20. The maximum capacity for reaching orgasm peaks in the late teens for males and occurs in the 30s for females. Sex hormone production is highest in the 20s but sex drive remains high in most persons for several decades, often into the 70s and 80s.

Observable behaviors and roles are easy for the young adult to evaluate and either incorporate or reject. However, intimate behavior is less observable and so less readily modeled. Discussion about comfort with **intimacy** is virtually unavailable to the young adult, and rarely addressed in clinical settings. Thus, many young adults abandon an otherwise promising relationship because of feeling unsure about how to achieve true psychosocial intimacy rather than merely perform intimate acts (e.g., fondling, intercourse).

Consolidation of **sexual identity** and **sexual orientation** occurs during late adolescence and early adulthood. For lesbians and gay males, defining oneself as homosexual internally and then to other homosexuals, is the first stage of disclosure called "coming out." Retrospective studies of adult homosexuals have found that gay males typically define themselves as homosexual between ages 19 and 21. Adult lesbians reach self-definition somewhat later, between ages 21 and 23. These milestones have been occurring earlier in some populations as a result of greater social acceptance of sexual minorities.

Sexual Relationships

At least 20% of young adults in their 20s and 30s do not marry; this number has been increasing since the 1970s because more women are choosing to delay marriage to take advantage of educational and career opportunities. *Living together* and sharing sexual activities without being married is common among both heterosexuals and homosexuals. In 2005, unmarried households became the majority of all U.S. households. Most of these relationships are short-term and average about 2 years.

Most individuals will marry eventually, but many choose long-term singlehood. **Singlehood** has the advantage of freedom to spend time, money, and other resources according to individual choice, more career opportunities, greater

geographic independence, enhanced sense of self sufficiency, and more psychological autonomy. About 80% of both male and female singles report some kind of coital activity between the ages of 25 and 50.

Although women in their 50s and 60s are capable of successful pregnancy, especially through *in vitro* techniques, most women prefer to bear their children before age 45 when the complication rate begins to increase dramatically. With higher average life expectancy, bearing children before age 45 also allows women to parent their children into middle adulthood.

Social Development

> **What is the major task of young adulthood?**

Erikson described the major task of young adulthood as intimacy vs. isolation**. Intimacy**, as defined by Erikson, includes the ability to form an interpersonal relationship characterized by commitment, reciprocity, attachment, and interdependency. Because intimacy entails self-disclosure, achieving a truly intimate relationship requires a strong sense of self (identity). Intimacy is not limited to sexual or spousal relationships.

Isolation, in contrast to intimacy, includes feeling victimized or exploited by others, experiencing difficulty cooperating with others, and having such a fragile sense of identity that the self-disclosure and analysis required in an intimate relationship are too threatening. Traditionally, women have been able to establish intimate relationships earlier than men, who usually find it easier to engage in intimacy after they develop a secure occupational identity. The increased number of occupational options for women has made this gender difference in timing less pronounced than in the past.

Collegiality with Parents

> **How do relationships with parents change during young adulthood?**

Once a stable and satisfying sense of *self* has developed, young adults begin to discover their parents as complex people. The change to exploring the interests, feelings, and values of parents is the beginning of a period of *mutuality* that extends until the individual assumes a caretaking role for the ill or elderly parent. In this initial stage, the young adult tentatively gives support and direction as well as receives it. The response of the parents can range from a reluctance to give up their authoritarian role to an appreciation for the contemporary perspective their children can provide. Members of the *Millennial Generation* (young adults reaching age 18 around the turn of the century) have been brought up by parents who generally have been more protective than parents of past generations. This protectionist relationship often continues during the college and post-college years as young adults continue to depend on parents for support and advice and, more recently, for access to health care insurance.

Intergenerational Relationships

- Young adults are most likely to form stable intergenerational relationships within their family of origin when they adopt a lifestyle similar to, but independent of, their parents, *if* that choice is an authentic reflection of what the young adult wants to do.
- Conflicted relationships occur when young adults reject parental values and adopt an antagonistic or antithetical lifestyle, or they adopt the lifestyle desired by the family of origin but wish they had chosen differently.

Gender and Career Choices

Today, many women have *occupational goals* that have traditionally been reserved for men. Many men prefer a partner with job aspirations for economic reasons and for the prospect of shared interests. Both men and women who are career oriented are more likely to postpone marriage, delay parenthood, and have fewer children. However, for women, commitment to a career remains problematic. Women are still vulnerable to an employer's concerns about the potential work-related effects of pregnancy, maternity leave, or relocation to accommodate the husband's career, and are occasionally asked many potentially discriminatory questions about marital status and family situation, even though such questions are unlawful.

Women who assume the multiple roles of wife/mother, homemaker, and career may find the combination too stressful for their physical and emotional health. On the other hand, the physical and emotional health of women who have no career other than wife and mother also may be in jeopardy. Women who work solely in the home have more depression, acute illnesses, chronic conditions, and health care visits than women who work both inside and outside the home.

Marriage and Parenthood

What is the correlation between divorce rate and age at marriage?

Having a satisfying marriage and family life is the goal of 80% of college students. Marriage partners typically share race, religion, age, social class, level of education, and mutual physical attraction. Although the durability of marriage is influenced by many factors, marrying later appears to lead to more stable and satisfying relationships. Over the past 50 years, the average age of first marriage for men has increased from 23 to 27 years and for women from 20 to 25 years.

Men who marry in their teens have twice the risk of divorce as those who marry in their late 20s.
  Women who marry between 14 and 17 have four times the risk of divorce as women who marry in their late 20s.

What are some of the risks and benefits of becoming a parent?

Life changes that challenge those who become parents include reduction in personal freedom, increased financial pressure, and concerns about being a good parent. The joys of parenthood stem from the pleasure derived from the child's development, the companionship, bonding, and awareness that the child is an extension of the parent's own self, even when a child is adopted, and the sense that children are the individual's link with immortality. Parenthood often promotes a sense of true adulthood.

Middle Age (40 to 65 Years)

After growth and development peak in the 20s and 30s, middle age declines in physical, cognitive, affective, and social functioning begin. Many declines are subtle, slowly progressive, and so universally anticipated that the changes are virtually imperceptible until the latter half of middle age. *Loss of neurons* and *degeneration of neuronal pathways* result in slower nerve conduction, which lengthens reaction times. Unless skills are practiced, they are lost because of active *dendritic pruning*. Relearning is possible, however, and may require less time and effort if remnants of the neuronal pathways are still functional. *Alzheimer* disease, *Parkinson* disease, and *Huntington* disease are specific neurodegenerative disorders. They have known autosomal dominant transmission patterns, although sporadic cases can occur, especially in Parkinson disease. These diseases typically have onset during late middle age and early old age. The pathogenesis of neurodegeneration remains unclear although research in this area is progressing rapidly.

> With age, the gradual lowering of *basal metabolic rate* results in reduced energy expenditure and caloric requirements. Although it may be typical to be overweight and less physically fit as a result of aging, research has shown that these body changes can be delayed by increased activity and better conditioning. Regular exercise slows both calcium loss from bones and the loss of muscle, helps maintain pulmonary functioning, and reduces kyphotic changes in the spine.

Although certain immunological responses (T-cell function, wound healing) and physiological functions (bladder reflex, hair growth) are diminished, the most significant change with age is the diminished ability of the body to *maintain homeostasis*, particularly during periods of stress. When confronted with temperature extremes, emotional strain, or physical injury, middle-aged adults recover less rapidly than younger adults. Many self-regulatory processes are under neuroendocrine control suggesting that either neurostimulation, end organ response, or both may be diminished.

Cognitive Development

Cross-sectional studies of traditional IQ test scores show that overall *intelligence* begins to decline at about age 30. However, while *"fluid intelligence"* (response speed, memory span), which depends on smooth functioning of the CNS, clearly declines beginning in the middle adult years, *"crystallized intelligence"* (reading comprehension, vocabulary), which depends on education and experience, may continue to increase throughout the adult years.

Affective Development

The middle adult years are characterized by *reflection about life goals*, assessment of personal and professional accomplishments, and critical thinking about the future. Some mid-life adults experience short-term distress over transition but ultimately handle and learn from the crisis. Other adults find that change cripples their decision-making skills, undermines their marriage or partner relationships, or interferes with their ability to be a parent. Good support systems enhance coping ability. Other positive factors include higher intelligence, flexible temperament, past successes in other areas of life, and absence of a significant mood disturbance.

Gender and Sexuality

The menstrual cycle becomes less regular in the late 30s and 40s and ceases for most women during the 50s. Factors associated with later **menopause** include child-bearing, early puberty, maternal history, thin physique, higher SES, northern European ancestry, and Caucasian race. The onset of menopause is associated with a decrease in the size of the reproductive organs and vaginal dryness and atrophy due to decreased estrogen production. This process is called the **climacteric**. Despite these changes, reproductive technology enables some postmenopausal women to bear children, suggesting that the pace of the aging process varies among different organs, even within a single system.

Men experience no single event to mark a "male climacteric." The circulating level of testosterone does, however, decline with age. Although men remain fertile until late in life, developing an erection requires more time and stimulation, and both the volume of seminal fluid and the force of ejaculation diminish with age. Men with low testosterone in middle age report lower energy and libido. The metabolic changes accompanying low testosterone explain a constellation of clinical symptoms and signs that mimic menopause.

Sexual Functioning

> How does sexual functioning in middle-aged men and women differ?

After the peak in male potency during the late teens and early adulthood, a decrease in interest and desire may occur at about age 50; a more significant drop in sexual activity occurs after age 70. Women, who reach peak sexual potency in the mid 30s, experience relatively little loss in capacity thereafter. However, the number of women who remain sexually active and the frequency of these activities decline with age and are correlated with the health of the spouse/partner. In contrast, partner health and marital status are poor predictors of sexual activity among older men.

The frequency of sexual intercourse drops to a level of 3–4 times/month among couples married 30 years. Older adults who have access to a regular partner report having intercourse about 2–3 times/month, even at the age of 70. There are limited data about the relationship between aging and homosexual activity. Older homosexual men report continued sexual activity and satisfactory relationships. Less is known about the sexual activity of older homosexual women.

Social Development

> Why do some people have a "mid-life crisis?"

Erikson proposed that the nuclear conflict of the adult years is generativity vs. stagnation. **Generativity** is concerned with guiding and contributing to the next generation. **Stagnation** refers to lack of productivity or creativity, self-centered behavior, and exploitation of others. Mid-life is typically the time for attaining maximal job/ career sat-

isfaction and achievement, especially among men. Prestige and power are at their peak, and many middle-aged adults mentor younger colleagues to achieve a sense of generativity. Jobs requiring heightened sensory capabilities may be subject to age-related performance decrements and provoke early retirement. In contrast, artists and musicians may continue to be creative into very old age.

Many factors, such as health, personality, social environment, income, and educational level, affect the feelings and behaviors of the mid-life adult. Marriage, parenthood, career, physical health, and general quality of life may be different from what was expected. Thus, many of the expectations of young adulthood must be reevaluated as time and energy become limited. Feelings of helplessness and a sense of being "trapped" can lead to a **mid-life crisis**, during which individuals reexamine themselves and the meaning of life. As reevaluation of life goals occurs, many people experience an "identity crisis" similar to that typically associated with adolescence. Extramarital affairs are common during this period, reflecting uncertainty and disappointment about the value of previous commitments, or the need to be reassured about physical attractiveness. If the original marriage/relationship survives, reorganization of roles, redirection of energy, and rejuvenation of sexual activity may result.

> Typical mid-life issues include increasing assertiveness and independence among women and increasing emotionality and sensuousness among men.

Parent-Child Relationships

> Why do some "empty" nests become "elastic" nests?

The period a married couple spends together from the time the last child leaves home to the time one spouse dies is known as the **"empty nest"** period. This can be a challenging time for both, but particularly for the woman who loses the role of mother. Although there is a sense of loss, there is also relief from the responsibility of daily child rearing, more opportunities to pursue other interests, and increased personal freedom and privacy.

The *"elastic nest"* describes the phenomenon of children leaving the family of origin and then returning *(boomerang effect)* in response to job changes, divorce, or other life changes. This intermittent dependency can be fulfilling to the parents who still feel needed; reassuring to the child who still feels protected; and frustrating to all as they struggle with the challenge of trying to move forward developmentally.

The poor financial climate that became clearly evident in 2008 with its uncertain resolution worldwide, led to the phenomenon of *household consolidation*, where parents <u>and</u> children with loss of job and benefits, depletion of life savings, and foreclosure made mutual decisions to pool resources in order to avoid poverty and homelessness. Whereas the elastic nest was usually seen as a temporary arrangement, the duration of household consolidation remains unknown, but is likely to be permanent in many instances.

The middle-aged population of the late 20th century has been called the *"sandwich generation,"* caught between the continuing needs of their children and the new needs of their now-aging parents. Assuming responsibility for social, financial, emotional, or physical aid to their parents can be stressful for adult children. Such role reversal requires giving up reliance and dependency on the aging parent. How aging parents and their adult children negotiate these changes depends on competing obligations (e.g., to other family members, work, social networks) and the previous parent-child relationship.

Later Life (65+ Years)

From a health standpoint, 65 is not old. For example, any man who reached the age of 65 by the turn of the century could expect to live into his early 80s; any woman could expect to live into her mid 80s. Factors that affect longevity include health and socioeconomic status, with higher levels of income and economic security being associated with longer lifespan. The elderly, especially those ≥ 80, are the fastest growing age group. In 2000, the number of Americans ≥ 65 exceeded the number ≤ 25. This trend has continued over the past 10 years with increasing numbers of *baby boomers* reaching retirement age.

Is There a Limit to Human Life Expectancy?

Certain molecular processes appear to regulate the lifespan of individual cells and the more complex tissues they comprise. These processes include:

1. the number of individual cell replications;
2. the production of free radical by-products of energy metabolism, which creates an intracellular electrical imbalance, that can damage other molecules (including DNA); and
3. glycosylation (attachement of glycans to proteins to form sticky, weblike networks or cross-linkages producing changes such as cataracts and arteriosclerosis).

What kinds of organ system changes occur with increasing age?

Changes in biological functioning due to aging are highly variable. Some elderly exhibit marked declines while others exhibit little or no diminution in organ system functioning. Although most people aged 65–80 are not significantly limited by a chronic physical condition, they do have *diminished reserve*, reduced ability to adjust to physical or psychological challenges, and prolonged recovery following injury or disease. Some problems create more widespread dysfunction. *Neurosensory system losses*, such as decreased hearing and vision, are common in the elderly and may cause significant difficulty with eating, following instructions, and ambulation. Impaired regulation of core body temperature may lead to reduced fever response to severe infection, increased risk for heat stroke during the summer, and increased risk for hypothermia during the winter.

While older individuals have essentially intact immune systems, there is some impairment in T-cell function and antibody responses are reduced. These and other changes in host defenses account for increased rates of infection of the skin and the urinary, gastrointestinal, and respiratory tracts in older adults, the latter resulting in increased mortality from pneumonia and influenza.

Reduced cardiac and pulmonary reserve, along with frequent coexisting medical conditions such as arthritis, decrease exercise tolerance, contributing to the more sedentary lifestyle typical of many older adults. Many older individuals show evidence of *coronary arteriosclerosis*, although this finding is not predictive of any particular functional limitations. Diminished lung elasticity and total lung capacity decrease respiratory reserve and increase vulnerability to the effects of otherwise minor pulmonary diseases or insults such as smoking.

Kidney function gradually diminishes with age, usually at a rate of about 0.6% per year. This loss of renal function is attributable to both a reduced number of nephrons and a decrease in tubular functioning. Structural and functional changes in the *gastrointestinal system* include reduced peristalsis and gastric acid secretion and slower emptying times, which contribute to indigestion. Because of slowed metabolic rate and more sedentary lifestyle, obesity is common. Decreased hepatic drug oxidation rates and renal function lead to slower drug metabolism and excretion and, thus, higher blood levels of medications and their active metabolites. Age-related changes in drug pharmacokinetics also include increasing tissue sensitivity, especially in the CNS, resulting in more drug side effects. Given that the standards for the use of most therapeutic agents were determined in younger adults, loading and maintenance doses of medication should usually be reduced when treating the elderly.

Cognitive Development

Deterioration of mental functioning, or **dementia**, is an acquired, chronic impairment in global cognitive functioning that affects comprehension, memory, communication, and daily activities. Fewer than 10% of individuals ≥ 65 have any form of measurable impairment in cognitive functioning. When dementia does occur, the patient's level of consciousness is usually normal and the onset of cognitive impairment is so gradual that it may not be noticeable until some consistent threshold of impairment is reached. The typical course is chronic and progressive.

The dementia associated with **Alzheimer** disease, which is diagnosable by classic symptoms, signs, course, and autopsy findings, accounts for about half to two thirds of all cases of dementia. A variety of other specific conditions, such as multi-infarct dementia, account for the remaining cases. Approximately 10–15% of patients with dementia have treatable, potentially reversible disorders

such as CNS tumors, subdural hematomas, hydrocephalus, drug toxicity, hypo- or hyperthyroidism, alcoholism, cerebrovascular insults, or depression. Recovery depends on successful treatment of the underlying condition.

Affective Development

Recognition of personal limitations in physical or mental ability, fear of inability to care for oneself, or fear of abandonment can lead to **anxiety**. Anxiety can also arise in association with specific conditions such as depression, dementia, and general medical illnesses. Thus, careful evaluation is critical for identifying potentially reversible causes of anxiety. As is true in other conditions, pharmacological treatment of anxiety should be cautious because of the increased incidence of medication side effects in the elderly.

> Individuals who developed insecure or mistrusting relationships early in life with their own parents appear most vulnerable to concerns about being taken advantage of by their children.

Loss plays a role in many life transitions, which the elderly increasingly experience with the death of spouse and friends. Feelings of loss occur not only in reaction to death but also in reaction to illness. Anger and resentment are early manifestations of concerns about long-term functioning. Later, preoccupation with health status can lead to depression. The grief process comes to closure as the individual adopts a realistic level of concern regarding the long-term consequences of the condition.

Depression is common in the elderly and may be due to serious medical conditions, deterioration in functioning, and social losses. Rates of completed **suicide** increase with age in both men and women. In women, the rate plateaus beginning in middle age. In men, it continues to rise slowly through old age.

The prevalence of **alcoholism** in the elderly is estimated to be 10–15%. Approximately one third of elderly alcoholics begin drinking excessively later in life. Those individuals who have a lifelong history of heavy alcohol intake may show evidence of *alcoholic dementia*.

Gender and Sexuality

The biological and social differences between men and women result in differences in their level of sexual activity during old age. In men, physiological degeneration of the *seminiferous tubules* causes decreased semen production and sperm quality. Although orgasm occurs, ejaculation is unlikely with every sexual act and retrograde ejaculation is common. The ability to develop an erection continues in old age, although the degree of tumescence is diminished. The concentration of circulating *testosterone* varies widely among elderly men, but, overall, serum levels decrease with age. Testosterone levels do not correlate well with impotence when it occurs in elderly men because certain medications (e.g., beta-blocking agents) interfere with erection. Medications to improve erectile function are generally safe and effective in older men.

Sexual functioning in women is less affected by age than it is in men. Although reproductive function ceases with menopause by the early to mid 50s, this process typically does not affect sexual desire. However, most surveys show that sexual activity is decreased among elderly women. Physiological changes (e.g., atrophy and drying of vaginal mucosa due to decreased estrogen levels) may play a role, but the decrease in sexual activity appears to be due more to *societal influences* than biological changes.

Social Development

> What are the common causes of despair in older adults?

The psychosocial challenge of late life was conceptualized by Erikson as ego integrity vs. despair. **Ego integrity** is maintained when the individual has overall positive feelings of self-worth and is able to view life as a series of personal achievements with challenges and failures in appropriate perspective. Those who do not view their life positively are likely to experience **despair**, isolation, melancholia, and depression. *Isolation* is the most significant threat to ego integrity. Stimulus deprivation can result from neurosensory deterioration (e.g., vision or hearing impairments) or from life in an institutional setting where opportunities for tender touch are limited. Elderly who lack a *support network* of familiar people and objects can lose the will to live.

Physical and neurosensory deterioration lead to reliance on others for normal activities of daily living. Many elderly are acutely aware of their loss of independence and ability for self-care. Family decisions about respite or nursing home care for elderly family members should include a professional assessment of level of functioning, ability to perform activities of daily living, and available family and community assistance.

Recommended Readings

Cavanaugh J, Blanchard-Fields F. *Adult Development and Aging*. Belmont, CA: Wadsworth Cengage Learning; 2006.

Connidis IA. *Family Ties and Aging*. Los Angeles, CA: Sage; 2010.

Thorson J. *Aging in a Changing Society*, 2nd ed. Philadelphia, PA: Brunner/Mazel; 2000.

Willis S, Martin M. *Middle Adulthood: A Lifespan Perspective*. Thousand Oaks, CA: Sage; 2005

Review Questions

1. For many women, the decision about when to have children is determined by their "biological clock." This term refers to the fact that the complication rate among pregnancies typically rises significantly after the age of
   A. 35.
   B. 40.
   C. 45.
   D. 50.
   E. 55.

2. Several different types of intelligence have been described to help explain how people function in different realms. Among the following types of intelligence, which is most likely to improve throughout the adult years?
   A. Bodily-Kinetic
   B. Crystallized
   C. Fluid
   D. Logical
   E. Mathematical

3. Which of the following best describes a typical health-related characteristic among the elderly?
   A. Decrease in completed suicides
   B. Decreased ability to eat
   C. Diminished physiological reserve
   D. Higher than 50% prevalence of dementia
   E. Increased pain

4. Among the following, the capability most likely to be spared in a person with dementia is
   A. activities of daily living.
   B. communication.
   C. comprehension.
   D. consciousness.
   E. mobility.

5. Following are some general statements about old age. Which one is best supported by current evidence?
   A. Decreased independence and isolation are major threats to maintaining ego integrity.
   B. Depression and dementia are inevitable consequences of aging.
   C. Frailty in old age is primarily associated with physical functioning.
   D. Old people typically complain a great deal to their doctors about their health problems.
   E. The physical and mental changes associated with aging follow highly predictable timelines.

Key to review questions: p. 407

15 The Family

J. LeBron McBride, PhD, MPH

- What are the varieties of contemporary families?
- What are the implications of viewing families as small social systems?
- What is the value of a genogram in family assessment?
- What are the stages of the family life cycle?
- What are respite care and custodial care?
- What are five types of post-divorce relationship?

As a new health care professional, you begin your practice with enthusiasm but are puzzled that many patients do not make the changes you encourage. During a visit with a patient and his wife, you find they have a traditional marriage. She does all the cooking, but the patient has concealed the need to change his diet "so as not to worry her." Therefore, you explain the goals of treatment directly to her. At his next visit, the patient has lost several pounds, is eating better, and walks daily with his wife.

Families play a significant role in the development and socialization of individuals and have a profound influence on the health and welfare of family members. Families embody *risk* and *protective factors* that can influence the onset and course of disease. Some, like genetic predisposition, shared family trauma, or family ethnic background, are unmodifiable. Others, like patterns of communication, power sharing, family structure, and belief systems, may be modified to reduce risk. And still other factors may or may not be modifiable, such as environmental circumstances that can place additional strains upon family systems and individual members. For example, the increasing costs of health care and other barriers to accessibility have resulted in families assuming greater responsibility for health care in the home, placing additional pressures on care givers and family relationships.

Varieties of American Families

The U.S. Census Bureau defines a **family** as two or more persons who live together and are related by blood, marriage, or adoption. By this definition, 81.2% of households in 1970 were family households as compared to about 68% currently. The number of married couples with children in the home declined from 40.3% of all households in 1970 to 22.5% in the early 21st century. This change reflects older age at first marriage, postponement of childbearing, children born to persons who are not married, and high rates of separation and divorce. The number of single parents rose from less than 3.5 million in 1970 to 13.7 million in 2010. About 84% of single-parent households are headed by mothers. Living in a *single-parent household* is an important risk factor for poor health outcome for both the mother and her dependents. Mediating variables include limited income, lacking time for medical appointments for themselves or others, the stress of being unable to meet basic needs due to illness, and/or carrying the burden of another's care without support. However, with adequate external support, the children of single-parent families do as well as those raised by couples or extended families.

Families may define themselves differently from how they are counted in the census. The **nuclear family** includes spouses and their children living together. An **extended family** includes three or four generations and encompasses aunts, uncles, cousins, and unrelated partners who come together out of affection, obligation, or economic necessity. The **family of origin** is the family into which a person was born, which may differ from the **family of procreation** or another current household.

Incorporating children from a previous marriage results in a "**blended family**." Varying loyalties to the divorced biological parents, anger about the dissolution of the previous family, blame directed at some or all of the involved adults, and guilt about personal responsibility for causing the divorce can foster confusion and conflict in the children. In addition, if the newly formed couple has biological children between them, the complexity of the pattern of relationships and loyalties is increased. Most parents and children are unprepared for the reorganization and adaptation required in a blended family structure.

Although only some states recognize same-sex marriage, the number of **same-sex families** is increasing. Both society and the families of origin may focus on the couple's sexuality, ignoring their social, financial, and emotional needs, which are similar to those of heterosexual couples. In general, children raised in gay and lesbian families do not experience negative effects due to the parents' sexual orientation, nor are they more likely to be gay or lesbian themselves.

The presence or absence of children does not define a family. The availability of safe contraception has made it possible for couples to choose *childlessness*. Reasons for this choice include dedication to career, concerns about personal resources or overpopulation, illness, and developmentally related desires not to be a parent. When young, such couples often face considerable social pressure to have children. For couples unable to have children, treatment for infertility, even if ultimately successful, may produce significant strains, making the couples' sexual life mechanistic and unsatisfying, and imposing large financial burdens.

Families as Social Systems

> What are the implications of viewing families as small social systems?

Considering the family as a small social system involves the concept of **boundaries,** both *external* boundaries between family and non-family, and *internal* boundaries between members. *Diffuse external* boundaries allow individuals to come and go at will. In such families, dependent members, especially children, may not have adequate protection and security. *Closed* boundaries make entering and exiting the family difficult, compromising the eventual emancipation of adolescent or adult children and preventing the acceptance of outside help, even including medical care. The open boundary around a healthy family can change, according to members' immediate needs. For example, a cousin or a friend can step in to care for a child who is ill and out of school, or the family may provide housing to an older member who can no longer manage alone.

Internal family boundaries, especially the boundaries between generations, significantly influence health and behavior. Emotional closeness or bonding among family members is termed **cohesion.** It ranges from *disengagement* (closed boundaries between individuals and low emotional reactivity) to *enmeshment* (diffuse boundaries between individuals and high emotional reactivity). Either extreme can affect family members' emotional well-being and self regulation. In well functioning families, adults support one another in setting expectations, applying age appropriate limits on behavior, and transmitting cultural values.

Boundary violations, for example, when a child allies with one parent against the other or when one parent relies on his/her relatives and excludes a spouse, contribute to a range of behavioral and health related problems. An adolescent boy who lives with his mother and hears constant disparagement of his father may struggle with self-esteem. A grandmother who undermines her son's relationship to his wife may complicate the couple's ability to manage their child's diabetes. The grossest violations of boundaries, intrafamily violence or incest (adult/child or within a generation), can contribute to unstable chronic disease, functional somatic disorders, violent behavior (including suicide), substance abuse, and psychiatric disorders.

Communication among family members can be *functional* (direct and clear) or *dysfunctional* (indirect and confused). Communication occurs on verbal as well as nonverbal levels. The actual words of verbal communication are modified by *prosody* (i.e., tone, volume, pitch of the voice) and *nonverbal behavior* (e.g., gestures, facial expressions, touches). Healthy families demonstrate congruent verbal and nonverbal communication, express emotion and caring, and share feelings and thoughts (see Chapter 9, Cognition and Social Interaction)

Overall, family functioning determines *familial power relationships*. Different family members may exert power in different domains: elders may establish cultural norms while other members provide emotional comfort and still others control how the family manages time, where they live, and how they meet financial obligations. Like boundaries, power arrangements within families may be chaotic, rigid, or flexibly adaptive to changing circumstances.

Changes within society and the place of the family within the **family life cycle** are normal modifiers of family systems. The need for two incomes and women's desires for broader social roles have led many families in the US to abandon traditional patriarchal configurations for more egalitarian ones. As children grow, family rules evolve to reflect changing capacities. Unexpected demands, such as job loss or providing care for a severely or chroni-

cally ill member, may require changes in who has power to do what and can induce both emotional distress and unstable behavior.

Family researchers assess families by interacting with them over time, eliciting different points of view, directly probing relationships, and observing patterns of interaction and communication. Most medical care providers assess families based on the descriptions provided by an individual patient or by a parent/child or spouse/patient dyad. In either case, construction of a family genogram uncovers and efficiently presents a wealth of information about family history, structure, and functioning.

What is the value of a genogram in family assessment?

Genograms (see Figure 15.1) are a type of family tree that can be used to diagram life events, illnesses, and interpersonal relationships. They may communicate ethnic, religious, and relationship histories as well as the patterns of occurrence of certain problems (e.g., substance abuse, marital conflict, a hereditary disease).

Figure 15.1. Selected examples of genogram symbols

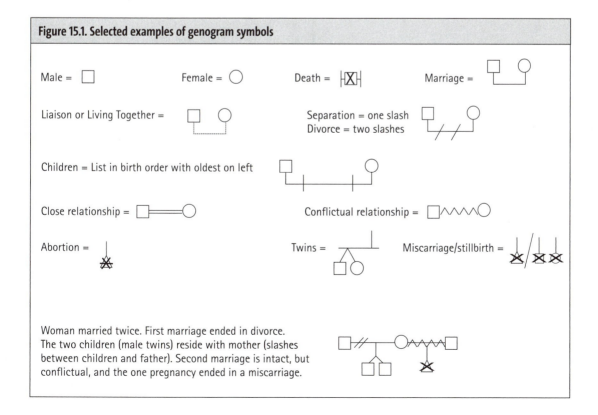

Woman married twice. First marriage ended in divorce. The two children (male twins) reside with mother (slashes between children and father). Second marriage is intact, but conflictual, and the one pregnancy ended in a miscarriage.

What are the stages of the family life cycle?

The concepts of the family life cycle derive from the study of nuclear families, although they can be applied to other family constellations.

The traditional family life cycle involves six stages: (1) between families: the single young adult; (2) joining: the newly married couple; (3) incorpo-

rating: the family with young children; (4) letting go/holding on: the family with adolescents; (5) launching children: the empty nest; and (6) withstanding time: the family in later life (see Table 15.1).

Transitions between life cycle stages require adaptation to new ways of functioning (e.g., changing the marital relationship to accommodate a child; accepting the independence of a child who

Table 15.1: Stages of the family life cycle

Family Life Cycle Stages	Key Principles of Emotional Process	Changes Required for Evolution
Between families: Single young adults	Accepting emotional and financial responsibility for self	a. Differentiation of self in relation to family of origin b. Development of intimate peer relationships c. Establishment of vocational and financial independence
Joining: Newly married couple	Committing to a new system	a. Formation of marital system b. Realignment of relationships with extended family/friends to include spouse/partner
Incorporating: Families with young children	Accepting new members into the system	a. Adjusting marital system to accommodate children b. Sharing childrearing, financial, and household tasks c. Realignment of relationships with extended family to include parenting and grandparenting roles
Letting go/holding on: Families with adolescents	Increasing flexibility of family boundaries to permit children's independence and grandparents' dependence	a. Shift in parent/child relationships to permit adolescents movement into/out of the system b. Refocus on midlife marital and vocational issues c. Beginning shift toward caring for older generation
Launching children: Empty-nest couples	Accepting exits from and entries into the family system	a. Renegotiation of marital system as a dyad b. Development of adult-to-adult relationships between children and their parents c. Realignment of relationships to include in-laws and grandchildren d. Dealing with disability and death of parents (grandparents)
Withstanding time: Couples in later life	Accepting shifting generational roles	a. Maintenance of functioning and interests despite physiological decline b. Support for central role of middle generation c. Adjustment to loss of spouse, siblings, and peers and preparation for death

Adapted from: Carter B, McGoldrick M (Eds.), *Expanded Family Life Cycle: The Individual, Family, and Social Perspectives.* 3rd ed. Boston, MA: Allyn and Bacon; 1999.

graduates from high school). Well functioning families that have anticipated these transitions and use effective coping strategies are most likely to maintain good individual and family health.

Between Families: Single Young Adults

This phase involves the young adult establishing independence and autonomy, separating from parents, establishing new relationships, and assuming responsibility for financial management, place of residence, and health care. In the US today, 50% of first marriages are preceded by cohabitation. In many societies, especially those that promote early arranged marriage, young people never live "between families" because they either bring a spouse into their family of origin or marry into their partner's family without living independently.

Joining: Newly Married Couples

The median age at first marriage in the US has increased over the past three decades (females from 23 to 26 and males from 25 to 28). Although illegal in this country, child marriages, often between a young girl and an older man, are common elsewhere. Such arrangements can have negative psychological and social consequences for the girls, who rarely complete their education and never develop the skills to support or protect themselves or their children. Child marriage customs also foster the transmission of sexually transmitted infections and maternal disability or death from early and frequent pregnancy.

The glossing over of conflicts or difficulties common in the early stages of a new relationship between adults is called *romantic idealization* or the "utopia syndrome." Eventually, the new couple must integrate the expectations they bring from their respective families. This stage often involves negotiation about contraception and child bearing, which may involve consultation with health care professionals.

Incorporating: Families with Young Children

With the arrival of children, the partners (or extended family) must adjust to meeting the child's needs, the resultant disruption in family routines, and decreased time alone. Differences in child rearing practices, thresholds for exhaustion and privacy, and balancing demands for time and attention required by the children must be negotiated. As children grow and develop, they interact with larger systems such as peer groups and schools. These experiences bring new ideas and energy into the family, but may lead the child to challenge the family's belief system and routines. Children of immigrants often function as cultural interpreters for their parents, which may be both a stress and source of enhanced self-esteem for them.

Letting Go/Holding On: Families with Adolescents

The major issue of western adolescence is **autonomy**. If the family has been authoritarian, rigid, or enmeshed, this life cycle transition may be difficult. Parents and adolescents who avoid extreme positions and negotiate compromises make the most successful transitions. Adolescents' difficulty assessing risk may require families to impose reasonable rules about acceptable behavior, especially about driving and substance use. Some adolescents react to the self consciousness that comes with the bodily changes of puberty or to rejection or non-acceptance by peers by retreating into the family, and may need encouragement to seek out new experiences and better peer relationships. Compared to Europeans, American families appear to have particular difficulty talking openly with their adolescents about sex, leading to higher rates of teenage pregnancy and sexually transmitted infections.

Launching Children: Empty-Nest Couples

While many couples derive satisfaction and relief from knowing that the phase of rearing dependent children is past, others experience feelings of uselessness ("**empty nest**"). Because of educational, financial, career, or marital considerations, adult children may return to their parents' home repeatedly, the so called "*boomerang effect*." This is a prime example of why the family life cycle is best viewed as a flexible series of stages and transitions, some of which are extended or repeated.

As parents enter middle age, they become aware of *health problems* in peers and experience their own *physical changes* (e.g., increased weight, decreased metabolic rate). This motivates many to initiate better health practices. Age-related bodily changes occurring at this stage typically signal decline. Coping with these reminders of mortality may adversely affect well-being and marital adjustment. Struggles with personal identity can produce a **mid-life crisis**.

This is also the period when most couples experience the loss of their parents and assume the roles of matriarch/patriarch for younger generations. The addition of grandchildren may bring the generations closer together as the new parents come to appreciate the contributions their parents made to their own care and upbringing. Grandparents can enjoy their grandchildren without the demands of parenthood, but must respect and support their adult children as parents.

Withstanding Time: Couples in Later Life

Adjustments during this period of life include retirement and shifting generational roles. *Physical* and *intellectual decline*, *custodial care*, *loss*, and *bereavement* become major issues. For some, the later stage of life involves enjoying accomplishments and finding satisfaction in the freedom to pursue new interests. For others, the transitions and adjustments are negative.

Retirement requires significant adjustment if the couple has difficulty tolerating the amount of time they now have together, or if the partners disagree about how to divide their time between outside interests and each other. Those who have derived their identity from their vocation miss the satisfaction of their job and may become isolated. Retirement can strain financial resources if income drops as assisted living and medical expenses increase.

The most significant loss experienced during this stage is the death of the spouse. When a death occurs, the extended family must realign and adjust to new relationships. If death followed chronic illness, burnout among caregivers may complicate the adjustment process, limiting support for the grieving spouse.

Many persons function well in old age but physical and intellectual declines eventually concern both the individual and the family. Some dependent individuals can be cared for within their family with periodic **respite care**. Others need partial or full **custodial care** in an **assisted living facility** or **nursing home**.

Assessing the attitudes of each family member about custodial care, the family's emotional and logistical resources without placement, the financial resources for placement, and timing of the placement is vital. Options such as home nursing care, bringing a full-time caretaker into the home, and accessing community services should be explored. Some individuals relocate to be near adult children, oftentimes after a long period of resistance, even when living independently is dangerous. Losing long established friendships and routines and trying to establish new relationships and habits may make such changes extremely stressful and poorly tolerated.

Special Issues of Contemporary Families

Occupation and Career

Two-career families must balance child rearing, household chores, and careers. Women generally retain the major responsibility for running the home even if they have other employment. Despite the added stress, women who work outside the home report enhanced self-esteem, but letting career obligations routinely take precedence over family life can produce tension in both marital and parental relationships.

More than 50% of mothers with children less than 1 year of age work outside the home. Comparisons between children raised by *"stay-at-home" mothers* and children placed in *child care* reveal that the effect of early child care on infant development reflects many factors such as group size, child-to-caretaker ratio, and consistency of the child care provider.

"Latchkey children" are youngsters less than 13 years old who care for themselves at home while their parents work. Although parents may be concerned about children at home alone, many

---

What are respite care and custodial care?

have few alternatives. Lack of appropriate super-vision increases the risk of behavioral problems as well as the risk of mistreatment or exploitation. Recognizing this, many schools and community agencies provide after school programs but cost may be a limiting factor for many families.

Geographic Mobility

Geographic mobility often results in separation from extended family that might otherwise pro-vide support and nurturance. Due to the ready-made network of the workplace, the one who accepts a job transfer may have less difficulty with the change than other family members who do not have the positive reinforcement of a promotion or

other career advancement. Indeed, they are likely to lose the community status they have achieved and the support provided by long-term relation-ships with friends and others, including health care providers. Recent moves and isolation from extended family are recognized risk factors for the incidence and perpetuation of domestic violence. New patient visits provide an excellent opportuni-ty for the health care provider to assess emotion-al health as well as physical health as the family acclimates to its charged environment.

Divorce

It is estimated that almost 50% of all U.S. mar-riages will end in **divorce.** The family life cycle of

Table 15.2. Phases of the family life cycle for divorcing families			
Phase		**Emotional Process of Transition: Prerequisite Attitude**	**Developmental Issues**
Divorcing	Decision to divorce	Accepting the relationship must end	a. Accepting personal responsibility for the failure of the marriage
	Planning the break-up of the system	Supporting viable arrangements for all parts of the system	b. Working cooperatively on problems of custody, visitation, and finances
			c. Dealing with extended family about the divorce
	Separation	Co-parenting cooperatively	a. Mourning loss of the intact family
			b. Restructuring marital and parent-child relationships
		Beginning dissolution of attachment to spouse	c. Realigning of relationships with own and spouse's extended family
	Divorce	Overcoming hurt, anger, and guilt	a. Mourning loss of the intact family; giving up fantasies of reunion
Post-divorce	Single parent (cus-todial household or primary resi-dence)	Maintaining cooperative co-parent-ing	a. Making flexible visitation arrange-ments with ex-spouse and family
			b. Rebuilding own social, financial, and emotional resources
	Single parent (non custodial)	Maintaining cooperative co-parent-ing Fulfilling financial responsibilities Maintaining parental contact and supporting custodial parent's relationship with children	a. Finding solutions to problems of visitation and distance parenting
			b. Fulfilling financial responsibilities to ex-spouse and children
			c. Rebuilding own social, financial, and emotional network

Adapted from: Carter B, McGoldrick M (Eds.), *Expanded Family Life Cycle: The Individual, Family, and Social Perspectives.* 3rd ed. Boston, MA: Allyn and Bacon; 1999.

divorcing families has different phases (see Table 15.2). As a result of family instability and disrupted parenting, children of divorced parents are at increased risk for depression and conduct problems, although not all children of divorce experience these difficulties. Family scholars have called divorce a "detour" for the family, with most eventually rejoining the "main road" of family development, although with greater complexity. Parents need to assure their children that the divorce is not their fault and to maintain as much stability as possible in their children's lives during the process. Ideally, they should refrain from criticizing or devaluing the divorced partner; children identify with both parents and having to divide loyalties is frequently troubling and disruptive for them until they reach a new equilibrium.

Litigation in court is the most common approach to divorce settlements and to child custody. It is typically costly, time consuming, and adversarial. *Divorce mediators* function as neutral parties in negotiating divorce settlements, seeking a mutually acceptable division of assets and authority. Successful mediation is contingent on both partners' willingness to negotiate without intimidation. The resulting agreement is usually reviewed by the attorney and financial consultant representing each party.

Legal custody can be sole (i.e., one parent has the legal right to make decisions regarding the child) or joint (i.e., both parents have the legal right to share in decisions). *Physical custody* can be either sole or joint. In sole physical custody, the child lives with one parent and the other parent may have visitation rights as determined by the court or the parents. In joint custody, the amount of time the child spends at each home is negotiated.

Health care professionals sometimes participate in custody negotiations. Joint custody may not be in the best interests of the child when one parent is clearly abusive, addicted, or unstable. Also, when caring for children of divorced parents, providers must know who has legal authority to consent to medical care.

Reduced standard of living is a major problem for the children of divorced parents. True financial hardship is a common result of the need to maintain two households. Nonpayment of child support is also a problem. Unresolved conflict between the former spouses is a primary motivation for nonpayment. Withholding child support is used to punish the former spouse, often without regard for

---

What are five types of post-divorce relationships?

Post-Divorce Relationships

Perfect Pals: Disappointment about the failed marriage does not impair positive elements of the relationship. Share decision making. Spend holidays together and maintain relations with extended families. Many feel they are better parents divorced than married.

Cooperative Colleagues: Work together around concerns of children and family, but are not close friends. Able to manage conflicts and separate spousal from parental issues.

Angry Associates: Like cooperative colleagues but not able to compartmentalize anger. Often tense, hostile, or in open conflict without former spouse.

Fiery Foes: Intensely angry and litigious years after the divorce. Unable to recall anything good about the marriage. Cling to very old wrongs. Still attached, but quick to deny it.

Dissolved Duos: After the divorce, have no further contact.

Adapted from: Ahrons CR. Divorce: Not the end, but a change in a relationship. *The Brown University Family Therapy Letter.* Providence, RI: Manisses Communication Group, Inc; 1990.

---

how nonpayment affects the child. From the children's perspective, financial support can be perceived as a measure of how much the noncustodial parent loves and cares for them.

People adjusting to divorce typically vacillate between relief and depression. Unless aware that this emotional turmoil is normal, they may feel they are becoming mentally ill. Rapid movement into another relationship provides escape from emotional pain. Such "rebound" relationships are usually short term, but typically act as conduits to the next phase of relationship building.

Although highly educated women are less likely to do so, most divorced persons remarry. Some persons experience feelings of loss when their former spouse marries because they must confront disavowed fantasies of reconciliation.

Surrogate Mothering

"**Surrogacy**" refers to bearing a child for someone else, usually in return for payment. Reasons for choosing a surrogate include infertility, repeated miscarriages, hysterectomy, or other health conditions. Whenever possible, the *commissioning couple* supply both sperm and egg, which, when fertilized *in vitro,* is implanted in the surrogate mother's uterus *(gestational carrier surrogate)*. This procedure circumvents the issue of whose child the woman is carrying, because all genetic material derives from the couple. In some situations, the sperm or egg may be provided by an anonymous donor bank. Potential confusion regarding parental rights, still debated in the court system, makes a gestational carrier the least desirable egg donor.

Moral, ethical, and legal issues raised by surrogate mothering include arguments that it is exploitative, particularly of poor women. "Renting" a woman's uterus places her at risk for pregnancy- and delivery-associated complications, for which financial gain seems inadequate benefit. Some surrogates, however, derive great satisfaction from helping infertile couples. For the couple seeking surrogacy, this technologic advance significantly lessens the emotional pain of infertility by allowing them to have a biological child.

Family Intervention in Contemporary Health Care

Recent trends in early hospital discharge have stimulated the growth of *home health agencies*. Agency personnel assist family members with caretaking responsibilities including home dialysis, home chemotherapy, and ventilator management. The patient may recover more function more quickly than in an institutional setting, and the family may experience a heightened sense of accomplishment. Parents of children, in particular, may feel in better control of the care and comfort their child receives. Even with good resources and the ability to give adequate care, however, **caregiver burnout** is common.

Families embodying relatively un-modifiable risk factors such as recent losses or highly dysfunctional structure may be referred to mental health providers for **family therapy**. However, all clinicians should learn simple family interventions, particularly how to educate family members about the medical conditions and needs of individual patients. They may enlist families directly for patients < 18

(except for **emancipated minors**, or where confidentiality is protected by law, as in the provision of reproductive health services in some states). Adults should always be asked to consent for physician communication with family members, who should be specifically identified by the patients.

Sophisticated clinicians intent upon changing modifiable risk factors learn to identify and ally with family members who have the respect and authority to arbitrate cultural boundaries, relieve others' emotional distress, and allocate resources. Different family members may have influence in different domains. For example, if a patient mistrusts the scientific explanation of a symptom, it may be most effective to engage the family member who is sympathetic to or shares the patient's concerns. Integrating competing medical and cultural perspectives within the family reduces conflict and facilitates treatment adherence (see Chapter 18, Culture and Ethnicity). When the patient and family share a pathological behavior or belief, such as abnormal eating or substance abuse, failure to involve family members inevitably undermines treatment unless the identified patient can be persuaded to detach from the family.

Recommended Readings

Cummings E, Davies P. *Marital Conflict and Children.* New York: Guilford Publications; 2010.

Dattilio F. *Cognitive Behavioral Therapy with Couples and Families*. New York: Guilford Publications; 2010.

McBride J. *Family Behavioral Issues in Health and Illness*. New York: Routledge Taylor & Francis Group; 2006.

Peterkin A. *Staying Human During Residency Training: How to Survive and Thrive After Medical School.* Toronto: University of Toronto Press; 2008.

Wiseman D (Ed.). *The American Family: Understanding Changing Dynamics and Place in Society.* Springfield, IL: Charles C Thomas Publishing; 2008.

Review Questions

1. A family does not provide protection or structure for its children from outside influences. What kind of boundaries is this family most likely to have?

A. Closed
B. Diffuse
C. Open
D. Rigid
E. Tight

2. Which of the following is considered a primary indicator of transition in the family life cycle?
   A. Birthdays
   B. Celebrations
   C. Closeness and distance
   D. Entering and exiting
   E. Rituals

3. The couple who seek a surrogate mother in order to have a child is called the
   A. biological couple.
   B. commissioning couple.
   C. embarking couple.
   D. enabling couple.
   E. gestational couple.

4. Intrafamilial violence is associated with
   A. childhood autism.
   B. childhood epilepsy.
   C. opportunistic infections.
   D. onset of cancer.
   E. unstable chronic illness.

5. What is the average age at first marriage for males in the US?
   A. 20
   B. 22
   C. 24
   D. 26
   E. 28

Key to review questions: p. 407

Section VI

Social and Cultural Issues

16 Social Behavior and Groups

Michael C. Hosokawa, EdD

- How do primary, secondary, and reference groups differ?
- What are the characteristics of a group?
- How does society differ from social class and culture?
- How do stereotypes develop?
- What stages do groups go through when challenged to change a core belief?
- How has technology affected the function of groups?

The evolutionary success of *Homo sapiens* is attributable in part to their ability to join together in social groups and collectively apply their adaptive skills to meeting the challenges of their environment. Their ability to remember past events, learn from those experiences, and use that knowledge to adapt to new situations enabled them to function across time and distance in increasingly complex societies and groups.

Thus, group identity and membership became important for both individual and collective survival, leading to the development of increasingly advanced and complex societies. In today's societies, we see various groups arise in response to perceived collective concerns including social, political, racial, religious, neighborhood, recreational, familial, cultural, and common interests.

Types of Groups

How do primary, secondary, and reference groups differ?

Primary groups are small and defined by face-to-face interactions among members. These groups provide basic food, shelter, love, acceptance, and comfort. The family and groups of friends may be included within this category. It is possible that a religious group, such as an Amish communi-

ty, may be a primary group because of the strong interdependence of members, the strong belief system, and the differences that exist between the Amish and the larger **reference group** (the general U.S. population).

Secondary groups are larger and may involve some members who do not interact directly with all other members. Typically, these groups serve a particular purpose or a particular interest, such as church groups or professional groups, and provide opportunities for enhancing personal satisfaction, sharing values, or changing society.

A **reference group** is any group with which an individual identifies, or uses as an anchor point, to define values or a standard against which to judge behavior. Individuals may identify with the beliefs of a reference group without belonging to the group. A senior citizen may believe in and agree with the work of the American Association of Retired People (AARP), but not be a member. Some groups are identified by their social distance from the reference group. Following the Vietnam war, many churches sponsored Southeast Asian families so they could begin a new life in the US. Many of these churches were in rural communities. Immigrant families were welcomed into the community, but the social distance caused many Southeast Asians to seek cities where refugee communities were able to form.

Under most circumstances, membership in a group does not preclude personal interpretations of the group's values or issues. For example, a person may identify as "pro-life" and yet favor the death penalty. In some groups, personal interpretation is not permitted; thus, believing wholly as the group believes becomes, in effect, a value of the group that must be held in order to be a member (e.g., a cult).

Characteristics of Groups

What are the characteristics of a group?

Any group has characteristics that make it unique. *Size* is a characteristic of a group. A group could be as small as two individuals or as large as a community or even a nation or civilization. Groups exist for a reason; thus, they have a *purpose,* such as a fund raising group for a family in need or a union that functions as an advocate for workers. *Solidarity* is another characteristic of a group. The strength of attraction among group members varies with the purpose. Religious groups vary greatly in solidarity from a world-wide identity in name only to a highly cooperative, interdependent Amish community. Sports fans show their solidarity by dress, vocal support, and enjoyment – or disappointment. The degree of *influence* group members have on others determines a group's solidarity. Influence can be seen in politics where some members vote a party line regardless of the merits of the issue. A discussion group is often based on diverse ideas rather than solidarity. A cult may demand complete solidarity or suffer consequences. The *stability* of a group determines what changes in membership, leadership, and purpose occur over time.

As social beings, humans adapt to and even change the environment, functioning as interdependent members of groups to solve problems and create an environment that fosters both group and self-identity. Emerging from the groups are beliefs, attitudes, and values that are the bases for perceptions, judgments, and ideas that govern the behaviors of group members, including health beliefs and practices. Beginning in childhood, socialization results in individuals acquiring an understanding and acceptance of the standards or norms expected and shared by the group. These *norms* are learned and adhered to through reinforcement for adherence and avoidance of reprimand for violation.

Of course, individuals can question and even reject the norms of a group. Adolescent "rebellion" against parental or societal norms is a developmental milestone where the adolescent begins to establish individuality and differentiate from the familial group. Members of religious or political organizations can challenge and seek to alter group norms such as religious dogma or political platforms. Failing that, they may seek membership in different groups.

Complex Social Groups

How does society differ from social class and culture?

Primary and secondary groups coalesce to form a larger network or **society**, defined as a population that occupies the same territory, is subject to the same political authority, and participates in a common culture. Individual relationship groups are the basic elements of a **social system**. They become organized into a pattern of relationships to form a **social structure**. Activities within the social system are governed by rules (e.g., marriage, education) that codify and preserve the social structure.

Social class is comprised of variables such as occupation, income, education, place of residence, memberships, social interactions, prestige, and self-identified status. **Socioeconomic status** (SES), based on income and years of education, may be a useful tool for purposes of research, but in day-to-day interactions has limited meaning. Categories specific to a particular issue are more helpful (e.g., "disadvantaged" meaning lacking opportunity to gain the same economic or educational levels as the general population, "working poor" meaning unable to meet basic needs despite having a job, and "undereducated" meaning not having the same educational opportunities as others).

Culture is the collective way of life that has evolved over numerous generations of a group living within a given ecological setting. Culture influences the development of the general beliefs and behaviors of its members. Although culture has constancy, it is not static but rather "shifts" in response to contemporary ecological, political, or economic challenges.

The US has been described as a "melting pot" of cultures. However, it is the recognition of multiple cultures that makes it possible for a society to be greater than the sum of its parts. Rather than homogenize the population into a single culture, there are aspects of life (e.g., health) that require different interpretations and applications. Patient-centered care is a popular concept that so far has defied a working description since health care providers persist in overlooking the social and environmental context of health and illness. The patient's beliefs, experiences, and interpretations of health and illness are influenced by the group but are unique to the individual. Health care strives to provide care to groups of patients taking into account the unique characteristics of the group. At the same time, by grouping individuals, the uniqueness of each patient may be compromised. Thus, health care providers walk a fine line between cultural sensitivity and stereotyping.

Stereotypes

| How do stereotypes develop? |

A **stereotype** is a generalization made by a person or group about the characteristics of another person or group. Stereotypes are usually oversimplifications, but may be based on salient physical or psychological features associated with the group, or on expectations regarding the beliefs or behaviors of the group. Unfortunately, stereotypes are most often negative and racially or culturally biased. As an example, at one time, the Irish were the target of strong prejudice and were viewed as primarily alcoholics and untrustworthy. In the early 1800s, signs in London said, "No Irish need apply." The same signs appeared in America in the mid-1800s as the Irish immigrated to the US.

Stereotypes focus attention on those characteristics that define the stereotype. Thus, members of different ethnic groups, regardless of professional success and social position, have been at increased risk for stereotyping and discrimination merely because of some perceived physical or behavioral characteristic. For decades, black football players could not be a quarterback because they were "not smart enough" and that extended to blacks not being head coaches. The Japanese have been viewed as "inscrutable," the English as "aloof," the French as "arrogant," Jews as "stingy," and

Latinos as "great lovers." Categorizing people into groups facilitates handling large amounts of information and can be useful if it reflects reality. However, cultural sensitivity demands that the categorization not be over-generalized and that characteristics assigned to a particular group are valid but also modifiable by new information.

Group Stereotyping in Health Care

In medicine, there is a strong movement promoting **cultural sensitivity**. Supposedly, cultural sensitivity recognizes the special characteristics and considerations required in the care of patients who are not in the mainstream of society. But cultural sensitivity, if applied indiscriminantly, can result in cultural insensitivity. A patient in a clinic may have the physical features of a person of Asian descent. Whether that patient has been in the US for a month or the family has been here for generations is unknown. Whether the patient's parents, grandparents, great-grandparents, or great-, great-grandparents came from Japan, China, Vietnam, Korea, or another country, is unknown. Whether that person is a service worker, a tradesman, or an engineer is unknown. Whether that patient is bilingual, or uses chopsticks or a knife and fork is unknown. Asian Americans represent many cultures, unique health-related risks, educational backgrounds, social positions, and professions. The same is true of Latinos, African and black Americans, and Native Americans. If the health care provider makes overly generalized assumptions (stereotyping), the quality of health care may be compromised, the patient may be offended, and the provider-patient relationship mitigated.

Related to stereotypes are **stigma** and **bias**. Historically, as groups developed, individuals less able to contribute to the survival of the group were stigmatized and often forced out of the group. Today, similar to stereotyping, individuals with different physical features, perceived character weaknesses, or other undesirable characteristics are assigned negative status. Physical features such as a limp, poor gait control, missing or deformed limbs, neurological disorders, vision problems, disfigurements, extreme height, or weight, or even signs of aging may be *stigmatized*. Although there are individuals with missing limbs who run marathons, as a group, amputees may be seen as less capable. Perceived character weakness may be assigned to individuals with a criminal record, substance abuse problems, divorce, or unemployment. Having received care from a psychiatrist or in a mental health facility is often included on personnel applications and background checks; identifying individuals who have been treated for depression, anxiety, alcoholism, or smoking cessation may stigmatize them as unreliable or having personality flaws. Stigma based on group membership, such as race, ethnicity, religion, gender, or sexual preference, is applied to all members of the group.

Bias is another form of generalization in which there is a positive or negative value placed on a characteristic. There may be a bias for or against hiring women for leadership positions. Physicians demonstrate a gender bias in the way they manage pain. A study in the *Journal of Pain* (2010; 11(8):746–754) showed blacks and women were more likely to receive inadequate pain management than other groups.

Changing Group Norms

What stages do groups go through when challenged to change a core belief?

Change in a group or an individual is not simply a decision to accept an alternative way of doing things, but a far more complex and sometimes chaotic process. Social psychologists, who

Example 1: For the past half century, there has been growing concern about the cost of health care and access to health care. President Clinton campaigned promising health care reform and, after he took office in 1993, set up the Task Force on National Health Care Reform headed by Hillary Clinton. From the Task Force came a bill that essentially required employers to provide health insurance coverage to all of their employees through competitive but closely-regulated health maintenance organizations (HMOs). Opposition to universal health care was intense even before the Task Force began its meetings. Health care interest groups in this country were not ready to "unfreeze" the way in which health care was being delivered or financed.

have studied the effects of social influence on attitudes and behaviors, describe three stages a group goes through in changing a belief. The first stage is *preparation for change*, or "unfreezing." Unfreezing refers to an emerging awareness that change may be necessary, and a willingness to consider weighing the pros and cons of change.

In 2010, President Obama was successful in getting Congress to pass legislation that would overhaul the nation's health care system and guarantee access to medical insurance for tens of millions of Americans. Republicans voted unanimously against the legislation, but since the Republicans were in the minority in both the Senate and the House, their opposition to the plan failed. Elections in the fall of 2010 shifted the balance of power toward the Republicans. While

Example 2: In 2009, the United States Preventive Services Task Force, a panel of experts appointed by the Department of Health and Human Services, recommended that screening mammograms be performed less frequently based on research data showing that *routine screening mammograms,* starting at age 40, saved relatively few lives and more often resulted in misdiagnosis, generating anxiety and debilitating treatment. Instead, the Task Force recommended that starting regular, biennial screening mammography before the age of 50 should be an individualized decision taking into account the patient's wishes and views regarding the benefits and risks of the procedure and the advice of her personal physician. The National Cancer Institute, the American Cancer Society, and the American College of Radiology opposed this recommendation and argued that the screening of patients with no risk factors or signs of abnormality does save lives, and strongly supported the existing guidelines for annual mammography beginning at age 40. Thus, the Task Force recommended beginning routine screening mammograms at age 50 rather than 40 based on the available data on breast cancer screening, and made a recommendation but did not mandate changes. "Unfreezing" the belief that annual mammograms should begin at age 40 will depend on the acceptance/rejection of the Task Force recommendation by practitioners, insurers, health care plans, and patients.

For details on the USPSTF report go to: http://www.uspreventiveservicestaskforce.org/uspstf/uspsbrca.htm

changes in the membership of Congress set the stage for "refreezing" opposition to universal health care, public opinion would ultimately determine whether the issue would be "refrozen" or partially "thawed."

The debate on these two examples constitutes the *force field analysis*, in which the members of the group (forces) for and against making change present their arguments. If unfreezing is successful (the pros for change outweigh the cons), then the second stage, or *change*, takes place. Thus, change is not an event but rather a gradual transition process often accompanied by chaos, as competing social interests within the group present and seek information, assurances, and compromise.

The recommendation to begin screening mammography in healthy women beginning at age 50 rather than 40 may take decades for adoption or rejection as best practice. Physicians may or may not advise their patients based on the new guidelines. Breast cancer is a frightening disease and a leading cause of cancer death so many patients will request screening mammograms beginning at age 40, especially since the value of early cancer detection has been emphasized for decades. For insurance companies, an ounce of prevention may be worth a pound of cure. The cost of the screening mammogram is far less than treatment after diagnosis. Research reports from a number of groups will continue to be published as they collect and analyze data to confirm or refute the recommendation.

The final stage is referred to as *freezing,* i.e., the change is generally accepted and becomes the new group norm. Smoking in public areas and on airplanes was once considered an individual's right. The first *Smoking and Health: Report of the Advisory Committee to the Surgeon General of the Public Health Service* was released in 1964, and was followed by at least 28 additional reports through 2006. Unfreezing public opinion has been very slow. The force field analysis was cluttered with data from the tobacco industry, health care professionals, voluntary health agencies, and other groups. Over some 50 years, legislation and policies have been enacted to limit or prohibit smoking in public areas. Although less than half of the population smoked, such behavior was viewed as an individual right of the smoker. Reports of the risks of "second-hand smoke" and public education from official and voluntary health agencies and other groups created an environment supporting non-smoking laws and policies. Although there are still groups opposed to legislating behavior, the issues around smoking are refreezing as bans on smoking on public transportation and in public buildings, restaurants, and even sports arenas are implemented.

Change is not easily predictable since each individual in a group may view the change in a different way. The adoption of the electronic medical record by clinics and hospitals has caused disruption, stress, anger, and frustration. The health professionals in a hospital, such as the physicians, nurses, ward clerks, technicians, social workers, and administrators, had become accustomed to and therefore comfortable with a paper documentation system even if it was slow, time-consuming, and unwieldy. A change away from paper charts, dictation systems, and filing cabinets to on-screen, computerized documentation with new terminology, on-line orders and scheduling, and electronic prescriptions and security systems has been stressful for most health care providers. It will take time, but the electronic health record will inevitably become the documentation system of the present and future. Today's students and trainees, knowing no other system, are likely to find searching for old paper information equally stressful and frustrating.

Social Networks

> How has technology affected the function of groups?

As Flight 001 lands and taxis toward the airport terminal, passengers are on their cell phones, greeting friends and family, making business contacts, accessing the hotel reservation desk, making dinner reservations, and checking the stock market, sports scores, and their e-mail. At that moment, some 300 passengers are communicating with someone who is not on the plane.

Membership in a variety of groups provides many positive outcomes. **Networking**, or developing social connections to many kinds of people in many contexts, contributes to broadening one's knowledge, skills, and attitudes in life. *Social contacts* can contribute to having a satisfying job, associating with interesting people, developing social supports, having a range of social and recreational interests, and developing meaningful relationships. Having a variety of group memberships is more important than just the number of groups. Advances in communications technology now make it possible for individuals to develop extensive networks of social connections and group memberships. In fact, one can develop group memberships around the world in an unlimited variety of cultures, occupations, beliefs, and lifestyles. As we enter the second decade of the 21st century, social networks such as Facebook, Twitter, MySpace, and LinkedIn are among the most popular on-line social networks in North America. There is also Cyworld in Asia, Skyrock in Europe, and Orkut and Hi5 in South America. How this technology will affect human behavior and groups in the future is yet to be determined.

Recommended Readings

Forsyth D. *Group Dynamics*, 5th ed. Beverly, MA: Wadsworth Publishing; 2009.

Funder DC, Krueger JI. Towards a balanced social psychology: Causes, consequences, and cures for the problem-seeking approach to social behavior and cognition. *Behavioral and Brain Sciences* 2004, 27:313–376.

Kaplan R, Sallis J, Patterson, T. *Health and Human Behavior*. New York: McGraw-Hill; 1993.

Levine R, et al. (Eds.). *Journeys in Social Psychology: Looking Back to Inspire the Future*. Boca Raton, FL: CRC Press; 2008.

Wedding, D, Stuber, M. *Behavior and Medicine*, 5th ed. Cambridge, MA: Hogrefe Publishing; 2010.

Review Questions

1. The group used for comparison purposes, such as the general U.S. population, is the
   A. data producing group.
   B. demographic group.
   C. primary group.
   D. reference group.
   E. secondary group.

2. A research study of smokers divides the subjects by socioeconomic status (SES). Designation of SES is typically based on
   A. characteristics of the primary group.
   B. education level and income level.
   C. income level and federal job classification.
   D. secondary group membership.
   E. social status in the community and income level.

3. Erik is an engineer who was recently diagnosed as HIV positive. The softball team on which Erik plays thought he was heterosexual, but now assumes he is gay. This is an example of
   A. bias.
   B. isolationist behavior.
   C. prejudice with malice.
   D. stereotyping.
   E. stigmatizing.

4. Erik has applied for a position with an engineering firm. He completed the application form and truthfully listed his HIV status. He has excellent evaluations from his present employer but he was not selected. This may be a case of
   A. bias.
   B. isolationist behavior.
   C. prejudice with malice.
   D. stereotyping
   E. stigmatizing.

5. At the country club, the person with a locker next to Erik's locker asked to move to the other side of the room. This may be an example of
   A. bias.
   B. isolationist behavior.
   C. prejudice with malice.
   D. stereotyping.
   E. stigmatizing.

6. "Native Americans are stoic, non-communicative, and alcoholics." This is an example of
   A. bias.
   B. isolationist behavior.
   C. prejudice with malice.
   D. stereotyping.
   E. stigmatizing.

Key to review questions: p. 407

17 Theories of Social Relations

Frederic W. Hafferty, PhD, and Brian Castellani, PhD

- How does a sociological analysis of behavior differ from a psychological analysis?
- How do implicit theories of life events differ from formal sociological theories?
- How does structural/functionalism theory differ from conflict theory?
- How does symbolic interactionism theory differ from utilitarianism/rational choice theory?
- How does the study of complexity facilitate our understanding of social relations?
- How does a sociological analysis of behavior differ from a psychological analysis?

No single theory of social relations adequately explains the evolving structure and social dynamics that make up "health care." The traditional physician-patient relationship has evolved into a more heterogeneous and distant provider-customer interaction. Complicating this picture are the interactions among different health care providers and the complex array of factors that attract a significant percentage of the population to alternative or complementary medicine (see Chapter 18, Culture and Ethnicity, and Chapter 31, Complementary and Integrative Medicine). The decision to seek health care, the type of provider seen, the diagnosis rendered, the therapy offered, and the resources ultimately used by the patient are determined by a complex interplay of social forces and special interests. More of these factors now operate at the organizational and institutional level than in the past. Multiple levels of analysis are required to understand the relationships that underscore the organization and delivery of health care services, as well as determine how "health" and "disease" are defined. In the following chapter, we examine several of the major theories of social relations and their applications to health care.

There are two ways to think about **social behavior**: (1) the actions and motivations of individuals, associated with the field of psychology; and (2) the interactions among individuals or collective behavior (**social relations**), associated with the field of sociology.

The lives of individuals are a product of social groups such as communities, or social institutions, cultures, and societies of which they are a part. Social relations determine the languages individuals speak, the religions they practice, the clothing they wear, and the ways in which they see themselves and the world around them. Sociologists refer to patterns of the social arrangements that exist among individuals and between individuals and their environments as **social structure**.

One of the earliest examples of a sociological approach to analyzing human behavior was Emile Durkheim's 1897 study of suicide in France. For Durkheim, individual psychological processes, such as mental illness, did not satisfactorily explain suicide rates. Instead, Durkheim considered suicide to be a "social phenomenon" and concentrated on the role played by factors such as social cohesiveness and integration. Durkheim hypothesized that individuals who had greater social isolation [anomie] were more likely to commit suicide than those with strong familial and personal bonds. At that time, Durkheim's findings were controversial because people in western society tended to think about suicidal behavior in psychological rather than sociological terms.

Levels of Analysis

How social relations and interactions that make up groups are viewed depends upon the *level of anal-*

ysis. Within the social and behavioral sciences, the smallest unit of analysis is the *dyad*. Other important social entities include *reference groups, communities, society*, and even *countries/nation states*.

Individual vs. Social

How a problem/issue is defined often determines what solutions are appropriate to apply. For example, when medical students and residents begin training, most attend an orientation session in which a member of the faculty discusses the "stresses and strains" of medical training, and how the school/program has multiple resources to help trainees "cope" with "their" problems. Unfortunately, any invitation to "feel free to visit if you have a problem" or "our door is always open" attributes both problems and solutions to the *individual* and his/her *psychological make-up* (e.g., personal stress, low self-esteem, depression). Pushed to the side is any notion that these same stressors may be associated with the *social-structural* elements of the institution and its policies, such as examination and course requirements, patient care responsibilities, and call schedules. The tendency to define problems – and their solutions – as "belonging" to individuals rather than **social systems** and structures is a core part of medicine's culture. As a consequence, trainees often come to define and approach patient health issues as problems of individuals and not of systems. This, in turn, has implications for how trainees learn to treat disease.

Elements vs. Systems

A similar problem is grounded in the culture of medicine. Traditionally, medicine has mimicked science by employing the logic and principles of "biological reductionism." Here the scientist/physician takes a complex problem (e.g., the biophysiological "nature" of a given disease) and reduces it to the most elemental part deemed responsible for disrupting system equilibrium. Treatment interventions thus attempt to correct or compensate for that disordered part, often via some outside agent or tool (e.g., drug, surgical intervention). As knowledge of disease etiology has accumulated, it has become apparent that a strategy of reducing problems to their most elemental parts – be that subcellular or genetic – is not sufficient to

understand many disease conditions. This is particularly true for chronic disease, which can manifest itself in a myriad of ways, among different people, over time. As a consequence, a paradigm has emerged where the focus is not on "parts" but on **system dynamics**, e.g., the fluctuating relationships that exist among elements in the system; on the malfunction, breakdown, and disequilibrium of interrelationships among the parts; and the developing strategies that will return the system to a state of equilibrium (**homeostasis**). As an example of this more comprehensive approach, Christakis and Fowler have examined the complex interplay of genetics, pathophysiology, lifestyle, and social relationships in the etiology of several health problems (smoking, obesity, alcohol consumption, depression, and infectious disease) by using the tools of social network analysis.

In addition to appreciating the ways in which different levels of analysis or different types of system thinking influence understanding and treatment of a medical problem, physicians need to appreciate the distinctions between their own *implicit theories* of the world and *formal sociological theory*. Sociological explanations may be difficult to apply, especially if they challenge an individual's already formed *implicit* understandings of the world, others, and themselves.

Implicit Theory

> How do implicit theories of life events differ from formal sociological theories?

Individuals develop personal understandings of their life-space and world as learned from, among others, family, community, teachers, movies, and religion. These beliefs about the way things are enable individuals and groups to make sense of, and thus master, the complexities of daily interactions with others and to anticipate and control future events. Without these implicit theories, individuals would be forced, each day, to reconstruct social understandings from scratch, much like Bill Murray's character in the movie *Ground Hog Day*.

Sociologists refer to an individual's assumption about the world as **implicit theory**, and they refer to an individual's views about others as the

generalized other. A first-time patient, for example, knows nothing about the particular physician she will be seeing, only about physicians generally. Similarly, the physician knows little about this particular patient. What both parties anticipate (consciously or not) is grounded in their knowledge or belief about patients or physicians in general and, given previous experiences, both parties will enter this first meeting with closely held expectations about how that interaction will (and should) evolve.

Health care providers need to acknowledge the power of implicit theories and understand how they influence expectations about social relationships in general and the provider-patient relationship, in particular. Sometimes, different occupational groups (e.g., physicians, nurses, therapists) will hold different ideas about how provider-patient and provider-provider relationships should be structured and unfold. The functioning of health care teams, clinic units, hospital services, and entire systems are shaped by these expectations. Part of this understanding includes recognizing that individuals do not generate implicit theories in an arbitrary fashion. Notions about what it means to be a "good" patient or "good" health care provider are *shared understandings*, developed through interactions and experiences with socially significant others, i.e., *reference group members* (see Chapter 18, Culture and Ethnicity).

While sociology studies these implicit theories, in many instances, formal sociological analysis uncovers causes and consequences that are invisible or otherwise hidden to those caught up in the details of daily life. C. Wright Mills refers to this process of formal theorization as the sociological imagination: formal theory expands our implicit theories into a larger frame of reference that demonstrates to us how our personal struggles are shared by others.

When a provider complains to a colleague about a "bad" patient or when a patient tells a neighbor about an "insensitive" provider, each party has some implicit understanding of what the other person means, even if the other person disagrees with that characterization.

Formal Theories of Social Relations

There are four major and one emergent theoretical schools within formal sociological theory. An out-

Five Formal Theories of Social Relations	
Structural/ functionalism	Systems seek dynamic equilibrium. Change is designed to preserve stability.
Conflict	Systems do not seek equilibrium. Conflict drives change.
Symbolic interactionism	Systems are dependent on microsocial interactions. Change is a function of actors making meaning.
Utilitarianism/ rational choice	Systems work best when individuals make informed choices to derive maximum personal benefit.
Complexity	Systems are best understood as complex networks built from the ground up through agent-based interactions.

line of these theories illustrates their similarities and differences by application to today's health care system.

Structural/Functionalism

Structural/functionalism (SF) emphasizes how *change* in one part of a group or social system has implications for other parts of that group or system. Structural/functionalism arose from an attempt to apply models of biological functioning to social action. Society is considered analogous to the biological organism, which is composed of various parts, each of which contributes to the functioning of the whole, and where all are needed to function in a state of **homeostasis**. Depending on the unit of analysis (e.g., individual, community, state, nation), the object is viewed as composed of interdependent and coordinated parts and, in turn, is itself part of some even larger *interdependent and coordinated* system. Change in one part generates reactive/adaptive change in another (note that the integrated sciences model described in Chapter 1 of this book is one such example). Parallels between SF theory and biological reductionism are not accidental. Early SF sociologists attempted to appear "more scientific" by modeling themselves after the dominant scientific paradigm of the time.

As a rule, individuals who apply a SF perspective to the analysis of social issues focus more on *outcomes/consequences* (e.g., homeostasis or its absence) than on cause. A pattern of social action is more likely to endure if a given social phenomenon contributes more to achieving system goals than to impeding them. Conversely, if the consequences are considered negative, then that pattern is likely to change. Thus, systems tend toward a pattern of dynamic equilibrium in which change is "met" by system adaptation in a manner designed to preserve stability and balance.

Application to Today's Health Care System

Evidence of a SF approach to health care can be seen in the emergence and failure of managed care to control the skyrocketing cost of health care. Experts defined health care as "out of control" and relied on a reductionistic approach to define both problem and solution as a problem of homeostasis and the need to reestablish a state of equilibrium. The imposition of practice protocols and guidelines (e.g., new standards for the treatment of diabetes), the initiation of new forms of paying for services (e.g., prospective payment), or the formulation of new forms of practice organization such as HMOs (health maintenance organizations), IPOs (independent practice organizations), and PPOs (physician practice organizations) were introduced to rationalize medical practice and to control costs (see Chapter 30, The U.S. Health Care System).

Initially, these structural and managerial solutions appeared to be effective as costs stabilized during the mid 1990s. However, new concerns emerged, e.g., the large number (about 47 million) of people who lack health care insurance and related problems of access and equity (see Conflict Theory below). Unfortunately, the initial "victory" of cost control gained by managed care proved to be only short-lived as costs began to spiral upward at the end of the 20th century. From a SF perspective, solutions other than cost controls are required to bring the health care system back into balance.

> How does structural/functionalism theory differ from conflict theory?

Conflict Theory

An example of **conflict theory** is Karl Marx's theory of class struggle in industrialized society. Those who control the means of production exercise social control and dominance. The *unequal distribution of authority* shapes, among other things, patterns of *social class*. Other examples include conflict between the sexes (part of the focus of feminist sociological theory), and between racial, ethnic, political, and religious groups.

Post-structuralism is a more recent version of conflict theory and focuses on the scientific and cultural institutions in society (such as law and medicine) and the power struggles that emerge as a function of the attempts by these institutions to structure daily existence. An example from medicine is *medicalization,* where certain "conditions" (e.g., alcoholism, drug addiction) are considered "diseases" rather than problems of a personal (e.g., lack of character/moral fiber), social (e.g., criminal), or religious (e.g., sinful) nature. In contrast to functionalism, conflict theory focuses more on issues of *inequities* and how the definitions of problems, and the solutions offered, serve the *vested interests* of "a few" (e.g., management and capital) rather than those of "the many" (e.g., workers/employees). A case in point is the fact that, historically, the use of addictive drugs was considered a crime and not a disease (drug addiction) until drug use moved from the inner cities to the suburbs and began to threaten the social stability and self-identities of the middle and upper classes.

Application to Today's Health Care System

A conflict theorist might focus on how the managed care system came to be defined as a problem (or not) and note that the original problem was that of "runaway" costs, not deficiencies in the quality of services. In turn, one might ask, "Whose interests were being served by this labeling?" Other areas of focus might be the efforts by health care corporations to identify their physicians as "providers" and thus group them with other health care workers such as nurses, therapists, and physician assistants/nurse practitioners, or for insurers to pay more for physicians to manage drug regimens rather than to do "talk therapy" with mentally ill patients. Conflict theorists also might study environmental factors such as patient rights legislation at the state and federal levels and question why legislation to protect patient interests has been so difficult to enact as law. The rise of corporate medicine and the consequent loss of status and influence by physicians are especially relevant to the conflict perspective.

Symbolic Interactionism

Symbolic interactionism and its related areas of inquiry (pragmatism, phenomenology, and ethnomethodology) begin with three assumptions: (1) people react to the world based on their understandings of it; (2) these understandings come from the interactions people have with others; and (3) people make these understandings on their own by filtering them through their own experiences. Symbolic interactionism gives microsocial relations a more powerful role in the construction of social reality. Not only does society shape the individual, but individuals shape society as well. As such, symbolic interactionism illustrates how individuals create and use the social structures of which they are a part.

Application to Today's Health Care System
Symbolic interactionists focus on the microsocial relations within the health care system, specifically the physician-provider relationship, interactions among providers, and the struggles between physicians and the health care systems in which they work. In studying microsystems, the goal is to understand how *social factors* such as the gender, age, and ethnicity of physicians, patients, and other health care workers influence the presentation of symptoms and the response/understanding of health care providers. The symbolic interactionist perspective would be concerned with how styles of interaction and use of language might differ when white male physicians interact with African American female patients, or whether physicians treat Latina women the same way they treat Asian American women.

> How does symbolic interactionism theory differ from utilitarianism/rational choice theory?

Utilitarianism/Rational Choice

According to **utilitarianism/rational choice theory**, social behavior is the result of rational actors agreeing to engage in goal-directed behavior via explicit rules regarding *individual interests* and the means of realizing those interests. Human relations are influenced by personal desires, objectives, and individual gratification and, therefore, have strong ties to behavioral psychology. Examples of this perspective include **exchange theory** where interaction is based on individuals weighing both past and potential rewards and costs, and **game theory** where individuals are rational actors making decisions based on information about the interactions in which they engage. Rational choice theorists assume that the system works best when patients are given access to all information necessary to make rational and decisions that are optimal for them.

Application to Today's Health Care System
An example of rational choice theory is the promotion of *health savings accounts* to replace work-based health insurance as a principal means of paying for health care services. Establishing a health care voucher system or a health care savings account system presumes informed rational choice at the individual level. Rational choice models underlie the movement to involve patients in managing their own health conditions and efforts to underwrite the costs of health education, particularly for patients with chronic disorders (e.g., diabetes or hypertension).

The push to educate patients assumes that there is a positive relationship between knowledge and compliance. Some rational choice theorists believe the only way to solve the problem of poor health behaviors (e.g., smoking) is to appeal more directly to self-interests. This might mean developing economic incentives to stop smoking rather than spending money "merely" educating people about the dangers of smoking. Taking this example a step further, a rational choice perspective would differentiate between first- and second-hand smoke. Incentives to stop smoking in the former instance (an appeal to self-interest) would be different from incentives for decreasing the dangers of second-hand smoke to protect the health of others. In the former case, education might work but would need to be changed to, for example, direct economic incentives when the goal is to improve the health of others.

Complexity Theory

Complexity theory has evolved from earlier systems theories in sociology, such as Parson's structural functionalism, as well as postmodernism, ecological systems theory, and systems biology. Its main theoretical lineage, however, comes from the recent interdisciplinary advances made in the study of complex systems, including such phenomena as six-degrees of separation (everyone in the world is connected by six or fewer people) and swarm behavior (complex group behaviors, such as large crowds leaving a baseball stadium can be modeled using simple rules, such as those followed by swarming bees).

The main focus of complexity theory is the complex system that is variously defined as self-organizing, adaptive, emergent, comprised of a large number of elements, nonlinear, dynamic, network-like in structure, open-ended with fuzzy boundaries, interdependent, agent-based, evolving, chaotic, comprised of feedback loops, historical, nodes within a larger network of systems, environmentally impacted, and so forth.

> How does the study of complexity facilitate our understanding of social relations?

Application to Today's Health Care System

Complexity theorists conceptualize public health systems, health care organizations, hospitals, physician's offices, outpatient clinics, and groups of health care providers as one big, complex, interconnected network functioning at multiple levels of scale, all interdependent upon one another. These complex networks, in turn, are situated within a wider network of systems, including the economy, politics, and culture of a particular region or society. The job of the complexity theorist is to figure out how these complex networks function and to examine the impact these networks have on the health and well-being of people. Examples include the study of communities and community health as complex systems, the examination of medical learning environments in terms of student networks, and the exploration of medical professionalism as a system comprised of several competing types.

Recommended Readings

Castellani B, Hafferty FW. *Sociology and Complexity Science: A New Field of Science.* New York: Springer; 2009.

Cockerham W. *Medical Sociology,* 10th ed. New York: Prentice-Hall; 2006.

Farmer P. *Infections and Inequalities: The Modern Plagues.* Berkeley, CA: University of California Press; 2001.

Lundberg GD. *Severed Trust: Why American Medicine Hasn't Been Fixed.* New York: Basic Books; 2000.

Patel K, Rushefsky ME. *Health Care Politics and Policy in America,* 3rd ed. Armonk, NY: ME Sharpe; 2006.

Review Questions

Directions: The items below consist of lettered headings followed by numbered descriptions. For each numbered description, choose the one lettered heading to which it is *most* closely associated. Each lettered heading may be used *once, more than once,* or *not at all.*

Match each scenario with the social relations theory it exemplifies.

A. Complexity
B. Conflict
C. Structural/functionalism
D. Symbolic interactionism
E. Utilitarianism/rational choice

1. To gain a broader patient base, a local chiropractor, Dr. Smith, has applied for privileges at Mercy Hospital, the newest hospital in Meta-General's national health care chain. Although Dr. Smith is a long time, well-respected local practitioner, there is considerable antagonism toward his application from within Meta-General's Board of Directors and the general physician staff. One overriding concern is that acting favorably on this request will allow non-physicians access to a "turf" traditionally controlled by physicians and open the hospital to requests for privileges from other non-physician practitioners. Alternatively, the Chief of Staff is aware of the successful 1990 antitrust suit brought against the AMA by three chiropractors as well as

that the AMA's Code of Ethics no longer prohibits physicians from consulting with chiropractors or teaching in schools of chiropractic.

2. To control costs, Good Samaritan Hospital reduced its nursing staff by 20%. Termination was based on seniority and degree status. Initially, the hospital enjoyed considerable savings. However, over the next several months, the number of hospital admissions decreased by almost 30%. A subsequent analysis found that most terminated nurses were admitting nurses, in charge of processing new patients. The efficiency of patient flow decreased, patients were dissatisfied, and the hospital's financial condition plummeted.

3. A patient is admitted to the neurological ICU with a complete C5 transection. The patient is intubated, placed on a ventilator, and connected to electronic monitors. Every few hours, the staff rolls the patient over to prevent bedsores. Over the ensuing two days, the patient becomes increasingly agitated and distressed, and resists falling asleep. Unable to speak with the patient because of his intubation, the staff calls for a consultant who can read lips. The patient, finally understandable, discloses that the reason the nurses keep turning him is to keep him awake because, "If I fall asleep, I will die." The nursing staff is surprised by this message and reassures the patient that this is not the case. The patient, to everyone's relief, finally falls asleep.

4. Acme Medical Supply Company offers its 30,000 employees several types of insurance coverage, each different with respect to levels of co-pay, access to specialists, and coverage of prescription drugs and mental health services. The rationale is that employees will assess their own needs, maximize the benefits they need, and choose the desired plan accordingly.

5. The Spoleto Health Care system — which provides extensive outreach services to its urban poor residents – wants its two free clinics to start a healthy eating campaign. The problem is they do not know where to start. The eating behaviors of local residents are influenced, in part, by a web of related factors, including household income, education, access to and quality of local grocery stores, cultural background, quality of food served in the local schools, and safety concerns about walking in the neighborhood at night.

6. Theoretically, the electronic medical record will provide instantaneous information about the health status, utilization of all health care-related services and visits to agencies or purveyors, number of hospitalizations and diagnostic testing and procedures performed with results, all medications with dosages taken over the individual's lifetime, insurance coverage and utilization, and health history of all first-degree relatives and other family members who have a genetic or heritable condition found in the proband. One problem to be solved is "garbage in; garbage out."

Key to review questions: p. 407

18 Culture and Ethnicity

Kathleen A. Culhane-Pera, MD, MA, and Jeffrey Borkan, MD, PhD

- What is "cultural humility" and how does it relate to "culturally competent" care?
- What are the four categories of disease causation common to many cultural groups?
- What are the distinctions between "popular," "folk," and "professional" treatments?
- Why are "explanatory models" important in health care?
- How do sick people decide on healers or specific healing methods?
- What is "culturally appropriate" communication?
- Why is it preferable to use professionally trained interpreters rather than family members?

Culturally Competent Care

> What is "cultural humility" and how does it relate to "culturally competent" care?

Biomedical physicians tend to focus on the pathological processes of *disease*; patients focus on the psychological experience of *illness;* and the patient's family and community focus on the patient's *sickness*, i.e., the social determinants and ramifications of disease and illness. **Cultural competence** in medical care requires that physicians understand cultural as well as social and psychological factors that influence how patients maintain health, experience illness, treat disease, and respond to suffering.

When physicians provide medical care that is *culturally competent* (similar terms include *culturally sensitive, culturally responsive,* and *culturally appropriate*) they inquire about, respond to, and respect the diversity of patients' beliefs and desires, regardless of the patient's age, gender, religion, ethnicity, or language. **Cultural humility** is a life-long attitude and approach to cultural competence that recognizes a provider's limited knowledge of a patient's beliefs and values, engages in self-reflection to increase awareness of personal assumptions and prejudices, and acts to redress the imbalance of power inherent in provider-patient relationships.

Dr. Jim Zedler, a new intern, had just begun his rotation in the Emergency Room. One of his first patients was Ms. Sovann Khoeun, a 62-year-old Cambodian woman, who walked in leaning on her son. Dr. Zedler took Mrs. Khoeun's history and examined her, using the son as an interpreter. She complained of abdominal pain and diarrhea that had been present for several months but had worsened in the past week. Ms. Khoeun and her son did not answer immediately when asked about her sexual history and there appeared to be some discomfort when Dr. Zedler examined her head, but he made nothing of it and proceeded. Her physical exam was normal except for some fading bruises on her stomach. He ordered a broad series of blood tests and imaging studies. All test results were normal. He told her, "You seem physiologically just fine. It's probably all in your head." He thought the mother and son were relieved, since they smiled and thanked him for his time. Given the presence of bruises on the patient's stomach, Dr. Zedler was concerned about the possibility of elder abuse, and called Protective Services. A few months later, the local Southeast Asian health agency filed a letter of complaint charging that the physician had not provided appropriate care.

How do you explain what happened? Could the intern have done anything to change the outcome of his interaction with the patient and the care he provided?

Each of the *core competencies* that have been identified as critical to patient care has objectives

Table 18.1. Core competencies and culturally competent care		
Expectations for Physicians		
Patient care	–	Communicate effectively and demonstrate caring and respectful behaviors
	–	Gather essential and accurate information
	–	Make decisions about diagnostic and therapeutic interventions based on patient information and preferences
	–	Develop and carry out management plans
	–	Counsel and educate patients and their families
	–	Use information technology to support education and patient care decisions
	–	Provide services aimed at preventing health problems or maintaining health
Medical knowledge	–	Know and apply clinically supportive sciences
Practice-based learning and improvement	–	Obtain and use information about their own patients and the larger populations from which their patients are drawn
Interpersonal and communication skills	–	Create and sustain therapeutic and ethically sound relationships
	–	Use effective listening, nonverbal, explanatory, questioning, and writing skills
Professionalism	–	Demonstrate respect, compassion, and integrity
	–	Demonstrate sensitivity to patients' culture, age, gender, and disabilities
Systems-based practice	–	Advocate for quality care and assist patients with system complexities

that prescribe culturally competent care (Table 18.1). One important skill is the ability to utilize culturally appropriate communication that is both respectful of the individual's beliefs, practices, and background, yet allows the health care practitioner to make precise diagnoses.

Culture influences beliefs about:
- bodily functions
- classification of disease
- disease causation
- treatment options
- the meaning of bodily signs and symptoms
- medical decision making
- healer/sick person relationships

Concepts of Bodily Functions

Each ethnic group has ideas about the functioning of the natural, social, and supernatural worlds that are germane to their ideas about health, illness, and healing. The *natural realm* includes ideas about the connections between people and the natural environment. The *social realm* includes ideas about how individuals interact with people of different ages, genders, lineages, and ethnic groups.

The *supernatural realm* includes beliefs about birth, death, afterlife, and interactions between the spiritual world and the human world.

Classification of Diseases

Since ethnic groups have differing classification systems for diseases, it is difficult to translate disease concepts across cultures. Entities that are recognized by certain ethnic groups and not others are often classified as **folk illnesses** or **culture-bound syndromes** (see Table 18.2) Such ailments have a defined etiology, course, and treatment, and include expressions of mental or social

Mr. Garcia Lopez, who recently came to the US from Mexico, was confused. His son was sent home from school with a draining ear. This condition is a common occurrence in Mexico and not a cause for alarm. But several weeks later, his son was not permitted to stay home from school after he was frightened *(asustado)* by a near-miss car accident that made him vulnerable to illness.

Table 18.2: Examples of culture-bound syndromes		
Culture-Bound Syndrome	**Ethnic Group**	**Description**
Empacho	Mexican, Mexican-American	An illness involving intestinal difficulties; believed due to lumps of food blocking the intestines
Nervios	Latino	"Nerves," a condition affecting both men and women and allowing expression of strong emotions
Susto	Latino	Illness resulting from a frightening experience; may also refer to illness due to soul loss
Mal de ojo	Latino, South American, Middle Eastern, North African	A look from an envious person resulting in a variety of ill-nesses, depending on the cultural group
Amok	Malaysian, Indonesian	Young men feeling excessive social pressures and role conflict experience a form of hysteria
Latah	Laotian, Malaysian, Indonesian	Exaggerated responses to startling stimuli; may be related to stress
High blood	African American	Blood that is too thick or too sweet; having too much blood; blood that is too high in the body

distress. Some previously considered folk illnesses, such as premenstrual syndrome and chronic fatigue syndrome, are now recognized as biomedical entities.

Theories of Disease Causation

> What are the four categories of disease causation common to many cultural groups?

Every cultural system links sickness to etiological events that provide an explanation for bodily dysfunction and treatments for human suffering. Determining etiology involves the interpretation of signs and symptoms, responses to therapies, the stature and reputation of the sick person, and historical events that have affected the individual, family, and community. Multiple etiologies may be considered even in a single sickness episode. While etiologies differ among ethnic groups, they typically fall into four categories:

1. *Individual etiologies* include behavioral risk factors for disease (e.g., lifestyle, diet, habits, sexual behaviors) and presume the individual is responsible for the illness.
2. *Natural etiologies* include germs, environmental factors, humoral factors (hot/cold elements), and the universe (stars, planets, constellations). Because these etiologies are seen as factors beyond human control, the individual has little personal responsibility for causing the illness.
3. *Social etiologies* arise from social interactions or conflicts (e.g., conflict between friends or family members; jealousy, envy, or hatred; giving someone the "evil eye").
4. *Supernatural etiologies* reflect religious beliefs. For example, sinful thoughts or actions may be punished by an angry God; *kharma* forces from previous lives will influence events in this life; or not displaying respect for ancestral spirits can cause sickness. Prevention or cure is provided by specific religious prescriptions about what constitutes appropriate behavior or contrition.

Biomedicine emphasizes individual and natural causes, but patients may consider other causes to be equal or more important. Thus, exploration of alternative etiologies based on cultural concepts or differences of opinion will help avoid miscommunication and conflict about appropriate diagnostic or therapeutic approaches.

Types of Treatments

> What are the distinctions between "popular," "folk," and "professional" treatments?

Popular or *lay treatments* are typically applied by the patient, family, or community to relieve symptoms or cure illnesses and include herbs, amulets, rituals, and massage or body work. Preventive practices include wise nutrition, sleep, and exercise; protective clothing; prayer or maintaining relations with spirits; and cleanliness to avoid spreading contamination.

> When Dr. Zedler examined Ms. Khoeun in the ER, he noted some fading bruises on her stomach. Had he asked the patient about them, he might have found that her family had been treating her with traditional cupping and coin rubbing. Traditional healers rub the skin with a mentholated cream and then either vigorously rub a silver coin over the affected area (coining) or create a suction with a cup (cupping), which is believed to relieve the pressure and thus improve the illness. The practices produce linear or circular bruises on the skin wherever the illness is (i.e., abdomen, back, chest, or extremities.) Unfortunately, Dr. Zedler, ignorant of the therapeutic bases of these practices, interpreted the marks as evidence of physical abuse and reported the family to Protective Services.

Folk treatments are applied by sacred or secular healers who have acquired authority through inheritance, apprenticeship, religious position, or divine choice. Their status is affirmed by their reputation for healing or by revelations. Healers include herbalists, bonesetters, traditional midwives, spiritualists, shamans, and injectionists. **Folk healers** tend to be holistic and deal with any natural, social, or supernatural forces that may be related to the sickness.

Professional treatments are applied by health care providers whose authority is recognized by formal education and official licensure or certification. This category of healer includes physicians, nurses, chiropractors, psychologists, physical therapists, and pharmacists. Complementary or alternative medical practitioners, such as acupuncturists, medical massage therapists, and reflexologists are also in this category. Although their training and licensure vary by field and governmental regulations, these health care providers maintain professional relationships, in which payment is exchanged for specialized services.

Interpretation of Bodily Signs and Symptoms

Individuals declare themselves "sick" when they interpret their signs or symptoms as abnormal. Socially, family members or healers must concur with the patient's interpretation before the patient can assume the **sick role**, legitimately withdraw from regular work and family responsibilities, and receive assistance from others.

> Why are "explanatory models" important in health care?

The significance patients attach to signs or symptoms of an illness is influenced by an individual's **explanatory models** (EM) about the sickness event. Kleinman defines EMs as people's beliefs about a specific illness, including etiology, symptoms, physiological processes, projected course, and appropriate treatments. People's EMs can change over time as symptoms change or as response to treatment occurs. The patient, family members, social network, and health care providers all have their own EMS for the sickness event, which may be congruent, complementary, or contradictory. When providers understand these diverse EMs, they can respond to patients' needs, expectations, and fears; aim educational messages at patient's uncertainties; and negotiate diagnostic and therapeutic approaches. See Table 18.3 for examples of questions that help health providers explore the explanatory models patients and their families may have.

Table 18.3. Eliciting the patient's and family's stories	
Story	1. Please tell me more about yourself? Please tell me the story of your illness? 2. How does this illness fit into or change your life story?
Illness/problem	3. What health problems or illnesses do you have, and for how long? What kind of care have you sought (conventional, complementary or alternative, traditional)? How has it been helpful? Not helpful?
Impact of the illness on the individual	4. How is this illness affecting your daily life and doing things important to you? 5. What do you miss most from before you were ill? 6. What do you think will happen in the future?
Impact of the illness on the family	7. What changes have occurred in the family since the illness began (daily routines, finances)? 8. How well do you feel the family is coping? Is there anything the family wishes they could do differently?

Medical Decision Making

> How do sick people decide on specific healers or specific healing methods?

Factors that influence medical decision making include *cultural beliefs*, *explanatory models*, *access*, *cost*, and *perceived efficacy*. **Ethnic identity** – the extent to which individuals align themselves with a sociocultural group – may influence people to seek healers or professionals from their ethnic background. The degree of **social dissonance** – the distance between the patient and the healer in terms of differences in ethnicity, socioeconomic class, language, or religion – may become important. The greater the dissonance, the less likely the patient will choose to see the healer or adhere to treatment recommendations.

When people relocate from one geographic area to another, ethnic identity may be modified through the process of **acculturation**. Acculturation is not a unidirectional phenomenon that necessitates changes in a person's orientation from traditional healing practices to the biomedical system. Rather, acculturation is a multifaceted and bidirectional process that varies among ethnic groups, individuals, and families and can lead to intra- and interfamilial conflicts regarding appropriate treatments.

Patients can seek assistance from the three types of treatment systems (lay, folk, and professional sectors). Following a **hierarchy of resort**, people often begin with lay treatments in the form of self-help or family remedies and then, if lay treatments are insufficient, they seek help from folk healers or professionals. Such patterns of resort may be sequential or simultaneous. Individual patients may make decisions themselves, or they may look to family members or to their social network to help them choose. A "therapy manager," such as a revered elder, may oversee the help-seeking process.

> Mr. Kang Tou Xiong is a 64-year-old Hmong man with persistent cough and weight loss despite treating himself with Hmong herbal medicines. His wife took him to her physician, who thought he had tuberculosis or cancer based on the chest x-ray and CT scan. When neither diagnosis could be proven, the doctor recommended an invasive procedure (bronchoscopy) to obtain sputum. Mr. Xiong discussed his options with his sons, and then consulted a shaman. The shaman determined that Mr. Xiong's illness was caused by his dead father's ghost wanting him to die so he could help his father in the afterlife. Mr. Xiong and his family refused the bronchoscopy, as it would render him vulnerable to his father's ghost. Instead, they performed a shamanic ceremony to appease his father's ghost.

In a society where multiple systems of healing co-exist, patients and their families may use specific healing practices without endorsing the entire healing system. That is, they seek assistance from different healing traditions depending on their interpretation of the situation, the fit between the sickness and the healing approach, the perceived effectiveness of the therapies, and their ethnic identity and degree of acculturation.

> Physicians should inquire about what healers have been seen, what treatments have already been received, and whom the patient will consult to make decisions.

Culture of Biomedicine

Like all healing systems, modern **biomedicine** is a cultural system influenced by historical, social, economic, political, religious, and scientific events. It has its own language, vocabulary, values, and concepts, which can be difficult to translate into lay terms. Each discipline (e.g., family physicians, surgeons, psychiatrists) is a cultural subgroup identifiable by its own perspective on biomedical practice, health and disease, and the profession as a whole. As a subculture of Western society, biomedicine reflects values of the larger society. For example, biomedical providers typically address patients as individuals rather than as people embedded in families; they often focus on diseased bodies as physiological and pathological processes, ignoring social and cultural contexts; they are likely to conceptualize defective body parts as mechanical objects that can be replaced; and they tend to approach natural processes of life and death as periods to be manipulated and controlled.

Healer-Sick Person Relationships

Every cultural system has social and cultural rules governing the healer-sick person-family relationship that influence the style of communication, the appropriateness of discussing certain topics, sharing or withholding information, and the authority of the healer.

The approach of mainstream biomedical providers may seem rude to patients from various ethnic groups. For example, providers may be seen as attempting to control nature, while patients may prefer to live in harmony with nature. Providers

may value direct communication, while patients may value indirect communication. Providers may emphasize the importance of the individual and focus on the physical, while patients may emphasize the importance of the group and focus on the social and spiritual. Providers may look to the future and exalt the young, while patients may look to the past and revere their elders.

Providers must be familiar with general information about a cultural group, but they cannot assume their patient's beliefs and values are based on this general cultural information (i.e., stereotyping). Rather, they should use general information about a group to generate hypotheses about an individual person or family, and then ask those people about their lives and their specific desires so the providers can (or not) validate these hypotheses.

> Mai Nguyen, a 29-year-old refugee from Vietnam, was being seen for a physical exam prior to starting a new job. She had numerous somatic complaints but was hesitant to talk about emotional, familial, or intimate matters, and refused a gynecological exam. Her physician consulted more experienced colleagues who advised accepting her complaints as consistent with Vietnamese "culture." However, after several encounters with the patient, the physician learned that the patient had escaped from Vietnam in a small overcrowded boat and had undergone significant trauma and sexual abuse while at sea. He came to realize her complaints were not just "cultural" but related to post-traumatic stress disorder that required social and psychiatric intervention.

Culturally Appropriate Communication

> What is "culturally appropriate" communication?

Communication between the provider and patient is significantly influenced by culture, as reflected in non-verbal expressions, manner of address, and appropriate styles and topics of communication. Nonverbal expressions can have different, even opposite, meanings in different cultures. Appropriateness of style and topic of conversation can vary widely and a provider's insensitivity to such differences can impair the provider-patient relationship. However, providers must be careful not to apply cultural generalities as stereotypes: cultural generalities about verbal and non-verbal communication, like all cultural generalities, will not apply to all patients. Providers must monitor

Sombit Suksanakha, a 48-year-old Buddhist monk, felt insulted after his first clinic visit in the US. In the waiting room, a female nurse called his name loudly and then indicated for him to come by pointing her fingers upwards (the way people call animals in Asia), rather than pointing her fingers downward (as appropriate to call people). Then she reached out to touch his arm when directing him to the exam room. In Buddhist society, a woman may never touch a monk. During history taking, his male physician looked directly in his eyes for a long period of time; he wondered if he were such an oddity that the physician would continue to stare at him. And then, during the physical exam, the physician touched his head without asking permission. In Buddhism, the head is the highest and most sacred part of the body and is treated respectfully.

Victoria Bearclaw, an 83-year-old Native American, feels insulted every time she attends the medical clinic in the city rather than the clinic on the reservation. The doctors and nurses talk quickly; they never wait even a full second before she can reply, and then they ask her another question as though she is dumb or deaf. They do not listen to her concerns as she tells the full story. Also, they look directly at her as though staring, and they call her by her first name rather than calling her Grandmother in a respectful tone of voice. She always feels as though they do not really care about her and her suffering.

their patients' responses, ask for their input, and seek assistance from bicultural colleagues.

Why is it preferable to use professionally trained interpreters rather than family members?

Although being proficient in a patient's language is optimal, providers are likely to work through interpreters. *Professionally trained interpreters* should be employed because they provide grammatically correct first-person verbatim translations for providers and patients, including explanations of medical language in lay terms. Using *family members* as interpreters is less desirable for several reasons. Differences in age and gender may mean that talking about some topics is inappropriate. Differences in acculturation may mean that the family interpreter prefers not to tell the provider what their relative said. Differences in language skills may mean the relative has inadequate knowledge of English medical terminology or medical terms in general to explain them in their own language. Whenever possible, providers should meet with the interpreter prior to the clinical encounter to clarify guidelines and expectations, ask for "word for word" translations, and listen to the interpreter's insights about relevant cultural practices, meanings, and idioms (see Table 18.4).

Applying Cultural Competence in Medical Encounters

Being sensitive to culturally relevant information in the clinical encounter requires multiple

Table 18.4. Working with interpreters

- Discuss expectations with interpreters before beginning, including first-person singular, verbatim translation.
- Assure that everyone has been introduced.
- Sit facing the patient and speak to the patient, not the interpreter.
- Use lay English terms and simple language structure.
- Pause intermittently to allow interpretation.
- Do not assume universal meanings to nonverbal gestures.
- Periodically check patient's understanding.
- Do not expect interpreters to resolve conflicts or disagreements or to actively negotiate outcomes.

tasks, which can be arranged into the acronym **LEARN**:

1. LISTEN with genuine interest to the patient's and family's stories about their illness experiences. Elicit the patient's and family's explanatory models. Be aware of whether direct questions are appropriate for obtaining information and gaining understanding.

2. EXPLAIN your views, building on the patient's and family's ideas, and address any fears or concerns. Use good patient education tools (e.g., understandable language and pictures), confirm the patient's understanding, and relate the current situation to a past experience.

3. ACKNOWLEDGE similarities and differences between the provider's and patient's concepts of bodily functions, disease states, etiologies, projected course, and preferred treatments.

4. RECOMMEND a course of action. Explain the treatment and ask permission to proceed. Give options whenever possible. Be prepared for the patient to choose not to proceed.

5. NEGOTIATE a plan. Acknowledge and build on a patient's own perspectives about the illness and how it should be treated. Promote active participation and create a sense of partnership. A plan that the patient has helped design is more likely to succeed (see Berlin & Fowkes, Recommended Readings).

Recommended Readings

Berlin EA, Fowkes WC. A teaching framework for cross-cultural health care-application in family practice. *Western Journal of Medicine* 1983; 139(6):934–938

Culhane-Pera KA, Vawter DE, Xiong P, Babbitt B, Solberg M (Eds.). *Healing by Heart: Clinical and Ethical Case Stories of Hmong Families and Western Providers.* Nashville, TN: Vanderbilt University Press; 2003.

Ember CR, Ember E (Eds.). *Encyclopedia of Medical Anthropology: Health and Illness in theWorld's Cultures,* Volumes I and II. Human Relations Area Files. New York: KluwerAcademic/Plenum Publishers; 2004.

Hark LA, DeLisser HM (Eds.). *Achieving Cultural Competency: A Case-Based Approach to Training Health Professionals.* Singapore: Wiley-Blackwell; 2009.

U.S. Department of Health and Human Services. National Standards on Culturally and Linguistically Appropriate Services (CLAS) in Health Care. Department of Health and Human Services, Office of Minority Health, Federal Register. 2000; 65(247): 80865-80879. Accessed on March 6, 2012 at: http://minorityhealth.hhs.gov/assets/pdf/checked/finalreport.pdf

One of the first patients Dr. Nancy Schaeffer, a new intern, saw in her primary care clinic was Sovann Khoeun, the 62-year-old Cambodian woman whom Dr. Zedler had seen in the Emergency Room. Ms. Khoeun complained of abdominal pain and diarrhea for the several months since arriving in the US. Dr Schaeffer took her history and performed a physical exam using a telephone interpreter, touched her head with permission, asked sensitive intimate questions without her son in the room, and asked about any traditional therapies she had used. Dr Schaeffer reviewed the ER records and added a few laboratory tests, including a colonoscopy. Relieved there appeared to be no life-threatening process, she speculated that Ms. Khoeun had lactose intolerance, exacerbated by her recent dietary changes including milk products. Her pains improved with a lactose-free diet but did not abate completely. Wanting to explore the sociocultural issues that could be contributing to Ms. Khoeun's distress, Dr Schaeffer and the family therapist preceptor held a family conference along with a Khmer interpreter. With a few simple questions ("When did this start? What do you think is causing it? How does it influence your life?"), Ms. Khoeun and her family described her refugee past and her experience of violence under Pol Pot. Suspecting PTSD, Dr Schaeffer referred Ms. Khoeun to a local refugee mental health clinic. Six months later, her symptoms had greatly ameliorated and the relationship between Dr. Schaeffer and Ms. Khoeun was comfortably established.

Online Recources

Country Studies, Library of Congress
    http://lcweb2.loc.gov/frd/cs
National Center for Cultural Competence
    www11.georgetown.edu/research/gucchd/nccc/
Provider's Guide to Quality and Culture
    erc.msh.org
Resources for Cross-cultural Health
    diversityrx.org

Review Questions

1. Explanatory models (EMs) are concepts that patients, family members, and healers form about a specific sickness. Which of the following statements is true about EMs?
   A. EMs are based primarily upon the pathophysiology of the disorder.
   B. EMs do not change once they are formed.
   C. EMs do not typically address the natural history of the disease.
   D. Eventually, patients, family members, and healers have the same EMs about the sickness.
   E. Greater agreement between people's EMs leads to fewer conflicts.

2. What is the LEARN model?
   A. A reminder that we must learn from our patients.
   B. An acronym for culturally sensitive approaches to patient education.
   C. An acronym for learning about cultural beliefs about health, disease, and treatment.
   D. An acronym for obtaining patients' cultural beliefs about their illness.
   E. An acronym for the sequence of events in a culturally appropriate clinical encounter.

3. A 4-year-old Cambodian girl has a temperature of 103.5° F and linear bruises on her chest and upper back. Her grandmother brought her to the clinic because of the fever. You do not have a Cambodian interpreter in the clinic. Among the following, which is the most likely cause of the girl's bruises?
   A. Child abuse
   B. Coagulopathy
   C. Coining
   D. Mongolian spots
   E. Sepsis

4. Which of the following is true about classification of diseases by different ethnic groups?
   A. A standard system of disease classification exists.
   B. All ethnic groups classify disease by physiological systems and etiologies.
   C. All ethnic groups classify disease in similar ways.

D. Classification systems are static.
E. Different disease classification systems contribute to miscommunication.

5. The primary reason the use of professional translators is preferred over family members or friends for provider-patient interactions is that they
   A. add background information they believe help explain symptoms.
   B. clarify or interpret questions and answers.
   C. embellish answers to provide additional information.
   D. translate conversations word for word.
   E. withhold information they feel may be too distressing.

Key to review questions: p. 407

19 Health Care in Minority and Majority Populations

Amanda K. Swenson, MD, MSPH, and Michael C. Hosokawa, EdD

- What are some causes of population differences in health care?
- What accounts for differences in infant mortality, life expectancy, and cause of death among minority and majority populations?
- Why do minority populations in the US have a higher death rate from cancer than whites?
- How does racism affect health outcomes?

Examination of health data reveals significant variations in mortality and morbidity based on race, education level, socioeconomic status, and sexual orientation. Advantaged groups, as defined by these factors, have better health and lower mortality than disadvantaged groups. The relationship between health and social position suggests hypotheses about the etiology of diseases, and strategies and policies for improving the health of the disadvantaged.

Minority Populations

Although the population of the US is growing more slowly than in the past, certain subgroups are growing rapidly. The white majority is becoming smaller and older relative to the black, Hispanic, Asian, and Native American populations. According to the 2009 census, of the estimated 307 million people in the US, 12.9% are **African American**, 15.8% are **Hispanic**, 4.8% are Asian/Pacific Islander, and 1.0% are **Native American/Alaska Native**. Thus, over one third of adults identified themselves as non-white. Projecting to 2050, whites will comprise 50% of the U.S. population, blacks 15%, Hispanics 24%, and Asians 8%.

With population changes, discussion of health care in **minority/majority populations** becomes more complex. There are communities where a "minority group" is really the majority. The Hispanic population of Los Angeles is larger than the white population; blacks are in the majority in Washington D.C., Cleveland, Detroit, and Atlanta; in Miami, the majority of residents are Hispanic. In many cities (e.g., New York City, Chicago, Dallas, Houston, Oakland) there is no majority racial group (www.city-data.com).

What are some causes of population differences in health care?

In addition to biological factors, economic status, education, and access to health care services are essential components in determining the overall health of the US. As single entities, *poverty*, *lack of education*, and *race* alone do not necessarily predict higher mortality, but combined, they have a synergistic and profound effect on health, disease, and access to health care services. Each minority group has unique health care challenges that a health care system attuned to the needs of the majority population may not serve adequately.

Black Americans

While most immigrant groups relocated to the US in search of better political, social, or economic circumstances, most black Americans are descendants of individuals imported as slaves. The rates of *poverty, crime,* and *inadequate education* are higher among the black population than among the majority population, in part due to state and federal laws that *denied equal access* to educational and social benefits until the mid 20th century. Although other immigrant groups have encountered these problems, most groups have been able to assimilate after one or two generations. In contrast, *discrimination, prejudice,* and *segregation* of black Americans have been more easily imposed and sustained because of skin color differences. Although millions of black Americans have moved up the socioeconomic ladder to create a stable and growing black middle class, black Americans still predominate in the lower socioeconomic classes.

Hispanic Americans/Latinos

Most of the more than 42 million Hispanic/Latino Americans living in the US in 2005 trace their ancestry to Mexico; the remainder to Puerto Rico, Cuba, and Central and South America. About 90% of Hispanic/Latino Americans live in metropolitan neighborhoods where language and customs are preserved. Many do not seek complete **acculturation** at the expense of relinquishing their culture. In fact, many Hispanic/Latino Americans have resisted giving up language and cultural traditions and in many parts of Florida, New Mexico, Arizona, Texas, Colorado, and California, the Hispanic/Latino culture is dominant. Bilingual (English-Spanish) signage is used in many government offices and other public accommodations throughout the US, although H.R. 3898 declares English as the official language and mandates that official governmental and legal business be conducted in English.

Asian Americans

China and Japan were major sources of indentured laborers for mining during the California gold rush. Nearly 200,000 Chinese laborers were brought to the western US to build railroads. Anti-Oriental sentiment grew when, despite completion of the railroads, which reduced manpower needs, the rail workers did not return to their home countries. Although some Chinese left the US in response to discriminatory practices, the majority remained and established self-contained Chinatowns in larger cities. Economically, the Chinese developed a robust tourist industry offer-

ing food and commodities and transforming work camp services such as cooking and laundry into lucrative businesses.

The Japanese were hired as field hands and workers for the railroads, canneries, lumber mills, mines, and smelters. They were particularly vulnerable to discrimination because they were scattered over the West, did not form an effective sociopolitical group, and were successful in competing with majority farmers. Anti-Japanese sentiment peaked after the bombing of Pearl Harbor. Approximately 110,000 men, women, and children, both Japanese aliens and Americans of Japanese ancestry, were *interned* in concentration camps. Although released at the end of the war, many Americans of Japanese ancestry lost their farms and businesses while in the camps. The dissolution of the Japanese American communities that had been centered along the West Coast forced those leaving the camps into the mainstream as they sought education and opportunity. While Chinese Americans were limited in their assimilation by the development of Chinatowns, the Japanese were launched into a rapid acculturation process.

By the end of the 20th century, Asians had become the *fastest growing minority* in the US. The 2000 census counted about 1,080,000 Korean Americans and 1,125,000 Vietnamese Americans. Many of the refugees and immigrants were helped to establish themselves by churches and community groups. The children of these families are well assimilated into American culture. Recent immigrants from Southeast Asia include Cambodians, Hmong, Laotians, Thais, Indonesians, Malaysians, and Myanmars.

Native Americans and Alaska Natives

Between 1990 and 2006, the Native American Indian and Alaska Native (NA/AN) populations increased from 2 million to 3.3 million, although some estimates put this figure at 4.4 million including individuals of mixed race. Most of these individuals are members of over 500 federally recognized tribes with distinctive cultures and histories. Contrary to popular stereotypes, approximately one fourth of NA/AN live on federal reservations. The *Bureau of Indian Affairs* encouraged Native Americans to leave the reservations and relocate in urban areas to find economic opportunities. However, poor education and lack of skills have resulted in unemployment. As a result, most urban Native Americans have dispersed rather than remaining in groups or ethnic neighborhoods where they might better be identified and obtain education, health care, and social services.

> Only one fourth of American Indians and Alaska Natives live on reservations, three fourths are living in rural areas and cities.

The *Indian Health Service* and *Tribal Council Health Care Administrations* provide tribes with outpatient and inpatient medical services. Tribes have three options for receiving health care: (1) from the Indian Health Service (IHS), (2) contracting with the IHS to have administrative control and funding transferred to tribal governments, or

> About 600 Indian Health Service and tribal health care facilities are spread over 35 states, most often in rural and isolated areas.

(3) an agreement with the IHS for the tribe to have autonomy in the provision of health care services. For many Native Americans, IHS or tribal health care facilities are the only accessible services. Unfortunately, much of the needed health care services, including specialty care, laboratory, imaging, and pharmacy services are not available through IHS or Tribal facilities and must be purchased under contracts with private sector health providers. While the Indian Health Service and tribal health services are often inadequate and underfunded, they also serve only 56% of the NA/AN population, leaving 44% of this group to receive health services through other means or not at all. Of particular concern are the rural poor and urban groups without access to services.

Health Status and Health Determinants

> What accounts for differences in infant mortality, life expectancy, and cause of death among minority and majority populations?

Infant Mortality

Infant mortality is an important indicator of health, as it reflects maternal health and health care resources. Infant mortality in the US has improved dramatically over the last 100 years. In 1900, 100 in 1000 infants died during the first year of life; in 2000, approximately 6.9 in 1000 infants died. However, the rate did not decline from 2000 to 2005, due in part to differences in infant mortality rates among racial/ethnic groups that have persisted and even increased.

During 2006, the infant mortality rate among African Americans was 2.4 times higher than the rate for whites. Compared with whites, infant mortality was higher for Native Americans and lower for Mexicans and Asians. These differences are due in part to African Americans often having lower incomes, lower education levels, and less access to medical care, all risk factors for infant mortality. The stress of minority group status and racism may also be factors that contribute to infant mortality. However, supportive cultural and family environments among Mexicans contribute to lower infant mortality rates despite lower income, lower education, and lower health insurance levels.

Prevention of preterm birth is critical to lowering infant mortality rates and reducing racial/ethnic disparities. Risk factors associated with infant mortality rates are also risk factors for preterm or low birthweight delivery. In 2007, the preterm birth rate for African American infants was 59% higher than the rate for white infants.

Life Expectancy and Causes of Death

> Why do minority populations in the US have a higher death rate from cancer than whites?

Life expectancy continues to improve but there are significant racial differences. In 2001, white Americans had a life expectancy 5.5 years longer than black Americans. By 2007, this disparity had been reduced to 4.6 years. Life expectancy in the US is 75.3 years overall for males and 80.4 years overall for females. However, among black males, average length of life is 70.2 years and for black females, 77.0 years.

Heart disease and *malignant neoplasia* are the two leading **causes of death** for males and females of all races, except Native Americans. Among Native American males, *unintentional injuries* are second to heart disease and claim more lives than malignancies. Heart disease and stroke are not only leading causes of death in the US but also account for the largest proportion of inequality in life expectancy between whites and blacks, despite the existence of low-cost, highly effective preventive treatment.

Cancer incidence and death rates vary considerably among racial and ethnic groups. For all cancer sites combined, black men have a 14% higher incidence rate and a 34% higher death rate than white men, whereas black women have a 7% lower incidence rate, but a 17% higher death rate than white women. All minority male populations have a greater probability of dying from cancer within 5 years of diagnosis than whites.

Stomach and liver cancer incidence and death rates are twice as high in Asian American/Pacific Islanders compared with whites, reflecting an increased prevalence of chronic infection with *Helicobacter pylori* and hepatitis B and C viruses in this population. Kidney cancer death rates are the highest among American Indians/Alaskan Natives; the higher prevalence of obesity and smoking in this population may contribute to this disparity.

Compared with whites, minority populations are more likely to be diagnosed at a later stage of disease. Decreased cancer survival is associated with being poor and less educated, and lack of access to health care and high-quality screening, leading to later diagnosis and treatment of cancer. Poor quality treatment and higher risk of exposure to occupational and environmental carcinogens also contribute to higher death rates.

Disparities in health status are related to income, education level, insurance status, access to health care, and racism. People who are negatively affected by one or more of these factors are more likely to live in environments with increased exposure to disease and limited access to health care.

Poverty is the biggest determinant of health status and access to care. It is present in all racial groups and negatively affects health, regardless of racial classification. In the US, the risk for sickness, death, unhealthy behaviors, exposure to environmental hazards, reduced access to health care, and poor quality of care increases with decreasing *socioeconomic status*. Income can also influence

Betty is a 55-year-old black female who is obese and a smoker. She works for a small floral business that does not offer health insurance. She lives in a neighborhood that borders the freeway and in the shadow of a coal burning power plant. She cannot afford health insurance and has been unable to see a doctor regularly. She has not had a preventive visit in 20 years and has never had a mammogram. She cares for her three grandchildren with no other family help. Betty had noticed a lump in her breast, but decided to wait to have it evaluated. Six months later, she notices a bloody discharge from her nipple. Betty takes a day off from work without pay and then rides on two city buses to go to the emergency room for evaluation. After the evaluation, she is told that she will need to be seen by an oncologist, have more tests, and then receive information about the most appropriate treatment. Overwhelmed by this information, Betty takes the bus home and decides to wait until she feels worse to go back to the doctor. Is this the best choice for Betty? What are her other options?

health by its direct effect on living standards (e.g., access to better quality food and housing, leisure time activities, and health care services, including preventive care).

In 2009, 14.3% of the U.S. population lived in poverty, up from 13.2% the previous year. In 2008, 34% of black children < 18 were living in poverty compared to 10% of white children. About 41% of families comprised of a female head-of-household and school-age children live below the poverty level, making this the single most impoverished population group.

Uninsured Health Care

In 2006, the estimated number of *uninsured* U.S. residents was 47 million and was projected to reach 52 million by the end of 2010. However, the 2010 estimate did not take into account the effect of across-the-board job loss that began in 2008, which added millions more to the number of uninsured. Millions of Americans continue to be *underinsured* and unable to afford essential medical services. Lack of health insurance is associated with reduced use of preventive services and early medical treatment, leading eventually to more costly care.

Approximately two of every five Hispanic persons and one of every five black persons were classified as uninsured during both 2004 and 2008. Both groups had significantly higher uninsured rates (average rates 42.7% and 22.6%, respectively) for 2004 and 2008 compared with Asians/Pacific Islanders and non-Hispanic whites (average rates 16% and 14.1%, respectively). Hispanics accounted for one third of the uninsured population.

Lack of insurance is most often due to lack of resources. The federal poverty level (FPL) is tied to a relative level of average individual income. The group with the highest rate of uninsurance is the near-poor (those at < 3.0 times FPL), accounting for about half (47.9%) of uninsured adults in the US. Adults who live at or below the FPL have more access to government insurance programs, whereas the *near-poor* do not. During 2008, income for the near-poor ranged from $22,000 to $66,000 per year for a family of four.

People in the near-poor group are often part-time employees and are not provided with health insurance by their employers. In particular, department stores, fast-food chains and restaurants, small businesses and convenience stores, and agriculture often do not provide benefits such as health insurance and pensions. Thus, an individual might hold two or three jobs and not have health

insurance, but have an income too high to qualify for Medicaid or services at a low-income community clinic.

> Hispanics are most likely to be uninsured, followed by Native Americans, black non-Hispanics, and white non-Hispanics. Many uninsured individuals are seasonal or part-time employment, or are unemployed.

Access to Health Care in Minority groups

Access to care is an important factor in determining health status, especially preventive care and timely treatment of illness and injury. The poor do not have access to regular preventive care and often seek care in the emergency room, the most expensive place to receive medical care. The poor often do not seek care when they are ill, and are less likely to get prescription drugs if they do get care because they frequently have to choose between buying food and buying medicine. Thus, their illnesses are often more serious, care is delayed until hospitalization is necessary, and the hospital stay is longer. Rates of preventable hospitalizations increase as incomes decrease. Eliminating these disparities would prevent approximately 1 million hospitalizations and save $6.7 billion in health care costs each year. There also are large racial/ethnic disparities in preventable hospitalizations, with blacks experiencing a rate more than double that of whites.

> Melody is a 25-year-old married female with an infant son. Melody and her husband are both college educated. Melody had trouble finding a job that paid more than the cost of daycare for her young son, so she decided to stay at home with him. Her husband works 35 hours a week at an auto parts store and at night as a waiter. His current wages place the family $100 above the FPL, so they do not qualify for any government assistance. Neither job provides health insurance, so the family has bought the only insurance they can afford, which does not cover any preexisting conditions. Melody has a history of depression and bulimia that had been under good control until the family's financial stresses increased. She is now severely depressed with suicidal ideation. She cannot be admitted to a psychiatric hospital because her insurance will not cover treatment for depression, which is considered a preexisting condition. The family declared bankruptcy a year ago due to medical bills. What is Melody to do?

> José is a 62-year-old Hispanic male who has had a cough, shortness of breath, and fever for the last week. He goes to the emergency room and is told that he has pneumonia. He is given a prescription for an antibiotic and sent home. José goes to the pharmacy to pick up the prescription and is told that the cost is $40. He cannot afford the prescription and goes home. A week later, an ambulance brings José to the emergency room due to worsening shortness of breath and unconsciousness. José is placed on mechanical ventilation and admitted to the ICU. After 3 weeks in the hospital, he is discharged home.

Educational Level

Education is an important determinant of future employment and income. Higher education usually leads to higher socioeconomic status and less poverty. Between 1997 and 2007, the percentage of 16- to 24-year-olds who had a high school degree increased from 89% to 91%. In 2007, a higher percentage of Hispanics did not have a high school degree (21%) than Native Americans/Alaska Natives (19%), blacks (8%), Asians/Pacific Islanders (6%), and whites (5%).

Among Asian subgroups, dropout rates for young adults in the Other Asian subgroup, which includes Cambodians and the Hmong, were 7%, significantly higher than the rates for Indian (1%), Filipino (1%), Korean (1%), Chinese (3%), Japanese (3%), and Vietnamese young adults (4%). Acculturation plays a major role in educational attainment among minorities.

In 2008, 29% of all U.S. adults $\geq$ 25 years old had a least a bachelor's degree, with Asian Americans having the highest percentage at 52%. The rates in other groups were: whites (33%), blacks (20%), Native Americans (15%), and Hispanics (13%).

Teenagers who have children are less likely to complete high school than peers who do not have children. In 2007, the birth rate was 43 births per 1,000 15- to 19-year-old females. The birth rates for Hispanic (82 per 1,000), black (64 per 1,000), and American Indian/Alaska Native (59 per 1,000) teenage females were higher than that of the general population of teenage females. Comparatively, the 2007 birth rate for white teenage females was 27 births per 1,000 females and that for Asians/Pacific Islanders was 17 per 1,000.

Racism

How does racism affect health outcomes?

Racism can have significant implications for overall health outcomes in low-income minority populations due to its effects on social and economic life. Communities that have a disproportionate amount of unequal health outcomes are often racially segregated and have fewer resources, including financial resources. These disadvantages, which contribute to the accumulation of stress over time, have a major influence on health.

Stress, especially when extreme or prolonged, has a significant influence not only on physical health but also on psychological health. It can lead to increased incidence, earlier onset, and greater severity of diseases and illnesses, such as hypertension and depression, as well as early death. Stress from frequent experiences of racism and discrimination, in addition to stressful work and living conditions, life events, and exposure to violence and interpersonal conflicts, may exacerbate racial and ethnic disparities in health outcomes. In looking for ways to reduce stress, people can engage in health-damaging behaviors such as smoking, drinking, physical inactivity, or risky sexual activities.

Sexual Orientation

Sexual orientation, like race and socioeconomic status, is an important sociocultural factor when evaluating health disparity. (See Chapter 21, Health Care Issues Facing Gay, Lesbian, Bisexual, and Transgender individuals).

Recommended Readings

Healthy People: Trends in Racial and Ethnic-Specific Rates for the Health Status Indicators: United States, 1990–98. Statistical Note No. 23, 2002–1237. Washington, DC: Public Health Service; 2000.

Proctor PD, Dalakar J. U.S. Census Bureau, Current Population Reports, pp. 60–219, Poverty in the United States. Washingtion, DC: U.S. Government Printing Office; 2002.

Winters LI, DeBose HL. *New Faces in a Changing America,* 3rd ed. Thousand Oaks, CA: Sage Publications; 2002.

Online Resources

CDC Health Disparities and Inequalities Report, *MMWR,* January 14, 2011. Current population statistics. Available at http://www.census.gov

Racism: Combating the Root Cause of Health Disparities: Grant Makers Health Issue Focus, April 19, 2010. Available from http://www.consumer-healthfdn.org/~conshfdn/images/uploads/files/issuefocusracism.pdf

Aud S. Status and Trends in the Education of Racial and Ethnic Groups, U.S. Dept of Education, July 2010: Available from http://nces.ed.gov/pubs2010/2010015.pdf

Review Questions

1. While health status for the U.S. population in general has shown substantial improvement, minorities have typically not enjoyed the same improvements. Among the following, the most likely reason for this disparity is
   A. a combination of factors including risk, access to care, and discrimination.
   B. better quality care for the wealthy and minimal health care for the poor.
   C. biological inferiority of patients in minority groups.
   D. discrimination against all but the wealthy and the insured.
   E. poor use of services by minorities who do not avail themselves of health care.

2. Among Native American males, the major cause of death is
   A. accidents.
   B. gunshot wounds.
   C. homicide.
   D. liver disease.
   E. suicide.

3. At the end of the 20th century, the fastest growing minority population was composed of
   A. Africans.
   B. Arabs.
   C. Asians.
   D. Native Americans.
   E. South Americans.

4. Discrimination is most often directed against minority groups
   A. from countries that were once enemies of the US.
   B. from underdeveloped countries.
   C. that do not contribute to the economy through gainful employment.
   D. that do not speak English.
   E. that were brought to the US as sources of cheap labor.

5. Native Americans and Alaska Natives
   A. are advantaged by the numerous tax-supported health and social services programs available to them.
   B. are encouraged not to work and to remain on reservations.
   C. are generally responsible for their health care since the majority are not covered by the Indian Health Service.
   D. have access to comprehensive health care through a nationwide system of Indian Health Service clinics.
   E. rely almost exclusively on their own health care system of healers and ceremonies.

Key to review questions: p. 407

20 Sexuality and Sexual Disorders

Charles P. Samenow, MD, MPH, and Nancy Eklund, MD

- What are the phases of the human sexual response?
- What is the most common sexual concern patients discuss with their physician?
- How do specific health situations affect sexuality?
- How do age and culture affect sexual health?
- How are sexual orientation and sexual identity defined?
- What are the major sexual disorders?

Sexual Health

Sexual health is defined as a state of physical, mental, and social well-being in relation to sexuality. It implies a positive and respectful approach to sexuality, the enhancement of life and personal relationships, and the possibility of having pleasurable and safe sexual experiences that are free of coercion, discrimination, and violence. Reproductive or sexual health services should provide basic information about biological and psychological aspects of sexual development, human reproduction, and the variety of sexual behaviors, dysfunctions, and disorders. The provision of such services requires health care professionals who possess positive attitudes toward sexuality, provide opportunities for discussion of sexual matters, and show understanding and objectivity in providing advice, information, and treatment.

Human Sexual Response

What are the phases of the human sexual response?

The human **sexual response** includes a cycle of *desire*, *excitement*, *plateau*, *orgasm*, and *resolution* phases.

- The *desire phase* involves spontaneous thoughts, fantasies, and biological urges to self-stimulate or initiate sexual activities with a partner.
- The *excitement (arousal) phase* is induced by sensory stimuli or mental imagery. Physical response includes male penile erection and female vaginal lubrication, erect nipples in both genders, and engorged clitoris and testicles. Respiration increases up to 60 breaths per minute and heart rate up to 180 beats per minute, and blood pressure may rise 40–80 mm Hg systolic and 20–50 mm Hg diastolic. In males, arteriolar dilation causes penile engorgement and obstruction of venous outflow. Engorgement is limited by the fascial sheath, causing rigidity. Other responses include scrotal engorgement, testicular retraction, and pre-ejaculatory secretion by the Cowper's glands. In females, vasoconstriction elevates the uterus, and increases the depth of the vagina, the upper two thirds of which expands while the lower third becomes engorged and narrowed.
- With the *plateau phase*, arousal levels off; it may be of varying duration depending on the experience of the individual.
- The *orgasmic phase* is a brief physiological response involving involuntary motor activity. Ejaculation occurs in males, as muscular contractions of the prostate, urethra, and perineum propel seminal fluid through the urethral opening. Up to 15 vaginal and perineal muscular contractions occur in females.
- In the *resolution phase*, physiological parameters return to normal. In males, orgasm is impossible until after completion of the *refrac-

tory period, which lasts minutes to hours depending on various factors, including age.

There are important differences between men and women regarding the sexual response cycle. A "new view of women's sexual problems" is based on a *circular model* of sexual response for women and postulates that the sexual response cycle differs for men and women. For example, sexual desire is not always necessary for nor does not always occur before arousal in women. Females are also capable of multiple successive orgasms. This has important implications on how practitioners view normal female sexual response.

Common Sexual Concerns of Patients

> What is the most common sexual concern patients discuss with their physician?

While patients may present their concerns and problems explicitly, in many cases these concerns may arise only when an astute clinician listens to the subtext of the patient's dialogue. Common concerns include:

- Am I normal? How do I compare?
- Sexual identity: lifestyle, orientation, preference
- Psychosexual development: over the life cycle
- Reproduction: infertility, family planning, contraception, pregnancy, abortion
- Sexual desire, satisfaction, and dysfunctions; couple's differences in desire; problems with vaginal lubrication, erections, orgasm, pain
- Sexual changes due to age, physical disability, medical illness, treatment
- Sexual trauma resulting from molestation, incest, rape
- Safe sex practices: HIV/AIDS, STIs
- Paraphilias and sexual compulsions

Situation-Specific Sexuality Issues

Contraception

Determining a method of **contraception** depends upon (a) type and frequency of intercourse (a

Table 20.1. Advantages and disadvantages of different types of contraception

Type of Contraception	Examples/Class	Advantages	Disadvantages
Hormonal	Progesterone implants/injections	Long Lasting Safer in hypertension and diabetes	Delayed return of fertility Irregular bleeding
Combined Pill	Estrogen/ Progesterone	Protects against cancers and osteoporosis Regulates period No long-term effects	Contraindicated in women >35 with smoking, hypertension, or diabetes Side effects
Mini Pill	Progesterone only	Good for women with contra-indications to combined pill	Must be taken at the same time each day
Condom (Male or Female)	Barrier	Easy to use Helps prevent STI's	Dulling of sensation Potential for failure
Intrauterine Device (IUD)	Barrier	No effect on hormones Works immediately	Risk of pelvic inflammatory disease
Diaphragm/Cap	Barrier	Inserted prior to sex No hormones	Can cause cystitis Can have failure
Rhythm/Fertility Awareness	Natural	No side effects	Restrictions on timing of sex

woman having infrequent intercourse may prefer a barrier to a continuous method); (b) number and type of partners (a woman with several partners is better protected using condoms and spermicide with oral contraceptives than oral contraceptives alone); (c) health history of the partner (the female partner of a man with genital herpes should use condoms rather than a diaphragm); (d) timing of a future desired pregnancy (a barrier method may be preferred to a long-term method such as injectable progesterone); (e) number of previous pregnancies (an IUD or relatively permanent contraception such as tubal ligation may be appropriate for a female in a mutually monogamous relationship); (f) degree of discomfort with touching one's body (oral contraceptives may be preferred to a diaphragm); and (g) concurrent medical conditions (oral contraceptives may be contraindicated).

Pregnancy

During early pregnancy, *fatigue, nausea,* or *breast tenderness* may interfere with sexual desire. In the second trimester, bothersome symptoms decrease, but issues of *body image* often arise. Some women feel unattractive, others feel more sexual. Some men are concerned about "hurting the baby" and avoid intercourse. Late in pregnancy, conditions may require abstaining from vaginal intercourse. However, in most cases, other forms of sexual intimacy are possible.

The discomfort of the healing perineum after episiotomy can interfere with resumption of sexual activity after childbirth. Sleep deprivation caused by an infant who awakens during the night can decrease libido.

Some women find breastfeeding to be sexually stimulating; others feel ambivalent about their partner touching or stimulating their lactating breasts. Marital strain can occur when a husband feels replaced by an infant who receives much of the mother's attention. Conflict can arise over the distribution of infant-related chores or the financial pressures of an expanded family.

Chronic Illness

How do specific health situations affect sexuality?

Medical conditions associated with changes in sexual functioning include: arthritis/joint disease, diabetes mellitus, endocrine problems, injury to the autonomic nervous system by surgery or radiation, liver or renal failure, mood disorders (including depression, anxiety, and panic), multiple sclerosis, peripheral neuropathy, radical pelvic surgery, respiratory disorders (e.g., COPD), spinal cord injury, and vascular disease.

Supportive therapy may be needed for patients experiencing physical limitations, changes in physical appearance or sexual functioning. Information about reproductive options such as electro-ejaculation is important for men with spinal cord injury. Patients may be embarrassed about appliances such as catheters, ostomies, artificial limbs, or about surgical scars. A postmastectomy patient's body image and relationship with her partner help determine whether reconstruction or a prosthesis should be considered. Antihypertensive drugs frequently cause erectile dysfunction, and although alcohol, sedatives, and narcotic analgesics may reduce inhibitions, they may also interfere with normal physiological functioning.

Infertility

Infertility and difficulty getting pregnant can cause conflict and concern. Monitoring, scheduling intercourse, taking medications, and undergoing testing are stressful. Respecting concerns, informing, counseling, and minimizing blame and guilt are essential components of managing infertility. Most couples have success using "low tech" options with a minority requiring *in vitro* fertilization. Success rates depend on type of therapy and age of the partners. Two thirds of couples being treated for infertility will conceive a baby.

Fertility treatment options include:
- *Fertility Drugs*: Clomiphene, letrozol (ovulation induction), anastrozol (ovulation induction), and gonadotropins.
- *Surgical Infertility Treatments*: Hysterosalpinogram (HSG) to determine blockage of the fallopian tubes followed by laproscopic surgery, if needed.
- *Intrauterine Insemination*: Artificial insemination, where sperm are placed into the uterus.
- *In Vitro Fertilization (IVF):* Fertility drugs are used to produce eggs. Eggs are removed,

inseminated outside of the female body until fertilization occurs, and then placed back into the uterus.

Termination of Pregnancy

Unplanned pregnancy is most common at the extremes of a woman's reproductive life. While political, religious, and ethical controversy surrounds this issue, providing information about alternatives is essential, even if that means referral to another provider. Familiarity with community resources and separating personal bias from the care of the patient are fundamental to good care. Current options include the "*morning after pill*," a high dose of oral contraceptives taken within 72 hours after sexual intercourse; an *abortifacient* like mifepristone, methotrexate, or misoprosol (to induce spontaneous abortion), and *vacuum aspiration*. *Adoption* should be considered as well.

Sexually Transmitted Infections (STI)

Common **sexually transmitted infections (STIs),** usually treatable with antibiotics, include gonorrhea, syphilis, and chlamydia. *Viruses* that cause STIs include human immunodeficiency virus (HIV), human papillomavirus (HPV), cytomegalovirus (CMV), and herpes simplex virus (HSV). Some strains of human papillomavirus have been associated with genital warts and with cervical cancer. Currently, it is recommended that the HPV vaccine be administered to all females between the ages of 9 and 26. For optimal results, the vaccine should be administered before the individual becomes sexually active. Public debate about immunizing young, prepubescent girls against an STI is ongoing as a primarily social rather than medical issue, especially in states like Texas where immunization has been mandated. Other sexually transmitted conditions such as trichomonas, molluscum contagiosum, pubic lice, scabies, and monilial vaginitis are bothersome, but rarely cause serious long-term problems. *Bacterial vaginosis*, frequently caused by *Gardnerella, Haemophilus*, or group B streptococcus, has been implicated in premature labor and small-for-gestational-age infants.

Prevention of STI requires candid communication between patient and partner and effective protection. Condoms, although not perfect, provide the best mechanical protection when combined with an appropriate spermicide. Latex gloves, finger cots, or condoms can be used for manual stimulation. Dental dams can be used during oral sex. In cases of latex allergy, non-latex skins can be applied over or under other coverings depending on which partner is allergic.

Least risky behaviors include gentle kissing, mutual masturbation, fellatio with a condom, and non-shared sex toys. *More risky behaviors* include oral sex on a male (fellatio) without a condom; oral sex on a female (cunnilingus) without a dental dam; and vaginal or anal intercourse using a condom and spermicide and withdrawing prior to ejaculation. *Most risky behaviors* include anal or vaginal intercourse without a condom, with or without ejaculation, and fellatio without a condom and with ejaculation. Correct techniques for condom use should be taught and reasons for not using condoms discussed. Role playing situations in which patients find themselves confronted by a partner who does not want to use a condom is helpful, particularly for adolescents.

Post-Exposure Prophylaxis (PEP) may be available for individuals exposed to HIV. Candidates are individuals who are HIV-negative, but have been in contact with a HIV positive individual, or an individual of unknown status in high prevalence areas. Such individuals must have engaged in a high risk sexual behavior and present for treatment within 72 hours of exposure. The course of therapy, lasting 28 days, usually involves 2 or 3 classes of antiretroviral therapy. Individuals who repeatedly engage in high risk behaviors are not good candidates for this treatment.

Emerging data also demonstrates that antiretrovirals can be effective in reducing the transmission of HIV in serodiscordant couples and high risk populations. This is known as pre-exposure prophylaxis (PrEP).

Age and Culture Specific Sexuality Issues

How do age and culture affect sexual health?

Childhood and Adolescence

Adolescent sexual behavior often includes masturbation and non-coital stimulation with partners of the same or opposite gender. Adolescents today engage in intercourse at an earlier age than their parents. By age 15, the majority of African American males and more than a quarter of African American females and Caucasian males and females have had coitus. By age 18, most adolescents have had sexual experiences including intercourse. Same-sex behavior in adolescence is not uncommon and does not necessarily predict future sexual orientation or behavior.

Adolescents know little about the risks of not using contraceptives or the types of contraceptives available. About 35% do not use contraceptives during their first sexual experience. Unfortunately, 20% of all pregnancies occur during the first two months of sexual activity. Adolescents are also at increased risk for STIs for biological (lower estrogen, immature lining of the cervix) or psychosocial (risky behaviors, embarrassment about contraception) reasons.

Many adolescents avoid consultation on sexual issues for fear of parental disapproval. Some states require parental permission while others allow treatment of minors for possible STIs without parental permission.

> When interviewing adolescents, use language/terms appropriate to their developmental age and provide a safe, non-judgmental environment to talk about sexual issues. This may involve time without a parent present.

Aging

Although sexual desire does not necessarily diminish with age, physiological function does change (see Chapter 22, Geriatric Health and Successful Aging). Postmenopausal women not taking *hormone replacement therapy* experience decreased vaginal lubrication, mucosal thinning, diminished vaginal expansion, and vasocongestion. Older men require longer to achieve penile erection and, if interrupted, may not gain full tumescence; ejaculation is less intense and forceful. Women typically cease to reproduce at *menopause*, but men have been reported to reproduce into their 90s. While older couples do not necessarily have less satisfac-

tion from intimate experiences, perceived diminution in function may inhibit activity. Medical conditions, medications, and physiological change can interfere with sexual functioning at any age, but these problems become more prevalent with age. Other issues for older persons include embarrassment, family disapproval, lack of privacy, and the illness or death of a partner. Given that older adults continue to engage in sexual practices, it is important to remember safer sex counseling and STI screening (including HIV) in this population.

Social and Cultural Expectations

Every culture has *norms* regarding sexual behavior. Sex may be acceptable only for procreation or only after a postmenstrual ritual cleansing bath. Extramarital sex or polygamy may/may not be acceptable. Some religions prohibit contraception unless the mother's life is at risk. In some cultures, unwed mothers are accepted; in other cultures, they are ostracized or killed. In 1999, the World Association of Sexual Health adopted a Declaration of Sexual Health that included:

- the right to sexual freedom, excluding all forms of sexual coercion, exploitation, and abuse;
- the right to sexual autonomy and safety of the sexual body;
- the right to sexual pleasure, which is a source of physical, psychological, and spiritual well-being;
- the right to sexual information – generated through unencumbered yet scientifically ethical inquiry;
- the right to comprehensive sexuality education; and
- the right to sexual health care, which should be available for prevention and treatment of all sexual concerns, problems, and disorders.

The declaration is not meant to impose upon cultural traditions, but certain customs, such as female genital circumcision, may be challenged under such a declaration.

Sexual Orientation and Identity

> How are sexual orientation and sexual identity defined?

Sex is the designation given at birth based on observed anatomy (genitalia) or biology (e.g., chromosomes).

Gender denotes the role assigned by society based on behavior and expression. **Sexual orientation** denotes the physical, romantic, or emotional attraction to another person (homosexuality, heterosexuality, bisexuality). **Sexual identity** describes the person's subjective experience of sexual orientation. Sexual behavior does not always indicate orientation or identity since individuals may be involved in same-sex activity, but not identify themselves as homosexual. However, the majority of people are consistent with self-identification, behavior, and attraction throughout their adult lives.

Homosexuality and Bisexuality

Most individuals develop a behavioral preference for the same or opposite sex partners during adolescence. While neuroscience and genetic research suggest a role for genes and neurobiological factors in determining sexual orientation, the actual determinants of sexual orientation remain unclear.

About 40% of males will have at least one *homosexual experience* leading to orgasm in their lifetime, but only about 10% of men practice homosexuality at any given time, and about 4% are exclusively homosexual for >10 years. **Homosexuality** appears to be less prevalent in women than men, but women are less genitally focused than men, and definitions related to the number of homosexually induced orgasms may not accurately reflect a person's perception of his or her own sexual orientation. Although 10–13% of women have had sexual experiences with other women, only 3% of all women describe themselves as lesbian.

Persons who identify themselves as **bisexual** are sexually attracted to members of both sexes. Although only a few people describe themselves as bisexual, many members of both genders have had sexual experiences with members of the same and the opposite sex in their lifetime.

Transgender

Transgender individuals feel an incongruity between their anatomic gender and their gender identity, often describing their problem as being "trapped in the wrong body." For some, this realization occurs during childhood; for others, it occurs during adolescence or later. **Gender dysphoria** refers to the discomfort or unhappiness experienced in the biologically assigned gender role. Some individuals choose to undergo hormone replacement or surgical correction; others live their lives in the opposite role without any anatomic changes. The term, **transsexual**, has been used to refer to an individual who desires gender-changing procedures to acquire a physical appearance consistent with their gender identity (see Chapter 21, Health Care Issues Facing Gay, Lesbian, Bisexual, and Transgender Individuals).

Sexual Disorders

> What are the major sexual disorders?

There are five categories of sexual disturbance: sexual response dysfunction; sexual pain; gender identity disturbances; paraphilia; and disorders due to a medical condition (see Table 20.2).

Disorders of Desire

Decreased libido (**hypoactive sexual desire**) is the most common complaint of women and may also be experienced by men. Decreased libido may be person-specific (a particular partner) or global, or reflect a discrepancy between partners' expectations of frequency or activity. Etiologies include dissatisfaction with a relationship, underlying medical or psychiatric problems, medications, substance abuse, stressors, and normal differences in desire. Sudden change in desire unrelated to a specific stress suggests an underlying medical or psychiatric problem. **Sexual aversion** is characterized by fear or repulsion of engaging in sexual activity in excess of normal fluctuations in sexual desire.

Disorders of Arousal

Erectile dysfunction is the inability to attain and maintain a penile erection sufficient to permit sat-

Table 20.2. Sexual and gender identity disorders: Definitions and estimated frequency

Disorder	Estimated Frequency	Definition
Sexual desire disorders Hypoactive desire disorder	20% of adults	Reduced desire for sexual contact or total aversion to sexual activity
Sexual aversion disorder	Unknown	
Sexual arousal disorders Female sexual arousal disorder	33% married females	Inability to attain or maintain sexual arousal sufficient to initiate or complete sexual acts
Male erectile disorder	2–4% < 35 years old 75% > 80 years old	
Orgasmic disorders Female orgasmic disorder	5% adult females	Excessive orgasmic delay, absence of orgasmic response, or premature orgasm
Male orgasmic disorder	4% adult males	
Premature ejaculation	30% adult males	
Sexual pain disorders Dyspareunia	Unknown	Pain in sexual organs during sexual activity that interferes with or prevents sexual activity
Vaginismus	Unknown	
Paraphilia Exhibitionism Fetishism Frotteurism Pedophilia Masochism/sadism Transvestic fetishism Voyeurism	Unknown	Deviant arousal patterns and object choices
Gender identity disorders	Unknown	Discomfort with or nonacceptance of primary sexual identification and desire to change sexual identification to the opposite gender
Sexual dysfunction due to medical conditions	Common	Variable sexual dysfunction resulting from identified medical conditions or treatment

Source: Sadock VA. Normal Human Sexuality and Sexual Dysfunction. In Sadock BJ, Sadock VA (Eds.), *Kaplan and Sadock's Comprehensive Textbook of Psychiatry*, 7th ed. Philadelphia, PA: Lippincott Williams and Wilkins; 2000.

isfactory intercourse. Up to 30% of men with erectile dysfunction have no identifiable organic basis for the problem. Differentiation of *psychogenically* based erectile dysfunction from *organically* based erectile dysfunction is critical to appropriate treatment. Individuals with psychogenic erectile dysfunction often have spontaneous nocturnal erections whereas those with organic etiologies do not. History and physical examination should identify medications (e.g., antihypertensive or antidepressant agents) or medical conditions (e.g., diabetes) that might cause dysfunction.

Vascular studies can uncover arterial or venous outflow problems. Oral medications that increase blood flow provide effective treatment in many cases. Surgical intervention may be necessary in more severe cases. Phosphodiesterase inhibitors such as sildenafil (tradename Viagra®) are usually effective. Endocrinological evaluation may indicate that administration of testosterone or alpha adrenergic receptor antagonists, penile self-injections, or use of urethral suppositories containing a vasodilator would be helpful. Vacuum pumps that provide negative pressure to obtain an erection that is maintained by an elastic band at the base of the penis, and various malleable or rigid penile implants are other options.

Non-organically based, or combined, erectile dysfunction in the male and disorders of arousal in the female often benefit from **sensate focus therapy**. This therapy includes having couples engage in progressive, sensual touching exercises with focus on the patient's sexual sensations. *Performance anxiety* is removed by initially excluding intercourse from the exercises.

Disorders of Orgasm

Rapid ejaculation (RE) is defined as ejaculation without sufficient voluntary influence over timing. For some men, ejaculation is considered rapid if it occurs within the first 2 minutes of vaginal intercourse; for others, it may be defined as ejaculation before 10 or more minutes of vaginal intercourse. Treatments to control the timing of ejaculation include the *"stop and start" technique* (repeated cycles of withdrawal of stimulation before ejaculation becomes inevitable) and the *"squeeze technique"* (application of pressure below the coronal ridge or at the base of the penis for 5 to 10 seconds until the urge to ejaculate ceases).

Men generally find vaginal intercourse an effective method of stimulation. Intercourse, however, is not the most effective means of stimulation for the female because the vagina is less sensitive to stimulation than the clitoris. Consultation for women who cannot achieve satisfactory orgasm includes learning direct methods of clitoral stimulation either by the patient or the partner, or use of appliances such as vibrators.

Psychological issues contributing to disorders of arousal include conflicts between an individual's level of sexual interest and perceived social "norms" (e.g., "nice girls don't have sex for orgasm"). Sometimes couples describe a change in their ability to "let go" when their role changes from date to spouse or from partner to parent. Sensate focus exercises may have the benefit of increasing the frequency of orgasm since less emphasis is placed on achieving it.

Sexual Pain Disorders

The **sexual pain disorders** affect women primarily. Common disorders are dyspareunia and vaginismus. Onset may follow sexual trauma or gynecological surgery, or have other physical or psychological origins. Discomfort during intercourse, **dyspareunia**, can occur at all times or only in certain situations or with certain partners. Discomfort due to inadequate foreplay, causing pain because of insufficient lubrication, must be differentiated from pain on deep penetration, or overt **vaginismus** (the inability to allow any object into the vagina due to involuntary muscular contractions).

Pain on intromission may be due to vaginal infection, irritation, anatomic abnormalities, changes resulting from irradiation, inelasticity, or trauma. Pain on deep penetration can be caused by infection or other conditions such as endometriosis. True vaginismus, or involuntary spasm of the perineal muscles, can be treated with graduated vaginal accommodators to a point where intercourse is possible. **Sexual trauma** must be ruled out as an etiological factor in any case of dyspareunia, but especially in suspected vaginismus.

Paraphilias

Paraphilia is defined by the presence of intense sexually arousing fantasies or sexual urges or behaviors to induce sexual excitement that occur over at least 6 months (see Table 20.3 for a list of common paraphilias). Many individuals who have thoughts or fantasies involving unusual settings, different partners, or bondage are concerned about being "abnormal in addition to differentiating between action and thought." It is also essential to distinguish between occasional behaviors and behavior that is repetitive/necessary for sexual arousal, and between consent versus non-consent by the partner.

Hypersexuality has been described as an addiction to sexual activity that temporarily allevi-

Table 20.3. Common paraphilias	
Paraphilia	**Behavior**
Exhibitionism	Genital exposure to an unsuspecting person or stranger
Fetishism	Use of non-living objects (e.g., pieces of apparrel of the other sex) for arousal
Frotteurism	Touching and rubbing against a non-consenting person
Pedophilia	Attraction to or behavior involving a prepubescent boy or girl
Masochism	Intense fantasies, urges, or behaviors, whether real or simulated, of being humiliated or made to suffer
Sadism	Arousal is achieved from the real psychological or physical suffering of the victim
Transvestic fetishism	Cross-dressing by a male in women's attire that produces sexual arousal
Voyeurism	Arousal while viewing nudity or sexual activity by others who have not given permission

ates anxiety, loneliness, and depression. According to some authorities, when the need to have sexual experiences interferes with normal activities and relationships, the condition should be viewed as similar to any addiction. Hypersexual individuals often feel unworthy and ashamed. Hypersexuality can present within the context of a committed relationship, as extramarital activity, or as a primary mode of sexual relations.

Potential Changes in Classification of Sexual Disorders – DSM-5

Definitions of "normal" vs. "abnormal" sexual behavior change across cultures and time. For example, homosexuality was considered a sexual disorder until 1973 when it was eliminated from the Diagnostic and Statistical Manual (DSM) of Mental Disorders. The American Psychiatric Association is considering the following changes to the classification of sexual disorders for DSM-5:

- The DSM-5 may distinguish *Paraphilia* from *Paraphilic Disorder*. Paraphilic Disorder will be reserved for individuals who present with distress/impairment related to a specific paraphilia.
- The DSM-5 will distinguish those paraphilias that involve non-consenting individuals (voy-

eurism, exhibitionism, and sexual sadism). Diverse sexual practices that do not cause distress, impairment, or harm will not be considered mental disorders but, rather, normal variants of sexual practice.

- A new diagnosis, *Hypersexual Disorder*, will be considered to represent individuals who engage in problematic or compulsive sexual behaviors. *Sexual Aversion Disorder* may be removed from the new DSM and reclassified under anxiety disorders as a specific phobia.
- Gender Identity Disorder may be replaced with *Gender Dysphoria*. Transgender advocates have argued that gender identity is more biological than psychological and that the term "Gender Identity Disorder" is stigmatizing.
- In women, hypoactive sexual disorder will most likely be changed to sexual interest/arousal disorder to reduce inflated estimates of disorders in women due to partner libido mismatching or cultural biases.

Sexual Exploitation

Rape is a legal rather than medical term. It is defined as penile penetration of the vagina without mutual consent or with a person who is less than a certain age (**statutory rape**). Although rape involves a sexual act, it is primarily an expression of violence or power (see Chapter 26, Interpersonal Violence).

Incest

It is estimated that one in four girls and one in five boys experience sexual abuse. Most perpetrators are known to the victim. **Incest** between siblings or child relatives is more common but less often reported than incest perpetrated by an adult relative. In some families, only one child may be victimized; in other families, many children may be abused. Although most sexually abused children are between 8 and 12 years of age, younger children, including infants, have been assaulted. Some children experience incest as a one time event; others may experience it on an ongoing basis for years.

Long-term *sequelae of incest* include difficulty establishing intimate relationships, sexual dysfunction during adulthood, and increased genitourinary complaints in later life. *Dissociation* is a common coping mechanism used by children while being assaulted. As a result, some victims never have memories of the events; others remember them years later either spontaneously or during the course of psychotherapy. While the effects of incest and child sexual abuse can be extremely traumatic, it is important to note that most individuals with trauma histories are able to live fulfilling, stable, and healthy lives.

Sexual Harassment

The legal definition of **sexual harassment** in the workplace includes sexual advances or conduct that interferes with the employee's working environment, performance, or conditions of employment. A study of federal employees found that 44% of women and 19% of men had felt sexually harassed at work during the preceding 24 months. Although regulations exist to prevent sexual harassment in the workplace, it is often subtle and difficult to prove. Most cases involve male perpetrators and female victims, although successful suits have been brought by men against women. Recent court cases have broadened the definition of sexual harassment to include unwanted sexual contact between members of the same sex.

Sexual Abuse in Intimate Relationships

Women who experience physical violence in an intimate relationship often experience being forced to have sex against their wishes. Before age 15, a majority of girls report that their first intercourse experiences were non-voluntary. Women in such situations may be at risk if they leave the relationship precipitously. Although reported less commonly, men can have similar experiences and are also at risk. Couples in a violent relationship should not be referred for conjoint counseling since the victim may not disclose information at all or the batterer may retaliate physically or emotionally if the victim does disclose. Referring the victim and the perpetrator individually to counseling services is imperative.

Prostitution

Prostitution involves the exchange of sex with another person for the explicit purpose of receiving immediate payment. Female prostitution for heterosexual activity is more prevalent than male prostitution, which is usually homosexual. Prostitution puts the individual at risk of sexually transmitted disease, assault or injury by customers, exploitation by pimps or other agents of organized crime, involvement of minors, and arrest for illegal activity.

Recommended Readings

Leiblum SR. *Principles and Practice of Sex Therapy,* 4th ed. New York: Guilford Press; 2006.

Sadock VA. Normal Sexuality and Sexual Dysfunction. In BJ Sadock, VA Sadock (Eds.), *Kaplan and Sadock's Comprehensive Textbook of Psychiatry,* 7th ed. Philadelphia, PA: Lippincott Williams and Wilkins; 2000.

Strong B, De Vault C, Sayad BW. *Core Concepts in Human Sexuality.* London: Mayfield; 1996.

Review Questions

1. Among the general population, the percent of males who have had at least one homosexual experience leading to orgasm is closest to

    A. 20%.
    B. 30%.
    C. 40%.
    D. 50%.
    E. 60%.

2. A man reveals that he sometimes rubs his chest with his wife's underwear in order to feel sexually aroused. This behavior is consistent with
    A. exhibitionism.
    B. fetishism.
    C. frotteurism.
    D. gender identity disorder.
    E. voyeurism.

3. Pedophilia is an example of which of the following sexual disorders?
    A. Gender identity disorder
    B. Obsessive-compulsive disorder
    C. Paraphilia
    D. Sexual arousal disorder
    E. Sexual desire disorder

Key to review questions: p. 407

21 Health Care Issues Facing Gay, Lesbian, Bisexual, and Transgender Individuals

David W. Pantalone, PhD, Douglas C. Haldeman, PhD, and Christopher R. Martell, PhD

- What is the difference between sexual orientation, sexual behavior, and sexual identity?
- Why are there limited research data on the health care problems of GLBT individuals?
- What are the major areas of GLBT health care concerns?
- What are the potential risk factors for cancer among GLBT individuals?
- What are the rates of anxiety and depression among GLBT individuals?
- What are the guidelines for providing informed care for GLBT individuals?

People who are sexual minorities (i.e., gay, lesbian, bisexual, or transgender – GLBT) face the same health care problems as the population in general. However, some GLBT individuals have additional, unique health concerns resulting from the societal discrimination they face because of their sexual minority status. These health issues may be the direct result of discrimination (e.g., lack of access or poor clinical care, physical assault via hate crimes) or result indirectly from psychological stress associated with being GLBT (e.g., realistic fears about coming out, societal messages about the immorality of same-sex sexual activity). The competent, ethical provision of physical and mental health care services to GLBT patients requires a basic understanding of these unique stressors as well as their health consequences. Empirical data indicate that many GLBT individuals have had negative experiences with health care providers in the past. Thus, it is critical that current providers deliver culturally-competent medical care in a professional and respectful manner.

Sexual Orientation and Sexual Identity

What is the difference between sexual orientation, sexual behavior, and sexual identity?

Sexual orientation is the most widely accepted term for referring to the way in which an individual defines his or her sexual identity. Examples of sexual orientation are "opposite sex" or "heterosexual," and "same sex" or "lesbian," "gay," or "bisexual." (Note that transgender individuals may have a sexual orientation that is same sex or opposite sex. Gender identity and sexual orientation are independent constructs). Sexual orientation is typically viewed more favorably than terms such as "sexual preference" or "gay lifestyle," which are seen as invalidating or trivializing an individual's sexual identity. It is also important to note that **sexual identity** and **sexual behavior** are not synonymous. Behavior is what people do, while identity is how people view themselves and how they represent themselves to the world. For example, a woman may engage in same-sex sex-

Historically, homosexuality had been included in the roster of mental illnesses, reflecting prevailing beliefs and biases on the part of society and the health care establishment. However, in 1973, the American Psychiatric Association removed homosexuality from the *Diagnostic and Statistical Manual of Mental Disorders* (DSM), and all other major medical associations followed suit. A vast literature supports the fact that there is no difference in any number of indicators of mental, emotional, or psychological adjustment between nonclinical samples of heterosexual and GLBT individuals.

ual behaviors but not identify as lesbian, or may self-identify as lesbian without engaging in same-sex sexual behaviors.

Despite the general reduction in cultural prejudice against GLBT individuals over the past 35 years, prejudice still persists in numerous social arenas. GLBT individuals who have internalized negative attitudes about their sexual orientation from their families or religious or other cultural groups may seek to change their sexual orientation through, for example, psychotherapy. Such "reparative therapies" have no credibility among mainstream mental health organizations given their astounding lack of success and potential to actually harm individuals seeking their services. These treatments are viewed by most providers as scientifically unfounded and professionally inappropriate attempts to oppress sexual minority individuals.

Many providers are uncomfortable working with patients whose cultural background (race, ethnicity, sexual orientation) is different from their own. As a result, a provider may avoid asking sensitive questions that are most important to the patient. Providers should become aware of this reluctance and strive to act in the best interests of the patient. In order to be respectful of patients who may be GLBT, providers should assess behavior and identity separately and use appropriately inclusive language when questioning patients. For example, it would be heterosexist (assuming heterosexuality universally) to say to every female patient, "Do you have a boyfriend?" and inclusive to ask, "Are you in a significant relationship right now?" Also, when a patient reports sexual activity, one could ask, "Were your partners men, women, or both?" in order to identify people who engage in same-sex sexual behavior but who do not necessarily identify as GLBT.

Why are there limited research data on the health care problems of GLBT individuals?

Epidemiologic research on GLBT populations, as hidden minority groups, is limited because large-scale surveys typically omit explicit questions about sexual orientation. Thus, the field lacks estimates of the size of the GLBT population overall (there is no sexual orientation question in the U.S. Census) as well as for relevant health and mental health factors. Because of the relatively small pro-

portion of GLBT people and the societal **stigma** attached to identifying as such, any data yielded by population-based studies must be viewed as an under-representation of the true figures. The most widely accepted prevalence figures for GLBT individuals range from 1.4% to 4.6% among women and 2.8% to 15.8% among men. Also, it is misleading to group together all GLBT individuals or, for example, to assume homogeneity within the "L" or "G" categories. It is more accurate to speak about GLBT communities (in plural) since there is substantial diversity in cultural background, ethnic or racial identity, age, education, income, place of residence, and many other characteristics. Individuals who engage in same-sex romantic or sexual experiences may not identify as GLBT (especially young people whose sexual orientation is not yet solidified) and would, therefore, be lost to researchers asking questions about this population in particular.

Patients who identify as GLBT can vary in the degree to which sexual orientation is central to their identity. Many GLBT individuals have other identity labels that they feel are more definitive such as being Latino, being a mother, or being Christian. Some young GLBT people may eschew identity labels altogether. To the extent that it is relevant to patient care, providers are encouraged to ask GLBT patients about their identity and its importance, and not make assumptions.

Major Health Care Concerns for GLBT Communities

What are the major areas of GLBT health care concerns?

The political climate of the early 21st century put a chill on funding for GLBT research, thus making this question more difficult to answer. Nevertheless, except for HIV/AIDS, data suggest that GLBT individuals do not generally experience any health-related concerns at rates different from heterosexuals, including alcoholism and drug abuse. When health disparities are seen, factors such as low socioeconomic status (SES), lack of connection with the health care system, and dealing with societal reactions to one's sexual minority identity all appear to contribute. For GLBT individuals, good health, fewer illnesses, and positive health behaviors have been shown to be associated with affirmative self-esteem, although these data are still being debated. Recent population-based research by Conron, Mimiaga, and Landers (see Recommended Readings below) found that bisexual individuals may fare more poorly than either heterosexuals or their gay and lesbian counterparts, as unemployment, lack of a primary health care provider, and no health or dental insurance is more common among this group.

A review of the literature to date has recommended six specific areas of GLBT health concerns to which health care providers should be especially attentive: (1) physical fitness and cardiovascular health, (2) sexual risk behaviors leading to HIV and other sexually transmitted diseases, (3) alcohol and substance use, including tobacco dependence, (4) interpersonal violence, (5) cancer, and (6) mental health issues, including depression and suicidality.

Physical Fitness and Cardiovascular Health

Emerging areas of interest among public health researchers are the health behaviors of GLBT individuals related to *physical fitness*, including *diet, exercise*, and overweight or *obesity*. Compared to heterosexual men, sexual minority men appear to have higher rates of body image problems and disordered eating, including purging behavior and binge eating episodes, in addition to clinically diagnosable eating disorders. Important consequences include blood pressure changes, osteoporosis, dehydration and electrolyte imbalance, muscle loss, and tooth decay. It has been suggested that sexual minority men identify more with the female gender and, thus, have taken on a stereotypical female quest for thinness. However, there is no universal support for this or any other single contributory mechanism.

In contrast, sexual minority women tend to report more satisfaction with their **body image** than heterosexual women. However, sexual minority women report less exercise than heterosexual women and are more likely to be overweight or obese. The consequences of these weight prob-

lems include increased risk of hypertension, heart disease, and diabetes. There is speculation that the specific cultural norms within lesbian groups (e.g., eschewing the drive for thinness) may contribute to a lack of motivation to avoid being overweight; but, again, there is no clear evidence in support of any single etiology.

Importantly, *heart disease* is the most frequent cause of death among women and, thus, risk factors should be monitored closely because lesbian and heterosexual women have similar risk profiles. Indeed, it may be especially important to be attentive to the cardiovascular health (including hypertension) of sexual minority women, given the higher rates of overweight, smoking, and elevated stress levels due to their sexual minority status. Given their higher rates of smoking and alcohol and substance use, sexual minority men may also be at increased risk of heart problems. Furthermore, because heart problems are prevalent among African Americans, African American GLBT women and men may be at particularly high risk and require especially vigilant screening.

Health Issues Related to Sexual Risk Behaviors

Since the initial clinical presentation of *HIV/AIDS* in 1981, it is estimated that up to 42 million people have been infected worldwide, with more than 1 million of those infections having occurred in the US. More than half of those people are thought to be men who acquired the virus through sex with other men (MSM) irrespective of their sexual orientation or sexual identity. Early in the epidemic, most affected men were white. However, the demographics of the U.S. epidemic have shifted and, beginning in 1998, the majority of people living with HIV/AIDS have been black and Latino MSM. Recent prevalence rates continue to show white, black, and Latino men at highest risk for incident infection. Recent data also indicate that many MSM of color do not identify as gay or bisexual. This is a crucial point, as most HIV prevention programs have erroneously equated behavior with identity, and have specifically targeted programs of men who identify as gay or bisexual by recruiting people from predominantly gay neighborhoods or bars. This recruitment strategy has made it difficult to generalize findings to MSM who do not identify as gay and has likely served as a barrier to effective HIV prevention efforts for that group.

The advent of *combination therapy* (protease inhibitors mixed with antiretrovirals) has made it possible for HIV/AIDS to be a condition with which many individuals can live productive, satisfying lives. Nevertheless, HIV continues to spread among gay men of all generations. A number of factors may play a role: some, especially younger, gay men may view HIV as a manageable condition and erroneously minimize their likelihood of exposure; some gay men abandon safe sexual practices because substance abuse impairs judgment or because of an unwillingness to relinquish the pleasure associated with unprotected anal intercourse, the primary high-risk sexual behavior within this group; and some men attach symbolic meaning to unprotected sexual behavior (i.e., having a trusting relationship with a partner).

HIV prevention programs have, in aggregate, shifted the trend in sexual behavior toward the use of barrier protection for gay or bisexual men. Successful prevention programs use targeted interventions focused directly on the behaviors of safer sex that are *culturally appropriate* (i.e., tailored to the unique barriers and strengths of a given subgroup). Several psychosocial factors that influence sexual risk taking are self-esteem, social support, mood prior to sexual encounter, overall optimism or fatalism, age, education, and alcohol or drug use before or during sex. The majority of patients do not discuss sexual activity with health care providers, which is a missed opportunity for education and intervention.

Men who have sex with men are also at risk of acquiring other STIs, including urethritis, proctitis, pharyngitis, prostatitis, hepatitis A and B, syphilis, gonorrhea, chlamydia, herpes, and HPV/anal and genital warts. Rates of some STIs are higher among MSM than among men who only engage in sex with women. Increasing rates of HIV infection parallel the rising rates of unprotected sex and other STIs.

There are no data showing that women who have sex with women have any higher rates of STIs; indeed, the opposite appears to be true. However, while sexual minority women are at lower risk for acquiring HIV, the risk is not zero. HIV could be spread through even occasional unprotected sex with a male partner (for behaviorally bisexual women) or through sharing sex toys.

Alcohol and Substance Use

Early research on *alcohol use* found GLBT individuals reporting significantly higher rates of problem drinking. However, these studies relied on sampling methods that may have artificially inflated prevalence estimates (e.g., recruiting participants at bars or gay pride events). More recent research has found no significant differences in rates of problem drinking (gay men, lesbians) or frequency of bar-going behavior (lesbians) compared to same gender, heterosexual counterparts. A few studies have found higher rates of heavy drinking or abstinence from alcohol among gay men, potentially related to the individual's past history of alcoholism or in response to a family history of alcoholism. Some studies have reported a higher incidence of binge drinking among bisexual women.

Research on substance use other than alcohol indicates higher rates of *smoking* among sexual minority men and women. Lesbians are the only demographic subgroup whose rate of smoking actually increases with age. Rates of *marijuana* and *cocaine* use are also higher in lesbians compared to heterosexual women. Compared to heterosexual men, gay men have higher rates of use of *inhalants* (e.g., amyl or butyl nitrite, also called "poppers," and usually used during sex), *hallucinogens*, and *illicit drugs* overall. Gay men and lesbian 18- to 25-years-olds report higher rates of substance use compared to older cohorts and to heterosexual peers.

Drug use is correlated with unprotected sex. Use of *ketamine* ("Special K") and *MDMA* ("ecstasy") and, more recently, crystal methamphetamine ("meth" or "Tina") are among the most commonly used substances. Gay men, in particular, may abuse crystal methamphetamine at high rates, especially in urban areas, because it increases the drive for sex over a period of many hours while simultaneously delaying orgasm. This combination is currently being investigated due to consistent reports that the drug facilitates HIV transmission and decreases the effectiveness of anti-HIV medication. While some groups of gay men use drugs, there is no evidence that gay men, in general, possess higher levels of drug addiction or dependence at threshold diagnostic levels.

Interpersonal Violence

The psychological and physical health consequences of **interpersonal violence** are well documented (see Chapter 26, Interpersonal Violence), and include emotional distress and mental disorders (depression, PTSD), acute health problems (fractures, lacerations) and chronic health problems (low back pain, fibromyalgia). Rates of traumatic victimization appear higher among sexual minority individuals, both during childhood (psychological, physical, and sexual abuse) and during adulthood (psychological or physical coerced sexual experiences, rape). It is possible that sexual minority individuals are targeted by perpetrators because of their perceived sexual orientation or gender nonconforming behaviors.

Screening for a history of abuse as well as current partner violence is critical. Data regarding violence perpetrated by a romantic partner suggest that the rates may be comparable in male-male, female-female, and male-female couples. Patients are often uncomfortable or fearful about disclosing abuse. However, in same-sex relationships, there is also another barrier to reporting: sexual minority women tend not to perceive their female partners as abusive and sexual minority men tend not to perceive themselves as victims.

Cancer

What are the potential risk factors for cancer among GLBT individuals?

Like all women, sexual minority women should be screened routinely for both *breast* and *colon cancer*. Like all men, sexual minority men should receive routine screening for *prostate, testicular, colon*, and *anal cancer*. In general, GLBT and heterosexual individuals are at equal risk for developing cancer. In some cases, however, individual health behaviors such as smoking or alcohol consumption may increase risk. Other potential problems may be lack of preventive health

care, since delayed detection and diagnosis are associated with negative outcomes; fear and distrust of health care providers based on previous negative experiences; and implicit or explicit discomfort among providers about working with sexual minority patients around topics like sex and reproduction.

Sexual minority individuals, especially men, do have an increased risk of anal cancer, possibly because of higher rates of HPV infection. Anal cancer can be detected through a pap smear-like test performed rectally.

Mental Health Issues

What are the rates of anxiety and depression among GLBT individuals?

Typically, major, large-scale studies of the prevalence of mental disorders in the general population have not included sexual orientation as a demographic variable, thus limiting information about mental health disparities among sexual minority individuals. Most of the work that has been done has looked at sexual orientation within populations meeting criteria for specific disorders or has used symptom scales that may be correlated with mental disorders at a diagnostic/criterion level. With these caveats, rates of mood and anxiety problems among GLBT individuals appear to be higher than among heterosexuals. This is most likely due to the social stigmatization, prejudice, and even violence that many sexual minority individuals encounter.

Rates of *anxiety* and *depression* among GLBTs are especially high if they are not "out" about their sexual orientation or if they lack adequate social support. The situation is likely compounded for younger GLBT individuals, who may lack role models and fear abandonment by their family of origin, and for GLBTs of color who face the additional stress of managing another stigmatized identity. The result is higher rates of health and mental health care utilization and, in some subgroups, higher rates of suicidal and self-harm behaviors. Screening for mental health problems, suicidal or self-harm behaviors, and psychosocial stressors should be a part of routine health care for GLBT individuals, with referral for culturally competent mental health services as needed.

Transgender Patients

The term **transgender** refers to a variety of identities and behaviors indicative of gender expression that does not conform to an individual's anatomically assigned gender. Unlike the same-sex attraction experienced by gay and lesbian individuals, transgender refers to a crisis of gender identity, the experience of being male or female. Further, some transgender individuals find that neither the male nor the female gender identity feels comfortable for them and, thus, question the notion of a binary gender categorization altogether.

The term transgender includes *transvestites*, who are individuals that derive pleasure, sometimes erotic, from *cross-dressing* (wearing attire of the opposite gender). Such behaviors may be episodic or regular; typically they are chronic and are experienced by heterosexually-identified persons, usually men. In and of themselves, transvestic behaviors do not pose unique health-related concerns, although sometimes the secrecy and shame associated with the behaviors can affect interpersonal relationships. In addition, the transgender category includes **intersex** individuals, whose anatomically assigned gender at birth is ambiguous. Such individuals may or may not claim a primary male or female identity in adult life, and may have had surgery during their youth to "correct" their ambiguous secondary sex characteristics. Adult intersex individuals may, thus, have positive, negative, or mixed feelings about their body and the decision-making process of their families and physicians in the past.

True transgenderism, or **transsexualism**, is characterized by a persistent sense of having been "born in the wrong body." This means that the individual likely exhibited gender atypical play interests in youth, feels most comfortable when attired in the manner of another gender, and seeks to evolve toward a stable life and presentation as the opposite gender. Transgender individuals may be either "M to F" (MTF; genetic males seeking to live as females) or "F to M" (FTM; genetic females seeking to live as males). Many, but certainly not all, transgender individuals have as their goal eventual sex reassignment through surgery. Prior to this, a series of medical and social prerequisites must be met (see Chapter 20, Sexuality and Sexual Disorders).

The transgender individual seeking *sex reassignment* must be under the care of a psychologist or psychotherapist in advance of initiating any changes in hormonal state or physiognomy. The first medical step for transgender individuals is usually hormone therapy, initiated after a 6- to 12-month period of psychological counseling. In the case of MTF transgender individuals, the person may seek removal of body hair through electrolysis or laser treatments, facial feminization surgery, and a number of other procedures prior to seeking sex reassignment surgery (SRS). According to the International Standards for Gender Change, the person should be living full time in the role of his/her desired gender for a period of one year prior to being eligible for the surgery. This usually includes living and working in role, as well as coming out to family and friends about one's thoughts and feelings. The process can be challenging, but the determination with which most transgender individuals approach it is testament to the deeply felt nature of the syndrome. The actual medical and psychological management of transgender cases usually requires specialized competence and training.

Tips for Providers Working with GLBT Patients

What are the guidelines for providing informed care for GLBT individuals?

Providers interested in more in-depth discussion of research findings related to GLBT health issues are directed to Conran et al. and Meyer et al. (see Recommended Readings). Those interested in more details about how to work with GLBT patients should consult *The Fenway Guide to Lesbian, Gay, Bisexual, and Transgender Health* or the Gay and Lesbian Medical Association's *Guidelines for Care of Lesbian, Gay, Bisexual, and Transgender Patients*. The following suggestions will help providers screen for problems and better understand their patients, who may have certain vulnerabilities because of their sexual orientation:
- Always take a thorough sexual history regardless of the partner/marital status of the patient. For example, ask a heterosexually married man if he only has sex with his wife and if he only has sex with women. Patients who identi-

fy as heterosexual may occasionally engage in same-sex sexual behavior (sometimes referred to in the public health literature as being "on the down low").

- Ask about the patient's understanding regarding safe sex practices and how successfully he or she follows his or her own sexual risk limits. Are there circumstances (certain places, certain partners, when feeling sad, when using drugs) under which he or she is more likely to engage in unprotected or otherwise risky sexual practices? Referral to a mental health professional or community clinic focusing on how to reduce sexual risk may be warranted.
- Sexually active patients should be screened for sexually transmitted diseases and encouraged to receive appropriate vaccinations (e.g., Hepatitis A and B, HPV).
- Be aware that GLBT individuals may be more vulnerable to certain psychological problems such as depression and anxiety disorders, including panic. GLBT adolescents may have higher rates of suicidal ideation than heterosexual adolescents. Understand the protective factors available to the patient. Inadequate social support is related to higher suicidality in GLBT adolescents and good social support can serve as a protective factor.

Many GLBT individuals have good reason not to trust the medical establishment. GLBT individuals have often been viewed as mentally disordered, and may currently be treated as sexually out-of-control. Transgender patients are often treated with intolerance or labeled as having a mental disorder. The GLBT patient's reluctance to be forthcoming with personal information may not be a sign of uncooperativeness or "resistance," but based on anti-GLBT attitudes from society at large. Providing high-quality, culturally competent care to this socially and medically vulnerable group require skill, objectivity, and compassion.

Recommended Readings

Conron KJ, Mimiaga MJ, Landers SJ. A population-based study of sexual orientation identity and gender differences in adult health. *American Journal of Public Health* 2010; 100:1953–1960.

Gay and Lesbian Medical Association. *Guidelines for Care of Lesbian, Gay, Bisexual, and Transgender Patients*. San Francisco, CA: Gay and Lesbian Medical Association; 2006.

Meyer IH, Northridge ME (Eds.). *The Health of Sexual Minorities: Public Health Perspectives on Lesbian, Gay, Bisexual and Transgender Populations*. New York: Springer; 2007.

Makadon HJ, Mayer KH, Potter J, Goldhammer H (Eds.). *The Fenway Guide to Lesbian, Gay, Bisexual, and Transgender Health*. Philadelphia PA: American College of Physicians; 2008.

Important Questions to Ask About Social Support

- Who knows about your sexual orientation/gender identity?
- What has their reaction been?
- What people are in your life that you trust and with whom you can share concerns? Who are they, and how often do you have contact with them?
- Whom do you consider to be family? Are they biological relatives or a network of friends with whom you share a particular bond?
- What substances (alcohol, tobacco, other drugs) do you use regularly? Are there others that you use only occasionally? Does your use of "substance" ever make you nervous or feel like it's difficult to control?
- How do you resolve conflicts with your romantic partner? Do arguments or fights ever become violent?

Review Questions

1. Of the following, HIV/AIDS is most prevalent among
   A. black and Latino lesbians.
   B. black and Latino men having sex with men.
   C. black and Latino transgendered people.
   D. white lesbians.
   E. white men having sex with men.

2. Sexual minority men are at risk for which of the following conditions?
   A. Anal cancer
   B. Drug abuse
   C. Eating disorders
   D. Suicidal death
   E. All of the above

3. Among the following, the major reason why GLBT people receive less-than-optimal preventive health care is
   A. appropriate care requires specialized training.
   B. gays and lesbians hide their sexual orientation.
   C. insurance does not cover atypical sexually transmitted diseases.
   D. practitioners are uncomfortable discussing sexual orientation and behavior.
   E. typical surveillance/screening tests are inadequate.

4. In comparing the risk of cancer in GLBT individuals with that in heterosexual individuals, research has shown that
   A. breast cancer is more common in lesbians.
   B. colon cancer is more common in gay men.
   C. ovarian cancer is more common in heterosexual women.
   D. testicular cancer is more common in heterosexual men.
   E. the risks for cancer are the same in both groups.

5. According to the International Standards for Gender Change, prior to being eligible for the surgery, a person seeking sex reassignment surgery should be living full time in the role of his/ her desired gender for a period of at least
   A. 3 months.
   B. 6 months.
   C. 12 months.
   D. 18 months.
   E. 24 months.

Key to review questions: p. 407

22 Geriatric Health and Successful Aging

Patricia Lenahan, LCSW, LMFT, BCETS, and Soo Borson, MD

- What are some of the physiological changes of aging?
- What are two common mental health problems of aging?
- What harmful substances are elders most likely to use?
- How does chronic illness affect sexual functioning?
- What living arrangement options exist for the elderly?

The world is experiencing an unprecedented increase in the aging population. China alone will have about 270 million people > 60 within the next 20 years. Census data reveal that the greatest advances in aging will be among people of color and in underdeveloped regions of the world. In the US, the population of individuals > 65 in 2030 will be approximately twice the number of those > 65 in the year 2000.

What are some of the physiological changes of aging?

The Aging Process

Aging produces variable physiological changes leading to gradual loss of functional abilities. Changes in connective tissue and the *fat/muscle ratio* lead to decreased flexibility, motor strength, and endurance, and affect how medications are distributed in the body. Decreased sensory system functioning increases with age. Decreased sensitivity to touch and to pain, hearing loss especially in high frequencies (presbycusis), diminished visual acuity (presbyopia), and greater sensitivity to light are common. Impaired visual acuity and mobility have an impact on an individual's ability to shop and cook, and can lead to falls, fear of falling, and loss of fitness due to reduced activity. Changes in taste occur as a result of illness, smoking, pollution, or medications. Dentures can make chewing food difficult, and loss of appetite is not unusual. Undetected, these changes can lead to malnutrition, decreased strength, functional disabilities, and mood disorders.

Sleep disturbances and changes in sleeping patterns are common in older adults. Insomnia and daytime naps disrupt normal circadian rhythm (see Chapter 6, Chronobiology and Sleep Disorders). This age group uses the highest percentage of sedative-hypnotic drugs, even though long-term usage of these medications is often ineffective and can even exacerbate insomnia. Caregiving responsibilities, chronic illness, mood disorders, caffeine, nicotine, and sedative-hypnotic drug and alcohol use all contribute to sleep disturbances.

Most individuals experience the onset of some chronic health condition during the fifth and sixth decades of life. Women, in particular, are at risk for hypertension, arthritis, diabetes, and osteoporosis. Heart disease, cancer, and stroke are the leading causes of death overall but pneumonia, influenza, and chronic obstructive pulmonary disease are also significant causes of death among older people.

The prevalence of **Alzheimer disease (AD)** is 1% among 65–74 year olds, but increases to at least 25% in people > 85. Currently, about 5 million people suffer from AD and the projections for the future are staggering. With the advent of aging baby boomers, it is expected that more than

14 million people will be diagnosed with AD by the year 2030. This means one in 45 persons will develop AD. While the probability of developing this disease is a function of advancing age and heredity, factors that mitigate the onset and severity of AD include education and diet. It is essential to raise this issue with patients during middle adulthood so that they can help themselves reduce their risk.

Individuals with a *thinner margin of health* (e.g., genetic predisposition to certain diseases) and lower income experience higher rates of disability due to greater exposure to risk factors and limited access to health care. Individuals who rely upon governmental insurance programs that pay only a fraction of health care costs receive less than optimal care. Members of minority groups receive fewer diagnostic tests and surgical procedures, thus subjecting them to greater risks of disability and premature death (see Chapter 19, Health Care in Minority and Majority Populations).

Diagnostic Assessment of Cognitive Functioning

Comprehensive assessment is required to differentiate among brain disease, substance-related disorders, delirium, and "masked depression." Comorbid dementia and depression are common and treating depression during the early and middle stages of dementia can help clarify the diagnostic picture. The **Mini Mental Status Exam** (MMSE) is among the most commonly used diagnostic tools for assessing cognitive decline, but newer tools such as the Mini-Cog and the Montreal Cognitive Assessment (MoCA) may have broad applications in screening for dementia and milder cognitive impairments. The *Cornell Scale for Depression in Dementia* has been validated for use with older individuals with and without dementia. Both the *Geriatric Depression Scale* and the *Center for Epidemiological Studies Depression Scale* are reliable tools for assessing depression in older adults; the latter also has been validated with Spanish-speaking samples and has been studied with Native American/Alaska Native populations. However, there may be significant limitations to the use of these instruments in minority populations due to language ability, translation

issues, educational levels, cultural concepts, and culturally appropriate expressions of mental health disorders. It is important to recognize how these factors may influence the results of testing and to develop alternative assessments. Clinicians should always familiarize themselves with the cultural variations in expression of symptoms characteristic of the ethnic group populations they serve (see Chapter 18, Culture and Ethnicity).

> What are two common mental health problems of aging?

Psychiatric Disorders

Wrinkles, graying or loss of hair, and decreased height are signs of normative aging and, although not life threatening, can result in loss of self-esteem. Declining physical and adaptive abilities make older adults more vulnerable to depression and other mental disorders. Many elderly patients take multiple medications for chronic conditions; side effects can contribute to depressive symptoms. Individuals who have suffered myocardial infarctions, stroke, hip fractures, or chronic illnesses such as arthritis and diabetes are especially at risk for depression.

Stressors associated with aging can exacerbate lifelong behavioral or mental health problems. Some elderly experience increased stress in family relationships if they become the primary caregiver for grandchildren or are affected by the successes/failures of children or grandchildren. Assimilation and acculturation stresses are common for foreign-born seniors who experience communication difficulties with grandchildren, whom they believe have abandoned traditional values, including respect for elders.

The experience of real or perceived *losses* (physical abilities, social status, relationships, income, pets) heightens vulnerability, and can result in isolation, withdrawal from usual activities, and loneliness. The loss of role and status associated with retirement can contribute to a lowered sense of self-esteem and personal competence. Bereavement is complicated by practical necessities, such as decisions to keep/sell one's home or distribute assets. If the deceased spouse was the primary caregiver, relocation can precipitate other losses (e.g., the neighborhood, support networks, sense of safety, transportation, health care).

> The U.S. Department of Health and Human Services (USDHHS) estimates that 20% of older adults will experience a mental disorder not associated with normal aging. The USDHHS projects that the prevalence of mental health problems in the elderly will double during the next 25 years, including significant increases in mood disorders, dementia, substance abuse, and schizophrenia.

Depression is one of the most common mental disorders in later life, especially among women. Bereavement, accumulated loss, and alcohol and medication abuse are contributing factors. *Masked depression* occurs when an individual or family member attributes symptoms of depression (e.g., memory problems) to the onset of cognitive impairment due to, for example, dementia. In fact, severe depression can be associated with sufficient cognitive impairment to raise the question of dementia. *Sub-threshold depression* is associated with a perceived sense of worsening physical health as well as decreased emotional functioning. Symptoms include increased anxiety and a history of mood disorders. Individuals with this symptom constellation have a pessimistic outlook and lowered sense of personal mastery and self-efficacy.

> Depressive disorders are common in patients with a wide variety of chronic medical and neurological diseases. "Masked depression" or "depression without sadness" is a variant of late-life depression with clinically significant cerebrovascular compromise. Characteristics include mild mood symptoms and prominent psychomotor retardation and executive cognitive dysfunction (poor insight, inability to plan, cognitive inflexibility).

Anxiety is under-diagnosed in the elderly due to overlapping symptoms with depression as well as some physical disorders. Many practitioners assume the symptoms are associated with the "normal" worries of aging (see Chapter 46, Anxiety and Dissociative Disorders). The underlying basis for somatic expressions of anxiety, such as somatoform disorders and hypochondria-

sis, can go unrecognized and be attributed to the aging adult's physical health status. However, approximately 10% of older adults, mostly women, appear to have some type of anxiety disorder. Older patients with both major depression and generalized anxiety have a worse prognosis than individuals who have either diagnosis alone. Patients with co-morbid disorders are more likely to have chronic functional impairments, higher utilization of health care services, and increased suicide risk. Aging individuals develop social phobias more frequently than younger people. This is related to self-consciousness about appearance, health conditions, and social fears (e.g., worrying about becoming incontinent in a social situation).

Posttraumatic stress disorder (PTSD) is seen in some older adults, especially those who have immigrated to the US from war-torn regions, who meet criteria for diagnosis at three times the rate of the general population. Older individuals who have witnessed or experienced torture or physical or sexual trauma as a result of political uprisings often present with multiple somatic complaints or culture-bound syndromes (see Chapter 18, Culture and Ethnicity).

High **suicide** rates exist for both older women and men. Individuals at particular risk are women, Caucasian males > 85 years old, and those with limited social supports, lower socioeconomic levels, and significant medical disability. High rates are also found among older Chinese women, older Japanese men, Native Americans, and Alaska Natives. Suicide is generally associated with depression related to poor health.

> In assessing suicide risk in the elderly, providers should be sensitive to behavioral changes such as disregard for personal hygiene or giving away prized possessions. Verbal expressions of suicidal thought ("You won't have me around much longer" or "I won't burden you much longer") should prompt an assessment of suicidality (see Chapter 28, Suicide).

"Rational suicide" and **physician-assisted suicide** appear to be particularly attractive for some older adults who reflect upon their desire for death with dignity and without pain, a need to preserve some degree of financial security especially for the remaining spouse, and a desire to avoid becoming incapacitated.

Violence and Abuse

Elder abuse includes *physical, emotional, psychological, and financial abuse,* as well as *self-neglect or neglect by caregivers.* Forms of self-neglect include failure to take medications, cluttering/hoarding, pet collecting, and poor hygiene. Fiscal or financial abuse includes Internet scams, solicitations for home repairs, and collections for charitable donations as well as stealing social security or pension checks by family and friends. Agencies working with victims of elder abuse include FAST (Financial Abuse Specialist Teams) that assess and intervene in such cases. The incidence of intimate partner violence and sexual abuse decreases in aging populations although the rates of psychological and emotional abuse do not decline with age. Chronic pain and depression are common diagnoses among victims of violence.

> What harmful substances are elders most likely to use?

Substance Abuse and Addictive Behaviors

Older people drink less *alcohol* than the general population but the physiological changes of aging promote intoxication at lower levels of intake. The prevalence of alcoholism among older adults in the general community appears to be about 5–10%, but the rate of current or prior alcoholism among individuals in hospitals, nursing homes, and other health care settings ranges from 15–58%. Some studies have found that up to 88% of nursing home residents have alcohol-related problems. Two thirds of older "early onset" drinkers (those who developed problem drinking behaviors before age 40) are men. Women are more likely to be "late onset" drinkers, whose drinking seems related to life stress events.

Nicotine is the most frequently used substance among current seniors with approximately 15% of older adults smoking. Next most common are alcoholism problems and prescription drug misuse. Illicit drug use is rare. However, it is anticipated that the use of marijuana, heroin, and cocaine will continue to rise among older adults as the next

generation ages. The belief that illicit drug use will decrease in older populations due to premature death, incarceration, or a switch to "legitimate" drugs such as prescription medications or alcohol is proving to be inaccurate. The legalization of medical marijuana and the proliferation of medical marijuana dispensaries may lead to increased marijuana use among the older population.

> The National Household Survey on Drug Abuse (NHSDA) and the National Survey on Drug Use and Health (NSDUH) predict that illicit drug use will increase significantly as baby boomers age due to the higher rate of lifetime use among that generation.

Older adults consume approximately one third of all *prescription drugs* and nearly two thirds of all *over-the-counter* (OTC) medications. It is not unusual for an older person to take seven or more prescription medications along with OTC medications, supplements, and herbal products. The alcohol contained in these medications can potentiate or diminish their effects.

Ideally, all adults should be screened for **substance use** disorders. The presence of severe cognitive impairment can complicate the assessment process. Treatment should be encouraged if problem drinking or drug misuse is detected. Age-specific group therapy is recommended as a part of an overall approach. Harm reduction techniques are generally successful with older alcoholics (see Chapter 25, Substance Abuse).

Gambling has emerged as an area of concern for older adults as lotteries, bingo, casinos, and online gaming have grown in popularity. Many senior centers and assisted living facilities offer day trips to local casinos. This new form of recreation includes a social aspect, relieves tension, provides an escape from day-to-day problems, and alleviates boredom. However, increased gambling may lead to problem or even pathological gambling disorders depending on the frequency of gambling, the number of gambling activities an individual engages in, and the amount of money spent on gambling.

The SOGS (South Oaks Gambling Screen) and the SOGS-R (Revised SOGS) are widely used to assess gambling problems. Another tool, the Gambling Motivation Scale (GMS), examines three aspects of gambling: for rewards, for release of tension and guilt, and for social recognition. While the rates of problem gambling among older adults appears to be lower than among younger adults, problem gambling disorders remain an area of concern, especially for individuals on fixed incomes and limited resources.

Psychotropic medications can be beneficial if applied judiciously. In general, older patients are more physically sensitive to medication side effects and require adjustment of standard dosages.

Psychiatric Treatments

Few clinicians would agree with Freud who stated that older patients were not appropriate candidates for therapy because they do not have enough life left to complete the process; yet, many clinicians are reluctant to treat what they regard as a difficult and challenging population. Reimbursement issues for practitioners and a lack of appropriate training and experience are concerns contributing to the limited number of therapists treating older adults.

Patient sensitivity to the stigma of mental disorders, the belief that personal problems should be solved within the home/family, sociocultural factors, and limited accessibility (transportation, mobility) contribute to low utilization of mental health services by older adults. Individuals in rural environments have limited access to qualified therapists, while those from other cultural backgrounds often lack confidence in the value of therapy. The advent of telemedicine may bring additional services to physically and linguistically isolated older adults who seek counseling.

Older adults are appropriate candidates for therapeutic interventions such as short-term, problem-focused individual counseling, cognitive-behavioral therapy (CBT), dialectical behavior therapy (DBT), group therapy, self-help groups, support groups, reminiscence groups, life review groups, book clubs and reading groups, couples' counseling, and family therapy. *Life review therapy* is especially beneficial to older patients since the primary goal is to facilitate the integration of past and present experiences through structured reminiscence, constructive reappraisal of the past, and recollection of previously used successful coping mechanisms. Life review therapy can include both individual and group activities such as writing a life history, sharing photo albums, or listening to music.

Medications in combination with psychotherapy, when administered by an experienced clinician, may produce results equal to or better than treatment regimes relying on medications or psychotherapy alone. Electroconvulsive therapy (ECT) is generally only considered in older adults who have unremitting depression despite adequate antidepressant and psychotherapeutic treatment, or those individuals whose complex medical conditions make ECT the safer choice for treating comorbid depression.

Non-Traditional Treatments

Community mental health centers located in ethnic communities often offer *culturally sensitive treatments* that may not be offered in the general therapeutic community (e.g., a community mental health center in Chinatown that offers acupuncture as a treatment for depression). Other alternative therapies include music, art, dance, and drama therapy. The health and mental health benefits of exercise (walking, Tai Chi, Qi Gong, longevity stick), touch, and aromatherapy are being studied. Many of these therapies embrace cultural values and forms of expression familiar to elders from varying backgrounds.

Studies of the therapeutic value of *companion animals* have demonstrated decreases in blood pressure and agitation among Alzheimer patients when animals are present. However, not all individuals or all animals should be included in a pet-facilitated therapy program. Organizations such as the Delta Society (which certifies a variety of animals other than dogs), Therapy Dogs International, Paws for Life, and Bright and Beautiful Therapy Dogs offer comprehensive testing of animals before they are approved as "therapists."

Sexuality and Sexual Health

Physiological changes in the sexual response cycle of aging women include decreased estrogen level, reduced elasticity and muscle tone, atrophy of the uterus, and loss of vulvar tissue. Vaginal lubrication is decreased, which may result in pain on intercourse and even bleeding. Changes in the intensity of orgasm and painful spasms during orgasm may occur. Aging women may need more direct manual stimulation to become aroused. Men may require more direct genital and mental stimulation, experience increased time to achieve an erection, and have decreased tumescence during penetration, decreased volume of ejaculate, and increased refractory time.

Chronic illness, disability, medications, mobility, psychosocial issues, and ageist beliefs can affect the sexual functioning of older adults. It is important to discuss sexual functioning in an open and sensitive manner, including the sexual orientation of the patient, although there has been little research on the sexual needs and health care concerns of aging gay, lesbian, bisexual, and transgender persons (see Chapter 20, Sexuality and Sexual Disorders and Chapter 21, Health Care Issues Facing Gay, Lesbian, Bisexual, and Transgender Individuals).

How does chronic illness affect sexual functioning?

Sexuality and Chronic Disease

Individuals who have had heart attacks, strokes, or chronic illnesses such as diabetes, pulmonary disease, and arthritis can maintain healthy and satisfying sexual lives. However, many of the medications used to treat these conditions can contribute to sexual dysfunction, e.g., selective serotonin reuptake inhibitors (SSRIs) used to treat mood disorders can have a significant negative sexual side effect. Older adults, who are counseled about adapting their sexual activities and are open to suggestions about timing and positional changes, can maintain satisfying sexual lives. Organizations (e.g., the Arthritis Foundation) often have information on disorder-specific sexual issues.

Sexual Expression in Dependent Living Facilities

Fears of liability (e.g., falls, other health consequences) along with biases of family, staff, and health care personnel, contribute to constraints on privacy and sexual expression in congregate living environments such as assisted living and nursing home facilities. Barriers to sexual expression include unavailability of a partner, physical and cognitive decline, inability to control the environment, lack of privacy, and body image concerns. Some facilities may consider appropriate sexual behavior to be acceptable as long as the individual understands what he/she is doing and respects the rights of others.

Sexuality and Dementia

Elderly residents with Alzheimer disease can participate in and even initiate sexual activity as long as certain criteria are met. For example, behavior should be consistent with lifelong sexual behaviors. Patients should also be cognitively able to engage in sexual activities, and be able to recognize the partner. However, patients and partners may experience conflict about continuing the sexual relationship. For example, role changes may take place in that the previously passive partner now becomes the initiator of sexual behavior, or a caregiving spouse is no longer able to see the partner as sexually attractive. The clinician should explore the sexual wishes and needs of the patient and partner and ascertain whether a sexual relationship is mutually beneficial. The provider must be alert to the possibility of abuse should one of the partners no longer consent to engage in sexual activities.

HIV/AIDS

The current cohort of seniors has been neglected with regard to prevention of sexually transmitted infections (STI) leading to a steady rise in the diagnosis of HIV and other STIs in the > 60 age group. Up to 15% of all new cases of AIDS and 25% of overall cases of HIV occur among people > 50. Many older individuals do not consider unprotected sex to be a high risk behavior since they are no longer concerned about the need for contraception. Therefore, they are less likely to use condoms. However, post-menopausal women are at greater risk for HIV infection – and re-infection – during heterosexual intercourse because of estrogen depletion resulting in fragile vaginal mucosa. Diagnosis of AIDS is complicated by early symptoms (fatigue, confusion, loss of appetite) that are common in other age-related illnesses. AIDS stigma among the elderly contributes to their under utilization of health and mental health services. Individuals are living longer with HIV and as a result are more likely to develop diseases associated with aging, perhaps at an earlier age. Recent evidence suggests that neurocognitive disorders may be increasing among older adults who have HIV.

Successful Aging

The term **successful aging** is used frequently by the baby boomer generation and is synonymous with U.S. cultural norms that emphasize the importance of maintaining independent functioning, continued physical mobility, social interactions with family and friends, ongoing interest in activities, and a sense of well-being. Successful aging is not related to age, ethnicity, or marital status, but describes an individual's ability to balance self-acceptance of who they are and "what" they are with a sense of engagement with life. Other factors that promote successful aging include adoption of healthier lifestyles, early detection of disease through screening, injury prevention techniques, and development of self-management strategies. The reality, however, is that many individuals may not be able to age well due to poverty, losses, lack of access to care, or lack of appropriately supportive neighborhoods and communities. Individuals who are frail may need another set of standards to be deemed as "aging well."

Retirement and Volunteerism

Many baby boomers plan to continue working after they reach the traditional retirement age of 65. Although some will make this decision because of personal preference, the recent downturn in the economy has had a significant impact on older adults who have seen the value of their retirement accounts diminish. These financial factors as well as the decline in employer-sponsored pensions are causing many older adults to re-examine the feasibility of retirement. Some will alternate between periods of working and leisure time, while others will embark on a second career. Still others who have adequate resources but want to maintain the mental stimulation and challenges associated with

working will volunteer. Currently, baby boomers have the highest rates of volunteer participation and volunteer for longer hours than any age group except the current older generation. Agencies as demanding as the Peace Corps are seeing an increase in volunteer applications from seniors.

> What living arrangement options exist for the elderly?

Long-Term Care: Conservative Care or Creative Options

Advances in medical treatment and the advent of managed care have complicated access to health care for seniors. A recent AARP survey indicated that 70% of its members believed that *long-term care insurance* was a good thing, yet only 17% had purchased any form of coverage, due in part to the high cost.

The continuum of care that is **long-term care** includes home and community-based services along a spectrum of specialized health, rehabilitative, and residential care. These services focus on the biopsychosocial, spiritual, residential, rehabilitative, and supportive needs of individuals and their families. Contrary to the belief of many elders, long-term care services are not synonymous with nursing homes; they may be delivered in a person's home, in the community (senior centers, mental health facilities, cultural clubs, churches, schools), or in residential care facilities (assisted living or nursing homes). A variety of factors determine the kinds of services needed, including income, type of housing/safety/ease of access, health status (including self-rated health), age/frailty, and availability of community resources.

Changes in public policies granting greater access to affordable community services are needed to alleviate the burden of long-term care borne by family caregivers. Governmental agencies (e.g., Veterans Health Administration, the Bureau of Indian Affairs) will be called upon to develop new approaches to service delivery to meet the burgeoning aging population. The *National Family Caregiver Support Program* (NFCSP) was established in 2000 to support education, information, support groups, and some limited services such as respite care in local communities (e.g., support to grandparents who are raising grandchildren).

Long-term care services in the home and the community provide many older adults with their first experience with aging-related services at a senior center where they attend exercise classes, participate in congregate meal programs, or select from a variety of other activities.

Home health care services provide a wide range of health-related services in the client's home including skilled nursing care, psychiatric nursing, physical therapy, occupational therapy, speech therapy, home health aides, and social work services.

In-home supportive services, a part of home health care, include help with meal preparation, shopping, light housekeeping, money management, personal hygiene, laundry, and chore services.

Adult day care/adult day health programs provide functionally impaired adults with daytime community-based programs in a protective setting. Therapeutic interventions can be adapted to focus on the behavioral and mood-related problems associated with psychiatric disorders, Alzheimer disease, and other health maintenance issues. Such programs support and provide respite for family caregivers of cognitively or physically disabled elders. Some of these services may be included in long-term care insurance benefits but most are not covered by general health insurance plans.

Respite Care

Respite care is short term and can be provided in the home or a facility. It allows family caregivers to take some time off to rest and relax and regain perspective on what they have chosen to undertake. Respite care services that acknowledge the significance of culture and provide volunteers or trained staff who speak the language of the patient are most likely to be used.

Types of Long-Term Residential Services

Long-term care options for individuals no longer able to live at home include *congregate housing* (including Section 8 rent-subsidized housing),

assisted living, board and care, intermediate care, and *extended care* facilities. Residents in extended care facilities are subject to pre-admission screening and annual reviews under the Omnibus Budget Reconciliation Act (OBRA) of 1987. OBRA closely regulates the quality of care in these facilities, including the use of psychotropic and other medications. This oversight is especially important since as many as 88% of nursing home residents exhibit symptoms of mental health problems.

The transition from living independently to life in an extended care facility is fraught with emotion for both the elder and the family. It amplifies the elder's fears of being abandoned and may trigger feelings of loss, anger, helplessness, and despair in the elder who is now viewed as old, sick, and frail. The older adult must also confront mortality, the reality of declining health, and realization that this may be the final move. Family reactions include guilt, anger, and resentment.

Hospice Care

Hospice care is based on the philosophy that death is a natural event and should be treated as a normal phase of life. It recognizes that through the provision of palliative care and pain management, individuals can be spared the pain of terminal illness and accorded death with dignity. Creative approaches to symptom control include acupuncture, massage, and exercise. Hospice care is provided in a comfortable home-like setting where care is focused not only on the dying person, but also on the family. A team of physicians, nurses, social workers, therapists, and pastors provide services that include assistance with funeral and burial preparations and help with the disposal of personal items. Ongoing bereavement counseling after the death of the family member is also an integral part of hospice care (see Chapter 31, Palliative Care).

Special Populations

Gay, Lesbian, Bisexual, and Transgender Elders

There are an estimated three million older gays and lesbians in the US. This number is expected to double by 2030. This has been a largely invisible group and little research has been devoted to aging in this population. Many of today's older gays and lesbians grew up when being homosexual was illegal and often considered immoral or sinful. Discrimination and stigma have resulted in marginalization from the health care and mental health sectors and disenfranchisement from aging organizations, housing, employment, and long-term care facilities (see Chapter 21, Health Care Issues Facing Gay, Lesbian, Bisexual, and Transgender Indivduals).

Future Outlook for Older Minorities

Minority elders are expected to account for 24% of the > 65 population in the US by the year 2020. Health care disparities, including access to care and lack of culturally appropriate services, are major concerns in addressing health outcomes and disease prevention (see Chapter 19, Health Care in Minority and Majority Populations).

Extended care facilities have been underutilized by minority populations due largely to cultural concerns (traditions of family care, lack of ethnic meals, few bilingual staff, inattention to traditions), social isolation, and access issues. *Medicare* and *Medicaid* are the primary payers for nursing home services, yet many minority families may not qualify for these programs. The Indian Health Service has never provided nursing home care although the Bureau of Indian Affairs has been charged with providing nursing home care. The first Native American/Alaska Native nursing home was founded in 1969. Today, there are fewer than 20 such facilities on tribal lands/reservations with extended care facilities located at great distances from reservations. This has prompted tribal groups to contemplate building their own facilities using money acquired from tourism or gaming.

While advancements are being made, the status of older minority members is not likely to improve significantly in the immediate future. In addition, the factors that determine quality of life (education, employment, income, health care) are not likely to vary much among any of the minority populations now approaching retirement age.

Recommended Readings

American Geriatrics Society. *Geriatrics at Your Fingertips.* Washington, DC: American Geriatrics Society; 2010.

Birren JE, Shaie KW (Eds.). *Handbook of the Psychology of Aging,* 5th ed. New York: Elsevier; 2006.

Capezuti EA (Ed.). *Encyclopedia of Elder Care.* New York: Springer; 2007.

Gillick MR. *The Denial of Aging: Perpetual Youth, Eternal Life, and Other Dangerous Fantasies.* Boston, MA: Harvard University Press; 2006.

Halter J (Ed.). *Hazzard's Geriatric Medicine and Gerontology,* 6th ed. New York: McGraw Hill; 2009.

Ham RJ. *Primary Care Geriatrics: A Case-Based Approach.* Philadelphia, PA: Mosby; 2007.

Kempler D. *Neurocognitve Disorders in Aging.* Thousand Oaks, CA: Sage; 2005.

Review Questions

1. Which of the following therapies is most effective in treating mood disorders in older adults?
   A. Combined drug and short-term psychotherapy
   B. Drug therapy
   C. Electroconvulsive therapy
   D. Problem-solving psychotherapy
   E. Psychoanalysis

2. Which of the following best describes HIV/AIDS in older adults?
   A. Aging heterosexual men are at greater risk of developing HIV than are older women.
   B. It occurs infrequently because of significantly decreased sexual intimacy.
   C. It occurs less frequently because older adults use safe sex practices.
   D. Symptoms of HIV/AIDS may mimic symptoms of other age-related disorders.
   E. Ten percent of new cases of HIV/AIDS occur in persons 60 and above.

3. Intimate partner abuse among older adults
   A. is most often manifested as psychological abuse.
   B. is perpetrated most frequently by the female partner.
   C. is routinely addressed as part of health care screening.

D. occurs more commonly among those with few resources.

E. occurs more frequently than among younger age groups.

Key to review questions: p. 407

Section VII

Societal and Behavioral Health Challenges

23 Obesity

Kristin A. Evans, MS, and Stephen R. Cook, MD, MPH

- How is obesity defined?
- What health consequences can result from obesity?
- How do individual and environmental factors interact to cause obesity?
- What can be done to reverse the current obesity epidemic?

The current national obesity epidemic is likely being driven by a combination of genetic and psychosocial factors occurring in an environment rife with calorie-dense/nutrient-poor foods. Efforts to reverse the trends in overweight and obesity in the US must include interventions at many levels, ranging from individual behavior modification to national policy changes.

What is Obesity?

How is obesity defined?

Simply defined, **obesity** refers to an excess accumulation of body fat that results in a body mass exceeding a recommended level. An individual's weight status is generally quantified by calculating their **body mass index** (BMI), which is a ratio of body mass (kilograms) to height (meters squared). Adults with a BMI between 25.0 and 29.9 kg/m² are classified as overweight, whereas those with a BMI $\geq$ 30.0 kg/m² are considered obese. Adults with a BMI between 35.0 and 40.0 kg/m² and $\geq$ 40.0 kg/m² are often referred to as severely obese and morbidly obese, respectively.

Children and adolescents are classified clinically as either normal weight, overweight, or obese based on age and gender-specific growth charts developed by the Centers for Disease Control and Prevention (CDC). Children $\geq$ 85th but < 95th BMI percentile for their age and gender are classi-fied as *overweight* and those $\geq$ 95th percentile are considered *obese*.

The Epidemic

According to the CDC's most recent estimates, more than two thirds (68.3%) of the U.S. adult population ($\geq$ 20 y.o.) is overweight or obese, with about one third of those (33.9%) falling into the obese category. Among children and adolescents (2–19 y.o.), nearly one third (31.7%) are overweight or obese, with more than half of those (16.9%) already falling into the obese category. These data reflect a 46% increase in adult overweight/obesity prevalence in the past four decades, and a greater than three-fold increase in child overweight/obesity over that same time period (Figure 23.1).

The proportion of Americans who are overweight and obese varies by race/ethnicity and gender. For example, a greater proportion of blacks and Hispanics are overweight or obese compared to white Americans (73.7% and 76.9% vs. 67.5%). Prevalence of a BMI $\geq$ 25 kg/m² is 72.3% and 64.1% among adult men and women, respectively, although this gender difference also varies with racial/ethnic group. Among whites, a higher percentage of men than women are overweight or obese; the opposite is true among blacks. More Hispanic men than women are overweight or obese, but the difference is less pronounced than among whites, and the pattern seems to shift with increasing age.

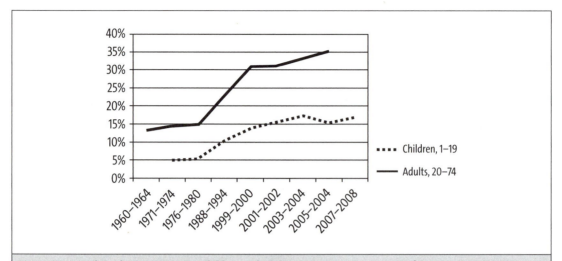

Figure 23.1. Trends in obesity among U.S. children and adults, 1960–2008. Sources: CDC/NCHS, National Health Examination Surveys I–III, and National Health and Nutrition Examination Surveys I–III, 1999–2000, 2001–2002, 2003–2004, 2005–2006, 2007–2008.

Among children (2–19 y.o.), approximately the same proportion (31–32%) of girls and boys have a BMI ≥ 85th percentile, and the racial/ethnic differences are similar to those seen in adults (whites 29.3%, blacks 35.9%, Hispanics 38.2%).

Consequences

What health consequences can result from obesity?

Over the past several decades, it has become increasingly evident that overweight and obesity are much more than just aesthetic problems. Excess body weight and fat significantly increase an individual's risk for a number of other diseases and conditions including insulin resistance, type 2 diabetes, heart disease, osteoarthritis, reproductive complications, and certain cancers including breast, uterine, colon, and kidney cancer. The risk of premature death from any cause is estimated to be 50–100% greater among overweight/obese individuals compared to those who are normal weight. For many diseases, the relative distribution of body fat is a more significant risk factor than BMI. Individuals with excessive *abdominal adiposity*, as opposed to more fat in the lower body (measured via the waist-to-hip ratio), are at greater risk of developing type 2 diabetes or suffering a heart attack.

Economically, the costs associated with obesity in the US are substantial. The most recent gov-ernment estimates indicate that medical spending attributable to overweight/obesity (including in/outpatient services and prescription drug costs) is nearly $150 billion per year, with a substantial portion of that being paid by government-funded insurance programs (Medicare, Medicaid). This total accounts for nearly 10% of all medical expenditures in the US.

What Causes Obesity?

How do individual and environmental factors interact to cause obesity?

At the most fundamental level, overweight and obesity result from an excess intake of food calories in relation to calorie expenditure (basal metabolic rate + physical activity). Although debated in the current literature, the prevailing evidence supports the idea that, on a population level, the positive energy balance associated with the high prevalence of overweight and obesity is due more to an increase in caloric intake than to a substantial decrease in physical activity. The following sections will describe the individual and social factors that influence this energy imbalance, as well as how these forces interact to create the population's weight crisis. Current evidence also supports the notion that obesity is the result of a complex interplay of genetic, environmental, and psychosocial factors.

Genetic Factors

Determining the precise contribution of genes to an individual's body weight and to the obesity epidemic has proven difficult. In only the rarest cases can any single gene explain obesity in a given individual – a phenomenon known as *monogenic obesity*. For the rest of the population, body weight and body fatness are regulated by complex gene-gene and gene-environment interactions. Estimates of the *heritability* of BMI and body fat range from 16–85%, and 35–63%, respectively. To date, more than 100 single genes have been positively associated with the development of obesity; many of them are involved in the regulation of energy metabolism, fat deposition, and hormone signaling. The most compelling evidence supports a role for genes encoding peroxisome proliferator-activated receptors involved in nutrient metabolism, melanocortin-4 receptors involved in feeding and metabolism, β_3-adrenergic receptors regulating lipid metabolism and thermogenesis, and uncoupling proteins involved in oxidative phosphorylation.

Genes associated with neurotransmitter action have also been linked to food intake and body weight/BMI (see Chapter 5, Nutrition, Metabolism, and Feeding Disorders). It has been propo,sed that for some obese people eating is a

> Research has shown that physicians and medical students who themselves engage in regular physical activity are more successful at motivating their patients to do so.

form of addiction in which food intake is reinforced by the pleasurable or positive feelings that follow. The action of the neurotransmitter dopamine is known to be associated with reinforcing/addictive behaviors, and individuals with a certain variant (A1 allele) in a gene that determines the density of dopamine receptors are more likely to experience the reinforcing value of food. Furthermore, obese individuals carrying that allele are more likely than non-obese people with the allele to receive positive reinforcement from food intake. In combination, high food reinforcement behavior and the presence of the A1 allele result in significantly greater food intake than either variable alone.

Psychosocial Stress in an "Obesogenic" Environment

Several conceptual theories have been used to explain the health behaviors that have led to the current obesity epidemic. One often cited theory is the *social ecological model* of behavior (Figure 23.2), which posits that individual health behaviors (e.g., eating, exercise) occur within a multi-layered context encompassing interpersonal relations within a community governed by public policies. In the past decade, much research has focused on the *built environment* (the man-made surroundings in which human activity takes place) regarding its effects on energy intake and expenditure.

In particular, the *retail food environment*, or the availability and types of food in a community, has received much attention as it relates to an individual's dietary practices and obesity risk. The main contention is that residents of communities with greater access to cheap calorie-dense/nutrient-poor foods (e.g., those available at convenience stores and fast food restaurants) compared to affordable healthy foods (e.g., fresh produce available in grocery stores and supermarkets) consume less healthful diets and are therefore at greater risk of obesity and its comorbidities. Large population studies have found that the presence of supermarkets in a community is positively associated with fruit and vegetable consumption, and a relatively greater number of convenience stores and fast food restaurants is associated with a greater prevalence of obesity and diabetes. These associations may partly explain the *racial and socioeconomic disparities* in obesity prevalence, as communities with larger minority populations and greater poverty rates often have less access to supermarkets and grocery stores. Paradoxically, the cost of available healthy food in low-income communities is often greater than the cost of the same food in more affluent areas, mainly due to the lack of supermarkets, which tend to have lower prices than smaller grocery stores.

Elements of the built environment have also been associated with physical activity levels. Environmental studies often categorize neighborhoods and communities based on their "walkability," that is, the extent to which the design of a community allows residents to walk to conduct their daily activities such as shopping. Highly walkable neighborhoods are generally densely populated,

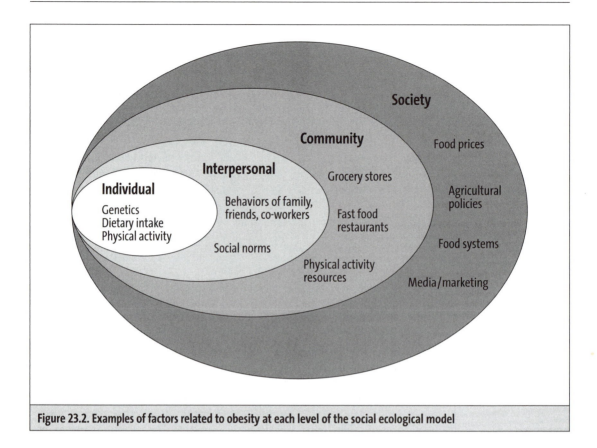

Figure 23.2. Examples of factors related to obesity at each level of the social ecological model

have commercial areas, and have grid-like street patterns. Studies have shown that residents of such neighborhoods tend to engage in more physical activity compared to those living in less walkable areas. There is also some evidence that overweight and obesity are less prevalent in neighborhoods of higher walkability and that neighborhood "greenness" and residential density are negatively associated with children's odds of becoming overweight.

Although overweight and obesity are ultimately a result of individual behaviors, other factors contribute as well. For example, technological changes in the food industry have decreased the time cost of food for consumers. Developments in areas such as food processing, preservation, and packaging allow manufacturers to produce an increasing variety of foods (often high fat/calorie meals and snacks) that require minimal at-home preparation. Proponents of this *"technical change theory"* point to two main facts to support it: (1) the consumption of calories from snacks (the "meal" in which the most technological changes have occurred) has approximately doubled since the 1970s with no compensatory decrease in calories from regular meals, and (2) the greatest increase in BMI

and proportion of obese individuals has occurred among married women, the group for whom the time cost of food has decreased the most (see Wisman et al. in Recommended Readings)

But it *sounds* healthy...

Did you know...?
Applebee's Pecan Crusted Chicken Salad packs a gut-wrenching 1,310 calories and 81 grams of fat – that's the equivalent of eating more than ½ dozen Krispy Kreme doughnuts!

Beware!
Restaurants often drown an otherwise healthy dish of fresh veggies in a fat- and calorie-laden sea of dressings, cheeses, and fried meats.

Try this...
Ask for grilled instead of fried meats, less of the "extras," and your dressing on the side. Many restaurants will also let you order a ½ size salad, automatically saving you ½ the fat and calories (and maybe even leave room for a *sensible* dessert!).

This increase in the variety and quantity of cheap, ready- (or nearly-ready) to-eat, unhealthy foods has occurred in tandem with a nationwide increase in everyday psychosocial stressors and economic insecurity. Studies have found several types of *psychosocial stress* to be associated with weight gain, including job demands, difficulty paying bills, depression, generalized anxiety, and perceived constraint in life. Chronic psychosocial stress may contribute to weight gain in two ways: by increasing pleasure-seeking behaviors that include the consumption of highly palatable but unhealthy foods, and by affecting the production of hormones involved in energy metabolism, namely cortisol and other glucocorticoids. *Acute and chronic stress* lead to elevated glucocorticoid levels, which, in turn, stimulate insulin secretion, promoting both emotionally-induced food intake ("comfort feeding") and fat deposition. Abdominal adipose depots are particularly sensitive to the combination of these hormones.

To burn off...	You would have to...
A McDonald's Big Mac®	Run for 56 min @ 5 mph (or only 26 min @ 10 mph!)
6 Oreo® cookies	Do 4,440 jumping jacks
A large movie theater popcorn	Dance for 2 ½ hours
A Grande Caramel Frappucino®	Shovel snow for 1 hour
3 Olive Garden breadsticks	Mow the lawn for 1 ½ hours (with a push mower!)

> The socioeconomic gradient in obesity observed in the US may be due in part to the chronic stress and insecurity experienced at lower income levels. The growing gap between the richest Americans and the rest of the country supports the notion that social and economic pressures are contributing to the obesity epidemic.

Curbing the epidemic

> What can be done to reverse the current obesity epidemic?

On the individual level, preventing overweight and obesity is conceptually simple: excessive weight gain can be avoided by maintaining energy balance through a healthy diet and regular physical activity. This advice, however, can be difficult to adhere to in an obesogenic environment. Although healthy eating and physical activity remain the mainstays of public health messages, higher-level interventions are needed to promote the nationwide change in individual behaviors that can curb and reverse the obesity epidemic. Recent community initiatives include improving healthy food options and physical activity in childcare and school environments, passing laws to limit sales and marketing of unhealthy foods and beverages to children, and making healthy foods more widely available in corner stores of low-income communities. Taxation of sugar-sweetened beverages and other unhealthy items has become a topic of national debate. Ending the country's weight problem must become a national priority, but it will require collaboration among many sectors of society to achieve.

Recommended Readings

Hu F. *Obesity Epidemiology*. New York: Oxford University Press; 2008.

Sallis JF, Glanz K. Physical activity and food environments: Solutions to the obesity epidemic. *Milbank Quarterly* 2009; 67:123–154.

White House Task Force on Childhood Obesity, Report to the President (May 2010). *Solving the Problem of Childhood Obesity Within a Generation*. Available at http://online.wsj.com/public/resources/documents/obesity May2010.pdf

Wisman JD, Capehart KW. Creative destruction, economic insecurity, stress, and epidemic obesity. *American Journal of Economics and Sociology* 2010; 69:936–982.

Yang WJ, Kelly T, He J. Genetic epidemiology of obesity. *Epidemiologic Reviews* 2007; 29:49–61.

Review questions

1. Children are classified as obese if they are at or above what age/gender-specific BMI percentile?
    A. 50th
    B. 66th
    C. 75th
    D. 85th
    E. 95th

2. Which BMI would classify an adult as overweight?
    A. 23.0
    B. 24.9
    C. 27.5
    D. 30.1
    E. 35.5

3. Which of the following has been identified as a contributing factor in the development of overweight and obesity?
    A. Environment
    B. Genes
    C. Hormones
    D. Stress
    E. All of the above

4. Which of the following is true about the retail food environment?
    A. Access to convenience stores and fast food restaurants is associated with lower risk of diabetes.
    B. Fresh produce and other healthy foods are generally more affordable than unhealthy foods.
    C. Low-income communities often have greater access to cheap unhealthy foods than to nutritious foods.
    D. Supermarket availability is associated with greater obesity risk.
    E. Technological advances have made healthy foods more affordable and easier to prepare.

5. All of these public health interventions have been proposed to address the obesity epidemic EXCEPT
    A. imposing taxes on unhealthy foods.
    B. improving access to and affordability of healthy foods in corner stores.
    C. improving food quality in childcare environments.
    D. requiring all schools to allow 10 hours of physical education or recess per week.
    E. restricting the marketing and sales of unhealthy foods and beverages to children.

Key to review questions: p. 407

24 Eating Disorders

Richard E. Kreipe, MD, Taylor B. Starr, DO, MPH, and Rachel E. Simeone

- How are eating disorders defined?
- What are the characteristic features of affected individuals?
- What are the causes of eating disorders?
- In assessing eating disorders, what other medical disorders must be ruled out?
- How are eating disorders treated?
- What is the prognosis for patients with eating disorders?

In the last 8 months, Brittany, a 14-year-old high school freshman, has joined the cross-country team, lost 9 lbs in an attempt to "get in shape," become a vegetarian, and has not menstruated after having normal periods for a year. Although her Body Mass Index (BMI) is at the 10th percentile, she reports feeling fat and needing to lose more weight. On examination, she is thin, cold with bluish hands and feet, and a low supine heart rate that almost doubles on standing. She notes feeling sad and worried that she will not be allowed to lose more weight. She also worries about her grades, although she is at the top of her class. Laboratory findings are all normal. She sleeps about 6 hours per night, and does not eat breakfast because she needs to get ready for school.

Definitions

How are eating disorders defined?

The predominant eating disorders (EDs) are **Anorexia Nervosa** (AN) and **Bulimia Nervosa** (BN). AN is characterized by overestimation of body size and shape, with a relentless pursuit of thinness that typically combines excessive dieting and compulsive exercising. AN is divided into a *restrictive* subtype in which caloric intake is severely limited, and a *binge-purge* subtype fea-

turing intermittent overeating followed by acts to rid the body of calories by vomiting or taking laxatives. Bulimia Nervosa (BN) is characterized by episodes of eating large amounts of food in a brief period (binge eating), followed by acts intended to eliminate or reduce the effects of ingested calories by vomiting, laxative use, exercise, or fasting. The majority of children and adolescents with EDs do *not* fulfill all of the criteria for either of these syndromes in the DSM-IV classification system. Instead, they fall into the category of Eating Disorder-Not Otherwise Specified (ED-NOS), which covers a wide variety of clinical presentations, including **Binge Eating Disorder** (BED), in which binge eating is not followed by compensatory behavior and, therefore, results in obesity. Proposed changes in the DSM-5 include less stringent criteria and BED as a separate category.

Characteristic Features

What are the characteristic features of affected individuals?

The distribution of EDs in the population is not uniform. AN typically is seen in white, early to middle adolescent females of above average intelligence and socioeconomic status, who are conflict-avoidant, risk-aversive, anxious, and perfectionist, and who often have depressed mood or obsessive-compulsive traits. BN tends to emerge in later adolescence, sometimes following AN, and is typified by impulsivity and difficulty in maintaining stable relationships, and depression. The 0.5–1% and 3–5% incidence rates among younger and older adolescent females for AN and BN, respectively, most likely reflect ascertainment bias in sampling and under-diagnosis in cases not fitting the typical profile. The same may be true of the significant gender disparity noted in affected individuals: females account for 90% of patients diagnosed with EDs. Among men, gay males are at increased risk due to the cultural emphasis on thinness and appearance. Other groups at risk include athletes, models, and dancers, regardless of gender. Male body builders are also at risk and can develop muscle *dysmorphia* or "reverse AN" in their desire to increase muscle and "get bigger." Depending on the sensitivity of the criteria used in diagnosis and the particular demographic features of the specific groups, ≥ 10% of some adolescent female populations may have ED-NOS.

Causes of Eating Disorders

> What are the causes of eating disorders?

Eating disorders are best viewed as a final common pathway, with a number of *predisposing* factors that increase the risk of developing an ED; *precipitating* factors often related to developmental processes of adolescence triggering the emergence of the ED; and *perpetuating* factors that cause an ED to persist.

Predisposing Factors

The range of heritability estimates for AN is 48%–76% and for BN is 54%–85%. **Genetic vulnerability** may be activated in girls at early and mid-stage puberty due to neuroendocrine changes. Speculations about what is inheritable include eating regulatory mechanisms, temperament and character styles, and biological predispositions such as ovarian hormone activity and serotonin system functioning that help regulate hunger, sati-

ety, and mood. For example, the dysregulation of **serotonin** systems appears to be involved in the development and maintenance of eating disorders. Recent studies also suggest that in AN there may be a dysfunction in the cortico-striatal-insular neural network, wherein the insula fails in its role as a connection and regulator between cortical and subcortical structures involved in AN (see Chapter 5, Nutrition, Metabolism, and Feeding Disorders).

Family influence in the development of EDs is complex because of the interplay of genetic, environmental, and developmental factors. Genetic research suggests that shared elements of the family environment and immutable genetic factors account for about equal variance in disordered eating. The emergence of EDs coinciding with the processes of adolescence (e.g., puberty, identity, autonomy, and cognition) indicates the central role of development in pathogenesis. Inherited genetic factors influence the emergence of EDs during adolescence, but only indirectly. A genetic predisposition to anxiety, depression, or obsessive/compulsive traits, modulated through puberty, appears to mediate the risk of developing an ED.

> There is little evidence that parents "cause" an ED in their child or adolescent. However, parental involvement in treatment is essential to successful recovery.

Research indicates a complex interplay of culture, ethnicity, gender, peers, and family on disordered eating. The gender dimorphism is presumably related to female perception of a relationship between body image and self-evaluation. Numerous studies demonstrate the influence of the Western cultural "thin body ideal" on the development of EDs. Race and ethnicity appear to moderate the association between risk factors and disordered eating, with African American and Caribbean females reporting lower body dissatisfaction and less dieting than Hispanic and non-Hispanic white females.

Peer acceptance is central to healthy adolescent growth and development, especially in early adolescence when the prevalence of AN initially peaks. Indeed, numerous studies, including experimental designs, support causal relationships among peer pressure, body image, and eating. Teasing by peers or by family members (especially males) may be a contributing factor for over-weight girls. Studies showing associations among parent and child eating behaviors, dieting, and physical activity levels suggest parental reinforcement of body-related societal messages.

> A history of sexual trauma is not significantly more common in individuals with eating disorders than in the population at large but, when present, makes recovery more difficult.

Precipitating Factors

Dieting is an especially significant precipitating factor in the development of disordered eating behavior. The causal relationship between dieting and eating disorders is unclear but may involve the physical effects of relative starvation and internalization of a "thin ideal," the experience of negative social comparisons, family or peer pressure to be thin, or peer teasing, all of which can create body dissatisfaction leading to dieting.

Perpetuating Factors

When persistent, the biological effects of significant starvation and malnutrition (e.g., true loss of appetite, hypothermia, gastric atony, amenorrhea, sleep disturbance, fatigue, weakness, and depression) combined with the psychological boosts that come from an increased sense of mastery and reduced emotional reactivity, actually "reward" and maintain pathological ED behaviors. This positive reinforcement of behaviors and consequences, generally viewed by parents and others as "negative," helps to explain why affected individuals characteristically deny that a problem exists and resist treatment. Though noxious, purging can be reinforcing due to a reduction in the anxiety triggered by over-eating; purging also can result in short-term, but reinforcing, improvement in mood that is related to changes in neurotransmitter levels. Recent studies indicate that an imbalance in neurotransmitters, most notably serotonin and dopamine, and possibly ghrelin and leptin, support the concept of EDs as both brain and behavioral disorders. However, the cause-effect relationship between CNS alterations and EDs is not clear, nor is reversibility.

Assessment

> In assessing eating disorders, what other medical disorders must be ruled out?

A careful history and thorough physical exam sometimes supplemented by self-report questionnaires help to target health care interventions. Thus, symptoms of excessive weight loss (feeling tired, cold, lacking energy, dizziness, and difficulty concentrating) can be linked to hypothermia with acrocyanosis and slow capillary refill, loss of muscle mass, and bradycardia with orthostasis. Table 24.1 details common eating and weight control behaviors and associated symptoms and signs that should be addressed in providing treatment.

Differential Diagnosis

Weight loss can occur in increased catabolism (e.g., malignancy or occult infection) or malabsorption (e.g., regional enteritis or celiac disease), but these illnesses are usually associated with other findings and are not typically associated with decreased caloric intake. However, the distinctions are not always clear cut. For example, patients with inflammatory bowel disease (IBD) experience abdominal cramping, and patients with AN may experience abdominal discomfort because of gastric atony.

Endocrinopathies can also share features with EDs. In BN, voracious appetite in the face of weight loss might suggest diabetes mellitus, but blood glucose levels are normal or low in EDs. Adrenal insufficiency mimics many physical symptoms and signs found in restrictive AN, and the overall presentation of AN can include symptoms of both under- and over-active thyroid function, such as hypothermia, bradycardia, and constipation, and weight loss and excessive physical activity, respectively.

In the CNS, craniopharyngiomas (Rathke pouch tumors) can mimic some of the findings of AN, such as weight loss and growth failure, and even some body image disturbances. However, the latter are less fixed than in typical EDs and are associated with other findings, including evidence of increased intracranial pressure. Any patient with an atypical presentation of an ED, based on age, sex, or other factors, deserves a scrupulous

Table 24.1. Eating and weight control habits, signs, and symptoms associated with eating disorders

Habits	Prominent Feature	
	Anorexia Nervosa	Bulimia Nervosa
Intake	Inadequate calories; low calorie and non-fat foods predominate	May restrict during the day, then binge at night on "forbidden" food.
Food	Monotonous "healthy" food/ beverages of low caloric density	Aware of calories and fat, but less regimented than AN
Beverages	Water or other low/no calorie drinks; non-fat milk	Variable, diet soda common; may drink alcohol to excess
Meals	Rigidly consistent schedule and structure to meal plan	Impulsive and unregulated binges followed by purging
Snacks	Reduced or eliminated	Large amounts common in impulsive or planned binges
Dieting	Initial habit that becomes progressively restrictive	Initial habit that gives way to chaotic eating and binges
Binge eating	Essential feature in binge/purge subtype	Essential feature, often secretive, followed by shame/guilt
Exercise	Compulsive, ritualistic, often linked to sport (dance, track)	Less predictable; may be athletic or avoid exercise
Vomiting	More common in binge/purge subtype; may chew, then spit out food	Most common means used to eliminate effects of eating/overeating
Laxatives	Restrictive subtype for constipation; binge/ purge subtype for catharsis	Second most common habit to reduce or avoid weight gain
Diet pills	Very rare except in binge/purge subtype	Used to reduce appetite or increase metabolism
Symptoms		
Body image	Distorted, feels fat/fears getting bigger; strong drive for thinness	May be overweight; desire to avoid weight gain predominant
Metabolism	Hypometabolic (cold, tired, weak, lacking energy)	Variable, depending on balance of intake and output and hydration
Skin	Cold, cyanotic extremities; dry, delayed healing, easy bruising	Self-injurious behavior (cutting, scratching) may occur
Hair	Lanugo-type hair on face/upper body; alopecia of scalp hair	–
Eyes	–	Subconjunctival hemorrhage from vomiting
Teeth	–	Enamel erosion with tooth decay/fracture/loss due to stomach acid
Salivary glands	–	Enlargement of parotid and/or submandibular glands
Heart	Dizziness, fainting, palpitations	Dizziness, fainting, palpitations
Abdomen	Full, bloated, discomfort after eating small amounts; constipation	Discomfort after a binge; cramps/diarrhea with laxative abuse
Mental status	Depression, anxiety, obsessive/compulsive symptoms	Depression, anxiety; borderline personality traits; substance use

search for an alternative explanation. Finally, individuals may have both an underlying illness and an eating disorder.

Laboratory Findings

Laboratory abnormalities, when found, are due to malnutrition, weight control behaviors, or medical complications; studies should be chosen based on history and physical examination. A routine screening battery typically includes: a complete blood count, an erythrocyte sedimentation rate (should be normal), and a biochemical profile. Common abnormalities associated with eating disorders include (1) low white blood cell count with normal hemoglobin and differential; (2) hypokalemic, hypochloremic metabolic alkalosis if there is severe persistent vomiting; (3) mildly elevated liver enzymes, cholesterol, and cortisol levels; (4) low gonadotropin and blood glucose levels with marked weight loss; and (5) generally normal total serum protein, serum albumin, and renal function. An electrocardiogram may be useful when profound bradycardia or arrhythmia is detected; the ECG typically has low voltage, with non-specific ST or T wave changes. Although prolonged QT_c has been reported, prospective studies have not found any increased risk associated with this finding.

Treatment

> How are eating disorders treated?

Health Care Monitoring

While explicitly linking ED behaviors to symptoms and signs may increase some patients' motivation to change, unresolved psychosocial conflicts in both the *intra*-personal (self-esteem, self-efficacy) and *inter*-personal (family, peers, school) domains may impede change. Weight control practices initiated as coping mechanisms become reinforced because of positive feedback. That is, "external" rewards (e.g., compliments about improved physical appearance) and "internal" rewards (e.g., perceived mastery over what is eaten or what is done to minimize the effects of

overeating through exercise or purging) are more powerful in maintaining behavior than negative feedback (e.g., conflict with parents, peers, and others about eating) is to change it. Thus, definitive treatment requires the development of more productive means of coping.

Health care visits should focus on behaviors, symptoms, and signs. Daily journals can be reviewed at each visit: caloric intake (food/drink, amount, time, location), physical activity (type, duration, intensity), and emotional state (e.g., angry, sad, worried). Focusing on recorded data helps to identify dietary and activity deficiencies and excesses as well as behavioral and mental health patterns.

Patients with AN tend to overestimate their caloric intake and underestimate their activity level. Thus, prior to reviewing journal entries, it is important to measure: (1) weight, without underwear, in a hospital gown after voiding, (2) urine specific gravity, (3) temperature, and (4) blood pressure and pulse in supine, sitting, and standing positions to provide objective data about health status. In addition, a targeted physical examination focused on hypometabolism, cardiovascular stability, and mental status, as well as any related symptoms should occur at each visit to monitor progress (or regression).

Nutrition and Physical Activity

The most important element of treatment for EDs is emphasizing that "*food is medicine.*" Framing food as fuel for the body and the source of energy for daily activities emphasizes health. For patients with low weight, the nutrition prescription should be designed to gradually increase weight at the rate of about ½ to 1 lb/week. This can be accomplished by increasing energy intake by ~200 kCal every few days toward a target of approximately 90% of average body weight for gender, height, and age. Weight gain will not occur until intake exceeds output. Intake for continued weight gain may exceed 3,500 kCal/day, especially for patients who are anxious and have high levels of non-exercise activity thermogenesis. Stabilizing intake is the goal for patients with BN, with a gradual introduction of "forbidden foods" while also limiting foods that may "trigger" a binge.

Dysfunctional cognitions include "all-or-none" thinking (related to perfectionism) with a tendency to over-generalize and jump to catastrophic con-clusions. Affected patients also believe that their body is governed by rules that do not apply to others. These tendencies lead to dichotomization of foods into "good" or "bad" categories, having a day "ruined" because of one unexpected food-related event, or choosing foods based on rigid self-imposed restrictions. These cognitions may be associated with neurotransmitter abnormali-ties related to executive function and rewards (see Chapter 5, Nutrition, Metabolism, and Feeding Disorders).

Patients with AN tend to follow highly struc-tured routines with markedly restricted intake; in contrast, patients with BN tend to lack structure, which results in chaotic eating patterns and binge/purge episodes. Patients with AN, BN, or ED-NOS all benefit from a structured plan for healthy eat-ing that includes three meals and at least one snack distributed evenly over the day and based on bal-anced meal planning. Breakfast deserves special emphasis because it is often the first meal elimi-nated in AN and is frequently avoided the morn-ing after a binge/purge episode in BN. In addition to structuring meals and snacks, patients should structure their activities. If appropriate, moni-tored exercise (≤ 45 minutes daily, at no more than moderate intensity) can improve mood and make increasing calories more acceptable.

Mental Health

Selective serotonin reuptake inhibitors (SSRIs) have minimal effect until weight is restored. With weight restored, however, SSRIs are effective in reducing binge/purge behaviors regardless of depression and are considered a standard element of therapy in BN. The dose of SSRI in the treat-ment of BN may require the equivalent of 60 mg of fluoxetine or more to maintain effectiveness.

Evidence-based studies indicate that *cogni-tive behavioral therapy* (CBT), which focuses on restructuring "thinking errors" and establishing adaptive patterns of behavior, is more effective than interpersonal or psychoanalytic approaches. *Dialectical behavioral therapy* (DBT), a form of CBT in which distorted thoughts and emotional responses are challenged, analyzed, and replaced with healthier responses, requires adult thinking skills and is useful for older patients with BN.

Group therapy can provide support, but requires skilled leadership because combining patients at various levels of recovery, who experience vari-able reinforcement from dysfunctional coping behaviors, can be challenging.

As a general principle, the younger the patient, the more intimately the parents need to be involved in therapy. The only approach with evidence-based effectiveness in the treatment of AN in children and adolescents is *family-based treatment*, exemplified by the Maudsley approach (www.maudsleyparents.org). This three-phase intensive outpatient model (1) helps parents play a positive role in restoring their child's eating pat-tern and weight to normal, then (2) returns "con-trol" of eating to the child who has demonstrated the ability to maintain healthy weight, and then (3) encourages healthy progression in the other domains of adolescent development. Features of effective family treatment include an "agnostic" approach in which the cause of the disease is irrel-evant to weight gain, emphasizing that parents are NOT to blame for EDs. Parents are taught to model healthy eating behaviors by sharing many meals with their affected child. They are also encouraged to be actively nurturing and support-ive of their child's healthy eating while reinforcing limits on dysfunctional habits, rather than assum-ing the role of authoritarian "food police" or main-taining a completely hands-off approach. Finally, parents are the best resource for recovery for almost all patients, and their positive role should be reinforced by professionals who serve as con-sultants and advisors.

Supportive Care

Support groups are often designed primarily for parents. Because their daughter or son with an ED typically resists the diagnosis and treatment, parents may feel helpless and hopeless. Because of the historical precedent of blaming parents for causing EDs (only recently recognized in the psy-chiatric literature as neither accurate nor useful), parents frequently express feelings of shame and isolation. Support groups and multi-family thera-py sessions bring parents together with other par-ents whose families are at various stages of recov-ery from an ED in ways that are both educational and encouraging. Because of residual body image or other issues, patients often benefit from support groups after intensive treatment or at the end of treatment.

Prognosis

With early diagnosis and effective treatment, ≥ 80% of youth with AN recover physiologically (i.e., develop normal eating and weight control habits, resume menses, maintain average weight for height, and function in school, work, and relationships), although some still have residual body image distortions. When weight is restored to normal, fertility appears to return as well, although the weight for resumption of menses (about 92% of average body weight for height) may be lower than the weight for ovulation. Unfortunately, up to 10% of severely affected patients die. The prognosis for youth with BN is less well established, but may be better than the prognosis for youth with AN. Death is a major risk when electrolyte abnormalities lead to cardiac arrhythmias or severe esophageal tears. Outcome improves with multidimensional treatment that includes SSRIs and attention to mood, past trauma, impulsivity, and psychopathology, if it exists.

Recommended Readings

Culbert KM, Slane JD, Klump KL. Genetics of eating disorders. *Annual Review of Eating Disorders* 2008; part 2:27–42.

Favaro A, Monteleone P, Santonastaso P, Maj M. Psychobiology of eating disorders. *Annual Review of Eating Disorders;* 2008; part 2:1–26.

Fisher M. Treatment of eating disorders in children, adolescents, and young adults. *Pediatrics in Review* 2006; 27:5–16.

Katzman DK. Medical complications in adolescents with anorexia nervosa: A review of the literature. *International Journal of Eating Disorders* 2005; 37:S52–S59.

Neumark-Sztainer D. Preventing obesity and eating disorders in adolescents: What can health care providers do? *Adolescent Health* 2009; 44:206–213.

Rosen DS. American Academy of Pediatrics Committee on Adolescence. Identification and management of eating disorders in children and adolescents. *Pediatrics* 2010; 126:1240–53.

Review Questions

1. A 17-year-old male with bulimia nervosa has been vomiting three times a day for the past two weeks so he can wrestle at a lower weight class. Of the following, which is the most common pattern of electrolyte disturbance that would be expected?
   A. Chloride high; Sodium high; Carbon dioxide high
   B. Chloride low; Sodium low; Carbon dioxide low
   C. Potassium low; Chloride high; Sodium high
   D. Potassium low; Chloride low; Carbon dioxide high
   E. Sodium low; Potassium high, Carbon dioxide low

2. A 15-year-old female is referred to a psychiatrist for evaluation and therapy after being evaluated by her primary care physician whose referral note describes her as a "classic case of anorexia nervosa." Which weight control methods were most likely reported by the patient?
   A. Appetite suppressants and vomiting
   B. "Fat burning" supplements and exercise
   C. High protein diet and appetite suppressants
   D. Low fat diet and exercise
   E. Metabolism stimulants and laxatives

3. A 14-year-old female cross-country runner with restrictive anorexia nervosa and a BMI below the 3rd percentile presents for a sports pre-participation evaluation. Which of the following would most likely be found on physical examination?
   A. Alopecia and tachycardia
   B. Dental enamel erosion and salivary gland enlargement
   C. Gingival hyptertrophy and cervical lymphadenopathy
   D. Hypothermia and bradycardia
   E. Knuckle calluses and self-inflicted cuts

Key to review questions: p. 407

25 Substance Abuse

Maria Fernanda Gómez, MD, João V. Nunes, MD, and Andre K. Ragnauth, PhD

- Which drugs are most likely to be abused?
- What dangerous health behaviors are associated with substance abuse?
- What physical and psychological factors contribute to substance abuse or dependence?
- What are some treatment approaches and how do they work?
- What is a "network intervention?"
- What is a "harm reduction" program?

Understanding **substance related disorders** requires a grasp of the following conditions. *Substance intoxication* develops soon after ingestion of a drug and reverses once the drug is metabolized and excreted. Its psychological signs and symptoms and maladaptive behavioral changes are due to the effects of the substance on the CNS. *Substance abuse* is maladaptive use that disrupts or impairs functioning at work, school, home, or leisure. It often causes or precipitates physical and psychological harm and persistent legal, social, and interpersonal problems. *Substance dependence* reflects the need to rely on a substance, marked by substance tolerance, substance withdrawal, and preoccupation with obtaining or recovery from the substance. *Tolerance* is a state of need for increased amounts of the substance to achieve a desired effect, or in which the same amount of substance produces a diminished effect. *Withdrawal* is the physical and psychological signs and symptoms that occur when a person dependent on a substance stops using it for a period of time. Withdrawal symptoms can be reversed if the drug or a suitable substitute is used.

The American Psychiatric Association is revising the diagnostic classification and terminology of the substance related disorders in the 5th edition of the DSM. The term *addiction* instead of *dependence* might better convey the appropriate meaning of compulsive drug-taking disorders and provides a better distinction from physical dependence, which is a normal consequence of continuous use of psychoactive substances.

Substance abuse and dependence lock persons into disordered, cyclical, and destructive patterns of behavior preventing them from exercising the sound judgment that enables them to resist. This leaves such persons vulnerable to risky behaviors such as sharing used needles. In "shooting galleries," drug users often engage in communal drug injecting through needle and syringe sharing, without cleansing or discarding them between uses. Such practices result in frequent micro transfusions accompanied by disease transmission. The risk is multiplied by the frequency of injections. Drug users who inject heroin alone or in combination with cocaine "shoot up," on average, three to five times a day. Intravenous cocaine users may inject every 15 minutes to maintain a "high."

Which drugs are most likely to be abused?

Alcohol, which is used by about 50% of the world's adult population, is the most commonly used psychoactive substance and alcoholism is the most common substance use disorder worldwide. In 2009, approximately 75% of Americans ≥ 12 years of age had used alcohol at least once in their lifetime and 51.9% reported being current drinkers of alcohol. This translates to an estimated 130.6 million people. About 15% of the U.S. health care dollar goes to treating alcohol-related disorders,

Commonly Abused Psychoactive Substances

- Alcohol
- Opioids (morphine, oxycontin, meperidine, methadone, oxycodone, heroin)
- Sympathomimetics/stimulants (amphetamine, methamphetamine or MDMA, cocaine)
- CNS depressants (barbiturates, methaqualone, benzodiazepines)
- Inhalants (nitrous oxide/volatile hydrocarbons)
- Hallucinogens (LSD, mescaline)
- PCP
- Belladonna alkaloids (atropine, scopolamine)
- Cannabis, nicotine, caffeine
- Designer/"club" drugs (MDMA, ketamine, GHB, rophenol)

and alcohol-related deaths rank third behind heart disease and cancer.

Marijuana use has increased in most areas of the US, primarily because of resurgence among adolescents. The rate of use of substances such as *inhalants* and *LSD* is also increasing among adolescents, and even preadolesents. Use of *crack cocaine* declined until the early 1990s. Since then, use has been rising again. The use of *heroin* is also increasing. It is available on the street in close to pure form, which makes the "high" conferred by inhalation (which is especially appealing to females) similar to that obtained by injection. The purer forms of both heroin and crack are often

sprinkled on marijuana and serve as an adolescent's introduction to the harder drugs of abuse.

What dangerous health behaviors are associated with substance abuse?

Intravenous drug use is an important vehicle for the acquisition and transmission of blood-borne infectious diseases (e.g., hepatitis B and C, HIV/AIDS), and ranks immediately behind unsafe sex practices as the most common risky behavior in which individuals with HIV/AIDS engage. More than 45,000 cases of AIDS in the US have been attributed to IV drug use. Although the rate of infection among IV drug users nationwide stabilized at approximately 40–45% in 2001, the rate of HIV infection among injecting drug users in New York City is estimated at 50%.

Etiological Factors

What physical and psychological factors contribute to substance abuse or dependence?

Understanding the bio-behavioral mechanism of alcoholism contributes to the disease model of addiction and greatly reduces the stigma attached to affected individuals.

Although imitation of peers is a potent factor in drug use, children and adolescents often first experiment with drugs as a way of coping with tension in the family. In such situations, drug use must be understood in the context of family dynamics. Adolescents sometimes use drugs to attract their parents' attention, as if to communicate that it is preferable to receive negative attention and punishment from parents than to be ignored. Conversely, drug use by acting-out adolescents may be encouraged covertly by the family so it can focus on the drug using behavior instead of focusing on underlying problems that threaten the integrity of the family.

Children may perceive parental substance use (alcohol included) as tacitly condoning such use by the children. If the parents prohibit and punish the children for behaviors the parents themselves exhibit, the children may dismiss the parents as hypocritical. Alcohol use poses an especially dif-

Effects of Alcohol on Different Organ Systems

Cardiovascular	Arrhythmias, cardiomyopathy
Gastrointestinal	Gastritis, bleeding, hepatitis, fatty liver, cirrhosis
Neurological	Neuropathy, dementia, cerebellar degeneration, Wernike-Korsakoff Syndrome
Immune	Suppression leading to increased infection
Neuroendocrine	Erectile dysfunction, testicular atrophy, feminization
Gynecological/ Reproductive	Infertility, fetal alcohol syndrome, other teratogenicity

Patterns of Substance Use and Misuse

- Experimental (may abate, intensify, or turn into other types of use)
- Social-recreational (may remain as such, intensify, or become compulsive)
- Circumstantial-situational (opportunistic; may intensify, or become compulsive)
- Compulsive (maladaptive)
- Intensified (often a quality of the other patterns)

Note: While all patterns of substance use may become maladaptive and impair functioning, a compulsive pattern is always maladaptive.

ficult challenge for adolescents. Because it is pervasive in all segments of society, adolescents may view drinking alcohol as an aspect of identity formation and as a marker of adulthood.

Family problems associated with substance abuse include neglect, marital discord, job loss and frequent relocations, and disrupted family dynamics, peer relationships, and social stability. Children of substance abusers may be stigmatized in school and the community. To cope with the resulting stress, some resort to abusing substances themselves. The children may understand this behavior as cognitively and emotionally maladaptive, but they may be unaware of resources that could allow them to break the behavioral cycle or they may not be in a position to access such resources without parental assistance.

Bio-behavioral Mechanisms of Dependence

Certain people appear to be at increased risk for developing alcohol misuse disorders. This risk presumably reflects the genetic variability of reward systems in the brain. Cross fostering studies revealed that genetic risk may be greater than social risk in offspring of alcohol abusers. Genes that influence the metabolism of alcohol (aldehyde dehydrogenase deficiency) may be protective because they induce a negative reaction (nausea, vomiting) to drinking alcohol. This gene is particularly prevalent among, for example, Asian populations.

The brain *reward circuit* includes dopaminergic neurons located in the ventral tegmental area (VTA). VTA neurons project to and modulate the neuronal activity of the nucleus accumbens (NAcc) neurons via the medial forebrain bundle. The NAcc has extensive connections with the prefrontal association cortices and basolateral amygdalae. These connections give this circuit wide influence on behavior, including behavioral responses to stimuli that promote feelings of pleasure, reward, and motivation. Most drugs of abuse (e.g., cocaine and amphetamine) produce marked episodic increases in dopamine levels in the NAcc, which disrupts the reward system. Psychoactive substance stimulation or disinhibition of VTA neurons, whose projections release dopamine in the NAcc, initiates what is perceived as a rewarding experience. Such reward positively reinforces the behavior. Reinforcement also occurs when the physical and psychological discomfort triggered by substance withdrawal is relieved by use of the same or similar substances.

This system is considered the final common pathway for reward and the regulation of motivation. The pleasurable signal drugs of abuse create in the brain reinforces their continued use, leading to further drug-seeking, which displaces more adaptive behaviors.

Substance Abuse Treatment Programs

What are some treatment approaches and how do they work?

Three principles guide the development of treatment for substance abusers:

1. Adverse physical symptoms must be minimal (few people knowingly put themselves in a position where discomfort and pain are likely).
2. The motivation for giving up the substance must be greater than the motivation for continued use.
3. Places, activities, and other situations strongly associated with using the substance (smoking while drinking a cocktail or coffee) must be avoided.

Treatment cannot begin until the patient takes initial steps toward recovery by voluntarily entering a program and developing a therapeutic relationship with a counselor. Recidivism is high even for those who take these steps, but it approaches 100% among those who are involuntarily enrolled in treatment unless they eventually participate voluntarily.

Supportive care for patients who are experiencing a "bad trip" from LSD may entail only a quiet space and a warm reassuring person to "talk them down." Supportive care during withdrawal depends on the type of drug the patient used and the patient's place within the withdrawal cycle. While hallucinogens, marijuana, and caffeine are exceptions, most drugs of abuse are associated with significant withdrawal symptoms. These may not be life threatening, but they do require prompt recognition and proper treatment. Withdrawal from cocaine may have serious emotional and psychological consequences, including risk for suicide.

Treatment Approaches

1 Detoxification (acute; 5–21 days)
2. Rehabilitation (short-term; 28 days)
3. Residential (long-term; 6–24 months)

Detoxification, employed to treat the acute physical effects of withdrawal from opiates, alcohol, and sedative-hypnotics, is provided in medical units. On average, length of stay for detoxification ranges from 5 days for alcohol and 14 days for opiates to 21 days for benzodiazepines. Detoxification programs are designed to prevent potentially life-threatening withdrawal syndromes through treatment prescribed by protocol. Affected patients are usually given a substance for which they have a cross tolerance that is administered in tapered doses over a defined number of days. As a rule, "detox" treatment teams include physicians, nurses, social workers, rehabilitation and occupational counselors, and certified alcoholism and substance abuse counselors. Most offer 12-step and other *relapse prevention* programs.

After detoxification, many patients enter 28-day *short-term rehabilitation programs* that offer a full schedule of structured activities to divert attention away from wanting or needing drugs, motivate continued progress toward recovery, and prevent early relapse. Typical activities include health education, HIV counseling, individual supportive or insight-oriented counseling, acupuncture, rehabilitation/vocational services, and groups that focus on support, spirituality, relaxation, meditation, and activities of daily living (personal grooming, housekeeping, recreational/gym activities).

Some patients enter *residential programs* for 6 months to 2 years of intense therapy and limited contact with the world outside. The goal is lifelong sobriety and abstinence from drugs through improvement in emotional state and belief system, while providing employment and education. Success requires commitment and adherence to strict rules. Many enroll in such programs as court ordered alternatives to incarceration. Those who are poorly motivated or who enroll only to satisfy others may be unable to engage in the required self-reflection or tolerate continuous scrutiny. Like most substance abuse programs, residential programs rely on peer counselors and role models.

Adjunctive pharmacological treatments are available to facilitate abstinence in alcoholics. These include disulfiram which induces aversive symptoms like nausea and vomiting after drinking; maltrexone, which reduces craving and the reward experience; and acamprosate, which reduces craving. The 12-step self-led program of Alcoholics Anonymous has also been adapted to the treatment of other addictions. Such programs require persons to participate in groups where members work through a hierarchy of spiritual, psychological, and behavioral steps to accept the reality of their loss of control and eventually recommit to a non-using lifestyle.

Network Intervention

What is a "network intervention?"

Network intervention generally occurs in treatment settings (residential, non-residential; short- or long-term). The therapist recruits and engages the addicted patient and the assistance of significant others (family, friends) to provide support, encouragement, and monitoring. Significant others provide accurate assessment of progress in recovery (e.g., quantity and pattern of use), while their involvement reinforces the message that the patient has not been abandoned and others are invested in the program and its success.

Smoking Cessation Programs

Smoking cessation programs follow the same tenets as programs designed to treat other drug addictions, emphasizing recovery and relapse prevention. Nicotine withdrawal produces uncomfortable symptoms that, like those from other drugs, need specific therapeutic attention. To aid recovery and prevention relapse, many smoking cessation programs use transdermal nicotine patches and nicotine gum as replacement therapy in addition to social support and motivational counseling. They also provide psychoeducational sessions designed to counter media messages promoting smoking. Many programs are located in schools and directed toward children and adolescents. Since peer pressure and curiosity are the most common reasons young people begin smoking, prevention is the key to anti-smoking programs in this age group.

Harm Reduction Strategies

What is a "harm reduction" program?

Harm reduction programs attempt to minimize the consequences of any psychoactive substance misuse. In particular, harm reduction is more successful than abstinence-based approaches for opiate addicts. For others substances, while abstinence is the best outcome, demanding an all-or-nothing commitment may not be possible for persons who fall into transition categories in their movement toward change. Encouraging and reinforcing smaller steps makes the ultimate goal – stopping usage – more attainable (see Chapter 36, Motivating Healthy Behavior).

If the individual wants to continue IV drug use, then stopping drugs by injection becomes the goal. If injection is desired, then not sharing injection equipment is the goal. If sharing will continue, using a decontaminating agent between users is the goal. In harm reduction, any positive steps are reinforced.

Needle exchange programs (NEP) are an example of a harm reduction method. At an NEP, addicts are given a supply of sterile needles in return for dirty used needles. At some NEPs, bleach kits are distributed for cleansing needles between injections. Condoms may be distributed. These programs often operate out of mobile centers that travel to high drug use areas on a regular schedule. To engage their clients, these centers also provide medical care, program referrals, and food.

Recovery readiness programs are similar to harm reduction programs. Program goals include outreach to users who are not yet responsive to overtures from drug treatment programs.

Methadone Maintenance Programs

Methadone is a synthetic narcotic that has pharmacological effects similar to those of heroin and morphine although it inhibits the euphoric effects of narcotic agents. Although it shares the addictive liability of the other narcotic agents, methadone has a 24- to 36-hour half-life, which permits once-a-day dosing.

Methadone maintenance programs provide daily doses of methadone to heroin addicts at a regular time and in a safe place, as they reinforce the person's steps towards recovery. The intent is to reduce the need to participate in criminal acts to fuel the addiction. Success is defined as reduction or cessation of heroin use, cessation of criminal activity, and appropriate productive functioning in the community. Recently, general medical practitioners have become authorized to prescribe buprenorphine, which is a partial opioid agonist that can be used without a structured social program.

Acupuncture in the Treatment of Addictive Behaviors

Auricular acupuncture, with needle insertion limited to defined anti-addiction points on the ear, is a popular therapy for alcoholism, smoking, and obesity. In Oregon, for example, where no methadone treatment programs are available, addicts receive regular periodic auricular acupuncture treatments. Anecdotal and small-scale case reports have described good success rates that are comparable to pharmacological and cognitive behavioral treatments. However, few randomized controlled trials exist.

Evidence for the effectiveness of various treatment approaches may be found in the evidence-based medicine literature. Unfortunately, the recidivism rates for all treatment approaches remain relatively high.

Recommended Readings

Galanter M, Kleber HD (Eds.). *The American Psychiatric Publishing Textbook of Substance Abuse Treatment,* 4th ed. Arlington, VA: American Psychiatric Publishing; 2008.

Rastegar DA, Fingerhood MI. *Addiction Medicine: An Evidence-Based Handbook,* 4th ed. Philadelphia, PA: Lippincott Williams & Wilkins; 2005.

Tucker JA, Donovan DM, Marlatt GA. *Changing Addictive Behavior.* New York: Guilford Press; 2000.

Online Resources

www.aa.org/bigbookonline

Review Questions

1. Among the following, which condition must be met for substance abuse treatment to be successful?
   A. Counselor must be available at all times of crisis.
   B. Family must insist on therapy.
   C. Individual must be motivated to change.
   D. Pain associated with abuse must be greater than the pleasure.
   E. Threat of legal action must be substantial.

2. The "network" referred to in network intervention programs consists of
   A. anonymous call-in lines.
   B. cooperating agencies.
   C. family and friends.
   D. former users or addicts.
   E. Internet resources.

3. The basic goal of harm reduction programs is
   A. development of supportive peer and family networks.
   B. improved education about the negative effects of drugs.
   C. minimization of the consequences of drug use.
   D. provision of assistance to recovering addicts.
   E. substitution of a less addictive drug.

Key to review questions: p. 407

26 Interpersonal Violence

Roland R. Maiuro, PhD, and Nancy K. Sugg, MD, MPH

- What are four major forms of abuse?
- What children are at risk for abuse?
- What are the clinical signs of partner abuse?
- What are the characteristics of the typical perpetrator?
- What is the Trauma Syndrome?
- What external factors contribute to violence?

What are four major forms of abuse?

A *violent act* is defined as any act of physical aggression or coercion toward a person, against their will. This definition includes psychological as well as physical *abuse* and emphasizes the issues of real or perceived power and control.

There are four major forms of abuse:

1. **Physical abuse** should be considered in any case of unexplained injury, as evidenced by bruises, welts, burns, lacerations, abrasions, fractures, bites (human or animal), or incidents of slapping, punching, kicking, choking, assault with a weapon, or tying down or otherwise restraining.

2. **Psychological/emotional abuse** is defined as controlling behavior where the perpetrator exercises power over another person or violates the person's rights and freedom through fear, degradation, threats of harm, extreme jealousy and possessiveness, deprivation, intimidation, or humiliation.

3. **Sexual abuse** includes acts of exposure, sexual exploitation (including childhood prostitution), and forced, coerced or any other unwanted sexual contact.

4. **Social/environmental abuse** is defined as behaviors that control a victim's activities including social contacts with other people, access to transportation, or withholding financial or other sources of support as a method of control.

According to the 2009 National Crime Victimization Survey, 4.3 million violent crimes were experienced by U.S. residents ≥ 12 years old, although rates of violent crimes have been dropping over the past decade (http://bjs.ojp.usdoj.gov/index.cfm?ty=pbdetail&iid=2217).

Types of Abusive Relationships

Family violence includes spouse/partner abuse, child abuse, child sexual abuse/ incest, sibling abuse, marital rape, and elder abuse. Family or **domestic violence** is characterized by a continuing relationship between the victim and the perpetrator. There is a high risk of repeated or increasingly violent encounters because of common living quarters and ongoing contact that provide easy access to a vulnerable victim. **Intimate partner violence** is violence between current or former spouses or romantic partners, girlfriends, boyfriends, and same-sex partners and non-cohabiting couples. *Power dynamics*, one partner controls the other through threats or physical violence, can render the victim dependent, fearful, and ambivalent about leaving the relationship or seeking and accepting help. Because many episodes of family violence or intimate partner violence occur in private, they are often undetected and unreported.

Child Maltreatment and Abuse

What children are at risk for abuse?

Child maltreatment includes both *physical, sexual, and psychological abuse* as well as *neglect* of children. It was the first type of domestic violence to be legally defined, legislated against, and designated as a violent act. It *must be reported* to the appropriate authorities (police, Child Protective Services) whenever suspected by an individual serving in health or educational capacities (physician, nurse, social worker, teacher).

Risk Factors for Child Abuse

- Difficult/unwanted pregnancy
- Traumatic delivery
- "Difficult" child
- Colic
- Hyperactivity
- Congenital abnormalities
- Chronic illness
- Physical disabilities
- Inadequate parental bonding or attachment

Clinical Signs Suggestive of Child Abuse

- Multiple injuries in different stages of healing
- Fractures caused by pulling, twisting, shaking
- Rib fractures in the absence of accidental trauma
- Multiple skull fractures suggesting repeated blows to the head
- Cerebral edema and retinal hemorrhages suggesting violent shaking
- Burns to the hands, buttocks, feet, and legs
- Scalding of the feet or lower legs or in a stocking/glove pattern suggesting immersion in hot water
- Grip marks on thighs, bite marks on breast or buttocks, perineal lacerations or scars, bruising of genitalia or anus suggesting sexual abuse
- Any unexplained injury

Child maltreatment refers to any act of omission or commission that endangers or impairs the child's emotional or physical heath and development. Typically, it is the intentional, non-accidental use of force by an adult caretaker aimed at injuring the child that is reported to authorities.

About 80% of reported perpetrators are parents of the abused child. However, **sibling abuse** (violence perpetrated by full siblings, half siblings, and adopted siblings) is very common and under-reported because the perpetrator is not a caregiver and, therefore, does not fall under the purview of CPS.

Sexual abuse refers to sexual acts perpetrated on children by adults or on any individual below the age of consent by another individual, who is at least 4 years older. **Incest** refers to acts perpetrated specifically by a family member on a child. It is estimated that each year more than 250,000 children are subjected to various acts of incestuous contact.

Children are especially vulnerable to **emotional abuse** because of their physical and emotional dependence and inability to protect themselves. Emotional abuse, although more difficult to identify and quantify than physical abuse, may be more profoundly damaging. Definitions of **neglect** (inadequate food, shelter, clothing, supervision) vary by state and may be mitigated by circumstances including intentionality, ignorance, poverty, and mental illness of the adult caretaker. In some states, children *witnessing violence* in the home is considered reportable child abuse since a growing body of evidence points to the long-term emotional damage experienced by children who witness violence. In 2008, Child Protective Services (CPS) estimated that 772,000 children were victims of maltreatment. This number represents only children brought to the attention of CPS and, therefore, represents a significant under-estimation of the real prevalence *(Child Maltreatment 2008.* U.S. Department of Health and Human Services, Administration on Children, Youth, and Families. Washington DC: U.S. Government Printing Office, 2010. Available at: http://www.acf.hhs.gov).

Discipline vs. Abuse

Determining when *parental discipline* is severe enough to be child abuse is complicated by socio-cultural factors. That is, disciplinary practices vary among ethnic groups and over time. Severe physical punishment was acceptable discipline to many parents in the US until the 1950s. Current standards of childcare, however, require the parent or guardian to meet the child's basic needs for shelter, nutrition, safety, and hygiene. These standards also require the parent or guardian to refrain from physical acts that may result in welts, bruises, or other enduring physical marks on the child. In cases where such injury is inflicted, the *health care professional* is obligated, by law, not only to provide care for the immediate injury, but also to intervene through mandatory reporting to protect the child from further abuse.

Child protective authorities must be notified in all cases of suspected child abuse by a caregiver so that a comprehensive investigation and assessment of future risk to the child can be performed.

Intimate Partner Abuse

Intimate partner abuse includes marital, non-marital, and same-sex adult partners and former partners. Although psychological and verbal abuse is the most common type of abuse in partner relationships, physical and sexual maltreatment as well as property damage are also included. Child abuse and pet abuse may also occur concomitantly.

Although the majority of partner/spouse abuse reported in the US is perpetrated by the male partner, a significant number of women are also verbally and physically aggressive in domestic settings. Furthermore, men often have difficulty asking for help when they are victims, resulting in under-estimation of female to male or male to male intimate partner violence. In some instances, abuse is bi-directional, further complicating the definitions of victim and perpetrator.

Intimate Partner Abuse

- 26% of women and 16% of men experience intimate partner violence in their lifetime (CDC data)
- 41% of rapes or sexual assaults against females were committed by an intimate partner (Bureau of Justice statistics)
- 45% of murdered women and 5% of murdered men were killed by an intimate partner (Bureau of Justice statistics)

Marital Rape/Date Rape

Marital rape and **date rape** are sexual acts forced on an individual without their consent. Marital rape definitions vary by state depending on whether, and to what extent, intention to have sexual relations is implicit in longer-term consenting adult relationships It is estimated that 10–14% of married women in the US have been raped by their husbands. Intimate partner rape can also be perpetrated by unmarried, long-term partners and former partners. The term "date rape" describes forced sexual acts perpetrated on an individual in a short-term, non-committed relationship. Almost 41% of all rapes are committed by an intimate partner, compared to 39% committed by an acquaintance and 21% committed by a stranger.

What are the clinical signs of partner abuse?

Many victims may mask interpersonal violence injuries as "accidents" or justify being hurt by blaming themselves. Attempting to avoid further threats and violence, some women restrict their activities and become less assertive. They accept apologies by their partner hoping the situation will improve. They may be reluctant to report battering because of financial dependency, immigration status, fear of police or the judicial system, religious or cultural constraints, or fear of retribution by the abuser, including further violence or

Physical Signs of Partner Abuse

- Multiple bruises, cuts, blackened eyes
- Defensive trauma to the hands, wrists, arms
- Cerebral concussion
- Strained or torn ligaments
- Fractures
- Blunt injuries to the chest or abdomen or back
- Loss of hearing, ruptured ear drum
- Loss of vision
- Burns or bites
- Knife or gun shot wounds
- Vaginal, perianal, and cervical tears and lacerations
- Recurrent STI
- Chronic pain syndrome
- Miscarriage, placental hemorrhage, fetal fractures, rupture of the uterus, and premature labor

death. Consequently, repeated injury is likely. It is essential to *examine the patient's entire medical history* for indications of previous abuse and to document findings and suspicions in those cases in which the patient's diagnosis cannot be made. Domestic violence cases can also present as stress, anxiety, PTSD, or depressive disorders and be characterized by over-utilization of medical services through vague, recurring complaints. Ending the relationship does not necessarily end the violence. Up to 40% of women without a current relationship are at risk of violence by a past partner as a result of persistent threatening behavior or stalking.

Elder Abuse

Elder abuse statistics generally involve adults > 60 years. There are approximately 500,000 to 1,000,000 victims of elder abuse each year. The National Center on Elder Abuse estimates that more than two thirds of elder abuse perpetrators are spouses, children, or other relatives (http://www.ncea.aoa.gov). Thus, although some abuse of the elderly occurs in institutional settings, the majority of abuse takes place in the home. Evidence of *physical assault* is often not visible to the casual observer and may become apparent only when assisting with bathing or performing a physical examination. Physical abuse must be differentiated from accidental falls and mishaps resulting from infirmity. Physical abuse is often

> **Types of Elder Abuse**
>
> - Failure to provide adequate food, clothing shelter, hygiene, or medical care
> - Verbal or non-verbal threats or acts that inflict pain, humiliation, or distress, including isolating or infantilizing the person
> - Misuse or illegal use of a person's money or property, including cashing checks without permission or deceiving them into signing documents.
> - Physical violence such as slapping or beating as well as inappropriate use of restraints or drugs to control the person
> - Any non-consensual touching or sexual act
> - Abandonment or threats of abandonment by a caregiver

coupled with neglect and can occur in the context of caregiving challenges (e.g., dementia, handicaps, self-care limitations) that the family member is poorly prepared to handle.

> Self-disparaging comments made by the victim regarding being old or of no value, communicating a sense of resignation, or acceptance of low self-worth may be signs of emotional abuse. Clinical signs of elder abuse include multiple bruises or fractures at different sites and of different ages; genital and urinary tract infections; bleeding; malnutrition; excessive or inadequate medication; and poor hygiene.

As in the case of child abuse, the elderly may be unable to report maltreatment because they are dependent on the perpetrator. Wrongdoing may be denied by the victimized elder and attempts made to cover for the offending family member.

Perpetrators of Interpersonal Violence

> What are the characteristics of the typical perpetrator?

Characteristics of perpetrators of domestic violence include exposure to family violence during childhood, drug or alcohol abuse, rigid assumptions about gender roles, denigration of women, exaggerated need to control, jealousy or paranoia, low self-esteem or depression, difficulty communicating feelings, anger, hostility, and aggressiveness verbally.

> Perpetrators of violence are found in every socioeconomic, educational, racial, ethnic, religious and political group and are of all ages and both genders.

Typically, *perpetrators of child abuse* have a history of violent treatment or neglect by their parents during their childhood, which then serves as their model for parenting behavior. As a result, there may be impaired bonding to the child, deficits in child rearing skills, or developmentally inappropriate expectations for the child's behavior. Stressors, such as socioeconomic pressure, lack of adequate family support, spousal discord, and conflicts over childcare responsibilities, are common in abusing families.

Stranger Violence

Stranger-to-stranger violence includes acts of workplace violence, gang violence, domestic and international terrorism, violent hate crimes targeting specific groups, and random violence associated with criminal activity. The Bureau of Justice statistics show that 52% of male and 31% of female violent crime victimization is from a stranger. Although stranger assault carries a lower risk of repetition and escalation than intrafamily assault, physical and psychological effects can be greater. Many victims become emotionally disabled by the apparently senseless and unpredictable quality of the violence and withdraw from what they perceive as an unsafe world.

Violence-Related Trauma Syndrome

> What is the trauma ayndrome?

The psychological effects of violence closely parallel those experienced by victims of other traumatic events. The *psycho-physiological distress* of the **trauma syndrome** is characterized by pervasive fear and anxiety and accompanied by sleep deprivation, early morning awakening, and recurrent nightmares. Losses of resiliency, inability to concentrate, and emotional instability are common. Somatic complaints may result from actual physical injuries, but more often are related to **stress**. Suspiciousness, anger, and rage can evolve into morbid hatred of the perpetrator. Grief, depression, and suicidal ideation, especially following multiple traumatic events, can occur. Avoidance, denial, emotional numbing or blocking, and, in some cases, detachment or psychogenic amnesia, may also occur.

Cognitive Signs

Cognitive distress is exhibited by viewing the world as unsafe, insane, and devoid of meaning; viewing oneself as damaged; feelings of guilt and self-blaming; a sense of personal powerlessness and limited hope for the future (**learned helplessness**); and acceptance of the inevitability of violence and abuse. *Disturbances in interpersonal relationships* include pathological detachment or dependency on the perpetrator after family violence; loss of emotional connection with loved ones after stranger assault; inability to trust or be intimate; emotional instability; avoidance of opportunities for new or more satisfying relationships; difficulty setting limits or establishing boundaries with others; and repetition of previous patterns of interaction.

Posttraumatic Stress Disorder

Although the diagnosis of **posttraumatic stress disorder (PTSD)** was initially given to survivors of natural disasters or war, the disorder is prevalent among individuals who experience interpersonal violence. Risk factors for developing PTSD include repeated severe psychological or emotional abuse, having experienced both physical and sexual assault, and a perception of life threat or sense of helplessness. Victims of violence experience a range of symptoms, but not all develop PTSD. The most common traumatic event listed for PTSD in the DSM-IV is "a serious threat to one's life or physical integrity; [or] a serious threat or harm to one's children" (see Chapter 46, Anxiety and Dissociative Disorders).

> **Common Features of PTSD**
>
> – Intrusive memories or flashbacks of the original trauma
> – Nightmares
> – Heightened arousal, such as exaggerated startle response
> – Hypervigilance to potential danger
> – Numbness
> – Disturbances in interpersonal relationships (mistrust, inability to become intimate)
> – Fear, anger, depression
> – Sexual dysfunction

Societal and Situational Factors

What external factors contribute to violence?

Violence is sanctioned and modeled in sports, the military, law enforcement, certain situations as self-protective acts by regular citizens, and the media. Institutional acts of violence also exist as sexism, sexual harassment, ageism, and racism. Violence is often precipitated by social and environmental events such as *interpersonal conflicts* with intimate family members, by *territorial disputes* between strangers, and by *domineering/unjust authority figures.* Recent job loss and relationship loss (due to separation or divorce) or being denied access to children can be major events and risk factors for intimate partner violence. Psychological factors such as acceptance of aggression as a means of resolving conflict, unrealistic expectations regarding certain types of relationships, prejudicial sentiments toward groups of people, and learned responses to stress and challenge also increase the risk of violence.

Influence of Drugs and Alcohol

Drug and alcohol intoxication increases the risk of violence. The severity of an assault is correlated with the use of alcohol or drugs by the perpetrator or the victim. In some instances, individuals with no history of violence, but who are taking benzodiazepines, can become violent, especially following the ingestion of alcohol. Careful history regarding current prescribed and OTC drugs can help detect potential chemical interactions and diagnose atypical reactions to medication. Abuse of illicit drugs such as cocaine, LSD, amphetamines, and phencyclidine hydrochloride (PCP) heightens the risk of violence by increasing arousal, irritability, and the possibility of inducing psychosis or paranoia.

Central Nervous System

Damage to the **hypothalamus** or **frontal** and **temporal lobes** of the brain increases the likelihood of assaultive behavior. The individual who has such brain damage may have limited ability to assess degree of threat, or to manage frustration or anger. Rarely, a seizure disorder (e.g., temporal lobe or complex partial seizures) can elicit violence, but this type of behavior is usually diffuse, disorganized, and stereotyped. The number of people who perpetrate violent acts due to neurological impairment may be limited but this etiology should be considered as it represents a potentially treatable cause of aggressive behavior.

Psychiatric Conditions

Violent behavior is not specific to individuals with psychiatric conditions. With the exception of intermittent explosive disorder, which includes violent behavior by definition, many diagnostic categories list aggressive behavior as one of many possible manifestations of emotional instability and impaired impulse control. Thus, psychopathology is best viewed as a vulnerability factor that makes anger and assaultive behavior more likely, rather than as a causal factor. That is, *the presence of a psychiatric illness is neither necessary nor sufficient for violence and victimization to occur.*

Violence as a Crime

The types of violence discussed above are crimes in most states. Some types, such as elder and child abuse, are considered crimes in all states. Although they are crimes, current professional policy dictates attention by both the criminal justice and health care systems. Health care providers must become familiar with reporting laws in the particular jurisdiction in which they practice to insure compliance with these laws. The Joint Commission on Accreditation of Hospitals requires the identification of abuse in clinical settings and the implementation of hospital polices that mandate protocols for identification, assessment, and diagnosis. Health care providers must be able to recognize cases of violence, assess the risk for further harm, and make reasonable efforts to protect the patient, family members, and potential victims from physical and emotional harm. Except for cases involving threats to life, serious bodily injury or harm, or use of a weapon, most states do not require mandatory reporting of spouse abuse. Such decisions are usually best made in collaboration with the victim in order to preserve trust and to avoid inadvertently exposing him or her to increased risk.

Intervention

The CDC has adopted the RADAR system to encourage health providers to intervene in cases of interpersonal violence:

R – **R**outinely screen for violence- and abuse-related injury and symptoms during the course of customary care.

A – **A**sk direct questions about violence in private, in a nonjudgmental manner. (See HITS below as an example of a screening tool.)

D – **D**ocument findings in the chart, preferably using body maps and photos for evidentiary purposes.

A – **A**ssess the patient's immediate safety and develop a safety plan.

R – **R**eview options and refer patient to in-house and community-based resources.

HITS is a 4-question screening instrument validated for both female and male patients.
How often does your domestic partner (or anyone else):
1. Hurt you physically?
2. Insult you?
3. Threaten you with harm?
4. Scream or curse at you?

Points: 1 = never, 2 = rarely, 3 = sometimes, 4 = fairly often, 5 = frequently
Score ≥ 10 for female patient indicates victimization
Score ≥ 11 for male patient indicates victimization

(Shakil A, Smith D, Sinacore JM, Krepcho M. Validation of the HITS domestic violence screening tool with males. *Family Medicine* 2005; 3:193–198.)

Education and Prevention

Tertiary prevention of violence and abuse requires crisis programs with trained professionals, shelters, emergency response communication, and clinical protocols to manage presenting problems. *Secondary prevention* requires education, particu-

larly among health care professionals, and effective public service campaigns. *Primary prevention* involves eradicating sexism, power imbalances, racism, ageism, and elitism, and increasing individual responsibility for promoting zero tolerance of violence. It also requires beginning early to educate children about healthy, non-violent relationships and conflict resolution.

Recommended Readings

Barnett O, Miller-Perrin CL, Perrin RD. *Family Violence Across the Lifespan.* Thousand Oaks, CA: Sage Publications; 2005.

Campbell J, Jones AS, Dienemann J. Intimate partner violence and physical health consequences. *Archives of Internal Medicine* 2002; 162:1156–1163.

Thompson RS, Rivara FP, Thompson DC, Barlow WE, Sugg NK, Maiuro RD. Identification and management of domestic violence: A randomized trial. *American Journal of Preventive Medicine* 2000; 19:253–262.

Internet Resources

CDC: Injury Center: Violence Prevention. www.cdc.gov/ViolencePrevention/pdf/NISVS_Report2010-a.pdf

Review Questions

1. Which of the following is the best estimate of how many children are subjected to various acts of incestuous contact annually?
   A. 25,000
   B. 100,000
   C. 250,000
   D. 500,000
   E. 1,000,000

2. The percentage of married women in the US who have been raped by their husband is closest to
   A. 5%.
   B. 15%.
   C. 25%.
   D. 35%.
   E. 45%.

3. In most states, it is mandatory to report which of the following?
   A. Child abuse
   B. Elder abuse
   C. Gun shot wounds
   D. Life threatening intentional injuries
   E. All of the above

4. The HITS is a 4-question screening tool that can be used to assess many forms of interpersonal violence, but it was originally designed to uncover
   A. child physical abuse.
   B. elder abuse.
   C. incest.
   D. partner abuse.
   E. stranger violence.

Key to review questions: p. 407

27 Poverty and Homelessness

K. Ramsey McGowen, PhD

- How is poverty defined?
- How many people are poor?
- What does it mean to be poor?
- What are the medical implications of poverty?
- What is homelessness?
- What is it like to be homeless?
- What are the medical implications of homelessness?
- What medical interventions might effectively address problems associated with poverty and homelessness?

Poverty and homelessness are powerful factors in the network of social determinants of health. They are complex social phenomena that can be aggravated or mitigated by other circumstances.

Poverty

How is poverty defined?

The U.S. Census Bureau establishes **poverty** *thresholds* based on data reflecting the amount of cash income required to support families of various sizes. Although these thresholds are adjusted annually for inflation, they are not adjusted for geographic variations in living costs. The Census Bureau thresholds are used primarily for statistical purposes to track poverty rates. The U.S. Department of Health and Human Services (HHS) issues *poverty guidelines*, which are simplified versions of the poverty thresholds. These establish separate figures for the 48 contiguous states and the District of Columbia, and separate sets for Alaska and Hawaii. The HHS guidelines are used for administrative purposes such as determining financial eligibility for a variety of federal programs (e.g., Head Start, food stamps, school lunch and other nutritional supplement programs, Legal Services for the poor, and the Job Corps). The guidelines are published annually in the Federal Register. The 2010 guidelines are listed in Table 27.1.

Table 27.1. 2010 HHS Poverty Guidelines

The 2010 Poverty Guidelines for the 48 Contiguous States and the District of Columbia	
Persons in family	Poverty guideline
1	$10,830
2	$14,570
3	$18,310
4	$22,050
5	$25,790
6	$29,530
7	$33,270
8	$37,010

For families with more than 8 persons, add $3,740 for each additional person.

How many people are poor?

According to the U.S. Census Bureau, in 2009, 14.3% of all persons in the US lived in poverty,

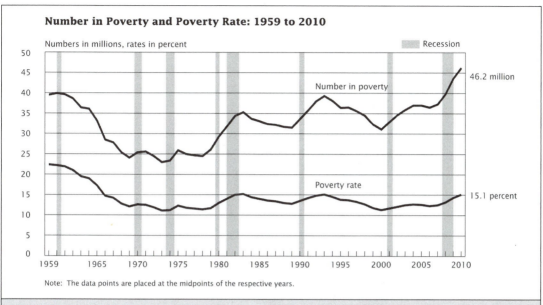

Figure 27.1. Overall U.S. poverty rates 1959–2009. Source: U.S. Census Bureau, Current Population Survey, 2009–2011, Annual Social and Economic Supplements

which is the highest percentage since 1994 (see Figure 27.1). The poverty rate for blacks was 25.8%; for Hispanics, 25.3%; Asians, 12.5%; and non-Hispanic whites, 9.4%. Although the rate of poverty is higher for blacks and Hispanics, the absolute number of individuals in poverty is higher for whites since they comprise the largest segment of the population. Therefore, the typical person living in poverty is white. In 2009, the poverty rate for children under the age of 18 was 20.7% (see Figure 27.2). In general, these numbers reflect increasing rates of poverty, partially due to the economic downturn that began in 2008, which produced higher levels of unemployment over a longer period of time.

There are significant variations in poverty by subpopulations and geographic areas. Poverty is

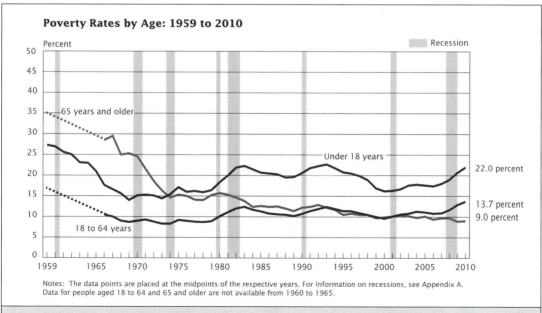

Figure 27.2. U.S. poverty rates by age 1959–2009. Source: U.S. Census Bureau, Current Population Survey, 1960–2011, Annual Social and Economic Supplements

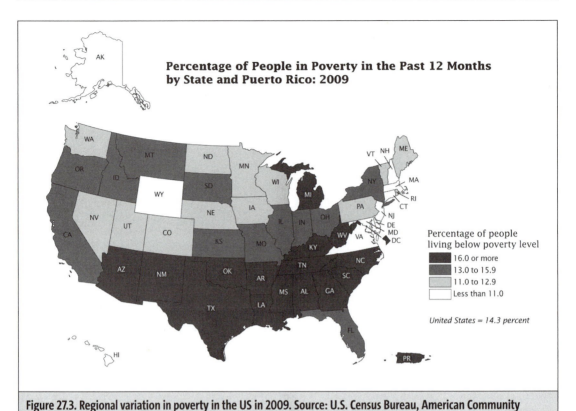

Figure 27.3. Regional variation in poverty in the US in 2009. Source: U.S. Census Bureau, American Community Survey, 2009 and Puerto Rico Community Survey, 2009

more prevalent in the Sunbelt although pockets of high poverty exist throughout the country (see Figure 27.3).

Demographics of Poverty

What does it mean to be poor?

Poverty is a multifaceted phenomenon that has both *objective* and *subjective dimensions*. Objectively, poverty is defined in economic terms by one of two means. Definitions using *absolute poverty* specify an income threshold considered the minimum amount necessary for survival (basic shelter, food, and clothing). *Relative poverty* defines poverty in comparative terms and stipulates poverty as a proportion of the median income in a society below which people are effectively excluded from acceptable living patterns (e.g., 60% of annual median income). The US uses an absolute standard to define poverty; the UK and European Union use a relative standard.

Poverty also has a subjective dimension, which should be incorporated into a more complete definition. *Subjective poverty* includes the sense of well-being (or its opposite: a compromised quality of life), social setting, cultural values, psychological resources, and context of an individual's experience. It includes the extent to which a person believes he or she is empowered or deprived in a society based on the resources available to them.

Poverty is not the same for everyone. Different forms of poverty are associated with different attitudes, beliefs, and outcomes. *Generational poverty* occurs when at least two generations of a family have lived on limited financial and other resources (e.g., psychological, educational, relational) and never owned property. Generational poverty is often accompanied by a family history of low educational attainment, a focus on survival, and *learned helplessness*. It is the form of poverty people are least likely to escape.

Situational poverty results from an event such as loss of employment, divorce, or chronic illness. People in situational poverty often have experienced stability and have a middle-class perspective. Situational poverty also is associated with having more resources in domains other than finances, such as prior educational attainments, supportive relationships, and an attitude that poverty is escapable. The number of individuals experiencing situational poverty increased dramatically after 2008.

> Working class poverty refers to those who are employed but do not earn enough to escape poverty. It involves never having extra money, living from paycheck to paycheck, and focusing on survival. Approximately 40% of those in poverty 18–65 years old are employed and therefore fall into the working class poverty category.

Health Implications of Poverty

> What are the medical implications of poverty?

Income is a significant determinant of both physical and mental health. Low income is associated with increased morbidity and mortality from a variety of conditions, especially chronic illness. Poverty also is linked to poorer mental health: those in the lowest income brackets have a two-to-three fold increase in psychiatric diagnosis.

> The social drift hypothesis states that the presence of mental illness leads to decline in socioeconomic status, but research suggests that poverty typically precedes mental illness.

Persistent poverty is the strongest predictor of age at death among low income persons. Individuals from the lowest income levels have an overall risk of earlier death from all causes 1.5–3 times higher than those at the highest socioeconomic levels.

The relationship between poverty and health is complicated. Poverty is associated with increased rates of problematic health behaviors such as smoking and poor dietary patterns. Individual health behaviors are affected by reduced access to health care, fewer interventions available in low income areas, and increased exposure to environmental hazards such as air pollution. In addition, low income areas typically have limited resources for healthy food choices, are characterized by unsafe surroundings, and offer few accessible green spaces, all of which create barriers to healthy lifestyles. Finally, those living in poverty face exposure to multiple sources of **stress**, including violence, financial stress, and chaotic life circumstances. They may use maladaptive behaviors that are detrimental to their health (e.g. smoking, alcohol, drugs, poor diet) to cope with these stressors. Thus, the relationship between poverty and health is bi-directional, with poverty leading to poorer health and poorer health contributing to poverty.

The effects of poverty on children are especially pronounced. A *life course perspective* suggests that children who grow up in poverty may experience lifelong detrimental effects. They are more likely to be exposed to second hand smoke, poor nutrition, and other health impairing circumstances. Children who experience extreme stress during development show structural changes in the CNS, neurobiological damage resulting in emotional dysregulation, and increased physical health problems. These not only disrupt childhood but may sow the seeds for chronic health problems in adulthood. The means by which this occurs may be through exposure to extreme stress during sensitive periods (e.g., nutritional deprivation, violence), the cumulative effects of stress over many years of exposure, or living in circumstances that create a social trajectory of disadvantage and limited options.

Homelessness

> What is homelessness?

By federal definition, **homelessness** occurs when an individual lacks a regular and adequate nighttime residence and has a primary nighttime residence that is either a supervised temporary shelter or a place not designed or ordinarily used for sleeping by humans. The exact number of homeless is difficult to document. The U.S. Department of Housing and Urban Development (HUD) obtains data on homelessness by collecting a point-in-time count from communities, usually conducted on a single night in late January.

According to the National Alliance to End Homelessness, approximately 700,000 people experience homelessness on any given night in the US; roughly 22 of every 10,000 people are homeless. Of that number, 37% are people in families while 63% are individuals; 18% of the homeless population is considered "chronic" and 20% are military veterans. "Chronic" homelessness is often the public face of homelessness despite being a relatively small proportion of the population. The ethnic make-up of the homeless population varies according to geographic location. In rural areas, homeless individuals are more likely to be Caucasian; in urban areas, the largest percentage (~40%) of homeless individuals are African American.

Families often become homeless after a financial setback such as a medical emergency. Youth frequently become homeless after a family disruption such as divorce or through neglect. Veterans may experience long-term adjustment problems leading to homelessness as a result of service-related disabilities.

Multiple factors lead to homelessness including poverty, unemployment, mental illness, domestic violence, and a lack of affordable housing. Many individuals who work but in low-wage jobs earn insufficient income to afford reasonable housing. National economic conditions also affect homelessness. For example, the recession beginning in 2008 led to increased homelessness, especially among families, due to higher rates of long-term unemployment leading to mortgage foreclosures.

What is it like to be homeless?

The biggest risk factor for homelessness is poverty and the factors associated with poverty are common in the homeless population. Homelessness also is associated with high rates of traumatic events. The typical homeless family is headed by a single mother with young children, who has experienced physical or sexual assault. Being homeless places families in situations where they are at greater risk of family dissolution, assault, or witnessing violence. Children are especially adversely affected by homelessness. They are sick and hungry twice as often as non-homeless children. Frequent moves disrupt their education. They are more likely to repeat a grade as well as more likely to have a learning disability.

Food insecurity is common among the homeless who often skip meals and have food choices that are nutritionally poor. Ironically, those who have limited access to food may be more likely to be obese because inexpensive, low nutrition foods tend to be high calorie.

Health Implications of Homelessness

What are medical implications of homelessness?

The National Healthcare for the Homeless Council lists major health concerns as exposure to the elements (e.g., frostbite, hypothermia), violence, stress, malnutrition, and unsanitary conditions. They state, "Healing and recovery are nearly impossible without a home." The homeless have increased rates of infectious diseases (HIV, tuberculosis, pneumonia), chronic diseases (cardiovascular disease, COPD), trauma, and skin disorders. They are less likely to have a place for routine care, such as standard preventive and health screening procedures. They also have difficulty obtaining prescription medications, dental care, eyeglasses, and surgery. In addition, keeping up with medications and appointments is complicated by poor communication by mail or phone with someone who is homeless.

The risk for early death is three to four times higher among the homeless and the average life expectancy is 42–52 years, approximately three decades less than that of the general population.

About 25% of the homeless population has some form of severe mental illness and a higher percentage experience other forms of psychiatric disorders. Serious mental illness is associated with impairments in functional abilities such as self-care and maintaining supportive social relationships, and a tendency to misinterpret efforts to assist them or provide treatment. Self-medication using street drugs or alcohol to the point of abuse or dependence is common. The combination of mental illness, substance abuse, and physical health problems makes it difficult for the homeless to obtain employment and stable housing.

Providing Health Care for the Poor and Homeless

> What medical interventions might effectively address problems associated with poverty and homelessness?

Providing health care for poor and homeless individuals is challenging and highlights the importance of an **integrated sciences model** of care that requires innovation at the individual and system levels.

On a system level, *integrated and collaborative care networks* that simultaneously address physical and mental health are essential. One solution for the homeless who are too frail to recover from medical problems on the street but too well to remain in the hospital is *medical respite care* or short-term residential care that allows recovery in a safe environment with access to medical care and other supportive services. Such care is offered in a variety of settings including freestanding facilities, homeless shelters, nursing homes, and transitional housing. Medical respite care has demonstrated cost savings and success in reducing readmissions.

Physician screening for factors such as poverty and food insecurity would promote better understanding of factors affecting the onset and maintenance of health concerns and facilitate the development of more appropriate interventions for poor and homeless patients. Training programs for health care professionals need to expand opportunities to learn about the complicated interrelationships that contribute to and make it difficult to escape poverty and homelessness. The norms, unwritten rules, and priorities for daily life upon which people must rely to survive in poverty and homelessness clearly interfere with the ability of the homeless and poor to comply with standard medical interventions that are based on middle class life circumstances. For example, complying with a recommendation for exercise by walking around the neighborhood is impossible for someone living in a high crime neighborhood. Working collaboratively to find practical interventions for patients who are homeless or financially limited is crucial.

Health care providers are susceptible to making a *fundamental attribution error:* minimizing the role of external factors and ascribing the cause of an individual's behavior or situation to his or her character or personality. This implicit cognitive disposition can lead to blaming individuals for the hardships they experience and creating barriers to effective care, empathy, and the patient-centered attitudes that are essential to professionalism. Developing training programs and interventions to address these barriers to adequate health care is critical to working effectively with these populations.

Recommended Readings

Braveman P. Do we have real poverty in the United States? *Preventing Chronic Disease* 2007; 4:A84.

Schanzer B, Dominguez B, Shrout PE, Caton CL. Homelessness, health status, and health care use. *American Journal of Public Health* 2007; 97:464–469.

Stringhini S, Sabia S, Shipley M, Brunner E, Nabi H, Kivimaki M, Singh-Manoux A. Association of socioeconomic position with health behaviors and mortality. *JAMA* 2010; 303:1159–1166.

Online Resources

National Alliance to End Homelessness
http://www.endhomelessness.org/
National Health Care for the Homeless Council, Inc
http://www.nhchc.org/
National Poverty Center
http://www.npc.umich.edu/

Review Questions

1. Which segment of the population has the highest rate of poverty?
   A. Asian
   B. Black
   C. Hispanic
   D. Native Americans
   E. Non-Hispanic white

2. A person living in homelessness most commonly
   A. grew up in homelessness.
   B. is a military veteran.
   C. is an adult with children.

D. is at increased risk of early death.
E. lives in homelessness as a chronic condition.

3. In what region of the US is poverty the highest?
   A. Central
   B. Northeast
   C. Northwest
   D. Sunbelt
   E. West Coast

4. Recent trends in rates of poverty indicate that poverty is
   A. highest among children.
   B. higher in 2010 than at any other time in U.S. history.
   C. highest among adults aged 18–64.
   D. highest for the elderly.
   E. leveling off over the past decade.

5. The life expectancy of those living in homelessness is approximately
   A. equivalent to those with homes.
   B. 10 years less than the non-homeless.
   C. 20 years less than the non-homeless.
   D. 30 years less than the non-homeless.
   E. 40 years less than the non-homeless.

Key to review questions: p. 407

28 Suicide

Alexander L. Chapman, PhD, RPsych, Charlotte R. McGinnis, MA,
Brianne K. Layden, BA, and Kristy N. Walters, MA

- How many people commit suicide each year?
- Why do people commit suicide?
- What are the major risk and protective factors related to suicidal behavior?
- When and how do I conduct a thorough risk assessment?
- What treatments or interventions are recommended for suicidal patients?

How many people commit suicide each year?

Suicide claims over 36,000 lives each year in the US and Canada and more than one million lives worldwide. Approximately 6 people are intimately affected by each suicide, for an estimated total of 216,000 people in North America. Completed and attempted suicides also place a heavy cost burden on the health care system, with approximately $37 billion spent each year in the US and Canada, as direct medical costs and as indirect costs such as loss of productivity.

Not all self-injurious behaviors are suicidal acts. *Non-suicidal self-injury* involves the direct and deliberate destruction of body tissue, without the intent to die. *Suicidal behavior* encompasses related yet distinct behaviors, including: *suicidal ideation* (e.g., thoughts, beliefs, cognitions, or images that involve the intention of ending one's own life); *suicide attempts*, or non-fatal self-inflicted harmful behaviors that involve intent to die as a result of the behavior; and *suicide*, which includes fatalities caused by self-inflicted behaviors with the intent to die.

Suicide ranks as the 11th most frequent cause of death in the US among individuals 15–24 years old, and the third leading cause of death overall. More people die by suicide than homicide, and the number of suicides in the US appears to be increasing. Approximately 10 times more people attempt suicide each year than those who complete suicide. *Completed* suicide is approximately three times more common among males than females;

however, *attempted* suicide is approximately three times more common among females than males. This gender difference may be due to males using more lethal means. For example, firearms are the most commonly utilized means in completed suicides, and are more commonly used by males, whereas poisoning (e.g., medication and drug overdose) is more common among females.

Caucasians commit suicide more frequently than non-Caucasians, with the exception of individuals aged 15–24. Among late adolescents/early adults, Native Americans have the highest rate of suicide. Suicide rates are the lowest among married people and highest among the divorced, separated, and widowed. Approximately 90% of those dying by suicide have a psychiatric disorder at the time of death, and as many as 60% of suicides are estimated to have occurred in the context of a mood disorder. Suicidal behavior, however, occurs across all demographic groups and, thus, suicidality should be routinely evaluated in every patient.

Theories of Suicide

Why do people commit suicide?

Thomas Joiner's *interpersonal theory of suicide* proposes that feelings of thwarted belongingness (the human need to belong is unmet), perceived burdensomeness (belief that one is a burden to others), desire for suicide, and the capability to complete suicide are four risk factors that predict suicidality. This theory recognizes that desire and capability of engaging in suicide are not the same, and posits that individuals who possess both factors are at greater risk than those with desire or capability alone. The *strain theory of suicide* is a sociological theory that suggests four competing pressures or strains in an individual's life usually precede suicide: value strain (conflicting values), aspiration strain (discrepancy between aspiration and reality), deprivation strain (e.g., poverty), and coping strain (lack of effective coping skills). *Diathesis-stress models of suicide* postulate that people with biological predispositions (e.g., serotonergic system dysfunction, elevated cortisol levels, hyperactive HPA axis) are especially vulnerable to develop suicidal behavior. According to these models, biological precursors are a necessary, but not sufficient, condition for suicide. Precipitating stressors must be present for an individual to attempt or complete suicide. By combining these theories, we conceptualize suicidal behavior within a transactional *biopsychosocial model.*

A biopsychosocial model conceptualizes suicidal behavior as the result of complex transactions among biological (e.g., genetics, brain and neurotransmitter functioning), psychological (e.g., hopelessness, depression), social, and environmental (e.g., deprivation, thwarted belongingness) factors. In this model, risk factors and suicidal behavior influence each other in a dynamic interplay. In a **diathesis-stress model**, an individual with elevated cortisol levels may be vulnerable to, or have a lower threshold for, suicide but does not engage in suicidal behavior unless faced with psychological or environmental precipitants. A biopsychosocial model, however, assumes a transactional relationship such that social or environmental risk factors increase an individual's stress levels (psychological factor), which then increase cortisol levels (biological factors), resulting in suicidal behavior. Over time, suicidal behavior may result in negative changes in the environment (withdrawal of support, conflict), neurobiological changes, and reduced capacity for effective problem solving, all further increasing the risk of suicidality. This framework acknowledges the reciprocal relationship among risk factors and recognizes that understanding the transaction among these factors is necessary to explain the complexity of suicidal behavior.

Risk Factors

> What are the major risk and protective factors related to suicidal behavior?

The probability that an individual will make a suicide attempt generally increases with the number of risk factors present. Not all factors, however, confer equal levels of risk. The single strongest predictor of completed suicide is a history of previous suicide attempts. About one third of individuals who have made a suicide attempt will make another attempt within a year. Further, recent exposure to the suicide of a friend or loved one also increases acute suicidal risk.

Acute risk factors indicate an imminent danger of suicide. When combined with other personal and biological predisposing factors, environmental

Acute/Imminent Risk Factors	
Unmodifiable	Recent/Past year: • suicide attempt • major life stress (e.g., divorce, job loss, death of a friend or family member) • discharge from a psychiatric hospital or abrupt clinical change • diagnosis of a terminal condition • imprisonment – *especially first night of incarceration*
Modifiable	Current: • suicidal ideation, intent, or self-harm • access to preferred or lethal means • specific suicide plan • feelings of hopelessness and burdensomeness • excessive or increased alcohol or drug consumption • insomnia, agitation, or panic • increased recklessness, impulsivity, or risk-taking – *especially if out of character*

stressors significantly increase the likelihood that an individual will engage in suicidal acts in the near future. Many stressors are intuitive, such as a recent loss or the diagnosis of a terminal condition. Suicide attempts tend to be highest within the first year following these stressors, however, some seemingly positive changes (e.g., improvement in depressive symptoms, release from a psychiatric hospital) actually increase the acute suicidal risk. In schizophrenic patients, it is estimated that one third of suicides occur during admission or within 1 week of discharge from the hospital. *Individuals presenting with acute risks warrant immediate risk assessment.*

Chronic risk factors are ongoing and put the individual continually at risk for suicidal behavior. In the absence of other influences, these individuals are typically not in immediate danger; however, a thorough risk assessment and possible referral for treatment to help manage suicide risk is still pertinent.

As with acute risk factors, some chronic factors are static, while others can be modified through intervention. Negative life events are often predisposing risk factors but differ from acute stressors by the amount of time that has passed since the event (i.e., > 1 year). Individuals who experienced maltreatment or abuse during childhood or whose parents were violent, abused substances, had psychiatric disorders (especially psychotic or mood disorders), or were divorced are also more likely to engage in suicidal behaviors.

Individuals with *chronic medical disorders* are also at increased risk of suicide, especially if the condition causes functional impairment or pain. Individuals with cancer, HIV, Parkinsons, or ALS typically have higher suicide rates than healthy individuals or individuals with less debilitating disorders like diabetes. Furthermore, there is evidence that hyperactivity in the hypothalamic-pituitary-adrenal (HPA) axis, through non-suppression of the cortisol response, may be a biological vulnerability to suicidal behavior. Hyperactivity of the HPA axis may occur in response to chronic stressors that lead to elevated cortisol levels, which, in turn, may inhibit neuro-protective brain trophic factors and neurogenesis. There is also evidence that genetic vulnerabilities contribute to reduced neurotrophic signalling, especially in the serotonin pathway, which can contribute to suicidal vulnerability.

Identifying and strengthening *protective factors* is critical to assessing suicidal risk. Having a strong social support system, feeling hopeful, having goals and reasons for living, and engaging

Chronic Risk Factors

Unmodifiable	A history of:
	• suicidal behavior or previous attempts
	• psychiatric treatment
	• Axis III medical disorder
	• parental psychiatric disorders, violence, divorce, or substance abuse
	• numerous or severe prior negative life events
	• childhood maltreatment
	• traumatic brain injury
	• reduced neurotrophic signalling – *especially the serotonin pathway*
	• hyperactivity in the hypothalamic-pituitary-adrenal (HPA) axis
	• genetic predisposition (protein kinase A dysfunction, BDNF 66MET allele)
	• old age
	• gender – *males are at higher risk*
Modifiable	• lack of social support
	• Axis I and II psychological disorders, especially mood, personality, psychotic, and substance abuse disorders – *risk increases 90 fold if more than one disorder is present*
	• feelings of hopelessness
	• unemployment
	• unmarried/single

Protective Factors

• Adherence to effective treatment
• Strong social support
• Hopefulness/goals/reasons for living
• Coping skills
• Stable relationships or responsibility to others
• Fear of suicide, death, or dying
• Fear of social disapproval/belief suicide is immoral
• Willingness to follow crisis plan
• Access to material resources (e.g., food, shelter, clothing)

in effective coping skills are strong protective factors and should be encouraged in suicidal patients. The majority of people contemplating suicide are ambivalent. Many do not actually want to die, but simply want to escape the pain of their current circumstances. Therefore, hope that the current situation will change, expectations that they will be able to cope and overcome difficulties in the future, and commitment to solving their current problems are all crucial protective factors.

Suicide Risk Assessment

> When and how do I conduct a thorough risk assessment?

The majority of health professionals will interact with a suicidal patient at least once, if not many times, during their career. This can be a highly stressful and challenging task because "missing" a suicidal patient can have tragic consequences. It is, therefore, essential that all clinicians are well-informed about how to assess suicide risk.

Warning Signs

All patients seeking treatment for, or complaining of, life stresses or mental health symptoms should be screened for suicide risk. This can be as simple as asking the patient if she or he has been having any thoughts about suicide. Often clinicians are hesitant to raise the topic of suicide for fear of giving someone the idea, but there is no evidence that asking the question influences patients that have not already thought about suicide. Doing so, however, does inform the patient that such concerns are appropriate to discuss. Questions should be direct and specific and include the words "suicide" and "death." Patients with acute or chronic risk factors should be screened for suicide risk on a regular basis, but how does the clinician know when a thorough risk assessment should be conducted?

Err on the Side of Caution

A **suicide risk assessment** should be conducted any time someone threatens self-harm or suicide,

talks openly about suicidal ideation, or gives any indication of imminent or long-term risk. Some individuals who are contemplating suicide will engage in behaviors to prepare for death, such as talking or writing a lot about death, acquiring firearms or stockpiling medications, writing a will, giving away possessions, or talking with loved ones in a way that sounds like a goodbye. Other individuals may not talk about or demonstrate any preparatory behaviors prior to a suicide attempt, but even if suicidal ideation is not expressed directly, there are often other signs that a patient may be at risk. The American Association of Suicidology has an acronym to help remember key warning signs: **IS PATH WARM?**

I	Ideation
S	Substance abuse
P	Purposelessness (saying things like "what's the point" or "it doesn't matter")
A	Anxiety (agitation)
T	Trapped (feeling like there is no way out)
H	Hopelessness
W	Withdrawal (from friends and family, as well as activities or commitments)
A	Anger
R	Recklessness (with personal safety or finances)
M	Mood changes (including suddenly seeming calmer and "better")

Conducting a Suicide Risk Assessment

When conducting a suicide risk assessment, remain calm, open, and supportive, asking questions in a non-judgmental and matter-of-fact manner. The goal is to get as much information as possible by asking follow-up questions and pressing for details. Use the risk factors to guide questioning. The risk assessment procedure can also be used to help lower or manage risk by helping patients find other solutions to their problems and pointing out or strengthening any protective factors.

Questions to ask:
- Have you thought about killing yourself recently/currently?

□ *If YES*: When? How often do you think about it? Do you think you can cope with or control these thoughts? How do you think you would do it? Do you have a specific plan? Can you carry out your plan (e.g., Do you have access to a gun? Are there bullets in it?) Have you written a suicide note or have one in progress? Have you taken any action towards carrying out this plan? Do you have a timeline in mind?

□ *If NO*: Have you <u>ever</u> had thoughts about killing yourself? (Then ask all the same questions listed above.)

■ *The more detailed the plan the higher the risk*

- Have you ever done anything to kill yourself?
  □ *If YES*: When? How many times? When was the most recent? When was the most serious? What did you do? What happened (e.g., did someone intervene, did you go to the hospital?) How did you feel about still being alive?
    ■ *The more numerous, recent, and lethal the previous attempts, the higher the risk*
- Have you ever intentionally hurt yourself? Have you ever cut, burned, or punched yourself or intentionally inflicted pain in another way?
  □ *If YES*: When? How often/how many times have you done this? How did you hurt yourself? What did you use to ____ (use patient's own words, e.g., cut, burn)? Why did you ____ (use patient's own words, e.g., cut, burn) yourself? Where were you? Were you alone?
    ■ *The higher the frequency and severity of these self-injurious acts the higher the risk*
- Have you ever had a time when you thought a lot about suicide but did not do anything to kill yourself?
  □ *If YES*: What helped get you through then? Why did you decide to choose life? What did you do to keep yourself safe while coping with that difficult time?
    ■ *The greater the number of strengths and attachments to life, the lower the risk*
- How do you feel about the future? Do you have personal goals?
    ■ *Help identify at least one reason for living. Goals and hopefulness about the future are strong protective factors*
- Do you drink alcohol? Do you use drugs (illicit or prescription)?

□ *IF YES*: What do you drink? What kind of drugs do you use? Why do you take them? How often/how many times a week do you drink alcohol/use drugs? How many drinks/how much ____ do you take per occasion? Has substance use increased or decreased recently? Why?

■ *Sudden increases in substance use habits or chronic substance abuse increase risk*

Determining Level of Risk

Relying on a single measure or source of information can lead to erroneous risk assignment. For

---

Suicide Risk Rating Classification

Very Mild/Non-Existent
- No identifiable suicidal symptoms
- No past suicide attempts
- No or very few other risk factors

Mild
- Multiple attempter with absolutely no other suicidal risk factors
- Non-multiple attempter with suicidal ideation of limited intensity and duration, no or only general plans or preparation, and no or few other risk factors

Moderate
- Multiple attempter with any other notable risk factor
- Non-multiple attempter with well-developed plans and some preparation
- Non-multiple attempter with no or mild general plans, but moderate to severe suicidal ideation and ≥ 2 other notable risk factors

Severe
- Multiple attempter with ≥ 2 notable risk factors
- Non-multiple attempter with well-developed plans, some preparation, and ≥ 1 other notable risk factor

Extreme
- Multiple attempter with well-developed plans and preparation
- Non-multiple attempter with well-developed plans and preparation, with strong or uncontrollable suicidal ideation, and ≥ 2 other notable risk factors

From: LaRicka R, et al. Empirically informed approaches to topics in suicide risk assessment. *Behavioral Siences and Health Care* 2004; 22:651–655. © John Wiley & Sons. Reprinted by permission of John Wiley & Sons.

example, the SAD PERSONS Scale would yield a higher score for a 50-year-old divorced male with diabetes and no suicidal ideation than for a 35-year-old woman with severe depression and an organized suicide plan. Clinical judgment is, therefore, essential. However, it is also important to recognize the limitations of clinical judgment and to use a variety of assessment methods that have empirical utility in suicide risk assessment. Based on current research, the sample profiles below provide an idea of what might be appropriately classified at each level of risk.

Next Steps

Consultation with colleagues regarding suicide risk and related interventions or precautions is essential. After appropriate interventions or actions have been undertaken, suicide assessments should be well documented, not only to protect the practitioner from malpractice, but also to provide information for future practitioners who may treat the patient. Clinicians should provide specific information (i.e., not just a general statement about risk level) about the factors considered in determining risk. Document the patient's own words as well as record any actions, consultations, and plans to follow up with the patient. Suicide assessment is ongoing and must be re-addressed regularly over the course of treatment, particularly following significant changes or times of stress.

General Steps in Conducting a Suicide Risk Assessment

1) Ask direct questions
2) Collect as much information as possible
3) Review history, current risk, and protective factors to determine level of risk
4) Consult when appropriate
5) Develop and implement an action plan appropriate to current level of risk
6) Document decisions and actions
7) Follow up and reassess

Intervening or Lowering Suicide Risk

What treatments or interventions are recommended for suicidal patients?

After determining a patient's level of suicide risk, steps must be taken to lower that risk. Move from the least invasive forms of intervention to more restrictive prevention methods as warranted by level of risk. Make every effort to have the patient actively participate in keeping her- or himself safe. This may include disposing of any lethal means, generating a crisis plan involving coping skills or strategies to modify or tolerate distress, encouraging communicating suicidal thoughts to a trusted friend, family member, or therapist, or having the patient stay with a friend or family member until the crisis has passed. Only if the patient is unable or unwilling to do these things should more invasive steps, such as breaking confidentiality to inform family members, or restrictive approaches, such as hospitalization, be considered.

A *crisis response plan* (CRP) should be the next step after a thorough risk assessment. A CRP provides specific directions to a patient on steps to take during a crisis. Write the plan down (e.g., on a 3 × 5 index card), have patients carry a copy with them, and put copies in their home, car, and anywhere else they might need to access this information. Some patients may prefer to store this plan in their phone, and even program alarms that remind them to read their crisis plan or use their coping skills.

There is no evidence that traditional "no suicide contracts" reduce the risk of suicide to the patient or liability to the practitioner.

The first steps in the CRP involve self-management by the patient to identify stressors and constructive coping options. If, after instituting self-management strategies, the patient is still feeling suicidal, he or she should act on accessing external interventions, such as identifying an emergency contact person, making note of that person's contact information, and including a backup plan such as going to the emergency room if the support person is unavailable.

Ways to Reduce Suicide Risk

1. Instruct the patient not to do it. (Now is the time to be firm and directive!)
2. Ask the patient to remove or stay away from lethal means.
3. Get the patient connected to a mental health provider, as well as trusted family and friends.
4. Have the patient stay with a friend or family member if possible or appropriate based on level of risk.
5. Get the patient to brainstorm ways he or she can cope with distressing thoughts or emotions. Simple suggestions include:
   - Distracting activities, such as spending time with other people, doing intense physical exercise
   - Progressive muscle relaxation, diaphragmatic breathing
   - Removing or lowering stressful events (e.g., vacation from work)
   - Making a plan for one small step toward solving the problem
6. Come up with a detailed plan of the strategies the patient will use to keep him- or herself safe (a CRP) including things he or she can do, whom to call, or where needed go to get outside help.
7. Obtain a commitment to this plan of action. This differs from a "no suicide contract" in that it involves a commitment to a personal plan to reduce suicide risk.
8. Troubleshoot this action plan. (What could go wrong or get in the way of this plan?)
9. Follow up or get the patient to check in with someone as they implement the plan.

Psychotherapy Interventions

The most effective *interventions* for patients in acute suicidal crisis are short-term, directive, crisis-focused, emphasizing problem solving, and skill building. An intensive behavioral approach to therapy, combined with ongoing outreach, has been shown to be effective for reducing future hospitalizations among suicidal patients. In this approach, patients are given greater access to a therapist or crisis mental health worker than in most standard forms of care (e.g., access to after-hours phone support). Effort is made to maintain contact with patients for an extended period of time (3–12 months), even if they are not receiving formal ongoing treatment. This may take the form of phone calls following missed appointments, or sending patients postcards at regular intervals to wish them well and remind them that help is available.

Cognitive behavioral therapy (CBT), where the primary goal is to manage the immediate risk by inducing hope, helping the patient to problem solve, creating a crisis intervention plan, and encouraging treatment compliance, is brief but effective therapy for treating acutely suicidal patients.

For patients who are more chronically suicidal, the immediate danger is lower and, therefore, may allow for relatively longer-term therapy, focusing more on the underlying issues of the individual's psychopathology (e.g., interpersonal communication, emotion regulation). *Dialectical behavioral therapy* (DBT) is a specialized form of treatment, originally developed to treat suicidal women, that has now become a well-researched treatment for borderline personality disorder (BPD). This intensive treatment includes individual therapy, group skills training, and telephone access to a therapist for crisis support and skills coaching. DBT has demonstrated efficacy among both adolescents and adults, and may be useful for patients struggling with emotional dysregulation, impulsivity, or self-destructive behaviors.

Recommended Readings

Granello D. The process of suicide risk assessment: Twelve core principles. *Journal of Counselling & Development* 2010; 88:363–371.

Jacobs DG. *The Harvard Medical School Guide to Suicide Assessment and Intervention*. San Francisco, CA: Jossey-Bass Publisher; 1998.

LaRicka R, Wingate LR, Joiner TE, Walker RL, Rudd MD, Jobes DA. Empirically informed approaches to topics in suicide risk assessment. *Behavioral Science and the Law* 2004; 22:651–655.

Meichenbaum D. 35 Years of working with suicidal patients: Lessons learned. *Canadian Psychology/ Psychologie Canadienne* 2005; 46:64–67.

Practice Guideline for the Assessment and Treatment of Patients with Suicidal Behaviors. *American Journal of Psychiatry* 2003; 160:Supplement 11.

Review Questions

1. Among the following, the strongest predictor of completed suicide is
   A. diagnosis of a terminal illness.
   B. discharge from a psychiatric hospital.
   C. major life stress.
   D. previous suicide attempt.
   E. suicidal ideation.

2. Which of the following statements about suicide is true?
   A. Completed suicide is more common among males.
   B. More people die by suicide than homicide.
   C. Suicide in the US appears to be increasing.
   D. Suicide is the third leading cause of death in the US.
   E. All of the above.

3. Which of the following are modifiable risk factors?
   A. Feelings of hopelessness
   B. Gender
   C. Lack of social support
   D. A and C
   E. All of the above

   Key to review questions: p. 408

29 Health Literacy

José L. Calderón, MD, and Sandra A. Smith, PhD, MPH

- What is literacy?
- How is literacy measured?
- How are literacy and health linked?
- What is health literacy?
- How is health literacy measured?
- What promotes health literacy?

What is literacy?

The meaning of **literacy** is constantly evolving. Just 100 years ago, although books were readily available, the ability to sign one's name was the commonly accepted measure of literacy. With the expansion of compulsory public education in the 20th century, literacy became equated with educational achievement. The Army required soldiers to have a 5th grade education while the Census Bureau established a 6th grade education as the standard for literacy in civilian life. By the middle of the century, the Department of Education recognized that years of education does not necessarily reflect literacy skills and changed the standard to an 8th grade *reading* level.

Literacy develops through social interaction and is defined by cultural forces and practices, such as class, race, ethnicity, and gender, which contribute to the meaning of literacy and how it is learned and applied. This makes literacy context-specific and leads to the idea of *multiple literacies*. For example, technological advances (e.g., computer literacy, digital literacy, media literacy), social developments (e.g., financial literacy, science literacy, health literacy), and specialization (e.g., diabetes literacy, mental health literacy, breast cancer literacy) all can lead to highly specific contexts, each with its own literacy domain.

The 1991 National Literacy Act established the concept of *functional literacy*. In this broader view, adult literacy level is determined not by skill level but by what those skills enable a person to *do*.

Literacy in America today means ability to:

- Read, write, and speak in English
- Compute and solve problems
- Function on the job and in society
- Achieve one's goals
- Develop one's knowledge and potential

U.S. Congress 1991 National Literacy Act

An individual's functional literacy level varies with circumstances and social contexts. For example, a man may function at a high level in familiar surroundings at home and on the job. He does not need to read a map or a bus schedule because he boards the bus at the same place and time each day. He does not need to read street signs because he knows what they say; instead, they serve merely as landmarks. Since he learned his job through demonstration and practice, he did not need to read an operator's manual. This man is functionally literate in his usual environment. However, in unfamiliar contexts, such as the health care environment, the same man's functional literacy plummets. He encounters difficulty at every level of the health care system from finding the institution and the clinic to filling out forms and adhering to treatment. In this context, he is said to have *low functional health literacy*.

Note that the National Literacy Act specifies proficiency in English as a component of the measure of literacy in the US. English is the most commonly spoken language and, since there is no official language in the US, where many languages are spoken, Spanish being the second most common, English is, in effect, *lingua franca* for business, education, and commerce. Therefore, regardless of a person's intelligence and literacy skills in other languages, limited English proficiency may result in low functional literacy. That is, a person with limited English proficiency may not have full access to the opportunities and benefits offered and may, therefore, be limited in functioning in American society.

Measuring Literacy

How is literacy measured?

The 1992 National Adult Literacy Survey (NALS) shocked the nation by demonstrating that nearly half (48%) of the U.S. population scored at a Literacy Level of 1 or 2. That is, they could read short simple text to locate a single piece of information, enter personal information on a form, and perform simple calculations with numbers provided. Most professionals scored at Level 3; they could make low level inferences, integrate information from lengthy text, and generate a response based on easily identifiable information. Less than 5% of adults scored at Level 5 indicating the abil-

Specific Skills Needed to Use the U.S. Health Care System

- evaluating information for credibility and quality
- analyzing risks and benefits
- calculating dosages
- interpreting test results
- locating health information
- locating providers and services
- understanding graphs or other visual information
- articulating health concerns
- describing symptoms accurately
- asking pertinent questions
- understanding spoken advice or directions
- engaging in self-care and chronic disease management

Literary Levels in 2003

NAAL Level	Capacity	% US Adults
Below Basic	Very simple, concrete tasks	14%
Basic	Simple everyday tasks	29%
Intermediate	Moderately challenging tasks	44%
Proficient	Complex tasks	13%*

* Significant drop from NALS estimates in 1992

ity to search for information in dense text, make high level inferences, use specialized knowledge, and use background knowledge to determine quantities and appropriate numerical operations. Using 1990 U.S. census data, these findings were extrapolated to estimate that about 90 million people lack sufficient literacy skills to negotiate health care delivery systems.

In 2003, the National Assessment of Adult Literacy (NAAL) introduced the current method of reporting literacy using four levels from Below Basic to Proficient. *Below Basic*, the lowest level of performance, means a person may be able to sign a form or add the amounts on a bank deposit slip. *Basic* means a person can perform simple everyday tasks such as comparing the ticket price of two sporting events or understanding a pamphlet that describes how a person is selected for jury duty. *Intermediate* means that a person can do moderately challenging tasks such as calculating the cost of an order from an office supply catalog or identifying a specific location on a map. *Proficient* means performing complex activities such as comparing viewpoints in two editorials or interpreting a table about blood pressure and physical activity. The NAAL found literacy levels to be essentially unchanged in the 10 years since the NALS except for a statistically significant drop in the percentage of adults proficient enough to complete complex literacy tasks.

Health and Literacy

How are health and literacy linked?

Research in several countries has repeatedly documented the negative effect of limited literacy on virtually all aspects of health, including over-all levels of morbidity and mortality, accidents, and a wide range of diseases that include diabetes, cardiovascular disease, and rheumatoid arthritis. Disease and violent death are more prevalent in areas with low levels of literacy. Hospital utilization by children is highest in communities with limited literacy levels.

Literacy affects health both directly and indirectly. Persons with less than proficient literacy skills (86% of the population) find it difficult to access, understand, and use health information and services at every level of the health care system, including completing forms, providing informed consent, and interacting with providers. They may have trouble seeking timely appropriate intervention, administering medication, following treatment regimens, engaging in self-care, and caring for others. Parents with low literacy skills and low functional literacy face significant barriers to fostering healthy development and school readiness in their children.

What is health literacy?

Health literacy is a type of functional literacy. Like computer literacy, it develops with need,

Definitions of Health Literacy

Institute of Medicine: "...the degree to which individuals have the capacity to obtain, process and understand basic health information needed to make appropriate health decisions."

World Health Organization: "...the cognitive and social skills which determine the motivation and ability of individuals to gain access to understand and use information in ways which promote and maintain good health."

AMA Council of Scientific Affairs: functional health literacy is "the ability to read and comprehend prescription bottles, appointment slips, and the other essential health related materials required to successfully function as a patient."

The Patient Protection and Affordable Care Act ("health reform") Title V, Section 5002 uses the legal definition: "Health literacy is the degree to which an individual has the capacity to obtain, *communicate*, process and understand health information and services in order to make appropriate health decisions."

opportunity, and experience. Regardless of their literacy level in general, nearly everyone has low functional health literacy; that is, they typically lack background knowledge, medical vocabulary, and experience in the health care system. For example, few people have the need or opportunity to learn and talk about diabetes until they experience it. It is only at diagnosis that their health literacy or, more specifically in this example, their "diabetes literacy" begins to develop. Similarly, until people have need of medical services, they lack the background knowledge and vocabulary to navigate the system efficiently. With experience, their health literacy, in particular their "health care literacy," improves and they progress toward higher levels of functioning in the context of that system.

Health Literacy Research

How is health literacy measured?

Studies in the last decade have focused on the individual patient's ability to read in the health care setting. Researchers have adapted reading and comprehension tests from the field of education to identify patients with low health literacy so that providers can tailor communications to increase understanding and compliance. Most commonly used are the REALM (Rapid Estimate of Adult Literacy in Medicine), a word recognition test, and the TOFHLA (Test of Functional Health Literacy in Adults). The latter has been administered in English and in Spanish. While these tests have established the foundation necessary for understanding health literacy, they are only useful for research purposes since they are stressful and embarrassing for patients, and time consuming for providers.

It is now recognized that the REALM and TOFHLA measure reading ability; they are not measures of functional health literacy. Although much evidence supports an association between ability to read (including printed health information) and a variety of health outcomes, the impact of the mismatch between the average literacy skills of U.S. adults and the sophisticated demands of the U.S. health care system has not been fully assessed. Better tools that reflect the reality of health literacy in people's lives are needed to measure health literacy beyond the current focus on reading. That is, instruments are needed that truly assess "the functionality of functional literacy."

What promotes health literacy?

Because the source of most health care communication problems is a mismatch between providers' and patients' logic, language, and experience, work to improve health literacy has focused on enhancing information delivery. Due to special training and vocabulary, physicians and other health care professionals think and talk about health, illness, and treatment in unique ways. Even among native-born patients who are not only proficient in English but also highly educated professionals in their own field, the culture and language of medicine can be barriers to efficient, effective care.

Federal and state law, Medicare and Medicaid regulations, and accreditation standards have placed responsibility for patient understanding squarely with the provider. For example, the Plain Writing Act of 2010 requires that government documents be written in "plain language," defined as "writing that is clear, concise, well-organized, and follows other best practices appropriate to the subject or field and intended audience." This law applies to health and medical information used in health care organizations that receive *any* federal funding.

- What do you call the problem?
- What do you think has caused the problem?
- Why do you think it started when it did?
- What do you think the sickness does?
- How severe is the sickness? Will it have a short or long course?
- What kind of treatment do you think the patient should receive?
- What are the most important results you hope to receive from treatment?

Adapted from: Arthur Kleinman as quoted in Fadiman A, *The Spirit Catches You and You Fall Down: A Hmong Child, Her American Doctors and the Collision of Two Cultures.* New York: The Noonday Press / Farrar Straus & Giroux; 1997, pp. 260–261.

Psychiatrist and anthropologist Arthur Kleinman developed a set of interview questions to elicit a patient's experience and perception of a condition and its treatment. Practitioners can use these questions to close gaps between a patient's logic, language, and experience and their own.

"... give it to them briefly so that they will read it, clearly so they will appreciate it, picturesquely so they will remember it, and above all accurately so they will be guided by its light."

Joseph Pulitzer

Over 300 studies have shown that most written health information exceeds patients' literacy skills and numerous guidelines have been published to increase the readability of health education materials (see Recommended Readings and Resources).

Improved information delivery alone, however, is not likely to mitigate the relationship between low literacy and poor outcomes. New studies suggest it is possible to promote functional health literacy through specific health education and direct assistance to a specific patient to personalize the information given and then to demonstrate how to apply it in context.

Support from family, friends, or social services providers can buffer the negative effects of low health literacy by enabling a person to understand information, enter and navigate the health system, and adhere to treatment regimens. Collaboration between health care organizations and literacy enhancing community services, such as adult basic education and English language learning classes, may also prove beneficial.

To facilitate understanding of the information you provide:
- become aware of the culture and language of medicine and of your institution
- become aware of your patients' culture and language
- use plain language (say "walk" instead of "ambulate")
- be aware of the pictures your words create in the patient's mind
- be especially aware of common words used as medical terms (e.g., stool, screen, cap)
- ask the patient to "teach back" to confirm understanding

- limit discussion to the "critical minimum" information the patient needs to cope and recover
- say the most important thing three times (adults, like everyone else, learn by repetition)
- invite patients to read aloud the most important part of treatment instructions, then ask what that means
- refer patients with less than a high school education who do not read for fun to literacy enhancing services
- encourage formal education
- encourage reading for fun, especially reading aloud (reading to children)
- never assume a patient understands your instructions or printed information
- instead of "Do you understand?" ask "Did I explain that clearly?"

To facilitate the use of information to maintain or enhance health:
- focus on behavior (what to do to cope, recover, or enhance health)
- ask the patient how and when to take the medicine
- include caregivers in the discussion
- connect the patient with institutional and community interpreter/case management/home health services
- follow up visits by phone to check how the patient is implementing the treatment plan
- be more concerned about what a patient does than about what a patient understands

Recommended Readings

Baker DW. The meaning and measure of health literacy. *Journal of General Internal Medicine* 2006; 21:878–883.

Calderón JL, Beltran R. Pitfalls in health communication: Health policy, institutions, structure and process of healthcare. *Medscape General Medicine* 2004; 6(1):9. Available at: http://www.medscape.com/view article/466016_5

Calderón JL, Smith S, Baker R. "FONBAYS": A simple method for enhancing readability of patient information. *Annals of the Behavioral Sciences and Medical Education* 2007; 14(1):20–24.

Doak C, Doak L, Root J. *Teaching Patients with Low Literacy Skills,* 2nd ed. Philadelphia, PA: JB Lippincott; 1996. Available online at http://www.

hsph.harvard.edu/healthliteracy/resources/doak-book/

Nutbeam D. The evolving concept of health literacy. *Social Science & Medicine* 2008; 67:2072–2078.

Paasche-Orlow, MK, Wolf MS. The causal pathways linking literacy and health outcomes. *American Journal of Health Behavior* 2007; 31(Suppl1):S19–S26.

Smith SA. *Promoting Health Literacy: Concept, Measurement & Intervention.* Cincinnati, OH: Union Institute and University, Publication No. AAT 3375168; 2009.

Online Resources

Medicare & Medicaid Services: https://www.cms.gov/WrittenMaterialsToolkit/Downloads/ToolkitPart01.pdf

MEDLINE/PubMed Search and Health Literacy Information Resources. National Library of Medicine. Available at http://www.nlm.nih.gov/services/health_literacy.html

U.S. Department of Health and Human Services, Centers for Medicare and Medicaid Services (2011). TOOLKIT for Making Written Material Clear and Effective. Available at https://www.cms.gov/WrittenMaterialsToolkit/

Ontario Ministry of Health. Literacy and Health Project. Phase One. Making the World Healthier and Safer for People Who Can't Read (1989) Available at http://www.eric.ed.gov/ERICWebPortal/search/detailmini.jsp?_nfpb=true&_&ERICExtSearch_SearchValue_0=ED346338&ERICExtSearch_SearchType_0=no&accno=ED346338

Review Questions

1. Which of the following statements is true?
   - A. A college education provides adequate literacy skills to negotiate health care systems.
   - B. Most health care documents are geared to the reading skills of the typical adult.
   - C. Strong reading skills ensure ability to direct the health care of self and others.
   - D. The World Health Organization definition of health literacy includes non-cognitive skills.

2. A 40-year-old parent with an elementary school education and her 7-year-old daughter took public transportation to visit the child's pediatrician for the girl's routine well-child

check-up. The child's immunizations are up to
date. She is meeting developmental milestones
and is doing well in school. This parent demonstrates functional health literacy by
A. maintaining a medical home for the child.
B. making and keeping an appointment on a
   timely basis.
C. obtaining preventive services for a well
   child.
D. supporting child health and development.
E. All of the above

3. The level of a person's functional health lit-
   eracy varies by the person's
   A. access to health care.
   B. current health status.
   C. experience with their condition.
   D. social skills.
   E. All of the above

Key to review questions: p. 408

Section VIII

The Health Care System, Policy, and Economics

30 The U.S. Health Care System

Jillian S. Catalanotti, MD, MPH

- What are the components of the U.S. health care system?
- What is continuity of care?
- How do we ensure competency of health care providers?
- How does the third party payment system work?
- What are the different forms of public health insurance?
- How does our health care system rate with regard to quality, cost, and access?
- What reforms are included in the Patient Protection and Affordable Care Act?

Components of the Health Care System

> What are the components of the U.S. health care system?

The infrastructure of the U.S. **health care system** provides for medical care and public health. Historically, the public health system targeted disease prevention and health promotion, while the medical system targeted treatment and cure of disease. Because our medical system has traditionally emphasized treatment rather than prevention, measures of quality generally show that the system performs better for acute care than preventive care.

Overall, the U.S. health care system is characterized by *fragmentation*. The system is divided into the *health care delivery* infrastructure, the *health care payment* infrastructure, and the *public health* infrastructure. The public health infrastructure is frequently viewed as parallel to the health care system rather than an integral part of it. Therefore, we will briefly describe the public health infrastructure, then focus mainly on the care delivery and payment components of the health care system.

Public Health Infrastructure

The public health infrastructure involves federal, state, and local levels. The federal infrastructure consists of the following agencies housed within the **Department of Health and Human Services**: Centers for Disease Control and Prevention (CDC); National Institutes of Health (NIH); Food and Drug Administration (FDA); Health Resources and Services Administration (HRSA); Agency for Healthcare Research and Quality (AHRQ); Substance Abuse and Mental Health Services Administration (SAMHSA); and Indian Health Service (IHS). Together, these agencies perform and fund health research, provide guidance for local health delivery, coordinate interstate surveillance efforts, ensure the safety of food, drugs, and durable medical equipment, and oversee the Federally Qualified Health Center (FQHC), Indian Health Service, and nationwide organ transplantation programs.

> Whereas federal public health agencies perform research and coordinate public health activities for the nation, most public health services (e.g., vaccination services, health promotion campaigns, and data collection) occur on a state or local level. Each state has a Health Department or Board of Health, and most states have one or more local health boards at the city or county level.

Levels of Health Care Delivery

Medical care is classified by the delivery setting (e.g., inpatient care, outpatient/ambulatory care, long-term care, or home-based care). *Inpatient care* involves admission to a hospital or extended care facility for more than one day, mainly for major physical or mental health problems that are potentially life-threatening or require services that cannot be provided at home. *Outpatient,* or *ambulatory care* is provided in office settings, ambulatory surgery centers (for procedures that do not require overnight observation), and urgent care clinics. *Long-term care* is intended to serve individuals who cannot care for themselves and is generally provided in extended care facilities with skilled nursing or residential staff (like nursing homes). *Home-based care* occurs along a continuum depending on the needs, disability, and infirmity of the patient. *Assisted living* may provide support for shopping, food preparation, household chores, or medication management. For disabled or homebound patients, who cannot easily travel but require services that can be provided outside of an institutional setting, nursing and other specialized care can be provided in the home.

Levels of health care include primary, secondary, and tertiary care. *Primary care* consists of preventive, diagnostic, and treatment services for common, uncomplicated medical problems (80% of health problems), typically delivered in an outpatient or home-based setting. *Secondary care* requires specialist physicians, and is delivered in an outpatient setting, or through short hospital stays, typically in smaller community hospitals. Secondary care addresses about 15% of health problems. *Tertiary care* involves complex medical management and newer medical technology delivered in large, specialized medical centers. Although tertiary care accounts for the bulk of health care costs, it addresses less than 5% of health problems.

Continuity of Care

What is continuity of care?

Ideal health care should be continuous, characterized by a seamless transition of patient and information between different settings and provid-

ers over time. The most continuous care possible would be provided by one health care provider with intimate knowledge of the patient's health history. To the extent that this is not possible in an era of medical specialization, **continuity of care** depends on good communication between health care providers. Breakdown in this communication has been identified as a common source of medical errors leading to unnecessary patient harm.

A barrier to continuity of care in the health care system is the degree to which care is fragmented among different providers, in different settings, affiliated with different hospitals or health care organizations, and different payers for health care with different priorities or contractual obligations. Each of these entities has its own system for record-keeping and variable availability of records to others. Even electronic medical records, which may improve completeness, accuracy, and legibility over paper charts, do not ensure accessibility of records to others.

Health Care Providers

How do we ensure competency of health care providers?

Health care providers include physicians, nurse practitioners, podiatrists, physician assistants, dentists, nurses, clinical psychologists, social workers, providers of ancillary services (e.g., physical and occupational therapists, speech therapists, respiratory therapists, nutritionists, optometrists, chiropractors, dental hygienists, pharmacists, case managers), and other allied health professionals (e.g., laboratory technicians, radiology technicians, phlebotomists, medical assistants, emergency medical technicians). In the 19th century, health professionals were variably trained with no system to ensure quality education and training. The 1910 *Flexner Report* called for higher standards of medical education and reform in training, giving rise to modern medical education. Currently, in order to ensure a competent workforce of health care providers, there are three main types of regulation: **accreditation**, **licensing**, and **certification**.

Educational and training programs, health care delivery organizations, and health insurance plans must be *accredited* as meeting certain pre-set criteria. Criteria for educational and training programs include required courses, duration of training or study, and faculty qualifications. Accrediting agencies for educational and training programs include the *Liaison Committee for Medical Education* (LCME), which accredits allopathic medical schools; the *Accreditation Council for Graduate Medical Education* (ACGME), which accredits allopathic residency programs; and the *American Osteopathic Association* (AOA), which accredits osteopathic medical schools and residency programs. In addition, *The Joint Commission* (TJC) accredits hospitals, medical offices, nursing homes, and home care organizations and the *National Committee on Quality Assurance* (NCQA) accredits health care plans.

Licensing of an individual health care provider requires completion of training at an accredited institution and meeting competency requirements in order to be granted legal permission to deliver clinical care.

> Licenses are granted by states. Health care providers can only practice in states in which they are licensed, although competency requirements often include meeting national benchmarks, such as passing the U.S. Medical Licensing Examination (USMLE) for physicians.

Certification is not a requirement for practice, but rather recognizes achievement of a higher standard of competency by a professional organization (*Board Certification*). In addition to meeting other requirements, certification requires passing an examination, and maintenance of certification may require re-examination at set intervals (e.g., annually, every 10 years).

Third Party Payment Systems

How does the third party payment system work?

Health care providers, institutions, and organizations are paid directly by individual patients (*out-of-pocket*) or by health insurance plans (private insurance or public, government-subsidized plans). This **third party payment system** adds to the complexity of the health care payment system, as there are many different health insurance companies, each offering different plans to their beneficiaries. The fragmented administrative requirements of this complex system significantly increase health care costs.

The main purpose of health insurance is to protect individuals from bankruptcy in the face of a medical catastrophe. A health insurance plan is a contract between the patient (*beneficiary*) and the insurer stipulating how much the individual must pay, and what care the health insurance plan will cover. Overall, a health insurer hopes to *pool risk* (i.e., collect payments from many beneficiaries in the hope that only some of them will incur health care expenses).

A *premium* is a beneficiary's monthly or annual payment for health insurance. Premiums may vary based on pre-existing health conditions, age, gender, or health behavior (e.g., smoking). Individuals deemed at higher risk, or more likely to utilize health care resources, may be charged higher premiums. A *deductible* is money the beneficiary must pay out of pocket for a health care service before their health insurance plan kicks in. In general, health insurance plans with lower premium rates tend to have higher deductibles, and those with higher premium rates tend to have lower deductibles.

Most health insurance plans require beneficiaries to pay *co-pays* when they receive certain health care services. A co-pay is a set amount paid out of pocket for a medical service. In addition to cost-sharing, co-pays influence the behavior of beneficiaries to prevent unnecessary use of health care resources or influence a beneficiary's choice of health care providers (e.g., charging a lower co-pay for care in a physician's office than in an emergency room, or for a visit with a primary care provider rather than with a specialist). When a co-pay is charged as a percent of total cost rather than a set amount of money (e.g., 10% rather than $10), it is called *co-insurance.*

Many health insurance plans are **managed care plans**, designed to control costs while still providing high quality medical care. The most common forms of managed care plans are **health maintenance organizations** (HMOs) and **preferred provider organizations** (PPOs). Traditional HMOs are both the insurer and provider of medical care. Beneficiaries may only see physicians employed by the HMO plan. If beneficiaries choose to see providers outside the HMO, they will have to pay for the service out of pocket. PPOs, in contrast, enroll physicians to become *in-network* providers with whom the PPO has a contract for services at a lower rate. Beneficiaries are given incentives to choose in-network providers, including lower co-pays. A beneficiary may choose to see an *out-of-network* provider, but will have to pay any charges beyond the amount paid by their insurance.

About two thirds of Americans have private health insurance plans, the majority of which are *employer-sponsored plans.* The advantages of employer-sponsored plans are: (1) part of the premium is paid by the employer; (2) employers purchasing a health plan on behalf of many beneficiaries have more bargaining power than individuals; and (3) for a large group of employees, the increased risk of one person's pre-existing medical conditions, new medical problems, or risk factors may be more easily absorbed by the large pool without dramatically increasing premiums. The main disadvantage is that a beneficiary can only select between plans offered by the employer, which may or may not suit individual needs. Additionally, the cost of providing health insurance can be significant for employers.

Individual private health insurance allows one to select a plan better suited to individual needs; however, the entire premium must be paid by the beneficiary alone. Health insurance plans may not insure or may require higher premiums from individuals with pre-existing medical conditions, who are deemed high-risk utilizers of health services, thus barring some individuals from affordable health insurance.

Evolution of the Health Care Payment System

During the Great Depression, the economic vulnerability of hospitals and the population at large led to the formation of private health insurance plans, in which participants paid monthly or annual premiums in exchange for a set amount of hospital days or medical care. Large-scale public works projects created jobs, fueled the economy, and improved the country's infrastructure. Kaiser Steel, founded by Henry J. Kaiser, produced much of the steel used on the West Coast for these projects. In response to employee injuries and the desire to maintain a healthy and efficient work force, Kaiser teamed with a local physician, Dr. Sidney Garfield, to pro-

vide medical care for his employees at a local hospital. Thus began the prominent role of the employer in the provision of health care.

During World War II, the Federal Government imposed wage and salary freezes on all workers. Benefits, including health insurance, were excluded from this freeze and employers expanded benefits packages in an effort to attract workers. Employer-sponsored health insurance plans allowed workers to pool their contributions with employer contributions to purchase health insurance and provide workers with financial protection in the event of medical illness.

After the war, returning veterans became entitled to a number of benefits, including insured health care, provided by the Federal Government at little or no cost, thus creating the first government-subsidized health program, under the Department of Veterans Affairs (VA).

The years leading up to and during WWII brought advances in the treatment of infectious diseases (e.g., the use of penicillin to treat bacterial infections). Subsequently, chronic diseases like heart disease and cancer became the leading causes of death. They proved not only difficult to prevent, but costly to treat, and U.S. health care expenditures increased dramatically. The increased incidence of chronic diseases, increased cost of health care, and central role of the employer in providing health insurance limited access to health care for three main groups of people: the elderly, the disabled, and the poor. By the early 1960s, half of all U.S. citizens older than 65 lacked health insurance.

In 1965, two programs were created to help these groups meet the rising cost of health care: **Medicare**, a federally funded health insurance plan for the elderly and permanently disabled; and **Medicaid**, a joint federal and state funded health insurance plan for the poor. The creation of these programs increased the Federal Government's role in paying for and monitoring the provision of health services.

Government Funded Health Insurance

What are the different forms of public health insurance?

Public (government-funded) health insurance is provided through five principle programs: Medicare, Medicaid, State Children's Health Insurance Plan, Tricare, and Veterans Affairs (VA).

Medicare and Medicaid are administered by an agency under the Department of Health and Human Services (HHS) called the Centers for Medicare & Medicaid Services (CMS). **Medicare** is an insurance plan to cover the elderly and disabled (See Table 30.1). It is funded by income tax paid to the Federal Government, and eligibility criteria, prices, and coverage are set by the Federal Government for the entire country. Medicare has limitations on annual and lifetime payments for any individual. In 2008, about 45 million Americans were covered by Medicare, about 85% of whom were aged 65 or older.

Medicare is a health care payment system (i.e., a form of health insurance not a health care delivery system). Beneficiaries can choose to see any health care provider who accepts Medicare coverage. Medicare is divided into four "Parts" (Parts A, B, C, and D) for coverage of different health services.

Medicare Part A covers hospital care, limited nursing home and inpatient rehabilitation services, and hospice care. It is available to every Medicare beneficiary without a premium. Deductibles and co-pays are set annually by the Federal Government. *Medicare Part B* covers outpatient care, medical equipment, and ancillary services. Any Medicare beneficiary may choose to purchase Part B for a premium, which is determined, along with deductibles and co-pays, by the Federal Government. Until 2011, Medicare Part B did not cover routine preventive physical examinations. *Medicare*

Table 30.1. Eligibility criteria for Medicare

Eligibility Criteria	Year coverage by Medicare began
1. Age 65 or older and you or your spouse have paid income tax for at least 40 quarters (10 years)	1965
2. Permanently disabled (any age)	1972
3. End stage renal disease requiring dialysis or kidney transplant (any age)	1972
4. Amyotrophic lateral sclerosis, also called "Lou Gehrig's disease" (any age)	2001

Part C consists of the Medicare Advantage plans, administered through private insurance carriers, with which Medicare beneficiaries may contract to receive Medicare benefits. Medicare Advantage Plans may offer additional benefits and may charge premiums, deductibles, and co-pays that are different from standard Medicare rates. *Medicare Part D* covers prescription medications and is administered through different insurance companies, each offering similar plans from which any Medicare beneficiary who would like Part D coverage may choose. The Part D coverage gap (the *"doughnut hole"*) refers to a $3,500 gap in coverage set by the original legislation (See Figure 30.1). After meeting the annual deduct-

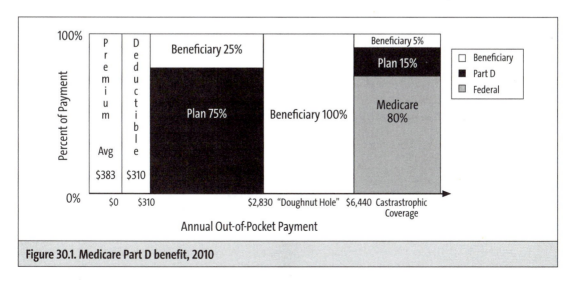

Figure 30.1. Medicare Part D benefit, 2010

ible, beneficiaries (patients) pay co-insurance (on average, 25%) for all medications up to a specified limit ($2,830 in 2010). Above this limit, the beneficiary enters the coverage gap in which the Part D plan pays nothing and the individual pays entirely out-of-pocket for all prescriptions until reaching a second total spending limit ($6,440 in 2010). Above this second amount (deemed "catastrophic"), beneficiaries pay very little (5% co-insurance on average) for additional medications. The remainder is shared by the Part D plan and the Federal Government.

Medicaid is an insurance plan for the poor who meet certain criteria (See Table 30.2). Funded by federal and state tax dollars, it covered approximately 40 million people in 2008. Eligibility, prices, and coverage are set by states in accordance with federal criteria. Thus, individuals may qualify in one state but not another, or eligibility may vary from year to year with state budget changes. States may expand coverage beyond federal minimums, but funding will not be matched by federal dollars.

Medicaid generally covers hospital care, outpatient care, skilled nursing home services, and dental care, and may or may not cover ancillary services, inpatient rehabilitation services, medical equipment, and prescriptions depending on the state. Deductibles and co-pays are relatively small and determined by state governments, and no co-pay may be charged for emergency services. Beneficiaries can see any providers who accept Medicaid, but the level of payment by Medicaid is often less than what is charged by providers with the result that many providers will not accept Medicaid.

The **State Children's Health Insurance Program (SCHIP)** is an insurance plan covering poor children who do not qualify for Medicaid. It is funded by federal and state governments, but administered by the state. Children whose families earn up to 200% FPL qualify for SCHIP. Many states combine their SCHIP and Medicaid programs.

Tricare is the health insurance plan for active and retired members of the military and their dependents. It is similar to an employer-sponsored health insurance plan, but the employees are military service members and the employer is the Federal Government. It is both a health payment plan and a health delivery system. Tricare ben-

Table 30.2. Eligibility criteria (minimum federal requirements) for Medicaid	
Children < Age 6	< 133% FPL* (optional expansion to < 185% FPL for children age 0–1 with federal matching funds)
Age 6–19	< 100% FPL
Foster care children	Any income level
Pregnant Women	< 133% FPL (optional expansion to < 185% FPL with federal matching funds)
Adults age 20–64 with dependent children	If qualify for Aid to Families with Dependent Children (AFDC) program
Certain poor Medicare beneficiaries	Varied criteria (Medicaid would pay for Medicare premium, deductible, and co-pays)
Poor blind or temporarily disabled	If qualify for Supplemental Security Income (SSI)
"Medically needy" (those who have incurred large medical expenses)	Defined differently by each state (optional, with federal matching funds)
Other adults	Not eligible for federal matching funds
*FPL = Federal Poverty Line for family or individual income as calculated by the U.S. Census Bureau	

eficiaries can see any health care providers who accept their coverage, or can see health care providers directly hired by the military health system.

Honorably discharged veterans are eligible for **Veterans Affairs** (VA) health services. The VA is a fully integrated health care delivery system with locations distributed across the country. Beneficiaries must be seen at VA facilities. The VA directly hires its own health care providers and runs its own ambulatory care centers and hospitals. Payment is internal via budgeting under the Department of Defense. In 2010, the VA treated nearly 6 million patients.

Safety Net for the Uninsured or Underinsured

Although Medicaid and SCHIP provide health insurance for many of the poor, as of 2009, there were still *50 million individuals without health insurance* according to the U.S. Census Bureau. Many cannot afford to pay health insurance premiums and are not poor enough to be eligible for Medicaid. Some choose not to purchase health insurance because they would prefer to pay out of pocket, or they perceive their personal risk as low compared to the cost of health insurance.

However, the uninsured fare worse than others on measures of health outcomes. The uninsured are less likely to receive recommended screening tests, and according to the Institute of Medicine, 18,000 persons die prematurely each year because they lack health insurance. The **Emergency Medical Treatment and Active Labor Act** (EMTALA), passed in 1986, stipulates that all hospitals that receive Medicare payments and have emergency rooms must treat all patients with emergency medical problems, regardless of ability to pay. Unfortunately, due to difficulty accessing health care in ambulatory settings, the uninsured tend to use emergency rooms unnecessarily for health care that could be delivered more cheaply and with greater continuity in an outpatient setting.

The **Federally Qualified Health Center** (FQHC) program was established in 1969 as part of President Johnson's War on Poverty to improve access to health care for the uninsured. FQHCs target high need communities and deliver culturally appropriate comprehensive primary health services. They include Community Health Centers, Migrant Health Centers, Health Care for the Homeless programs, and Public Housing Primary Care programs. Designation as an FQHC means that the center meets program criteria and receives several benefits, as outlined in the Table 30.3.

In 2002, President George W. Bush's President's Health Center Initiative doubled funding for the FQHC program from $1 billion to $2 billion and created 1,200 new health centers. The 2008 American Recovery and Reinvestment Act (ARRA) designated an additional $2 billion for investment in FQHCs over two years. The 2010

Table 30.3. Eligibility criteria for and benefits of designation as a Federally Qualified Health Center	
Eligibility Criteria	**Benefits**
1. Located in or serve a community with limited access to health care	1. Federal grant money and federal loans for capital improvements
2. Provide comprehensive primary health care services and support services to promote access to care	2. Improved reimbursement rates for Medicaid and Medicare payments
3. Provide health care to all with sliding-scale fees based on ability to pay	3. Ability to hire National Health Service Corps providers
4. Governed by a board, at least 51% of whom are patients who represent the target population	4. Medical malpractice for providers paid by the Federal Government
5. Meet certain clinical, administrative, and financial performance and accountability requirements	5. Special price discounts for pharmaceutical products for patients of the center

Patient Protection and Affordable Care Act (ACA) designated $11 billion for investment in FQHCs over five years. As of 2010, there were 8,530 FQHC sites that served over 19 million patients across the country. The FQHC program is estimated to save the health care system $9.9 billion to $17.6 billion per year by helping patients access preventive medical services and avoid unnecessary emergency room use.

Grading the U.S. Health Care System

> How does our health care system rate with regard to quality, cost, and access?

The US spends more than any other country on health care. In 2008, total U.S. health expenditures were $2.3 trillion. About 48% was paid by public funds, 40% was paid by employers, private insurance companies, and other private sources, and 12% was out-of-pocket payments by individuals. Federal Government spending on Medicare, Medicaid, and SCHIP together represents about 20% of total federal spending. Health care costs have risen rapidly, outpacing inflation. According to HHS, premiums for family health insurance have increased 131% since 1999. Many experts agree that the high cost of health care is unsustainable and that reform is needed. Serious discussion on this topic has historically been hindered by concerns about the rationing of health care services and political priorities.

Unfortunately, high costs have not guaranteed high quality. In its report, *To Err is Human*, the Institute of Medicine (IOM) reported that medical errors cause 98,000 deaths in the US annually. In a subsequent report, *Crossing the Quality Chasm*, the IOM defined quality care as safe, timely, effective, efficient, equitable, and patient centered. Although there are no standards for evaluating health care systems, the World Health Organization (WHO) suggested such criteria include *infant mortality* (in 2000, the US ranked 19th worldwide), *maternal mortality* (ranked 32nd), and *life expectancy* (ranked 24th). Of course, the quality of the health care system depends on which outcomes are valued. The U.S. health care system fares well on outcomes such as survival after myocardial infarction and traumatic injuries, yet many people do not have access to these services. In its rankings for overall quality of care, the WHO highly valued *equal access* to health care services, a criterion on which the U.S. health care system performs relatively poorly because access to health care is uneven and closely related to insurance status. Studies have repeatedly shown that those without health insurance forgo needed medical care and have higher mortality rates for many conditions than those who are insured. Additionally, health care providers and facilities are not evenly distributed across the country; common shortage areas include both rural and inner city localities. *Overall, the WHO ranked the U.S. health care system 37th in the world in quality.*

Health Care System Reform

> What reforms are included in the Patient Protection and Affordable Care Act?

For decades, there have been attempts to reform the health care system, decrease costs, improve quality, and increase access to care. President Barack Obama signed the **Patient Protection and Affordable Care Act** (ACA) into law on March 23, 2010. This comprehensive law seeks to overhaul the health care system by focusing on several objectives, with components scheduled to begin at different times between 2010 and 2019 (See Table 30.4).

The Congressional Budget Office (CBO) estimates the ACA will provide coverage to an additional 32 million Americans when fully implemented in 2019, and estimates its cost at $938 billion over 10 years. Due to proposed financing through savings from Medicare and Medicaid, as well as new taxes and fees, the CBO further estimates that the law will reduce the deficit by $124 billion over 10 years.

Unfortunately, health care reform has been politically divisive and the ACA passed without a single Republican vote. At the time of this writing, several provisions of the ACA (including Medicare coverage of preventive exams, the requirement that health insurance companies cover dependent children until age 26, and the inability to deny coverage to children based on pre-existing conditions) are already in effect. Overall however, the fate of

Table 30.4. Components of the Patient Protection and Affordable Care Act (ACA)

Reduce the number of uninsured
- Expands Medicaid eligibility to all citizens and residents up to 133% of FPL
- Requires U.S. citizens and legal residents to have health insurance coverage
- Requires employers with ≥ 50 employees to offer health insurance coverage

Reform health insurance industry
- Prohibits rescissions of coverage or dollar value limits
- Outlaws pre-existing condition exclusions
- Establishes Health Benefit Exchanges allowing individuals/small businesses to purchase insurance
- Sets minimum coverage requirements for all health plans
- Requires all plans to cover dependent children up to age 26
- Requires insurance companies to spend 85% of premium income on clinical services and quality

Improve preventive care
- Requires Medicare and Medicaid to cover preventive services with no cost-sharing
- Requires all health plans to cover a minimum level of preventive care
- Establishes the Independence at Home program to provide home-based primary care services for high-need Medicare beneficiaries

Improve health care quality
- Requires physician reporting on certain outcome measures
- Provides incentives for providers in Accountable Care Organizations that meet quality thresholds
- Reduces Medicare payments for hospital-acquired infections and preventable hospital readmissions
- Funds comparative effectiveness research for direct comparisons of treatments and medications

Decrease health care costs
- Increases oversight to reduce waste, fraud, and abuse in Medicare and Medicaid
- Slowly decreases co-insurance rate in the "doughnut hole" from 100% to 25% over 10 years
- Establishes the Independent Payment Advisory Board to reduce growth in Medicare spending

Increase access to care
- Increases Medicaid payment rates for primary care services to Medicare rates for 2 years
- Increases funding for the Federally Qualified Health Center program
- Recruits providers to primary care: loan repayment and training incentives, especially for rural/underserved areas; 10% bonuses on Medicare payments for 5 years

Decrease administrative overhead
- Streamlines and standardizes health insurance claims processing

Pay for health care reform
- Increases Medicare payroll taxes, reduces tax relief from health savings and flexible spending accounts
- Imposes fees on health insurance and pharmaceutical companies
- Levies tax on certain employer-sponsored health plans with very high levels of coverage

Improve public health
- Creates the Prevention and Public Health Fund, the largest public health fund in U.S. history
- Requires restaurants and vending machines to publish calorie information

the ACA is uncertain. Some lawmakers support a full repeal of the ACA, others hope to seriously amend parts of it, and still others propose denying funding to carry out various provisions of the act.

Perhaps the most controversial part of the ACA is the requirement that all Americans have health insurance (the "*individual mandate*") as of 2014 or pay a penalty. In order to assist with this requirement, the ACA establishes *state-based Health Benefit Exchanges* through which individuals can purchase coverage. Each exchange must have at least two health insurance plans providing varying levels of coverage above a minimum standard. The CBO estimates that the national average annual premium for coverage in a health benefit exchange would be $4,500–5,000 for an individual and $12,000–12,500 for a family for the minimum coverage available. Those individuals with income levels between 133–400% FPL will be granted *cost-sharing credits* to assist in purchasing health insurance through the exchanges. Separate but similar exchanges will also be available for employers who own small businesses. At the time of this writing, several legal cases have challenged various provisions (most notably the constitutionality of the individual mandate in a case brought by 26 states against the Federal Government) with differing outcomes in the federal court system. The question has been accepted by the Supreme Court and as scheduled to be heard in March 2012.

A second common area of controversy is the expansion of Medicaid eligibility to cover all citizens and permanent residents with incomes up to 133% FPL. The largest newly eligible group is adults *without* dependent children. Although the ACA offers 100% federal funding for the initial expansion of Medicaid coverage, this percentage will decrease over time. Several states have resisted the ACA's large expansion of Medicaid eligibility, citing financial hardship. The effect of state resistance to enforcing this and other parts of the law remains to be seen.

Recommended Readings

The Institute of Medicine. *To Err is Human: Building a Safer Healthcare System*. Released on November 1, 1999. Report Brief available at http://www.iom.edu/Reports/1999/To-Err-is-Human-Building-A-Safer-Health-System.aspx

The Institute of Medicine. *Crossing the Quality Chasm: A New Health System for the 21st Century*. Released on March 1, 2001. Report Brief available at http://www.iom.edu/Reports/2001/Crossing-the-Quality-Chasm-A-New-Health-System-for-the-21st-Century.aspx

Sultz HA, Young KM. *Health Care USA: Understanding Its Organization and Delivery,* 7th ed. Boston, MA: Jones and Bartlett; 2010.

Online Resources

The Henry J. Kaiser Family Foundation. Health Reform Source. Available at http://healthreform.kff.org/

U.S. Department of Health and Human Services. Information about the Patient Protection and Affordable Care Act. www.healthcare.gov

U.S. Department of Health and Human Services. The Official U.S. Government Site for Medicare. www.medicare.gov

Review questions

1. The amount of money that health insurance beneficiaries must pay regardless of whether or not they seek health services is called a
   A. co-insurance.
   B. co-pay.
   C. deductible.
   D. premium.

2. Which of the following groups of U.S. citizens or permanent residents is not eligible for Medicare?
   A. Individuals > 65 who have paid income tax for 10 years
   B. Individual with amyotrophic lateral sclerosis
   C. Individuals with end-stage kidney disease requiring dialysis
   D. Permanently disabled individuals
   E. Poor pregnant women

3. The Patient Protection and Affordable Care Act
   A. expands Medicaid eligibility to all individuals with income up to 133% of the federal poverty level.
   B. offers limited bonuses to primary care physicians treating Medicare patients.

C. requires all health plans to cover a minimum level of preventive care.

D. requires all individuals to have health insurance.

E. all of the above

Key to review questions: p. 408

31 Complementary and Integrative Medicine

Hilary McClafferty, MD, and Olle Jane Z. Sahler, MD

- How do complementary medicine and conventional medicine differ?
- Why is the popularity of complementary medicine increasing?
- What is integrative medicine?
- How is complementary medicine classified?
- Which complementary medicine practices are licensed in the US?
- What distinguishes behavioral science-based treatments from complementary medicine treatments?
- Why do some proponents of complementary medicine reject accepted scientific standards for research?
- How should CAM therapies be evaluated for usefulness?

Defining Complementary and Alternative Medicine

> How do complementary medicine and conventional medicine differ?

Conventional medical practice in the US is based on the biomedical model that had its origins in the 1911 *Flexner Report* recommending more scientifically-based training and practice for physicians. **Complementary and alternative medicine** (CAM) refers to models, practices, and procedures that are generally regarded as lying outside the domain of contemporary biomedicine. CAM covers a broad range of therapeutic modalities, some of which have demonstrated efficacy, while others do not. Some forms of CAM are medical systems encompassing many treatment modalities while others are specific treatments for select disorders. In general, complementary implies treatments used *in conjunction with,* while alternative implies treatments used *instead of* conventional medicine.

CAM Therapies as listed by the National Center for Complementary and Alternative Medicine include:

- Acupuncture
- Alexander technique and other movement therapies (Feldenkrais method, pilates, Rolf structural integration, Trager psychophysical integration)
- Aromatherapy
- Ayurveda
- Biofeedback
- Chiropractic
- Energy medicine
- Healing and therapeutic touch
- Herbalism
- Holistic nursing
- Homeopathy
- Hypnosis
- Massage Therapy
- Mind-body practices (breathing exercises, guided imagery, mindfulness, hypnotherapy, progressive muscle relaxation, meditation)
- Naturopathy
- Nutritional therapy
- Osteopathic manipulative therapy
- Qi gong
- Reflexology
- Reiki
- Spiritual healing
- Tai Chi
- Traditional Chinese medicine
- Yoga

> **Why is the popularity of complementary medicine increasing?**

Increased interest in CAM has been attributed to a variety of factors including the *high cost, invasive nature,* and *noxious side effects* of many conventional treatments, greater interest in prevention, and the more user friendly, palliative nature of complementary care practices. In 1993, Eisenberg et al published a landmark study in the *New England Journal of Medicine* reviewing the demographics of users, utilization of treatments and consumer goods, motivation for use, and financial expenditures for complementary medicine, and found that usage was significant.

> The Eisenberg et al study in 1993 concluded that one third of the U.S. population used some form of CAM therapy. A repeat study by the same authors in 1997 reported increased utilization and estimated that $47.5 billion was spent out of pocket annually on CAM treatments.

Critics of these studies point out that, because the definition of CAM is so non-specific and includes practices that are tangential to health care (e.g., food supplements, weight management activities, exercise regimens) or practices and procedures that are already part of some conventional medical practice (e.g., biofeedback, clinical hypnosis, support groups, breathing exercises, relaxation training, guided imagery), the use of CAM is greatly overestimated. Interestingly, and perhaps in support of that contention, prayer is included in many classifications of CAM. When it is, it is the most commonly used modality.

> **What is integrative medicine?**

The incorporation of CAM treatments into conventional medicine has led to the development of the concept of **integrative medicine**, which the University of Arizona Center for Integrative Medicine has defined as "...healing-oriented medicine that takes account of the whole person (body, mind, spirit), including all aspects of lifestyle... [and] ...makes use of all appropriate therapies, both conventional and alternative." The National Center for Complementary and Alternative

Medicine (NCCAM) offers a more precise definition that speaks directly to the inherent controversy about the efficacy of CAM by defining integrative medicine as combining"... conventional practices with CAM therapies *for which there is demonstrated evidence of safety and effectiveness.*"

CAM and Public Policy

The National Institutes of Health (NIH) established the Office of Complementary and Alternative Medicine (OCAM) in 1991 with a budget of $2 million to support research on various complementary medicine treatment approaches. In 1998, the office was upgraded to and renamed the **National Center for Complementary and Alternative Medicine** (NCCAM) with a budget of $110 million.

In March, 2000, the *White House Commission on Complementary and Alternative Medicine Policy* was established to review this body of medical care and develop administrative and legislative proposals aimed at creating safe and effective complementary medicine opportunities for the public.

> The Commission on Complementary and Alternative Medicine is accountable for: (1) establishing equal standards for both conventional and complementary medicine; (2) educating health care practitioners and consumers regarding high quality research in complementary medicine; and (3) proposing insurance coverage policies.

In 2005, the Institute of Medicine recommended that health profession schools incorporate CAM subject matter into training curricula. A year later, the AMA recommended CAM education be included in medical school curricula. Most medical schools now include instruction in some aspect of complementary medicine. A few schools offer specialized fellowship training, and continuing medical education offerings are common. Although few MD physicians are trained to deliver complementary care, many are increasingly involved in integrative care, offering their patients information or referrals, especially in situations where biomedical therapies have not been successful or where patients are interested in non-pharmacological or non-surgical approaches to treatment.

Classification of CAM Practices

Initially, the NIH defined complementary and alternative medicine as "health care practices not taught in conventional western medical schools." However, the NIH has subsequently developed a more descriptive and useful taxonomy with five classifications of complementary medicine practices identified by the CAM Advisory Board in 2001–2002 (see Table 31.1).

Complementary medicine includes traditional medical theories and practices such as the Ayurvedic, Chinese, Greek, and Arabic systems formulated over the past several millennia (see Chapter 1, Evolving Models of Health Care). Folk medicine, homeopathy, chiropractic, and naturopathy, as well as more limited practices that have specific therapeutic goals and are adjuncts to a larger system of care (e.g., creative arts therapy, acupuncture, therapeutic touch) are also typically encompassed by the description CAM. Many traditional health care systems and CAM practices share several basic holistic assumptions such as (1) individuals possess a life force and seek balance among physical, spiritual, emotional, social, mental, and environmental factors through diet, family, lifestyle, spirituality, and culture; (2) illness is a complex manifestation of imbalance within the person's life experience; and (3) restoring and maintaining balance among mind, body, and spirit induces wellness. In attempting to achieve wellness, the holistic practitioner's goal is to assist patients in creating and maintaining well-being by providing education, encouraging personal responsibility, and enhancing innate strengths to maximize their own healing potential.

Since a comprehensive review of all CAM systems and therapies is beyond the scope of this chapter, we will focus upon licensed CAM practices.

Licensed CAM Practices

At the time of this writing, four complementary medicine practices were recognized as *licensed professions* by many, if not all, states in the US: chiropractic, acupuncture, naturopathy, and massage. To be licensed as a professional in one of these four areas, most states require that a practitioner graduate from an accredited school recognized by the U.S. Department of Education and pass a standardized national examination. In addition to these four professions, there are a number of other CAM treatment approaches that are *certified* by states or professional interest groups,

Table 31.1. Classifications of complementary medicine with examples				
Alternative Medical Systems	**Mind-Body Interventions**	**Biologically-Based Therapies**	**Manipulative/Body-Based Methods**	**Energy Therapies**
– Homeopathy – Naturopathy – Ayurveda – Traditional Chinese medicine	– Meditation – Prayer – Mental healing – Creative outlets (art, music, dance)	– Dietary supplements – Botanical Medicine	– Chiropractic – Osteopathy – Massage	– Biofield therapies (Qi gong, reiki, therapeutic touch) – Bioelectromagnetics (electromagnetic fields)

but certification requirements vary considerably between CAM approaches, and from state to state.

Acupuncture

Acupuncture is a component of **traditional Chinese medicine**, which classically consists of a broad spectrum of interventions including herbal therapy, dietary therapy, Qi gong exercises, tuina massage, and acupuncture/moxibustion. Acupuncture treatment involves the insertion of fine needles (typically 0.25 mm in diameter) into defined acupuncture points at specific anatomic locations. These points lie along 14 main *meridians* (energy pathways) that are thought to run parallel to but are distinct from the circulatory and nervous systems. There are 361 primary points corresponding to different organ systems and functions of the body. **Acupressure** is a variant of acupuncture. In this case, pressure, rather than skin puncture, at the primary points is used to obtain effect

The goal of acupuncture is to promote the smooth flow of energy, or *Qi* (pronounced "chee"), throughout the body to restore balance and good health. Needles placed in the appropriate acupuncture points are presumed to facilitate energy flow along the meridians. In certain cases, **electroacupuncture**, the application of a weak electric current to an inserted needle to strengthen the degree of stimulation, is used.

Efficacy

In November 1997, the NIH convened an expert, multidisciplinary panel to determine the effectiveness of acupuncture as medical treatment. The panel determined that there was evidence of treatment effectiveness for nausea associated with chemotherapy, pregnancy, post-operative recovery, and motion sickness; analgesia for dental pain, headaches, menstrual cramps, fibromyalgia, osteoarthritis, and low back pain; and anesthesia for certain surgical procedures. Mechanisms underlying pain relief appear to involve the activation of the body's own pain relief systems: research has shown acupuncture-stimulated changes in opioid receptor binding in brain networks associated with the sensory and affective aspects of pain, especial-

ly the right medial orbitofrontal cortex. How acupuncture affects other disorders is unknown.

> The mechanism of action of acupuncture in pain management appears to be enhancement of specific neurotransmitter activity within the CNS, particularly through increased circulatory release of endorphins and enkephalins, opiate-like peptides that have analgesic and anxiolytic properties.

Training and Licensure

Some states include acupuncture in MD and DO licensure, but most require additional training or an examination. *Physician acupuncturists* take a 300-hour structured acupuncture course that provides a measure of standardization, and there is now an American Board of Medical Acupuncture, established in early 2000, that provides physician acupuncturists the opportunity to obtain board certification. The American Academy of Medical Acupuncture is a physician organization that supports the integration of acupuncture with Western Medicine and promotes an all-encompassing approach to health care.

For *non-physician acupuncturists*, licensing requirements are set by individual states, but typically include graduation from an accredited school (typically three- to four-year master's level programs) and passing a national standardized exam. As of 2011, there were approximately 50 accredited non-physician acupuncture schools in the US and 42 states and the District of Columbia licensed acupuncturists. Most states require successful completion of the National Certification Commission for Acupuncture and Oriental Medicine (NCCAOM) written examination, or a state written exam. Some states also require the Practical Examination of Point Location, or a state practical exam.

Chiropractic

Chiropractic was founded in the late 1800s by a layman, Daniel Palmer. It is concerned with the relationship between the structure and function of the spine, and how it affects the nervous system and body functioning. Loss of structural integrity, termed *subluxation,* is presumed to result in loss of normal physiology or function. The goal of chiropractic therapy is the correction of subluxation with resulting restoration of function. This goal is accomplished primarily through the use of *adjustment* (joint manipulation), which involves a high velocity, low amplitude maneuver to restore normal joint alignment and mobility. The site of adjustment is determined by symptoms, clinical examination (e.g., palpation), or diagnostic assessment (e.g., thermographic patterns, radiologic imaging).

Biological Basis

The biological basis for the structural and physiological effects of chiropractic is not entirely understood. Reported responses to manipulation include elevation of serum beta-endorphin levels, increased joint mobility, enhanced neutrophil activity, and attenuation of spinal electromyographic activity.

Contraindications

Contraindications to chiropractic care include conditions caused by serious underlying disease (cancer and cardiac disease), unfavorable response to manipulation, fractures, ligament injury, inflammatory arthritis, ankylosing spondylitis, bone disease, osteoporosis, infection, disc prolapse, and bleeding disorders.

Complications

The most serious complication of cervical manipulation is injury to the vertebrobasilar artery resulting in a cerebrovascular accident (CVA). The incidence of developing a CVA after cervical manipulation is estimated at 1 in 500,000 to 1 in 2 million manipulations. Lumbar manipulation carries a lower risk for serious complication than cervical manipulation.

Training and Licensure

Chiropractic is licensed in all states, but there is significant variation in the scope of practice. Some states allow only spinal manipulation (adjustment), and restrict the use of clinical examination procedures. Other states permit chiropractors to perform certain laboratory procedures (e.g., venipuncture), practice acupuncture, give nutritional advice, and dispense supplements.

Chiropractic training requires four years. All schools currently have at least a two-year undergraduate requirement that includes prescribed hours in the sciences and humanities. A bachelor's degree is becoming an increasingly common requirement for admission. There are 18 chiropractic colleges in the US accredited by the Council on Chiropractic Education (CCE), the accrediting agency recognized by the Department of Education. Thirteen colleges are also accredited by regional accrediting agencies for secondary and post-secondary colleges. At least one college offers a 7-year combined BA-DC program. Following the completion of educational requirements, the chiropractor must pass state and national examinations to become licensed. Postgraduate level studies that lead to specialty certification include sports chiropractic, rehabilitation, chiropractic sciences, orthopedics, neurology, and nutrition.

Efficacy

Most conditions treated by chiropractors involve low back complaints. Non-low back complaints are usually musculoskeletal conditions involving neck pain, mid-back pain, arm or leg pain, and headache. Non-musculoskeletal complaints such as asthma, otitis media, and gastrointestinal distress account for less than 3% of all patient visits to chiropractors. Uncomplicated low back pain is the most widely researched condition commonly treated by manipulation.

> Based on reviews of published research findings, spinal manipulation has been shown to be of short-term benefit in the alleviation of acute low back pain, neck pain, and headaches.

The Agency for Health Care Policy and Research has recommended spinal manipulation in its published guideline on the management of acute low back pain. A five-year pilot program, initiated by Congress in 1995 to assess the effectiveness of chiropractic care in the military, concluded that patients with neuromuscular complaints had: (1) better outcomes with chiropractic care, (2) increased satisfaction with medical care, (3) less lost duty time, and (4) reduced hospitalization time and costs. NCCAM and the National Institute of Arthritis and Musculoskeletal and Skin Diseases have provided funding for chiropractic research.

Naturopathy

While **naturopathy** had its origins in the natural healing movements of the 18th and 19th centuries, its establishment in the US is associated with the work of Benedict Lust. Dr. Lust, an immigrant from Germany, came to the US in the 1890s, completed his own medical training (studying allopathic [conventional Western], chiropractic, osteopathic, and homeopathic medicine), and established the first school of naturopathic medicine in New York City. About the same time, Dr. James Foster established a school of naturopathic medicine in Idaho. These two individuals subsequently collaborated in establishing the new profession of naturopathy, which drew on an array of natural healing interventions derived from traditional Chinese, Ayurvedic, and Greek medicine, Native American healing systems, and modern scientific principles and technology.

Six Basic Principles of Modern Naturopathy

1. Nature has the power to heal and it is the physician's role to enhance the self-healing process.
2. Treat the whole person so that every aspect of a patient's natural defenses and function is brought into harmonious balance.
3. "First, do no harm" reflects the Hippocratic creed that the physician should utilize methods and substances that are non-toxic and non-invasive.
4. Identify and treat the cause, in contrast to suppressing symptoms.
5. Prevention is an important aspect of care that the physician should promote.
6. Doctors should be teachers and educate the patient about his/her personal responsibility to maintain health.

Naturopathic Modalities

1. Clinical nutrition and the therapeutic use of diet, including drug-nutrient interactions
2. Physical medicine procedures such as hydrotherapy, exercise, massage, manipulation, immobilization, braces, splints, ultrasound, diathermy, heat therapy, electrical stimulation, and balneology (therapeutic use of thermal/mineral baths)
3. Homeopathic treatments that simulate the body's own natural forces
4. Botanical medicine including the use of herbs and other natural substances to maximize desirable effects and minimize undesirable side effects, including drug-herb interactions
5. Natural childbirth
6. Traditional Chinese medicine including the use of Chinese herbs and acupuncture
7. Ayurvedic medicine
8. Mind-body techniques that emphasize the facilitative effects of counseling, psychotherapy, behavioral medicine, hypnosis, stress management, and biofeedback

By the 1920s, there were approximately 20 colleges of naturopathy in the US and licensure in most states. As a result of the increasing influence of biomedicine, however, naturopathy declined in popularity until the 1970s when it experienced a resurgence due, in part, to the high costs of biomedicine and changes in health care financing. Currently, there are six recognized colleges/universities of naturopathic training accredited by the Council on Naturopathic Medical Education and recognized by the U.S. Department of Education.

Drawing on effective treatments from a wide range of healing approaches, naturopathy has been shown to be an effective *complement to biomedicine* in disease prevention, the treatment of acute illnesses, and supportive treatment of chronic and degenerative conditions. Naturopathic physicians recognize that conventional medicine is essential in addressing more complex medical crises such as acute trauma, childbirth emergencies, fractures, corrective surgery, and acute life-threatening illnesses. Recognition of their relative strengths and limitations has led to increasing collaboration between biomedical and naturopathic physicians.

Training and Licensure

There are three categories of naturopathic practitioners: naturopathic physicians, traditional naturopaths, and other health care providers who offer naturopathic services as part of their practice.

Naturopathic physicians complete a 4-year, graduate level program. Admission requirements generally include a bachelor's degree and standard premedical courses. Naturopathic physician students receive training in anatomy, cell biology, physiology, pathology, neuroscience, histology, genetics, biochemistry, pharmacology, clinical and physical diagnosis, laboratory diagnosis, biostatistics, and epidemiology. Graduates receive the degree of ND (Naturopathic Doctor) or NMD (Doctor of Naturopathic Medicine) depending on where the degree is issued. Although it is not required, some graduates pursue residency training.

As of 2010, 15 states, the District of Columbia, and two U.S. territories (Puerto Rico and the Virgin Islands) had licensing requirements for naturopathic physicians. In all of these places, naturopathic physicians must graduate from a 4-year naturopathic medical college and pass the naturopathic licensing exam (NPLEX). A graduate's scope of practice is variable and defined by law in the state or territory in which he or she practices. For example, a naturopathic physician may or may not be allowed to prescribe drugs, perform minor surgery, practice acupuncture, or assist in childbirth. In 2006, it was estimated that there were approximately 3,000 naturopathic physicians practicing in the US.

Traditional naturopaths emphasize naturopathic approaches to a healthy lifestyle, strengthening and cleansing the body, and non-invasive treatments. Prescription drugs, injections, x-rays, and surgery are not included in their scope of practice. Several schools offer training for this type of naturopathy, but the programs are highly variable, and are not accredited by organizations recognized by the U.S. Department of Education. Admission requirements for these schools can range from minimal to a high school diploma to specific

> According to the 2007 National Health Interview Survey, an estimated 729,000 adults and 237,000 children had used a naturopathic treatment in the previous year.

degrees and coursework. Traditional naturopaths are not eligible for licensing.

Efficacy

Naturopathy appears to be increasingly integrated into conventional medicine due to cost effectiveness and the relatively less distressing nature of its natural treatment alternatives. It has received increasing respect from the health care consumer, government bodies, and the biomedical community. There is positive evidence for the effectiveness of some of the common naturopathic interventions. However, because of its wide-ranging nature (i.e., drawn from a large number of healing systems), it cannot be assumed that this provides conclusive evidence of the efficacy of all naturopathic or associated complementary healing systems. Well designed and controlled research is required to determine the efficacy of specific techniques for specific disorders.

Massage Therapy

Massage therapy is defined as the systematic, therapeutic stroking, rubbing, or kneading of the skin and underlying muscle and other soft tissue of the patient for the purpose of physical and psychological relaxation, improvement of circulation, relief of sore muscles, and other therapeutic effects. There are multiple forms including *relaxation*, *Swedish*, *sports*, *deep tissue*, and *trigger point massage*. According to the 2007 National Health Interview Survey, an estimated 18 million adults and 700,000 children received massage therapy in the previous year.

Efficacy

Although data are limited, studies support the effectiveness of massage therapy in reducing anxiety, blood pressure, and heart rate, relieving pain, and reducing stress and feelings of depression. In 2008, a review of 13 clinical trials showed massage to be useful in the treatment of low back pain. The *gate control theory* suggests that massage stimulation may help to block pain signals sent to the brain. Massage is known to release endorphins and serotonin that can positively affect mood. Massage is also effective in hospice and neonatal ICU settings.

Licensure and Training

In 2010, 43 states and the District of Columbia offered licensure in massage therapy. Training requirements ranged from 100 to 1,000 hours, with most states requiring ≥ 500 hours. Some states require graduation from a training program approved by the Commission on Massage Therapy Accreditation (COMTA) or an equivalent program, or training in a specific area such as anatomy. Most states that license massage therapists require a passing grade on the Massage and Bodywork Licensing Examination (MBLEx), or one of two exams provided by the National Certification Board for Therapeutic Massage and Bodywork.

CAM and the Behavioral Sciences

> What distinguishes behavioral science-based treatments from complementary medicine treatments?

In his book, *The Best Alternative Medicine,* Pelletier states: "Of all the CAM interventions, mind-body medicine is supported by the greatest body of scientific evidence for the greatest number of conditions for the largest number of people. It has also gained the widest acceptance within the conventional medical system." (p. 59). He then traces the evolution of **mind-body medicine** from its origins, the revolt against the reductionism of biomedicine, through the shifts in focus from infectious diseases to lifestyle and public health-based disorders, to the increasing recognition of the interplay of environmental, psychological, social, and lifestyle factors in health. What Pelletier is describing is, in fact, the emergence of the **biopsychosocial model**, although he does not use that term. Since its inception, the biopsychosocial model has gained increasing acceptance, largely through the supporting empirical evidence accumulated via research on the role of the behavioral sciences in medicine. These research efforts have given rise to the emerging fields of behav-

ioral medicine, health psychology, and psychoneuroimmunology, all of which have focused on identifying the mechanisms of bio-behavioral interaction.

Empirically-based treatment modalities developed out of these research efforts include relaxation, meditation, hypnosis, imagery and visualization, cognitive behavioral therapies, and biofeedback. All are forms of treatment based on research into the role of behavioral and cognitive factors in the etiology of select medical disorders. As Pelletier points out, they are now widely accepted within the conventional biomedical system so, by definition, they should not be subsumed under the complementary medicine rubric.

Complementary Therapies and the Scientific Method

> Why do some proponents of complementary medicine reject accepted scientific standards for research?

Some proponents of complementary medicine argue that accepted standards of scientific investigation are not appropriate for evaluating CAM methods and treatments. The argument is based on two assumptions.

(1) The first assumption is that CAM treatments are individualized and, therefore, cannot be fairly assessed by large sample randomized controlled trials. The argument is not unique to CAM adherents as biomedical researchers in general realize that large-scale studies do not enable the clinician to make predictions about individual case responses, especially those requiring individualized treatment. At the same time, biomedical researchers believe that the efficacy of any treatment approach must first begin with demonstrated effectiveness within population samples.

(2) The second assumption is that CAM approaches are based on explanations fundamentally different from those of conventional biomedical approaches and, therefore, should not be judged on the same biomedical criteria. This argument implies that the theoretical causal explanations of CAM are not biological, cognitive, behavioral, sociocultural, or environmental in nature,

but rather attributed to phenomena that lie outside the realm of generally accepted scientific explanations for human functioning, disease, and disorder. Not all adherents of CAM agree with this position. Naturopathic physicians, for example, recognize and undergo stringent training in the biomedical and behavioral sciences.

While there is evidence that certain CAM therapies can be effective in the treatment of selected disorders and can serve palliative and supplementary roles with biomedical approaches, continued research into the efficacy of specific treatments for specific disorders and their mechanisms of effect is required. In 2005, the Institute of Medicine report on complementary and alternative medicine in the US stated that health care should be both comprehensive and evidence based with biomedicine and CAM following the same research principles but recognizing that new research methods need to be developed to test some therapies in *both* conventional and complementary medicine.

These arguments aside, why has there been so little substantive research into CAM modalities? At least part of the answer lies in the degree of financial support that has been earmarked for CAM research. As noted above, the NCCAM budget in 1998 was $110 million. Eight years later, the 2006 budget was $121 million. In 2010, the NCCAM budget was $127 million, or an increase of 4.7% over 4 years. The total NIH budget during those years increased from $28.7 billion to $31 billion, or an increase of 8%. Looked at another way, the NCCAM budget represents 0.4% of the NIH budget. Granted, many of the individual institutes (e.g., National Cancer Institute, National Institute of Nursing Research) also help support CAM research, but the overall funds available are extremely small and cover all of the modalities and the various permutations recognized by the NCCAM. Unlike pharmaceutical industry research, which can lead to financially lucrative patents, there is little or no financial reward associated with, for example, finding a better way to teach self-hypnosis, especially if it results in less need for anxiolytic or antidepressant medications, mainstays of drug sales.

Thus, lack of good data for or against efficacy is the result of many factors, some based in theoretical and methodological differences about what constitutes "good" data and how to obtain it, and some based on the very practical issues of financing credible research in an era of dwindling resources.

Integrative Medicine

RJ is a 41-year-old construction worker who hurt his back 8 months ago when he fell from some scaffolding. Although disabled for a month, he has been working full time since. He has, however, continued to have moderate to severe back pain at L4 – S2 that has been minimally responsive to over-the-counter analgesics. He does not want to take any stronger medication. He comes in today to ask you about other possible treatments: a chiropractic adjustment, a weekly massage, and using a TENS unit. How do you respond?

As complementary medicine modalities have become more mainstream, and the efficacy of many has begun to be demonstrated scientifically, physicians are incorporating more treatment modalities into a patient's overall health care plan. Concurrently, more opportunities are evolving for training in CAM and integrative medicine for health care practitioners and students. The integration of CAM into the conventional medical model will be facilitated by:

– Improvements and innovations in research methods to study CAM therapies
– Increased federal and state funding for the study of CAM
– Expanded educational opportunities about CAM for medical professionals
– Improved organization and standardization of training, credentialing, and licensing of CAM practitioners
– Improved insurance reimbursement for CAM therapies

How should CAM therapies be evaluated for usefulness?

In assessing the usefulness of CAM therapy in integrative care, practitioners must address the following questions:

– What is the evidence?
– What is the potential harm?
– Does the therapy resolve the underlying problem or merely suppress symptoms?
– Is the therapy consistent with the patient's culture and belief system?
– What is the cost?

- Will CAM divert the patient from receiving necessary conventional treatment?
- Is the treatment clinically responsible, ethically appropriate, and legally defensible?

This risk/benefit table is appropriate for evaluating any treatment, including CAM therapies and conventional treatments.

		Benefit	
		Y	N
Risk	N	Use	Use if patient strongly desires
	Y	Use cautiously and monitor carefully	Do not use

Recommended Readings

Eisenberg DM, Davis RB, Ettner SL, et al. Trends in alternative medicine use in the United States, 1990–1997. *JAMA* 1998; 280:1569–1575.

Faass N. *Integrating Complementary Medicine into Health Systems.* Gaithersburg, MD: Aspen; 2001.

Pelletier KR. *The Best Alternative Medicine.* New York: Fireside; 2000.

Robson T (Ed.). *Introduction to Complementary Medicine.* London: Allen & Unwin; 2004.

Wisneski L, Anderson L. *The Scientific Basis of Integrative Medicine,* 2nd ed. Boca Raton, FL: CRC Press; 2009

Review Questions

1. Which of the following is **not** included in the National Center for Complementary and Alternative Medicine (NCCAM) classification of complementary medicines?
   A. Chelation therapy
   B. Dietary supplements.
   C. Energy therapies
   D. Mind-body medicine
   E. Whole medical systems

2. Which of the following CAM modalities does **not** offer national examinations?
   A. Acupuncture
   B. Ayurveda
   C. Chiropractic
   D. Massage
   E. Naturopathy

3. According to Pelletier, the efficacy of which of the following CAM therapies is supported by the most evidence?
   A. Chiropractic
   B. Homeopathy
   C. Mind-body medicine
   D. Music therapy
   E. Traditional Chinese medicine

4. Which is **not** a key question in assessing the usefulness of a CAM therapy?
   A. How often must the patient be treated?
   B. Is the therapy culturally appropriate?
   C. What is the cost?
   D. What is the evidence?
   E. What is the potential harm?

Key to review questions: p. 408

32 Palliative Care

Timothy E. Quill, MD, and Mindy S. Shah, MD

- What are palliative care and hospice care?
- When is palliative care appropriate?
- What are the four main end-of-life trajectories?
- What are common events during the dying process?
- What is complicated grief?

The role of **palliative care** is to provide patients with relief of physical, psychological, spiritual, and social suffering. Unlike hospice, which is reserved for patients in the last months of life and focused exclusively on comfort, palliative care can be initiated at any point in the illness and given in tandem with disease-directed treatment.

What are palliative care and hospice care?

Inpatient palliative care services consult with the attending physician and treatment team on symptom management, medical decision making, prognosis, and end-of-life issues when required. Some hospitals have designated inpatient units for patients receiving primarily palliative treatments. *Outpatient clinics* provide palliative care consultation for outpatients not admitted to the hospital, and offer follow-up care for those who need

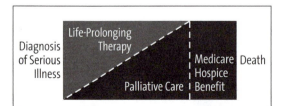

Figure 32.1. The place of palliative care in the course of illness. Adapted from National Consensus Project for Quality Palliative Care. *Clinical Practice Guidelines for Quality Palliative Care.* 2004.

ongoing treatment and support. *Home visit programs* provide palliative care for patients in their own homes, and are often the best option for those who cannot physically tolerate being transported to and from an outpatient clinic. Ideally, the *palliative care team* is interdisciplinary and, at minimum, includes physicians, nurses, social workers, mental health professionals, and pastoral caregivers providing coordinated multi-faceted care.

Hospice

If cure is not possible or life-prolonging treatment too burdensome, palliative care may become the sole focus of therapy. In such cases, the patient may be a candidate for **hospice** programs funded by Medicare and designed to provide palliative care for terminally ill patients. To qualify, a patient must have an expected survival of less than six months, and forego disease-directed therapies. The situation for pediatric patients is sometimes different, and continued disease-directed therapy may be permitted.

For many patients, **home hospice** is their first choice. However, home hospice provides only a few hours of hands-on patient care each day. For many families unable to shoulder the remaining caregiving requirements, hospice houses and hospice care at nursing homes are alternatives. *Hospice houses* are staffed by trained volunteers and provide a home-like environment. *Nursing* *home hospice care* provides custodial care paid for by patients or other sources, as well as daily extra aide service covered by the hospice benefit. *Acute hospice units* provide intensive nursing care and physician oversight for patients with recalcitrant symptoms who are imminently dying.

Clinical Application – Part I

Joseph Amato is a 71-year-old man with idiopathic pulmonary fibrosis. Prior to his diagnosis 4 years ago, he was an avid golfer but increasing shortness of breath has limited his recreation to monthly fly-fishing outings with his granddaughter. Mr. Amato has been on corticosteroids and immunosuppressant therapy with only marginal benefit. He understands he has "some sort of lung disease" and is glad it is not emphysema, which his brother died from 2 years ago. At that time he remarked to his wife, "When my time comes, just let me go." Mr. Amato goes to his pulmonologist for routine follow-up. After a hurried exam, the physician reports that "nothing's really changed" since the last visit and gives a relieved Mr. Amato medication refills. Mr. Amato has significant shortness of breath but believes that nothing can be done about it.

When is palliative care appropriate?

Unlike hospice, patients receiving palliative care can have an expected prognosis of > 6 months, and may pursue disease-directed treatments. Early palliative care can be appropriate for a patient with a wide range of illnesses. In addition to careful symptom management, palliative care providers can offer added family and patient support, guidance in medical decision making, and assistance in clarifying treatment goals. Palliative care practitioners can facilitate communication between patients, families, and medical staff, which is critical when a patient is seeing multiple subspecialists. "Triggers" for urgent *palliative care consults* include imminent death, increasing patient suffering in the face of a poor prognosis, or decreasing response to aggressive treatment. Many have advocated early palliative care involvement for virtually all serious illness, and there is now some preliminary evidence that early involvement may potentially increase length as well as quality of life for some serious illnesses.

The Palliative Care Interview

In preparing for an initial palliative care interview, information is gathered from all involved medical teams regarding the disease process, treatment options, and prognosis. Making note of areas the teams agree on and determining what information has already been shared with the patient limits miscommunication and enables the provider to synthesize information with the patient and family.

After introductions, an *explanation of palliative care* should follow, such as *"We help relieve pain and other uncomfortable symptoms, and we also help patients and families with difficult decision making."* The patient and family should be asked to tell their story about how the illness is affecting them including a careful review of potentially uncomfortable symptoms. Their perception of events and their expectations for the future should be explored. The treatment team should *clarify misunderstandings*, and try to reconcile the patient's understanding with the information gathered by the team. At the end of the interview, the discussion should be summarized, options described, recommendations shared, and a follow-up meeting arranged.

Delivering Bad News

One of a physician's most daunting tasks is **delivering bad news**, such as when a serious illness is first diagnosed or with each decline in the patient's condition. Before meeting with the patient, facts about the patient's illness, prognosis, and treatment options must be reviewed to ensure accurate discussion. The meeting should be held in a quiet, private setting and everyone the patient desires should be present. If the patient's health status impairs understanding, the health care proxy or other surrogate should be present.

Begin by assessing what the patient and family understand about the area to be discussed (e.g., test results, treatment options, prognosis). Helpful statements to prepare them for hearing the news include, *"The test results didn't turn out as well as we'd hoped,"* or *"I'm afraid I have some news".* *Give information in small chunks* to avoid overwhelming the patient or family with details. *Allow time for the patient's response*; be prepared for grief, anger, denial, anxiety, or acceptance. No matter what response the news elicits, *acknowl-*

edge and legitimize emotions: "This must seem so unfair." *Encourage questions.* Repeat key points and assess for understanding. Provide detailed information if requested. Before concluding the meeting, determine if the patient is at risk for self-harm. Ensure a safe ride home, as patients can be too distracted to drive safely. Offer to call relatives or friends to provide support. Establish a clear follow-up plan, such as another visit or a phone call the next day. If any appointments for subspecialists, tests, or procedures are needed, offer to arrange them. Finally, reassure the patient that you will continue to work with him or her no matter what the course of the disease.

Clinical Application – Part II

Two months later, Mr. Amato is hospitalized with pneumonia. He requires supplemental oxygen and desaturates with minimal exertion after 2 weeks of treatment. During a conversation with his primary care physician of 20 years, Mr. Amato talks about his plans to attend his granddaughter's college graduation in 6 months. Not wanting his patient to lose hope, his physician keeps silent about the low likelihood of Mr. Amato's surviving until then. After the visit, the physician requests a palliative care consult to clarify prognosis and treatment options.

Dr. Keats, on the palliative care service, sees Mr. Amato and asks that his wife and his three children be present. Dr. Keats asks Mr. Amato to describe the events that led to his hospitalization. It becomes clear that Mr. Amato does not know the nature of his illness or prognosis. When he asks for more information, he is told what his disease is called and how it affects the lungs. Mr. Amato says he has never heard the term idiopathic pulmonary fibrosis and that he thought his illness was "not that serious." "I'm afraid it can be serious for many patients," Dr. Keats replies. Mr. Amato indicates that he wants to hear more and is given a "typical" scenario of worsening dyspnea and fatigue. After a period of silence, Mr. Amato asks, "Will this kill me?" "Eventually, yes. I wish I could tell you differently," is Dr. Keats' response.

Mr. Amato seems stunned. The patient, physician, and family sit quietly for several seconds. Mr. Amato asks for time alone with his family. Dr. Keats, the patient, and family agree to talk again that afternoon. Dr. Keats tells Mr. Amato how to reach him in the interim, should he have questions.

Giving Prognosis

Patients and families generally value a *balance of realism and compassion.* A realistic understanding of the disease course and timeline can aid patients in prioritizing family visits, vacations, financial issues, spiritual/religious needs, or guardianship arrangements. Before giving a prognosis, it is critical to determine the likely course of the patient's disease, including the average length of survival. Certain illnesses, such as cancer, congestive heart failure, and dementia, have distinct trajectories and uncertainties that can lead to better understanding of the prognosis. Some patients, upon hearing their initial diagnosis, may ask, "How much time do I have?" Others may want little or no information. Ask the patient if information about prognosis is desired before providing it. If a timeline is requested, give averages and allow for outliers in both directions. "The average person with your illness will live 3 to 9 months. It could be longer if treatment is successful, but unfortunately it could also be shorter…" Note the possibility for longer survival than average, which allows for hope, but also shorter survival, which encourages preparation. "Let's hope for the best but prepare for the worst."

Clinical Application – Part III

On his return visit, Dr. Keats explains to Mr. Amato that some patients want estimates of how much time they have left. Mr. Amato doesn't want much detail, but does want to know his chances of surviving until his granddaughter's graduation in 6 months. Dr. Keats explains, "Although I hope you make it to the graduation, you could die before then. In a disease like yours, the odds of living 6 months are about 50/50. You might live considerably longer than 6 months, but it could also be quite a bit shorter if you get another pneumonia or some other complication."

What are the four main end-of-life trajectories?

Disease Trajectories

The four main end-of-life trajectories are: (1) terminal illness, (2) organ failure, (3) frailty, and

(4) sudden neurological impairment (see Figure 32.2). Palliative care is appropriate in all four of these trajectories. The first trajectory is one that many cancers follow: a relatively rapid predictable decline over weeks to months. This trajectory best fits the hospice option since, once the decline begins, death is likely within 6 months. The second trajectory, sudden decline with intervening periods of relative stability, is more characteristic of organ failure such as congestive heart failure or pulmonary fibrosis. For these patients, one cannot reliably predict if the prognosis is 1 day or 6 months. Exacerbations tend to come suddenly, and the patient either recovers or dies, or potentially becomes dependent on mechanical ventilation. The third trajectory, gradual progressive decline resulting in an often lengthy period of frailty, is characteristic of Alzheimer dementia. Here the prognosis can be years, depending on how aggressively illnesses and complications are treated. The fourth trajectory is for patients with acute CNS injury from trauma and bleeding. Such patients sometimes die suddenly; if they survive the initial phase, they may have variable degrees of neurological recovery over days to weeks and sometimes longer. It is critical that patients and families understand which trajectory applies to their illness, and use that information in decision making.

Do-Not-Resuscitate Orders

Responsible care for seriously ill patients requires a candid discussion of **do-not-resuscitate** (DNR) and **do-not-intubate** (DNI) orders. Misconceptions about the effectiveness of cardiopulmonary resuscitation (CPR) have been fueled by media depictions of miraculous, highly successful interventions. In fact, < 5% of cardiac arrest victims survive to hospital discharge. Of those who do survive, many have neurological impairments and are not able to live independent-

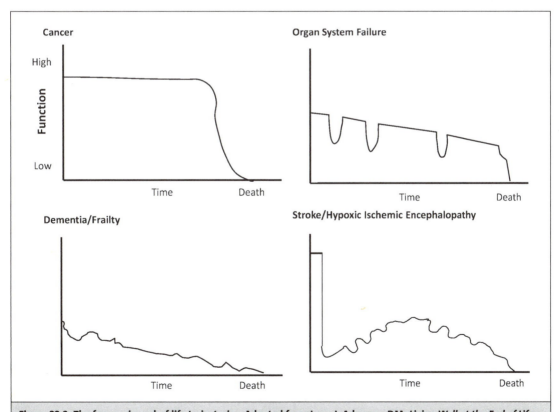

Figure 32.2. The four main end-of-life trajectories. Adapted from Lynn J, Adamson DM. *Living Well at the End of Life: Adapting Health Care to Serious Chronic Illness in Old Age*. Santa Monica, CA: The RAND Corporation; 2003. © 2003 by The RAND Corporation. All rights reserved. Reproduced with permission.

ly. In the setting of severe chronic illness, CPR is even less effective. If the patient survives the initial event, the underlying disease process still progresses. Similarly, patients with chronic illness who are intubated and on a ventilator have difficulty being weaned.

When discussing *resuscitation status for patients with serious chronic or terminal illness*, physicians should inform the patient if CPR is likely to result in outcomes most patients would find unacceptable. The patient should understand that a decision to withhold CPR or intubation does not preclude other more efficacious aggressive medical interventions. "Given your desire to live as long as possible, but not to lose your independence, I suggest we try all potentially effective treatments, but I also recommend that you avoid CPR and breathing machines. They are harsh treatments and are unlikely to work in your circumstance."

Clinical Application – Part IV

Mr. Amato is ready for discharge. He has decided to continue disease-driven treatment so he can have his "best shot" at seeing his granddaughter graduate. In the hospital, Dr. Keats began treatment with low-dose around-the-clock opioids to help relieve Mr. Amato's dyspnea, and arranges to see him in the outpatient palliative care clinic. He and Mr. Amato will re-evaluate his treatment plans as his health status and goals evolve. Prior to discharge, Mr. Amato agrees to a DNR order since he understands such efforts would likely be futile. He considers a trial period of intubation, then decides against it after his physicians explain that the most likely outcome would be lifelong mechanical ventilation.

Presenting the Hospice Option

Since a hospice patient must have a prognosis of < 6 months and be willing to forgo disease-directed treatment, often the patient is confronting the prospect of impending death for the first time. The physician should emphasize that choosing hospice is not "giving up." Rather, the goal of care shifts from disease-driven treatments that may add to a patient's suffering, to maximizing quality of life. This means aggressive symptom control and giving patients the opportunity to gain emotional, spiritual, existential, and social closure. The physi-

cian promises to not abandon the patient and to use all of his or her expertise to maximize the patient's quality of life; the patient-physician partnership is maintained, and sometimes even strengthened, until the end of life.

Clinical Application – Part V

Mr. Amato returns to the hospital several times over the next few months because of respiratory insufficiency. He and Dr. Keats continue to talk about the benefits and burdens of disease-directed treatment versus hospice. Mr. Amato holds firm to his goal of seeing his granddaughter graduate. Dr. Keats lets him know he supports this decision, and works aggressively to reduce Mr. Amato's dyspnea with opioids while searching for reversible elements of the underlying disease. Mr. Amato's appetite has been poor. The hospital nutritionist notes Mr. Amato's weight has declined sharply and recommends placement of a feeding tube. Dr. Keats discusses the risks and benefits with Mr. Amato who decides against tube placement at this time.

Experimental Treatments

Academic centers and other institutions occasionally offer qualified patients *experimental therapy* as part of clinical trials, when standard therapies are no longer effective. For patients unlikely to do well with conventional treatments, such opportunities offer the possibility of controlling the patient's disease and prolonging life. However, potential downsides to experimental therapy must be carefully considered. First, what is the *toxicity of the treatment?* Many patients will not want to pursue treatments that have severe side effects if the benefit is small or unknown. Second, *time* is precious for seriously ill patients who may not want to spend it in medical settings. Third, what *outcome* does the therapy offer? If the treatment extends survival by a few months, those months may or may not be worthwhile if quality of life is poor. On the other hand, if side effects, time commitment, and possible benefits are acceptable, experimental treatment can be compelling. Experimental therapy may be important to patients who have invested hope in the possible efficacy of medical treatments. Such patients prefer to "go down swinging" and would see stopping disease-directed treatment as "giving up." Patients need realistic information about the potential benefits and burdens of treatments available, and what their physician recommends. Those who put their hope in experimental therapy should also be given the opportunity to prepare for the possibility that the treatment will not work, and make back-up plans accordingly.

Clinical Application – Part VI

Mr. Amato's son, while searching the Internet, finds several clinical trials for patients with pulmonary fibrosis. After he reviews the information with Dr. Keats, it becomes apparent that Mr. Amato is not a good candidate because he has late-stage disease and the side effects of the experimental therapy would be beyond his tolerance.

The Family Meeting

Family meetings should be conducted in a quiet conference room or the patient's room if he or she is too ill to be moved. Ensure critical family members are present; especially the health care proxy in the event the patient is or is likely to become unable to make his or her own decisions. Other important figures (e.g., clergy person, matriarch, patriarch, primary care physician) whose input would be valued by the rest of the family should be invited if the patient and family wish.

All who attend should be encouraged to contribute their perspective of the present situation and develop a collective understanding of the illness and its prognosis. If the patient is unable to make personal medical decisions, surrogates should be encouraged to think in terms of *what the patient would want* rather than what they want for the patient. This can be challenging if the patient never expressed any wishes regarding end-of-life care. Sometimes a patient's wishes must be inferred from prior health decisions or personal values. Sometimes patient preferences clash with those of the proxy or family. It is important to remind decision makers to make decisions as they imagine the patient would (using "**substituted judgment**"), and not decide based on their own wishes or values. "What would you do, doctor?" is a common question. If the practitioner believes

that certain choices are best for the patient, given what is known of his or her clinical circumstances and values, the proxy and family should be so informed. Often a physician's recommendation is not only welcome but can also ease the uncertainty and guilt that can accompany end-of-life decisions.

Clinical Application – Part VII

During Mr. Amato's last admission, hypoxia renders him drowsy and unable to participate in medical decisions. The palliative care team meets with his family and primary care physician, whose opinion the family trusts. Dr. Keats explains that the frequent hospitalizations, delirium, and hypoxia are all indicators of approaching death. Mrs. Amato, who is her husband's health care proxy, and their children review Mr. Amato's goals. Attending his granddaughter's graduation is no longer possible. Recalling his statements at the time of his brother's death, Mrs. Amato is sure her husband would "just want to be made comfortable." His primary care physician recommends hospice, a recommendation echoed by the palliative care team. Reassured that Mr. Amato will receive diligent attention to his symptoms and quality of life, the family chooses a home hospice program.

Pain Management

Pain is rated on a scale of 0–10, with 0 being no pain and 10 the worst pain imaginable. Mild pain (1–3) can be treated with non-opioid medications such as acetaminophen and nonsteroidal anti-inflammatory drugs (NSAIDs). Moderate to severe pain (4–10) is treated with opioids, with doses titrated according to pain intensity. Adjuvant pain medications (drugs not usually used for analgesia that have benefit for specific types of pain) can be used at any level of discomfort. Often, an alert patient with mild or intermittent pain can be treated with *prn (as-needed) analgesics.* However, patients with moderate to severe constant pain require a combination of *scheduled pain medication* as well as prn dosing. Providers may hesitate to schedule opioid medications fearing respiratory depression. However, since sleepiness almost always precedes respiratory depression, the next scheduled dose can be withheld if lethargy develops and the following doses adjusted accordingly.

Exaggerated fear of using opioids often stems from a misunderstanding of tolerance, dependence, addiction, and pseudoaddiction. *Tolerance* means that increasing doses of opioids may be required over time to achieve the same analgesic effect; fortunately, opioid tolerance is usually limited. *Physical dependence* is an expected result of chronic opioid use and means the body has adapted to its opioid use. In the physically dependent patient, abruptly decreasing the opioid dose can result in a withdrawal syndrome. Both tolerance and dependence are expected parts of chronic opioid use, and should be anticipated and compensated for. *Addiction* is characterized by impaired control over drug use, craving, erratic behaviors, and continued use over time despite harm. True addiction is infrequent in palliative care in the absence of pre-existing alcohol or substance abuse problems. If such problems coexist, involvement of a pain or palliative care specialist is advised. *Pseudoaddiction* appears similar to addiction, but is, in fact, a result of inadequate pain relief. The behavior disappears when the patient's pain is properly treated. Tolerance, dependence, and pseudoaddiction can be managed by careful dose adjustments.

Clinical Application – Part VIII

Dr. Keats receives a call from the home hospice aide the day after Mr. Amato is discharged. The aide reports that the patient is complaining of severe pain in his lower back and anxiety due to feeling short of breath. After examining Mr. Amato, Dr. Keats suspects compression fractures and increases the opioid dose. Although opioids may reduce any anxiety associated with uncontrolled pain or dyspnea, Dr. Keats also prescribes a benzodiazepine prn as a back-up medication if the anxiety persists.

Finding the right regimen of pain medications can be a complex task. Chronically ill or dying patients often require dose titration and adjuvant therapies. Converting from one opioid to another is frequently necessary to minimize side effects or to optimize the dosing regimen. Calculating the **equianalgesic dose** of a strong opioid with a variable, dose-dependent half-life such as methadone, requires considerable expertise. Enlisting the aid

of palliative care or other pain management specialists is advisable in more complex cases.

Special Issues in Terminal Care

Balancing Aggressive Management and Alertness

If a dying patient experiences increasing pain, strong opioids in increasing doses may be necessary, although such treatment may be accompanied by decreased mental status. Since some patients prefer to be as alert as possible, even if it means they experience more discomfort, it is important to ascertain the patient's preferences. Such preferences often evolve over time, and may need to be revisited, especially as the patient is approaching death. The patient and family should be reassured that, should suffering become severe, the team will seek solutions that keep the patient in charge of pain relief.

Artificial Nutrition and Hydration

In many cultures, preparing and serving food is an expression of caring. Withholding food can seem unforgivable, even though many dying patients experience anorexia. Providing the family with information about the natural aspects of diminished need for food and fluids as death approaches, while exploring and empathizing with their concerns, can help with decisions regarding *feeding tubes* and *intravenous fluids*. First, feeding through a gastric tube has not been shown to prolong the life of most patients, except those with select cancers (e.g., of the oropharynx or esophagus). Second, tube feeding and intravenous fluids can increase the discomfort of actively dying patients as they lose the ability to mobilize fluids and handle respiratory secretions, resulting in significant generalized edema and increasing respiratory distress and congestion. Third, delirious patients often pull at intravenous lines and feeding tubes, necessitating the use of restraints. Finally, the taste and texture of food and the social engagement that occurs at mealtime make eating enjoyable; artificial feeding offers none of these benefits.

Patients and families should be reminded that not eating or drinking much toward the end of life is a *natural process,* and does not result in increased suffering. People who have voluntarily fasted have reported that, as long as their mouth was kept moist, the experience was not unpleasant. Some describe an almost euphoric state after a few days without food. Furthermore, dying patients who do not receive tube feeds or intravenous fluids can still take small amounts of whatever food or beverage they desire. The mouth of a patient who is unable to eat or drink at all can be kept clean and moist with diligent mouth care.

Clinical Application – Part IX

According to his daughter, Mr. Amato will no longer take any food or drink and "looks like a skeleton." She is concerned that he is suffering from thirst and hunger, and asks if tube feeds can be started. Dr. Keats reassures her that her father is likely not experiencing any discomfort as a result of not eating or drinking. He also explains that starting tube feeds would actually cause discomfort through fluid overload, resulting in edema and worsening shortness of breath. The daughter feels more at ease after these reassurances. She increases the use of moist mouth swabs and puts balm on her father's lips, which becomes one of the ways she expresses her love for him.

Delirium and Agitation

Delirium is generally addressed by an extensive metabolic and anatomic work-up. Toward the end of life, however, delirium can be a natural phase in the dying process, and should be handled more symptomatically. Aggressive treatment, however, may be necessary if delirium and agitation are extremely distressing for both the patient and the family. In the later stages of disease, symptoms can be handled with *antipsychotics* or *benzodiazepines.* Environmental modifications, such as a quiet atmosphere with limited interruptions and the regular presence of family and staff, can also decrease agitation. The removal of any equipment such as intravenous lines, telemetry, or nasogastric tubes can help calm the patient. Physical restraints should rarely be used but, if needed, should be transitioned to continuous

family presence with gradually increasing sedation if needed.

On rare occasions, delirium is intractable and requires **palliative sedation**. The administration of proportionately dosed sedatives can relieve extreme degrees of suffering by reducing the patient's level of consciousness and is used as a *last resort* once conventional management has failed. Before implementation, informed consent is obtained from the patient (if capable) or the proxy. The patient, proxy, family, and medical staff should develop a clear plan that includes the reasons and endpoints for sedation. The patient is sedated until restlessness and agitation cease, and then is maintained at that level of sedation. Frequent reassessment is needed to ensure the level of sedation is adequate to relieve distress. Support should be provided to the family throughout the process. Heavy levels of palliative sedation should generally be utilized under the guidance of a palliative care specialist.

Clinical Application – Part X

After a week of home hospice, everyone in the family is exhausted. Mr. Amato has become increasingly agitated despite medication, attempting to strike his caregivers and occasionally injuring himself. He appears to be "seeing things" in his room that frighten him. Dr. Keats adds an antipsychotic medication and gives directions for regular around-the-clock dosing and as-needed ("breakthrough") doses for persistent agitation. He asks the family to call with a progress report in 24–48 hours, and offers the possibility of admission to an acute hospice unit for symptom management.

Requests for Physician-Assisted Death

Individuals are divided on the ethics of **physician-assisted death**. Requests for such assistance often result from intolerable symptoms or fear of future (physical, emotional, spiritual, or psychological) suffering. The patient's request should be explored and triggering symptoms aggressively managed. The possibility that underlying delirium, depression, or anxiety are contributing to the request should be carefully evaluated. After careful evaluation, most suffering can be addressed within the bounds of standard palliative care. However, the patient should be informed that, if suffering becomes intolerable, palliative sedation or voluntary cessation of eating and drinking are legal options of last resort. Many patients find comfort in knowing they have some control over the manner and timing of their death with such options, which, in fact, most never choose to activate (see Chapter 33, Ethical and Legal Issues).

Clinical Application – Part XI

Mrs. Amato asks the hospice nurse, "Can't we just end it all? I can't stand to see him like this." Dr. Keats speaks at length with Mrs. Amato and learns that she is most bothered by her husband's extreme agitation, which has not responded to increasing doses of antipsychotics and anxiolytics. The family decides that Mr. Amato's needs can no longer be met at home despite their efforts. Mr. Amato is admitted to an acute inpatient hospice unit. Although the family is relieved, they feel guilty that they were unable to let him die at home. The hospice team reassures them that they have made the most loving decision in bringing him to the inpatient unit where he can be made as comfortable as possible. In the acute hospice unit, his antipsychotic regimen is proportionally adjusted so that he is calmer, but also more sedated. All agree that this is acceptable.

What to Expect during the Dying Process

What are common events during the dying process?

Because many people have not witnessed death, they may be anxious and uncertain as it approaches. Preparing the family can alleviate their concern. Generally, a dying patient will become more

Clinical Application – Part XII

Aggressive symptom management brings Mr. Amato's agitation and delirium under control. Opioids provide good relief of his dyspnea. Mr. Amato dies quietly a few days later surrounded by members of his family and the medical team.

somnolent, and may develop congested breathing (irregular, gasping) because of secretions. The family may interpret this as suffering and should be reassured that such signs are usually more distressing for onlookers than for the patient.

Grief and Bereavement

Grief is the emotional response to loss. A dying patient not only experiences loss of life but loss of employment, family, self-image, and independence. During **anticipatory grief** (prior to death), some patients review their life while the family adjusts to the idea of a future without their loved one. There is opportunity to ask for, give, and receive forgiveness or to express thanks and love. Some have described this as a time of personal growth.

What is complicated grief?

Grieving survivors usually move, eventually, toward accepting their loss. Their sense of self is intact, life retains meaning, and relationships with others are resumed.

Clinical Application – Part XIII

A few days after the death, the hospice bereavement counselor contacts Mrs. Amato. Although she feels some lingering doubts about the decisions she made on behalf of her husband, her overall sense is one of relief, especially that her husband is no longer suffering. Dr. Keats calls Mrs. Amato the following week, which is much appreciated by Mrs. Amato and also helps to provide Dr. Keats with some closure.

In comparison, **complicated grief** is characterized purposelessness, disbelief, and emotional detachment. Emotions such as unrelenting loneliness, anger, and bitterness become prominent. The bereaved may experience intrusive thoughts of the deceased. While complicated and uncomplicated grief can both demonstrate these features, in complicated grief, the symptoms last longer and cause a high degree of impairment. *Risk factors* for complicated grief include unexpected or traumatic death, a history of mental illness, family dysfunction, low self-esteem, prior dependency on the deceased, and isolation.

Bereavement, the state of loss that occurs after death, is a health risk, and can result in increased use of medical services. Most palliative care teams and all Medicare-certified hospice programs include bereavement specialists who monitor families for complicated grief and use preventive measures, such as counseling, for survivors at risk. Expressions of condolence from the medical team (sending a card, making a phone call, attending the funeral) can be powerful gestures that are appreciated by the bereaved. Clinicians may need to grieve after they have lost a patient with whom they were very close, or for whom they provided care through a medically complex illness. It is useful to find safe places (e.g., talking with colleagues or a counselor, participating in a team meeting) to express and explore such feelings. Leaving such feelings unaddressed may lead to isolation and problems for the clinician as time passes.

Recommended Readings

Holloway RG, Quill TE. Palliative Care. In TE Andreoli (Ed.), *Andreoli and Carpenter's Cecil Essentials of Medicine*. Philadelphia, PA: Elsevier; 2010, pp. 1210–1217.

McPhee SJ, Winker MA, Rabow MW, Pantilat SZ, Markowitz AJ (Eds.). *Care at the Close of Life: Evidence and Experience*. JAMA Series. New York: McGraw Hill Medical; 2011.

Morrison RS, Meier DE. Clinical practice: Palliative care. *New England Journal of Medicine* 2004; 351:1148–1149.

National Consensus Project for Quality Palliative Care. *Clinical Practice Guidelines for Quality Palliative Care*. 2004. Available at http://www.nationalconsensusproject.org/guideline.pdf

Quill TE, Holloway RG, Shah MS, Caprio TA, Olden AM, Storey P. *Primer of Palliative Care*, 5th ed. Glenview, IL: American Academy of Hospice and Palliative Medicine; 2010.

Quill TE, Lo B, Brock DW. Palliative options of last resort: A comparison of voluntarily stopping eating and drinking, terminal sedation, physician-assisted suicide, and voluntary active euthanasia. *JAMA* 1997; 278:2099–2104.

Temel JS, Greer JA, Muzikansky A, et al. Early palliative care for patients with metastatic non-small-cell lung cancer. *New England Journal of Medicine* 2010; 363:733–742.

Review Questions

1. A patient with cancer has bone metastases and 8–10/10 pain. According to the WHO, the best pain management is likely to result from the administration of
   A. adjuvant modalities.
   B. non-opioid medications.
   C. opioid and non-opioid regimens.
   D. strong opioids.
   E. strong opioids and adjuvant modalities.

2. Which of the following people is MOST likely to experience complicated grief?
   A. 58-year-old woman whose husband dies peacefully at home after a 2-year battle against cancer
   B. 62-year-old mother of two young adults who participates in a bereavement support group
   C. 75-year-old man whose 99-year-old mother dies in a nursing home
   D. 86-year-old childless man whose wife of 60 years dies suddenly of a stroke

3. Palliative care is appropriate for which of the following patients?
   A. 20-year-old woman with aggressive leukemia being treated with chemotherapy and bone marrow transplantation, who has uncontrolled pain and nausea
   B. 55-year-old man in the ICU following a car accident, who it not improving despite maximal treatments, and whose family is undecided about continuing ventilator support
   C. 73-year-old woman with advanced heart failure requiring frequent admissions to the hospital, who is considering hospice care
   D. 88-year-old woman with moderate Alzheimer dementia, living in a nursing facility, who is slowly losing weight and spending more time in bed
   E. All of the above

Key to review questions: p. 408

33 Ethical and Legal Issues in Patient Care

Jeffrey P. Spike, PhD

- What is informed consent?
- What are legitimate exceptions to patient confidentiality?
- Under what conditions do minors have authority to make their own medical decisions?
- What are the two types of advance directives and how do they differ?
- What is the difference between "do not resuscitate" and "comfort care" orders?
- What are the arguments for and against physician-assisted suicide?
- What is the standard of clinical equipoise in research?

Traditional medical ethics emphasized two principles: beneficence and nonmaleficence. **Beneficence** requires that the physician provide for the patient's best interest, balancing potential benefits and risks. **Nonmaleficence** requires that the physician avoid heroic efforts, if they inflict unnecessary suffering or promote unrealistic hope, and to focus on comfort care and relief of pain or other symptoms.

These principles left decision-making responsibility to the physician, which some interpreted as license for unquestioned authority for the patient's medical care. During the 1970s, as questions were being raised about who had decision-making authority, treatment options were rapidly expanding. Thus, more was at stake and more responsibility fell on the decision makers.

patient to all relevant facts before deciding on a course of action, and the right to *refuse* treatment as well as consent to it.

A fourth principle, **justice**, concerns populations, guaranteeing access to care as a right of citizenship akin to public education.

Codes of ethics, written by the American Medical Association, the American College of Physicians, and most other specialty groups typically incorporate these ethical principles. Each principle is recognized to be *prima facie* (i.e., have "face" validity, though not always the final say), independent (i.e., yield recommendations that potentially conflict with the other principles), and serve as guidelines designed to help analyze and clarify complex ethics cases.

Informed Consent

What is informed consent?

Patient autonomy, the third principle of medical ethics, requires patients be given complete information about diagnosis, prognosis, and treatment options, in understandable terms, and affirms their right to make their own health care decisions. The legal doctrine of **informed consent** entitles the

Malpractice, Negligence, and Good Samaritans

Laws that govern physician practice are primarily state laws or case law based on precedents established by court decisions.

Malpractice is, in legal terms, a civil claim, not a criminal offense. The standard of evidence is lower (preponderance of the evidence rather than beyond a reasonable doubt), the jury smaller (if there is one), and the penalty less severe (financial award to the plaintiff rather than a prison sentence for the guilty party). To win the case, a plaintiff must prove negligence or substandard care, and an injury caused by the substandard care.

Civil law is intended to compensate a victim for being wronged, not to punish the wrong-doer. To be found guilty of malpractice, a physician must not only have harmed a patient, but it must be shown that the doctor was negligent in knowledge or performance and failed to meet the accepted standard. This can include not explaining known risks and side effects of a treatment or procedure (i.e., substandard informed consent). Expert witnesses are needed to define the standard of care, and upholding those standards is considered an obligation of members of a profession (hence, physicians should be willing to act as expert witnesses in cases involving other physicians).

Many states grant immunity from malpractice when a physician encounters a medical emergency such as a vehicular accident (**Good Samaritan Law**). In fact, there is no real difference between states with and without these laws. The risk of being sued is minuscule and the risk of being found at fault is defensible by the claim that the physician acted in good faith.

Confidentiality

> What are legitimate exceptions to patient confidentiality?

Physicians must never reveal information about a patient except to other members of the health care team or a professional to whom the patient is being referred. There are *legitimate exceptions*, all related to the potential for danger to the patient or others. If a patient admits to planning to kill someone, it must be reported to the proper authority. Suspected child or elderly abuse and neglect must be reported to the appropriate agency. Sexually transmitted infections should be reported to the Department of Health, which can then locate and inform sexual contacts anonymously if the patient chooses not to do so. In each case, the patient's confidentiality is compromised to protect someone else from known danger, but exceptions should be kept to the minimum to preserve patients' willingness to confide in their physicians.

Decision-Making Capacity

> Capacity requires that a patient understand the nature of the illness, the treatment options available, and the consequences of the decision.

Capacity is presumed present in all adults and any clinician can determine a given patient's capacity. Psychiatric illness does not categorically rule out capacity to make medical decisions. (For example, most psychiatric illnesses, if well controlled by medication, or if classified mild, are compatible with capacity.) In addition, psychiatric consultation is not usually required to determine capacity.

The physician should obtain **informed consent** from the patient before doing any procedure that involves touching the patient. It is not necessary that a written form be signed. Such forms were developed as a reminder for physicians of which topics should be discussed with the patient and to provide documentation that the discussion took place. The only *exceptions* to the rule of informed consent are if the patient is clearly incapacitated (e.g., unconscious) or there is a life-threatening emergency and no time for explanation before taking action. As soon as the patient regains capacity or the danger passes, the patient should be informed about what has been done and included in discussions about further treatments. Any treatment begun can be stopped. This option for the patient to forgo the treatment later is the basis for the ethical and legal justification for unilateral decision making by the physician when the situation demands such action. When there is a difference of opinion between the physician and patient, respect for the patient's preference should be an overriding concern.

Minors and Capacity

> Under what conditions do minors have authority to make their own medical decisions?

Parents of minors have the authority to make decisions about medical treatment for their children, but this authority is not absolute. Children develop capacity as they mature. Teenagers can be determined to have capacity by their clinician using the same criteria as for adults. This process, known as the **Mature Minor Doctrine**, provides for minors to participate in decisions about their medical treatment. Age 14 is a commonly used criterion to include the patient in the decision-making process alongside parents or guardians, but the age may vary depending on the particular child and the specific circumstance. Teens may be in need of direction, and the input of the physician can be as important as that of their parents.

In most states, a statute known as the **Emancipated Minor Doctrine** empowers minors to make their own medical decisions if they are married, live independently of their parents, have children of their own, or are in the military.

Religious Beliefs

Religious beliefs are valid reasons for adults to refuse treatment (e.g., Jehovah's Witnesses' refusal to accept blood transfusions and Christian Scientists' refusal of some medical treatments). Whereas adults are assumed to be capable of making their own decisions based on religious conviction, minors are normally protected from decisions by their parents based on the parents' religious beliefs. As a judge once said, "Parents have the right to make martyrs of themselves, but not of their children." Thus, if reasonable treatment of a minor is refused by parents solely on the basis of the parents' religious beliefs, a *court can authorize* such treatment. Infants and children are considered members of the human community first, and cannot be presumed to understand and accept their parents' religious beliefs (and refuse reasonable treatment on religious grounds) until they also understand the alternatives and consequences.

Efforts at persuasion that arise from sincere concern are commendable, but must never become coercive. While the physician urges the patient to consider the issue with an open mind, the physician must be prepared to accept the patient's decision *not* to accept treatment.

The *standard of capacity* is the ability to understand alternatives and the consequences of one's choice. A teenager who meets that standard can be determined a mature minor by the clinician and his or her choice respected on that basis. Only individuals who *lack capacity* due to developmental age should have their parents make decisions on their behalf. For cases in a gray area, including most school-age children, the minor should be included in the decision-making process and, at least, give their *assent* to the outcome.

Psychiatric Illness and Capacity

Capacity is frequently questioned in psychiatric or brain injury cases. Unless it is clear that a condition is affecting the patient's judgment, all adults are presumed to have capacity, including those who have mental or physical illness. If a patient can participate in a conversation with family or caregivers about their illness, treatment choices, and the consequences of their choice, they are demonstrating capacity. If the reasons behind their decisions are understandable, these decisions should be accepted even if they are not those that most people would make. Conversations to collect relevant information about the history and values of the patient (e.g., what is meaningful in life, what constitutes the moral of his or her life story, and what goals are sought) enable the physician to resolve ethical dilemmas. When a person's decision is consistent with past decisions, it is generally a violation of the integrity of that person's life for the decision to be overridden.

Neurological Illness and Capacity

The capacity of patients who have a neurological disease such as dementia is virtually always questioned. However, early dementia can coexist with capacity. Patients with mild but progressive neurological illness are the *sine qua non* of individuals for whom **advance directives** would be appropriate. The most likely course of a disease can be predicted, enabling patients to complete advance directives before they lose capacity. Because such discussions are uncomfortable, they are frequently deferred – by clinicians and family – until too late for the patient to exercise the right to self-determination.

Unconsciousness

Coma, vegetative state, and brain death are three types of unconsciousness. **Coma** is an unconscious sleep-like state lasting from hours to weeks and, in rare instances, months to years. Patients in coma may die, regain consciousness, or emerge into a **vegetative state** in which there is no conscious activity but there is a continuation of vegetative or involuntary functioning (e.g., breathing without assistance, some reflexes). There can be meaningful improvement from a vegetative state but the longer the state continues, the less likely improvement will occur. The vegetative state is considered "persistent" after 1–3 months of unconsciousness and "permanent" after 6–12 months, depending on whether the cause was anoxic or traumatic.

After 1–3 months, the chance of significant improvement or meaningful recovery is small. However, patients can live for decades with little more support than full nursing care and a feeding tube. The issue to be determined is whether the patient would have wanted that protracted period of severely debilitated life, or would have preferred to avoid it as undignified or not worth the small chance of improvement (especially given quality of life even if a minimally conscious state [MCS] is regained).

Brain death (technically, "death diagnosed by neurological criteria") is a lack of brainstem and cortical functioning. There is no breathing, eye movement, sleep-wake cycling, or reflexive activity, and no chance of regaining consciousness. The diagnosis is usually made by electroencephalography that reveals no electrical activity in a 30-minute tracking obtained in the absence of hypothermia and central nervous system depression from drugs or other substances. The physiological functions of brain dead patients can be maintained indefinitely with the use of ventilators, vasopressors, and other supportive therapies.

Some sects of ultraorthodox Jews assert that their beliefs demand that treatment continue despite a diagnosis of brain death. New York and New Jersey have recognized the need to "reasonably accommodate" these beliefs without defining that phrase further.

Maximizing Patient Self-Determination

The physician's duty is to counsel the family about the *primacy of the patient's wishes* so that, if a conflict arises, no family member can usurp the patient's right to choose. If the patient has some understanding but it is compromised, undeveloped, wavering, or uncertain, the physician must seek to achieve a *collaborative partnership*. In these situations, patients often require advice from the physician, but the goal of the partnership is to maximize the patient's input into decisions about care. Initiation or withdrawal of some treatments that will enhance, even temporarily, the patient's decision-making capacity may be justified in this situation.

All patients should be encouraged to complete a **living will** and a **health care proxy** to name a surrogate decision maker. All patients should be asked under what conditions they would want possible future treatments to be discontinued. Answers should be recorded in the patient's chart

---

The consensus among ethicists is that families do not have the authority to request continued treatment for patients who are brain dead. Usually, a day or two for family to travel to see the patient is provided, although there is disagreement about whether this aids or delays their comfort and closure.

Factors to Consider in Making a "Best Interests Decision" for a Patient

- Interests exist only where there can be an awareness of a *benefit*; thus, if a patient cannot experience the benefit from a procedure, then it has none.

- If a patient can experience pain or discomfort from either a procedure or the continued existence it would produce, then it is a *burden* and should not be done, unless balanced by equal or greater benefits gained from continued life.

- *Primum non nocere*, "First, do no harm," means the physician must maximize quality, not just length of life, and prohibits lengthening the process of dying.

The objective benefits and burdens measure of the patient's best interest is justified where there is lack of direct or indirect evidence of the patient's values and preferences.

and living will. Patients unable to discuss these issues should still be encouraged to select the surrogate they would most trust to make these decisions for them.

Ideally, the *surrogate* chosen by the patient understands the task to make a choice as the patient would have done if the patient were capable of decision making. Input from family and friends may be solicited (e.g., to shed light on what the patient would want) but should be limited. The physician serves as educator and collaborator. The physician's goal is to determine, together with the surrogate, what the patient would have wanted in this situation, not what the surrogate wants. An important formulation of this suggests the physician must ask the surrogate what the patient would say if he or she could suddenly sit up and speak, knowing that returning to his or her current state was inevitable. The source of justification in this situation is respect for the patient's values and preferences, although they are determined indirectly.

If the patient was never capable of decision making (e.g., is a newborn or is severely mentally handicapped), then the focus of the physician's partnership with the family is to determine what is in the best interests of the patient.

Advance Directives, End-of-Life Decisions, and Futility

What are two types of advance directives and how do they differ?

Physicians frequently rationalize withholding information to avoid harming a patient who would be psychologically devastated by the truth. No empirical research has ever supported this claim. The only exceptions are patients who requested that they not be told and that someone else be told instead, or patients who are members of groups known to fear the supernatural effects of spoken bad news (e.g., the Navajo). For most patients, informing them of their condition contributes in the long run to a *sense of control* and participation in health care decisions.

Advance directives enable individuals to ensure that their health care wishes are carried out. There are two major types of advance directives: proxy and living will. In the **proxy**, the patient names a

surrogate who will make decisions if the patient loses capacity. The surrogate should be someone who knows the patient's wishes and who can advocate for them, even in difficult emotional situations.

In completing a **living will**, the patient describes treatments he or she would or would not want under specified circumstances. Regardless of the kind of advance directive, the physician should discuss with the patient any likely future scenarios given the patient's diagnosis. The patient can then discuss these issues with the surrogate or leave written instructions. For most patients, filling out both types of advance directives is best, as living wills are often too vague to stand alone but provide important helpful guidance to the proxy.

What is the difference between "do not resuscitate" and "comfort care" orders?

Some authorities interpret patient self-determination to mean that even *futile treatments* must be offered to patients and provided if requested. In general, this is not true: futile treatments should not be offered, and any request for them should be patiently and sympathetically denied, with a clear explanation. Compassion does not require compliance but, rather, concern and guidance. **Futility** is difficult to define. Some physicians use "futile" in a value-free physiological or biological sense (i.e., cannot maintain or extend life); others intend a more value-laden or biographical sense (i.e., cannot offer an acceptable quality of life).

When further treatment is *biologically* futile, a **"do not resuscitate"** (DNR) order should be recommended and attention paid to pain control, palliative care, and avoidance of unnecessary tests and procedures. In contrast, when further treatment is *biographically* futile, which refers to quality of life, the patient or surrogate must determine the values inherent in an acceptable quality of life, and caregivers must respect those choices. **Quality of life** is a key ethical concept, as long as the authority in deciding is the patient rather than the physician or society. What is acceptable to one person may be a demeaning loss of dignity and independence for another, and vice versa.

When the family, rather than the patient, demands treatment, the ethical problem is the same, although the situation is emotionally more complex. Such demands are best understood as expressions of love in a context of despair and denial. Patience and compromise may be appropriate temporary measures, with firm time limits ("We can continue this treatment for 24 hours and see if she improves"). The question to ask the family or proxy is whether "doing everything" is what the patient would want.

DNR and comfort care are closely related but distinct concepts. A *DNR* order simply states that, should a cardiopulmonary arrest occur, resuscitation efforts (commonly, cardiopulmonary resuscitation, cardioversion, intubation) will not be performed. The patient could still consent to individual components of resuscitation (e.g., intubation if it is likely to be only a temporary measure). DNR orders can be rescinded by the patient at any time and any patient, no matter how healthy, may choose not to be resuscitated.

DNR orders cannot be rescinded by the physician unilaterally; for the physician to do so imposes an unwanted aggressive intervention on the patient. Furthermore, DNR has no bearing on the treatment plan; it only specifies treatment to be withheld in the event of an actual arrest. Thus, DNR is best thought of as another type of advance directive, although one that requires a physician's order.

Patients must understand the process of *advanced cardiac life support* (ACLS), including intubation, cardioversion, and ventilation, as well as the alternatives, before their consent for a DNR order can be considered informed and valid. The chance of a successful outcome, as defined by the patient, is critical information and must be included in the consent process. Many patients do not understand that ACLS survivors often suffer neurological compromise, may not ever "wake-up," and if they do, will most likely be intubated and in the ICU.

Comfort care implies a general withdrawal of curative or *life-prolonging* care in favor of making the patient's comfort the primary treatment goal. Comfort care includes aggressive pain management, balancing the patient's desires to be pain free but alert to people and events. Inconveniences such as monitoring vital signs and phlebotomy are eliminated. Diagnostic efforts are abandoned unless a condition that is easily treatable but causing undue discomfort is suspected. These elements constitute good **hospice care**, which can be provided in the home, a freestanding hospice, or the hospital as part of a comprehensive **palliative care** treatment plan (see Chapter 32, Palliative Care).

Death and Dying

Medicine cannot prevent death, but it can make death less frightening by giving patients control over its manner and timing. Any treatment that can be started can be stopped to **allow natural death** (AND). Withdrawal of ventilatory and nutritional support is now accepted as ethically and legally proper, given clear understanding that withdrawal represents the patient's wishes. Often, discontinuing a medical treatment will ease a patient's suffering, sometimes hastening a painless death, and sometimes actually lengthening life.

The most common obstacles to death are continuation of life-sustaining treatments, administration of antibiotics, and insertion of feeding tubes. Some authorities argue that **physician-assisted suicide** would never be necessary if withdrawing of feeding tubes or refusal of food by patients capable of eating were considered appropriate options. Studies show that terminally ill patients do not experience pain or suffering when feeding is discontinued. Proper comfort care also requires discontinuing hydration at the same time to prevent fluid overload, fluid collection, urinary tract infections, and aspiration pneumonia.

Semantics can be crucial. A "natural process of malnutrition and dehydration" leading to a gradual increase in endogenous endorphins, loss of consciousness, and a quiet death over the course of a week or two is an accurate description of this situation; "starvation" is not.

A painless and dignified death is an important value to most people in the US. Patients have the right to refuse life-sustaining treatments. A physician may prescribe a treatment for palliation of suffering and that treatment may have the unintended consequence of shortening a patient's life. For example, a terminally ill cancer patient with multiple bone metastases and severe pain may require such high doses of narcotics to manage the pain that the medication eventually suppresses the respiratory drive. Under such circumstances, the use of high doses of medication can be justified by the **doctrine of double effect**. Besides the ethical justification for whatever risk is involved, it is also true that, while many family members fear narcotics will shorten life, evidence does not support such fears. Most importantly, "First, do no harm" would prohibit limiting treatments that might reduce or eliminate suffering at the end of life.

What are the arguments for and against physician-assisted suicide?

Withdrawal of life-sustaining treatment must be distinguished from physician-assisted suicide (PAS) and euthanasia. Physician-assisted suicide involves a physician *prescribing* a drug to a mentally competent patient who has requested the prescription for the sole purpose of self-administering the medication to cause death. PAS is, in turn, distinguished from **voluntary euthanasia**, in which the physician *administers* the lethal drug *with* the patient's consent and cooperation. **Involuntary euthanasia** is physician *administration* of a lethal drug *without* the patient's consent or cooperation.

Neither PAS nor any form of euthanasia is sanctioned by any medical governing body in the US. However, organizations such as the American College of Physicians have recognized the existence of medical situations where such action "needs to be explored in depth." In 1997, the U.S. Supreme Court ruled that assisted suicide is not a constitutional right, but did allow states to decide whether to legalize it.

For those who defend assisted suicide as a reasonable means for a patient to achieve a pain-free death *actively* (through the knowing use of medication to cause death) instead of *passively*

Arguments Favoring PAS:
(1) Mentally competent individuals have the right to self-determination, even regarding the timing of their death, and they should be able to do so legally with the aid of their physician; and
(2) a physician is acting humanely by helping otherwise terminally ill persons die before they experience extreme physical pain, debility, or loss of personal dignity, and they should be able to do so legally with the aid of their physician.

Arguments Opposing PAS:
(1) It violates many religious prohibitions, the Hippocratic Oath, and, in most states, legal statues;
(2) patients may be coerced into PAS for financial or other self-serving reasons by families, insurance companies, or institutions; and
(3) the distinction between "mentally competent" or "rational" suicidal thoughts and depression in people with terminal illness is unclear.

(through withdrawal of life-sustaining measures), certain safeguards to prevent abuse are generally insisted on: (1) the patient must request assisted suicide without outside pressure, on more than one occasion, over a sustained period of time; (2) the patient cannot be suffering from any mental illness that impedes judgment; and (3) assisted suicide should be contemplated, if ever, only when all other avenues to relieve suffering have been tried and failed.

It has been argued that, in sanctioning PAS, the definition of who would be allowed to commit suicide could be expanded without justification creating a "slippery slope." Physician-assisted voluntary euthanasia has been officially tolerated for some time in The Netherlands, Belgium, and Switzerland for patients who are terminally ill, and some have claimed that patients with severe debilitating chronic illnesses are also "being euthanized" in those countries. But in Oregon, which legalized PAS in 1997, data have shown no indications of abuse or a "slippery slope" after more than 10 years of experience. Washington followed suit in 2009. There are no laws against PAS in Wyoming, North Carolina, and Utah.

Social Justice and Access to Health Care

Though subject to partisan debates, the Affordable Care Act was passed in 2010 with the broad support of most ethicists, hospitals, and medical societies. The ethical issues it addresses are related to justice, the fourth of the four principles: (1) cutting the number of people who are uninsured by 30 million (by eliminating pre-existing conditions as a legal cause for exclusion, eliminating high expenditures as a reason to refuse continued coverage or to raise rates, raising the age of dependents who can be on parents' policies up to the age of 26, charging a small penalty for those who choose not to be insured, and creating a subsidy for those who earn less than 400% of the poverty level); (2) increasing the influence of evidence-based medicine and, thus, lessening the overuse of often costly non-evidence-based interventions (by creating the Patient-Centered Outcomes Research Institute and encouraging data entry and reimbursement systems that incorporate the results of such research); and (3) adding new tools to regulate private for-profit insurance plans and protect against fraud by curtailing the development of new physician-owned specialty hospitals, mandating that insurance plans spend 80–85% of their income on medical payments for patients and limiting wasteful overhead and salaries for CEOs and CMOs, expanding Medicare to more hospitals, especially small rural hospitals to decrease urban-rural disparities, and re-funding the Indian Health Service.

All of these measures can be seen as attempts to address ethical problems within the U.S. health care system, which, on the basis of many important measures (e.g., average lifespan, infant mortality), is no longer in the top 30 systems in the world.

Academic and Financial Conflicts of Interest

> What is the principle of clinical equipoise in research?

> The first basic principle of the Nuremberg Code (1948) begins with the statement: "The voluntary consent of the human subject is absolutely essential."

Patients have the right to participate, fully informed, in research that has little hope of helping them. The researcher must ensure that the patient does not participate because of false hope (*therapeutic misconception*).

In some instances, the research protocol may have a likelihood of greater benefit compared to a known treatment in a double-blind trial. In this situation, where the patient's enrollment in the study with possibly better efficacy is determined by chance, the physician's obligations to the patient are balanced with the opportunity to improve patient care in the future. The investigator must meet the standard of **clinical equipoise**, waiting until sufficient data are collected to draw a sound conclusion, *but no longer than necessary* because of the risk to patients. If the information gathered indicates the new treatment is significantly better, or more dangerous, than the established treatment, then it is the obligation of the investigator to end the trial, but only after the evidence has scientific credibility beyond mere anecdotal reports.

Gifts and Financial Incentives

Accepting *gifts* from pharmaceutical or medical supply companies must be balanced against the compromise to objective judgment such gifts are meant to create. Larger gifts (e.g., vacations) are now illegal. Smaller gifts (e.g., pens, note pads) probably damage the physician's image more than his or her objectivity. Free lunches or dinners with an educational talk delivered by a speaker paid by the company typically involve biased information being provided with positive reinforcement (food) to enhance susceptibility to the marketing message.

Medication samples, used to help patients who cannot afford needed drugs, can be defended on the principle of justice. However, if the patient is saddled with an expensive medication when a generic would suffice, justice would suggest providing samples of generics instead. Use of samples by the physician's family cannot be justified since the cost of medication is then increased for others to cover the cost of these "freebies."

Financial interest in a facility (laboratory, clinic) to which a physician refers patients should be revealed to the patient (on the consent form, consultation request, prescription pad, and in public advertising), and the facility must offer services that meet accepted standards of care and charge reasonable fees.

Trainees

Trainees should accurately describe their status and role, and avoids euphemisms like "doctor-in-training" for medical students. Patients appreciate honesty and concern for their well-being while also understanding the students' need to learn. Of all the members of the team, trainees are often the ones who have the time to talk with the patient and answer questions, and, in many cases, provide one of the most valuable services the system has to offer – listening.

Recommended Readings

ACP Ethics Committee. *Ethics Manual*, 6th ed. *Annals of Internal Medicine* 2012; 156:73–104.

Barsky AE. *Clinicians in Court: A Guide to Subpeonas, Depositions, Testifying and Everything Else You Need to Know*, 2nd ed. New York: Guilford Press; 2012.

Beauchamp TL, Childress JF. *Principles of Biomedical Ethics*, 6th ed. New York: Oxford University Press; 2008.

Lo B. *Resolving Ethical Dilemmas: A Guide for Clinicians*, 4th ed. Philadelphia, PA: Lippincott Williams & Wilkins; 2009.

Review Questions

1. Informed Consent, as a legal doctrine, is based on which of the following principles of biomedical ethics?
    A. Autonomy
    B. Beneficence
    C. Fiduciary
    D. Justice
    E. Nonmaleficence

2. Which of the following groups of patients are legally presumed to lack capacity, but may be determined to have capacity by a clinician?
    A. Bipolar
    B. Dementia
    C. Elderly
    D. Minor
    E. Schizophrenic

3. The best tool for capacity assessment is
    A. comprehensive DSM-IV Axis I and II evaluation.
    B. discussion with the patient about her values and treatment goals.
    C. Mini Mental Status Exam.
    D. the Rorschach Test.
    E. the Stanford-Binet Test of Intelligence.

4. DNR orders are
    A. a statement of "giving up" when nothing more can be done.
    B. a type of advance directive.
    C. revocable by any physician.
    D. revocable by the patient's attending physician.
    E. revocable by the patient's primary care physician.

5. Comfort care for patients in the last days of life typically includes
    A. continuing artificial hydration and aggressive symptom management while discontinuing artificial nutrition and other life-sustaining treatment.
    B. continuing artificial nutrition and aggressive symptom management while discontinuing artificial hydration and other life-sustaining treatment.
    C. continuing artificial nutrition and hydration and aggressive symptom management while discontinuing other life-sustaining treatment.
    D. discontinuing artificial nutrition and hydration and other life-sustaining treatment while continuing aggressive symptom management.
    E. discontinuing all interventions.

Key to review questions: p. 408

Section IX
The Clinical Relationship

34 The Physician-Patient Relationship

Dennis C. Russo, PhD, and Lars C. Larsen, MD

- What are the responsibilities and rights of physicians?
- What are the responsibilities and rights of patients?
- What is "informed consent?"
- What is the difference between transference and countertransference?
- What are patients' two main fears?
- What influences patients' adherence to treatment recommendations?
- What are six methods for supporting participatory decision making?

The **Hippocratic Oath** required physicians to be responsible for the patient's well-being, but did not require the physician to inform the patient or follow the patient's wishes. In fact, the physician could deceive the patient if the deception was intended to offer hope. By the end of the 18th century, Benjamin Rush, a physician and signer of the Declaration of Independence, was urging physicians to share information with patients while John Gregory, of the University of Edinburgh, proposed that patients be more responsible for their own health education and that physicians aid their efforts.

Today, the physician-patient relationship is based on a *mutual exchange of information* and *participatory decision making*. The patient's right to determine his or her care is a core element of the implicit physician-patient contract. The patient's values and preferences are to be discussed and incorporated into the treatment plan that the physician and patient share responsibility for developing and implementing. While the dominant culture of the US emphasizes patient autonomy, active involvement, and independent functioning, patients from more family-oriented cultures may find this type of physician-patient relationship offensive or discourteous. In many of these cultures, the family is viewed as the agent of decision making, although negotiating treatment is still a major element of determining care. Hence, the physician should be especially sensitive to cultural differences and the effect they will have on patient expectations and practices (see Chapter 18, Culture and Ethnicity).

Responsibilities and Rights of Physicians

What are the responsibilities and rights of physicians?

The physician has a responsibility to inform the patient, to the best of his or her ability, regarding the nature of the disorder, probable course if untreated, and available and recommended treatments. The physician also has an obligation to elicit and listen to the patient's concerns, address them objectively and sensitively, and respect the patient's decisions even though the physician may disagree with them. Above all, the physician has a responsibility to use his or her authority in the best interests of the patient and avoid abuse of this authority that can result when there are conflicts of interest.

Refusal to Perform Certain Procedures

The physician may refuse to perform any act that conflicts with personal moral or ethical principles (e.g., performing an abortion or withdrawing life support). However, the physician has the responsibility to *respect the patient's wishes* and make a referral to another physician who is more comfortable and responsive to the patient's wishes.

Recommending Appropriate Treatments

Although treatment costs must be considered in medical decisions, the most important principle is that patients receive *appropriate care*. For example, a 60-year-old, otherwise healthy patient who has suspected pneumonia expects, and should receive, appropriate diagnostic studies and medication. Among terminally ill patients, whose feelings regarding prolongation of life vary, however, the same situation may raise complex ethical dilemmas that require balancing expectations for cure against the realities of quality of life.

Rights and Responsibilities of Patients

> ### What are the responsibilities and rights of patients?

In 1972, the American Hospital Association developed the **Patient's Bill of Rights** that details the patient's right to receive complete information, to refuse treatment (unless the patient is incompetent or the decision poses a threat to the community), and to know about a hospital's possible financial conflicts of interest. **Informed consent** is the patient's right to know all treatment options and to decide which care is appropriate for him or her. To empower the patient to make a rational decision,

---

Informed Consent

The Patient Self-Determination Act requires health care institutions to advise patients that:
1. they have the right to refuse or accept medical care; and
2. they have the right to execute an advance directive concerning their care or to designate a person (proxy) to make decisions for them if they are unable to do so.

---

the physician must provide information and full, accurate, and understandable explanations. Until the late 1970s, decisions regarding life-sustaining treatment were considered the domain of physicians. Respect for patient participation in such decisions led to the passage of the **Patient Self-Determination Act** in 1991.

> ### What is "informed consent?"

Informed consent is an open communication process between the patient and physician that results in the patient approving or not approving a medical intervention or course of action. Under most circumstances, care can be withdrawn at a patient's request. However, it is illegal in most states for a health care worker to actively hasten death even at the patient's explicit request (e.g., **physician-assisted suicide**). Parents are empowered to make legal decisions for their children, but over the past 30 years, there has been a movement to allow children to participate more actively in medical decision making. In the case of experimental protocols, children as young as 7 years of age are mandated by some institutions to give **informed assent** prior to being accepted as a participant and their parents must give *informed consent*. Adolescents may make their own decisions regarding sexual matters (e.g., contraception, STI treatment, abortion) although some states require parental notification or involvement.

Establishing Limits of Confidentiality

Except in situations where the physician is concerned that the patient will harm him- or herself or others, or in situations that involve mandatory reporting (child abuse, communicable diseases), patient information may not be shared with others without the patient's expressed consent. Patient information may be discussed without explicit patient consent only with professional individuals who are involved in the patient's care, or with members of a teaching group (all of whom have been instructed in the principles of confidentiality) in a controlled environment away from areas where the discussion could be overheard.

The **Health Insurance Portability and Accountability Act (HIPAA)**, which took effect in 2003, provides new standards to protect patients' written and electronic medical records and other health information that is provided to health plans, physicians, hospitals, and other health care providers. These standards give patients access to their medical records and more control over how their personal health information is used and disclosed.

Guidelines for Protecting Confidentiality

- Conduct the interview in private.
- Tell patients with whom and under what circumstances information will be shared.
- Teach or consult about patients in private.
- Override confidentiality when safety of the patient or others is a concern.

With the development and promulgation of electronic health records (EHR), **Protected Health Information** (PHI) is more available to members of the patient's health care team but, at the same time, more vulnerable to access by a variety of individuals and organizations. HIPAA requires that individually identifiable health information be protected and includes all written, numeric, or pictorial information related to physical or mental health that would allow a patient to be identified. With the development of models of health team-based care (e.g., the Patient-Centered Medical Home), communications between providers, both verbal and written, must comply with HIPAA regulations.

Factors Influencing the Physician-Patient Relationship

Accurate empathy is the ability to understand the patient's illness experiences from the patient's perspective, to communicate this understanding to the patient, and to have this understanding confirmed by the patient. Patients list kindness, understanding, interest, and encouragement as primary expectations they have of their physicians. They want their physical, interpersonal, and emotional needs met in a mutually under-

stood, courteous, warm, and personal manner that permits them to feel they are partners with the physician.

Hippocrates emphasized the importance of relationship by admonishing the physician to: bear in mind his manner of sitting, reserve, arrangement of dress, decisive utterance, brevity of speech, composure, bedside manners, care, replies to objections, calm self-control ... his manner must be serious and humane, without stooping to be jocular or failing to be just; he must avoid excessive austerity; he must always be in control of himself.

Whereas "empathy" is *understanding* the patient's experience, "sympathy" is *feeling* and *experiencing* the emotions expressed by the patient. This distinction is important because it is not necessary to experience the patient's feelings to be helpful. In fact, over-identification with the patient can lead to ineffective communication or complicate the relationship.

What is the difference between transference and countertransference?

Transference refers to the beliefs, expectations, and perceptions from previous relationships that influence current life experience. For example, a patient with insulin-dependent diabetes has not complied well with dietary restrictions. The patient grew up in a household with a harsh, critical parent. If the physician attempts to counsel the patient about proper dietary habits and expresses these recommendations in a firm fashion, the patient may become angry and feel belittled because the physician has not appreciated the patient's efforts to control her diet. In this instance, the patient is reacting as if the physician were a parent (transference).

Countertransference refers to inappropriate reactions the physician has to a patient. If the physician perceives the patient as a "nice little old lady" who is just like a favorite aunt, the physician may find it difficult to ask her questions that seem intrusive (e.g., about how frequently she voids or if she has urinary incontinence). Effective medical care involves being objectively vigilant and aware that the patient <u>and</u> physician may bring past emotional experiences to each encounter.

Impediments to Communication

Sensory Impairment

Communication is likely to be inhibited to some degree by impaired hearing, sight, or verbal expression. *Hearing-impaired individuals* may need to use sign language, require a signer to translate, or be able to read the lips of a physician who speaks clearly and slowly. For patients with hearing impairment who are literate, the interview may be facilitated by the use of written material. The *visually impaired* patient's need for verbal explanation and description exceeds that of all other patients. The patient who is mute may be able to sign and, therefore, may require a translator. When any patient has an impairment, the physician must inquire about the extent to which physical or cognitive assistance will be required to adhere to the therapeutic plan and if that assistance will be available.

Language and Cultural Differences

Virtually every physician will need to communicate with a patient through a *translator* or an *interpreter* at some time. Because of differences in language structure, literal translations may not be possible or accurate. Efforts should be made, however, to ensure that the patient's complaints and condition are clearly communicated. An interpreter, in contrast to a translator, brings his or her own cultural and ethnic background values, knowledge, and belief system to the exchange. In effect, *the role of the interpreter triangulates the encounter*. For example, if the patient is angry, but the interpreter feels that displaying anger is inappropriate, the physician will not be told and the patient's answers will be softened or references to anger, blame, or guilt removed. If the translator or interpreter is a child or family member of the patient, issues such as confidentiality become especially important.

The time needed for an interview involving a translator or interpreter is usually twice as long as one solely between physician and patient. The physician should acknowledge to the patient that there may be difficulty in arriving at a diagnosis and management plan as a result of the language difference but that they will work together to overcome these problems.

Cognitive differences include the disparity between how the patient and the physician *conceptualize experiences*, and how they understand and explain the world, including the disease and its treatment. Misconceptions, often made at first glance, can affect subjective assessments of the patient's race, ethnic origin, cultural values, appearance, demeanor, and reason for seeking care. This profile, possibly due to a lack of cultural awareness and poor communication, may lead to misdiagnosis and inappropriate care of the patient. Awareness of personal bias and prejudice, coupled with attention to the patient and a willingness to listen and understand his or her concerns, is requisite for providing quality treatment for every individual (see Chapter 9, Cognition and Social Interaction, and Chapter 18, Culture and Ethnicity).

Age Effects

Because age is associated with increased experience, younger physicians are sometimes challenged for being too young and may need great patience to win a patient's confidence. Seeing themselves as children or even grandchildren, younger physicians sometimes have difficulty advising older patients.

Gender Effects

Male physicians offer the same number of explanations to men and women patients but explanations to women are given in less technical language. Female patients are more likely to ask questions and receive more information. The male physician is likely to be more empathic toward female patients.

Male and female physicians have different communication styles. Female physicians are less likely to interrupt patients. Although male and female physicians do not appear to ask different questions of men and women patients, patients are more likely to initiate discussion of both medical and psychosocial issues with female physicians than they are with male physicians. Men patients are more likely to bring up personal habits with female physicians.

Other Factors

Psychosocial stresses and *psychiatric disorders* may pose an impediment to the interview. Psychosis, paranoia, and some personality disorders may stop the physician from being able to form a therapeutic relationship with the patient. Children or individuals with developmental or cognitive disorders may have difficulty understanding complex issues and decisions related to their health care. Also, patients with various types of *dementia*, especially in the early stages, may confabulate or provide unreliable or inaccurate medical information. In these cases, having family members involved in the interview to confirm information and assist in the care plan for the individual can be valuable. In trauma situations, such as rape or domestic violence, the physician must be aware of the need for privacy and support. The patient should be given clear guidance concerning the process of the physical examination and other data collection, and should not be left alone in the exam room.

Physician-Patient Relationships and Changes in Medical Care Models

Changes in the physician-patient relationship are likely with the implementation of the Patient-Centered Medical Home. Within this model, the physician becomes the primary caregiver and the primary agent for preventing illness, promoting wellness, and managing chronic conditions. The model assumes a strong relationship between the patient and a personal care physician who, like the family doctor of the past, will be responsible for tending to a patient's overall health and well-being as well as working with other health care professionals who implement various parts of the care plan.

Understanding Patient Fears

What are patients' two main fears?

A patient typically has two main fears: *losing bodily integrity* and *becoming dependent*. The degree

to which these fears affect the patient depends on the patient's age and stage of development, personality, and life experiences. Young athletes are usually able to tolerate injury and pain, yet they have little tolerance for discomfort or inconvenience if an illness limits their activities or makes them dependent on others. In contrast, older persons with a chronic illness may accept limited independence, being more concerned about maintaining at least the basic functioning essential for maintaining their own home.

Acceptance of Dependency Is Influenced by Life Stage

1. Young children are used to being dependent on others, but may be fearful because they do not understand illness.
2. Adolescents struggle to establish their identity and may find any threat to independence difficult to accept.
3. Adults may find it difficult to tolerate absence from work or isolation from friends, especially if they define themselves in terms of their work or relationships.
4. The elderly may experience illness as a signal that their healthy life is jeopardized and there may be no hope of recovery.

Ensuring Treatment Plan Success

The success of any intervention depends on the physician and patient reaching agreement about the nature of the problem and its proper treatment (see Chapter 18, Culture and Ethnicity). The patient's explanation of the illness, or **explanatory model**, influences beliefs about causation and determines what assistance he or she will seek and accept. Therefore every effort should be made to accurately explain the nature of the illness, its etiology, and its treatment in terms that are in keeping with the patient's explanatory model, culture, and treatment expectations.

What influences patients' adherence to treatment recommendations?

It is rare for patients to follow treatment recommendations rigorously. The adherence rate for

---

Adherence to Treatment Will Depend on the Patient's Belief that:

1. the illness warrants treatment,
2. the treatment is effective,
3. the cost of treatment is reasonable given the benefits, and
4. the treatment is feasible.

---

prescribed medications is about 50% even in the treatment of acute illness, and the proportion of patients completing treatment decreases as the duration of treatment increases. Thus, higher dose but shorter course treatments are used for a wide variety of infections.

Patient **adherence** to therapy recommendations typically depends upon: (1) the complexity of the regimen, (2) the persistence of symptoms, and (3) the frequency and quality of contact with the physician. In cases of chronic illness, the physician can help to ensure that patients have the proper skills to manage the "prescription" through a careful explanation of the agreed upon care plan, the specific behaviors required by the patient, and an ongoing assessment of patient adherence as a regular part of repeated clinical encounters. Providing specific benchmarks for patient compliance, frequent feedback, and praise for success in meeting adherence goals should replace general statements of support.

Participatory Decision Making

What are six methods for supporting participatory decision making?

Patients who participate in the decisions regarding their care are more likely to adhere to the treatment plan. Successful **participatory decision making** requires that the patient be fully informed about the clinical findings (i.e., the nature of their condition), the treatment options available, and the efficacy and risks associated with each option.

Effective participatory decision making inevitably depends upon the physician's interpretation and presentation of the effectiveness of available treatments. How the information is interpreted will be influenced by:

Methods for Supporting Participatory Decision Making:

1. Present options for how the patient can participate in the decision-making process.
2. Present options for how clinical detail is presented to the patient.
3. State information regarding clinical procedures in terms of absolute risk since relative risk-reduction statements may be confusing and misleading.
4. Carefully weigh the order in which information is presented.
5. Carefully present the time frame of treatment outcome.
6. In presenting outcome rates, use proportions rather than percentages, especially with less educated or older patients

---

– Patient knowledge, fears, and prioritized treatment goals. It is imperative that the physician be familiar with the patient's level of knowledge, concerns, and treatment goals, and be prepared to inform and advise the patient when necessary.
– Physician knowledge, resources, biases. The physician should insure that his or her knowledge base is current, resources are indeed available, and that personal biases are openly discussed and fairly presented.
– External resources, accessibility to facilities, limitations in time and practice. The physician should insure in advance that external resources and facilities are available, and that practice constraints and demands will not impede patient care.

Recommended Readings

Levinson W, Roter DL, Mullooly JP, et al. Physician-patient communication. *JAMA* 1997; 277:553–559.

Rosser RR, Kasperski J. The benefits of a trusting physician-patient relationship. *Journal of Family Practice* 2001; 50:329–330.

Roter DL, Stewart M, Putnam SM, et al. Communication patterns of primary care physicians. *JAMA* 1997; 277:350–356.

Sapien RE, Commentary: Profiling by appearance and assumption: Beyond race and ethnicity. *Academic Medicine* 2010; 85:580–582.

Travaline JM, Ruchinskas R, D'Alonzo GE. Patient-physician communication: Why and how. *Journal of the American Osteopathic Association* 2005; 105:13–18.

Review Questions

1. Dr. Johnson was approaching retirement and, at the age of 67, had provided care for patients in a rural town in South Dakota for almost 35 years. Although felt by patients to be "a bit old fashioned," he was respected as capable, caring, and always available to meet his patients' needs. His preferred role in relationships with patients was a paternalistic one, a role encouraged during his medical school education. Among the following, a common characteristic of paternalistic physician roles is
   A. deferring decision-making authority to the patient's family.
   B. mutual exchange of information between physician and patient.
   C. patient passivity during encounters with a physician.
   D. physician respect for patient autonomy.
   E. sharing of medical decision making between physician and patient.

2. Among the following, an example of transference in career decision making is choosing
   A. a career in biomedical research after winning many science awards.
   B. a health care career after a significant childhood illness.
   C. a helping profession because of a family history of alcoholism.
   D. medicine based on a physician role model outside the family.
   E. to be a physician after being raised in a physician's family.

3. Which of the following best describes the basic requirement of informed consent?
   A. The patient must have a designated proxy to make decisions if the patient becomes incompetent.
   B. The patient must have all necessary information before agreeing to medical treatment.
   C. The patient's family must be advised before medical procedures are undertaken.
   D. The patient's primary care physician must be informed before a subspecialist performs a procedure.
   E. The physician must be well informed before consenting to perform a procedure.

4. The presence of empathy is crucial in the development of the physician-patient relationship. The core element in the establishment of empathy focuses on
   A. avoiding excessive emotional detachment.
   B. mastering active or reflective listening.
   C. modeling how to remain in calm self-control.
   D. providing reassurance about a positive outcome.
   E. using exclusively open-ended questioning.

5. Encouraging patients to participate in the clinical decision-making process
   A. complicates and impedes the treatment course.
   B. decreases patient confidence in physician competence.
   C. increases patient adherence to treatment regimens.
   D. increases the risk of poor outcomes and litigation.
   E. raises ethical issues with regard to clinical responsibility.

Key to review questions: p. 408

35 The Medical Encounter and Clinical Decision Making

Lars C. Larsen, MD, Dennis C. Russo, PhD, Frank C. Seitz, PhD, and John E. Carr, PhD

- What is rapport?
- What are the two types of clinical reasoning?
- What kinds of questions should be avoided?
- What are eight data gathering techniques?
- What is included in the comprehensive medical history?
- What is the Mental Status Examination?
- What are the six steps in the clinical decision-making process?
- What are eight sources of error in clinical decision making?

The Medical Encounter

Setting, time constraints, and purpose determine the structure of each provider-patient medical encounter. In an emergency or triage situation, the interview is limited to essential information sufficient to initiate care. In contrast, in a new patient office visit, data collection is more thorough and comprehensive, requiring sufficient time to accomplish the goals of the visit. In a continuing care encounter, addressing issues to keep the patient healthy or managing chronic illness become important parts of the agenda. Whatever the circumstance, every patient encounter should be documented in writing to facilitate communication and consistency of care.

Introductions

The interviewer should always introduce him- or herself, even if wearing a name tag. The patient should be addressed using a formal title (i.e., Mr., Mrs., Ms.) and the patient's last name, unless the patient is a child or has asked to be addressed in another way. Many clinicians shake hands with the patient and anyone accompanying the patient. However, care should be taken to respect differences in social practices and expectations if the patient is from another culture.

Developing Rapport

What is rapport?

Rapport is a state of mutual confidence and respect between two people. Because the provider is perceived as being in a position of authority, developing rapport is essential to establishing a mutually respectful relationship. The development of trust comes when patients believe the provider understands and respects their concerns.

Sensitivity to Emotions

Responding appropriately to an expression of emotion by the patient can be reassuring and facilitate the interview. It is important for the provider to be comfortable with emotion in order to allow the patient to be comfortable expressing it. When a patient cries, showing respect and caring by waiting or offering a tissue can be comforting even if nothing is said. With an angry or hostile patient, acknowledging the anger, remaining calm and listening reflectively, and encouraging the patient to discuss what is causing the anger are likely to diffuse the situation. Above all, care should be taken to avoid taking the patient's display of anger as personal.

Cultural Appropriateness

Every patient has a set of culturally based *health beliefs*, *illness behaviors*, and *explanatory models* for what is normal or abnormal. Understanding and respecting the patient's cultural context increases the likelihood of full participation in developing and adhering to an effective treatment plan.

Establishing Limits of Confidentiality

The medical encounter involves the patient sharing large amounts of personal information with the physician. The patient must feel confident that the provider will treat that information in a manner consistent with accepted standards and guidelines for confidentiality (see Chapter 34, The Physician-Patient Relationship).

Attentive Listening

Attentive listening communicates interest, concern, and understanding about what the patient is saying and feeling. The provider's interest enhances the patient's impression of professional competence, which, in turn, facilitates trust and prompts the patient to be more open and candid.

To Promote Attentive Listening:

1. the setting should be comfortable,
2. the provider should face the patient with an erect but relaxed posture,
3. eye contact should be frequent or culturally appropriate,
4. the provider should use gestures and facial expressions that are congruent with what is being said, and speak in a pleasant voice,
5. the provider should address the topic the patient has introduced and encourage the flow of information by using occasional facilitative words and phrases

Observation

Careful observation is an important part of a patient's evaluation and should begin the moment the provider first sees the patient. How is the patient groomed? Does the patient appear comfortable? Relaxed? Impatient? Frightened? When the patient is accompanied by others, their interaction can provide important information on interpersonal or family relationships. Initial hypotheses begin to form as the provider notes apparent age, gender, race, dress, affect, and whether the patient appears healthy, ill, or in distress.

Touching

Touching between the provider and the patient in the interim between shaking hands during introductions and the physical examination may or may not be appropriate. Although touching can be interpreted as empathetic by some patients, others can construe it as intrusive or seductive. Backing away, stiffening, or becoming silent are clues that a patient prefers not to be touched. Most experienced clinicians use measured, appropriate physical contact to reassure patients and enhance rapport unless the patient signals that this is unwelcome.

Clinical Reasoning

What are two types of clinical reasoning?

Central to the clinical decision-making process is the provider's expertise in clinical reasoning, of which there are two types: *non-analytic*, where previous experience and other intrinsic factors enable the clinician to quickly understand the patient's case and make correct decisions, and *analytic*, where deliberate and thoughtful consideration of all aspects of the patient's case is required for correct decisions. Both types are used in the clinical decision-making process, with analytic reasoning typically being more reliable in cases where the provider has less experience, the clinical presentation is more complex, or the case does not fit a characteristic disease pattern.

Conducting the Interview

Interviewers usually begin with open-ended questions, follow with more focused questions, and end with closed-ended questions to confirm data. *Open-ended questions* ("How have you been getting along?" "How can I help you?") signal the provider's interest in the patient, and allow patients to present issues they wish to address. Although it may seem paradoxical, open-ended questions elicit the maximum amount of information in the minimum amount of time because they impose few values or expectations, involve the patient in the interview and problem-solving process, and allow the patient to reveal information not apparent from the presenting complaint or medical history.

Focused questions narrow the area to be explored, but still give the patient latitude in answering (e.g., "What is your understanding of your situation?" or "How do you think this happened?"). Questions to help *clarify certain points* are "What do you mean when you say ...?" or "What are some examples of ...?"

Closed-ended questions prompt specific responses and are appropriate for clarifying details, facilitating decision making in triage or emergency situations, or directing the interview. Questions that elicit *specific information* are "Where does it hurt?" or "What did you eat today?"

Open-Ended Questions Can Quickly Elicit:

1. major concern or most pressing or potentially serious problems,
2. triggering events that led the patient to seek help,
3. attributions or explanatory models for the symptoms, and
4. expectations about what can or should be done.

What kinds of questions should be avoided?

Questions to be *avoided* include *compound questions*, which are several questions asked together (e.g., "Tell me what happens when you have chest pain, does it come after you've eaten something, or when you're feeling anxious?") and *leading questions*, which prompt the patient to give a specific response (e.g. "You haven't been drinking alcohol again, have you?").

What are eight data gathering techniques?

Eight Successful Data Gathering Techniques

1. *Nonverbal techniques* – head-nodding and verbal cues ("Tell me more about that") prompt the patient to expand and report what he or she feels is most important.
2. *Checking* – reviewing or repeating to ensure accuracy ("You think this started last Thursday?").
3. *Clarification* – asking the patient to restate or give examples, or paraphrasing what the patient has said ("So, your headaches occur both day and night, but are the absolute worst when you wake up. Is that correct?").
4. *Interruption* – breaking the flow if the patient is rambling. Acknowledge the importance the patient attaches to the information being given, then provide a transition to another topic ("Mrs. Jones, your son's school problems are certainly worrying you, but how about you? How's your arm healing?").
6. *Transition* – linking what the patient has been saying with a change in direction ("What you've been talking about reminds me to ask you....").
7. *Reflection* – paraphrasing what the patient has said to demonstrate attention ("You've told me a lot of things. Let's see if I've understood them all.").
8. *Information sharing* – interpreting and explaining the problem to clarify goals and expectations for outcomes. Written information should be culturally appropriate and suitable for the patient's literacy level.
9. *Giving directions* – clearly explaining various tasks and who has responsibility for completing them and checking for understanding.

Defining the patient's condition and concerns requires two kinds of information: **subjective data**, such as the description and history (chronology) of the symptoms; and **objective data**, such as observations during the interview, the physical examination, and results from laboratory tests/studies.

The History

What is included in the comprehensive medical history?

A Comprehensive Medical History Includes:

1. *Identifying data:* name, age, gender, occupation, and a brief statement of the major presenting problem in one or two sentences
2. *Reliability of the source of data:* patient, family member, chart records, letter of referral
3. *Chief complaint:* the reason for seeking care in the patient's exact words
4. *History of the present illness:* narrative account of each current problem including its beginning, course, diagnosis, and management; the patient's explanation for the problem and how it has affected his or her life ("Diabetes runs in my family." "I can't sleep at night."); characteristics of each symptom: timing or chronology, quality or character, quantity or severity, location, aggravating/alleviating factors, associated manifestations
5. *Past medical history:* medical, surgical, obstetrical, and psychiatric problems not currently active, including injuries and hospitalizations
6. *Current health status and habits:* prescription, over-the-counter, and herbal or supplemental medications, allergies, habits (including substance use), environmental exposures, travel, diet, immunizations, exercise, and health maintenance and prevention
7. *Family history:* narrative and genogram of the family, including as many generations as possible, with dates of birth and death, causes of death, and illnesses
8. *Social history:* biographical sketch including birthplace, parents, education, places of residence, work, marital status/relationships, children, hobbies, satisfactions/stresses
9. *Review of systems:* standard set of questions about common symptoms associated with each organ system that help to disclose any disease not yet discussed

Mental Status Examination

What is the Mental Status Examination?

The **Mental Status Examination** (MSE) bridges the history and physical examination. It begins with observation and assessment throughout the encounter and concludes with a more formal evaluation of the cognitive status of the patient. The formal evaluation of mental status includes assessment of level of consciousness; attention; memory (short- and long-term); orientation to time, place, and person; thought processes; thought content, insight, and judgment; affect; mood; language; vocabulary; fund of knowledge; and ability to abstract, calculate, and copy.

The Physical Examination

The physical examination elicits *signs* (observable objective data) indicative of disease. Signs primarily confirm hypotheses that have been generated during the interview process. The physical examination, like the history, may be complete or focused. When a patient has *symptoms* (subjective complaints) that are limited to a specific region or organ system, the examiner may decide to limit the examination to that area. The risk is that a significant finding will be undetected (e.g., a heart murmur in a child with acute rheumatic fever who presents complaining only of a limp). Physical alterations can occur over the natural course of a disease, and can be detected by observation, palpation, percussion, or auscultation.

Generally, a complete physical examination is conducted by region, starting with the head and neck and concluding with the extremities. The recording of the findings should begin with a descriptive general statement followed by a listing of the vital signs. The remainder of the data is usually organized under the following categories: skin, head, eyes, ears, nose, mouth and pharynx, neck, lymph nodes, thorax and lungs, cardiovascular system, breasts, abdomen, genitalia, rectum, peripheral vascular system, musculoskeletal system, and neurological system.

Laboratory Investigation

Necessary laboratory studies may be ordered after data from the history and physical examination have been collected and an initial *differential diagnosis* (list of diagnostic possibilities with their relative probabilities) has been generated. Diagnostic laboratory studies are likely to be most helpful when the probability of a particular disease is in the intermediate range, although some diagnostic tests are obtained to confirm a highly likely diagnosis. Tests should be ordered based on *predictive value* (likelihood of providing diagnostic help) as well as *cost benefit*. It is poor medical practice to order tests automatically, or to order an entire panel of tests merely because they can be processed simultaneously.

The Six Steps in the Clinical Decision-Making Process

What are the six steps in the clinical decision-making process?

The provider's role in the clinical decision-making process begins before the patient's appointment. It is initiated through a self-made appointment or a professional referral seeking answers to questions about the patient's condition. These questions determine the parameters of the provider's role in dealing with the patient, and the decisions the provider will be asked to make. *Referral questions*,

The Six Steps of the Clinical Decision-Making Process

1. *Defining the problem* – clarifying the nature of the problem, including an appreciation of the patient's cognitive context (i.e., beliefs, assumptions, expectations).
2. *Defining outcome goals* – defining the desired resolution of the problem in attainable terms.
3. *Generating alternative solutions* – identifying possible alternative solutions to resolve the problem.
4. *Selecting the best solution* – conducting a "cost-benefit" analysis based on the merits of each alternative solution (probable consequences; good vs. adverse effects; approximation to desired outcome), developing a strategic plan for the implementation of each solution (how much will it "cost" in time, money, energy), and then choosing the solution not only most likely to produce health but also most likely to be followed.
5. *Implementing the solution* – carrying out the plan.
6. *Evaluating the outcome* – determining if the goal was achieved and the problem solved. If not, reformulating the plan to reach a desirable end. Sometimes, as in chronic illness, the patient must redefine "health" to reach an accessible end point.

either from the patient or from a referral source, such as another provider, define the initial problem. The clinician develops a set of hypotheses that determine what information will be required and how it will be obtained. For example, if the patient is a hyperactive child being seen because a teacher has expressed concern to the parent, the clinician may seek assessment of school performance, gather data about behavior at home, and meet with the child's parents and teachers in addition to examining the child in the office.

Defining the Problem

The *problem list* serves as an organizing point for clinical problem solving. The list is a compilation of all the symptoms, signs, problems, and issues

Clinical Application – Part I

A 41-year-old female engineer who has had increasingly severe migraine headaches with shoulder and facial pain for which no medication has been helpful in reducing her symptoms is referred to the Behavioral Medicine Clinic by a neurologist. History and physical examination reveal no other past or current medical problems. The patient experiences headaches most frequently mid-morning, Monday through Friday, and occasionally in the evening. Personal and social history reveals the patient is married to another engineer, a "Type A workaholic." They both leave for work at 6 a.m. and return home at 6 p.m., at which time the patient prepares dinner. After dinner, they prepare construction materials for two cabins they are building on weekends. The patient reports no personal time, no recreational activities, and feeling pressured to work as hard as her husband. Her job as a middle manager in a large firm requires her to manage contract negotiations between the company and government agencies. Her office is in a large manufacturing plant, with continuous exposure to production noises (e.g., metal saws, riveting) that can interfere with concentration, dust, and debris. The initial referral hypothesis, that her headache problem may be stress related, is supported by: (1) she is working in a physically stressful work environment; (2) she is working in a psychologically stressful work environment; (3) her home environment is stressful; (4) she reports that she experiences pain in her shoulders and face, and difficulties concentrating; and (5) she has no private/personal time or recreation (e.g., family incidence of breast cancer) of concern. As the list is developed, symptoms and signs may cluster under a single diagnosis, hypotheses become better defined, and certain problems may be eliminated as new data are acquired.

Tentative hypotheses generated by the referral question are tested and refined in light of the information obtained from history taking and physical examination. These, in turn, are subjected to verification through the selection of appropriate tests. The clinician should be knowledgeable about the validity and reliability of each potential test to ensure that the selected test measures what needs to be measured, and does so in a consistent, accurate, reproducible, and conceptually meaningful way.

Defining Outcome Goals

Initial diagnostic impressions based on referral questions, history, and examination may rule out some diagnoses but raise questions about others. Further data gathering and laboratory and other tests will produce a limited set of problems and diagnoses. The provider and patient must carefully weigh realistic and attainable *outcome goals* – what is the patient's desired health condition at the conclusion of treatment? Once these goals have been negotiated and agreed to, the provider and patient generate alternative solutions in the form of various treatment modalities.

Clinical Application – Part II

Outcome goals for the patient's defined problems were discussed and agreed to as follows: (1) reduce work environment stress; (2) reduce work-related psychological stress; (3) reduce stress at home; and (4) increase personal/private time and recreation.

Prevention and Early Intervention as Targets of Care

Upon initial examination, some patients may exhibit physical and laboratory findings consistent with imminent or early chronic illness. Careful observation of patients with chronic ill-

ness may reveal significant emotional distress (depression, anxiety) and somatic symptoms that reflect the patient's reaction to his or her medical illness as opposed to a primary psychological disorder. In such cases, the physician should consider prevention or early intervention as a primary goal of treatment. Identification of lifestyle factors such as poor diet, lack of exercise, or somatic complaints such as headache or insomnia should alert the practitioner to add these issues to the problem list with specific consideration about their treatment.

Generating Alternative Treatment Solutions

Given the symptom complaints and diagnosis, what solutions or *intervention strategies* can the patient use to remediate the problem and achieve her outcome goals? The decision-making process focuses on how to (1) modify behavior or cognitions, (2) alter biological functioning, (3) facilitate changes in the environment, and (4) tap social resources. This stage of the decision-making process is critical to eventual treatment outcome. The physician's training and experience, command of a repertoire of treatment alternatives, intellect, clinical reasoning skills, and pragmatic creativity are brought to bear on helping the patient find favorable cost/benefit solutions to the problems inherent in her situation.

Clinical Application – Part III

The provider and patient together decided on the following solutions for each of the patient's outcome goals: (1) develop a scenario for requesting enclosed sound and dust-proof office space; (2) develop a scenario for requesting staff support to cope with government contracts; (3) meet with the patient and her husband to discuss reducing stress at home by limiting the number of evenings devoted to cabin preparation work, and planning one "no work" weekend a month for getting away together; and (4) assist the patient in arranging to attend aerobics class after work two nights a week, and allowing sufficient time for a relaxing bath before bedtime.

Selecting the Best Solution

In developing the treatment plan, the provider must review the defined problems with the patient and together determine the *best methods* for resolving these problems and the order of *priority* in which various problems should be addressed.

Clinical Application – Part IV

The patient decided the home situation was the most critical. Hence, she made the implementation of solutions 3 and 4 top priority. She further decided that because solutions 1 and 2 would require time to develop, prepare, and rehearse, she would take time to give some thought to how to approach her supervisor and plan to do so in about a month.

Implementing the Solution

The treatment plan, thus formulated, is ready to be implemented. The various steps should unfold in logical sequence (i.e., each step setting the stage for the next step). The strategy is to have the treatment course build to a final resolution of the patient's problem.

Clinical Application – Part V

The patient's husband initially failed to see the link between his own behavior and his wife's medical condition. Once aware, however, he became alarmed, concerned, and highly cooperative. He was supportive of her having more personal recreation time and opportunities for relaxation. Both goals 3 and 4 were implemented immediately.

Ending the Clinical Encounter

Before ending the clinical encounter, the provider should review the relevant clinical information, the diagnosis and explanation of the patient's problem, and the mutually agreed upon step-by-step plan for treatment, ending with scheduling the next appointment.

Evaluating the Outcome

The decision about whether treatment has been successful and the outcome goal achieved will be determined by the selection and assessment of appropriate *outcome criteria.* Optimally, outcome criteria should be observable and quantifiable (e.g., symptom reduction, measurable changes in biological function, behavior, or cognition). However, qualitative assessments are also legitimate (e.g., assessing changes in quality of life, feelings of self-control, competency, or perceived intensity of pain). A fully successful outcome, including the resolution of the original problem and the termination of treatment, is the final goal. However, if assessment reveals that treatment has not been successful, the treatment plan must be modified or alternative solutions developed. The revised solutions are then implemented and the outcome again assessed. This "back to the drawing board" process continues until the treatment goals are attained.

Clinical Application – Part VI

Both goals 3 and 4 were achieved for the patient who went to her aerobics class 2 days a week and took a relaxing bath before bedtime each evening. The couple rediscovered their love of walking and bicycling on their monthly weekend holiday. The patient's husband was also helpful in formulating strategies and scenarios for requesting changes in his wife's work situation. Her requests for changes (solutions 1 and 2) were responded to favorably by the company, resulting in a more quiet office, and a part-time assistant to help with contract negotiations. The intensity and frequency of the patient's headaches began to decrease almost immediately, and within 8 weeks after the initial referral she was experiencing only occasional minor headaches.

Sources of Error in Clinical Decision Making

What are eight sources of error in clinical decision making?

1. **The provider's theoretical and personal biases:** interpreting medical information in accordance with personal orientation can distort clinical data. The traditional biomedical model biases judgments toward (a) reduction of clinical phenomena to anatomic structure and biological function; and (b) mind-body dualism, which draws a distinction between the physical and the nonphysical, the observable and the subjective, the material and the spiritual, and the "medical" and the "psychiatric." Cognitive, emotional, and sociocultural factors are not distinct from biological factors in determining disease and illness.

2. **Diagnosis by formula:** trying to fit patients into preconceived categories.

3. **Optimism/pessimism:** the provider's desire to seek the best for the patient may result in explaining problems and their treatment too optimistically. Conversely, fearing litigation, providers may over emphasize the worst case scenario.

4. **Too many hypotheses:** only a limited number of hypotheses can be adequately examined simultaneously. Thus, the provider should systematically rule out the most improbable hypotheses as soon as possible.

5. **Oversimplification:** the provider may assume that all the patient requires is a simple explanation and treatment plan, when, in fact, the patient's concerns are more complex, emotionally based, and resistant to intervention.

6. **Reorganizing the abnormal:** the provider should avoid making personal judgments about the "normal limits" of test values, the behaviors or beliefs of patients from different sociocultural backgrounds, or patients with an unusual genetic history.

7. **Provider-patient interactions:** dislike, distrust, and disdain can breed distortion and defective decisions. Patients who question the physician are sometimes labeled as "crocks" or uneducated. Such attitudes and labels do not promote objective clinical judgment.

8. **Mistaking correlation for causation:** clinical phenomena are rarely straightforward, linear, cause-and-effect processes. Instead, patients live within complex interactive systems (see Chapter 1, Evolving Models of Health Care).

Recommended Readings

Bowen JL. Educational strategies to promote clinical diagnostic reasoning. *New England Journal of Medicine.* 2006; 355:2217–2225.

Epstein RM, Alper BS, Quill TE. Communicating evidence for participatory decision making. *JAMA* 2004; 291:2359–2366.

Gunn W, Blount A. Primary care mental health: A new frontier for psychology. *Journal of Clinical Psychology* 2009; 65:235–252.

Kassirer JP. Teaching clinical reasoning. *Academic Medicine* 2010; 85:1118–1124

Platt FW, Gordon GH. *Field Guide to the Difficult Patient Interview,* 2nd ed. Philadelphia, PA: Lippincott Williams & Wilkins; 2004.

Robinson G. Effective doctor-patient communication: Building bridges and bridging barriers. *Canadian Journal of Neurological Sciences* 2002; 29:S30–32.

Review Questions

1. Which one of the following statements is consistent with the guidelines for protecting confidentiality?
   A. Conduct interviews in a setting where privacy can be maintained.
   B. Hallway discussions are preferable to talking in front of an anxious patient.
   C. Keeping confidentiality overrides any other agreement between patient and physician.
   D. Only family members should have the opportunity to review files without patient consent.
   E. The patient should be protected from knowing who has access to his or her medical record.

2. Which of the following is an open-ended question?
   A. Are you sexually active?
   B. Do you have any questions?
   C. How can I help you this morning?
   D. Where is the pain?
   E. You don't smoke, do you?

3. Of the questions below, which one would you use to begin a clinical encounter?
   A. "Do you get the pain when you eat or when you walk?"

B. "Just give me the short list of your prob-
lems."
C. "What brings you in to see me today?"
D. "Where does it hurt?"
E. "You haven't been drinking, have you?"

4. An assessment of the patient's attention, mem-
ory, orientation, and judgment is part of the
A. examination of the head.
B. mental status examination.
C. past medical history.
D. review of systems.
E. social history.

5. Which of these steps comes first in the clinical
decision-making process?
A. Acting on the proposed solution
B. Defining outcome goals
C. Defining the problem
D. Evaluating the outcome
E. Selecting the best solution

6. The differential diagnosis is a list of
A. all the patient's active and inactive medical
problems.
B. diagnostic possibilities and their probabili-
ties.
C. diagnostic tests to be ordered.
D. reasons the patient is being seen at this
visit.
E. symptoms present for at least 1 month.

7. Which of the following is a type of clinical
reasoning used in making clinical decisions?
A. Abstract
B. Concrete
C. Interpretive
D. Non-analytical
E. Theoretical

Key to review questions: p. 408

36 Motivating Healthy Behavior

Richard Botelho, BMedSci, BMBS

- What are the leading causes of preventable death associated with lifestyle?
- How is the decision balance helpful in promoting behavior change?
- What is the stages of change model?
- What is motivational interviewing?
- How do self-efficacy and outcome expectancy influence behavior change?
- Why are intrinsic motives more effective than extrinsic motives in changing behavior?

What are the leading causes of preventable death associated with lifestyle?

In 2000, almost 50% of the causes of preventable death in the US were related to lifestyle behaviors. Almost a decade later, an international collaborative group determined that deaths attributable to tobacco (467,000) and high blood pressure

Cause of Death in 2000	Number of Deaths	% of Preventable Deaths
Tobacco	435,000	(18.1%)
Poor diet & physical inactivity	400,000	(16.6%)
Alcohol consumption	85,000	(3.5%)
Microbial agents	75,000	(3.1%)
Toxic agents	55,000	(2.3%)
Motor vehicle	43,000	(1.8%)
Firearms	29,000	(1.2%)
Sexual behavior	20,000	(0.8%)
Illicit drug use	17,000	(0.7%)
Total	1,159,000	(48.2%)

(Adapted from: Mokdad, et al. Actual causes of death in the United States: 2000. *JAMA* 2004; 291:1238–1245.)

(395,000) each accounted for one-fifth of all mortality associated with lifestyle. Obesity (216,000) and physical inactivity (191,000) each accounted for one-tenth of preventable deaths. Thus, despite considerable attention being focused on the risks of unhealthy habits in the professional literature and public media, information alone is often insufficient to change a patient's behavior.

Practitioners generally pay limited attention to changing patients' unhealthy habits, other than giving information and advice about their negative consequences, and appealing to patients' rationality and good intentions to pursue healthier lifestyles. Good intentions, like New Years's resolutions, soon dissipate.

Such intentions are usually short lived because the short-term emotional rewards of unhealthy habits (e.g., smoking to relax) outweigh the rational, long-term benefits (e.g., avoiding preventable diseases and living longer). Knowledge of the risks of unhealthy habits and good intentions to change are prerequisite but insufficient to change unhealthy habits for most patients. The traditional "fix-it" health education role of the primary care physician may be sufficient to influence change for the minority of patients who are *ready to change*, but it is only the first of many steps required for the majority of patients who are reluctant or ambivalent about change. In fact, promoting behavior change requires the development of motivational strategies for:

1. Shifting patient perceptions toward healthy change
2. Maximizing the harms and minimizing the benefits of their risk behaviors
3. Minimizing the risks and maximizing the benefits of change
4. Lowering resistance and enhancing patient motivation
5. Enhancing intrinsic motives to change
6. Enhancing patient self-efficacy
7. Addressing discrepancies between what they say and what they do

How is the decision balance helpful in promoting behavior change?

Clinical Application – Part I

Mrs. S., a 45-year-old woman, went to her family physician, Dr. M., for a follow-up to her HIV test. Two years ago, she remarried after being divorced for many years. She had recently moved back to her home town after her husband broke his parole and was returned to jail. Mr. and Mrs. S. had regularly attended an HIV clinic because Mr. S. was HIV positive. Mrs. S. deferred to her husband's wishes to not wear a condom and, fortunately, she remained HIV negative even without practicing safe sex. The doctor at the HIV clinic advised Mrs. S. to have an HIV test done every 3 months. Dr. M. ordered the HIV test and asked her to fill out a *decision balance form* to better understand why she did not want to use condoms. She agreed and provided the following:

Reasons not to use condoms

1. *What are the benefits of not using condoms?*
   - Not make him feel he is failing at being sexually competent
   - He feels secure that I will stay with him

3. *What are your concerns about using condoms?*
   - He will have erection problems and it will make him sad
   - He will wish he were with his ex-girlfriend (who is HIV positive) so he won't have to use them

Reasons to use condoms

2. *What concerns you about not using condoms?*
   - Don't want HIV
   - Don't want my family hurt
   - Maybe people will think he doesn' t care to protect me

4. *What are the benefits of using condoms?*
   - Won't get HIV so won't upset family
   - Won't get sick myself so I can take care of him when he gets sicker
   - Will feel that he cares enough about me and will not allow me to get sick

An effective practitioner acts as a consultant or coach in motivating patients to participate in and take charge of their decision-making process. The practitioner also helps the patient address the targeted health care problem and negotiate the behavioral changes required to address the problem, and then explores the patient's ambivalence by looking at the "pros" and "cons" of the behavior change being considered. To accomplish this task, the practitioner can use the *decision balance* methodology to help the patient explore and clarify issues about the status quo versus change. After completing the decision balance, the practitioner engages the patient in a change dialog to help decide if and when he or she would like to change perceptions about behavior change. This exploratory process helps the patient examine the rational and emotional aspects of the reasons to stay the same (sustain talk) versus the reasons to change (change talk).

Clinical Application– Part II

Assessing resistance and motivation
Dr. M. asked her to use a scale from 0 to 10 (0 = not important, 10 = very important) to rate her reasons for not using condoms. Mrs. S. had a *resistance score* of 9. Dr. M then asked to rate her reasons for using them. She had a *motivation score* of 4.

Assessing thoughts and feelings about change
Mrs. S. stated that her scores were based on her feelings. In other words, she was an *emotional decision maker* on the issue of condom use; her scores represented how she *felt* about change, rather than what she *thought* about it. Dr. M. then asked her to rate her overall reasons to stay the same versus her reasons to change based on what she thought. Mrs. S. had a score of 6 for cognitive resistance and a score of 8 for cognitive motivation. This process helped her to better

understand how much her emotions ruled her decision making. Emotionally, she felt that she should stay the same, but rationally she thought she should protect herself.

Understanding her emotions and values
Looking over her decision balance, Dr. M. said that Mrs. S. must really love her husband. Mrs. S smiled in total agreement and expressed devotion to her husband, stating that she wanted to care for him when he gets terminally ill. Dr. M. asked her how she valued her relationship with her husband in comparison to her own welfare and her relationship with her children. Mrs. S. loved her husband so much that she was willing to sacrifice her life for him, but admitted to having mixed feelings when thinking about her children.

Stages of Change Model

What is the stages of change model?

Typically, patients maximize the benefits of their risk behaviors and minimize the risks. Conversely, practitioners minimize the benefits of the risk behavior and maximize the risks (see Figures 36.1 and 36.2).

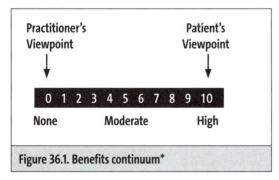
Figure 36.1. Benefits continuum*

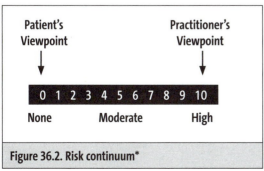
Figure 36.2. Risk continuum*

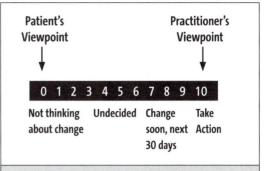
Figure 36.3. Readiness for change continuum*

Given these discrepancies in perceptions, practitioners and patients are often at different stages in terms of their responsiveness to the need to take action. Thus, unless practitioners make appropriate accommodations, they can run the risk of making patients more resistance to change (see Figure 36.3)

The **stages of change model** provides a framework for understanding how patients' perceptions about the pros (motivation) and cons (resistance) of behavior change can shift in favor of healthy change.

In the *precontemplation stage*, the cons (reasons to stay the same) far outweigh the pros (reasons to change). Some precontemplators, such as die-hard smokers, are fully aware of the risks, but disregard them, while others are unaware of the risks (heart disease) of a particular behavior (smoking). In the *contemplation stage*, patients are ambivalent because the strengths of the pros and cons are about the same. For example, many smokers think about quitting for 2 years before making a serious quit attempt. Practitioners can actually help patients reduce duration of the contemplation stage (before they make a seri-

Stages of Change Model

- **Pre-contemplation:** has no intention of changing within the next 6 months
- **Contemplation:** intends to make change within the next 6 months
- **Preparation:** intends to change within the next 30 days
- **Action:** has changed for < 6 months
- **Maintenance:** has changed for > 6 months

ous attempt to quit). In the *preparation stage*, the pros outweigh the cons such that patients are willing to set a date to change within 1 month. In the *action stage*, the pros far outweigh the cons such that patients put their short-term or long-term goals into action. Patients are in the *maintenance stage* when they have achieved their goal for ≥ 6 months. A "lapse" at this stage is a temporary setback, such as smoking a couple of cigarettes over a few days, whereas a "relapse" is complete reversion to a previous pattern of behavior, such as smoking a pack of cigarettes daily. Usually, when patients relapse, they must re-cycle through the change process again.

Clinical Application – Part III

The *stages of change model* facilitates understanding practitioner-patient differences in perceptions about the risk, benefit, and harm of change. Mrs. S. was cognitively in favor of change but emotionally against it. The practitioner did not fall into the trap of responding to her cognitive inclination but responded instead to the emotional factors that were holding Mrs. S. from protecting herself. Dr. M. used motivational interviewing techniques to address Mrs. S.'s ambivalence and shift her perceptions in favor of change.

Motivational Interviewing

What is motivational interviewing?

Motivational interviewing (MI) is "a collaborative, person-centered form of guiding designed to help patients elicit and strengthen motivation for change." Patient motivation is a "change-able" state that is influenced by the nature of the patient-practitioner interaction and the practitioner's interviewing style. An empathic and non-confrontational style can facilitate change whereas a controlling or confrontational style can make patients regress and become more resistant to change. Practitioners use five basic strategies for enhancing the patient's motivation and commitment to change:

1. Expressing empathy through listening rather than telling

2. Identifying discrepancies between where patients are now (i.e., risk behavior) and where they want to be
3. Avoiding argumentation (i.e., trying to convince patients by force of argument)
4. Rolling with the patient resistance rather than challenging it head-on
5. Supporting self-efficacy, instilling hope, and encouraging patients' belief that they can change

Motivational interviewing (MI) is divided into two major phases: (1) *building motivation* to change, and (2) *strengthening commitment* to change. MI techniques include **o**pen-ended questions, **a**ffirmations, **r**eflections and **s**ummaries (OARS). Practitioners can effectively implement OARS by using the spirit of MI. This spirit includes *empathy*, *collaboration*, *autonomy-supportiveness*, *directness*, and *evocation*.

With a non-judgmental, genuine, and positive regard for their patients, practitioners are more likely to empathize with their emotional and cognitive experiences. This collaboration also involves guided decision making with practitioners respecting their patients' autonomy to choose. Practitioners are directive, in terms of advocating for healthy change, but without persuading, coercing, or forcing any commitment. Evocation involves practitioners exploring patient ambivalence about change, with the goal of shifting the dialogue from "sustain talk" to "change talk." Practitioners can elicit change talk about desires, abilities, reasons, and need to change. This strategy can help patients build commitment to change. The amount of change talk within a session can predict patient outcomes.

Clinical Application – Part IV

The practitioner adopted a non-confrontational stance in his interaction with Mrs. S. He empathized with her decision-making process, even though he did not agree with her decision. Rather than confronting her, he "rolled with" (did not challenge) her resistance and began to explore her ambivalence about change, based on how she felt about not using condoms and what she thought about using them.

Enhancing Self-Efficacy

> How do self-efficacy and outcome expectancy influence behavior change?

Self-efficacy is patients' confidence in their ability to achieve a behavioral goal. When patients have low self-efficacy, practitioners seek to boost their confidence in their ability to change through empowerment strategies such as: setting incremental goals with achievable outcomes, identifying and linking patients' strengths and past successes to goals, blocking self-defeating thoughts, and focusing on solutions rather than problems.

Outcome expectancy reflects the patient's belief that a given behavior (e.g., a low-calorie diabetic diet and physical exercise) will produce a particular outcome (e.g., normal glucose levels and weight reduction). Patients may have high self-efficacy about sticking to a low-calorie diabetic diet and exercise program but doubt that these lifestyle changes will produce the desired change (40-lb weight loss and normalized blood glucose levels). Thus, patients with low outcome expectancies may not bother making lifestyle changes, even when they have high self-efficacy.

> **Clinical Application – Part V**
>
> Self-efficacy is a key predictor of behavior change. Mrs. S. knew how to use condoms. She believed that condoms would protect her from getting HIV from her husband, but her reasons for not using condoms reflected her insecurity and low sense of self-efficacy and low outcome expectancy as manifested by fear of losing her husband if she used them.

Motives for Change

> Why are intrinsic motives more effective than extrinsic motives in changing behavior?

A psychosocial assessment can help practitioners and patients appreciate the factors that influence patients' motives to change and their challenges in managing their health care issues. Life circum-

Table 36.1. Motivational principles*

A. Support and respect autonomy
- Invite participation
- Gain consent
- Be non-judgmental
- Offer choice

B. Understand patients' perspective
- Develop empathic relationships
- Clarify roles and responsibilities
- Clarify patients' issues about change
- Work at a pace sensitive to patients' needs
- Understand patients' perceptions, motives, and values

C. Adopt a positive stance
- Focus on strengths rather than weaknesses
- Focus on health rather than pathology
- Focus on solutions rather than problems
- Provide constructive feedback
- Help patients believe in healthy outcomes
- Encourage patients to do emotional work

D. Elicit patients' problem-solving skills
- Enhance patients' confidence and ability
- Increase supports and reduce barriers
- Negotiate reasonable goals for change
- Develop plans to prevent relapses
- Use "failures" as learning opportunities

E. Maintain long-term engagement
- Maintain a learning partnership
- Monitor resistance and motivation
- Negotiate frequency of follow-up
- Adjust goals to changing circumstances

stances can make the change process more challenging as patients generate a blend of motives in response to their stresses, competing priorities, and life circumstances:

- *Indifferent motives* – "I don't care if I live or die." Indifference may be due to factors such as: stress, depression, or environmental or social barriers.

---

* Reproduced with permission from Botelho R. Motivational Practice: Promoting Healthy Habits and Self-Care of Chronic Disease. Rochester, NY: MHH Publications, 2004

- *External (controlled) motives* – "I'm only changing because my family wants me to." A patient may only comply because he does not want to upset his wife or doctor. Relapse may occur when external reinforcement is absent or insufficient to maintain the behavior desired by others.
- *Introjected (controlled) motives* – "I ought to quit smoking." Individuals act out of a sense that they should change their behavior. Outwardly, they appear to have autonomous motives (see below), but inside they feel conflicted because of ambivalence. They initiate and maintain change by internally prompting themselves. Relapse may occur in the absence of such internal reinforcement.
- *Integrated (autonomous) motives* – "I love to exercise. It makes me feel great." With autonomous motives, individuals experience a true sense of volition about their behavioral choice. The initiation and maintenance of behavior change is self-regulated and driven by the patient's values and freely chosen motives, as opposed to being influenced by others.

If practitioners act in autonomy-supportive ways, patients are more likely to develop autonomous motives for change. Conversely, if practitioners act in controlling ways, they are more likely to stifle patients' sense of autonomy and generate indifference or resistance. Paternalism and authoritarianism can make patients feel pressured, resentful, and resistant to change.

Clinical Application – Part VI

Mrs. S. came from an abusive family and suffered from chronic low self-esteem. As an adult, she became an alcoholic and raised her children with her first husband. She divorced, recovered from her alcoholism without treatment, and remarried. Mrs. S. has felt overwhelmed most of her life and has had chronic anxiety and recurrent bouts of depression. She cares for her second husband and was willing to help him until his death from AIDS, but she had little time and energy left to address her own needs.

Mrs. S. was not indifferent about the prospects of getting HIV. She did not want to get AIDS, but did not use condoms, deferring to her husband's wishes. She felt conflicted and knew her children would disapprove,

but she did not tell them about this situation. Mrs. S. lacked self-esteem. Her decision was greatly influenced by her valuing her husband's wishes more than her own health. Her external motives were more powerful than her introjected (controlled) or integrated (autonomous) motives.

Dr. M. asked Mrs. S.'s husband to attend a session to discuss her HIV status but he did not respond. Soon after, Mrs. S. separated from her husband and had an alcoholic relapse for several months following the separation. She stopped drinking without professional help, and became involved with another man who was also HIV positive. This time, however, she insisted on using condoms with her new partner.

Recommended Readings

Alvarom S, Grandes G, Cortada JM, Pombo H, Balague L, Calderon C. Modelling innovative interventions for optimising healthy lifestyle promotion in primary health care: "Prescribe Vida Saludable" Phase I Research Protocol. *BMC Health Services Research* 2009; 9:103.

Johnson BT, Scott-Sheldon LAJ, Carey MP. Meta-synthesis of health behavior change meta-analyses. *American Journal of Public Health* 2010; 100:2193–2198.

Prochaska JJ, Prochaska JO. A review of multiple health behavior change interventions for primary prevention. *American Journal of Lifestyle Medicine* 2011; 5:208–221.

Schwarzer R. Modeling health behavior change: How to predict and modify the adoption and maintenance of health behaviors. *Applied Psychology: An International Review* 2008; 57:1–29.

Online Resources

To join a learning community about health behavior change, go to www.familyandpeerhealthcoaching.com

Review Questions

1. Warning an obese patient about the risks and consequences of an unhealthy diet and lifestyle is generally not effective unless the
   A. health care provider is willing to offer an effective treatment plan.
   B. health care provider specializes in nutritional and life style counseling.
   C. patient has health insurance that covers preventive care.
   D. patient has social support from friends and family.
   E. patient is ready to change his or her behavior.

Directions: The items below consist of lettered headings followed by numbered descriptions. For each numbered description, choose the *one* lettered heading to which it is *most* closely associated. Each lettered heading may be used *once, more than once,* or *not at all.*

In items 2–5, match the scenario with the stage of change
A. Action
B. Contemplation
C. Maintenance
D. Precontemplation
E. Relapse

2. A 29-year-old woman who smokes a pack of cigarettes per day tells her doctor that her grandfather smoked cigars all his life and lived to be 95.
3. A 30-year-old man arrested for a DWI reports he has not had a drink in more than a year.
4. A 40-year-old woman checks herself into a residential detoxification program.
5. A 62-year-old woman who lost 40 lbs in the past 8 months is now down to her target weight of 160 lbs but continues to attend weight watchers meetings.

Key to review questions: p. 408

37 Physician Health, Impairment, and Misconduct

Charles P. Samenow, MD, MPH

- What are the major types of impaired behaviors?
- What are the common traits that predispose physicians to unhealthy behaviors?
- What substances are most commonly abused by physicians?
- What are the most common psychiatric problems found in physicians?
- What physical illnesses can lead to impairment?
- How does physician misconduct differ from physician impairment?
- What responsibility do colleagues have to report an impaired physician?
- What resources are there for the treatment and monitoring of impaired physicians?

Physician Impairment

What are the major types of impaired behaviors?

While *alcohol* and *substance abuse* remain major public health problems among practicing physicians, **impairment** actually encompasses a wide variety of behaviors and conduct. According to the Federation of State Medical Boards' (FSMB) *Essentials of Modern Medical Practice Act* (p. 26):

> Impairment should be defined as the inability of a licensee to practice medicine with reasonable skill and safety by reason of: 1) mental illness; or 2) physical illness or condition, including, but not limited to those illnesses or conditions that would adversely affect cognitive, motor, or perceptual skills; or 3) habitual or excessive use or abuse of drugs defined by law as controlled substances, or of alcohol, or of other substances that impair ability.

Simply having a disability, mental disorder, or alcohol or drug use does not automatically imply impaired physician behavior. In fact, many physicians who are under treatment for such conditions, or who may have mild variants, are known as exceptional practitioners. Rather, the underlying disorder must jeopardize the safety of medical practice to be considered true impairment.

It is believed that 7–12% of practicing physicians are impaired at some point in their careers. About 75% of cases are due to alcohol or drug use. Up to 20% of physicians report impairment due to mental health problems. In many instances, mental health problems and substance use are present as co-morbid conditions. The remaining cases are due to cognitive impairment and physical disability. There has been a rising number of reported cases of behavioral problems (e.g., anger outbursts, sexual harassment, misprescribing controlled substances) that straddle the line between professional misconduct and markers of potentially impaired functioning.

Physician impairment presents a direct risk to patient safety. Furthermore, physicians are valuable human resources deserving of good health and well-being. Finally, the public places great trust in the hands of physicians. Hence, even the appearance of impropriety should be avoided because it detracts from the overall confidence people have in the medical profession.

Risk Factors for Impairment

What are the common traits that predispose physicians to unhealthy behaviors?

Often, traits that the public values most are what place physicians at greatest risk. The public demands *meticulousness* and *perfectionism*. At healthy doses, these traits can lead to exceptional clinical care. However, when these traits are inflated or out of control, they place physicians at risk of isolation and feelings of inadequacy.

Gabbard has defined the compulsive traits among physicians who commonly present with problems as: *self-doubt*, *guilt*, and an *exaggerated sense of responsibility*. These physicians often struggle with rigidity, stubbornness, inability to delegate tasks, and neglect of self and family. Given the complexity of medical systems, and the inevitability of sickness and death, such physicians set themselves up for failure because of unrealistic expectations. Shame, guilt, and feelings of failure can predispose certain physicians to anxiety and depression, which they self-medicate with alcohol and other substances.

Multiple biological, psychological, and social factors can contribute to physician impairment. Similar to the general population, risk factors such as family history, gender, or a history of trauma can predispose a physician to certain psychiatric disorders. There is evidence that those who select a career in medicine may have certain psychological vulnerabilities. The culture of medicine may exacerbate these vulnerabilities by modeling unhealthy behaviors, abusive relationships, and financial, emotional, and physical demands and expectations.

> The question arises whether it is those who enter the profession that are most at risk, or whether it is the training process and professional life that leads to impairment. Most likely it is a complex combination of both.

An important risk factor for physician impairment, particularly depression, is **burnout**. This syndrome is marked by emotional exhaustion, cynicism, ineffectiveness, and depersonalization of relationships. Up to 60% of physicians have reported experiencing burnout during their careers; women appear to be especially at risk. Burnout has been associated with poor health behaviors and changes in practice behaviors such as ordering more tests, writing more prescriptions, having less empathy, and receiving more patient complaints.

Alcohol and Drug Abuse

> ## What substances are most commonly abused by physicians?

The rate of physician *alcohol abuse* and dependence is equal to the general population when matched for age, sex, and socioeconomic status, with an estimated lifetime prevalence of 8–15%. However, physicians are overrepresented in terms of *opiate addiction* and other prescription drugs, probably because they have easier access to these drugs. Substance related disorders cross all medical specialties, although anesthesiologists, emergency medicine physicians, and surgeons tend to have a higher rate of opiate dependence than other physicians.

The use of *psychostimulants* (e.g., amphetamine salts, methylphenidate) is increasing among physicians, particularly trainees. What little data exist suggest that use is mostly situational (e.g., around examinations) and not at a level causing impairment.

Finally, there is increasing recognition of *behavioral addictions* including pathological gambling and sexually compulsive behaviors such as viewing pornography. Both of these behaviors are facilitated by access to the Internet throughout the hospital or in medical offices. In their most severe form, sexual compulsions can lead to *sexual boundary violations*.

Mental Health

> ## What are the most common psychiatric problems found in physicians?

Mental health problems can lead to impairment through multiple mechanisms. *Depression* can lead to difficulty concentrating, inability to complete tasks due to low energy, poor memory, and problematic judgment. *Mania* can lead to distractibility, impulsiveness, irritability, and grandiosity that can compromise patient care and relationships with the health care team.

Recent studies have found that almost 25% of medical students report having been depressed. Among practicing physicians, the rate of depression is similar to the general population. Anxiety disorders are common. Psychotic disorders are less common, probably because the initial presentation of such disorders typically occurs during the second decade of life, and it is unlikely that someone with a serious mental disorder would meet the requirements for admission to medical school.

Suicide

Physicians have an elevated rate of **suicide** compared to the general population. Unlike the general population, where men are more likely to complete suicide, the gender distribution among physicians is approximately equal. This equates to a 4-fold risk for female physicians when compared to the general population. Other risk factors include older age (> 45 years for females, > 50 years for males), Caucasian race, decreased social support, presence of psychiatric or physical illness, and access to lethal means, as well as physician-specific factors such as professional isolation and coping with malpractice suits and licensure investigations. While physician suicide crosses all medical specialties, recent studies report that psychiatrists, anesthesiologists, and general practitioners have the highest rates. Overdose of a prescription drug is the most common method of suicide.

Physical Illness

What physical illnesses can lead to impairment?

In general, *physical illness* does not limit a physician from practicing for prolonged periods of time. Certain illnesses, however, may prevent a physician from practicing safely. Examples include neurological degeneration (e.g., Parkinson disease, multiple sclerosis) or traumatic injuries that affect manual dexterity or cognitive functioning. Of particular concern with the aging workforce is the onset of dementia and other cognitive disorders. Such cases can be particularly difficult to recognize because of physician denial or compensatory behaviors by loyal staff, who may have worked with the physician for years.

Physician Misconduct

How does physician misconduct differ from physician impairment?

Over the past several decades, increasing numbers of physicians have been summoned by medical licensing boards due to disruptive behaviors, misprescribing controlled substances, and sexual boundary violations. Similar to physician impairment, these behaviors stem from a complex interaction of physician factors and environmental factors. While many of these physicians have underlying mental health issues including both Axis I (e.g., depression) and Axis II (e.g., personality disorders) pathology, the profession, to date, has not viewed these as traditional forms of physician impairment.

Disruptive physician behavior is defined by the American Medical Association (AMA) as "Personal conduct, whether verbal or physical, that negatively affects or that potentially may negatively affect patient care." Examples can be verbal (foul, intimidating, belittling, or demeaning language) and non-verbal (facial expressions or other body language). They are classified as aggressive (throwing objects, striking out), passive (chronically late, failure to write chart notes), or passive-aggressive (hostile or inappropriate notes, derogatory comments about colleagues or institutions).

Misprescribing controlled substances is a form of physician misconduct. It may be the result of poor education about pain management or being victim to drug-seeking patients. In other cases, it may be indicative of personality issues (inability to say no), family of origin issues (addiction history), or poor practice organization.

Sexual boundary violations are defined by the AMA as "sexual contact or a romantic relationship concurrent with a physician-patient relationship." Such behavior is considered unethical. Sexual relationships with former patients are also generally unethical but depend on specialty, type of medical encounter, and jurisdiction. The Federation of State Medical Boards (FSMB) subdivides sexual relationships into two categories: *sexual violation* and *sexual impropriety* (see Table 37.1). These behaviors often begin with non-sexual boundary violations such as accepting gifts from patients, engaging in business affairs, and excessive self-disclosure.

Table 37.1. Examples of sexual boundary violations by subtypes	
Sexual Violation	**Sexual Impropriety**
Frank physical contact of a sexual nature: – Oral sex – Penetration – Sexualized kissing – Touching of the breasts or genitals for any purpose other than a clinical exam	Making sexually demeaning comments to or about a patient
	Not using appropriate disrobing or draping techniques
Encouraging the patient to masturbate in front of the physician or masturbation by the physician in front of the patient	Subjecting a patient to intimate examination in front of students without informed consent
	Performing an intimate examination without explaining the need for the examination
Exchanging practice-related services (e.g., drugs) for sexual favors	Requesting details of the sexual history when not clinically indicated
	Using sexually suggestive expressions
	Using the physician-patient relationship to solicit a date
	Discussing personal sexual problems, preferences, or fantasies

Sexual harassment, according to the U.S. Equal Employment Opportunity Commission, is any unwanted and repeated verbal or physical advances, derogatory statements or sexually explicit remarks, or sexually discriminatory comments made by someone in the workplace. Such behavior or comments are considered harassment if the recipient (patient, employee, trainee) is offended or humiliated or job performance suffers. In almost all cases of physician misconduct, it is the physician who is held accountable for the behavior due to the inherent inequity in power in the physician-patient relationship.

Physician misconduct does not only cause potentially serious harm to the physical and mental health of both patients and staff, but it can also cause serious repercussions for the physician including loss of licensure, restriction in practice, loss of relationship, and even public humiliation. While mental health issues may underlie certain unprofessional behaviors, these are usually seen as mitigating factors and areas for rehabilitation as opposed to excuses or reasons not to discipline the physician. A comprehensive evaluation by trained professionals can help determine to what extent misconduct may stem from impairment or a clinical disorder.

Reporting Impaired Colleagues and Unprofessional Conduct

> What responsibility do colleagues have to report an impaired physician?

The AMA is explicit in stating that it is the duty of colleagues to report any suspected impaired behavior. The primary goal is to protect the safety of the public from dangerous clinical practice. With that said, the AMA and other regulatory agencies also recognize the importance of rehabilitation and non-punitive approaches toward foster-

> AMA ETHICAL PRINCIPLE 9.031 – Physicians have an ethical obligation to report impaired, incompetent, and unethical colleagues in accordance with the legal requirements in each state..."
>
> JCAHO MS 2.6 – "Medical Staff implements a process to identify and manage . . . physician health that is separate from Medical Staff disciplinary function."

ing a culture of health and wellness. Hence, both the AMA and The Joint Commission (formerly, the Joint Commission on Accreditation of Healthcare Organizations; JCAHO) require that hospitals have a mechanism in place to detect, handle, and rehabilitate impaired physicians that avoids disciplinary procedures except when absolutely necessary.

Resources for Identification, Treatment, and Monitoring

> What resources are there for the treatment and monitoring of impaired physicians?

Most impaired physicians can return to clinical practice after rehabilitation. In fact, the recovery rate for physicians with substance-related disorders is 85–90%, which far exceeds the general population. Physicians tend to be a highly motivated group and there are multiple incentives that can be used to facilitate recovery, including restriction of clinical practice and licensure, which has serious personal, career, and financial implications.

Most states have professional organizations that can help intervene, refer, advocate for, and monitor impaired physicians. These organizations, known as *physician health programs* (PHP), may be administered by boards of licensure, branches of state medical societies, or independent agencies. A physician who is referred or self-refers to such organizations will generally receive a comprehensive evaluation by an objective multidisciplinary team of individuals who can provide a clinical diagnosis and treatment plan. In some cases, hospital employee assistance programs or physician wellness programs can serve as a referral or monitoring resource.

The physician health program can use the information from the comprehensive exam to refer an impaired physician to a local professional for monitoring and treatment. In the case of a physician with a substance-related problem, this may include *residential treatment* at a program that specializes in treating impaired professionals, followed by *random urine drug screens*, psychotherapy, and participation in a *Caduceus group* (a 12-step recovery program specifically for health care professionals). A physician with mental

health problems may be required to see a psychiatrist or therapist, and to have a *360-degree behavioral evaluation*, which involves colleagues, staff, and sometimes patients providing an anonymous report on the physician's behavior. A physician with physical disability or cognitive impairment may be required to undergo an intensive retraining program to ensure clinical proficiency.

Generally, a physician will sign a 5-year contract to work with a physician health program. By doing this, the physician's medical record and treatment plan remains confidential from the licensing board and employer. The physician health program may advocate on the physician's behalf so that the physician may return to practice as soon as possible and avoid restrictions or other disciplinary action. A physician who is noncompliant with treatment, relapses without seeking help, or demonstrates unsafe behavior will ultimately be reported to the medical board and employer for disciplinary action.

Many physicians fear seeking help because of concerns about their medical career. Physicians in a number of states have challenged questions asked by licensing boards that seem to stigmatize against individuals with mental health problems; some have prevailed in lawsuits under anti-discrimination clauses in the Americans with Disabilities Act. In theory, licensing boards may only ask questions that assess for impairment of function. Hence, a physician who is undergoing treatment or who has had treatment in the past should not be at risk of having his or her license restricted. Finally, given the tremendous success physician health programs have had in assisting physicians to re-enter practice, the risks associated with impairment far outweigh the risks of seeking help.

Physician Health and Patient Care

In recent years, physicians have shown an overall improvement in their own healthy behaviors. They have been found to exercise more, eat better, and smoke less than the general population. Yet, physicians still lag behind the general population in terms of not going to work when sick, having their own personal doctors, and not self-treating rather than seeking professional help.

Instilling healthy behaviors in physicians is important, not only for the individual physician, but for society at large. There are data to suggest that physicians' own health behaviors affect their professional behaviors. Physicians who have better personal health practices tend to recommend better health practices to their patients. Furthermore, patients who perceive that their physician is healthy are more likely to implement healthy lifestyle changes when their doctor recommends them.

Recommended Readings

Knight JR. A 35-year-old physician with opioid dependence. *JAMA* 2004; 292:1351–1357.

Leape LL, Fromsan JA. Problem doctors: Is there a system-level solution? *Annuals of Internal Medicine* 2006; 144:107–115.

McLellan AT, Skipper GS, Campbell M, DuPont RL. Five year outcomes in a cohort study of physicians treated for substance use disorders in the United States. *British Medical Journal* 2008; 4:337.

Myers MF, Gabbard GO. *The Physician as Patient: A Clinical Handbook for Mental Health Professionals*. Washington, DC: American Psychiatric Publishing; 2010.

Papadakis MA, Teherani A, Banach MA, et al. Disciplinary action by medical boards and prior behavior in medical school. *New England Journal of Medicine* 2005; 353:2673–2682.

West CP, Huschka MM, Novotny PJ, et al. Association of perceived medical errors with resident distress and empathy: A prospective longitudinal study. *JAMA* 2006; 296:1071–2078.

Review Questions

1. Which of the following best describes the rates of physician alcohol and drug abuse compared to the general population?
   A. Physicians abuse alcohol and drugs at rates higher than the general population.
   B. Physicians abuse alcohol and drugs at rates lower than the general population.
   C. Physicians abuse alcohol and drugs at rates similar to the general population.
   D. Physicians abuse alcohol at rates higher than the general population, but abuse drugs at rates similar to the general population.
   E. Physicians abuse alcohol at rates similar to the general population, but abuse drugs at rates higher than the general population.

2. Compared to the general population, physicians are at greater risk for which of the following conditions?
   A. Alcohol abuse
   B. Anxiety
   C. Cocaine abuse
   D. Depression
   E. Suicide

3. Which of the following behaviors is an example of sexual violation according to the Federation of State Medical Boards?
   A. Making sexually suggestive comments
   B. Not using proper robing techniques
   C. Performing an unnecessary exam
   D. Touching a patient's genitals outside the physical exam
   E. Using a clinical encounter to solicit a date with a patient

4. Which of the following is a form of physician impairment?
   A. Engaging in sexual relations with a patient
   B. Making sexually suggestive comments to staff
   C. Prescribing too many narcotic drugs
   D. Tremulousness
   E. Yelling profanity at nurses

5. Among the following, which organization can help with the treatment of an impaired physician?
   A. National Practitioner Data Bank
   B. Specialty Society
   C. State Medical Board
   D. State Medical Society
   E. State Physician Health Program

6. What is the relationship between physician health behaviors and medical practice?
   A. Improved personal health habits are only important if a patient is struggling with a similar problem.
   B. Improved personal health habits are only important if patients see that their physician appears healthy.
   C. Improved personal health habits benefit a physician's office staff members the most.

D. Improved personal health habits lead to better health promotion in the clinical setting.

E. While improved personal health habits benefit the physician, they are unrelated to clinical practice.

Key to review questions: p. 408

Section X

Psychopathology

38 Introduction to Psychopathology

Julia Frank, MD

- How are psychiatric syndromes defined?
- What are the five axes of the multiaxial diagnostic system?
- How does diagnosis relate to etiology?
- How are philosophy, medical science, psychoanalysis, and naturalistic observation related to psychopathology?

Diagnosis and Psychopathology

How are psychiatric syndromes defined?

As the scientific study of mental disorders and the factors that influence their onset and natural history, **psychopathology** relies on the assumption that regularly occurring phenomena reflect universal processes rooted in bodily processes and organs. Although some psychopathological phenomena are unique to individuals or to cultural context, many fundamental patterns of dysfunction reflect disordered activity within the executive systems of the body, especially the nervous system and the associated neuroendocrine system. These systems coordinate and regulate mental and physiological functions with the ultimate purpose of meeting challenges to survival.

The modern study of psychopathology grew out of diverse sciences, traditions, and methodologies. The search for a unifying language has prompted contemporary researchers and clinicians to base the characterization of psychopathology on shared observations, without requiring adherence to any particular theory or evidence of an organic footprint. Thus, the current system of diagnosis represents an uneasy and forced consensus that defines psychiatric disorders as *syndromes,* or patterns of symptoms and signs that have a characteristic onset, course, and duration. Descriptive classification offers little insight into the *etiology* or *pathogenesis* of disorders. At its most extreme, diagnosis becomes an end in itself, divorced from

the theories that link causes and effects and permit the development of effective treatment.

A 17-year-old girl has a body mass index of 16.5 kg/m^2. She expresses motivation to stay thin and is unconcerned, even pleased, that she looks emaciated. Her BMI and excessive desire for thinness merit the *diagnosis* of anorexia nervosa, but the term does not provide any information about developmental experiences (bullied? criticized by her parents?), psychological qualities (perfectionism?), social factors (media images of thinness?) or pathophysiology (effects of starvation on thought and behavior?) that may have contributed to the disorder and which could open avenues of treatment.

Multiaxial Diagnostic System

The American Psychiatric Association's (APA) *Diagnostic and Statistical Manual of Mental Disorders*, currently in its fourth edition, text revision (DSM-IV-TR), provides the dominant classification of psychopathology in the US and other industrialized nations. The *International Statistical Classification of Diseases and Related Health Problems* (ICD 10), published by the World Health Organization (WHO), and now in its 10th edition, lists behavioral and mental problems as well as general medical conditions. It is also widely used in the US and in other countries.

The DSM-IV-TR defines syndromes on the basis of observable features. Many DSM categories require that a syndrome be present for a specified period of time (e.g., 2 weeks for major depression; 6 months for schizophrenia) and follow typical patterns (e.g., sudden or gradual onset; persisting, or waxing and waning course). Syndromes fall into domains (mood disorders, anxiety disorders) according to their observable similarities.

The ICD 10 merely lists symptoms, signs, and other justifications for intervention without specifying criteria. Despite these differences, the two systems are generally compatible.

The DSM has been revised three times since 1978 in response to advances in epidemiological and clinical research. The descriptions of psychopathology in this textbook derive from the current version, DSM-IV-TR.

> What are the five axes of the multiaxial diagnostic system?

In DSM-IV-TR, a patient's problems are coded on five axes. Axes I and II cover diagnoses per se. Axes III, IV, and V cover related medical condtions, social factors, and severity.

Axis I: Clinical disorders

Axis I codes for all psychiatric disorders except personality disorders and mental retardation. Defining disorders by their symptoms and course implies that they are superimposed on, rather than reflective of, the fundamental qualities of the person who has them. We say a person *has* an obsessive compulsive disorder, not that the person *is* an obsessive compulsive. By convention the codes of Axis I also cover conditions such as relational problems or bereavement that are not mental disorders, but which may be grounds for treatment by a mental health professional.

Axis II: Personality Disorders and Mental Retardation

The conditions coded on Axis II are assumed to be relatively stable qualities of the individual. Axis

II also codes for maladaptive personality *traits* in persons who do not meet the full criteria for a personality *disorder*.

Axis III: General medical conditions

Axis III codes for medical conditions causally linked to the syndromes coded on Axis I (e.g., anxiety secondary to hyperthyroidism, or delirium secondary to hypoxia). By convention, practitioners also use Axis III to record medical problems that may be stressors or that may constrain treatment (e.g., heart disease that precludes the use of certain medications).

Axis IV: Psychosocial and environmental problems

Axis IV codes for non-medical stressors related to a patient's disorder (e.g., recent loss of a spouse) or social factors that shape the presenting symptoms or may complicate care (e.g., homelessness, social isolation).

Axis V. Global Assessment of Functioning (GAF)

Axis V rates the severity of impairment by assigning a number between 1 and 100 on the Global Assessment of Functioning (GAF), a specific scale that provides anchor points describing general relational, occupational, and academic functioning.

A major revision (*DSM-5*, slated for publication in 2013) may combine Axis I and Axis II, an acknowledgement that the same genetic, developmental, and environmental factors that interact in the genesis of Axis I disorders also contribute to the personality disturbances of Axis II. DSM-IV-TR currently separates disorders of children and adolescents into its own domain, but DSM-5 is likely to remove this division, adding descriptions of adult disorders as they appear in children and adolescents, and putting other childhood disorders into already existing categories.

Syndrome Components

The signs and symptoms that comprise the DSM *syndromes* include both unusual experiences and ones that are normal, but excessive in degree or inappropriate to context. The criteria for a single disorder may include atypical *emotional states* (sadness, anxiety, euphoria, irritability), *thoughts* (helplessness, hopelessness, guilt, low self-esteem, suicidal or aggressive thoughts), *beliefs* (delusions), *perceptions* (hallucinations), *vegetative functions* (sleep, appetite, pleasure), and *patterns of behavior* (avoidance, impulsivity, compulsivity, aggression). To receive a *diagnosis*, the patient's signs and symptoms must fall into characteristic patterns of onset and duration.

Since many individual symptoms (e.g., depressed mood, poor sleep) are not inherently pathological, making a formal diagnosis further requires that the defining symptoms cause significant *functional impairment*. For example, periodically enjoying a few drinks too many does not qualify a person for the diagnosis of alcohol abuse. DSM-IV-TR criteria for that diagnosis specify that the drinking must also cause problems with health, relationships, or occupational function.

The DSM does incorporate some hierarchies. The diagnoses of syndromes "secondary to general medical conditions" and syndromes related to the effects of substances supersede the diagnoses of idiopathic syndromes with identical symptoms. Some syndromes (e.g., "brief psychotic episode") may be a diagnosis per se, or be subsumed within a broader category such as schizophrenia.

Overall, diagnosing a psychiatric disorder depends not only on responding to what a person spontaneously reports as a problem, but also on systematically gathering information about symptoms and behavior. This information must then be matched against specifically stated criteria for a particular disorder, including criteria that specify impairment and involve ruling out medical etiologies.

Relating Diagnosis to Etiology

How does diagnosis relate to etiology?

While the current diagnostic system facilitates research by standardizing patient diagnoses across studies, it overlooks, and can even obscure, important questions of pathogenesis and etiology. Thus, while the DSM achieves reliability (agreement between different observers), it does not necessarily enjoy validity (the degree to which observed syndromes identify and correspond to the mechanisms and processes that produce them). It is the search for these links between diagnosis and etiological factors, rather than diagnosis itself, that both structures meaningful scientific investigation and determines the nature and outcome of treatment.

The ultimate goal of psychopathology should be to relate identifiable dysfunctions to the multiple elements that underlie successful adaptation, and the complex mechanisms by which those factors interact. In section I, we defined an **integrated sciences model** and the diverse domains of variables that may contribute to pathogenesis when adaptation fails. In the following chapters on psychopathology, we focus on applying this model to clinical problems, emphasizing how multiple perspectives go beyond description to contribute a more valid understanding of disorders and underlie the development of effective treatment.

Evolving Models of Psychopathology

How are philosophy, medical science, psychoanalysis, and naturalistic observation related to psychopathology?

Many intellectual disciplines, including religion and moral philosophy, have been concerned with understanding the determinants of human behavior. From the time of **Descartes** in the 1600s until the latter half of the 20th century, the prevailing view ascribed some mental disorders to manifestations of organic disease, but related many others to divine or demonic influence, moral weakness, or social processes (e.g., malevolence and witchcraft).

Such dualistic approaches to behavior have unfortunate consequences. Many mental disorders include experiences and behaviors that escape conscious control or violate social norms, causing the person to act inappropriately towards others because of psychosis, compulsions, or strong impulses. Conceptualized in non-medical terms, these qualities are judged harshly as evidence of sin or weakness, evoking negative **stigma**. Even with a modern, rational approach to mental illness, many psychiatrically disordered individuals experience stigma, being viewed askance or overtly mistreated or rejected by family, prospective employers, and others. Stigma is institutionalized in how the media portray psychiatric problems. Wittingly or unwittingly, medical professionals cannot avoid stigma as they practice in a system that raises barriers between medical and mental health care. The effort to cast mental and behavioral difficulties in strictly medical terms, however imperfect, is in part a compassionate attempt to make disorders less mysterious and reduce stigma by finding common mechanisms underlying normal and abnormal behavior.

Psychoanalysis was the first widely disseminated, systematic, post-Enlightenment attempt to explain subjective human experience and erratic or irrational behavior in scientific terms. Its founder, **Sigmund Freud**, studied neuroembryology and evolutionary science early in his career. His system of explanation involved often unrecognized leaps from verifiable fact (e.g., consciousness represents only a fraction of brain activity) to sheer speculation (e.g., all children develop a conscience by mastering sexual and murderous impulses towards their parents – the "Oedipal complex"). A major weakness of psychoanalysis was its reliance on theoretically driven inferences about the meaning of an analyst's interactions with a small number of patients.

The enduring contributions of psychoanalysis include the recognition that the irrational aspects of human behavior may serve identifiable purposes in stabilizing adaptation and that adult experience is shaped by the person's childhood and adolescence (see Chapter 10, Selected Theories of Development). Freud's focus on the unique human capacity for symbolic thought, so essential to meeting the fundamental demands of adaptation, anticipated many current perspectives of psychopathology and paved the way for the development of **psychotherapy** as a legitimate medical activity.

Taking a more standard medical approach, **Emil Kraepelin** and other late 19th and early 20th century physicians studied the natural history of psychiatric conditions in institutionalized patients. They identified patterns linking bodily

function, behavior, and psychological experience, and described how these patterns changed in predictable ways over time. For example, Kraepelin recognized the cycles of mood that characterize *manic depressive* (now *bipolar*) *disorder*. He and other investigators hoped to correlate observed symptoms with brain pathology found on post mortem examination but lacked methods that could identify the complex genetic, neurochemical, and microscopic derangements contributing to the behavioral patterns they identified. The patterns themselves, however, strongly influenced the current nosology of psychiatric disorders.

A number of mid- and late-20th century psychiatrists, particularly **Adolf Meyer**, and the internist **George Engel**, advocated particular ways of integrating the sciences that explain disordered behavior. Engel's **biopsychosocial model**, presented as an alternative to the biomedical model, calls attention to the many different factors that contribute to psychiatric and medical problems and disorders without laying out in detail how these factors interact. More recently, Phillip Slavney and Paul McHugh have proposed a heuristic scheme they term the *perspectives of psychiatry*, emphasizing *phenomenology* rather than description. They group problems into the clinically relevant domains of *diseases, dimensions of personality*, *goal-directed behaviors*, and *life stories*. Each domain incorporates biological, social and psychological factors that may be the targets of further investigation using modern scientific methods and tools, leading eventually to the adoption of evidence-based (or evidence-informed) approaches to treatment.

Ultimately, the study of psychopathology belongs within the domain of evolutionary scienc-

In studying macaques, Stephen Suomi has demonstrated that when mothers have little need to forage for food, or when food is consistently scarce, their infants form stable attachments. However, under variable foraging conditions, when mothers oscillate between nurturing behavior and finding food, the infants demonstrate endocrine and autonomic signs of stress and unstable attachment (clinging or rejecting behavior). Genetic qualities of both mothers and infants, interacting with environmental conditions, affect the development of behaviors that are primate versions of human psychopathology.

es, in which knowledge of the evolving interaction of genetic, environmental, and social factors explains how behavior evolves over time from its simplest elements.

At the same time, the most sophisticated genetic, tissue, or animal models cannot capture the complex *meanings* that human beings derive from experience and that profoundly influence behavior. Multiple avenues of investigation, ranging from cognitive and social neurosciences to reflective interactions with troubled people, are needed to discern how meaning and disorders of meaning relate to functions of the nervous system, learning, and elements of the surrounding environment and culture.

Recommended Readings

American Psychiatric Association. *The Diagnostic and Statistical Manual-IV-TR* Washington, DC: American Psychiatric Publishing Inc; 2004.

Slavney P, McHugh P. *The Perspectives of Psychiatry,* 2nd ed. Baltimore, MD: John Hopkins University Press; 1998.

Smith R. The biopsychosocial revolution; Interviewing and provider relationships becoming key issues for primary care. *Journal of General Internal Medicine* 2002; 17:309–310.

Stevens HE, Leckman JF, Coplan JD, Suomi SJ. Risk and resilience: Early manipulation of macaque social experience and persistent behavioral and neurophysiological outcomes *Journal of the American Academy of Child and Adolescent Psychiatry* 2009; 48:114–127.

Review Questions

1. A 45-year-old man with well controlled schizophrenia is denied housing because of his history of a mental disorder. This is an example of
   A. a life problem that would be coded on Axis V.
   B. the effect of genetic vulnerability in generating maladaptive behavior.
   C. the functional impairment required for all DSM diagnoses.
   D. the impact of stigma.

2. The main advantage of the DSM-IV-TR over other systems of classification is
   A. its simplicity of application.
   B. its wide availability.
   C. its diagnostic reliability.
   D. its diagnostic validity.

3. The DSM-5 is likely to eliminate distinctions between
   A. child or adolescent and adult forms of disorder.
   B. different cultural expressions of similar disorders.
   C. male and female presentations of particular disorders.
   D. medically related and idiopathic psychiatric disorders.

Key to review questions: p. 408

39 The Psychiatric Evaluation

Julia B. Frank, MD

- Which histories are required to make an accurate diagnosis?
- What are the components of the Mental Status Examination?
- What are three uses for psychological testing in clinical evaluation?
- What is a case formulation?

A complete **psychiatric evaluation** should elicit information needed to make a DSM diagnosis, and to *assess* the person's *risk* for suicide or aggressive behavior, crucial in decisions about whether care should be inpatient or outpatient, and voluntary or involuntary. Evaluation should also bring out information about risk factors, stressors, and exacerbating or mitigating factors, the elements necessary for formulating a treatment approach.

Since making a diagnosis depends on matching the patient's experience to defined criteria, assessment begins with eliciting the patient's concerns. Complete evaluation combines systematic questions with the interviewer's observations of the patient, often supplemented by information obtained from other people. All patients require physical and neurological screening. Laboratory tests may rule out possible contributing medical conditions, but unlike other branches of medicine, they cannot confirm a suspected psychiatric diagnosis.

All clinical psychiatric diagnoses are initially provisional. *Confirming* a diagnosis involves answering five questions:
Is this the right...
1. person (correct age/gender/developmental stage) for this diagnosis?
2. symptom and course constellation (matched to DSM criteria)?
3. backstory (typical developmental history)?
4. family history?
5. response to past or current treatment?

The information elicited should be clearly documented in whatever format the setting requires (paper chart, electronic medical record) to insure communication with other health care providers and justification of care to third-party payers.

History Taking

Which histories are required to make an accurate diagnosis?

History of the Present Illness

It is essential to determine the *onset, quality, duration, intensity,* and *ameliorating, and aggravating factors* of any clinical finding. Regardless of presenting symptom, every patient should be asked about vegetative signs, mood, risk factors for suicide and aggression, and recent behavior. The interviewer also looks for commonly comorbid symptoms (e.g., anxiety in the course of depression). Because psychiatric patients may lack insight and because memory of emotional states is unreliable, soliciting information from someone close to the patient improves the accuracy of diagnosis.

Understanding the sequence and environmental context of symptoms is essential. For example, after 3 months of sleeplessness, sadness, and social withdrawal, a person develops delusions and hallucinations. The sequence makes *major depression with psychotic features* a more likely diagnosis than *schizophrenia.*

Even if the disorder clearly fulfills diagnostic criteria, context is needed to answer the crucial clinical question: "Why now?" For example, when someone presents with signs and symptoms suggesting *major depression* a month after the death of a spouse, *bereavement* is a better description of the person's state than major depressive disorder.

Past psychiatric history should cover previous psychiatric diagnoses and treatment as well as untreated or unrecognized prior episodes of illness. The best predictor of any patient's likely response to treatment is his or her past response.

Other Histories

A *general medical history* reduces the likelihood of missing a physical or substance use disorder that may account for the patient's psychiatric condition. This history reviews current health status, reproductive health, previous illnesses, use of prescribed, over-the-counter, and herbal medicines, and allergies to medication.

Family history provides information about family members with diagnosed mental illness. The goal is both to uncover clues about genetic **predisposition** and to describe patterns of family interaction. Family members' medication responses suggest what drugs might be effective. Information concerning familial behaviors (e.g., poor impulse control, suicidal behavior) can be useful in risk assessment. Familial relationships may be triggers for relapse. For example, in families of people with schizophrenia, high levels of *expressed emotion* or "in-your-face" expressions of negative emotions, especially anger, correlate with frequency and severity of relapses.

Social and developmental histories provide information about the patient's sociocultural context and the experiences, patterns of behavior, social networks, and personality characteristics involved in the *pathogenesis* of the present illness. This history covers past academic and occupational performance and briefly surveys the person's relationships with parents, siblings, friends, colleagues, intimate partners, and children. Other elements are ethnic identification, religious practices and affiliation, legal involvement, and military service. By convention, medically trained people typically include habits – drug, alcohol and tobacco use – in the social history. In a psychiatric evaluation, these may be listed separately or in the history of the present illness. A comprehensive social and developmental history is crucial for recognizing personality disorders, understanding developmental impairments, and assessing the person's resources and resilience.

Mental Status Examination

> What are the components of the Mental Status Examination?

The **Mental Status Examination** (MSE) evaluates the patient's appearance, motor activity, mood and affect, speech and language, thought form and content, perception, capacity for insight and judgment, and cognitive functioning. Although the MSE is reported as a distinct section of the psychiatric evaluation, assessment of the patient's mental status begins during the initial contact and continues throughout the interview.

Appearance

Appearance includes observations of the patient's posture, motor activity, general state of health, body weight, grooming, and dress. Clinical examples include the exhausted demeanor and poor grooming of a severely depressed patient and the odd, eccentric dress of the patient with schizophrenia. General activity level, eye contact, gait, abnormal movements (e.g., *tremors*, *tics*, *dyskinesias*, *choreoathetoid movements*) offer clues to diagnosis and to underlying brain function.

The patient's *body language* offers clues suggesting possible moods, attitudes toward the interviewer, and cultural identification. The patient's attitude toward the examiner may be recorded under appearance or in a separate category.

Mood is a *sustained subjective emotional state as reported by the patient.* Moods that correlate with **limbic system** function, and are most affected in psychiatric disorders, are euphoria/excitement, sadness, worry/fear, anger, and disgust. Some people have little subjective emotion and describe only indifference. **Affect** is an observed emotional state, more immediate and transitory

Mental Status Examination Format

Appearance	Attitude toward the examiner, grooming, appropriateness of dress
Motor behavior	Level of activity, gait, eye contact, body language, abnormal movements
Mood	Patient's subjective emotional state
Affect	Observations of patient's emotional state
Speech & language	Rate, prosody, modulation of tone and volume, articulation, spontaneity
Thought content	Amount of thought, themes, abnormal content (e.g., delusions, obsessions, preoccupations, overvalued ideas)
Thought form	Rate and flow of ideas, organization of thought
Perception	Nature and quality of perceptual disturbances in any of the five senses (illusions and hallucinations)
Insight/ judgment	Nature and quality of insight and judgment
Cognitive functioning	Level of consciousness, attention/ concentration, memory, language functions, calculation, praxis
Risk assessment	Ideation, motivation, intention, and planning of suicidal or violent behavior

than mood. Facial expression and rate and tone (prosody) of speech convey affect, which is rated as being *full range*, *constricted*, *blunted*, or *flat*. The examiner should specifically note *incongruence*, when mood and affect are not consistent with the patient's expressed thought.

Speech and Language

A full psychiatric examination also includes assessing the amount, rate, tone, volume, fluency, articulation, and spontaneity of the patient's speech. Deviations from normal include the slow,

monotonic answers and lack of spontaneity seen in major depression, contrasted with the loud, rapid, difficult-to-interrupt (pressured) speech of mania.

Thought Form and Content

Normal thought is "logical and goal directed," flowing easily from one idea to the next and communicating ideas clearly. Disorders of thought form include *tangentiality* (wandering from a topic), *circumstantiality* (providing excessive detail), rapid jumps from one idea to the next ("*flight of ideas*"), and complete lack of logical connectedness ("*derailment*" or "*loose associations*"). Some patients with psychosis link words by their sounds (*clanging*) rather than their meaning. Others create new words (*neologisms*). More subtle abnormalities include *blocking* (going blank) and *perseveration* (the inability to move from one idea to the next). Many people have mildly disorganized thought that does not seriously impede communication. Significant disorders of thought form are prominent in psychosis, mania, severe depression, delirium, and dementia.

Abnormalities of *thought content* include **rumination** (preoccupation with distressing thoughts, as seen in depression and anxiety), **obsessions** (unwanted concerns, ideas, images, or impulses intruding into consciousness), and **delusions** (false beliefs foreign to the individual's sociocultural or religious background that persist despite evidence to the contrary). Delusions may be *fixed* (unshakeable and consistently present) or *fluctuating* (changing in response to circumstances). They are also rated as *mood congruent* or *incongruent*, *plausible*, or *bizarre*. Schizophrenic delusions are often bizarre such as, for example, belief that an alien force has turned others into robots. Delusions in severe mood disorders may reflect (and justify) the underlying mood. Delusionally depressed patients believe they are poverty stricken, or dying of some unknown disease, or guilty of a terrible crime. *Mood congruent manic delusions* include the belief that one has special powers, can control others, or has unlimited resources.

Perception

Perceptual disturbances occur in any sensory modality. **Illusions** are perceptions that are misinterpreted (e.g., thinking a coat rack is a threatening person). **Hallucinations** are sensory experiences that occur without external stimulation (e.g., hearing voices when no one else is present).

Executive Functions tested on MSE

Insight is subjective awareness and understanding. Judgment is the capacity to organize and manipulate information to make appropriate decisions and regulate behavior. Lack of insight fosters poor judgment, but intact insight does not guarantee good judgment. Many psychiatric conditions impair both insight and judgment.

Cognitive Functioning

Testing cognitive functioning involves inferring the adequacy of patients' orientation, memory, concentration, and capacity for abstraction from how they report their experience, supplemented by standardized probes. It begins with assessment of the patient's level of consciousness or *sensorium.* Patients must be fully alert for cognitive tests to be valid. Fluctuating level of consciousness is the cardinal sign of **delirium**.

Many probes of cognition begin with screening for the integrity of intellectual functions. Patients are asked to tell who they are and where they are, and give the day, date, season, or time of day (*orientation*). They are given the names of 3 objects to repeat (*registration*) and then asked to restate them a few minutes later (*recall*). They perform serial subtractions of 7 from 100 (test of *concentration*), remember increasingly long strings of numbers forward and backward (*digit span*; a test of *attention*), interpret common proverbs (*abstraction*), and describe the best response to particular situations (*judgment*).

The **Folstein Mini Mental State Examination (MMSE)** is a more specific bedside test of cognition. In addition to quantifying orientation, registration, recall, and serial calculations, it screens for **aphasia** by testing the patient's ability to name objects, follow a written command, and write a sentence, **apraxia** (having the patient copy a drawing), and **executive function** by testing sequencing (having the patient follow a three-step command). The MMSE is quantitative and scores have been normed in healthy and clinical populations. It does not facilitate the diagnosis of disorders generally, but it is especially powerful in identifying and following the course of *delirium* and *dementia of the Alzheimer type* and in differentiating these from severe *depression*. A perfect score is 30. Patients who score less than 20 are nearly always delirious or demented.

Beyond beside evaluation, various **psychological test batteries,** administered under carefully standardized conditions, assess cognitive function in more precise detail (see below and Table 39.1).

Table 39.1. Psychological tests		
Test	**General Description**	**Common Uses**
Intelligence or ability tests – Wechsler Scales (WAIS-IV, WISC-IV) – Stanford Binet-5 – Kaufman Scales (KBIT-2)	– Standardized tasks of cognitive abilities that represent "intelligence" – Scales yield an intelligence quotient (IQ), and index scores of major cognitive domains (e.g., verbal, visual, quantitative, sequential reasoning) – IQ & index scores reflect individual's performance compared to others of similar age. IQ 100 is the 50th percentile compared with the general population of age peers; the standard deviation is 15	– Diagnosis and classification of mental retardation and other developmental cognitive disorders – Determination of general cognitive ability to guide treatment planning and disposition – Academic placement and vocational planning – Assessment of cognitive dysfunction due to acquired brain damage/disease (as part of larger neuropsychological battery)

Table 39.1. (continued)

Achievement tests – Wide Range Achievement Test (WRAT4) – Woodcock Johnson-III – Wechsler Individual Achievement Test (WIAT II)	– Tests of academically based skills and knowledge (e.g., reading, spelling, mathematics, written expression) – Scores are typically reported as grade levels and age percentiles	– Diagnosis of learning disability – Academic placement and vocational planning
Neuropsychological tests – Halstead Reitan Battery – Wechsler Memory Scales – Boston Naming Test – Rey Complex Figure Test – Dementia Rating Scale – Verbal Learning Tests	– Standardized tests of memory, language, attention, concentration, spatial abilities, sensory/motor integrity, and frontal executive functions – Administered as a fixed battery or tailored to the purpose of an assessment – Scores reported as age percentiles, index scores, or impairment index	– Assessment of cognitive dysfunction due to acquired brain damage or disease for diagnosis or treatment planning – Assessment of developmental cognitive disorders for academic and vocational planning
Objective tests of personality and psychopathology – MMPI-2 – MCMI-III – Beck Depression Inventory (BDI-II) – Beck Anxiety Inventory – State-Trait Anxiety – Symptom Checklist-90-R	– Assess emotional states, attitudes, behavioral traits/tendencies, interpersonal relations, motivation, and presence/severity of psychopathology – Standardized questions and response options (e.g., true-false or structured ratings) – Self-report tests subject to response bias (e.g., social desirability, symptom exaggeration, defensiveness) – MMPI-2 and MCMI-III include validity scales to determine test-taking attitudes	– Assessment of personality structure and presence or severity of psychopathology — Screening for psychopathology (e.g., mood or anxiety disorders) – Assessment of malingering or symptom exaggeration
Projective tests of personality and psychopathology – Rorschach Test – Thematic Apperception Test – Projective Drawings – Sentence Completion	– Use of ambiguous test stimuli to assess unconscious motives, feelings, or response tendencies – Based on the *projective hypothesis* that response to an ambiguous stimulus will be a projection of person's perceptual style, feelings, thoughts, attitudes, desires, experiences, problem-solving skills, and needs – Subjectivity in interpretation limits reliability and validity	– Diagnosis of psychopathology – Assessment of emotional needs, reality testing, organization of thought, and attitudes regarding interpersonal relationships

Risk Assessment

Every evaluation should include assessment of *risk of harm* to or by the patient (e.g., suicide or violence). Conditions such as major depression, psychosis, and intoxication are particularly associated with high-risk behavior. Assessment involves directly questioning the patient about *feelings*, *attitudes*, *ideas*, *motives*, and *intentions* to harm self or others. It is also essential to ascertain whether the patient has means and opportunity to execute the behavior and the extent of planning that the patient has already done. Because past behavior is the best predictor of future behavior, impulse control and past suicidal or violent behavior must be explored. A family history of poor impulse control, suicide, or violence increases the patient's risk of carrying out a violent act (see Chapter 26, Interpersonal Violence, and Chapter 28, Suicide).

Physical and Neurological Examinations including Laboratory Tests

Examiners must consider neurological and endocrine disorders, and toxic metabolic states (including drug intoxication) that mimic psychiatric disorders. Blood or urine tests can uncover or rule out possible endocrine or metabolic factors and identify conditions that constrain pharmacological treatment (e.g., renal impairment may contraindicate the use of lithium).

Functional neuroimaging (fMRI, SPECT, and PET scans) are commonly used in research but only rarely in general psychiatric assessments. When a neurological lesion is suspected (e.g., when an adult develops epilepsy or when depression or mania begins after head injury), magnetic resonance imaging (MRI) is the imaging study of choice. MRIs can reveal masses, vascular abnormalities, and inflammatory or demyelinating processes that may cause psychiatric symptoms. Other typical research methods, including studies of *sleep architecture* (sleep EEG) and genetic testing, may answer specific questions in selected patients.

Psychological Testing

Various psychological tests (see Table 39.1) measure emotions, cognition, behaviors, and personality characteristics. Tests are designed to ensure that they measure what they purport to measure (*validity*) and that they do so consistently (*reliability*). Each test has operating characteristics (*psychometric properties*) defined by specificity, sensitivity, and standard measurements of error. Formal psychological tests should be performed and interpreted by licensed psychologists trained in test selection, administration, and interpretation.

> What are three uses for psychological testing in clinical evaluation?

A full battery of psychological testing is expensive and time consuming. It is used strategically to define/refine a *diagnosis* in cases with ambiguous symptoms. For example, a patient with a history of poor school and social performance may also exhibit odd speech, incongruent affect, disturbed behavior, and preoccupation with idiosyncratic religious ideas. Psychological testing could determine this patient's level of intellectual functioning and clarify whether findings reflect mental retardation/developmental disability, personality disorder, or psychosis.

Psychological testing is also used to define a *baseline* or to follow *change over time*. Neuropsychological measurement of cognitive functioning after head injury may be compared to previous testing done in academic settings. Repeated testing at set intervals identifies progress during the course of rehabilitation.

Psychological tests are also used in *screening* to determine whether a given patient is likely to have a particular mental disorder. Screening tools range from lengthy tests requiring expert interpretation (e.g., personality inventories such as the Minnesota Multiphasic Personality Inventory [MMPI]) to simple checklists (e.g., Beck Depression Inventory, Symptom Checklist [SCL 90]) – Revised; Alcohol Use Disorders Identification Test [AUDIT]) that take little time and may be self administered. Many screening tools (e.g., the Patient Health Questionnaire [PHQ 9] or PRIME MD) have been modified for use in primary care settings. All require follow up questioning to confirm or refute the suggested diagnosis.

Case Formulation

What is a case formulation?

A *case formulation* represents a concise summary of the biological, psychological, and social factors that account for the patient's development of a clinical psychiatric disorder, and provides the basis for decisions about treatment.

> Mrs. R. is a 58-year-old married woman with diabetes who has symptoms of a major depressive episode with anxiety.
>
> Mrs. R.'s family history of depression (mother and sister) suggests genetic predisposition. Periods of hypoglycemia may be contributing to her anxiety. She has disturbed sleep and tearfulness, presumably reflecting an imbalance of neurotransmitter activity. She was abused as a child and now describes longstanding low self-esteem and difficulty making friends. Her recent retirement and move to a new city where she feels isolated have precipitated this episode.
>
> She would benefit from intensive outpatient treatment, including an antidepressant and either individual or group psychotherapy. Consulting an internist about her hypoglycemia is also recommended.

Recommended Readings

American Psychiatric Association. *Practice Guidelines. Psychiatric Evaluation of Adults*, 2nd ed. 2006. Available online at psychiatryonline.org/content.aspx?bookid=28&sectionid=2021669

Campbell WH, Rohrbaugh RM. *The Biopsychosocial Formulation Manual: A Guide for Mental Health Professionals* New York: Routledge; 2006.

Review Questions

1. A 28-year-old former Marine Sergeant who fought in Iraq is being seen for what his wife describes as a change in personality after a closed head injury. Although he was typically cheerful, optimistic and energetic, he is now lethargic, apathetic, and irritable. He complains of difficulty with concentration and poor memory, but is able to work at his present job as a stock clerk. The most useful approach to further evaluation would be
   A. assessing response to trial of medication.
   B. obtaining more history from other relatives.
   C. ordering functional neuroimaging.
   D. requesting psychological testing.
   E. reviewing military records.

2. A 20-year-old woman who seems excited and unrealistic in her thinking is brought to the Emergency Department after making a scene in a department store. She denies that she has any problems and asks to be discharged. The next step in her evaluation should be to
   A. administer medication and re-interview her when she is calmer.
   B. obtain information about her from a family member.
   C. order a brain scan.
   D. request psychological testing.
   E. request records from the security guards.

3. The Folstein Mini Mental Status Examination screens for which of the following conditions?
   A. Cognitive impairment
   B. Movement disorders
   C. Personality disorders
   D. Psychotic symptoms
   E. Risk of violence or suicide

4. Among the following, the neuroimaging study that is most sensitive in the evaluation of patients with psychiatric complaints is
   A. computerized axial tomography.
   B. magnetic resonance imaging.
   C. positron emission tomography.
   D. single photon emission computed tomography.
   E. Ventriculography.

Key to review questions: p. 408

40 Principles of Psychotherapy

Julia B. Frank, MD, and John E. Carr, PhD

- What is psychotherapy?
- Who provides psychotherapy?
- What distinguishes first-, second-, and third-generation psychotherapies?
- Which therapies are empirically validated?
- What are the components of the therapeutic alliance?

What is psychotherapy?

The unique evolutionary development of the human brain's facilitation of social processes enabled *Homo sapiens* to collaborate, communicate, and adapt in order to survive as a species (see Chapter 9, Cognition and Social Interaction). Humans' extraordinary capacities for understanding, supporting, nurturing, teaching, and caring for one another foster attachments, affiliative relationships, empathy, and communication more sophisticated and complex than those of any other species. Since the dawn of recorded history, affiliative and empathic relationships have been essential tools in every health care system, including modern medicine. As medical science applies the knowledge of biological processes to the development of biological interventions to restore health, so do the neurosciences, psychology, and other behavioral sciences apply knowledge of intra- and interpersonal processes to the development of social and behavioral interventions that improve general adaptation and enhance individual well-being or even survival.

Human societies typically create roles and methods for certain members to apply the interpersonal elements of healing to relieve distress or disability in other members. Psychotherapy constitutes a specialized form of interpersonal helping relationship offered to individuals with impaired adaptive functioning, typically attributable to diagnosable psychiatric or behavioral disorders.

Who provides psychotherapy?

Psychotherapy is provided by professionals who are highly trained in the use of specialized interpersonal skills.

The accrediting bodies for clinical psychologists, psychiatrists, psychiatric social workers, and psychiatric nurse practitioners all require postgraduate training for general expertise in psychotherapy. Addiction specialists, pastoral counselors, and various other licensed professional counselors are trained in therapeutic skills but target more specific issues or populations.

While accrediting bodies promote high standards for training, studies have shown that formal training in mental health has only a limited effect on outcome. Research on "placebo effects" and "non-specific factors" in psychotherapy has revealed that essential components of effective psychotherapy include the therapist's capacity for accurate empathy, genuineness, respect for the patient, and interpersonal skills. These skills are the core principles of the provider-patient relationship in all health care settings.

Evolution of Psychotherapeutic Systems

What distinguishes first-, second-, and third-generation psychotherapies?

All systems of psychotherapy are based on developmental, psychological, interpersonal, behavioral, and existential or humanistic concepts and principles. Beginning with psychoanalysis, contemporary psychotherapeutic systems reflect the evolution of theories of psychopathology and efforts to understand how "normal" human functioning can go awry. In the evolution of these therapies, we identify three stages of development: *first-generation therapies* that represent the foundations from which subsequent therapies generally derive; *second-generation therapies* whose procedural innovations reflect conceptual advances in the underlying theories; and *third-generation therapies* that integrate elements of the major therapeutic systems into new, innovative, and complex amalgams of empirically validated treatments.

First-Generation Therapies

Psychodynamic psychotherapy, derived from **psychoanalysis**, is based on the concept that much of a patient's behavior reflects unconscious processes influenced by childhood experiences. To uncover these processes, psychodynamic treatment typically encourages patients to talk freely about their distress, symptoms, inability to achieve psychologically important goals, self-defeating behaviors, or failures to adapt (see Table

40.1). The therapist looks for patterns of interactions between the patient and others, including the therapist, that derive from the person's early experience (**transference**), and evidence that the patient is using unconscious psychological operations (**psychological defenses**) in ways that impair adaptive coping. Therapists help patients identify past failed efforts, modify them, and develop more realistic, present-focused ways of understanding and reacting to their life circumstances. Although therapists often withhold direct advice, they encourage patients to make behavioral experiments to identify coping strategies, effective or not, and to test and reflect on new ones.

Behavioral Therapy

While researchers explored the clinical application of behavioral techniques as early as the 1920s, **behavioral therapy** emerged as a significant therapeutic modality in the early 1950s. Behavioral therapies apply learning theory, especially the role of classical and operant conditioning in acquiring and modifying maladaptive behavior (see Chapter 8, Emotion and Learning).

Behavioral therapy techniques target specific maladaptive behaviors, identifying the stimuli or cues that trigger the behavior, and directing patients to make the behavioral changes required to achieve a more adaptive outcome.

Table 40.1. Elements of psychodynamic psychotherapy

- Focus on affect and underlying emotion
- Exploration of avoidance of distress
- Identification of recurring themes
- Discussion of past experience as shaper of the present
- Focus on relationships
- Attention to therapeutic relationship
- Acceptance and exploration of fantasies, dreams, desires, and fears

Adapted from Shedler (2010) and reprinted with permission from Wells, LA and Frank, JB. Psychodynamic Psychotherapy: *From Psychoanalytic Arrogance to Evidence Based Modesty.* In Alarcon RD and Frank JB (Eds.), *The Psychotherapy of Hope;* 2012. © 2012 John Hopkins University Press. See Recommended Readings.

Second-Generation Therapies

Gestalt Therapy

Gestalt therapy originated in the late 1940s in part as a reaction to the extensive exploration of the unconscious and the past that characterized psychodynamic therapy. Experiential/humanistic in nature, it focuses more on the immediate life experience of the individual and emphasizes subjectively feeling and objectively observing experience without interpretation. Such focused awareness on how a person experiences a situation and how he or she reacts to it *(mindfulness)* fosters insight, similar to that achieved in psychodynamic therapy. Change is encouraged by experimenting, through dialogue and behavior, with different approaches to a situation. In a sense, Gestalt therapy is an existential or phenomenological behaviorism that recognizes the influence of cognition on behavior but focuses on behavioral experience as the source of change.

Client-Centered Therapy

In the early 1950s, **Carl Rogers** developed **client-centered therapy**, calling attention to the importance of the therapist-client relationship. He was among the first to identify essential qualities of an effective therapist: *congruence* (i.e., authenticity, genuineness), *respect* for the client, and *empathy*. Rogerian therapists demonstrate empathy through reflective, non-judgmental responses to clients' self disclosures. Rogers followers later emphasized the importance of "accurate" empathy, modifying the technique to stress that therapists should communicate their understanding to the client, and that the client should confirm the therapist's understanding.

Cognitive Therapy

Psychology in the 1950s stressed the importance of cognitive processes in influencing behavior. In developing **Rational Emotive Therapy** (RET), Albert Ellis affirmed that how an individual responded to a stimulus or challenging event depended upon the individual's conscious beliefs about such events. If those beliefs were distorted, then the respondent's behavior would be maladaptive. Thus, RET focuses upon identifying and correcting distorted belief systems through encouraging and teaching patients to make rational choices about more adaptive beliefs and behaviors.

In the early 1960s, Aaron Beck developed **cognitive therapy**, which also focuses on the influence of cognition on behavior, specifically, distorted beliefs about oneself, the present, and the future. Cognitive research suggested that patients with different disorders manifested distortions in different belief systems or *schema*. Treatment teaches the patient to recognize and correct distorted cognitions that contribute to maladaptive social relations and dysfunctional behavior. Beck and his colleagues played a major role in the development of standardized treatment protocols and the establishment of cognitive therapy as an empirically supported treatment modality.

Cognitive Behavioral Therapy

Cognitive behavioral therapy (CBT) represents an integration of cognitive and behavioral therapeutic modalities. The underlying theory posits a circular process in which distorted beliefs (**cognitions**) and ways of thinking (**schema**) impair coping ability so that distressing symptoms persist, resulting in dysfunctional and maladaptive behaviors. For example, people who are depressed make inaccurate *appraisals* of the challenges they face, systematically underestimating their ability to handle stress, over-personalizing negative information, and making negative assumptions about the future and significant others in their lives. These inaccurate appraisals lead to *maladaptive coping behavior* and *dysfunctional social relations*, which become self-fulfilling prophecies that then contribute to the persistence of the person's depressed mood. The therapist explicitly helps the person to recognize distorted thinking, more accurately appraise situations and relationships, and learn from behavioral experience by trying out new strategies and behaviors. After evaluating the outcome, the individual further modifies cognitions/behaviors as needed.

Which therapies are empirically validated?

Interpersonal Psychotherapy

Interpersonal psychotherapy (IPT), initially developed as a treatment for depressive disorders, evolved from psychodynamic therapy, but focuses less on past experiences and more upon current

> The focus of CBT on targeted problems, the specific situations in which they occur, and the factors that determine them has led to the development of many variants. Each approach is standardized and designed to address a specific disorder, syndrome, or patient population. Since so many CBT variants are "manualized" and involve detailed data collection, they readily lend themselves to clinical investigation. As a result, statistical and quantitative research provides stronger evidence for the effectiveness of CBT, when comparing it to psychotherapies applying more variable techniques to less well defined problems.

social relationships as factors that precipitate and sustain depression. Like CBT, IPT is a targeted and short-term treatment that has been manualized for research purposes. IPT directs patients' attention to one of four interpersonal crises: loss, social conflict, role transitions (job change, graduation, becoming a parent), or developmental deficits (inability to establish appropriate relationships). Extensive, well controlled research studies support the efficacy of IPT for the treatment of mild to moderate depression, bulimia nervosa, and several other conditions.

Third-Generation Therapies

The standardized protocols of second-generation therapies readily lend themselves to investigations of which elements are effective and essential to successful outcome, and which are not. Such transparency allows clinicians and researchers to integrate theories and elements of different treatments into new, eclectic approaches meant to maximize the benefits of therapy. Dialectical behavior therapy and the cognitive behavioral analysis system of psychotherapy are two examples of such integrated approaches.

Dialectical Behavior Therapy

Developed by Marsha Linehan, **dialectical behavior therapy** (DBT) applies methods of CBT to the treatment of suicidal or self-injurying people, typically those diagnosed as having **borderline personality disorder**. Linehan incorporated concepts and methods from multiple modalities to target specific maladaptive practices or dysfunctions in this population. DBT emphasizes that *acceptance*, defined as respect for the patient's perspective and experience, is essential. The therapist does not need to agree with the patient's perspective, but does need to *empathically understand* what the patient is experiencing and why. Fostering change is a *dialectical process* in which discussion, reflection, and accommodation may transform the patient's views of self and others. DBT helps patients to: (1) develop self control, (2) experience and tolerate emotion (*mindfulness*), (3) solve problems, (4) accurately infer the emotions and motives of others (*mentalize*), and (5) enlist these skills in further existential development.

The techniques are used within multiple contexts (e.g., individual therapy sessions, skills training groups, and phone coaching in emergent situations). Research has shown DBT to be an effective treatment system for its target population and has prompted researchers to examine its applicability in other disorders.

Cognitive Behavioral Analysis System of Psychotherapy (CBASP)

In the 1980s, James McCullough developed the CBASP approach for the treatment of chronic depression incorporating psychodynamic, IPT, and CBT concepts and methodologies. McCullough targeted the interpersonal dysfunction of the chronically depressed individual as the focus for intervention. The therapist encourages patients to review past significant transference relationships to uncover the sources of deviant and maladaptive interpretations (cognitions) of events and beliefs about significant others. Focusing on here-and-now social interactions, patients are trained to (1) assess social interactions more objectively, (2) distinguish between maladaptive and adaptive interpretations, (3) identify maladaptive and adaptive behavioral responses, (4) explore realistic and unrealistic expectations about the outcome of social interactions, and (5) learn from the analytic process in order to modify future behavior.

In a major multi-site, double blind study comparing CBASP and an antidepressant medication, both were effective alone (52–55% improvement), but their combination yielded a much higher improvement rate (85%). This finding has stimulated further research on combination therapies and the mechanisms of bio-behavioral interaction in the treatment of depressive disorders.

Components of the Therapeutic Alliance

What are the components of the therapeutic alliance?

While psychodynamic, cognitive behavioral, and interpersonal therapists may view themselves as different, research into the outcome of psychotherapy consistently finds that these and other variants all induce similar improvements. This finding is known as the *equal outcomes phenomenon.* It has prompted investigation into what actually contributes to successful outcomes in psychotherapy.

According to Wampold (see Recommended Readings), the answer to that question depends upon the model of health care upon which the research is based. The model, in turn, determines which outcomes are measured.

A *medical model* assumes that specific actions in specific therapies are necessary to produce specific results. Research based on the medical model, therefore, tends to favor therapies such as CBT and IPT.

In contrast, a *contextual model* assumes that the healing context (the therapist's confidence and the patient's belief in the treatment, the therapist-patient relationship, the rationale for the treatment and actions consistent with that rationale, and the meaning the patient attributes to the therapy) are critical. Wampold reviewed the research evidence related to absolute efficacy, relative efficacy of different methods, specificity of components, effects due to common factors, effects due to adherence, and differential therapist effects, and concluded that, in each case, the evidence supported a contextual model rather than a medical model.

Overall, the most consistent findings in psychotherapy research have been that the efficacy of any psychotherapeutic modality is dependent upon a strong **therapeutic alliance** that derives from (1) *conceptual compatibility* between the patient and the therapist, thereby facilitating communication and collaboration; (2) the patient's feeling *respected* without judgment, by a (3) caring, *empathic, genuine* therapist, and (4) the therapist's skill in using *empirically validated therapeutic tools*. These qualities instill *hope* and foster patients' *self-efficacy* or sense of *mastery*, two other factors critical to successful outcome (see Frank and Frank, 1991, Recommended Readings). These characteristics constitute the fundamental requirements of an effective therapist-patient relationship, whether between a mental health specialist and psychiatric patient or between a primary care physician and a general medical patient.

Recommended Readings

Alarcon RD, Frank JB. *The Psychotherapy of Hope: The Legacy of Persuasion and Healing.* Baltimore, MD: Johns Hopkins University Press; 2012.

Elkin I, Shea MT, Watkins JT, et al. National Institute of Mental Health Treatment of Depression Collaborative Research Program. General effectiveness of treatments. *Archives of General Psychiatry* 1989; 46:971–982.

Frank JD, Frank JB. *Persuasion and Healing: A Comparative Study of Psychotherapy.* Baltimore, MD: John Hopkins University Press; 1991.

Leichsenring F, Rabung S. Effectiveness of long-term psychodynamic psychotherapy: A meta-analysis. *JAMA* 2008; 300:1551–1565.

Roth A, Fonagy P. *What Works for Whom? A Critical Review of Psychotherapy Research.* New York: Guilford Press; 2005.

Shedler J. The efficacy of psychodynamic psychotherapy. *American Psychologist* 2010; 65:98–109.

Wampold BE. *The Great Psychotherapy Debate: Models, Methods, and Findings.* Mahwah, NJ: Lawrence Erlbaum Associates; 2001.

Review Questions

1. A therapist treating a depressed man gives him a daily homework assignment to record his thoughts about doing a pleasurable activity, do the activity, and record his reactions. This therapist is using
   A. cognitive behavioral psychotherapy.
   B. existential psychotherapy.
   C. psychodynamic psychotherapy.
   D. interpersonal psychotherapy.
   E. strict behavioral psychotherapy.

2. An otherwise healthy woman consults a physician because of insomnia related to a tendency to brood over disappointments and past mistakes. In recommending psychotherapy, the physician should stress that she should see a therapist
   A. of her own gender.
   B. who inspires trust and demonstrates understanding.
   C. who will focus on behavioral change.
   D. who will focus on family relationships.
   E. with training in a particular discipline.

3. The capacity to be therapeutic with patients seems to deteriorate during the course of gen-

eral medical education. This deterioration may reflect an educational approach that stresses

A. the importance of adopting a theory that explains distress in terms that make sense to the patient.
B. considering multiple contributors to a dysfunctional state.
C. focusing solely on the objective realities of a disease.
D. having a diverse medical workforce.
E. respecting patient confidentiality.

Key to review questions: p. 408

41 Pharmacological Interventions for Psychiatric Disorders

Julia B. Frank, MD

- What are the main types of psychotropic drugs?
- What is the response latency of a drug?
- What is the therapeutic index of a drug?
- What are the ethical issues associated with psychopharmacological treatment?
- Can pharmacological and non-pharmacological treatments be combined?

Psychotropic Medications

Psychotropic drugs are those that target the mind, systematically changing thought or emotion. The first modern psychotropics were drugs given for other conditions that coincidentally modified psychiatric symptoms. The tuberculosis drug isoniazid, for example, was found to relieve depression, and the adjunctive anesthetic chlorpromazine also suppressed hallucinations and other psychotic symptoms. These unexpected effects of drugs have focused attention on disordered brain activity in mental disorders, but our knowledge of pathogenesis remains too rudimentary to explain fully the actions of commonly prescribed medications. **Rational pharmacology**, developing a drug based on understanding the pathophysiology of a disorder, is an unmet goal for psychiatry. With a few exceptions, *empirical remedies*, backed by systematic study of pharmacological mechanisms and treatment outcome, form the basis of psychopharmacology.

What are the main types of psychotropic drugs?

Psychotropic drugs are classified by their **chemical structure** (e.g., tricyclics, phenothiazines, opiates), by the symptoms they target (e.g., **antidepressants, antipsychotics, anxiolytics, mood stabilizers, sedative hypnotics, stimulants**), or by some element of their mechanism of action (e.g., **selective serotonin reuptake inhibitors** or **SSRIs, dopaminergics**). Classifying drugs by target, though clinically useful, may be misleading because drugs that target one symptom may coincidentally modify others, both positively and negatively. Antidepressants, for example, both relieve and exacerbate anxiety. Antipsychotics typically relieve anxiety but may induce severe dysphoria. Each clinical grouping includes drugs from different chemical classes and some drugs fall into several classes.

The majority of prescriptions for psychotropic drugs are written by non-specialists, especially primary care clinicians. Providers in all specialties receive training in basic pharmacology, covering the chemical properties and mechanisms of action, absorption, distribution, metabolism, half life and excretion, toxicity, and the positive and adverse effects of a drug throughout the body. While this chapter focuses on more clinical issues, such basic understanding is important, particularly since many psychotropic drugs are prescribed "off label." Therefore, responsible prescribers need to be fully aware of the research literature or clinical evidence when prescribing a drug not certified by the FDA for use for a particular condition. Note: *None of the material in this chapter should be taken as advice to prescribe a particular drug for a particular patient or condition.*

Antidepressants

What is the response latency of a drug?

The 25 currently available antidepressants fall into seven classes (see Table 41.1). The choice of an antidepressant (or any drug) for a particular patient depends on the target symptoms, medical contraindications such as allergy, acceptability, and safety. Older antidepressants such as the tricyclics are about as effective as newer agents but have more troubling side effects. The major advantage of the most commonly prescribed antidepressants, the *SSRIs*, is that they are not lethal in overdose. The *dual acting agents* that block the reuptake of both serotonin and norepinephrine (SNRIS) fall between tricyclics and SSRIs in terms of both safety and side effects. These drugs help some people who do not respond to SSRIs.

Response latency characterizes all antidepressants. They must be taken consistently for several weeks before the response can be differentiated from a **placebo** response or clear non response. This highlights the importance of *measurement based care* where clinicians record patients' symptoms over time, with reliable and valid instruments used in research on the drug in question. Patients have difficulty accurately reporting symptoms retrospectively over periods longer than a few weeks. Thus, having patients or clinicians regularly fill out a depression rating scale (e.g., the self-reported *Beck Depression Inventory II* or *Patient Health Questionnaire* [PHQ 9] or the clinician-rated *Hamilton Depression Scale*) helps define the level of response and leads to more appropriate management decisions. Trials of different medications may be needed to identify the most effective, best tolerated medication(s) for a given patient.

Patients who respond to an antidepressant should continue on it for 4–6 months. Premature discontinuation can result in relapse. Because some patients take antidepressants indefinitely, concern for side effects and long-term consequences (e.g., weight gain) becomes important in the management of depression and other chronic conditions.

Antipsychotic Medications

The accidental discovery that *chlorpromazine* relieves some psychotic symptoms revolutionized psychiatry. Since this drug blocks **dopamine receptors** (DA) in the **nigrostriatal pathway** between the **basal ganglia** and the **prefrontal cortex**, many assumed that dopamine blockade was a necessary mechanism for all antipsychotic drugs (see Chapter 48, Schizophrenia and Other Psychotic Disorders). In the normal brain, DA and **acetylcholine** (ACh) counterbalance each other. Unfortunately, drugs that block DA activity can lead to motor dysfunction mimicking the symptoms of Parkinson disease (*extrapyramidal side effects*, or EPSE), or "drug induced *Parkinsonism*." This negative drug effect can be partially buffered by *anticholinergic* drugs that simultaneously block the effects of ACh.

Until the mid-1980s, there were classes of antipsychotic drugs (see Table 41.2) similar to chlorpromazine, now called **typical antipsychotics**, that reduced EPSE, but caused anticholinergic side effects such as sedation, dry mouth, hypotension, tachycardia, and constipation (see Table 41.2). New drugs (e.g., butyrophenones) were developed to reduce these side effects, but they increased EPSE, which then had to be counteracted by adding an anticholinergic drug. After antipsychotic drugs had been in use for two decades, DA blockade was also found to be associated with *tardive dyskinesia* (TD), an irreversible movement disorder that causes involuntary lip pursing and mouth smacking, sometimes choreoathetoid movements (e.g., writhing, twitching) of the hands, and, rarely, abnormal movements of the trunk. Patients on typical antipsychotics sometimes felt the cure was worse than the disease.

Newer drugs, called "second generation" or **atypical antipsychotics**, modulate DA activity less directly by blocking specific serotonin receptors. The adverse effects of atypical antipsychotics differ somewhat from those of earlier drugs (see Table 41.2). Their increased tolerability, especially reduced EPSE, makes it easier for patients to take them consistently, and they have an extended range of action (i.e., most also relieve acute **mania**, and some are now used for sedation or severe anxiety).

However, atypical antipsychotics do have some significant side effects, which must be taken into account. All antipsychotics (except **quetiapine**) increase prolactin levels, inhibiting fertility in women and contributing to breast enlargement in men. To varying degrees, all lengthen the QTc interval on EKG, some to the point of raising concern about arrhythmias, including the fatal *torsade des pointes*, if the drug is combined with other drugs that also prolong the QTc interval. In addition, widespread and long-term use of the atypical antipsychotics contributes to the development

Table 41.1. Antidepressant medications: Common and serious side effects by class

Class/Example Medications	Common Side Effects	Serious Side Effects	Special Concerns
Tricyclic (TCA) Amitriptyline Desipramine Imipramine Nortriptyline	Blurred vision Dry mouth Orthostatic hypotension Sedation Sexual dysfunction Weight gain	Cardiac conduction defects Seizure provocation Increase in glaucoma/urinary retention Drug-drug interactions	Very dangerous in overdose Elders and youths more sensitive to side effects
Selective serotonin reuptake inhibitor (SSRI) Citalopram Escitalopram Fluoxetine Paroxetine Sertraline	Nausea Diarrhea Sedation or insomnia Sexual dysfunction Headache Weight gain in long term	Drug-drug interactions for some Agitation Increase in suicidal ideation or behavior in youth	Withdrawal syndrome (fluoxetine is an exception due to long half-life)
Serotonin and norepinephrine reuptake inhibitor (SNRI) (Dual Acting Agent) Venlafaxine Duloxetine	Similar to SSRI profile	May cause sustained BP elevation Hepatic toxicity (duloxetine)	Withdrawal syndrome
Dopamine and norepinephrine reuptake inhibitor (DNRI) Buproprion	Insomnia Anxiety Agitation	Seizure risk escalates when maximum recommended doses is exceeded and if excessive single doses are taken Psychosis in elders and those with risk factors like schizophrenia	Seizure risk in overdose Relatively contraindicated in eating disorders
Serotonin antagonist and reuptake inhibitor (SARI) Nefazodone Trazodone	Sedation	Hypotension for trazodone at higher doses Hepatic toxicity and drug-drug interactions for nefazodone Priapism	
Norepinephrine and specific serotonin receptor modulator (NaSSA) Mirtazapine	Sedation Weight gain		Sedation or weight gain leads to discontinuation in ~10% of exposures
Monoamine oxidase inhibitor (MAOI) Phenelzine Selegiline transdermal Tranylcypromine	Sedation or insomnia Weight gain Orthostatic hypotension Sexual dysfunction	Dangerous hypertension with tyramine ingestion Drug-drug interactions require dietary restrictions and careful patient education	Selegiline transdermal does not require dietary restrictions at low doses (6 mg)

Table 41.2. Selected antipsychotic drugs: Adverse effects and special considerations

Typical Antipsychotic	Common Adverse Effects	Serious or Toxic Adverse Effects	Special Considerations
Chlorpromazine (cpz)	++EPSE ++++ACh +++Sedation	Hypotension Jaundice	Other drugs dosed in "CPZ equivalents" Threshold of efficacy roughly equivalent to 400 mg of cpz
Thioridazine	+ EPSE +++++ACh Retrograde ejaculation +++Sedation	Hypotension Jaundice	Pigmentary retinopathy at doses > 800 mg/day
Clozapine	0 EPSE +++++ACh +++Sedation	Agranulocytosis Jaundice	Monitor blood counts frequently *Reduces suicide rate in schizophrenia*
Perphenazine	++++EPSE ++ACh ++Sedation		
Fluphenazine	+++++ EPSE ++ACh +Sedation		Given by IM injection every two weeks; enhances adherence
Haloperidol	+++++EPSE +ACh +Sedation		May be given IM once per month
Atypical Antipsychotic			
Olanzapine	+ EPSE +ACh ++Sedation	Dramatic weight gain	
Risperidone (also paliperidone, iloperidone)	+EPSE +ACh +Sedation		Risperidone available in depot form (very expensive) Given every two weeks At doses > 6 mg/day, more EPSE
Quetiapine	+ EPSE +ACh +++Sedation		Does not raise prolactin levels May be monotherapy for bipolar depression
Ziprazodone	+EPSE +ACh +Sedation		Does not typically cause weight gain Possible increase in risk of arrhythmia due to prolongation of QTc interval
Aripiprazole	+EPSE +ACh +Sedation		Does not typically cause weight gain May be used to augment SSRIs in refractory depression
Asenapine	+EPSE + ACh +Sedation		

of obesity and its complications (e.g., metabolic syndrome, diabetes). Finally, these drugs are very expensive compared to earlier drugs.

Mood Stabilizers

What is the therapeutic index of a drug?

Treating **bipolar disorder** requires strategies to both relieve and prevent acute **mania, hypomania**, or **depressive episodes**. Antipsychotics all have anti-manic properties, even when the person is not psychotic. They are often prescribed for bipolar patients, for both acute treatment and prevention of mania, but generally do not prevent depression. Several *anticonvulsants* and the ion *lithium,* termed *mood stabilizers*, also relieve manic symptoms and may have some benefit for bipolar depression.

Lithium empirically reverses acute mania, has some antidepressant effects, and is *the only drug that clearly reduces the suicide rate in bipolar disorder*, but it is difficult to use safely. The difference between a therapeutic dose and a toxic dose (**therapeutic index**) is very narrow, and the side effects, especially with chronic use, include troubling tremor, polydipsia/polyuria, thyroid dysfunction, kidney dysfunction, and weight gain. Patients taking lithium must have their blood levels monitored carefully to keep them in the range of therapeutic effect and to avoid toxicity.

The search for alternatives to lithium led to the hypothesis that bipolar episodes resemble epileptic fits, in that sub-threshold symptoms may accumulate until a threshold is reached that precipitates the full-blown mood episode. This *"kindling hypothesis"* led to trials of *anti-epileptic drugs* (AEDs) in the treatment of bipolar patients. Various forms of valproic acid, carbamazepine and its metabolite oxcarbazepine, and lamotrigine were found to relieve acute bipolar states. Lamotrigine seems to have special benefit in treating bipolar depression. It has few side effects but is not helpful in acute episodes because the dose has to be titrated to a therapeutic level very slowly to minimize the risk of the rare but possibly fatal complication, known as *Stevens-Johnson syndrome.*

Valproic acid and carbamazepine are used mainly to treat mania. They have more side effects than lamotrigine, and both also have potentially fatal, rare toxicities (i.e., hemorrhagic pancreatitis and bone marrow failure, or agranulocytosis, respectively). However, these complications are not related to rate of introduction, so the drugs can be used in situations requiring immediate effect. Patients taking AEDs need laboratory monitoring, as therapeutic effects are dose related, and the complications can be identified in serum chemistries and blood counts.

Anxiolytics, Sedatives, and Stimulants

Many psychotropic drugs moderate anxiety. For example, the antidepressants and antipsychotics can reduce chronic anxiety associated with their target disorders in some patients. The response latency of these drugs makes them less useful for acute anxiety, although taken over time, the SSRIs and *dual acting agents* do prevent panic attacks.

Sedatives have been known in medicine since antiquity. Early antianxiety drugs (barbiturates) modulated the brainstem areas involved in general arousal. As a result, high doses could induce lethal respiratory suppression. Newer anxiolytics target mainly *cortical* areas in which the neurotransmitter gamma-aminobutyric acid (GABA) balances the activity of the excitatory neurotransmitter **glutamate**. The brain has endogenous benzodiazepine receptors that regulate the expression of GABA. The benzodiazepines, affecting only the cortex, are safe in overdose.

Benzodiazepine drugs work immediately to relieve the unpleasant state of anxiety. This reinforcing action makes them quite addictive and susceptible to abuse, and subject to withdrawal effects, especially when stopped abruptly. Judicious use during periods of high stress or short courses of these drugs while waiting for another drug to take effect are well tolerated and do not generally lead to addiction.

Modified benzodiazepines (e.g., flurazepam) given to improve *sleep* have similar problems and advantages. They work initially, but patients may develop *tolerance* requiring higher doses to get the same effects. Discontinuing sedatives after regular use typically leads to recurrent sleep problems. Newer agents (e.g., zolpidem) preserve normal *sleep architecture* and are less associated with tolerance or withdrawl effects. For both anxiety and sleep, the early implementation of cognitive behavioral strategies (**sleep hygiene**) may help patients minimize their use of medication and its associated risks.

Stimulant drugs (e.g., methylphenidate, dextroamphetamine) improve concentration and attention in people with attention-deficit disorder. Although they may be abused, and are distantly related chemically to the highly addictive drug cocaine, research has demonstrated that appropriately diagnosed children who take stimulants improve in general adaptation and are less likely than their untreated peers to abuse drugs in adolescence or adulthood. Stimulants that are less rapidly absorbed, longer acting, or made from precursors reduce the potential for abuse.

Drugs for Other Conditions

Currently, pharmaceutical firms are actively pursuing novel therapies for challenging clinical and public health problems, especially dementia and addiction. Drugs that increase ACh activity have some limited value in treating dementia. Alcoholics may benefit from *disulfiram*, which induces nausea and vomiting in response to alcohol; *naltrexone*, which reduces craving and the tendency to binge drink; and *acamprosate*, another drug that reduces craving. Psychotropic drugs play an important role in **harm reduction** in *opiate addiction*, where substitution therapies like *methadone* (a long-acting opiate agonist) and *buprenorphine* (a mixed agonist/antagonist) are demonstrably superior to abstinence strategies in reducing criminal behavior and functional impairment.

Ethical Issues in Psychopharmacotherapy

> What are the ethical issues associated with psychopharmacological treatment?

Advances in psychopharmacology have clearly benefited patients with severe, previously untreatable illness. However, the use of psychotropics raises many questions about the meaning of personal experience, patient autonomy, and the boundaries of normal and disordered functioning.

The logic of using medication to relieve a psychological symptom confuses some patients. Symptoms have meaning in people's lives. When offered medications to relieve nightmares and intrusive recollections, military veterans with PTSD from combat trauma have accused doctors of "drugging the vet to make him forget." They questioned whether the treatment was intended to relieve their suffering or to absolve the military of the responsibility for causing it.

Using medication to change a person's thoughts or perceptions can be perceived as *undermining autonomy* and a form of social control, even when intended for the good of the person. Obtaining *consent* after fully explaining treatment risks, benefits, and alternatives, is essential to preserving autonomy. However, psychiatric disorders may compromise patients' cognitive capacities and judgment, making it difficult for them to give fully informed consent. Conversely, patients who are competent to make decisions may have their judgment questioned because of their psychiatric diagnosis. The use of psychotropic drugs in children, who lack legal capacity to consent and whose conditions may respond differently from those of adults, poses ethical and clinical concerns. While the problem of overuse has received widespread attention, withholding effective therapies merely because of a patient's age is also inappropriate.

Professional training teaches practitioners to assess competency and symptoms separately, and to negotiate with patients to obtain consent. States legally restrict who can be medicated without consent, generally allowing this only in situations of immediate risk of harm to self or others.

Many psychotropic drugs resemble drugs that are taken illegally to induce particular states or enhance normal performance. Deciding whether a patient who must take a drug over a long period of time to control symptoms or prevent relapse is addicted – as opposed to physiologically dependent – is not straightforward. Some psychotropic drugs are susceptible to abuse or non-medical use; others are rarely misused. Determining which drugs may be abused requires studies of basic mechanisms, animal testing, and, finally, surveillance for diversion and the development of a street market.

Drugs that enhance the function of pathways that mediate pleasure (mainly the mesolimbic DA pathway), stimulate opioid receptors, or modify arousal (stimulants or sedatives) are the most often abused. In animal studies, if an animal prefers a drug to food or water, humans are likely to abuse it. The development of a street market, another marker of a drug's abuse potential, may or may not relate to a drug's basic mechanisms of action. The antihypertensive clonidine, for example, may be sold illegally because it relieves the effects of opiate withdrawal. At the same time, there is almost no illegal diversion of antidepressants because, for most people, antidepressants are not fundamental mood elevators; they only relieve symptoms of depression when present. Patients need to be warned about the dangers of certain drugs, but often those concerned about becoming addicted to an appropriately prescribed medication can be reassured that a drug is not addicting in the sense that most people use the term.

Combining Pharmacotherapy and Psychotherapy

> Can pharmacological and non-pharmacological treatments be combined?

Some psychiatric phenomena, especially persistent psychosis, mania, and melancholic depression, are basically unresponsive to psychotherapy. Other conditions, such as *dissociative disorders*, do not respond to currently available medications. Effective drug and non-drug treatments exist for many other conditions, especially anxiety disorders, mood disorders, and facets of addictions.

Considerable evidence supports the efficacy of combined treatment for certain disorders. For example, patients with severe anxiety disorders may experience few symptoms while medicated, but will remain avoidant and disabled without therapy that encourages exposure to, and mastery of their fears. Patients with schizophrenia benefit from having a consistent therapeutic relationship with their prescribing provider, and may also benefit from specific rehabilitative interventions and encouragement to socialize. Using medication to rapidly control symptoms can inspire patients' trust in therapy, making them more open to therapeutic influence.

Drug treatment tends to work only while the drug is taken. The benefits of psychotherapy tend to persist, even become greater, after the end of a course of therapy. Drugs do not teach patients anything, although having access to an effective drug can be empowering and therapeutic in itself.

In the end, the choice of treatment reflects many factors, including patient preference, the setting of treatment, available expertise and resources, and contraindications to the use of particular medications. For therapists, it is most important to know what the goals of a particular intervention are at a given time in the course of a patient's illness, and to match these to the appropriate modality. The single best predictor of any patient's response to treatment is his or her prior response or non-response.

Recommended Readings

Hoop JG, Spellecy R. Philosophical and ethical issues at the forefront of neuroscience and genetics: An overview for psychiatrists. *Psychiatric Clinics of North America* 2009; 32:437–449.

National Institute of Mental Health. Mental Health Medications 2008. U.S. Dept of Health and Human Services. Available at http://www.nimh.nih.gov/health/publications/mental-health-medications/complete-index.shtml

Preston J, Johnson J. *Clinical Psychopharmacology Made Ridiculously Simple,* 6th ed. Miami, FL: Medmaster; 2011.

Review Questions

1. A 34-year-old married woman who takes depot fluphenazine to prevent relapse of schizophrenia has been unable to conceive a child. Her medication should be changed to
    A. aripiprazole.
    B. chlorpromazine.
    C. depot haloperidol.
    D. quetiapine.
    E. ziprazidone.

2. A psychiatrist is trying to persuade a middle-aged man who is acutely manic to take medication. The man refuses. In this circumstance, medication may be administered immediately only if

    A. a competent family member authorizes the administration of the medication.

    B. the man has previously responded well to the recommended medication.

    C. the man is on the verge of attacking staff members or other patients.

    D. the man is refusing because of side effects.

    E. the psychiatrist declares the man incompetent to make decisions.

3. A 23-year-old man with schizophrenia has gained 50 pounds since starting treatment with olanzapine. His medication should be changed to

    A. asenapine.

    B. haloperidol.

    C. perphenazine.

    D. risperidone.

    E. ziprasodone.

Key to review questions: p. 408

42 Somatization and Somatoform Disorders

Julia B. Frank, MD

- What is somatization?
- What are the mechanisms of somatization?
- What are psychosomatic and somatoform disorders?
- How does understanding somatization help determine treatment?

Somatization

What is somatization?

In pediatric and adult general practice, many care seekers present with two complementary conditions: (a) physical complaints without any demonstrable physical findings, and (b) the presence of psychosocial factors sufficient to initiate, maintain, or worsen the physical complaints. These conditions define the phenomenon of **somatization**. Many of the *non-localizing symptoms* presented by affected patients are physiological components of the individual's *stress response* to disruptive life situations or other psychosocial factors (see Chapter 7, Stress, Adaptation, and Stress Disorders). In some cases, the symptoms can increase in severity and fit the pattern of vegetative signs for known psychiatric disorders (e.g., the insomnia or fatigue of major depression or the rapid heart rate, shallow breathing, and dizziness of an anxiety disorder).

Children too young to express emotional distress in words often complain instead of stomachaches, headaches, and feeling sick. In many cultures, focus on a physical symptom is a legitimate way of avoiding inner or interpersonal conflict. For people of low SES and others who live in persistently stressful conditions, health care is one of the few avenues of available help. Somaticizing patients may acknowledge psychological concerns, but may not appreciate the connection between their symptoms and precipitating stress conditions.

Our medical system discourages professionals from taking the time to understand the developmental, personal, and sociocultural contexts of illness. Providers fear patients will resent questions about psychological stress. Patients expect extensive testing, and providers are under pressure to order tests to avoid missing subtle or serious disease. As a consequence, somatization consumes billions of health care dollars. Medical journals and popular media abound with stories of common complaints turning out to be something unusual, but the media rarely report, and providers spend little time uncovering and helping patients resolve, the emotional problems that account for the vast majority of non-specific somatic distress.

S.F. is a 34-year-old, recently married, professional woman with persistent, diffuse lower abdominal pain that she attributes to self-diagnosed "polycystic ovaries." She worries this means she is infertile. She expects to be sent for an ultrasound and multiple blood tests and to receive a definitive answer about her fertility. When asked, she acknowledges ambivalence about getting pregnant, although she has always thought she wanted to. Her ultrasound shows normal ovaries. She responds, not with relief, but with further questions about rarer disorders.

Bio-Behavioral Mechanisms of Somatization

Understanding how prior experience and social context influence the generation and interpretation of *somatosensory* information helps providers avoid frustrating interactions with patients who focus on physical symptoms without clear organic pathology. Similar mechanisms apply when a patient's distress and disability far exceed that expected in someone with proven disease, a common form of **somatization**.

Stress-related somatic distress involves several *neuroendocrine* and *neuroregulatory systems*: the *autonomic nervous system*, the *hypothalamic-pituitary-adrenal (HPA) axis*, the *enteric nervous system*, and pathways that mediate the recognition of *pain*. Somatization typically involves headaches, abdominal, pelvic, or muscle/joint pain, and disrupted bowel function (e.g., flatulence, bloating, diarrhea, constipation, cramping). Less commonly, patients will have cryptic or "pseudoneurological" symptoms, such as an isolated area of numbness or paralysis, abnormal gait, or a "fit" or "spell" that resembles a seizure or fainting. Somatization does not apply to patients with uncontrollable hypertension or diabetes, although psychological stressors may affect autonomic and endocrine function in these conditions.

The **autonomic nervous system** (ANS) mediates both stress responses and maintenance functions such as digestion, sexual behavior, circadian rhythms, and immune responses (see Chapter 7, Stress, Adaptation, and Stress Disorders). Severe or chronic stress may disrupt the normal balance of sympathetic/parasympathetic activity, generating symptoms. Even stressors from the remote past may contribute to such disruptions. Women with bowel related complaints, for example, have high rates of prior sexual trauma, but not necessarily of current stress. Since people do not have conscious awareness of homeostatic regulation, somaticizing patients may have no awareness of the role of the genetic sensitivity or life stressors involved. In explaining the connections between stress and symptoms to patients who have no insight into the connections, providers must take great care to avoid leaving patients feeling misjudged and as though the provider feels their symptoms are "not real" or not worthy of medical attention.

The early characterization of somatization as *hysteria* (causally attributed to a "wandering" uterus) was based on the observation that most forms of somatization are 2–10 times more common in adult women than adult men. Female reproductive hormones affect the activity of serotonin and other neurotransmitters. Estrogen and serotonin co-vary in the nervous system, and somatization in females is especially prevalent during the reproductive years, when hormone levels fluctuate. Women are also more vulnerable to certain sensitizing or precipitating stressful experiences, including childhood sexual abuse, interpersonal violence, low social status, and lack of perceived control over threatening or aversive circumstances. Seeking medical care is often their only avenue of help in such circumstances. Stressed women may become sensitized to the effects of normal hormone flux and seek medical care for complaints related to otherwise physiologically normal functioning.

Symptom interpretation or the meaning assigned to a symptom determines associated distress and care-seeking. This meaning is often strongly influenced by familial experience. Individuals who experienced serious illness in themselves or a close family member during childhood are more inclined to interpret a sensation as ominous and a reason to seek help, or to adopt the *sick role*. A person who experiences dizziness on standing but expects this as the result of taking antihypertensive medication will accept the problem without distress. Someone whose mother died of a stroke may react to a dizzy spell by going to the emergency room, where he or she will be viewed askance as someone who is "somaticizing." In fact, the decision to seek medical care is part of the pathology of somatization; what differentiates these patients from the general population of people who suffer headaches, GI symptoms, pain, or fatigue is typically their amplified level of concern and their decision to pursue relief through medical care.

Psychosomatic Medicine

Table 42.1. DSM-IV-TR diagnostic categories for somatoform disorders

Disorder	Defining Criteria	Epidemiology, Comorbidity, Associated Findings	Comment
Somatization disorder	Distressing symptoms in four domains: – GI – sexual function – "pseudoneurological" – pain	– Must begin before age 30 and persist – F >M: 1% general population males; 2% general population females	– Recommended treatment: avoid unnecessary testing, offer routine visits to show concern and availability – May respond to CBT
Conversion disorder	Alteration or loss of physical functioning without explanatory pathology (e.g., focal paralysis, non-epileptic seizures)	– Common in children – Associated in time or symbolically to a psychological stressor	– Symptoms assumed to be unconsciously generated – May remit with hypnosis or other psychotherapy – May require physical therapy or other ritual of care – Can become chronic
Body dysmorphic disorder	Pre-occupation with minor or imagined physical flaw, deformity, "imagined ugliness"	– M=F – Face most often involved – Comorbid with anxiety disorders	– Associated with shame, low self-esteem – May lead to repeated medical/ surgical procedures – Responds somewhat to SSRIs, CBT
Factitious Disorder	Purposeful self infliction of signs of illness or injury to elicit medical attention and care	– F > M – Patients are often experienced in health care or are themselves health care professionals – Severe, persistent disorder termed "Munchausen's Syndrome"	– Desire for care assumed to be unconsciously motivated – May respond to empathic interview targeting stresses – "Munchausen's Syndrome" by proxy is when parent makes child ill or reports illness
Malingering	Purposeful self injury, infliction or feigning of illness to escape punishment or achieve financial or other compensation	– Common among prisoners and soldiers – Otherwise associated with antisocial personality disorder	– Aberrant illness behavior, not a mental illness
Somatoform disorder NOS	Somatization that does not meet criteria for another disorder	– Most common somatoform disorder – Person does not have enough symptoms of sufficient duration to be otherwise diagnosed	
Hypochondriasis	Conviction one has a particular disorder despite no evidence	– May lead to aggressive organ focused testing, which can cause damage, increasing anxiety	– Providers typically dismissive and judgmental, increasing patients' anxiety and resentment – May respond to CBT

In the mid 20th century, Franz Alexander proposed a category of **psychosomatic disorders**, listing colitis, arthritis, asthma, ulcers, neurodermatitis, hypertension, and anorexia as conditions in which **stress** played a major *etiological* role. As medical science and technology focused more upon the biological origins of disease, the etiological role of psychological factors became discredited. More recent epidemiological studies and new technologies illuminating the mind-body interface offer new support for the role of stress as both an etiology by itself and as a consequence of various biological disorders, especially those involving pain and GI dysfunction.

The DSM-IV-TR diagnostic categories for **somatoform disorders** sidestep controversial questions of pathogenesis, basing the diagnoses entirely on patterns of symptoms and the association of some behavioral patterns with particular motivational factors (see Table 42.1). While the DSM diagnostic categories are relatively reliable, they do little to guide treatment. The DSM-5 is likely to substantially revise many of these criteria and rename several disorders.

Non-psychiatric clinicians often diagnose patients who meet criteria for a somatoform disorder with irritable bowel syndrome, migraine or tension headaches, cystitis, fibromyalgia, or chronic fatigue syndrome. Dividing patients between different specialties impedes treatment. In fact, psychotherapy may benefit sufferers from all these conditions. Conversely, patients in psychiatric treatment may benefit from medical remedies for specific syndromes, especially IBS and migraine headaches.

Treatment Begins with Educating the Patient

> How does understanding somatization help determine treatment?

Simple reassurance typically fails to relieve somatization as it does not acknowledge the reality of the subjective pain and dysfunction for which the person is seeking relief, nor does it address the connection between the symptom and the precipitating stressor, which may be critical for resolution. **Cognitive behavioral therapy** focuses on

(1) educating people about the functioning of the body's stress response, (2) explaining that "symptoms" patients are experiencing are normal stress responses, (3) helping patients accept that they are misinterpreting bodily sensations as ominous, (4) acknowledging stressor events as contributory causes of distress, and (5) suggesting that focusing on resolving or managing the stress will relieve the problem.

Conversion symptoms often respond to the exploration of underlying conflict when the person is in a deeply relaxed state such as **hypnosis**. Symptom relief or management of other stress responses may be achieved through aerobic exercise, focusing on breathing, changing patterns of anxious thought (as in CBT), or less specific psychological interventions (other psychotherapies) that allow the person to express and then modify emotions associated with the symptom. *Meditation* and other *integrative medicine* interventions may help patients temporarily focus away from their symptoms or engender **relaxation** (increased parasympathetic tone) that relieves stress and tension whether or not they also address the precipitating psychosocial factors. Similar mechanisms may account for the "healing" that occurs through religious rituals.

For some patients, *antidepressant medication*, especially tricyclics and dual acting agents, may relieve many functional symptoms, even though they do not address the stressful conditions that are the source of the problem. Once symptoms are controlled, the person may view stressors as less damaging. Decreased stage 4 sleep also contributes to symptom formation. Although few medications improve this phase of sleep, behavioral interventions (**sleep hygiene**) may be helpful.

Which interventions to offer which patient is less a function of diagnosis than of the patient's willingness/ability to trust the physician or therapist enough to accept that troubling symptoms are not what they seem to be. A consistent, concerned but medically conservative approach is essential. Practitioners must learn to recognize the patterns and circumstances that suggest somatization and avoid unnecessary tests or overzealous treatments that only reinforce patients' catastrophic thinking. At the same time, providers must be willing to change their view of a patient and pursue other diagnostic possibilities if new symptoms arise or if efforts to manage somatization do not have the expected effect.

Recommended Readings

Allen LA, Woolfolk RL. Cognitive behavioral therapy for somatoform disorders. *Psychiatric Clinics of North America* 2010; 33:579–593.

Harding KJK, Hyler S. Somatoform and Factitious Disorders. In Cutler JL, Marcus ER (Eds.), *Psychiatry,* 2nd ed. New York: Oxford University Press; 2010, pp. 331–357.

Warnock JK, Clayton AH. Chronic episodic disorders in women. *Psychiatric Clinics of North America* 2003; 26:725–740.

Review Questions

1. After going to the emergency room one night for severe epigastric pain that was eventually attributed to reflux, a 45-year-old man becomes convinced he suffers from heart disease and that the diagnosis was missed. He continues to feel chest discomfort and visits several cardiologists, requesting a stress test, an echocardiogram, and blood tests. Finally, he is referred to a cognitive behavioral therapist. The rationale for this referral is that
   A. he is indirectly expressing distress over some upsetting problem from his early life that the therapist can explore.
   B. his requests for multiple consultations are likely to prompt his insurance company to reject further claims.
   C. it is inappropriate to use medical resources for someone who clearly has no organic disease.
   D. sending him to therapy is a tactful way of communicating that he does not have a real medical problem.
   E. therapy will help him change his focus and correct his interpretation of his symptoms.

2. A young woman asks her primary care physician to recommend a plastic surgeon. She spends 2–3 hours every day checking her reflection in the mirror because she is sure that her jaw is lopsided. She avoids socializing because of this imagined deformity. This is an example of
   A. body dysmorphic disorder.
   B. factitious disorder.
   C. hypochondriasis.
   D. malingering.
   E. somatoform disorder NOS.

Key to review questions: p. 408

43 Adjustment Disorders, Bereavement, and Demoralization

Julia B. Frank, MD

• What is an adjustment disorder?
• What makes particular events stressful?
• What is resilience?
• Is grief a psychological disorder?
• How can health care professionals help bereaved or demoralized people?

Adjustment Disorders

What is an adjustment disorder?

The **adjustment disorders** are defined as reactions to an identifiable stressor event or situation. To be a disorder, the reaction must exceed a normally expected response, in either intensity or duration, although not necessarily in kind. Patients may demonstrate disturbed behavior (e.g., angry outbursts, impulsivity, social withdrawal), anxiety, or mood symptoms that do not reach the diagnostic threshold for another disorder. Adjustment disorders occur within 3 months of an event, and chronic forms last > 6 months.

A 50-year-old woman cannot stop thinking about the death of her ailing cat 3 months ago, a loss that coincided with the finalization of her divorce. She has withdrawn from friends because condolences irritate her, and she has sudden crying spells at work. She can cheer up when she is busy, and her sleep is only disrupted by awakenings when she thinks she hears a cat crying.

People who develop symptoms in response to events that are not intrinsically traumatic, or who respond to trauma with symptoms other than those of a recognized PTSD, may be diagnosed with an *adjustment disorder*. In the example, a diagnosis of *adjustment disorder with depressed mood* would be appropriate.

The vagueness of the adjustment disorder diagnoses highlights the indistinct boundary between normal and abnormal states. Nevertheless, common sense and common experience, coupled with research into the impact of stressful life events, support the need for this diagnostic category.

What makes particular events stressful?

The impact of a stressor depends on the person's appraisal of its *meaning*. Events perceived as negative and not under a person's control have the strongest predictive value. The particular symptom patterns needed for diagnosing an adjustment disorder are, however, unspecified, because such a wide range of stressors induce such widely differing symptoms in various individuals.

The adjustment disorder diagnoses are particularly useful in medical settings. People under stress seek help for difficulty sleeping, functional GI symptoms, increased chronic or non-specific pain, fatigue, and similar vague complaints. Medical diseases themselves may serve as the stressors that induce an adjustment disorder. Having a diagnostic term for an excessive and maladaptive reaction to an illness is helpful, as it is can justify a referral for mental health treatment.

Psychotherapy of many sorts (see Chapter 40, Principles of Psychotherapy) can be useful in relieving adjustment disorders, even those related to ongoing or irreversible stressors. Problem solving, encouragement of more adaptive coping, and mobilizing social support are especially helpful. Although drugs may be given for anxiety symptoms or disrupted sleep, they tend to be of limited value and may even impede other coping unless coupled with psychological intervention.

Resilience

What is resilience?

Good general health, adequate social resources, and the psychological qualities of sociability, humor, flexibility of thought, perseverance, emotional self awareness, and an internal locus of control all contribute to **resilience** in the face of stress. General medical clinicians are uniquely positioned to foster resilience in people with serious or chronic diseases by providing explanations and teaching patients how to manage, self regulate, and better control their conditions. Empathic listening to patients' concerns during medical encounters also lessens stress and helps prevent the development of stress-related disorders.

Bereavement

Is grief a psychological disorder?

Loss through death ranks high on the list of pathogenic stressors. People also experience **grief** in relation to losses other than death, including divorce or separation, loss of a job or community, or loss of a pet. Normal **bereavement** may evolve into a disorder requiring treatment to forestall or relieve prolonged disability or severe complications, such as suicidal behavior. As with stress, it is the meaning or significance of the loss, rather than the loss itself, that determines the person's response.

Attachment theory is particularly relevant to understanding grief. Like other mammals, humans react to disrupted attachment with fluctuating arousal, protest, agitation, withdrawal, sometimes aggression, and eventual reorganization of behav-

ior. Normal grief is built upon these ingrained reaction patterns.

> The typical qualities of grief include preoccupation with the loss, searching for the person, sadness, guilt, anger, despair, anxiety, and a desire for comfort or consolation from others coupled with a need for time alone, difficulty concentrating, anorexia, restlessness, and poor sleep. Fleeting experiences of hearing or seeing the lost person are not uncommon. Symptoms tend to come in waves and may recur unexpectedly when some person or event triggers a memory.

The loss of a parent during childhood, the death of a child, and the loss of a spouse/life partner during early and middle adulthood can have particularly devastating effects. Sudden losses, especially if due to suicide, violence, accident, or disaster, typically trigger severe reactions. So called *complicated* or *pathological grief* may have lasting effects on a survivor's overall adaptation. Grief may exacerbate trait vulnerabilities, such as tendencies to internalize or externalize distress, poor self-esteem, and negative expectations of the future. Anxiety over the material consequences, for example, after the loss of a primary earner or caregiver, can exacerbate distress. In individuals genetically vulnerable to psychiatric illness, loss may trigger an initial episode or a relapse. Social isolation can complicate the normal process of recovery from grief.

Age, gender, and culture influence the experience and expression of grief. Bereavement may precipitate an existential crisis or spiritual alienation. Mourning rituals – funerals, a defined period of withdrawal from social activities, memorial gatherings – are important for restoring meaning and helping a bereaved person to structure his or her experience and to re-connect to other people.

The time course of normal grief is variable. Rather than relying on an arbitrary time frame, clinicians should recognize signs and symptoms of **complicated grief** that may appear at any point. Signs of complicated grief include intense guilt, prolonged anhedonia, inability to find any meaning in life, and suicidal ideation. Increased use of drugs or alcohol is an intrinsically maladaptive response to grief that can have serious consequences.

Palliative care practitioners routinely address **anticipatory grief** as well as grief following a loss. Other medical practitioners, however, may overlook preparing patients and their families for these reactions, which can be far more intense and troubling than expected. Although specialized counselors including nurses, social workers, and clergy may be available, all practitioners should be familiar with the basic phenomenon of grief and the need to provide support and guidance. Clinicians help by expressing sympathy while explaining and predicting the eventual resolution of grief based on their knowledge of its natural history. They can further assist by relieving symptoms such as sleeplessness and monitoring for complications, including lack of attention to health needs.

Demoralization

The psychological literature identifies **demoralization** as a form of patterned maladaptation in circumstances that overwhelm normal coping. By definition, demoralized people feel trapped, experience *subjective incompetence*, and believe they cannot master what troubles them. Serious chronic medical disorders are among the most demoralizing stressors people face. In fact, life threatening or disabling medical conditions often trigger demoralization as patients contemplate their own impending death with its associated loss of plans, capacities, activities, and relationships.

> How can health care professionals help bereaved or demoralized people?

The qualities that differentiate depression, grief, and demoralization have important implications for treatment. People who are *depressed* lose the capacity to enjoy anything (anhedonia) and generally isolate themselves from others. Their symptoms are persistent and feel unrelenting. Medication and intensive psychotherapy may be needed. *Grief* is a more fluctuating state, involving a desire for and ability to respond to empathic social interactions. People find consolation in the normal rituals and practices of mourning and in supportive interactions with caregivers. People who are mainly *demoralized* may improve when they are given more control over their circumstances, such as when they are allowed to make

choices about their care or to self-administer treatment. They also improve when aversive symptoms like pain and nausea are treated, and in response to helpful information and empathic support.

Psychotherapy can be effective in ameliorating all three conditions.

Recommended Readings

Clarke DM, Kissane DW, Trauer T, Smith GC. Demoralisation, anhedonia and grief in patients with severe physical illness. *World Psychiatry* 2005; 4:96–105.

Defiguereido JD. Deconstructing demoralization: Subjective incompetence and distress in adversity. In Alarcon R, Frank JB (Eds.), *The Psychotherapy of Hope: The Legacy of Persuasion and Healing.* Baltimore, MD: Johns Hopkins University Press; 2012.

Jamison KR. *Nothing Was the Same: A Memoir.* New York: Knopf; 2009.

Review Questions

1. Five months ago, a 62-year-old man lost his wife of 30 years to cancer. He finds it impossible to force himself to clean out her closet. He has lost 15 pounds and oscillates between bouts of restlessness and lethargy. He is unproductive at work. Initially, he could sleep for only 4-5 hours at night, but this seems to be improving. The appropriate professional advice would be:
   A. "Feel free to ask me questions about your wife's illness and treatment."
   B. "I am sorry for your loss but, over time, I feel confident you will learn to live with it."
   C. "I wonder if you can't get over this because you have unresolved guilt about this relationship."
   D. "It's time to bite the bullet, give away your wife's things, and start to rebuild your life."
   E. "You should be over the acute mourning by now. You seem to be getting depressed."

2. A soldier feels numb and sad after his second deployment overseas is extended. He believes

the leadership of his unit is unresponsive to his need to get back to his family. He cannot imagine feeling better when the deployment ends, since he considers himself unemployable outside the military. This soldier is likely to respond best to

A. antidepressant therapy.
B. leave for recreation and relaxation.
C. more contact with his family.
D. motivational talks from his commanding officer.
E. psychotherapy.

3. Among the following, the most appropriate description of this soldier's condition is
   A. adjustment disorder with mixed emotional features.
   B. demoralization.
   C. depressive disorder NOS.
   D. inability to adjust to military life.
   E. malingering.

Key to review questions: p. 408

44 Dementia

Julia B. Frank, MD

- Is dementia one syndrome or many?
- What is the role of gene-environment interaction in dementia?
- What are the consequences of dementia for the individual and society?
- What treatments affect the course and outcome of dementia?
- Is dementia preventable?

Is dementia one syndrome or many?

Dementia is a syndrome of general loss of cognitive functions and significant functional deterioration. In contrast, in developmental disorders, cognitive functions lag behind or never reach expected levels. The actual deficits found in the two groups – slowing of thought, poor memory and concentration, deterioration of personality, and diminished ability to learn, manipulate information, or perform basic tasks of self-care – overlap. Persons with dementia may also experience delusions and hallucinations. Although normal aging is associated with some cognitive decline, the symptoms of dementia are qualitatively different and more severe.

Dementia may result from genetic processes that are expressed directly in neurological tissue (primary degenerative dementias), from progressive deterioration of the blood supply to the brain (vascular dementia), and/or from the effects of metabolic, infectious, toxic, traumatic, autoimmune, or endocrine insults to the brain (see Table 44.1). Many cases involve mixed etiology (i.e., vascular or other disease processes may trigger the expression of genetically regulated cell damage and death).

Dr. M. suffered from *dementia of the Alzheimer type* (DAT) or **Alzheimer disease**, a primary degenerative dementia first described by Alois Alzheimer in 1906. Alzheimer and other German pathologists correlated cognitive and behavioral deterioration with characteristic lesions of cortical

Dr. M. was a 53-year-old physician who retired because she could longer remember the details of patients she had just examined. Over the next 5 years, she developed severe deficits of memory and judgment, documented on neuropsychological tests. Her affect became shallow and labile. She stopped being able to dress or feed herself, slept erratically through the day, suffered from visual hallucinations, and became nearly mute. She died, 7 years after diagnosis, from aspiration pneumonia.

tissue: plaques made of beta amyloid, neurofibrillary tangles (later found to include tau proteins), and granulovacuolar degeneration. Alzheimer's proof that disorders of mentation stem from damage to the brain guides the current effort to identify the molecular and chemical derangements that underlie all mental and behavioral disorders.

Early research classified dementias based on pathological changes. Because many patients are never autopsied, bedside classification, although less precise, is the usual approach to diagnosis. The observable differences between, for example, DAT and Lewy body dementia (diagnosed based on the presence of Lewy bodies in brain tissue) are too subtle to be recognized by most clinicians. In addition, currently available neuroimaging does not differentiate between various microscopic pathological findings, which co-occur in many patients.

A more useful, mixed classification categorizes dementias based on clinical course, neuro-

Table 44.1. Varieties of dementia

	Known genetic factors	Distribution of lesions	Pathological findings	Symptoms	Comments
Dementia of the Alzheimer type (DAT)	– ApoE4 genes, chromosome 19 – Also chromosomes 1,4,21	Cortical radiations of cholinergic neurons, esp. hippocampus and parietal and occipital lobes	– Beta amyloid, tau proteins, granulovacuolar degeneration, neurofibrillary tangles; – Presenilin 1 and 2 (amyloid precursor proteins)	– *Early* short-term memory loss, apraxia, progressive confusion, inability to sequence, learn, or recognize people – *Later* personality changes, depression, paranoia, visual hallucinations	– Most prevalent – Incidence increases with age
Vascular dementia ("multi-infarct dementia")		Diffuse cortical in vascular distribution	– Small infarcts	– Variable, stepwise deterioration	– Often co-exists with DAT – Second most prevalent – Related to other cardiovascular risk factors
Huntington disease (HD)	– 36–250 repeats of CAG on chromosome 4	Destruction of caudate, radiations of caudate	– Increased huntingtin protein	– Paranoia, impulsive dyscontrol, memory loss, psychosis, chorea	– Characteristic "Butterfly" pattern on neuroimaging – Autosomal dominant
Parkinson disease (PD)		Cortical radiations of dopamine neurons originating in basal ganglia	– Lewy bodies (alpha synuclein) – Changes due to cholinergic deterioration	– Tremor, rigidity, cogwheeling; memory loss, paranoia, apathy; aggression	– Occurs late in 24–31% of PD
Lewy body dementia		Similar to PD but spares temporal areas	– Lewy bodies (alpha synuclein)	– Severe motor symptoms, visual hallucinations early, memory loss, personality change	– Much rarer than DAT but second most common *primary* degenerative dementia
Pick disease (primary frontotemporal dementia)		Frontal and temporal lobe atrophy		– Impulsive/ disinhibited or anergic/ apathetic, poor hygiene, loss of social skills, aphasia, no insight; memory may be spared	– Subclassified: with or without aphasia
Dementia secondary to other diseases/ deficiencies/injury (see Table 44.2)		Mixed, frontotemporal symptoms may predominate early on		– Memory loss, personality change, often motor abnormalities, depression	– Partly preventable – Progression varies with underlying condition

pathology, or etiology. Parkinson disease (PD), Huntington disease (HD), Pick disease, and DAT are primary degenerative neurological conditions, recognized in part by patterns of symptoms and in part by pathological lesions. The etiology of these conditions is variable. For example, HD is caused by a recognized autosomal dominant genetic lesion (see Table 44.1). DAT and dementia in PD result from the interaction of genetic risk factors with known/unknown environmental conditions. Creutzfeldt-Jakob disease (CJD), a dementia that also follows a relentless degenerative course, is caused by a neurotropic virus.

Vascular dementia, usually a disease of old age, differs clinically from the dementias above by following a stepwise, rather than steady, downhill course. The distribution of the degenerative changes in vascular dementia follows the distribution of the small arteries and arterioles blocked by atherosclerosis. Vascular dementia is often a late life complication of diabetes, hypertension, or other cardiovascular conditions.

Table 44.2. Examples of dementias of known etiology		
Etiology	**Pathology**	**Symptoms and Progression**
Primary HIV infection of CNS or AIDS-related infections	– Damage may be focal or diffuse	– Typically prominent frontal symptoms: personality change, movement disorders – May remit with treatment of underlying infection
Multiple sclerosis	– Characteristic scattered lesions throughout the brain	– Symptoms worsen during flares – May be partially reversed or arrested by treatment
Autoimmune disorders (systemic lupus erythematosus)	– Effects of vasculitis	– Rapidly progressive in uncontrolled disease (seizures)
Alcohol related	– Diffuse toxic damage, sometimes prominent cerebellar damage	– Permanent but may not progress if drinking stopped
Thiamine deficiency (related to alcoholism or malnutrition)	– Selective deterioration of mamillary bodies	– Early acute stage, "Wernicke's encephalopathy," reversible with treatment – Later "Korsakoff's psychosis" irreversible, severe loss of short-term memory
Following closed head injury	– Diffuse axonal injury, cerebral contusions and scarring – Acceleration of DAT type changes	– Often frontal damage, personality change, and diminished executive functions – Younger people may recover considerable function – Depression, mania, or psychosis may occur, depending on site of injury
Hypothyroidism		– Sluggishness, loss of motivation, slowed thought – May be reversible with thyroid replacement
B12/Folate deficiency (intrinsic or secondary to alcoholism)		– Often associated with anemia or peripheral neuropathy – May be improved with vitamin replacement
Normal pressure hydrocephalus	– Compression of cortical tissue surrounding cerebral ventricles	– Prominent gait disturbances and incontinence, personality changes – May remit with early diagnosis, shunting

Dementias of other etiologies produce different patterns of tissue damage, and different patterns of symptoms, and have different prognoses (see Table 44.2).

Clinically, the distribution of pathological changes in dementia corresponds broadly to two distinct patterns of symptoms and behaviors. DAT begins with short-term memory loss and includes early perceptual disturbances, while other dementias may begin with personality changes or mood symptoms. The initial lesions of DAT appear in the hippocampus and posterior brain. Other dementias (classified variably as *subcortical dementia*, *frontotemporal dementia*, FTD, or simply *non-DAT*) first damage the prefrontal and temporal cortices, basal ganglia, and associated limbic areas. Such distinctions are most meaningful early on. In later stages, severe dysfunction and widespread destruction result in global impairment.

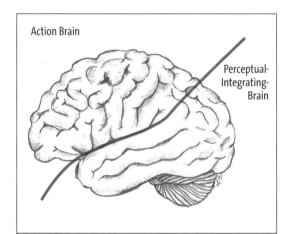

Figure 44.1. Components of the action brain and perceptual brain. Based on Vaidya NA and Taylor MA. *Psychiatry Rounds: Practical Solutions of Clinical Challenges*. Miami, FL: Medmaster; 2004.

The distribution of early lesions explains why the initial symptoms of dementia differ, depending on etiology. The posterior brain, the region first affected in DAT, is particularly specialized for receiving and beginning to process stimuli and associating them with memory (see Figure 44.1). It has been termed the *perceptual integrating brain*, in contrast to the *anterior* or *action brain*. FTDs first affect the action brain, which is specialized for inhibiting or moderating emotion and action, conscious cognitive processing, expressive language, social skills, and executive functions

(e.g., sequencing, holding information in a buffer zone so that it can be manipulated, abstraction).

Widely separated areas of the perceptual integrating brain are linked by a neuronal network whose primary neurotransmitter is *acetylcholine*. These neurons originate in the nucleus basalis of Meynert. DAT, in particular, results from a selective, possibly genetically programmed, deterioration of this network. The plaques and neurofibrillary tangles of DAT cluster in the limbic and cortical areas where these cholinergic axons terminate.

The pathological changes of FTDs appear in the frontal and temporal areas that receive both cholinergic and adrenergic input from sub-cortical centers and from dopaminergic neurons in the basal ganglia, including the caudate (Huntington disease) and the substantia nigra (Parkinson disease).

Phenomenology, Genetics, and Assessment of Dementia

Many older adults show *mild cognitive impairment*, including slowed mentation and decrease in short-term memory. Research is ongoing to determine how often this progresses to diagnosable dementia, since intervention is useful only at the earliest stages. DAT begins with severe short-term memory loss and progresses with apraxia, aphasia, and agnosia, eventual loss of normal circadian rhythms, paranoia, and visual hallucinations. FTDs begin with deterioration of attention, moderate short-term memory loss, sometimes marked aphasia, changes in personality, and disordered motor function (chorea, gait disturbance, incontinence). As deterioration becomes global, clinical distinctions between DAT and FTDs disappear.

What is the role of gene-environment interaction in dementia?

The folksinger Woody Guthrie became impulsive, paranoid, and demented in his late forties. His mother and several of his children had similar symptoms and died young. During his lifetime, his condition was recognized as Huntington disease, a dementia and movement disorder that follows a clear pattern of autosomal dominant inheritance.

The distinctions between familial, as opposed to sporadic, forms of dementia have led to studies in neurogenetics. Specifically, variants exist in the gene on chromosome 19 that codes for Apolipoprotein E (APOE), which accumulates in amyloid plaques. The inheritance of two alleles coding for APOE 4 (APOE 4/4) is associated with widespread formation of plaques (but not neurofibrillary tangles) by age 70. The brain of those with APOE2/3 shows diffuse plaques only in extreme old age (> 90 years), if at all. Those with one APOE4 allele form plaques between these ages. The presence of the APOE4 gene is, thus, a risk or susceptibility factor for the early onset of DAT. Mutations or abnormalities of chromosomes 1, 14, and 21 (including *trisomy 21*, the genetic lesion of *Down syndrome*) are associated with other abnormal proteins (presenilin 1 and 2, also called amyloid precursor proteins) that contribute to the onset and course of DAT. In people with these rare genetic variants, DAT may occur as an autosomal dominant, and appear at an early age.

Huntington disease follows the pattern of autosomal dominant inheritance. A gene on chromosome 4 codes for the protein huntingtin. This gene has an abnormally high number (> 35) of repeats of the sequence CAG. Although the normal functions of huntingtin are unknown, in HD, the presence of the abnormal protein correlates with destruction of the caudate nucleus of the basal ganglia. This produces a characteristic "butterfly pattern" visible on CT or MRI scans. As the caudate deteriorates, beginning in middle age, patients develop chorea, severe dysregulation of emotion, psychosis, and significant losses of cognitive function.

Among the dementias, only HD results entirely from known genetic factors. In all probability, the pathogenesis of most other dementias relates to the *allostatic load* of accumulated risk factors, the piling up of multiple minor or moderate CNS insults such as head injury, vascular blockage, nutritional deficits, infections, or autoimmune processes. Factors such as the presence of the APOE4 gene may determine the capacity of individuals to compensate for or repair damage, accounting for the time of onset and initial distribution of lesions.

People with dementia need medical, neurological, and behavioral assessment. Repeated Mini Mental Status Exams document baseline cognitive deficits and their progression over time.

Clinical Recognition of Dementia

A 75-year-old woman is brought to her physician's office after she left a pot on the stove, then locked herself out of the house because she could not remember where she kept her extra key. Her daughter says that her mother has become gradually more forgetful over the past 2 years, although she covers up her lapses by asking questions, often repeatedly. At times, her mother is anxious about her memory loss, but more recently seems to not recognize her deficits. On the Mini Mental Status Exam (see Chapter 39, The Psychiatric Examination) the woman cannot identify the exact date or day of the week, forgets two of three objects, can do only two serial subtractions, cannot follow a three- step command, and cannot write a grammatically correct sentence, yielding a score of 20. The daughter notes that beyond memory loss, her mother has trouble making decisions, may not recognize people she does not see frequently, easily gets lost, and makes mistakes with daily tasks like cleaning or shopping.

A 40-year-old man infected with HIV takes antiretroviral medication erratically. He shows personality changes with irritability and apathy replacing a normally cheerful, curious, and outgoing disposition. He has considerable loss of short-term memory and difficulty manipulating information as measured by serial subtractions, but no disorientation or aphasia. His score on the Mini Mental Status Exam is 24. His partner reports other impairments, including sleeping at odd hours, loss of balance, paranoia, and weight loss.

Concurrently eliciting input from caregivers using measures like the Dementia Severity Rating Scale is essential to identify the functional deficits that may benefit from rehabilitative or supportive care. In younger patients with FTD, neuropsychological tests may uncover preserved functions that can be strengthened by treatment. Evaluators should repeatedly ask about or measure behavioral deficits and psychopathological symptoms (e.g., extreme or labile moods, hallucinations, paranoia) as these are possibly treatable sources of disability and also major contributors to caregiver burden. General medical assessment and treatment are essential. Neuroimaging, CSF examination, or other invasive testing may confirm the presence of particular dementing conditions (infections, HD, or MS). Genetic studies may be important to family members.

What are the consequences of dementia for the individual and society?

DAT alone is an enormous and growing public health concern. Incidence rises with age, with 20% prevalence in people age 80. The rate doubles roughly every 5 years, so that up to 50% of people > 85 may have some degree of dementia. Currently, 4 million people in the US and 29 million people worldwide are affected. By 2030, if current trends continue, 8–14 million people in the US will be demented. The cost of dementia (reflecting both care and the lost productivity of patients and caregivers) exceeds $100 billion annually in the US. The worldwide cost of dementia care was $604 billion dollars, or 1% of the world's GDP, in 2010.

Many conditions of modern life (e.g., widespread HIV infection, increased survival from closed head injury, and epidemic alcohol abuse, diabetes, and atherosclerotic cardiovascular disease) increase the incidence and prevalence of dementia, including in younger people.

What treatments affect the course and outcome of dementia?

Some dementias (e.g., those resulting from CNS HIV infection) may be stopped from progressing or reversed by treating the underlying cause. The lesions of DAT cluster in areas of the brain where acetylcholine is most common. Drugs that potentiate acetylcholine may slow the progression of DAT and other dementias. The dementia of PD responds partly to drugs that increase brain dopamine. Older patients who are depressed often have prominent cognitive impairments ("pseudodementia" or *dementia syndrome of depression*) that may improve when the depression is treated. When depression occurs secondary to dementia, treatment may improve function and reduce caregiver burden. Psychotic symptoms in dementia or uncontrolled aggressive behavior may respond to low doses of antipsychotic medication. Psychotropic drugs should only be used to control clear target symptoms, as use of antipsychotic drugs in dementia may increase mortality. Elderly patients are especially sensitive to drug side effects such as falls and drug-drug interactions.

Although abnormal proteins accumulate in the brain of people with dementia, no currently available drugs or therapies target this process.

Supportive medical, behavioral, and family interventions may improve the lives of people with dementia. Treatment of concurrent infections, bodily organ dysfunctions, and good nutrition help maintain cognitive function. Providing a safe and adequately, but not overwhelmingly, stimulating environment preserves the autonomy of patients with mild to moderate dementia. Encouraging whole families to participate in the maintenance of a demented person is crucial to prevent the development of depression or uncontrolled medical illness in caregivers, especially elderly spouses, who shoulder the full burden of dementia care. Offering prepared meals and day treatment also helps keep patients with dementia in community settings. Anything that delays the point at which patients require nursing home care improves quality of life and can lessen financial hardship. However, complete care is often necessary in the last year or so of life. Medical professionals must help families recognize when they have arrived at that difficult point.

Is dementia preventable?

The prevention of dementia is a crucial public health goal. The tissue changes associated with dementia occur late and typically represent irreversible damage. Pre-morbid neurochemical imbalances and genetic abnormalities are future targets for preventive treatment. Existing public health initiatives aimed at preventing head injury and aggressively treating hypertension, diabetes, endocrinopathies, vitamin deficiencies, autoimmune diseases, alcoholism, and other chronic conditions are important strategies for preventing dementia.

Recommended Readings

Clark CM, Ewbank DC. Performance of the Dementia Severity Rating Scale: A caregiver questionnaire for rating severity in Alzheimer disease. *Alzheimer Disease and Associated Disorders* 1996; 10:31–39.

Huey ED, Putnam KT, Grafman J. A systematic review of neurotransmitter deficits and treatments in frontotemporal dementia. *Neurology* 2006; 66:17–22.

Mace NL, Rabins PV. *The 36 Hour Day: A Family Guide to Caring for Persons with Alzheimer Disease, Related Dementing Illnesses, and Memory Loss in Later Life,* 5th ed. Baltimore, MD: Johns Hopkins Press Health Book; 2011.

Taylor MA. Dementia. In Taylor MA, *Fundamentals of Clinical Neuropsychiatry,* New York: Oxford University Press; 1999.

Review Questions

1. A 77-year-old woman is caring for her 82-year-old husband who has DAT. She is uncomfortable going out of the house with him for fear he might become confused or agitated. She asks the physician to prescribe something that will "knock him out," since worrying about him wandering at night has made her own sleep fragmented and unrestful. She acknowledges feelings of sadness and worthlessness, along with some loss of weight. The physician should
    A. counsel her that placement in a skilled nursing facility will soon be necessary.
    B. make a referral to adult protective services to protect the husband.
    C. prescribe a sleeping pill for her to take and consider offering an antidepressant.
    D. send her for psychiatric evaluation.
    E. urge her to ask other family members to help care for him.

2. A woman diagnosed with hypertension when she was 64 began to show personality changes around age 75, becoming anxious and forgetful. At age 77, her mini mental status score was 18, with her most marked deficits being disorientation to time and inability to do a three-step command or copy a figure. Retest at age 78 was unchanged, but at 79, she developed aphasia, with a drop in score to 12. Her caregiver confirmed that loss of function was erratic (e.g., she would be stable, then· suddenly lose a capacity such as knowing where she kept things, or how to put on clothes). After her death at age 80, her family requested an autopsy. This would likely show
    A. diffuse lesions containing presenilin and huntingtin.
    B. enlargement of the fourth ventricles and diffuse cortical atrophy.
    C. Lewy bodies clustering primarily in frontal and temporal lobes.
    D. plaques, granulovacuolar changes, and neurofibrillary tangles.

    E. signs of infarction of medium and small blood vessels, with lesions of different ages.

3. A 49-year-old man with trisomy 21 (Down syndrome) and an IQ of 65 lives in a group home and works assembling packages in a sheltered workshop. Over the course of a year, he loses the ability to work, becomes withdrawn and uncooperative, and speaks much less than before. This deterioration should be considered
    A. delirium of unknown etiology.
    B. dementia since he has lost previously acquired capacities.
    C. expected neurodevelopmental degeneration.
    D. organic personality syndrome.
    E. psychosis secondary to trisomy 21.

Key to review questions: p. 408

45 Delirium and Secondary Syndromes

Peter D. Zemenides, MD, and Julia B. Frank, MD

- What is meant by altered mental status?
- What are the key clinical features of delirium?
- What causes delirium?
- What brain dysfunctions produce delirium?
- How is delirium managed?
- What are secondary syndromes?

Altered Mental Status

What is meant by altered mental status?

Altered mental status (AMS) is a non-specific clinical term describing acute (hours to days) changes in an individual's baseline awareness, attention, perception, memory, language, personality, or behavioral responses to various internal and external stimuli. AMS is not, itself, an actual diagnosis because it does not distinguish primary (idiopathic) psychiatric disorders from psychological and behavioral symptoms that result from acute brain dysfunction. While primary psychiatric disorders are not usually life threatening, delirium and other psychiatric disorders due to general medical conditions (secondary syndromes) may be. Thus, optimal management of patients presenting with altered mental status requires careful diagnostic evaluation and differentiation among primary psychiatric disorders, delirium, and secondary syndromes.

Delirium

Mr. Brown brings his 74-year-old mother to the Emergency Department because she has been behaving strangely for 2 days. He reports that she seems confused about events that happened during the day and has had trouble with tasks such as dressing, preparing meals, and using the telephone, which she normally does without difficulty. She has been in good health and has had regular routine medical screening tests with negative results. She takes only calcium and vitamin D supplements for osteopenia. In the ED, the patient's pulse and blood pressure are normal but her temperature is 39°C. On exam, she is lethargic and answers questions slowly and unreliably. She is disoriented to time and situation and has trouble recalling recent events. Her physical examination is unremarkable. Urinalysis reveals many white blood cells consistent with a urinary tract infection. Following treatment with antibiotics, the patient gradually returns to her baseline level of functioning.

What are the key clinical features of delirium?

Delirium is a disorder characterized by an *acute alteration of consciousness* with fluctuating disturbances in cognition, perception, behavior, affect, and sleep due to an underlying physical cause (see Table 45.1). These global disturbances, which can be subtle or obvious, mark an abrupt change from baseline functioning. Although many of the symptoms resemble those of idiopathic psychiatric disorders (especially mood and psychotic disorders), delirium reflects brain dysfunction verifiable by

Table 45.1. Clinical features of delirium

Acute Onset: Symptoms develop over hours to days and represent a clear change from baseline functioning. The time between the onset of the cause of the delirium and the appearance of symptoms varies widely, depending on the specific cause and the presence of other risk factors.

Fluctuating Course: The quality and intensity of disturbances can vary within a 24-hour period and between consecutive days. Periods of transient improvement may be mistaken for resolution. Patients suspected to have delirium should be examined multiple times a day.

Impaired Attention: Difficulty in focusing, sustaining, and shifting attention is typically present. Marked distractibility is a cardinal feature. The absence of attentional impairment makes the diagnosis of delirium unlikely.

Altered Level of Consciousness: Often described as a change in consciousness, a more accurate description is "abnormal level of arousal" that varies from somnolence to hypervigilance disproportionate to environmental stimulation.

Memory Deficits: Impairment in the registration, consolidation, retention, and retrieval of information appear as poor performance on tasks that assess immediate, short-term, and remote memory. Verbal and nonverbal memory is affected; severe cases may impair procedural memory. Autobiographical memory is usually preserved, but retrieval may vary, leading patients to provide misleading or inaccurate information.

Disorientation: Delirious patients are usually disoriented to time, place, and situation but rarely to self. Marked impairment in tracking the passage of time may be one of the earliest signs. Disorientation to time typically fluctuates within a day and may respond to environmental cues such as verbal reorientation, clocks, and calendars.

Disorganized Thoughts: Thoughts may be tangential or circumstantial and demonstrate an illogical flow of ideas. Severe cases include significant paucity of content and lack of spontaneous speech. Thought disorder may make patients' communication incoherent or hard to follow.

Perceptual Disturbances: Initially, delirious patients may perceive sizes, shapes, and colors abnormally. They can develop illusions or gross misinterpretations of external stimuli in any sensory modality, most often vision and hearing. Misperception of *internal* stimuli is expressed as hallucinations. These are typically auditory or visual, although tactile and olfactory hallucinations may occur. The presence of vivid and bizarre visual hallucinations is more common in delirium and other secondary syndromes than in primary psychiatric disorders.

Delusions: Delusions are common and often lead to misdiagnosis of a primary psychotic disorder such as schizophrenia. Delusions in delirium are usually paranoid and bizarre but are not typically fixed or well developed. Delusions may be a form of confabulation, as the patient tries to make sense of internal and external stimuli in the face of distractibility, disorganization of thought, and perceptual disturbances.

Language Disturbances: Slow, slurred speech, paraphasias, dysgraphia, word-finding difficulty, and reduced comprehension may be present. Full-blown expressive or receptive aphasia may develop in severe or prolonged delirium.

Psychomotor Disturbances: Behavior may vary from absence of voluntary movement to restlessness with purposeless or inappropriate motor activity. Patients may injure themselves or others as a result of clumsiness, agitation, or purposeless aggression.

Sleep Disturbances: These include daytime drowsiness with frequent napping, followed by nighttime insomnia and fragmented sleep. Symptoms of delirium typically worsen at night ("sundowning"). Dreamlike experiences may occur when awake.

Disturbances in Affect: Affect may be constricted or flat. Labile expressions of anxiety, depression, euphoria, and irritability are common, reflecting underlying unstable mood. These emotional states may also be responses to the cognitive and perceptual disturbances that impair the patient's appreciation of reality.

objective evaluation, such as electroencephalography (EEG). In addition, patients may have physical signs associated with the underlying etiology, such as postural tremors in alcohol withdrawal, fever in infection, or pupillary signs in intoxication. Because the disturbances in delirium fluctuate, features may not always be present at the same time or with the same intensity.

What causes delirium?

Delirium is usually the result of multifactorial processes, including general medical conditions, metabolic derangements, the effects of medical treatment or street drugs, and even prolonged stress in vulnerable populations (see Table 45.2). While these etiologies are diverse, all have the potential to disrupt normal neuronal activity. Delirium indicates that this disruption has affected the brain on a global scale, impairing neuronal circuits that sustain consciousness, higher level cognitive functions, and even those regulating vital functions such as temperature, circulation, and respiration. Intervention is urgent, as further deterioration may result in death. As illustrated in the case of Mr. Brown's mother, effective treatment of the underlying condition, when possible, usually reverses delirium, although full resolution of symptoms is not always attainable.

The mature human brain has multiple overlapping functions and dense connections that make it resilient to physical stressors. Very young and very old people lack this "cognitive reserve" and may become delirious with little provocation. Other major risk factors that reduce cognitive reserve include preexisting medical conditions and functional impairments (see Table 45.3). Patients in

---

Table 45.2. Causes of delirium

1. Drugs
Sedatives
- Opioids
- Anticholinergics
- Alcohol intoxication/withdrawal
- Illicit drug intoxication/withdrawal
- Polypharmacy
- Misc: corticosteroids, fluoroquinolones, dopamine agonists, muscle relaxants

2. Metabolic/electrolyte abnormalities
- Hypoglycemia/hyperglycemia
- Hypoxia
- Hypercapnia
- Hypernatremia/hyponatremia
- Hypercalcemia/hypocalcemia
- Acid-base disturbances
- Fever/hypothermia

3. Endocrine disorders
- Hypothyroidism/hyperthyroidism
- Cushing's syndrome
- Adrenal insufficiency

4. Nutritional deficiencies
- Wernicke's encephalopathy
- Vitamin B12 deficiency

5. Infections
- CNS infections - meningitis, encephalitis, AIDS, neurosyphilis, Lyme disease
- Any infectious process (e.g., UTI, pneumonia)

6. Systemic inflammatory disorders/vascular disorders
- Systemic lupus erythematosus
- Paraneoplastic syndromes
- Disseminated intravascular coagulation
- Thrombotic thrombocytopenic purpura

7. Organ system failure
- Uremia
- Hepatic encephalopathy
- Hypoperfusion (e.g., shock, congestive heart failure)

8. Primary neurological disease
- Head trauma
- Elevated intracranial pressure
- CNS neoplasms
- Seizures - ictal, postictal, and interictal states
- Vertebrobasilar stroke
- Right (nondominant) parietal lobe infarct

9. Severe stress states
- Surgery
- Prolonged sleep deprivation
- Prolonged immobility, physical restraints
- Severe pain

hospitals and nursing homes are especially vulnerable. Awareness of these risk factors is critical to responding early and implementing preventive measures.

Table 45.3. Risk factors for delirium

– *Extremes of age* (very young/very old)
– *Preexisting cognitive impairment* (dementia or intellectual disability)
– *Preexisting medical conditions* (especially neurological conditions such as head injury, stroke, epilepsy)
– *Baseline poor health or disability*
– *Environmental conditions* – sensory deprivation, meaningless stimulation, overstimulation (e.g., impaired vision/hearing, intrusive medical procedures: fecal disimpaction, bladder catheterization)

What brain dysfunctions produce delirium?

Delirium is the consequence of changes in neuronal function, including alterations in neurotransmitter and chemical signaling. The variety of clinical features in delirium reflects disturbances in multiple brain regions and neurotransmitter sys-

---

Table 45.4. Neuroanatomical correlates of the clinical features of delirium

Frontal lobe/prefrontal cortex – inattention, thought disorganization, delusions, perceptual disturbances, disorientation/memory deficits, language impairments, psychomotor disturbances
Basal ganglia/thalamus/hippocampus – inattention, thought disorganization, delusions, perceptual disturbances, disorientation/memory deficits, disturbances in affect, psychomotor disturbances, sleep disturbances
Cingulate gyrus – psychomotor disturbances, language impairments
Temporal lobe – delusions, perceptual disturbances, memory deficits
Parietal lobe – inattention, delusions, perceptual disturbances, disorientation
Occipital lobe – perceptual disturbances
Brainstem – inattention, altered level of consciousness, sleep disturbances

---

tems. Correlating functional neuroimaging, brain lesion studies, and performance on neuropsychological tests in delirium helps clarify the specific brain regions involved (see Table 45.4).

Several neurotransmitter systems have been implicated in delirium (see Table 45.5). Neurons that synthesize and release these neurotransmitters are clustered mainly in brainstem and other subcortical nuclei; their axons terminate in dispersed cortical and subcortical areas, where receptors that respond to a particular neurotransmitter regulate their excitatory or inhibitory effects. This interaction is reciprocal, as subcortical input influences cortical output, and vice versa. Cortical neurons also directly regulate one another by releasing and responding to GABA (generally inhibitory) and glutamate (generally excitatory). The coordinated activity of a particular network of neurons is necessary for complex functions such as cognition, emotion, personality, language, perception, and behavior. In addition, chemical signals originating outside the brain, such as cytokines and corticosteroids, affect the activity of these networks.

Table 45.5. Neurochemical alterations in delirium

– Acetylcholine deficiency
– Dopamine excess
– Serotonin excess or deficiency
– Norepinephrine excess
– Histamine excess or deficiency
– GABA excess or deficiency
– Glutamate excess or deficiency
– Glucorticoid excess
– Cytokine (IL-1, IL-6, TNF-alpha) excess

The end result of all of these potential derangements is diffuse *hyperpolarization* of neurons that makes them less likely to generate action potentials. This pattern of *hypoactivity* typically appears on an EEG as *diffuse slowing* of the dominant rhythms, generalized delta waves, and loss of reactivity of the EEG to eye opening and closing. The EEG is the only objective test with *specific* findings in delirium and correlates well with the degree of cognitive impairment.

Managing Delirium

How is delirium managed?

There are four components to the optimal management of delirium: (1) treatment of the underlying cause, (2) modification of risk factors, (3) environmental interventions, and (4) pharmacological management of symptoms (see Table 45.6). Given that delirium is associated with high morbidity and mortality, rapid intervention is critical to successful outcome. In addition, management must be flexible as symptoms fluctuate in quality and severity.

Table 45.6. Management of delirium

1. **Treatment of underlying cause:** Identifying and correcting the physical cause is essential, although spontaneous resolution of delirium may occur. Examples include antibiotic treatment for infection, discontinuation of medication, and correction of metabolic/electrolyte abnormalities. Often causes cannot be identified or treated directly, requiring other measures to improve prognosis, as listed below.

2. **Modification of risk factors:** Examples include simplifying complicated medication regimens, improved management of preexisting medical conditions, including pain and discomfort, and correction of sensory deficits with eye glasses and hearing aids. Ideally, these risk factors should be addressed preemptively rather than reactively.

3. **Environmental interventions:** These include controlling external stimuli to promote relaxation and uninterrupted sleep, using cues such as clocks and calendars to help orientation, utilizing familiar persons such as family or consistent staff as caregivers, maintaining a comfortable environment by optimizing temperature and lighting, and encouraging mobility and activity. Physical restraint may be necessary if the patient poses a risk to self or others, but this is a last resort. Physical restraints can actually worsen the course of delirium, and expose the patient to other complications.

Table 45.6. (Continued)

4. **Pharmacological management:** Certain medications may attenuate symptoms of delirium and improve the overall prognosis. Medications are primarily used to control acute agitation but may have value in scheduled dosing to manage thought disturbances, inattention, paranoid delusions, mood lability, and insomnia. Medications used in delirium include: high potency typical **antipsychotics**, atypical antipsychotics, short-acting benzodiazepines, and nonbenzodiapine **hypnotic agents** (e.g., trazodone). The choice of medication depends on the underlying cause and coexisting factors. Benzodiazepines should not be used alone except in delirium due to alcohol or benzodiazepine withdrawal. In all cases, dosing should begin low and be titrated slowly upward, especially in the elderly.

Secondary Syndromes

S. L., a 23-year-old Iraq War veteran, was brought to his primary care physician by his wife. Since returning home following rehabilitation from a concussive injury to his head, he has had significant changes in his personality. Despite his physical recovery, he stopped showing interest in any activity, often sitting for prolonged periods staring at the television. His wife described him as impulsive, with poor table manners and socially inappropriate behavior, and subject to wide mood swings with little to no provocation. An MRI of the patient's brain revealed white matter loss in the frontal lobe with old microhemorrhages.

What are secondary syndromes?

Secondary syndromes are typical psychiatric syndromes (*psychosis*, *major depression*, *mania*, *anxiety*, *catatonia*, *personality changes*) or specific patterns of *cognitive impairment* (e.g., frontal lobe syndrome) that occur in the course of various medical conditions. Clinicians may be distracted by the psychiatric symptoms (hallucinations, delusions, extreme mood) and overlook the underlying disorder. A differential diagnosis that includes the possible medical etiologies of every psychiatric syndrome, at least when it first appears, is essential to avoid this serious error.

Differentiating secondary syndromes from delirium is particularly important. Some chronic conditions, such as endocrine or vitamin deficiencies or structural insults (especially to the head), may damage neuronal networks without the same spreading of dysfunction that occurs in delirium. In consequence, secondary syndromes typically spare vital functions and lack signs of diffuse cortical impairment, making recognition less urgent. Key differentiating factors are that these secondary syndromes tend to occur without alterations in consciousness or significant fluctuations in symptoms. Also unlike delirium, which typically occurs in conjunction with an acute cause and remits following treatment, secondary syndromes may be due to chronic processes that cause permanent brain damage and, therefore, persisting symptoms (see Table 45.7 for examples). Although certain symptoms may respond to psychotropic medication, treatment of the underlying medical condition, where possible, is essential to recovery and future well-being.

Table 45.7. Etiologies of secondary syndromes
– Neurodegenerative conditions (Alzheimer disease, Parkinson disease, Pick disease, Huntington disease) – Multiple sclerosis – Traumatic brain injury, stroke/multi-infarct dementia or other focal brain lesions – Epilepsy (especially complex partial seizures) – AIDS – Systemic inflammatory disease (sarcoidosis, systemic lupus erythematosus) – Obstructive sleep apnea – Pheochromocytoma, other endocrine tumors or endocrinopathies (hypo/hyperthyroidism; adrenal insufficiency/ hypercortisolemia) – Vitamin deficiencies (thiamine, folate, B12) – Chemotherapy (e.g., for cancer) – Iatrogenic (drug side effects)

Recommended Readings

Burns A, Gallagley A, Byrne J. Delirium. *Journal of Neurology, Neurosurgery, and Psychiatry* 2004; 75:362–367.

Inouye S. Delirium in older persons. *New England Journal of Medicine.* 2006; 354:1157–1165.

Kay J, Tasman A (Eds.). *Essentials of Psychiatry.* West Sussex, UK: John Wiley & Sons; 2006.

Maldonado J. Pathoetiological model of delirium: A comprehensive understanding of the neurobiology of delirium and an evidence-based approach to prevention and treatment. *Critical Care Clinics* 2008; 24:789–856.

Trzepacz P. The neuropathogenesis of delirium: A need to focus our research. *Psychosomatics* 1994; 35:374–391.

Review Questions

1. Which of these clinical features does NOT suggest the diagnosis of delirium?
   A. Altered level of consciousness
   B. Distractibility
   C. Fluctuating course
   D. Identifiable physical cause
   E. Insidious onset

2. Typical EEG patterns in delirious patients include which of the following?
   A. Diffuse slowing of dominant rhythm
   B. Focal increase in delta wave activity
   C. High-frequency wave patterns
   D. Increased reactivity to eye opening and closing
   E. Increased sleep spindles

3. Secondary syndromes may usually be distinguished from delirium by
   A. absence of altered consciousness.
   B. disorganized thought.
   C. disturbances in affect.
   D. hallucinations.
   E. paranoid delusions.

Key to review questions: p. 408

46 Anxiety and Dissociative Disorders

Julia B. Frank, MD, and Rory P. Houghtalen, MD

- What are the major anxiety disorders?
- How does understanding pathogenesis contribute to the treatment of anxiety?
- How are medication and CBT effective in treating anxiety?
- What are normal and pathological dissociation?
- Why are dissociative disorders controversial?
- What are common treatments for dissociative disorders?

Human adaptation to any challenge begins with the arousal of the entire organism, mediated by a unique blend of cortical regulation and neurobehavioral fight/flight/freeze responses. Through activation of the **autonomic nervous system**, and elements of the **HPA axis**, the individual mounts *differentiated* responses to environmental dangers, social threats, internal physiological signals, and idiosyncratic challenges related to prior experience.

Moderate arousal fosters cortical activity that enhances learning, planning, and the weighing of positive and negative outcomes. However, overwhelming, unduly persistent, inappropriate, or misunderstood arousal compromises effective adaptation and constitutes the defining characteristics of **anxiety disorders**. Even the "normal" peripheral manifestations of arousal (e.g., increased or pounding heartbeat, shortness of breath, gastrointestinal distress, dizziness) can alarm individuals unfamiliar with the body's arousal mechanisms and prompt requests for medical care. Individuals who are naïve with regard to normal functions of arousal, or who lack experience in coping with anxiety-provoking situations, can develop *anticipatory fear* of arousal episodes ("fear of the fear") which, if continuously reinforced by avoidance behaviors, paradoxically bring on the feared panic attacks.

Whereas anxiety activates a response in the *amygdala* mediated by input from the hippocampus and prefrontal cortex, **panic** triggers an amygdala response that is generally unmodulated by limbic system/cortical regulation (see Chapter 7, Stress, Adaptation, and Stress Disorders). When the person is unaware of the stimulus condition triggering the anxiety/panic, the emotional arousal feels uncued, as though coming "out of the blue," resulting in increased anticipatory fear.

Major Anxiety Disorders

What are the major anxiety disorders?

Anxiety disorders are the most common form of psychopathology with a prevalence of about 18%. However, the number of people who seek treatment for anxiety is far smaller. The symptom clusters defining anxiety disorders all embody the following basic elements: (1) *arousal* that may be tonic, paroxysmal, or mixed, (2) *negative expectation* and interpretation of situations as ominous or overwhelming, and (3) *avoidance* of situations perceived as dangerous. See Table 46.1 for an overview of the major anxiety disorders.

Panic disorder is characterized by recurrent panic attacks, occurring over at least 1 month, involving *anticipatory anxiety* (the fear of having an attack) and *avoidance* of situations where panic is likely to occur or help is unavailable. A panic attack is defined in the DSM-IV-TR as a discrete period of intense fear or discomfort during which at least four of the following symptoms develop abruptly and reach a peak within 10 minutes:

– Palpitations, pounding heart
– Sweating
– Trembling, shaking
– Dyspnea, feeling smothered
– Choking sensation
– Chest pain, tightness
– Nausea, abdominal distress
– Dizziness, fainting
– Paresthesias
– Chills, hot flashes
– Fear of dying/ going crazy
– Depersonalization/derealization

Social phobia refers to fear (sometimes panic), often with blushing, of anticipated humiliation or rejection by others in social situations. While the person desires social activities and relationships, the dread of embarrassment leads to avoidance. As with panic disorder, the avoidance prevents corrective learning and sustains impairment.

Research has correlated social phobia and the related diagnosis of **avoidant personality disorder** to developmental experiences, ranging from familial modeling of social avoidance to more adverse experiences such as being subjected to humiliation as a form of discipline, being isolated or bullied, especially as an adolescent, or disfiguring lesions that provoke disgust or rejection. A less generalized form, *performance anxiety* (or *stage fright*), is more common and responds to more limited treatment.

Developmental Experiences Contributing to Social Phobia/Avoidant Personality Disorder

– Familial modeling
– Being bullied
– Humiliation as a form of discipline
– Disfiguring lesions (visible burns or deformities)

Simple phobias are characterized by fear responses to specific cues, encountered during a particularly frightening experience (e.g., animals [snakes, insects, dogs], environment [darkness, heights], situations [flying, riding an elevator], blood, injury, or needles). Phobias only require treatment when they inhibit some necessary activity, such as air travel or seeking health care, or create excessive distress. Blood, injury, and injection

phobias are uniquely associated with fainting due to reflexive *vasovagal* responses.

According to the DSM-IV-TR, to qualify for the diagnosis of **posttraumatic stress disorder** (PTSD), a person must experience, witness, or be confronted with an event or events that involve actual threatened death or serious injury, or a threat to the physical integrity of oneself or others, and to which the person responds with intense fear, helplessness, or horror (in children, agitated, disorganized behavior). The three symptom clusters needed for diagnosis are *intrusion*, *arousal*, and *avoidance*. Intrusion symptoms include forced recollection (remembering when one does not want to), nightmares, flashbacks (reliving the traumatic situation in the present), and bodily reactivity to reminders (a form of arousal). Other arousal symptoms include poor sleep, inability to concentrate, irritability, and enhanced startle response. Avoidance is both behavioral and cognitive. The person avoids cues to traumatic recollection or actual situations where trauma might recur, and makes conscious efforts not to think about what happened. Internal avoidance involves numbing (i.e., inability to experience normal emotion), amnesia for some or all of the experience, a sense of estrangement from others, loss of interest in former activities, and an inability to imagine a positive future.

Although not part of the diagnostic criteria, nonspecific somatic distress (headaches, pain, or GI dysfunction) is common in PTSD and often prompts the search for medical care. The person may not disclose the precipitating traumatic event unless asked.

When the immediate reaction to the trauma involves dissociation followed by all three types of PTSD symptoms and lasts up to one month, the diagnosis would be **acute stress disorder** (ASD). ASD is likely to be subsumed under PTSD in DSM-5.

Physiologically, PTSD has a unique pattern of endocrine dysfunction, with low urinary cortisol and high norepinephrine metabolite excretion. Neuroimaging has also shown partly reversible shrinkage of the hippocampus. One postulated mechanism is the failure of glucocorticoid receptors to inhibit the initial intense alarm response, first to the trauma and then to recollection of the trauma.

Social support, including medical care, and returning to usual meaningful activity after a trauma buffer the impact and may prevent development of PTSD. In the US, the most typical trauma affecting women is rape or family violence, while for men it is combat or accidents. Natural and man-made disasters expose males and females equally.

Obsessive compulsive disorder (OCD) is characterized by intrusive, arousal, and avoidance symptoms. Intrusive symptoms include obsessive thoughts, typically fears of contamination or danger, and unjustified guilt. More rarely, patients describe fears of doing something violent or sexually or socially inappropriate. The compulsions are acts (e.g., counting, repeating phrases) or behaviors (e.g., washing, cleaning, checking locks or outlets, creating symmetry) that the person does to neutralize the fear of doing something

wrong, making a mistake, or being criticized. Compulsions may or may not be related to obsessions. Adults with OCD typically recognize their thoughts are irrational but still feel compelled to neutralize them. Relief of the arousal reinforces the compulsions, causing the behaviors to proliferate until they become disabling.

Generalized anxiety disorder (GAD) is defined as a persistent (> 6 months) pattern of uncontrollable worries about health, safety, access to resources, and threats to other people. The person shows multiple signs of arousal and autonomic dysfunction (e.g., muscle tension, headaches and backaches, sighing, difficulty concentrating). Generalized fearfulness leads to constriction of behavior, avoidance of risk or novelty, and inhibi-

Table 46.1. Onset, course, and epidemiology of anxiety disorders

Disorder	Onset, course	Epidemiology
Panic disorder	Onset: early teens through age 40 Chronic, relapsing (may remit)	Prevalence: 1–3% community, 3–8% in primary care Female:Male 2:1
Social phobia/social anxiety disorder	Bimodal onset; age 5 or early adolescence Chronic, but may remit with positive social experiences	Prevalence varies: 3–4% severe; performance anxiety more common Female:Male 3:2 (more males seek treatment)

Simple phobia	Onset:
	  Animals, age 7
	  Blood, age 9
	  Situations, age 2–7 and early 20s
	May remit with experience
		Prevalence: 11% (most common anxiety disorder)
		Blood, injury, injection phobias more common in males

Posttraumatic stress disorder	Onset: any age, after trauma May begin at variable intervals Intensity waxes and wanes with experience	Population prevalence: 8%, varies by exposure risk With equal exposure to trauma, females more likely than males to develop PTSD
Obsessive compulsive disorder	Onset: males age 6–15; females 20–29 (especially post partum) Onset gradual, 5% episodic, 15% severely deteriorate (early onset worsens prognosis) Waxes and wanes with stress	Estimated prevalence: 2% Prevalence in pediatric population: 0.3–1% Childhood onset: males > females Adult onset: males = females
Generalized anxiety disorder	Onset: mid teens to mid 20s May occur after onset of chronic illness Duration > 6 months	5% prevalence Female:Male 2:1

tion of normal curiosity. GAD may develop at any age, often following the onset of chronic disease. If untreated, GAD may cause or exacerbate disability.

Three other anxiety disorders are: *agoraphobia*, defined as fear of situations where the person might be embarrassed, humiliated, and unable to escape or find help if anxious; *substance-induced anxiety disorder*; and *anxiety disorder secondary to a general medical condition*.

Because any stressor, challenge, or threat to the integrity or survival of the individual prompts arousal, anxiety is commonly *comorbid* with other psychiatric disorders. As a dysphoric state associated with helplessness, anxiety is especially associated with *major depressive disorders*. Indeed, up to 60% of depressed patients have previously experienced, or will eventually develop, an anxiety disorder (see Chapter 47, Major Mood Disorders).

2. A 30-year-old woman experiences nightmares after being raped in a dark room. She breaks into a sweat whenever it is dark. She feels constantly threatened, jumpy, and unable to concentrate. She avoids talking about the rape or reading the newspaper or any other possible reminders. By avoiding discussing her experience, her belief that she was somehow responsible and doomed to another attack goes uncorrected and contributes to persistent hyperarousal.

3. A 16-year-old boy is distressed by intrusive thoughts that his hands are dirty. Even if he has washed them recently, he feels uneasy until he washes them thoroughly again. He develops skin irritation from using caustic soap but cannot stop himself from using it.

Treatment

> How does understanding pathogenesis contribute to the treatment of anxiety?

While *genetic factors* influence the sensitivity of the arousal response, it is epigenetic factors that determine which environmental conditions or psychological factors trigger panic. An individual's lack of familiarity with the normal stress response sets the stage for misconstruing arousal states. Familial modeling and training are also critical risk factors (e.g., hypervigilant or fearful parents). Once established, the perpetuation of an

Clinical Examples

1. Metabolic acidosis following exercise triggers a panic attack in a 32-year-old woman, who has no explanation for it and fears she has a life-threatening medical condition. She broods on her fears, constantly scanning her body for signs of disorder. As her anticipatory fear increases, she avoids places where she might not be able to get to a hospital, or where she would be embarrassed by fainting, or losing control in front of other people. Repeated emergency room evaluations for cardiac disease are normal but not reassuring, until she receives a diagnosis of panic disorder and pursues treatment.

anxiety disorder results from continued reinforcement of the misperceptions, behavioral symptoms and emotional responses, generally via avoidance. Fortunately, these responses can be modified by treatment.

Psychotherapy

> How are medication and CBT effective in treating anxiety?

Anxiety disorders involve characteristic **cognitive distortions** (e.g., overestimating the danger or likelihood of a feared event, underestimating self control or capacity to cope, and self-fulfilling negative prophecy). All also involve **avoidance**, which prevents corrective learning and perpetuates the symptoms.

Even when medication modifies neuroendocrine arousal, cognitive distortions and crippling avoidance can persist. **Cognitive behavioral therapy** (CBT) addresses these factors by educating the patient about how anxiety develops and persists. Successful treatment involves helping patients identify and confront their misperceptions, learn relaxation exercises to reduce, tolerate, or control arousal, and interrupt and modify the avoidance behaviors that perpetuate their symptoms.

The woman with panic (Example 1) might be taught to interrupt her thoughts when she starts to anticipate panic and to challenge the perception that her condition is dangerous. After learning slow breathing, she could practice *interoceptive exposure*, purposefully inducing feared bodily sensations and recognizing that she can experience them without panic. After treatment, she will be able to successfully tolerate the periods of heightened arousal when they occur.

The woman with PTSD (Example 2) should be encouraged to repeatedly recount the memory of the trauma to a calm and nonjudgmental therapist (*imaginal exposure*). The degree of unpleasant arousal typically lessens with each retelling. The person begins to remember the trauma more normally by *redefining the contextual time and place of the trauma*, reducing factors that trigger recurrence, and resolving feelings of guilt and estrangement.

For the 16-year-old boy with OCD (Example 3), treatment would involve *exposure and response prevention*, uncoupling the intrusive thought from the compulsive response by, for example, purposefully dirtying his hands and resisting the compulsion to wash until the distress subsides.

Similar principles underlie the cognitive behavioral therapy of *specific phobias*, in which people progressively expose themselves to a feared situation or object. Social phobia responds equally well to CBT, especially when the corrective learning occurs in group therapy and real social situations (see Chapter 40, Principles of Psychotherapy).

> The success rates for various cognitive behavioral treatments for anxiety vary from 60–90% for people who complete a full course of treatment.

Pharmacotherapy

Medication that modulates the serotonin/norepinephrine system, especially **SSRIs, monoamine oxidase inhibitors**, and **dual acting antidepressants** (see Chapter 41, Pharmacological Interventions for Psychiatric Disorders), are useful in preventing panic and reducing anticipatory anxiety. **Benzodiazepines** are effective in reducing anticipatory or generalized anxiety but only the most potent benzodiazepines (e.g., alprazolam) quickly and directly relieve panic. *Performance anxiety* responds well to lipophilic

beta-adrenergic blocking agents, such as propanolol.

Although medications are effective for reducing the physiological symptoms associated with anxiety, relapse often follows the discontinuation of medication. Optimal treatment should always also include basic principles of CBT, especially exposure, which teaches the patient how to understand, tolerate, and self regulate arousal responses. However, patients on clinically effective doses of benzodiazepines (i.e., experiencing <u>no</u> anxiety symptoms), may not respond to CBT because they cannot learn to regulate an anxiety response if it is not occurring. In such cases, a reduction in benzodiazepine dosage to allow for a limited anxiety response enables the exposure therapy to have its effect by facilitating the development of more adaptive coping skills.

Dissociative Disorders

> ### What are normal and pathological dissociation?

Dissociation is the disruption, loss, or absence of the usual integration of memory, consciousness, and personal identity. *Normal* dissociation commonly occurs, for example, when a person is absorbed in a book and unaware of the surrounding environment. Dissociation also occurs during periods of fatigue and monotony, such as driving a long stretch of highway without remembering doing so. **Hypnosis** is believed to be dissociation induced by intense concentration.

Dissociation can be a protective response to trauma or intense and recurrent *fear*, allowing the individual to ignore pain or anxiety and cope with the emergent situation. *Pathological dissociation* is dissociation that occurs repeatedly and out of context and results in impaired functioning, primarily in close personal relationships and stressful environments. Pathological dissociation

> A woman involved in a multi-car accident stands beside her car directing traffic until the police arrive. Only then does she realize she has a broken arm. At the time, she had felt herself standing outside her body, watching the scene from a distance.

Table 46.2. Dissociative phenomena and related disorders

Dissociative Disorders NOS	Description	Example	Comment
Dissociative Fugue	– Departs from usual activity with patchy loss of personal memory – May be subtly confused or in no distress	– Woman wakes up in a hotel room wearing unfamiliar clothes; does not recall traveling there; remembers her name, age and profession, but not a recent violent confrontation with her partner	– Often occurs after a traumatic event – Can last hours to months – F > M ratio 3:1
Dissociative Amnesia Note: fugue and amnesia may be combined in *DSM-5*	– Inability to remember important stressful personal events	– Veteran cannot recall witnessing death of friend in combat, time in training together, or his own last months of deployment	– May involve patchy gaps in remembering personal history, details of an event, or period of time – Lasts minutes to years
Depersonalization	– Detachment from one's own body and emotions – Feels robotic, as though describing someone else	– After receiving a kidney transplant, a man feels no spontaneous joy or interest. He feels like he's watching himself from a distance	– Persistent or intermittent – No memory loss – May occur in reaction to medical procedures or states of severe anxiety (e.g., fear of closed spaces) – Person typically has insight into condition
Derealization Note: may be combined with depersonalization in *DSM-5*	– Person sees self as separate from environment, as if in a movie	– Sleep deprived intern in ER feels as if working behind a glass curtain in two dimensional space; puzzled by familiar equipment, although uses it correctly	– Usually a transient symptom, not a disorder per se
Dissociative identity disorder (formerly *multiple personality disorder*)	– Person has two or more subjectively felt identities, each typically expresses a particular affect – Person is aware of being divided, but may not know all the states or that they operate independently	– A woman in psychotherapy varies from session to session, by turns giddy, cheerful, miserable, childlike, sullen, angry, and terrified; emotional states shift abruptly; refers to herself in the third person and is unaware of her inconsistency	– Different states called "alters" – Person is unable to integrate unacceptable emotions tied to memories not normally available – Alters may claim their own personal histories, identities, and names – Often associated with severe early trauma such as sexual abuse – Frequent switching among alters occurs during increased stress – Patients may meet criteria for *borderline personality disorder*

is generally experienced as occurring randomly or "out of the blue," although it may be triggered by cues related to prior trauma of which the patient is unaware. See Table 46.2 for an overview of dissociative disorders.

Dissociative disorders have been reported worldwide, frequently manifested as dissociative trance and states of possession, reflecting culturally-specific *explanatory models*. Dissociation can occur in other psychiatric disorders, for example, *schizophrenia*. However, the mechanisms underlying dissociation are likely to vary in different contexts. Rarely, dissociation is a sign of serious neurological disorder (e.g., *partial complex epilepsy*).

Risk Factors

A history of severe family dysfunction and poor premorbid emotional, social, or occupational functioning predisposes people to pathological dissociation. Repeated dissociation beginning early in life, especially in abused children, affects the child's ability to form realistic perceptions of other people. This primes catastrophic responses to hints of separation or disconnection. The person may develop a tendency to see others as either all good or all bad, even holding contradictory views of a single person.

> Susan, a 32-year-old woman, seeks treatment for chronic depression, anxiety, and thoughts of suicide. She reports being sexually and physically abused as a child and being raped during adulthood. She complains of "spacing out" and experiences minutes to hours of amnesia, after which she may find herself walking unfamiliar streets or wearing clothing in a style different from her own. She reports hearing angry voices inside her head. One day, she tells her therapist to call her Kim. "Kim" says Susan knows nothing about her, mocks Susan's timidity, and is irritable and aggressive, especially when discussing fears. Later in the session, Susan returns, has no memory of Kim, but is aware of a time gap in the session.

> Why are dissociative disorders controversial?

In dissociated states, especially dissociative identity disorder, fugues, and dissociative amnesia, people may act in ways that violate their own and other's sense of social appropriateness and morality. The person can carry out complex behaviors, but may not remember, or claim not to remember, doing them. For this reason, people who dissociate are sometimes suspected of malingering or falsifying their history to avoid punishment or responsibility.

The phenomenon of dissociation raises questions about the validity of all memories. Researchers have shown that memory of an event can change in response to questioning by authority figures. Thus, "therapists" who assume that all dissociation results from unremembered victimization may in fact inadvertently foster the development of false memories. This has led other researchers to question, in particular, whether **dissociative identity disorder** occurs spontaneously or is taught by therapists as a "way of explaining" contradictory or incompatible aspects of one's personality. A person may "remember" a daydream, or something witnessed or described by others, as personally experienced. This can disrupt whole lives, especially if a person tries to get confirmation – or seek legal justice – against someone remembered, long after the fact, as a perpetrator of abuse. Family informants and hospital and legal records should be carefully researched to objectively verify the reports of patients with dissociation who claim early victimization.

Bio-Behavioral Mechanisms of Dissociation

The mechanisms underlying dissociation are not fully understood. Some psychotropic drugs, particularly ketamine, phencyclidine (PCP), and LSD can induce dissociative states. Neurochemically, this suggests that dissociation relates to disruptions of the subcortical/cortical networks that express monoamine neurotransmitters (dopamine, serotonin, norepinephrine, acetylcholine) and endogenous opioids. Dissociation may also involve imbalances of GABA and glutamate in the cortex.

Treatment

> What are common treatments for dissociative disorders?

Although treatment for depression or anxiety sometimes relieves moods that induce dissociative states, no psychotropic drug to prevent dissociation is currently available. Someone suffering fugue or amnesia typically can benefit from reassurance and an exploration of possible triggering events. **Psychodynamic psychotherapy**, which explores emotional memories of triggering events and their meaning, may be effective. **Hypnosis** to induce dissociation therapeutically is potentially helpful in facilitating intervention while the person is in the dissociated state. However, it can also be harmful because people under hypnosis are suggestible and may generate memories or states in response to the therapist's inquiries and assumptions. *Mindfulness*, a technique used in **dialectical behavior therapy**, has been shown to facilitate awareness of one's own bodily state and more realistic perceptions of others.

Recommended Readings

Bell V, Oakley DA, Halligan PW, Deeley Q. Dissociation in hysteria and hypnosis: Evidence from cognitive neuroscience. *Journal of Neurology, Neurosurgery, and Psychiatry* 2011; 82:332–339.

Fricchione G. Generalized anxiety disorder. *New England Journal of Medicine* 2004; 351:675–682.

Jenike MA. Obsessive-compulsive disorder. *New England Journal of Medicine* 2004; 350:259–265.

Katon WA. Panic disorder. *New England Journal of Medicine* 2006; 354:2360–2367.

Yehuda R. Post-traumatic stress disorder. *New England Journal of Medicine* 2002; 346:108–114.

Review Questions

1. Walter, a 25-year-old medical student, is mortified by racing heart beat, shaking voice, and dizziness when he has to make presentations or respond to questions from his superiors. When observed doing procedures, his hands shake. He wonders if he can finish his training. He has friends and a solid marriage. He might respond quickly to
    A. cognitive behavioral therapy.
    B. prolonged exposure.
    C. reassurance that he is doing well.
    D. treatment with a beta blocker.
    E. treatment with an SSRI.

2. Esther, a college educated woman of normal intelligence, cannot hold a job. She expresses initial enthusiasm for new colleagues, but quickly begins to feel misunderstood, mistreated, and exploited. She finds it hard to concentrate and has angry outbursts at work, then becomes a model employee for a few weeks before reverting to disruptive behavior. The therapist who evaluates her should
    A. administer a dissociative experiences scale.
    B. attempt to gather objective information about office conditions.
    C. offer hypnosis to quickly uncover early traumatic memories.
    D. order an EEG and an fMRI to look for imbalances of cortical activity.
    E. suggest medication to reduce her impulsivity.

3. A nursing student is invited to observe the repair of a large laceration. Eager for the experience, he glances at the injury and faints. His supervisor should
    A. advise him to see a psychiatrist and get medication.
    B. reassign him to an office position.
    C. say that blood/injury phobia is not uncommon.
    D. suggest that he is unsuited for a health related profession.
    E. tell him to wear support stockings to prevent fainting.

Key to review questions: p. 408

47 Major Mood Disorders

Julia B. Frank, MD, and Rory P. Houghtalen, MD

- What is a mood disorder?
- How is the current classification of mood disorders likely to change in DSM-5?
- How do gender, genetic risk, and environmental stress interact in the development of mood disorders?
- How are mood disorders diagnosed?
- What treatments are effective for mood disorders?

Introduction to Mood Disorders

What is a mood disorder?

Moods are persistent subjective states, expressed in thought, emotion, behavior, and bodily functions. Moods are not inherently pathological. Sadness in response to deprivation, loss, or disappointment is an expected, generally self-limited state. Euphoria is an appropriate response to entering a desired relationship, achieving a goal, or surviving a threat. Fear or anxiety is an appropriate adaptive response to unknown or dangerous situations.

A **mood** (or **affective**) **disorder** is diagnosed when an unusually intense and persistent mood occurs out of context, compromising self-care, adaptive functioning, and the ability to relate to others. A precipitating event may or may not be involved. Moods become disorders based on the duration, intensity, and pattern of symptoms during an episode. **Mania** describes a mood state that is elevated, expansive, or irritable, with accompanying *vegetative* symptoms (disruptions of **homeostasis**). Signs of mania include behaviors such as excessive output of speech and thought, distractibility, racing thoughts, excessive pleasure seeking, impulsive and sometimes aggressive acts, and, in extreme cases, delusions or hallucinations. By definition, mania must last a week or more. Severe symptoms may lead to hospitalization. By definition, **hypomania** describes a mood with some or all of the features of mania, except

psychosis. Although it may be intense, hypomania either lasts less than a week, or does not meet all of the other criteria for mania. Hypomania does not lead to hospitalization.

Mood disorders have been recognized since antiquity. The alternation of mania with depression was described by the early 20th century empiricist Emil Kraepelin as "*manic depression*" (DSM **bipolar disorder**). Classic presentations are fairly easy to recognize. The mnemonic SIG: E CAPS (**S**leep, loss of **I**nterest, **G**uilt, decreased **E**nergy, **C**oncentration difficulty, **A**ppetite disturbance, **P**sychomotor retardation/agitation, **S**uicidal thoughts) helps to systematically elicit the nine vegetative symptoms of which the DSM requires five for the diagnosis of a **major depressive episode**.

SIG: E CAPS

In a physician's prescription, the abbreviation **SIG** means "directions." E CAPS reminds the prescriber to write **E**nergy **Cap**sules for depression (antidepressants).

Diagnostic Criteria

Current criteria for the diagnosis of mood disorders can be found in the DSM-IV-TR of the American Psychiatric Association and the ICD-10 of the World Health Organization. Both orga-

Table 47.1. Core signs and symptoms of mood disorders

Pathological moods
Depression: sadness, negative mood, inability to experience pleasure (anhedonia), anxiety (generalized, panic, or both)
Mania: euphoria, expansiveness, irritability, anger
Mixed: oscillating sadness, euphoria, anger and anxiety

Neurovegetative (chronobiological/homeostatic) dys-regulation
Depression: difficulty falling or staying asleep, early morning awakening, exhaustion, loss of appetite or overeating, loss of sexual interest, crying spells, bodily symptoms of anxiety, pain sensitivity, slow gastrointestinal activity/constipation
Mania: Lack of need for sleep, increased energy, increased sexual interest and acitivity, impulsivity; hyperphagia

Cognitive qualities
Depression: guilt, worthlessness; hopelessness, helplessness, suicidal thoughts; difficulty concentrating or remembering; memory biased toward negative experiences
Mania: grandiosity, suspiciousness or paranoia; catastrophic loss of judgment with overspending; thought disorder (circumstantiality, tangentiality, flight of ideas)

Motor behavior (including speech)
Depression: slow thought; slow, sparse speech; "leaden paralysis" *(psychomotor retardation)*; agitation
Mania: restlessness, hyperactivity; rapid, "pressured" speech, difficult to interupt

In depressed children, irritability and labile sadness are more typical than prolonged, persistent sadness or anhedonia. Mania in children is difficult to differentiate from attention-deficit disorder with hyperactivity.

nizations have worked to establish conformity in the two diagnostic systems, but some differences remain. Because the DSM is the predominate system in the US, DSM IV-TR criteria are used for the descriptions below.

Major Depressive Disorder (MDD): The diagnosis of MDD requires the presence of major depressive episodes, characterized by severely depressed mood persisting for at least 2 weeks. Episodes may be isolated or recurrent, and are categorized as mild (few symptoms), moderate, or severe (marked effect on social/occupational functioning).

Bipolar Disorders: *Bipolar I disorder* is diagnosed if the person has one or more episodes of mania with recurrent depressive episodes. *Bipolar II disorder* is diagnosed if the person has recurrent depressive episodes and one or more episodes of hypomania (periods of elevated mood that do not fulfill the criteria for mania). *Cyclothymic disorder* is characterized by rapidly alternating mood states occurring continuously over a period of 2 years. The moods include symptoms of hypomania or depression but do not meet criteria for a full episode of either one.

Dysthymic Disorder: diagnosis is made in individuals who persistently experience symptoms of depressed mood and at least two of the other characteristics of major depression. By DSM-IV-TR definition, dysthymic symptoms must be present for ≥ 2 years. Clinically, dysthymia may be a lifelong quality or "personality trait." Superimposed episodes of major depression may occur, resulting in *double depression*.

Mood Disorder due to a General Medical Condition (GMC): For diagnosis, the pathological mood must be the direct result of an endocrine, metabolic, or autoimmune disorder, chronic infection, cancer, nutritional deficiency, head injury, or other condition affecting brain function. Depressive psychological reactions to illness do not meet these criteria.

Other mood disorders include *Substance-Induced Mood Disorder* and *Mood Disorder* NOS (Not Otherwise Specified).

Issues in Diagnosis

How is the current classification of mood disorders likely to change in DSM-5?

The criteria for many mood states and disorders are "heterothetic" and threshold based (i.e., formal diagnosis requires the person to endorse a certain number of symptoms from a list). Many combinations "meet criteria," so persons with markedly different symptoms may receive the same diagnosis. Also, DSM IV-TR does not provide diagno-

Table 47.2. DSM qualifiers of mood states (coded with main diagnosis)	
Atypical features	Overeating, oversleeping while depressed; preserved reactivity to reward.
Catatonic features	Detachment from the environment while awake; negativism including immobility, mutism, refusal to eat or drink. May be life-threatening.
Melancholic features	Dense anhedonia, lack of response to reward, terminal insomnia (early morning awakening), diurnal variation (mornings worse).
Postpartum onset	Depressive episode within 1 month of childbirth by definition. Clinically, this period of markedly increased risk may be ≥ 3 months. Often includes marked anxiety.
Psychotic features	<u>Mood congruent in depression</u>: Delusions of poverty, guilt, nihilism, illness, self-disgust; derogatory auditory hallucinations. <u>Mood congruent in mania</u>: Delusions of special powers or unlimited resources, paranoia, auditory hallucinations.

ses for many recognized patterns of pathological mood (e.g., recurrent mania without depression, marked depressive symptoms entrained to the menstrual cycle [*premenstrual dysphoric disorder* or PMDD]). Thus, the current diagnostic criteria do not accurately reflect the complex clinical phenomena of mood disorders, raising the risk of misdiagnosis and inappropriate or ineffective treatments.

The stability of mood diagnoses is also questionable. Up to 60% of people with depression experience co-morbid anxiety disorders. This relationship to anxiety is bidirectional, since anxiety disorders frequently evolve into episodes of depression. Anxiety that co-occurs with depression can significantly increase the risk of **suicide**. DSM-5 may expand the definitions of mood disorders to acknowledge these clinically important facts.

Clinical Course

How do gender, genetic risk, and environmental stress interact in the development of mood disorders?

At least 10% of people in the US experience an episode of depression in their lifetimes. Women have twice the rate of depression as men, due to increased incidence during the reproductive years. Once established, depression *recurs* in men and women with equal frequency. Mood disorders often begin in late adolescence or early adulthood. Early onset, especially in childhood, may reflect greater genetic influence and often predicts a highly recurrent course. Onset in late life suggests depression (rarely mania), *secondary to a general medical condition*, although depression as a primary disorder may develop at any age. Major depressive disorder is about 10 times more common than bipolar disorder (10% versus 1% prevalence, respectively).

After a first episode of major depression, 50% of patients experience recurrence within 2 years unless on maintenance treatment; after a third episode, the rate of recurrence is 90%. Bipolar patients experience more frequent episodes of depression than mania or hypomania. After any bipolar episode, the risk of recurrence increases from 50% at 1 year to 90% at 3 years if mood stabilizing treatment is not continued. Four or more episodes of either mood within a year is called *rapid cycling*. The consequences of untreated or inadequately treated depression include disability and suicide. Even with treatment, 30–40% of people with bipolar disorder are unable to work at their pre-illness

According to the World Health Organization (2008), Major Depressive Disorder ranks 3rd among the leading causes of disability worldwide (1st in high and middle income countries, and 5th in low income countries). It is the *leading source of disease burden among women*, regardless of country income.

level. In mood disorder generally, rates of completed suicide range between 3% and 15%.

Psychotic symptoms occur in 10–15% of severely ill patients with MDD or bipolar disorder. Psychotic symptoms can increase the risk for dangerous behaviors and often lead to hospitalization.

Bio-Behavioral Mechanisms of Mood Disorders

Having a first-degree relative with *MDD* doubles a person's risk of developing MDD, while having a first-degree relative with *bipolar disorder* repre-

sents a 5–10 times greater risk for that disorder. Although multiple genes have been implicated in the etiology of depression, unmodified, direct genetic influence is limited. Research on gene-environment interactions has been more promising. Early traumatic life events appear to have negative epigenetic effects on genes that encode glucocorticoid receptors, corticotrophic releasing factor (CRF), and serotonin transporter systems, all of which are essential to adaptive functioning and the ability to cope with stress (see Chapter 2, Predisposition). The need to consider both genes and environment emerges from the research finding that in patients with a specific genotype regulating the serotonin transporter (5-HTT) system

Table 47.3. Role of brain structures in relation to normal function and mood disorders

Structure	Normal Function	Symptoms/Signs of Mood Disorder
Hippocampus	Short-term memory	Cognitive inefficiency, recollection bias (depressed people cannot access happy memory; mania makes sad memory inaccessible)
Thalamus	Individual thalamic nuclei are part of three distinct circuits that link cortical areas with sensory cortices and subcortical structures. These regulate emotion, motivation, arousal, and attention.	Erratic arousal, subjective distress, compromised attention/concentration; Loss of pleasurable responses to sensation in depression; Sometimes associated with hypersensitivity to sensory input in mania
Dorsolateral prefrontal cortex	Conscious thought, executive functions (selection among alternatives, anticipation, inhibition of impulses, sequencing)	Helplessness, indecisiveness, hopelessness, distorted sense of time (slowed in depression, accelerated in mania)
Orbitofrontal cortex	Assess risk in pursuit of reward, relate new information to context (memory and environment)	Overestimation of risk and reduced reward in depression; underestimation of risk in mania
Anterior cingulate gyrus	Integration of emotion and cognition	Abnormal motivation (apathy in depression); Dysregulation of arousal
Amygdala	Fear, rage, selective attention	Anxiety, irritability, vigilance, hypersensitivity to negative environmental cues
Nucleus accumbens	Reward	Lack of pleasure (depression), decreased or increased motivation
HPA axis	Sleep, appetite, sexual behavior, metabolic rate, adaptation to acute or chronic environmental or social stress	Insomnia/hypersomnia, lack of or increased sexual interest, hyperphagia or anorexia

and a history of severe emotional neglect in childhood, the hippocampus and prefrontal cortex were smaller than in patients with only one of these risk factors. This finding highlights the role of gene-life stress interaction leading to a decrease in serotonin receptor response, impaired glucocorticoid receptor response, and a decrease in brain-derived neurotrophic factor (BDNF), an essential element for neurogenesis. Decreased BDNF results in thinning of the neuronal structures in the prefrontal regions receiving input from the limbic system, resulting in reduced hippocampal/PFC volume. Reduced volume in these areas is associated with decreased function (i.e., impaired adaptive and coping skills and depression). Antidepressant medications appear to restore BDNF levels, glucocorticoid receptor response, and serotonin receptor response, enhancing neurogenesis and facilitating new and adaptive learning.

Recent research also suggests that stress-induced increases in the MPK-1 gene contribute to depressive symptoms by negatively regulating a key signaling pathway (MAPK) involved in neurogenesis. Antidepressant medication appears to reduce the expression of the MPK-1 gene.

Thus, mood disorders are associated with genetically regulated dysfunction in a number of brain structures and neuronal systems that coordinate cognitive, vegetative, and motor activity critical for adaptation and survival (see Table 47.3). These brain areas are linked by networks of neurons that respond to circulating neuropeptides, releasing factors, and hormones. Moderate to severe depression also involves dysregulation of the catecholamine (*norepinephrine* and *dopamine*) and indolamine (*serotonin*) systems, and disturbances in hypothalamic activity, especially the regulation of thyroid and glucocorticoid hormones. Stress-induced elevations in glucocorticoids also have a catabolic effect upon the hippocampus, impairing the individual's ability to learn from experience and adapt to new stressful situations. Thus, genetically predisposed individuals are vulnerable to psychosocial stressors, especially social or interpersonal challenges or losses (see Chapter 7, Stress, Adaptation, and Stress Disorders).

Research also implicates *female reproductive hormones* in the pathogenesis of depression. Periods of hormonal flux (postpartum, premenstruation, and perimenopause) are all associated with mood symptoms that may reach the threshold for diagnosis of a mood disorder. Established

mood disorders in women typically worsen during these phases.

Sleep regulation is also a factor in the development and maintenance of mood disorders. Disordered sleep is common in major depression, with patients showing increased and intensified REM sleep, early onset of REM (decreased REM latency), and relative lack of stage 4 sleep. Sleep deprivation can bring on mania in genetically vulnerable people (see Chapter 6, Chronobiology and Sleep Disorders).

Screening for Depression in Primary Care

How are mood disorders diagnosed?

A 24-year-old woman asks her primary care physician for sleeping medication. She reports that life seems flat and that she wants to break up with her fiancé, because she feels unworthy of his love. She cannot sleep past 4 a.m. and has lost 10 lbs. A similar episode resulted in a leave of absence during her junior year in college. Her mother has recurrent depression.

Pain, fatigue, or changes in sleep and appetite often prompt people to seek help from primary care providers. Major depression is present in roughly 20% of patients in general medical offices. Unfortunately, only half of these patients are diagnosed correctly, leading to expensive unnecessary testing and inadequate treatment. In addition to overtly depressed mood, "red flags" that should prompt exploration for depression are a past personal history of mood disorder, family history, recent loss, or severe stress, and frequent ER or office visits. Many valid screening techniques exist to identify patients in need of further question-

Parents bring their 17-year-old son to an emergency room. For the last 6 weeks, he has slept less than 2 hours a night. He claims he has developed a revolutionary operating system for computers. He has been telephoning strangers in the middle of the night to sell his idea. He is irritable and has threatened his father. In the interview, he laughs frequently, cannot stay still, is hard to interrupt, and shouts at his parents.

ing. The simplest is to ask, "Have you felt down, depressed, or hopeless, or had little interest or pleasure in doing things during the past 2 weeks?"

Mania is usually diagnosed on behavioral, rather than medical, grounds. People with mania often lack insight and resist the suggestion that they are ill. Although confidentiality is important in dealing with psychiatric disorders, the accuracy of recognizing bipolar disorder increases dramatically when a friend or family member contributes information to the assessment of a person in a depressed or manic phase.

Careful assessment to rule out underlying medical causes is essential every time a person experiences a mood episode, but repeating expensive invasive diagnostic tests is neither necessary nor helpful.

> **Medical screening for mood episodes should include:** review of systems, physical exam, blood count and chemistries, thyroid function tests, and tests for autoimmune factors. Other studies (EKG, neuroimaging) should be obtained only if indicated by specific symptoms, not just abnormal mood.

Treating Mood Disorders

> What treatments are effective for mood disorders?

Psychoeducation, explaining a diagnosis in terms of etiology and particular symptoms while offering ways to improve coping, is critical to the success of any treatment. Psychoeducation should start during the first encounter. Treatment selection should be determined by the nature and severity of the patient's symptoms, frequency of recurrence, precipitating stress, developmental concerns, and individual preferences.

Evidence-based medicine strongly supports the use of psychotherapy, medication, or both in the treatment of mild to moderate depression. Complementary approaches, including light therapy, massage, or acupuncture, can also help. The evidence supporting the efficacy of bright (but not full spectrum) light is particularly strong.

Melancholic depression, depression with psychotic or catatonic features, highly recurrent depression, and mania initially require somatic intervention, usually medication (see Chapter 41, Psychopharmacological Interventions for Psychiatric Disorders). These conditions also respond well to *electroconvulsive therapy* (ECT), the safest and most rapidly effective treatment for mood disorders, with a ≥ 90% success rate. Some newer brain stimulation technologies also show promise. *Vagal nerve stimulation* is now an FDA-approved treatment for *refractory* depression. Transcranial magnetic stimulation also has been approved for treatment of depression, and deep brain stimulation is under investigation.

After an episode of depression responds to initial treatment, maintenance medication is used to prevent recurrence, while psychotherapy supports adherence to treatment and introduces new and more adaptive coping strategies and social skills. Family involvement in treatment (when possible) is critical, as patients often lack insight and motivation to seek help when ill.

Psychotherapies for Depression

Psychodynamic approaches that encourage patients to review past experiences and relationships can be helpful if the person is able to avoid becoming further pre-occupied with prior experiences that appear to justify the current mood.

Multiple, rigorous evaluation studies demonstrate the efficacy of **Interpersonal Psychotherapy (IPT)** and **Cognitive Behavioral Therapy (CBT)** for depression. IPT focuses on the link between depression and four interpersonal issues: (1) loss, (2) conflict or detachment, (3) a life transition such as new job or move, and (4) deficits in social skills. Patients learn to recognize and change their patterns of interpersonal activity, and then to apply therapeutic insights to future situations as a form of *relapse prevention*.

CBT involves identifying distortions of thinking and maladaptive behavior that contribute to depressed mood, then altering the reinforcing conditions that sustain it. Cognitive behavioral therapists teach patients more adaptive appraisal, problem solving, and interpersonal skills (see Chapter 8, Emotion and Learning), prescribing exercises that require the patient to challenge and change patterns of negative thought, and to increase rewarding activities (*behavioral activation*). In comparison to psychodynamic psychotherapy, CBT is more present-oriented and eschews any inferences about the role of unconscious processes.

Recent developments in psychotherapy have led to the integration of elements of psychodynamic psychotherapy, IPT, and CBT into "third-generation" systems of psychotherapy, sometimes in combination with medication. One such modality, *cognitive behavioral analysis system of psychotherapy* (CBASP) was developed specifically for the treatment of chronic depression. While it is still under investigation, the combination of CBASP and antidepressant medication has been shown to be especially effective in chronic severe depression. While the effects of medication alone may disappear once treatment ends, improvement from psychotherapy persists or even increases as patients continue to apply what they have learned to new situations. In combination therapies, medications apparently "jump start" neuroendocrine processes to promote plasticity and make the brain more receptive to the learning provided by psychotherapy.

Medication for Mood Disorders

Antidepressant medications include serotonin reuptake inhibitors (SSRIs), tricyclics, and monoamine oxidase inhibitors (MAOIs). Newer drugs act on predetermined neurobiological targets that are known to be involved in the etiology of mood disorders (rational psychopharmacology). SSRIs are the most frequently prescribed antidepressant medications because they are easy to use and their side effects are usually well tolerated. Despite their common action on 5-HT uptake, the structural heterogeneity in these compounds results in varied pharmacological properties (e.g., plasma half life, liver metabolism, protein binding, receptor affinity), inducing different drug responses in different patients. As a result, determining the appropriate medication for a given patient involves both selection based on the patient's particular history and, sometimes, trials of several drugs before the most effective medication for a specific patient is identified (see Chapter 41, Psychopharmacological Interventions for Psychiatric Disorders).

Antidepressant medications may take up to 3 weeks to have any clinical effect (**response latency**) and must be taken consistently for 6-8 weeks before a full therapeutic response can be differentiated from a placebo or non response. Since patients have difficulty accurately reporting symptoms retrospectively, clinicians periodically evaluate patients' symptoms with instruments validated in research studies (e.g., *Beck Depression Inventory II, Patient Health Questionnaire, Hamilton Depression Scale, Montgomery Asberg Rating Scale for Depression, or Young Mania Rating Scale*). Such "measurement based care" improves clinical decisions, especially during protracted episodes that require sequential trials of different drugs.

Patients who respond to an antidepressant should continue it for at least 4–6 months. Stopping earlier can result in relapse. In recurrent mood disorders, mood stabilizing medications, which may include antidepressants, lithium, anticonvulsants, and some atypical antipsychotics, must be continued indefinitely to prevent relapses. Concern for side effects and long-term consequences such as weight gain thus becomes important in the management of recurrent depression, bipolar disorder, and all other chronic conditions.

Patient and Family Education

Engaging and maintaining patients in treatment requires collaboration between them, their physicians, and their family, when available. Adherence improves when patient and family fully under-

---

Key educational issues in mood disorders:

- describing the nature of mood disorders and rationales for treatment
- dispelling myths and stigma
- reviewing potential harmful consequences of substance use
- increasing knowledge about healthy sleep-wake cycles and sleep hygiene
- understanding the importance of taking medication reliably and not stopping medication prematurely
- encouraging patient and family to talk openly about the disorder, develop symptom management techniques, and reduce unnecessary stress
- improving early identification of signs of recurrence
- developing a crisis plan to respond to new or increased suicidal ideation

stand the patient's psychiatric condition and treatment.

Organizations like the *Depression and Bipolar Support Alliance* (DBSA) offer patients educational materials, measurement tools, and support groups. Peer-led programs such as *Recovery International* (formerly *Recovery, Inc.*) may also be helpful in inducing and sustaining recovery.

Recommended Readings

Elkin I, Shea MT, Watkins J, et al. NIMH Treatment of Depression Collaborative Research Program: General effectiveness of treatments. *Archives of General Psychiatry* 1989; 46:971–982.

Frank JB. Perinatal Depression. In Battle C. (Ed.), *Essentials of Public Health Biology: A Guide for the Study of Pathophysiology.* Sudbury, MA: Jones & Bartlett; 2008.

Sher L, Kahn D, Oquendo I. Mood Disorders. In Cutler JL, Marcus ER (Eds.), *Psychiatry,* 2nd ed. New York: Oxford University Press; 2010, pp. 53–98.

Online Resources

Office of Mendelian Inheritance in Man (OMIM) Major Affective Disorder 1 MAFD1, Bipolar Disorder BPAD Major Depressive Psychosis, Autosomal. Available at http://omim.org/entry/125480

Review Questions

1. The mnemonic SIG: E CAPS covers
   A. anxiety symptoms commonly comorbid with depression.
   B. common side effects of antidepressants.
   C. DSM criterion symptoms of major depression.
   D. suicide risk factors.
   E. symptoms differentiating mania, hypomania, and depression.

2. Mania is required for diagnosis of which of the following disorders?
   A. Bipolar I disorder
   B. Bipolar II disorder
   C. Cyclothymic disorder
   D. Dysthymic disorder
   E. Mood disorder with psychotic features

3. Maintenance treatment (continuing antidepressant medication for years) should be considered in
   A. patients who have attempted suicide.
   B. patients who prefer medication to psychotherapy.
   C. patients with a history of post-partum depression.
   D. patients with severe comorbid anxiety.
   E. patients with three or more episodes.

4. Once depression is identified, medical evaluation should include
   A. examination of CSF for protein.
   B. functional neuroimaging.
   C. Halstead-Reitan Battery.
   D. thyroid function tests.
   E. 24-hour urine cortisol excretion.

Key to review questions: p. 408

48 Schizophrenia and Other Psychotic Disorders

Sonja M. Lillrank, MD, PhD, and Rory P. Houghtalen, MD

- What are the characteristic features of psychotic disorders?
- What are the symptoms of schizophrenia?
- What is the natural history of schizophrenia?
- What factors have been hypothesized to contribute to the etiology of schizophrenia?
- What are four psychotic disorders other than schizophrenia?

Psychotic Disorders

> What are the characteristic features of psychotic disorders?

Psychosis is a generic term for a state in which reality testing is impaired. Psychotic disorders are characterized by *delusions* or *hallucinations,* and varying degrees of *disorganized thought*, *speech*, *behavior*, and *social impairment* that affect the patient's ability to meet the ordinary demands of life. Psychotic disorders are differentiated from one another by the quality and quantity of the clinical findings manifested by the patient, by the impact of the disorder on personality and social functioning, and by etiology, if known.

The cardinal symptoms of psychosis are internally generated perceptions (*hallucinations*) and fixed, false beliefs (*delusions*). Depending on the type and nature of the psychosis, varying degrees of disorganization of thought and behavioral and social impairment are seen. Psychotic symptoms may occur in mood disorders, drug intoxication, dementia, delirium, various medical conditions, and developmental disorders. *Primary psychotic disorders* are classified by the nature, severity, and pattern of symptoms and behavior, rarely by known etiology.

Schizophrenia

Schizophrenia, the most common psychotic disorder, affects about 1% of the world's population. Both genders are equally affected, but the disorder tends to present earlier in life in males. It can have pervasive effects on the person including the loss of ability to perceive and express emotion normally (i.e., dysregulation of affect) and deterioration from baseline personality. To varying degrees, schizophrenia compromises motivation, self-care, and the ability to work, occupy oneself, and relate to other people. Schizophrenia is usually chronic, with periods of remission and exacerbation. When not overwhelmed with psychosis, people with schizophrenia can recover significantly and lead gratifying and productive lives.

Worldwide, management of schizophrenia accounts for more inpatient treatment days per year than any other condition. Schizophrenia also accounts for roughly 2.6% of the total years lost to disability (YLD) calculated by the World Health Organization. Statistically, persons with schizophrenia have a reduced life expectancy of about a decade and often suffer from comorbid problems including substance use, tobacco use, difficulty accessing primary care, and obstacles to managing chronic health conditions that likely contribute to early mortality. Death by suicide occurs in 10–15% of cases.

Previously fastidious and outgoing, a 20-year-old college sophomore now rarely comes out of his room, is unkempt, is preoccupied with the meaning of life, mumbles to himself, and is expressionless except for bursts of inappropriate speech. His speech is sparse. He talks about his "vision quest" to find "the inner soul of the patrician monarchy." He becomes hostile when questioned and accuses the interviewer of attempting to "steal my mind to insert your sins." Physical examination and screening laboratory studies reveal no obvious medical problems and urine drug screen is negative.

Symptoms of Schizophrenia

What are the symptoms of schizophrenia?

The symptoms of schizophrenia are divided into three groups: positive, negative and cognitive. Each group implicates dysfunction in different brain regions and neurotransmitters.

Positive symptoms include *delusions, hallucinations, thought disorder,* and *movement abnormalities.*

Delusions are false beliefs that are not changed by reason or evidence that controvert them. In schizophrenia, these erroneous beliefs are often bizarre and incongruent with mood, and tend to guide how the individual interprets reality and behavioral responses. Examples include beliefs that one's body, mind, or soul has been mysteriously changed and beliefs that supernatural or alien forces are influencing events, inserting or removing one's thoughts, or causing one's thoughts to be broadcast without speaking them. Some delusions are less bizarre and involve themes of persecution, grandiosity, jealousy, illness, guilt, or sin. Convictions that random events such as a man tipping his hat or that news stories, television, radio programs, or religious texts are directed toward oneself are called *delusions of reference.*

Auditory hallucinations are the most common type of hallucination, although any of the five perceptual senses may be involved. The hallucinations are typically more complex and bizarre than those of other psychoses. Auditory hallucinations may be experienced as conversations between several different voices that talk together about the individual, comment on his or her thoughts,

or command the person to behave in a way that is uncomfortable and uncharacteristic. Other odd experiences include perceptions that someone or something is controlling the thoughts, emotions, and behaviors of the patient.

Thought disorder (see Table 48.1) is characterized by the absence of linear and logical connections between ideas. Communication in speech or writing is also disorganized and may become incomprehensible. The classic thought disorder of schizophrenia is characterized by *loose associations (derailment)* where ideas are strung together in a random, convoluted manner such that the listener cannot understand or make sense of the person's conversation. Other named thought disorders observed in schizophrenia include tangential and circumstantial thought.

Table 48.1. Typical descriptors of abnormal thought form in schizophrenia

Name	Description
Derailment	Loss of meaning due to random connections/loose associations between ideas
Tangential	Responses to questions are only partially or remotely connected to the topic
Circumstantial	Excessively detailed or circuitous speech, yet still responsive to the question
Neologism	Creation of words with unique meaning understood only by the individual (e.g., "predentity" or "tragement")
Blocking	Losing track of the goal of speech and not being able to return to the topic
Word Salad	Complete disregard for conventions of word usage or grammar, incoherence
Clanging	The sounds of words, instead of the meanings or conventions of speech, determine the flow of speech
Perseveration	Repetition of words or phrases

Positive symptoms of schizophrenia include *movement disorders* such as purposeless movements repeated over and over (stereotypy) and catatonia in which both spontaneous and volitional movement is dysregulated along a continuum of retardation to the point of stupor, and extreme excitement.

Negative symptoms are aspects of normal function that schizophrenia impairs. These include *disturbances of affect or emotional tone* (e.g. flat, blunted or labile affect), *poverty of speech* (alogia), *inability to experience pleasure* (anhedonia), *lack of motivation* (avolition) and *social withdrawal* (asociality). Though less dramatic than positive symptoms, negative symptoms are typically persistent and often account for much of the actual disability of schizophrenia.

Cognitive symptoms can be subtle or dramatic deficits in higher intellectual or executive functions that often impair adaptive function and decision making. These include *impaired focus and attention* and marked *deficits in working memory*, or the inability to use recently learned information. Cognitive symptoms may make tasks of everyday life difficult and affect patients' ability to work or study.

Natural History of Schizophrenia and Making the Diagnosis

What is the natural history of schizophrenia?

Schizophrenia typically first appears in adolescence or young adulthood, rarely beyond the fourth decade of life. The usual course proceeds through three distinct phases: *prodromal*, *active*, and *residual* (see Table 48.2). The prodrome of subtle peculiarity of thought, social oddity, and diminished motivation often begins in adolescence or early adulthood. Most patients begin treatment in the active phase, when psychotic symptoms appear. The residual phase, when negative and cognitive symptoms persist, may be punctuated by one or more recurrences of active psychosis in the absence of prominent delusions or hallucinations.

To make the diagnosis of schizophrenia, two criteria must be met:

1. an active phase with prominent psychotic symptoms lasting > 1 month, unless symptoms are interrupted by effective treatment; and

Table 48.2. Phases of schizophrenia

Phase	Features
Prodromal	Gradual change in behavior that may appear as personality or mood change (aloofness, preoccupation, moodiness, oddities of thought or behavior) lasting weeks to months.
Active	Classic findings of delusions, hallucinations, disorganized thinking and behavior. May include agitation, sleeplessness, and dangerous behaviors.
Residual	Continuing oddities of thinking and behavior, often with prominent negative and cognitive symptoms. Delusions or hallucinations are typically absent.

Table 48.3. Key features of schizophrenia subtypes

Subtype	Key features
Paranoid	A central delusional theme predominates, without prominent disorganization of thinking or behavior
Catatonic	Prominent psychomotor changes including stupor, excessive excitement, posturing, mechanical speech
Disorganized	Disorganized thinking and behavior; multiple delusions are often poorly formed into fragmentary themes
Undifferentiated	Insufficient differentiation of symptoms to classify
Residual	Persistent, incapacitating negative symptoms; social and emotional disabilities; without prominent delusions or hallucinations

2. a total duration of symptoms, regardless of phase, of ≥ 6 months.

The DSM-IV-TR further defines five subtypes of schizophrenia: (1) *paranoid,* (2) *catatonic,* (3) *disorganized,* (4) *undifferentiated,* and (5) *residual* (see Table 48.3). The paranoid subtype has the best prognosis and the disorganized subtype the worst.

In cross section, many types of psychosis can appear consistent with the acute phase of schizophrenia. Various factors including the temporal association with mood findings, inciting factors in the history (e.g., active substance use) and family history can help differentiate schizophrenia from other conditions with psychotic symptoms. The mental and behavioral effects of persistent endocrine or nutritional deficiencies, neurological disorders, CNS infections, drug or alcohol abuse, and structural brain abnormality are some of the possible causes of symptoms appearing as schizophrenia that should be ruled out during initial evaluation.

Etiology: Gene Environment Interaction

> What factors have been hypothesized to contribute to the etiology of schizophrenia?

While the etiology of schizophrenia is not known, research implicates both *genetic* and *environmental* factors. The concordance rate for developing schizophrenia is 45–65% in monozygotic twins and 10% in first-degree relatives. The genetic factors are thought to be multiple genes of small effect. Environmental factors including birth injury or intrauterine malnutrition, exposure to cytokines, or infections in the 2nd trimester have been correlated with schizophrenia. The full range of possible causal factors – either specific genes or experiences in pre- and postnatal development – is not yet fully known.

Although no single biological abnormality is diagnostic, major *neuroanatomical changes* have been observed repeatedly in some or most schizophrenic brains. These include decreased blood flow to the *frontal lobes*, thinning of the medial *temporal lobe cortex*, the *frontal cortex*, and small anterior portions of the *hippocampus*, and enlarged *lateral and third cerebral ventricles.*

While most cases of schizophrenia begin in early adulthood, longitudinal studies of populations at risk find subtle problems well before classic symptoms appear. This recognition has led to the suggestion that schizophrenia is a *neurodevelopmental* disorder. Various brain regions, especially the human prefrontal cortex, continue to develop into adolescence and early adulthood. A pre- or perinatal genetic or environmental insult to the still-developing brain could cause a cascade of negative neurobiological effects that do not produce overt symptoms until adult level competencies in cognitive tasks are reached. Some histological findings and expression profiles of schizophrenia susceptibility genes support this hypothesis. Problems stemming from faulty neuronal proliferation, migration, or synapse formation in late-maturing areas of the prefrontal cortex and hippocampus, or disordered connections in the circuits between them, seem part of a neurocognitive system that is impaired in schizophrenia. Abnormal neuronal development in the prefrontal association areas, in particular, may account for the negative symptoms of impaired executive functioning and planning.

While research focuses on brain circuits and genetic vulnerabilities, current treatment targets neurochemical abnormalities. Drugs that relieve positive symptoms all block the dopamine DA-2 receptors. This finding underlies the so called "dopamine hypothesis of schizophrenia," which suggests that increased activity of dopamine (DA) in subcortical mesolimbic brain regions produces positive symptoms, while hypofunction or alterations of DA and other neurotransmitter systems in the prefrontal cortex correspond to negative and cognitive symptoms. New antipsychotic drugs manipulate serotonin (5-HT) activity to partly rebalance dopamine systems. Other research implicates an imbalance in the complex, interrelated chemical reactions of the neurotransmitters 5-HT, GABA, and glutamate. Recently, hypofunctioning of the glutamate system in the prefrontal cortex has also been suggested as an etiological factor in schizophrenia. For example, when given to healthy volunteers, low doses of the glutamatergic NMDA receptor antagonists produce select aspects of schizophrenia, including attentional and memory problems.

Treatment

Antipsychotic medications are the mainstay of medication treatment. They relieve positive symptoms but do not improve negative or cognitive symptoms to the same degree. All have significant adverse effects and risks (see Table 48.4). Those with catatonia may also benefit from ECT.

Psychosocial interventions remain essential in schizophrenia. Empathic and consistent psychiatric care is needed to foster adherence to medication and attention to patients' concurrent medical complications and conditions. Evidence-supported psychosocial treatments include teaching illness management skills, addressing co-occurring substance abuse, rehabilitation to preserve or enhance social and vocational skills, family education, and cognitive behavioral therapy. People whose schizophrenia has driven them into homelessness, or who are at risk of becoming homeless, need special attention. Supported individual or group housing reduces hospitalizations and the overall costs of care and is critical to recovery, relapse prevention, and limiting chronic disability.

Prognosis

Prior to the development of effective antipsychotic agents, multiple recurrences, unremitting psychoses, and gradual deterioration of mental and social abilities leading to institutionalization were common. Today, the active phase of the illness almost always remits within a few days or weeks after treatment begins. However, the active psychotic phase is still a highly recurrent problem for most patients, unless maintenance treatment with antipsychotic medications continues. The prognosis for recovery, supported or independent community living, and employment is better than it once was. However, sustained recovery occurs in < 14% of patients within 5 years of diagnosis; an additional 16% of patients show late-phase recovery.

Table 48.4. Antipsychotic medications
Typicals: haloperidol, chlorpromazine, fluphenazine, and others
Atypicals: olanzapine, risperidone, quetiapine, clozapine, aripiprazole, ziprasidone, and others

	Typical antipsychotics	Atypical Antipsychotics
Mechanism of Action:	Blockade of DA-2 receptors	Blockade of DA-2 and serotonin receptors
– *Extrapyramidal symptoms* (acute dystonia, muscle rigidity, tremor, akathisia)	More common	Less common
– *Tardive dyskinesia* (involuntary movements usually presenting first in the face, lips, or tongue, typically occurs after long-term use)	More common	Less common
– *Metabolic syndrome* (weight gain/problems with glucose/lipid metabolism)	Less common	More common
Toxicity:		
– *Neuroleptic malignant syndrome* (fever, muscle rigidity, delirium, autonomic instability; potentially lethal)	Risk exists	Risk exists

Psychotic Disorders Other than Schizophrenia

> What are four psychotic disorders other than schizophrenia?

People with **schizophreniform disorder** have all the cardinal manifestations of schizophrenia, but recover in less than the 6 months required to diagnose schizophrenia. Family history of schizophrenia is less common than in patients with schizoaffective disorder, but more common than in the general population. The prognosis for full recovery is better than in schizophrenia. Treatment with an antipsychotic medication is usually brief, followed by monitoring for recurrence off medication.

In **schizoaffective disorder**, major depression or mania co-occur with psychotic symptoms characteristic of schizophrenia. Psychotic symptoms persist during periods when the mood symptoms are absent for > 2 weeks. Acute treatment typically includes combining antipsychotic medication with an antidepressant or mood stabilizer. Antipsychotic maintenance is required as in schizophrenia; antidepressant or mood stabilizer maintenance is also necessary in many cases. The psychosocial treatments are the same as those for schizophrenia. Schizophrenia and bipolar disorder appear to share genetic roots; the overlap in the genetic risk for both disorders may explain this "in between" diagnosis.

Delusional disorders present with an isolated non-bizarre delusion of a persecutory, jealous, somatic, or grandiose type. Organization of thought, personality, and social functioning remain relatively unaffected. Onset is typically later in life than schizophrenia, schizophreniform disorder, or schizoaffective disorder. Antipsychotics and serotonin-specific antidepressants (SSRIs) have been used alone and in combination with variable success. The persecutory subtype is particularly resistant to treatment.

Brief psychotic disorder is a transient psychosis that develops suddenly, usually after a highly stressful life event. It remits rapidly with minimum intervention, and does not typically develop a pattern of recurrence. Treatment is symptomatic, generally including a brief course of antipsychotic medication.

Recommended Readings

American Psychiatric Association. *Practice Guideline for the Treatment of Patients with Schizophrenia*, 2nd ed. Arlington, VA: American Psychiatric Association; 2004.

Lieberman JA, et al. Effectiveness of antipsychotic drugs in patients with chronic schizophrenia. *New England Journal of Medicine* 2005; 353:1209–1223.

Nature 2010 Nov 11; 468(7321) Special edition on schizophrenia.

Torrey EF. *Surviving Schizophrenia: A Manual for Families, Consumers, and Providers*, 5th ed. New York: Harper & Row; 2006.

Review Questions

1. A 35-year-old man presents with bizarre delusions, auditory hallucinations, disorganized thinking, insomnia, and agitation. These changes in personality and behavior began nearly a year ago when he lost his job. He became obviously ill in the last month, but resisted evaluation until he assaulted his wife. Neurological examination, screening laboratory tests, urine drug screen, and substance use history are negative. The most likely diagnosis is
   A. bipolar disorder, manic phase, with psychotic features
   B. brief psychotic disorder
   C. major depression with psychotic features
   D. schizophrenia
   E. schizophreniform disorder

2. Which of the following symptoms of psychosis would be most responsive to treatment with antipsychotic medication?
   A. Delusions
   B. Depressed mood
   C. Negative symptoms
   D. Social withdrawal
   E. Thought disorder

3. The prevalence of schizophrenia in the US is closest to
   A. 0.1%.
   B. 1%.
   C. 5%.
   D. 10%.
   E. 15%.

4. In the last 6 months, a 50-year-old, employed woman has become convinced that relatives are swindling her out of her savings. Her bank manager found no evidence to support her contention. A comprehensive medical work-up shows no evidence of medical or neurological disease, dementia, or substance abuse. She has no signs of a thought disorder. Relationships with people other than family are intact. The most likely diagnosis is
    A. brief psychotic disorder.
    B. delusional disorder.
    C. major depression with psychotic features.
    D. schizophrenia.
    E. schizophreniform disorder.

5. A 44-year-old man presents with intense delusional thinking and signs of major depressive disorder. The family reports that he began describing delusional ideas about 3 weeks before his mood changed. Two years ago he had a similar episode. After the major depression remitted, he continued to express delusions for 2 months before these also remitted. The most likely diagnosis is
    A. delusional disorder.
    B. major depression with psychotic features.
    C. schizoaffective disorder.
    D. schizophrenia.
    E. schizophreniform disorder.

6. Which group of symptoms characterizes the prodromal phase of schizophrenia?
    A. Agitation, insomnia, negative thinking
    B. Delusions, hallucinations, disorganized behavior
    C. Disorganized thinking, hallucinations, loss of appetite
    D. Odd behaviors, aloofness, preoccupation
    F. Posturing, mechanical speech, agitation

Key to review questions: p. 408

49 Personality and Impulse Control Disorders

Julia B. Frank, MD, and Joseph C. Viola, PhD

- How are personality disorders defined in the DSM-IV-TR?
- What are the axis II personality clusters?
- How are the definitions of personality disorders being revised?
- What is the dimensional approach to personality?
- What does research reveal about the formation of personality?
- How does the DSM classify behaviors related to impulsive dyscontrol?

Personality Disorders

Warren, a 41-year-old, married college graduate trained in tech support, consults a psychotherapist after losing his job. When interacting with new people, he fears he will say or do something embarrassing. He believes others see him as "weird." Interviewing for new jobs seems overwhelming; he never applied for promotion in the firm where he worked for 15 years. Warren has been anxious since age 14. After his parents divorced, he moved often and was bullied in several of the high schools he attended. Then, as now, he managed to have one or two friends. His wife would like them to socialize more. He has mild insomnia, but otherwise has symptoms only when in a new social situation or preparing for one.

How are personality disorders defined in the DSM-IV-TR?

The DSM-IV-TR, published in 2000, identifies 10 specific personality disorders based on behavioral criteria that encompass difficulties controlling thoughts, regulating mood, and relating to others across multiple domains of the person's life. This *categorical classification*, coded on *Axis II* (Developmental Disorders and Personality Disorders), represents a compromise among adherents of neurobiology, descriptive psychopathology, and psychoanalysis, and contrasts with the *dimensional assessment of personality*, a primary focus of current psychological research. The two approaches agree that temperament and traits that are predominately genetic in origin appear early in development and are then modified by experiences occurring during formative periods. By early adulthood, the qualities of personality have become relatively fixed, although some changes may occur.

The definitions of the DSM-IV-TR all require that a person display core maladaptive characteristics in multiple contexts, such as in both social and occupational functioning. The qualities themselves are mostly *ego syntonic*: they seem part of the self – not in conflict or incongruent. Elements must appear before age 18, but the diagnosis of a personality disorder is not applied until adulthood, when patterns of behavior become more stable. Most DSM personality disorders relate systematically to Axis I disorders, with some overlapping symptoms and partly shared genetic risk factors, as shown in Table 49.1. This overlap or continuity calls into question the validity of separating the two axes. People with personality disorders differ from those with related Axis I disorders in terms of their relatively preserved capacity for appropriate behavior, and absence of marked vegetative signs. Many other elements of Axis I and Axis II disorders differ in degree, rather than kind. These relative differences are not recognized in the current arbitrary categorical definitions.

Type of Disorder	Brief Description
Table 49.1. DSM-IV-TR Axis II personality disorders and related syndromic diagnoses	
Paranoid	Views others as unstrustworthy, exploitative; sees self as victim; responds with behavior aimed at protecting self against the devious intentions of others
Schizoid	Aloof, prefers to be alone and does not enjoy interpersonal encounters; unable to reach intimacy with others
Schizotypal	Eccentric, often odd speech and behavior; may believe self to have special abilities, although not delusional
Histrionic	Excessive emotionality disrupts healthy relationships
Antisocial	Exploits others; manipulative and irresponsible; difficulties maintaining relationships and adhering to societal standards; may participate in criminal activity
Borderline	Constantly shifting mood; prominent anger, fear of abandonment; pushes and pulls others simultaneously; self-destructive; dysphoric
Narcissistic	Grandiose, self-important, generally disdainful of others
Obsessive-compulsive	Perfectionistic, orderly; driven by logic rather than emotion
Avoidant	Wants relationships but fears rejection, humiliation; lacks self-esteem
Dependent	Relies on others to make decisions; fears loss of emotional support; may stay in destructive relationships

Differences in the duration and level of distress and degree of impairment distinguish normal personality variation from personality disorder. Only the most severe personality dysfunctions appear in the DSM-IV-TR. It follows that by the time someone's difficulties reach the threshold of diagnosable personality disorder, those difficulties have become highly resistant to change.

Personality Clusters

What are the Axis II personality clusters?

Because the individual personality disorders overlap, the DSM-IV-TR groups them into **Cluster A** (odd-eccentric), **Cluster B** (dramatic-emotional), and **Cluster C** (anxious-emotional), as described in Table 49.2. A shorthand way of remembering the clusters is to think of them as "mad, bad, and sad" reflecting the negative social judgments that

people with personality disorders typically elicit from others.

Although these clusters are more diagnostically reliable than the individual disorders, problems of validity remain. While genetic and longitudinal studies support the validity of schizotypal, antisocial, and avoidant personality disorders, the validity of the other personality disorders is questionable.

Personality: Continuum or Categories

How are the definitions of personality disorders being revised?

Real world phenomena have challenged the assumptions of the DSM-IV-TR categorical system. Two people who "meet criteria" for the same disorder often differ markedly in other aspects of their personality, while two people who share important, defining characteristics could receive

Table 49.2. The clustered classification of DSM personality disorders		
Classification	**Traits**	**Disorder**
Cluster A	Suspicious, mistrustful Alienated Odd ideas and behaviors	Paranoid Schizoid Schizotypal
Cluster B	Amoral, destructive Unstable mood and relationships Dramatic, flamboyant Inflated self-image	Antisocial Borderline Histrionic Narcissistic
Cluster C	Excessive anxiety Pervasive reliance on others Perfectionistic, inflexible	Avoidant Dependent Obsessive-compulsive

different diagnoses. People with avoidant, borderline, or dependent personality disorders, for example, may all experience rejection sensitivity and troubling mood symptoms. In addition, criteria that rely on observable patterns of behavior without regard to etiology may tell the clinician nothing about pathogenesis and offer little guidance for treatment.

A further problem is that the DSM-IV-TR definition of personality disorders medicalizes cultural differences. For example, dependent personality disorder, defined as reliance on others for decision making or staying in relationships to avoid being alone, describes traits and behaviors that are encouraged, even enforced, in cultures that assign women to subordinate roles. Qualities such as aggressive competitiveness or devaluation of family and social ties may be adaptive in Eurowestern cultures but would be signs of personality dysfunction, if not disorder, in more patriarchal cultures.

Dimensional Approach to Personality

What is the dimensional approach to personality?

An alternative to the categorical approach to diagnosis involves defining personality disorders in terms of variability in the multiple *dimensions of personality* that contribute to personality types. One domain of dysfunction does not automatically imply difficulty in another. Characterizing an individual on multiple dimensions allows for a broad and nuanced classification of personality and places personality disorders on a continuum that ranges from variations of normal to clear psychopathology.

A long tradition of research and practical application, mainly within the field of psychology, supports a dimensional classification of personality. An emerging consensus groups large numbers of traits, measured in subtly different ways, into a small number of domains that are then related to the categories described in DSM-IV-TR. These *hierarchical models* depend on complex methods of factor analysis. One proposed version, the *five factor model* has gained widespread acceptance, and may be incorporated into DSM-5, in which Axis II may no longer be separate from Axis I, and dimensional measurement (i.e., quantitative ratings of symptoms and behavior) will be part of both personality assessment and the characterization of some of the major mental disorders.

Each of the *five factors* represents a continuum between opposite qualities, with multiple specific facets that relate to the broader construct. Each facet is measured by patterns of answers on various interview protocols or self-reports. The Dimensional Assessment of Personality Pathology, or DAPP, aligns with the current DSM classification, and measures personality dysfunction within clinical and normal populations. Factor analyses then identify domains, which may be related to but do not duplicate or confirm the current DSM-IV-TR personality disorders (see Table 49.3).

Table 49.3. Five personality factors and their associated behavioral patterns and dysfunctions

Basic Trait Continuum	Personality/behavioral patterns	Dysfunctions
Emotional stability-neuroticism	Anxious-submissive	Dependency, indecisiveness, low self-esteem, pessimism
Agreeableness-antagonism	Psychopathic Socially exploitive/hostile	Manipulativeness, deceitfulness, aggressiveness
Extraversion-introversion	Socially withdrawn	Low self-esteem, disagreeableness
Conscientiousness-constraint	Compulsive	Rigidity, coldness
Empathic-eccentric No clear normal analog (possibly openness, creativity, eccentricity)	Oddness	Schizotypal patterns of thought Suspiciousness

Gene-Environment Interaction and Personality

> What does research reveal about the formation of personality?

Research on the determinants of personality illuminates the relative contributions of *genetic predisposition* and the moderating effects of *experience*. Twin studies have shown that traits like social avoidance, oppositionality, and affective lability are more than twice as common in monozygotic than dizygotic twins. Studies of rhesus monkeys, humans' closest cousins, can identify differences in thresholds and persistence of arousal in the neonatal period, when genetic influence is most obvious.

Other biological studies in both animals and humans have demonstrated links between behavioral patterns and genetic variations. For example, several studies have related aggressiveness to variations in the inheritance and expression of a promoter gene region that determines the function of the *serotonin transporter receptor protein* (5-HTT). Comparisons between individuals with two long, one long and one short (polymorphism), or two short alleles of this gene find that those with the two long alleles are highly resistant to developing antisocial behaviors in childhood, while those with two short alleles show such behaviors significantly more often than those with polymorphism. (These data support the finding that aggressive individuals and those who attempt

or complete violent suicide have low levels of the serotonin metabolite 5-HIAA in their spinal fluid.) Although these studies clearly identify genetic factors in personality, they also show that the expression of a genetic trait reflects environmental influence on gene activity and the formation of networks of neurons during development. Early parental loss, parental neglect, and traumatic events have discernible impact on development in many species. In humans, early loss and persistent physical or sexual abuse clearly foster the expression of maladaptive personality traits.

Treating Personality Disorders

Current efforts to treat or modify personality disorders fall mainly within the realm of long-term psychotherapies that, in attempting to relieve multiple dysfunctions, require radical changes in the whole person. "Trait-based" diagnoses suggest more strategic interventions (e.g., modifying behavior patterns related to decreased serotonin acitivty with drugs; using mood stabilizers when unstable moods do not reach the threshold for diagnosable depression or mania). Assessment across dimensions helps to identify adaptive and maladaptive functioning, encouraging clinicians to build on strengths, rather than focus on longstanding deficits that resist direct modification. Targeting specific traits/behaviors helps clinicians tailor treatment directly and efficiently to an individual, rather than simply imposing a treatment modality on a syndrome, the specifics of which may be different depending on the patient in question.

In general, the treatment for personality disorders relies on *supportive, psychodynamic, interpersonal, and cognitive behavioral approaches*. Evidence-based studies of outcome particularly support **dialectical behavioral therapy** (DBT), informed by an understanding that many patients with personality disorders, especially those diagnosed as borderline, have experienced trauma or abuse. Therapy enables patients to come to terms with their victimization, exert self control, and develop self awareness. Specific elements of treatment include confronting distorted cognitions, stabilizing self-destructive behavior before necessarily exploring its roots, helping patients develop mindfulness of their own bodily reactions, and helping them to interpret the behavior of others more accurately (*mentalization*). Peer groups that offer both support and confrontation can be particularly useful for patients who can tolerate them.

Psychopharmacological treatments for personality disorders are mainly adjunctive to psychosocial treatments. The affective symptoms of borderline personality disorder may be somewhat responsive to antidepressants, mood stabilizers, or low-dose antipsychotics. Elements of schizotypal and paranoid personality disorders may respond to antipsychotics. Some avoidant and dependent patients respond to antidepressants, especially those that modify serotonergic functioning.

Impulse Control Disorders Not Elsewhere Classified

> How does the DSM classify behaviors related to impulsive dyscontrol?

Although similar, if not identical, to other personality traits, impulsive dyscontrol is either recognized as an element of many Axis I disorders (e.g., mania, substance dependence), or classified within a separate domain. The category of **impulse control disorders, not elsewhere classified**, comprises six disorders:

- impulse, temptation, or drive to act in a manner harmful to self or others
- intermittent explosive disorder

- kleptomania
- pyromania
- pathological gambling
- trichotillomania

Impulse, Temptation, or Drive to Act in a Manner Harmful to Self or Others

Affected persons report that, on occasion, they consciously resist the impulse and on other occasions plan the act. Prior to committing the impulsive act, they feel increased tension or arousal; afterwards, they feel pleasure or release, thus reinforcing the impulse and resultant behavior. Still later, they typically feel regret and guilt.

Intermittent Explosive Disorder

Patients who have **intermittent explosive disorder** experience sudden bursts of anger, assault of others, or destruction of property. The aggressive display is disproportionate to the triggering event. These "attacks" or "spells" remit spontaneously, usually followed by deep regret. No aggressiveness or impulsivity is seen between episodes. The disorder may begin at any age, but most commonly has its onset during the second and third decades. Men are affected more than women. First-degree relatives of affected persons are at increased risk for the disorder.

Persons who have impulse disorders tend to be hyperactive and accident prone. They may describe aura-like experiences, hypersensitivity to photic and auditory stimulation, and post-ictal-like changes such as partial memory loss. The EEG may show nonspecific abnormalities. *Predisposing factors* during childhood include perinatal trauma, head trauma, encephalitis, and hyperactivity. However, a disruptive psychosocial environment (e.g., exposure to alcoholism, child abuse, neglect, promiscuity, and threats to life) is considered a more important precipitating factor.

The diagnosis of intermittent explosive disorder requires multiple episodes of loss of control and the exclusion of a psychotic disorder, attention-deficit/hyperactivity disorder, conduct disorder, substance intoxication, personality change due to a general medical condition, and antisocial or borderline personality disorder. The most effective treatment is a combination of psychotherapy and medication. Anticonvulsants, antipsychotics, propranolol, and lithium have been used with mixed results. Selective serotonin reuptake inhibitors (e.g., fluoxetine, paroxetine, sertraline) have produced the best results.

Kleptomania

Persons with **kleptomania** cannot resist the impulse to steal things they do not need. Stolen objects are returned, given away, or hidden. Tension mounts before the act; relief of tension is experienced immediately after the act and reinforces future behavior. Guilt, anxiety, and remorse follow. For affected persons, the act of stealing is an end in itself. The objects they steal are items they could easily purchase. Although they do not plan to steal, they avoid situations in which the danger of being caught is obvious. Despite this, they usually get caught multiple times, causing humiliation.

Women suffer from kleptomania more often than men. The frequency of stealing episodes can range from less than once per month to more than 100 times per month. Although the disorder waxes and wanes, it tends to be chronic and recurs during periods of stress.

Brain disease, mental retardation, faulty monoamine metabolism, cortical atrophy, enlargement of the lateral ventricles, and focal neurological signs have been associated with kleptomania. However, *reinforcement* through tension reduction appears to be significant in the maintenance, if not the onset, of the disorder. Fewer than 5% of shoplifters have kleptomania. Therefore, kleptomania should not be diagnosed if stealing is a symptom of another disorder (e.g., conduct disorder, mania, or antisocial personality). Behavior modification can be effective even when motivation is low. The use of SSRIs helps in some cases.

Pyromania

Repetitive, deliberate fire setting that relieves tension or produces arousal and attraction to fires and firefighting equipment characterize **pyromania**. Affected individuals usually make elaborate preparations prior to setting a fire. This disorder often begins in childhood and its consequences become more destructive over time. It is more common in men than in women and is frequently associated with mental retardation, alcoholism, or delinquent traits such as truancy or cruelty to animals.

Pyromania should not be diagnosed if there is another motivation for fire setting (e.g., sociopolitical beliefs, personal gain, vengeance) or if the fire setting is a symptom of a major psychiatric disorder (e.g., a response to schizophrenic hallucination).

Legal problems are a compelling force for seeking help, but often only incarceration controls the behavior of adults. Children are likely to respond to intensive, non-punitive behavioral therapy. Due to its potentially devastating consequences, pyromania must be treated as soon as it is diagnosed. An affected child will generally make a full recovery.

Pathological Gambling

Pathological gambling includes preoccupation with gambling, increasing stakes to achieve excitement, gambling to escape problems and recoup losses, lying to hide the magnitude of the problem, supporting gambling through illegal but usually nonviolent means (e.g., embezzlement and fraud), and relying on others to pay gambling debts.

> Pathological gambling is estimated to affect up to 3% of the adult population in the US, men more than women. Among men, the disorder typically begins during adolescence; among women, it begins during middle age. Sons of affected fathers and daughters of affected mothers are at risk for the disorder. Affected women are likely to be married to alcoholic, generally absent men.

Pathological gambling may coexist with mood and anxiety disorders. *Predisposing factors* include childhood attention-deficit disorder, loss or absence of a parent before age 15, inappropriately harsh or lax parental discipline, parental modeling with exposure to gambling during childhood or adolescence, lack of family emphasis on financial planning, and excessive emphasis on material goods.

Impaired metabolism of catecholamines (especially norepinephrine) has been associated with the development of pathological gambling. The reinforcing effects of self-stimulation and tension reduction (relief) serve to maintain and increase the behavior. The most effective treatment is the 12-step peer group support offered by **Gamblers Anonymous** (GA).

Trichotillomania

Persons with **trichotillomania** regularly pull out their hair, producing noticeable hair loss. Hair pulling episodes are preceded by mounting tension and followed by relief of tension, thus reinforcing the behavior. Although any area of the body may be involved, the scalp is the most common site of hair pulling.

Examination of an affected area reveals normal hairs, broken strands, and bald spots without evidence of skin disease. Biopsy shows characteristic histopathological changes of the hair follicle *(trichomalacia)*, which helps differentiate trichotillomania from other types of alopecia. Associated signs include evidence of self-mutilation such as scratches, nail biting, and head banging.

Trichotillomania usually begins during childhood or adolescence but may begin later; remission and relapse are common. Trichotillomania is more common in women than in men. It is comorbid with obsessive-compulsive disorder, borderline personality disorder, and depression. Separation anxiety, strained mother-child relationships, loss in childhood, depression, and self-stimulation are possible contributing factors.

The disorder is difficult to treat. Hypnosis, insight-oriented psychotherapy, behavior therapy, biofeedback, general dermatologic treatment (e.g., topical corticosteroids and oral hydroxyzine), SSRIs and other antidepressants, anxiolytics, antipsychotics, and pimozide have each been reported to have some efficacy.

Recommended Readings

Costa PT Jr, Widiger TA. *Personality Disorders and the Five Factor Model of Personality,* 2nd ed. Washington, DC: American Psychological Association; 2002.

Gabbard GO. Mind, brain, and personality disorders. *American Journal of Psychiatry* 2005; 162:648-655.

Hollander E, Stein DJ. (Eds.). *Clinical Handbook of Impulse-Control Disorders.* Washington, DC: American Psychiatric Press; 2006.

Kushner SC, Quilty LC, Tackett JL, Bagby RM. The hierarchical structure of the dimensional assessment of personality pathology (DAPP-BQ). *Journal of Personality Disorders* 2011; 25:504–516.

Review Questions

Directions: The items below consist of lettered headings followed by numbered descriptions. For each numbered description choose the *one* lettered heading to which it is *most* closely associated. Each lettered heading may be used *once, more than once,* or *not at all.*

Match the case scenario with the personality disorder type it describes.

A. Antisocial
B. Borderline
C. Histrionic
D. Obsessive-Compulsive
E. Paranoid

1. A.H., a 39-year-old woman with a history of turbulent relationships and frequent job changes, recently made her fourth suicide attempt. Her current partner describes her as excessively demanding, angry, reckless, alcoholic, extremely possessive, and very fearful that he will "abandon" her.

2. L.B. is a 26-year-old graduate student who was recently placed on administrative leave after breaking into a professor's office to read his teaching assistant evaluations. On several occasions, he claimed the professor was falsifying his evaluations and recently accused the professor of substituting the evaluations of another graduate student, being investigated for theft, for his as a way of ruining L.B.'s career.

3. R.S. is a 20-year-old waitress who is fearful of losing her job because she cannot take orders quickly. She always starts at the right back corner of a table to take orders and gets frustrated when the manager tells her to always start with the oldest-appearing woman regardless of seating.

4. J.B. is a 45-year-old salesman, who was fired last month from his job with a local insurance company. He was accused of selling policies to unqualified buyers, taking credit for sales made by other sales

representatives, abusive relationships with staff, and padding his expense account. When confronted with these offences, he shrugged them off, his only concern being that he was caught.

Key to review questions: p. 408

50 Disorders of Infancy, Childhood, and Adolescence

Richard R. Pleak, MD, and João V. Nunes, MD

- How is mental retardation classified?
- What is the definition of a learning disorder?
- How are language disorders related?
- What are some examples of autism spectrum disorder?
- When does oppositional defiant disorder become conduct disorder?
- What is a tic?
- How should enuresis be treated?

The disorders of infancy, coming early in the individual's developmental course, reflect the greater influence of genetic and biological predisposition. Disorders of childhood and adolescence reflect the increasing influence of environmental, social, and experiential factors with age.

Developmental disorders are characterized by limitations in academic, communication, social, motor, and intellectual functioning. The limitations are apparent in infancy or childhood as delays in the acquisition of **developmental milestones** and developmental gaps become more noticeable. In 2013, the DSM-IV-TR diagnostic criteria are scheduled to be replaced by DSM-5. Therefore, both classifications are given for each disorder, if a change is anticipated.

Mental Retardation (MR)/ Intellectual Disability (ID)

William is a 13-year-old boy who lives with his mother who can no longer control his outbursts since he entered puberty and has become larger and stronger. She struggles with whether to send him to a residential treatment center. Pregnancy was normal but as an infant, he did not smile or babble, and had marked delays in speech. He then began to bang his head and flap his hands, sometimes injuring himself. He does not play with other children, wants to do the same things repeatedly, and becomes aggressive in school when a new teacher is present or when there are changes in his class schedule. His IQ is 45.

How is mental retardation classified?

Mental retardation (MR)/**intellectual disability** (ID) is defined as intellectual functioning below an IQ of 70; impaired functioning in two of the following areas: communication, social skills, self-direction, health and safety, academics, leisure, work, activities of daily living, or use of community resources; and onset before age 18. MR is difficult to diagnose in children < 5 years of age since test results are less reliable in younger children, and difficulties often do not appear until the child enters school. The degree of MR has been defined by the number of standard deviations (1 SD = 15 IQ points) below the mean IQ (100) at which the child scores (see Table 50.1), but these designations will not be used in the ID diagnosis in DSM-5.

MR/ID is associated with autism spectrum disorders, Down syndrome (DS), fragile X syndrome (FXS), cerebral palsy, and intoxication by

Table 50.1. Functional capacity by approximate IQ as defined in DSM-IV-TR		
115–85	Average	Mean IQ = 100; SD = ±15; normal functioning
85–70	Below average	1–2 SD below 100; borderline intellectual functioning
70–55	Mild MR	Can develop language and social skills although delayed; good motor development; academic achievement < 6th grade by late adolescence; can be self-supporting
55–40	Moderate MR	Can talk or sign; fair motor development; some self-help skills; academic achievement < 2nd grade; may find employment in sheltered settings
40–25	Severe MR	Can profit from systematic habit training; can use words or gestures but few expressive skills; needs supportive living arrangement
<25	Profound MR	Minimal functional capacity in sensorimotor areas; indicates wants/needs with sounds or body movements; needs support for basic functions

environmental agents such as lead. Around 95% of DS cases are caused by trisomy of chromosome 21; 4% by fusion of chromosome 21 with chromosome 13, 14, or 15; and 1% by mosaicism. FXS is an X-linked dominant disorder. It is the most common inherited neurodevelopmental disorder, is twice as prevalent in males (1:4,000 births) as in females, and is associated with autistic symptoms. In this disorder, the CGG nucleotide sequence is exaggeratedly repeated in the FMR1 gene, which reduces production of the protein FMRP, resulting in abnormal brain development with cognitive, emotional, behavioral, and neurological impairments. The wide range of degree of impairment in children with FXS may be explained by mosaicism (i.e., the presence of both normal and abnormal cells in the same individual). Although the distinguishing features of the disorder (i.e., long face, prominent jaw and forehead, large ears, and large testicles in males) become most apparent around puberty, they are not reliable as a basis for diagnosis.

In a large percentage of cases, the cause of MR/ID remains unknown. Potential causes include maternal abuse of alcohol (fetal alcohol syndrome) and other substances during pregnancy; metabolic disruption involving mother or fetus (e.g., congenital hypothyroidism); trauma; and CNS infections such as toxoplasmosis and rubella. MR/ID is often associated with autism spectrum disorders and neurological disorders like epilepsy.

About 85% of persons with MR fall in the mild/educable range. Although no intervention will significantly alter IQ, most people with mild mental retardation can find suitable vocations and function to maximal capacity with proper behavioral management, social support, and education.

Learning Disorders (LD)/Learning Disabilities (LD)

What is the definition of a learning disorder?

The diagnosis of LD is based on scores on standardized tests of reading, written expression, or mathematics that are ≥ 2 years below age, schooling, and intellectual ability levels.

Reading Disorder/Dyslexia

Reading disorder/dyslexia is manifested by slow inaccurate reading characterized by letter reversal and poor word recognition, reading comprehension, and spelling in the absence of MR/ID or sensory deficits. Additional diagnoses of expressive, receptive, or mixed language disorders or disorder of written expression may be warranted.

Dyslexia is often apparent by age 6, although recognition may be delayed in children of above average intelligence. About 5–10% of school-aged children are estimated to have dyslexia, with boys affected more often than girls. Although prevalence of dyslexia in families of affected individuals is increased, a genetic link has not been confirmed.

Intervention, including remedial education, management of any emotional problems, and parent counseling, should begin by 3rd grade. Otherwise, reading is likely to remain impaired, with consequent low self-esteem and poor school attendance.

Mathematics Disorder/Dyscalculia

Mathematics disorder/dyscalculia is characterized by deficiencies in four arithmetic-related skill areas that are not explained by poor education or neurological, sensory, or cognitive impairments: 1) *linguistic skills* – understanding mathematical terms and conversion of verbal instructions into mathematical symbols; 2) *perceptual skills* – recognition of symbols and ordering of number clusters; 3) *performance skills* – carrying out and appropriately sequencing the four basic arithmetic operations; and 4) *attention skills* – exact copying of figures and performance of operations designated by symbols. Diagnosis is usually made during or after the 2nd grade. Almost 5% of school-aged children of average intelligence are affected.

Remedial education is the treatment of choice. Undiagnosed or inadequately treated children will continue to perform poorly, and may develop poor self-esteem, depression, anger, frustration, disruptive behavior disorders, or school refusal.

Disorder of Written Expression/Learning Disability

Disorder of written expression/learning disability is characterized by poor spelling, frequent grammatical and punctuation errors, and poor handwriting. The disorder becomes evident around the 3rd grade, appears to be familial, and affects 3–10% of school-aged children. Boys are affected more than girls. The etiology is unknown although dysfunction in cerebral information-processing areas is suspected because it often accompanies expressive and mixed receptive/expressive language disorders and reading disorders.

Communication Disorders/Language Impairment

How are language disorders related?

Expressive Language Disorder (ELD)/Language Impairment

Expressive language disorder, to be subsumed under **language impairment** in DSM-5, is characterized by limited vocabulary, inability to produce complex sentences, inability to use correct tenses, and impaired word recollection. The diagnosis is confirmed by expressive language test scores significantly below receptive language scores. ELD affects 3–10% of school-aged children; boys are affected two to three times as frequently as girls. While the etiology is unknown, the disorder is prevalent in families with a history of communication disorders. ELD is usually a developmental disorder, but it may also result from a neurological insult (e.g., trauma, seizure disorder).

About 50% of affected children recover spontaneously. Severely affected children will have mild to moderate language impairment if the ELD is untreated. Speech and language therapy is essential. Psychotherapy and parent counseling may be needed to cope with for associated low self-esteem, frustration, performance anxiety, and depression.

Mixed Receptive/Expressive Language Disorder (R/ELD)/Language Impairment

Because **receptive language disorder** impairs development of **expressive language**, the DSM-IV-TR classification combined these two disorders. DSM-5 is expected to further combine expressive and mixed R/ELD into one diagnosis of **language impairment**. Mixed R/ELD is usually developmental but may be learned. The criteria for diagnosis of R/ELD include disrupted academic achievement and social communication, receptive and expressive language test scores significantly below age and developmental expectations, and language scores significantly below performance scores on standardized IQ tests, without evidence of autism spectrum disorder or functional impairment not due to MR/ID, neurological disorder, or sensory defect.

> For both ELD and R/ELD (i.e., language impairment), audiologic evaluation is essential to rule out hearing impairment, the most common sensory defect contributing to poor language development.

Mild R/ELD may not be identified until adolescence and may produce minimal long-term language impairment. Although the etiology is unknown, children with R/ELD respond more to environmental sounds than to speech sounds, suggesting auditory discrimination difficulties. Ambidexterity and left-handedness are increased among affected individuals.

Phonological (Articulation) Disorder / Speech Sound Disorder

Phonological disorder (articulation disorder)/ speech sound disorder is characterized by speech sounds that are incorrectly produced, omitted, or substituted for appropriate sounds. The diagnosis is made in the absence of anatomical-structural, physiological, neurological, or sensory (e.g., auditory) abnormalities. The disorder occurs in 5% of children, although it may be present in up to 10% of children < 8 years old. Boys are affected more than girls and first-degree relatives are at increased risk.

Although the etiology is unknown, phonological disorder is probably caused by *maturational delays* in the brain processes underlying speech. Phonological disorder is correlated with large family size and lower SES, suggesting insufficient stimulation of speech development as an etiological factor. Spontaneous remission is common before age 8, but rare thereafter. *Speech therapy* provides the most successful treatment. Parent counseling and education are helpful adjuncts.

Stuttering

Stuttering/childhood-onset fluency disorder is speech that lacks fluency and temporal patterning, resulting in repetition and prolongation of sounds and syllables. Deficits must exceed any disturbance produced by a speech-motor, neurological, or sensory impairment. Stutterers develop anticipatory anxiety and avoid situations in which they expect they will stutter. Many develop tics, eye blinking, or trembling of the lips and jaw in anticipation of speaking.

The etiology is probably multifactoral, with *significant learning and anxiety components.* Spontaneous remission occurs in up to 80% of cases. Children who do not recover may experience months of remission but relapse at times of stress. Treatments focusing on stuttering as a learned behavior and restructuring speech fluency are most successful. Children and adolescents recover better than adults.

Developmental Coordination Disorder

Developmental coordination disorder is manifested by delayed developmental milestones such as sitting, crawling, standing, and walking, clumsiness, accident proneness, and poor fine motor skills such as tossing a ball or fitting puzzle pieces together. The disorder may interfere with academic progress and trigger emotional and behavioral disorders. Standardized evaluations of a child's age skill level help establish the diagnosis. Boys are affected 2–4 times as frequently as girls. The etiology is unclear but risk factors include hypoxia at birth, prematurity, low birthweight, and perinatal malnutrition.

Effective treatments include physical therapy to enhance gross motor skills, occupational therapy to enhance fine motor skills, perceptual motor training, neurophysiological exercise techniques, and modified physical education.

Autism Spectrum Disorder (formerly, Pervasive Developmental Disorders)

Pervasive developmental disorders (PDD)/**autism spectrum disorder** (ASD) are characterized by disruption in attaining behavioral milestones and impaired development of language and social skills during childhood. Four of the five separate PDD diagnoses including PDD NOS in DSM-IV-TR will be subsumed into the one autism spectrum disorder in DSM-5.

> What are some examples of autism spectrum disorder?

Autistic Disorder/Autism Spectrum Disorder

Autism spectrum disorder appears before age 3 and is characterized by:
1. impaired social interactions (e.g., lack of eye contact, inadequate peer relationships, and lack of social/ emotional reciprocity);
2. communication deficits (e.g., delay or lack of verbal skills; repetitive, stereotyped, and idiosyncratic language; and absence of spontaneous symbolic play); and
3. repetitive, stereotyped, and idiosyncratic behaviors, interests, and activities (e.g., exclusive dedication to a particular interest; rigid adherence to routines; and motor mannerisms such as hand flapping or head banging).

Recent studies suggest that autism spectrum disorder has increased in prevalence to as many as 1 in 110 individuals, with autistic disorder (DSM-IV-TR) being 1 in 1,000. Boys are affected more than girls (1 in 70 boys), but girls are more likely to have a family history of serious cognitive impairment and their symptoms are more severe. Two thirds of autistic children have some degree of MR/ID.

Autistic children with IQ > 70 and reasonable language skills by age 5 have the best prognosis. A few autistic children with high IQ improve to the point of no longer meeting criteria for the disorder, even though they retain some manifestations. Up to 2% of affected children become independent and 5–20% become semi-independent. Some, termed high functioning, can be productive and achieve major accomplishments. However, > 70% will require family or institutional care as adults.

Treatment includes educational and behavioral techniques that encourage normal social interactions, discourage bizarre behaviors, and improve interpersonal communication. These interventions

Findings Suggestive of Possible Etiologies for Autism

- Prenatal and perinatal complications
- Minor congenital anomalies, abnormal dermatoglyphics, and ambidexterity
- Higher concordance rates among monozygotic compared with dizygotic twins
- Fifty times greater risk among siblings
- Autistic-like behavior in some persons with temporal lobe lesions, severe tuberous sclerosis, or fragile X syndrome
- Decreased numbers of Purkinje cells in the cerebellum
- Grand mal seizures, EEG abnormalities, and ventricular enlargement
- Diminished response to infection and pain
- Mild facial dysmorphia (e.g., wide-set eyes, widened philtrum)

are most effective when begun in the pre-school years. Autistic children function in structured settings. Psychopharmacological agents are useful for treating severe perseverations, impulsivity, aggression, and self-injurious behavior.

Asperger Disorder/Autism Spectrum Disorder

Asperger disorder, to be subsumed under ASD in DSM-5, is a less severe type of autism, without extensive cognitive and language disturbances. It is more common than autistic disorder (1 in 300 children), and boys are affected more than girls. Children who have Asperger disorder typically have abnormal communication, with stilted or monotonous speech. They often have trouble developing social relationships, are awkward in reciprocal interactions, and lack emotional sharing, although, unlike children with autism disorder, they generally desire social interactions. They have difficulty with transitions and are sensitive to changes in routine. Most do not have MR/ID, and some develop particular or peculiar areas of strength or skills.

Affected children often become very shy adults, are uncomfortable in social interactions, may exhibit thinking oddities, and choose careers in areas with limited human contact. High IQ and high-level social skills predict a good prognosis.

Rett Disorder (to be removed from DSM-5)

In **Rett disorder**, development may be normal for several months after birth but begins to decelerate at 5–8 months. Loss of hand skills occurs at 5–30 months and is replaced by repetitive wringing of hands, fingers in front of the mouth, and other stereotypic behavior. Other manifestations include loss of social engagement, poorly coordinated gait and trunk movements, and impaired development of receptive and expressive language. *Rett disorder is found almost entirely in girls* (1 in 23,000 females) and is 100% concordant in monozygotic twins. A mutation in the X chromosome methyl-CpG binding protein 2 (MECP2) gene, essential for neuronal maturation, is the basis for the disorder.

Physical therapy can help ease discomfort from muscular maladaptation and behavioral techniques can be useful in controlling self-injurious behavior. Rett disorder is now considered a medical rather than psychiatric condition and is due to be removed from DSM-5. Instead, it will be placed into the section on neurological disorders in the International Classification of Diseases (ICD).

Childhood Disintegrative Disorder

Childhood disintegrative disorder, to be subsumed under ASD in DSM-5, is characterized by the deterioration of social, cognitive, and language functions after 2 years of normal development. The onset may be abrupt or, more often, insidious over several months. The child loses skills usually acquired before the age of 10, such as expressive and receptive language, bladder control, and ability for social interaction. Diagnostic features include impaired social interaction and communication skills, stereotypical behavior, and seizures. The disorder is more common in boys (1 per 100,000).

Attention-Deficit/Hyperactivity Disorder (ADHD) and Other Disruptive Behavior Disorders

Attention-deficit/hyperactivity disorder (ADHD, sometimes known as ADD) is characterized by

> Dean is a 9-year-old boy whose parents have been told he cannot return to school until he is evaluated by a physician for disruptive behavior. Dean talks excessively with peers during instruction time, is inattentive to the teacher, and inappropriately calls out answers. He squirms in his seat and frequently asks to go to the bathroom but, once in the hall, he runs around. He has run into chairs and tables causing bruises to the extent that a neighbor considered reporting the parents for abuse. His friends no longer wish to play with him because he cannot wait his turn and constantly interrupts them. He is failing several classes because he does not complete projects or homework. A year ago, Dean began having twitching of his mouth, eyes, and neck, and making sudden odd sounds; he reports, "I have to do this – I can't help it."

attention problems and motor/verbal overactivity. ADHD has three subtypes: predominantly hyperactive-impulsive, predominantly inattentive (sometimes referred to as attention-deficit disorder or ADD), and combined hyperactive-impulsive and inattentive. Girls are more likely to have the inattentive type; boys are more likely to have the combined type.

ADHD affects 10–15% of children. Two thirds have significant symptoms into adulthood. Youth with ADHD are at risk for dropping out of school, substance abuse, motor vehicle accidents, higher rates of emergency room visits, and difficulty sustaining employment.

The etiology of ADHD is unclear although frontal lobe and reticular activating system dysfunction and deficiency of noradrenergic neurotransmitters are suspected. Genetic vulnerability is suggested by evidence that children with ADHD are likely to have parents/relatives who have ADHD. In fact, heritability may be as high as 80%. Vulnerability is increased by environmental factors, such as intrauterine exposure

Characteristics of ADHD

- Impulsivity
- Distractability / inattention
- Difficulty following directions
- Fidgety/disruptive
- Trouble taking turns and sharing
- Difficulty completing tasks without supervision

to tobacco smoke or cocaine. Treatment includes tutoring, behavioral incentive programs, limit setting, and structured settings and times for school work and chores. Most respond well to stimulant drugs. Parent support and education should be provided by the clinician. Additional assistance is available through national support groups such as CHADD (Children and Adults with Attention Deficit Disorder, www.chadd.org).

Oppositional Defiant Disorder

Oppositional defiant disorder (ODD) is persistent (> 6 months) negativistic, and defiant behavior in a child ≥ 3 years old. Symptoms include frequent loss of temper, defiance, irritability, spitefulness, and vindictiveness. ODD should be considered when symptoms impair functioning and are not due to a mood disorder or psychosis. ADHD and LD are common co-morbidities.

Suspected etiological factors include inconsistent caretaking, poor limit setting, neglect, abuse, and family dysfunction. Assessment includes a careful history from parents or caregivers focusing on discipline and conflicts within the family. Treatment includes parenting education and treatment of co-morbid disorders.

> When does oppositional defiant disorder become conduct disorder?

Conduct Disorder

Conduct disorder (CD) is more severe and socially destructive than ODD. Onset may occur during childhood or adolescence. Symptoms include aggression or cruelty toward people or animals, bullying, using weapons, vandalism, fire setting, deceitfulness, forgery, and rule violations. Approximately 6% of children have some degree of conduct disorder; boys are affected four times as frequently as girls.

CD is generally co-morbid with ADHD or LD. Children with CD are also at risk for substance abuse, homelessness, prostitution, incarceration, suicide, and homicide. If symptoms persist beyond age 18, the person is re-diagnosed as having antisocial personality disorder in adulthood (see Chapter 49, Personality and Impulse Control Disorders). The diagnosis of **antisocial personality disorder** is dependent on a history of conduct disorder, but only 50% of adolescents who have CD will be diagnosed with antisocial personality disorder. Others remit, become less symptomatic, or die as a result of homicide, suicide, or other violent events. Prosocial outcomes can occur in careers such as the military and law enforcement.

The etiology of CD is unclear. Fathers are likely to be alcoholic with a history of violence and incarceration. The child may have been abused, grossly neglected, harshly or inadequately disciplined, and have no consistent role models for moral behavior. Developmental markers of conduct disorder in boys include low serum levels of dopamine beta-hydroxylase and muted galvanic skin responses to noxious stimuli.

Treatment includes management of comorbid disorders such as ADHD, which, unfortunately, is best achieved using highly abusable and salable agents such as stimulants. Affected children respond best to immediate and concrete reward. Intensive behavioral modification may be transiently effective. Placement in a long-term treatment facility is beneficial in some cases.

Tic Disorders

> What is a tic?

Tics are recurrent sudden, rapid, nonrhythmic stereotypical movements or vocalizations.

Tourette Disorder

Tourette disorder appears before age 18 and consists of multiple motor tics and at least one vocal tic. Tics occur numerous times daily for at least 1 year, impair functioning, and are unrelated to medical disorders. Tourette disorder occurs in 2% of the population and males are affected three times more often than females. Motor tics are evident by age 7 and vocal tics by age 11. *Coprolalia*, or socially inappropriate words or phrases, occurs in a minority of affected persons. Patients have some control over their tics, which they describe as "compelling" rather than totally involuntary. Tourette disorder appears to have a *genetic component* and exists on a continuum with chronic motor tics and vocal tic disorder. It is an autosomal disorder transmitted in a bilinear mode (i.e., between recessive and dominant).

Although the etiology is unclear, dysfunction of the dopamine system may be involved. The endogenous opiate system is likely involved in cases of comorbidity with obsessive-compulsive disorder, and the adrenergic system appears to be involved in cases that respond to alpha-2 adrenergic agonists such as guanfacine and clonidine.

Pharmacotherapy is the most effective form of treatment. Behavioral therapy can be of benefit in reducing reactivity to urges and stress.

Motor or Vocal Tic Disorder

Chronic motor or vocal tic disorder is manifested by motor or vocal tics but not both. Onset is before age 18, prevalence is estimated at 1–2%, and school-aged children are at highest risk of developing the disorder. Children who have onset of motor or vocal tics at 6–8 years are likely to become symptom free an average of 4 years after onset. Patients with facial tics have a better prognosis than those with tics involving larger muscle groups. Treatment depends on severity and degree of academic, social, and emotional impairment.

Behavioral techniques and pharmacotherapy can be effective. Supportive psychotherapy is helpful in the management of secondary emotional problems, difficulties coping with peer reactions, and low self-esteem.

Transient tic disorder consists of one or more vocal or motor tics or both that begin before age 18. The tics occur many times a day for at least 1 month, but last no longer than 12 months. Up to 25% of school-aged children have a history of tics that intensify or reappear at times of stress.

Tics with *a psychogenic origin* may remit spontaneously; those with a *biological origin* tend to be familial. Patients with tics that progress to a chronic motor or vocal tic disorder are thought to have a mixed organic and psychogenic condition. If symptoms are mild with little or no functional impairment, no treatment is needed and parents should be counseled to ignore the problem. If the problem does not remit quickly, or the person declines in social, emotional, or academic func-

tioning, pharmacotherapy and behavioral treatment should be considered.

Stereotypic Movement Disorder

Stereotypic movement disorder is manifested by repetitive movements that impair age-appropriate activities and cause injury to the child. Examples include self-biting, self-hitting, head banging, handshaking, and picking at skin. For diagnosis, these behaviors must be present for ≥ 1 month and not explained by drug effects or medical conditions, compulsions, or developmental disorders. The disorder is more common in boys, and up to 20% of children with mental retardation are affected. Prognosis is correlated with the frequency and intensity of self-injurious behavior. Control often requires the use of physical restraints. Pharmacotherapy and behavioral treatment such as reinforcement and behavioral shaping are the most effective strategies available.

Elimination Disorders

Encopresis

By age 4, more than 95% of children in Western cultures have acquired bowel control via myelination of the nerves controlling the anal sphincter. By age 5, 99% have acquired bowel control.

Encopresis is repeated, intentional, or involuntary passage of feces in inappropriate places. Diagnostic criteria include ≥ 1 episode per month for 3 months, developmental age ≥ 4 years, and no substance or medical condition to account for the behavior.

The etiology is multifactorial and includes power struggles over toilet training and inefficient/ineffective sphincter tone. Most affected children do not have a psychiatric disorder associated with the encopresis. For many, the disorder is *behavioral*. In contrast, persons who can control their bowel but voluntarily deposit feces in inappropriate places should be suspected of having a primary psychiatric disorder. Developmental and maturational difficulties such as distractibility, poor frustration tolerance, and poor motor coordination are common in affected children. After bowel control has been established, regressive reactions to life stressors may precipitate a recurrence of encopresis.

Many children with encopresis develop **psychogenic megacolon**, which arises when painful defecation or voluntary withholding leads to fecal impaction. This, in turn, produces colonic enlargement. Loss of colonic tone reduces sensitivity to pressure that signals the need to defecate. In many cases, encopresis remits spontaneously and rarely persists beyond adolescence.

Nonpunitive parental involvement is essential for a favorable outcome. Reward-based behavioral techniques, psychotherapy, and family therapy are indicated.

Enuresis

Enuresis is repeated involuntary or intentional urination into clothes or the bed by an individual ≥ 5 years old *developmentally*. The behavior must occur at least twice weekly for 3 consecutive months or be accompanied by emotional distress or functional impairment. The behavior cannot be explained as the effect of a substance or a physical dysfunction. Failure to acquire bladder control at the appropriate age, and loss of bladder control after it is acquired, are both defined as enuresis.

Although there is some *genetic* predisposition, *psychosocial factors* such as family toilet training practices and family distress are also etiological. *Enuresis is unrelated to sleep stages.*

> How should enuresis be treated?

Many cases remit spontaneously so that prevalence drops to about 1% in young adults. In persistent cases, restricting liquids close to bedtime, encouraging urination at bedtime, waking the child to urinate, and having the child be responsible for cleaning soiled sheets are useful. Operant reward systems (e.g., charting and rewarding dry nights) can be useful, as can classical conditioning, using a device that detects urine dampness and triggers an alarm that wakens the child. Supportive and family therapy can also promote constructive coping. Pharmacotherapy with synthetic vasopressin may be helpful for when the child is sleeping away from home or when starting behavioral ther-

apy, but symptoms may recur when the medication is discontinued unless the behavior itself has changed.

Other Disorders of Infancy, Childhood, and Adolescence

Separation Anxiety Disorder (SAD)

Separation anxiety disorder (SAD) is the *most common anxiety disorder in children*, occurring with equal frequency in boys and girls (4% of school-aged children and 1% of adolescents), with onset at about 7 years of age. The etiology is multifactoral and includes abnormally intense but developmentally appropriate fears (e.g., of bodily harm or losing the mother) and heightened response to environmental stressors. The principal factor is *parental modeling* by an anxious or depressed parent.

> **Diagnostic Criteria for Separation Anxiety Disorder**
>
> At least three of the following behaviors must be displayed when separation is occurring or anticipated:
> - Recurrent distress
> - Persistent worry about losing the attachment figure
> - Persistent fear of separation from the attachment figure
> - Reluctance or refusal to go to school
> - Reluctance or refusal to go to sleep
> - Nightmares about separation
> - Physical complaints (e.g., headache, stomach ache)

Treatment includes psychotherapy, family education, and therapy addressing the parent's anxiety/depression. Pharmacotherapy with anxiolytics can be useful in refractory cases. The presence of school refusal requires prompt intervention. The goal of treatment is to return the child to school immediately, at least part time, and then gradually increasing the time spent in school to achieve full attendance.

Selective Mutism (SM)

Selective mutism is consistent refusal to speak in social situations where speech is expected, when the child is known to speak in other situations and to have age-appropriate language skills. The difficulty must be present for ≥ 1 month and interfere with academic and social functioning. The diagnosis should be reserved for children whose symptoms are not explained by a communication disorder, developmental disorder, or psychotic disorder. SM usually remits within weeks, but may persist for years. Children who do not improve by age 10 have a worse prognosis. Up to one third of children with selective mutism develop other psychiatric disorders, especially anxiety disorder.

Prevalence is estimated at less than 1 per 1,000 children and affects girls more frequently than boys, and up to 90% of children with SM have a history of social phobia. Early psychological trauma is a significant risk factor.

Treatment includes cognitive behavioral psychotherapy and pharmacotherapy for the child, and counseling and supportive therapy for the parents.

Reactive Attachment Disorder

Reactive attachment disorder (RAD) occurs before age 5 and is associated with moderate to grossly *apathetic caregiving*, such as neglect by parents or by orphanage staff. Affected children demonstrate inappropriate social relatedness not fully explained by developmental delay. The child may fail to thrive physically and have delayed motor and psychosocial milestones. There are two types of reactive attachment disorder:

1. *Inhibited type*: consistent failure to initiate or respond to social interactions in a developmentally appropriate fashion, with limited positive affect.
2. *Disinhibited type*: unselective, undifferentiated, and uninhibited social relatedness. This type of reactive attachment disorder will become a separate disorder in DSM-5, called **disinhibited social engagement disorder**.

Family disorganization, single parenting, psychosocial deprivation, and poverty increase vulnerability to RAD.

Children with RAD may eventually behave normally. However, depending on severity and duration of pathological caregiving, manifestations can progress to inanition and death.

Treatment includes hospitalization if the child is at risk. The therapeutic goal is normalization of the child-caregiver relationship. Management includes support services (e.g., child care, improved housing, financial assistance), decreasing social isolation of the family, comprehensive medical and psychiatric care, parent counseling, education and skills training, and close supportive follow-up. Long-term placement may be in the best interests of the child.

Recommended Readings

Cheng K, Myers KM. *Child and Adolescent Psychiatry: The Essentials.* Philadelphia, PA: Lippincott Williams & Wilkins; 2005.

Dulcan M. (Ed.). *Dulcan's Textbook of Child and Adolescent Psychiatry.* Washington, DC: American Psychiatric Publishing; 2010.

Martin A, Volkmar FR (Eds.). *Lewis's Child and Adolescent Psychiatry: A Comprehensive Textbook*, 4th ed. Philadelphia, PA: Lippincott Williams & Wilkins; 2007.

Review Questions

1. Sammy is a 14-year-old boy who has been cruel to animals and aggressive toward his brother and his friends since he was in the 3rd grade. This pattern has intensified over the past year and now includes lying, running away from home, and stealing. Yesterday, he was caught vandalizing and setting a fire in a neighbor's house. The symptoms are most suggestive of
   A. attention-deficit/hyperactivity disorder.
   B. autism spectrum disorder.
   C. conduct disorder.
   D. mental retardation.
   E. oppositional-defiant disorder.

2. Arthur is 9 years old. Although he says he wants friends, he has difficulty developing social relationships, and is especially awkward in reciprocal interactions and emotional sharing. His communication is characterized by stilted and monotonous speech. He has difficulty with transitions and is especially sensitive to any change in routine. At age 18 months, he became isolated, appeared not to

enjoy playing with adults, and ignored other children. He played with toys in an unusual fashion, as though he did not understand their purpose. He flapped his hands frequently and had severe temper tantrums if his routine was changed. His speech consisted of a few words repeated from games and television. Over time, he has become emotionally unresponsive to his parents and other family members. He has never developed good peer or adult relationships. The most likely diagnosis is

A. Asperger disorder/autism spectrum disorder.
B. attention-deficit/hyperactivity disorder.
C. learning disorder not otherwise specified.
D. oppositional defiant disorder.
E. reactive attachment disorder.

3. Rachna is a 10-year-old girl who is the class clown, always joking and talking to peers when the teacher is trying to instruct and during tests. She has been suspended for refusing to follow the teacher's directions and for trying to hit the principal. She scored 2 years behind her age level on recent reading tests. Rachna failed 4th grade and is repeating it since her parents refused summer school; she rarely wants to go to school. She was in the ER recently for the third time since she was hit by a car after running into the street without looking. Her father drinks heavily and is punitive. Her mother cannot keep a job and is lax with limit setting. Rachna ignores her mother and does whatever she wants until her father gets home. She has been experimenting with cigarettes and alcohol that she finds in the house. The most likely diagnoses are

A. Asperger disorder and learning disorder, NOS.
B. attention-deficit/hyperactivity disorder, oppositional defiant disorder, and dyslexia.
C. childhood disintegration disorder and separation anxiety disorder.
D. conduct disorder and developmental coordination disorder.
E. Tourette disorder and enuresis.

4. Lila is 10 years old and the youngest child within an intact caring family. She was apparently normal at birth. At age 2 months, Lila suffered atypical seizures followed by crying spells. Neurological consultation revealed nonspecific static encephalopathy. Her development has been slow. She has never been capable of understandable speech and cannot meet her basic needs. Her mother bathes, dresses, and feeds her, although Lila can eat finger foods independently. She has been unable to learn and the primary goal of schooling has been basic socialization. The most likely diagnosis is

A. attention-deficit/hyperactivity disorder.
B. learning disorder.
C. mental retardation/intellectual disability.
D. reactive detachment disorder.
E. Rett syndrome.

Key to review questions: p. 408

Review Questions – Answer Key

Chapter 1
1. E
2. B
3. E

Chapter 2
1. B
2. E
3. C
4. C
5. D
6. B

Chapter 3
1. E
2. C
3. B
4. D

Chapter 4
1. E
2. D
3. E

Chapter 5
1. B
2. D
3. D

Chapter 6
1. C
2. C
3. D
4. C

Chapter 7
1. E
2. A
3. D
4. A

Chapter 8
1. E
3. B
4. A
5. E

Chapter 9
1. A
2. C
3. A

Chapter 10
1. E
2. D
3. B
4. A
5. D
6. E

Chapter 11
1. A
2. E
3. A
4. C

Chapter 12
1. D
2. D
3. B
4. A

Chapter 13
1. A
2. E
3. B
4. B

Chapter 14
1. C
2. B
3. C
4. D
5. A

Chapter 15
1. B
2. D
3. B
4. E
5. E

Chapter 16
1. D
2. B
3. D
4. A
5. E
6. D

Chapter 17
1. B
2. C
3. D
4. E
5. A
6. A

Chapter 18
1. E
2. E
3. C
4. E
5. D

Chapter 19
1. A
2. A
3. C
4. E
5. C

Chapter 20
1. C
2. B
3. C

Chapter 21
1. B
2. E
3. D
4. E
5. C

Chapter 22
1. A
2. E
3. A

Chapter 23
1. E
2. C
3. E
4. C
5. E

Chapter 24
1. D
2. D
3. D

Chapter 25
1. C
2. C
3. C

Chapter 26
1. C
2. B
3. E
4. D

Chapter 27
1. B
2. D
3. D
4. A
5. E

Chapter 28
1. D
2. E
3. D

Chapter 29
1. D
2. E
3. E

Chapter 30
1. A
2. B
3. C
4. A

Chapter 31
1. E
2. D
3. E

Chapter 32
1. A
2. D
3. B
4. B
5. D

Chapter 33
1. C
2. C
3. B
4. B
5. C

Chapter 34
1. A
2. C
3. C
4. B
5. C
6. B
7. D

Chapter 35
1. D
2. E
3. E

Chapter 36
1. E
2. A

3. E
4. C
5. D

Chapter 37
1. E
2. E
3. D
4. D
5. E
6. D

Chapter 38
1. D
2. C
3. A

Chapter 39
1. E
2. B
3. A
4. B

Chapter 40
1. A
2. B
3. C

Chapter 41
1. D
2. C
3. E

Chapter 42
1. E
2. A

Chapter 43
1. B
2. E
3. B

Chapter 44
1. E
2. E
3. B

Chapter 45
1. E
2. A
3. A

Chapter 46
1. D
2. A
3. C

Chapter 47
1. C
2. A
3. E
4. D

Chapter 48
1. D
2. A
3. B
4. B
5. C
6. D

Chapter 49
1. B
2. E
3. D
4. A

Chapter 50
1. C
2. A
3. B
4. C

Apendix A: Epidemiology

Steven R. Daugherty, PhD, and Peter P. Vitaliano, MS, PhD

Epidemiology is "the study of the distribution and determinants of health related states in a defined population" (Last JM (Ed.). *A Dictionary of Epidemiology*. Oxford, UK: Oxford University Press; 2001). The tools of epidemiology are ratios or rates. In their simplest form, ratios are the number of people with a condition, divided by the number of persons in the population who are at risk for having that condition. **Risk** means a person is vulnerable to a condition. It does not mean that the person will get the disease, only that it is a possibility.

> Ten senior high school girls were diagnosed with dysfunctional menstrual bleeding during the last school year. The school had 275 senior girls. The ratio 10/275 defines how many of the individuals at risk actually have the condition. The numerator (N), 10, is the number of diagnosed cases, and denominator (D), 275, is the number of females at risk. This ratio, N/D or 10/275, defines what proportion of the at-risk community has the condition.

Most risk estimates use a *standardized denominator*. This is done by multiplying the ratio by a constant, usually 100,000, yielding a rate per 100,000 of the persons at risk (N/D × 100,000). The ratio of students who have dysfunctional menstrual bleeding over all students at risk, 10/275 or 0.036, now becomes 10/275 x 100,000 or 3,636 per 100,000. Thus, among a group of 100,000 high school senior girls, about 3,636 are likely to have dysfunctional menstrual bleeding. This estimate for the entire US is limited by how closely the female high school senior population at the local city high school resembles the population of female high school seniors in the US. We would expect this number to be representative if the distribution of local high school senior girls was ethnically, racially, and socioeconomically similar to the US population.

Incidence and Prevalence

The two most widely used types of rates are called incidence and prevalence. **Incidence** is the number of new cases in a given time period divided by the number of persons at risk for contracting the disease. **Prevalence** is the total number of cases that exist in a given period, whether the cases are new or old. This value is then divided by the number of persons at risk who *have* the disease. **Period prevalence** is the number of cases of a disease divided by the population at risk over a given *span of time*. **Point prevalence** is the number of cases of a disease divided by the population at risk at a given *moment in time*.

Incidence is the rate at which people *acquire* a disease, while prevalence is the total number of people who *have* the disease or condition. Thus, incidence is a good index for tracking the course of acute conditions such as influenza while prevalence is more suited for tracking chronic conditions such as hypertension.

The relationship between incidence and prevalence is shown by the formula: *Prevalence = Incidence × Duration*, where duration is the length of time that someone has the disease (see Figure A.1.). As either incidence or duration rises, prevalence rises. Conversely, a decline in either incidence or duration reduces prevalence.

Screening Tests

Screening tests are designed to identify who has a disease and who does not. In developing screening criteria, a sample of the target population is measured on a key dimension. Scores on this dimension are used to classify people as having the disease or not, according to predefined criteria. People who meet the criteria are considered to have the disease, while those who do not are assumed to not have the disease.

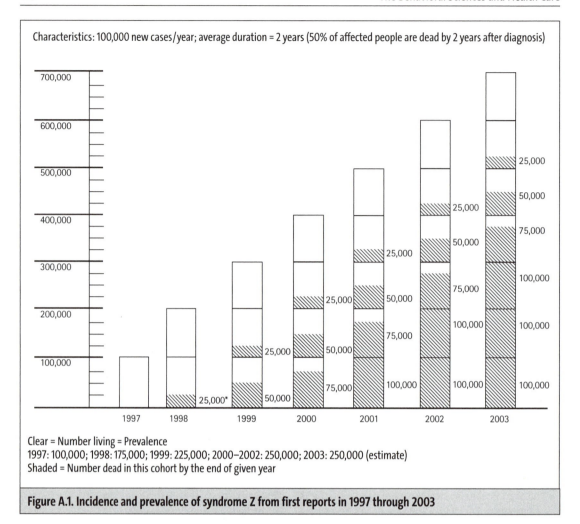

Characteristics: 100,000 new cases/year; average duration = 2 years (50% of affected people are dead by 2 years after diagnosis)

Clear = Number living = Prevalence
1997: 100,000; 1998: 175,000; 1999: 225,000; 2000–2002: 250,000; 2003: 250,000 (estimate)
Shaded = Number dead in this cohort by the end of given year

Figure A.1. Incidence and prevalence of syndrome Z from first reports in 1997 through 2003

To detect hypertension in the population at large, a researcher might take the blood pressure of a sample of people. People with a systolic blood pressure higher than 130 mm Hg might be defined as hypertensive, while those who have a systolic blood pressure lower than this cut-off score would be considered to be in the normal range.

A key consideration in constructing a screening test is that the measure must be as *accurate* as possible. The best test would detect all of the people with the disease and correctly exclude the healthy people. A screening test should also be *less expensive* and *easier to administer* than a definitive evaluation. The results of a screening test, when compared with the "gold standard" evaluation can be displayed as a simple 2 × 2 table (see Figure A.2.). This figure contains all the logical possibilities for matching screening classifications with the gold standard diagnosis. Optimally, there is agreement between the results of the screening test and the gold standard as to who has disease (*true positives*) and who is disease free (*true negatives*). Persons classified by the screening test as diseased who are really disease free are called *false positives*; they are positive on the screening test, but are false (not confirmed) on the gold standard. Persons classified by the screening test as disease free who really have disease are called *false negatives*; they are negative on the screening test, but are false in that the gold standard says they have the disease.

Certain characteristics are used to determine the quality of a screening test. **Sensitivity** concerns the detection of disease: out of all the persons with disease in the population, what propor-

True Disease Status

		Yes	No	Total
	Yes	(a) True Positives	(b) False Positives	a + b All subjects with + screening
Screening Tool Results	No	(c) False Negatives	(d) True Negatives	c + d All subjects with − screening
	Total	a + b All subjects with disease	b + d All subjects without disease	a + b + c + d All subjects

a/(a + c) = Sensitivity
d/(b + d) = Specificity
b/(b + d) = False-Positive Error Rate (alpha or Type 1 Error)
c/(a + c) = False-Negative Error Rate (beta or Type 2 Error)
a/(a + b) = Positive Predictive Value
d/(c + d) = Negative Predictive Value

(a + c)/(a + b + c + d) = Prevalence

Example: 2 x 2 table for screening for hypertension

Hypertension

		Yes	No	
	Positive	TP **90**	FP **20**	110
Screening Test	Negative	FN **10**	TN **80**	90
		100	100	200

Sensitivity $= \dfrac{TP}{TP + FN} = \dfrac{90}{100} =$ 90%

Specificity $= \dfrac{TP}{TN + FP} = \dfrac{80}{100} =$ 80%

Positive Predictive Value $= \dfrac{TP}{TP + FP} = \dfrac{90}{110} =$ 81.8%

Negative Predictive Value $= \dfrac{TN}{TN + FN} = \dfrac{80}{90} =$ 88.8%

Accuracy $= \dfrac{TP + TN}{TP + TN + FP + FN} = \dfrac{170}{200} =$ 85%

Figure A.2. Standard 2 x 2 table comparing test results and true disease status (gold standard)

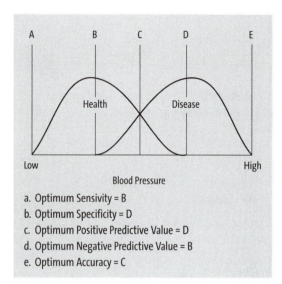

a. Optimum Sensivity = B
b. Optimum Specificity = D
c. Optimum Positive Predictive Value = D
d. Optimum Negative Predictive Value = B
e. Optimum Accuracy = C

tion was identified correctly? **Specificity** targets the healthy people: out of all the healthy people in the population, what proportion was labeled correctly? If the disease for which the screening is being done is some type of virulent, contagious disease, a screening test with high sensitivity would be preferred. If, in contrast, the disease requires painful, expensive medical treatment, a highly specific test would be preferred. Sensitivity and specificity are properties of the screening test itself and are unaffected by the underlying prevalence of disease in a population.

When a screening test identifies a patient as a positive (has the disease), most patients will ask, "Are you sure?" **Positive predictive value** of the test answers this question. Positive predictive value is the percentage of all people who will test positive who actually have the disease. **Negative predictive value** is the degree to which a negative on the test identifies a person who is disease free. In a population with a high prevalence, a positive test is more likely to be accurate than a positive test

A researcher screened two populations, one with a prevalence of 1 out of 2 and one with a prevalence of 1 out of 1,000,000. Given a positive test from both samples, the researcher should feel more confident about the positive result from the 1 in 2 population because, just by random selection, any given person has a 50% chance of having the disease, compared to the 1 in a million chance for the positive test in the person from the other population.

in a population with a low prevalence. Conversely, in a population with high prevalence, a negative test is less likely to be true than a negative test in a population with a low prevalence of disease.

Screening is only appropriate when attempting to detect a disease with relatively high prevalence. That is, screening for a disease with a prevalence of 1 per 100,000 would require screening approximately 100,000 people to detect just one case. This is not a good use of time or resources. Screening is also only appropriate when there is a clear action for those who are identified as having the disease (e.g., receiving treatment for an infectious disease).

Observational Study Designs and Comparative Risk

Risk factors identify who is more likely to develop a disease. However, individuals with risk factors do not necessarily develop the disease; in fact, often they do not. Being able to identify persons who are more likely to develop the disease allows prevention and monitoring efforts to be focused where they will do the most good. Risk factors are discovered by observation. Three basic types of observational research are cohort studies, case-control studies, and cross-sectional studies.

Cohort Studies

In a **cohort study**, the researcher follows two samples of persons over time, those with and those without the risk factor, to compare the onset of disease within these two groups. By comparing the incidence rate in people with the risk factor with the incidence rate in people without the risk factor, it is possible to estimate the relative importance of the risk factor as a precursor of the disease. The temporal sequence inherent in a cohort study helps to reveal any causal linkage between having the risk factor and developing the disease. The results provided by a cohort study are not subject to distortion due to biased recall because the outcome (i.e., the onset of disease) is assessed at the time it first appears.

The *relative incidence* of the disease between the two groups in a cohort study can be compared

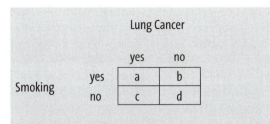

a. <u>Cohort Study</u>: Tracking incidence related to risk factor
   calculation = relative risk = (a/a+b) / (c/c+d)

b. <u>Case-Control Study</u>: Assessing retrospective occurrence of risk factor given existence of disease
   calculation = odds-ratio = ad/bc

c. <u>Cross-Sectional Study</u>: Measuring the association between disease and risk factor at a single point in time
   calculation = chi-square = $\chi^2 = \Sigma\ [(O\text{-}E)^2/E]$
   where O = Observed value for cell
   E = Expected value for cell

by calculating the **relative risk**. Relative risk is simply the ratio of the incidence rates of the two groups. This comparison yields the probability of acquiring the disease in one group compared to another. The difference between the two groups in terms of the actual number of persons who catch the disease can also be calculated. **Attributable risk** is computed by subtracting the incidence rate of the unexposed group from that of the exposed or at-risk group. In more general terms, attributable risk is the incidence rate of one group subtracted from the incidence rate of the second group.

If infant mortality in a given community is 14 per 1,000 live births for the African American population, and 6 per 1,000 live births for the white population, the relative risk of death in the first year of life for blacks compared to whites is 14/6 or 2.33. That is, an African American child has more than twice the chance of dying in the first year of life as does a white child. The results of cohort studies such as this alert epidemiologists to possible risk factors (e.g., socioeconomic status or access to pre- and perinatal health care).

Case-Control Studies

A **case-control study** compares a sample of people who have a disease (cases) with a group of comparable people drawn from the same population who do not have the disease (controls). Historical features that distinguish the disease group from the control group can be identified as possible risk factors. An example of a case-control study would be selecting a sample of people who have lung cancer and a comparable group of people without lung cancer. From interviews with both groups, it would be possible to determine the percentage of each group who had smoked cigarettes (and how much) in the past.

Data from a case-control study are usually analyzed by calculating an **odds ratio**, or the odds of the risk factor appearing in the disease group divided by the odds of the risk factor appearing in the control group. The odds ratio provides an estimate of the likelihood that a risk factor is more common in the cases than in the controls. The larger the number produced by the odds ratio, the greater the difference between the two groups. Factors that significantly differ in incidence between the two groups can then be explored further to see how they contribute to the onset of disease.

Case-control studies are the research design of choice to study low frequency events such as suicide. For example, given a suicide rate of approximately 13 per 100,000, many hundreds of thousands of people would have to be followed prospectively in a cohort study to have a sufficient number of incidence cases to be analyzed. However, in a metropolitan area of 2.5 million people, 250 cases of suicide could be identified quickly. The only challenge would be to find 250 individuals, each of whom matched one of the cases on certain selected variables (e.g., age, race, gender, socioeconomic class, education). The weakness of a case-control study is that recollections are subject to some decay over time. What participants recall at the time of the study may be different from what actually happened in the past.

Cross-Sectional Studies

The goal of a **cross-sectional study** is to establish the prevalence of disease and associated risk factors within a specific time frame. A sample, drawn from the population of interest, is analyzed to determine (1) who has the disease, (2) who does not, and (3) what characteristics distinguish the persons who have the disease from those who are disease free. Of great importance in cross-sectional studies is that they provide an estimate for the most important cell of a two-way table (i.e., the intersection of those who are exposed and those who have the disease). If this proportion of the sample is very tiny, then prospective studies may be difficult to do and one may need to sample on the disease and retrospect back to the exposure (e.g., case-control study).

Because data regarding both disease prevalence and risk factors are collected at the same time, a cross-sectional study is not useful for determining cause and effect. *In a cross-sectional study, it is impossible to determine whether the risk factors preceded the onset of disease, or whether they are the consequence of the disease.* The results of a cross-sectional study are usually analyzed by means of a statistical test called a chi-square (see Appendix B, Biostatistics) which determines if the patterns seen in the data collected are meaningful, or merely the result of random chance. Note that longitudinal and prospective studies also cannot determine causality, but at least they can speak to the direction of the pathways of influence.

Reliability and Validity

The quality of a measure is judged in terms of its **reliability** (i.e., is it consistent within itself and/or over time?) and its **validity** (does it measure what it purports to measure?). Reliability is a necessary but not sufficient condition for validity. Hence, a test can be reliable without being valid but, except in some cases where multidimensional measures are used – which is beyond the scope of this discussion – it is very difficult for a test to be valid without being reliable.

Types of Reliability

Reliability is assessed in four ways: (1) how consistent the measure is over time (test-retest reliability), (2) how consistent the test is within itself (homogeneity of items, using Cronbach's alpha), (3) how consistent and stable the test is (by using parallel forms of a test across time), and (4) inter-rater reliability (the degree to which different raters diagnose a group of persons similarly). Hence,

a measure given on two separate occasions should give consistent results if it has **test-retest reliability**. The caveat here is, if the ability or construct that is being assessed changes, changes in scores may be difficult to interpret. Hence, one should not examine stability (e.g., test-reliability) in persons who are expected to change on the underlying construct being assessed For example, cognitive ability should not be assessed for test-retest reliability (stability) in persons with Alzheimer disease (a moving target). Rather, it is best used for ability or trait measures.

Types of Validity

Validity is assessed by how well the test measures what it purports to measure. For an instrument to have **face validity**, individual items should appear to reflect the variable in question (e.g., to find out about depression, items should ask about mood).

Content validity requires that a measure directly assess the construct of interest (e.g., asking questions about heart sounds on a cardiology test). It asks whether the test samples from the universe of features that represents the contruct of interest. For example, depression symptoms can be viewed in terms of duration, intensity, and frequency, and their relative importance depends on the type of depression that is of interest. Thus, clinical depression is determined by duration; depressed mood in response to acute stress may be best viewed in terms of intensity; and depressed mood in response to chronic stress can be viewed in terms of duration, intensity, and frequency.

Construct validity requires that the theoretical construct being assessed is consistent with the measurement (e.g., if schizophrenia is hypothesized to be genetic, items would not be expected to relate to child rearing practices).

Convergent validity stipulates that any new measure correlate positively with existing measures that purport to assess the same thing. **Divergent validity** stipulates that any new measure correlate less or negatively with existing measures that purport to assess different things.

To establish **criterion-related validity**, the results of the measure must agree with some existing feature of reality or observable criterion (e.g., doing well on an examination that purports to assess knowledge in anatomy should be related to being ranked high in anatomy by an expert).

Criterion validity is, in psychometrics, the analog to diagnosis in medicine. An example of criterion validity in psychiatry is showing that a cognitive measure is related to cerebral blood flow.

Predictive validity is criterion-related validity over time (e.g., doing well on an entrance examination that purports to assess how well a student will do at a particular school should be correlated with rank in the graduating class four years later). Predictive validity in psychometrics is the analog to prognosis in medicine. In obstetrics, an example of predictive validity would be that degree of cervical effacement is predictive of the imminence of delivery.

Appendix B: Biostatistics

Steven R. Daugherty, PhD, and Elizabeth J. Dansie, PhD

While **epidemiology** defines and measures the distribution of diseases and their risk factors, **biostatistics** enables the researcher to analyze the significance of these measures.

The Normal Curve

Distributions vary in size and shape, but the **normal distribution (Gaussian curve)** is the most common and is easily recognized by its "bell shape." The frequencies of many things (e.g., height, weight, intelligence, blood pressure) are more or less "normally" distributed. When graphed, these distributions are generally balanced or symmetrical, with the bulk of cases in the middle (center) and relatively few at the extremes (tails) of the distribution. If split down the middle, the two resulting halves will generally match. The normal distribution serves as the central organizing element for a large number of statistical methods.

Measures of Central Tendency

A distribution can be summarized by two sets of parameters: central tendency and variability. **Central tendency** identifies the center of the distribution and its position along the dimension that defines it, although there may not be a single value that is precisely at the center. **Variability** defines the degree to which the distribution spreads out from the center.

Central tendency is established by three parameters: the *mean,* the *median,* and the *mode.* The mean is the average, or the sum of the scores divided by the total number of scores ($\Sigma(x)/n$). The median is the middle score or the score that has 50% of the scores below it and 50% above it. In the case of an even number of scores, the medi-

an is estimated by adding the middle two scores together and dividing by two [$(xml + xm2)/2 =$ median]. The mode is the most frequently occurring score regardless of its position with respect to the mean and the median.

> Given the following set of numbers [2, 2, 2, 3, 3, 4, 4, 6, 7, 7, 8, 8, 8, 8, 8, 9], the mean is 5.4, the median is 6, and the mode is 8.

The shape of the distribution influences which measure most appropriately describes a distribution (Figure B.1.). In a normal distribution, the mean, median, and mode are all the same num-

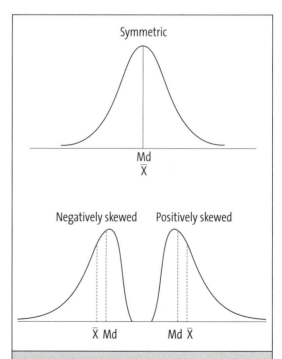

Figure B.1. The top panel depicts a normal distribution; the bottom panel depicts a negatively skewed (left) and positively skewed (right) distribution.

ber. If the mean, median, and mode are not all the same number (i.e., the majority of the scores are concentrated on one side of the distribution), then the curve is *skewed.* A distribution can be skewed with the tail extending to the right (positive skew), or with the tail extending to the left (negative skew). With a skewed distribution, the median is typically more appropriate for describing the distribution, because the mean is highly influenced by extreme scores in the tails of the distribution.

Measures of Variance

Various measures exist to measure the *variability* present in a distribution of scores. The most simplistic is the *range*, or the difference between the lowest and highest scores in the distribution. The range describes the width of the distribution, or how spread out the distribution is along the dimension of measurement.

The **standard deviation** (represented by lower case sigma, below), provides a method for calculating a standardized measure of the variance in any distribution. To compute a standard deviation, the mean is subtracted from each individual score of the distribution (x − mean). These differences, or deviations, are then squared $(x - mean)^2$, and the squared deviations then added, $\Sigma(x - mean)^2$. The sum of the squared deviations is then divided by the sample size (n) minus 1 (n − 1) and the square root taken of the whole quantity.

$$\text{Standard deviation} = \sigma = \sqrt{\frac{\Sigma(x - mean)^2}{(n - 1)}}$$

A larger standard deviation signifies that the scores are more spread out. A smaller standard deviation means that the scores are more compact. In any normal distribution, approximately 68.0% of the cases lie between 1 standard deviation (SD) above the mean and 1 SD below the mean. Approximately 95.5% of cases lie within ± 2 SD of the mean and 99.7% of cases lie within ± 3 SD of the mean. These numbers are constants and will always apply for any normal distribution. "Within two standard deviations of the mean," or 95.5% of the cases, is typically used to define "within normal limits." Scores + 3 SD from the mean are considered "*outlying*" values.

Inferential Statistics

Descriptive statistics are useful for summarizing sample data. **Inferential statistics** permit drawing reasonable conclusions about a population based upon the sample data. The estimates generated from a sample are an approximation of the whole, but they are not exact. Statistical calculations enable the researcher to determine how good the approximation is likely to be.

Confidence Intervals

Confidence intervals provide a sense of how close estimates are to reality. Basically, a confidence interval begins with the number provided by the sample (the point estimate), and then adds and subtracts from that number to create a range within which the true parameter is believed to lie.

The formula for calculating the *confidence interval of the mean* is comprised of the *sample mean*, which anchors the estimate, a *standard error*, which serves as an index of the quality of the sample, and a *standard score*, which indicates the degree of confidence the interval is to have.

The **standard error** is a measure of how far off the sample estimate of the population is likely to be from the true value. This error is estimated using two factors: the sample size and the standard deviation. The larger the sample, the better the estimate is likely to be. The standard deviation indicates how much variation there is in the sample. If there is little variation, then the cases are generally alike and any sample will offer a good approximation of the whole. If, on the other hand, the population is highly variable, then the chance of selecting unrepresentative cases in the sample rises, and the chance of error in the estimate increases. Thus, as the standard deviation increases, the standard error also increases.

If repeated random samples were taken from a population, 95% of the time the means computed from each of these samples would fall into the range defined by ± 2 SD or the 95% confidence interval. The true mean is somewhere in the computed range. The confidence interval does not specify where in the given range it is most likely to be, only the likelihood that it falls somewhere within that interval.

Standard Score Distribution

Any normal curve distribution can be analyzed more easily by converting it to a **standard score distribution**. A standard score distribution is a normal distribution with a mean equal to zero and a standard deviation equal to 1. Any number, in any distribution, whatever the computed mean and standard deviation, can be converted to a *standard score* by the simple formula:

$$\text{Standard score} = Z = (x - \text{mean})/\sigma$$

Because the mean is equal to zero, any positive number is greater than the mean, and any negative number is less than the mean. By making the standard deviation equal to 1, the basic unit on the **z-score** distribution becomes the standard deviation. The value of any score on the distribution tells us exactly how many deviations it is above or below the mean. This means that a z-score of 2.6 is exactly 2.6 standard deviations above the mean, and that a z-score of -1.3 is exactly 1.3 standard deviations below the mean. The standard distribution is useful because you can compare scores from any distribution when they are converted to z-scores.

In summary, the standard deviation is a measure of the variability or spread of the distribution; the standard error is an index of the quality of the parameter estimate (e.g., the mean) and is calculated using both the standard deviation and the sample size; and the standard score is a value taken from a normal distribution that has been standardized to have a mean equal to zero and a standard deviation equal to 1.

Confidence Intervals for Relative Risks and Odds Ratios

Confidence intervals can be computed for **relative risks** and **odds ratios**. However, both the calculation and the interpretation will be different from that of a mean because these values are ratios. In any ratio, a value of 1.0 means that the numerator and the denominator are the same. Therefore, the number 1.0 is a critical value, which implies no difference between the two populations being compared. Thus, when interpreting the significance of a confidence interval

Using Confidence Intervals

A researcher wishes to assess the efficacy of a new anti-hypertensive medication. Two groups of patients are randomly selected for this study. Both groups have the same level and severity of hypertension at the start of the study. One group is given the new antihypertensive medication over a 6-month trial, while the second group is given a placebo. At the end of 6 months, the blood pressures of both groups are assessed.

The results are shown below, plotted as means with bars representing the 95% confidence intervals. Note that the mean diastolic blood pressure for the treatment group is lower than that for the placebo group. Does the new antihypertensive drug work better than the placebo?

The best estimate of the effects of the medication in the population is defined by the confidence interval. An examination of Figure B.2 shows that the bars overlap. That is, the upper boundary of the treatment group is higher than the lower boundary of the placebo group. Because the true mean has a 95% chance of being within the confidence interval, and the intervals overlap, the true means could be the same. Therefore, as the graph shows, the best estimate is that, if used in the population at large, the effectiveness of the new antihypertensive will be no different from the placebo for lowering blood pressure over a 6-month trial.

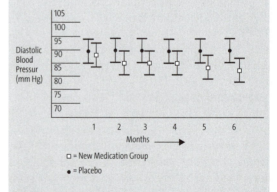

Figure B.2. A comparison of means scores for the new medication group versus the placebo group indicates no true difference between groups because the confidence bars overlap.

of a relative risk or odds ratio, if the value 1.0 falls within the confidence interval, the possibility exists that the groups being compared are the same.

The Null Hypothesis

Consider the example of a clinical trial testing a new antidepressant drug against existing standard pharmacotherapy. How will it be determined if the new drug is more effective? The design involves the selection of two groups of comparably depressed patients, one of which will receive the new drug and the other the standard approved therapy. The group treated with the new drug should show more or faster relief from their depressive symptoms if the drug is more effective. But how much more or faster relief would be needed to determine that the drug is better?

> Every statistical analysis begins with a question. What this question is and how it is framed are critical to determining the type of answer that will be found.

The question "Does the new antidepressant drug work better than the standard therapy?" is transformed into the **null hypothesis**: "The group receiving the new drug will not show significant symptom reduction relative to the standard treatment group." Note that the null hypothesis is stated exactly the *obverse* of the original question. To gain evidence that a given proposition is true, evidence is gathered to reject its opposite, in this instance, to disprove the null hypothesis.

> The logic of statistics dictates that because nothing can be really proved, it is necessary to try to disprove its opposite.

The null hypothesis states that the results of the study are due to chance only and that any differences are the result of random variations within the data. Disputing this null hypothesis requires finding differences that are large enough that the researcher can be confident that they represent real differences. Statistical analysis provides information about just how large those differences must be to be interpreted as real at, for example, the 95% confidence level.

Probability

On what basis do we conclude that the null hypothesis can be rejected? The key to this deci-

sion lies in two specific characteristics of the p-value (a probability ranging from 0 to 1.0). The first is the **p-value criterion**, or the standard against which the results of the statistical analysis will be judged. Most often, the standard of $p < .05$ is used. This corresponds to the 95% confidence interval, just as $p < .01$ corresponds to the 99% confidence level. The second is a **computed p-value**, generated by statistical analysis using data from the sample. The decision whether or not to reject the null hypothesis is made by comparing the computed p-value with the .05 or .01 criterion selected. If the computed p-value is less than the criterion, then statistical significance is achieved and the null hypothesis is rejected. If the computed value is higher than the chosen criterion, statistical significance has not been achieved and the null hypothesis cannot be rejected. Thus, if the criterion is set at $p < .05$, then a computed p-value of $p = .03$ allows rejection of the null hypothesis while a computed p-value of $p = .09$ does not. Note that the null hypothesis is not accepted, it is either "rejected" or "failed to be rejected." The distinction is similar to the difference between knowing that a person is innocent and not having enough evidence to prove guilt.

Type I (α) and Type II (β) Errors

If the cut-off for significance (criterion) has been set at $p < .05$, and a computed p-value is less than .05, the null hypothesis is rejected. However, because the data from the sample may not accurately reflect the real world population, rejecting the null hypothesis may be wrong. How likely is it to be wrong? If $p = .02$, the interpretation will be wrong 2% of the time, or 2 out of 100 times. This type of error, rejecting the null hypothesis when it is really true, is called a **Type I error**. Note that the researcher never knows if a Type I error was made, only the chance that one was made. A Type I error is only possible when the null hypothesis is rejected.

If the null hypothesis is not rejected, a Type I error is impossible. However, by failing to reject it, a **Type II error** may have been made. A Type II error is a failure to reject the null hypothesis when it should have been rejected.

Returning to the example of the study of a new antihypertensive medication, the null hypothesis would be that the medication fails to relieve high blood pressure better than the placebo. A Type I error would occur if it were decided the drug is more effective, when in fact it is not. A Type II error would occur if it were decided the drug is not more effective, when in fact it is. Generally speaking, a Type I error is worse than a Type II error. A Type I error is an error of *commission* (the drug is said to be more effective when it is not); while a Type II error is an error of *omission* (failure to discover that the drug, in fact, is better). A computed *p*-value gives the chance of a Type I error. It does not indicate what proportion of the patients will benefit from the treatment, nor the probability that a single patient will benefit.

Scaling of Data

To conduct statistical analyses, things, events, and people must be converted into numbers. This is done by scaling.

Nominal or **categorical scaling** divides data into discrete groups that are mutually *exclusive* and *exhaustive*. Mutually exclusive means that each observation fits into one and only one category. Exhaustive means that every observation can be clearly classified into some category. A categorical or nominal variable contains two or more groups into which data can be classified. Numbers assigned to groups are solely used to identify groups and are assigned arbitrarily. Thus, they cannot be used for mathematical operations. "Gender," a single nominal variable comprised of two groups, male and female, is one example.

Ordinal scaling organizes data along a given dimension. Ordinals provide information about the relative relationship between things (e.g., something is bigger, faster, or better). Although ordinal data give the order of things, the actual distance between them is not specified (e.g., how much bigger, faster, or better).

Interval scaling organizes data along dimensions with equally spaced gradations or intervals,

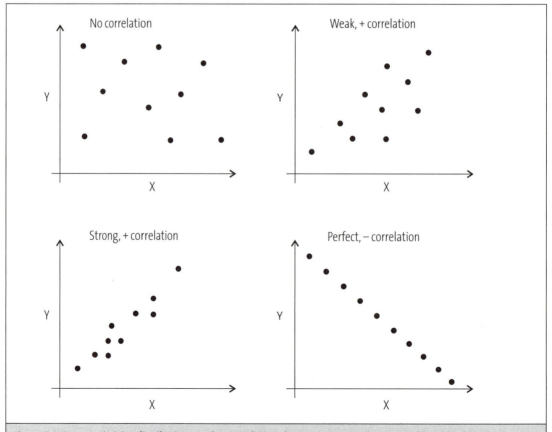

Figure B.3. Patterns in joint distribution graphs: Correlations between two continous variables, X and Y

which allows for more accurate comparisons (e.g., "A measurement of 4 units is exactly halfway between 2 units and 6 units"). Interval scales can provide means and standard deviations, which nominal and ordinal scales cannot. For example, "What is the mean of gender?"

A **ratio scale** has all the properties of an interval scale, plus one more: a *true zero point*. A true zero sets an absolute floor to the scale below which no lower values are possible. For example, when temperature is measured using the Fahrenheit scale, which is an interval scale, zero does not mean absolute zero. By contrast, when temperature is measured using the Kelvin scale, a ratio measurement is produced. Zero Kelvin means absolute zero – no molecular movement. It cannot get any colder than zero degrees Kelvin. This absolute zero point allows for taking ratios of measurements (e.g., "He is twice as tall as she is"), while this cannot be done using the interval scale.

The four types of scales, *nominal, ordinal, interval*, and *ratio*, form a hierarchy from the least specific information to the most specific information. Data can be degraded (e.g., interval data can be treated as ordinal data or ordinal data can be treated as nominal data) but cannot be upgraded. That is, interval data lack the information that ratio data provide and nominal data provide no information about the rank order necessary for ordinal data. For purposes of statistical analysis, ratio level data are generally treated as interval level data.

Statistical Tests for Interval and Ratio Data

The type of data determines which statistical test is appropriate to use. If data are measured on an interval or ratio scale, two basic statistical tests are available: Pearson correlation and regression analysis.

A **Pearson correlation** answers the question, "Is there a linear relationship between these two variables?" The Pearson correlation tests the degree to which a line can be found to represent the data and is expressed as a number between –1.0 and +1.0, where 0 represents no linear relationship

between two variables (see Figure B.3). The further the value of the correlation is from zero, the stronger the linear relationship represented. Thus, a correlation of –.76 is a stronger correlation than a correlation of +.67. The + or – sign indicates the direction of the relationship; a + indicates a positive relationship, a – indicates an inverse relationship. A strong correlation says that two variables are associated and that they vary together, it does not say that one causes the other.

A **regression analysis** answers the question, "What exactly is the relationship between these two variables?" Regression analysis specifies the slope (i.e., the angle of the regression line) and the intercept (i.e., the point at which the line hits the Y-axis) to describe any linear relationship between two interval level variables. Regression analysis can be used to make predictions; that is, given a value for one variable, what is the expected value is for the other?

Statistical Tests for Nominal Data

If all the data in the study are nominal, three basic statistical tests are available: *chi-square analysis, Fisher's exact test*, and *McNemar's test with matched pairs data*. These statistical tests are sometimes referred to as non-parametric since the data are not measured in continuous parameters but rather discrete categories.

The most commonly used test statistic for the analysis of nominal level data is the **chi-square** (χ^2). A chi-square analysis tests whether two nominal sets of data are independent. For example, a chi-square analysis would be used to determine if there is any relationship in the data collected from a cross-sectional study between gender and hair color.

When sample sizes are small, a chi-square test may be inappropriate and the **Fisher's exact test** can be used. Fisher's exact test does not derive a test statistic, but rather computes the p-value directly from the data. For this reason, a Fisher's exact test is used only when the sample size is less than 20 and when the nominal variables each have only two groups (2×2 design).

McNemar's test is used in those instances when the data in two of the nominal groups are joined or linked in some way.

Statistical Tests for Combined Interval and Nominal Data

If the study uses a combination of interval and nominal data, the basic statistical tests are either the student's *t*-test *(t*-test*)* or an *analysis of variance* (ANOVA). The **student's *t*-test** compares differences in the mean values of a single interval variable between two independent groups defined by a single nominal variable (e.g., a study comparing the mean heights of men with those of women).

If the nominal variable has more than two groups, a *t*-test is no longer possible. Instead, a one-way **analysis of variance (ANOVA)** would be used to determine if there are any mean differences among any of the groups that comprise the nominal variable. The test is called a *one-way*

ANOVA because it uses only one nominal variable with more than two levels to analyze the included interval variable. For example, a study of differences in patient satisfaction ratings among five local hospitals (hospital is the single nominal variable with five levels) would make use of a one-way ANOVA. A *two-way ANOVA* is used to analyze two nominal variables combined with a single interval variable. It yields three separate, independent statistical tests that answer the questions, what is the effect of each of the two nominal variables considered separately (*main effects*), and what is the effect of them both taken together (*interaction effect*), where the combined effect of the nominal variables may differ from either effect considered separately. A two-way ANOVA would be appropriate to assess whether men and women (1st nominal variable) from the north and south

Table B.1. Statistical analyses		
Data to Be Analyzed	**Test Statistic**	**Key Features**
Interval Data Only		
Pearson correlation	*r*	Test for linear relationship only, be cautious about attributing causation
Basic regression analysis	*b*	Specifies exact nature of relationship, used for prediction
Nominal data only		
Chi-square	χ^2	For any size table, tests for independence
Fisher's exact test	*p*-value	For 2 × 2 table only, $N < 20$
McNemar's test		For 2 × 2 table only, with matched pairs
Interval and nominal data combined		
Student's *t*-test	*t*	Compares means of two groups
Matched pairs *t*-test	*t*	Subjects are linked or matched, or subjects assessed over time
Analysis of Variance (ANOVA)	*F*	When a *t*-test will not do
One-way		Only one nominal variable
Two-way		Two nominal variables
Repeated measures		Assess subjects over time
Ordinal data only		
Spearman's rank correlation	rho	Tests for relationships within group
Ordinal and nominal data combined		
Mann-Whitney *U*	*U*	Compares ordered scores of two groups
Wilcoxon's matched pairs signed-ranks test		For matched pairs

(2nd nominal variable) had different mean anxiety levels (interval level variable).

If the persons in the separate groups of a nominal variable were non-independent (e.g., siblings or husbands compared with wives) then a **matched-pairs *t*-test** would be used if there were only two groups and a **repeated measures ANOVA** would be used if there were more than two groups. Data from persons assessed repeatedly over time would be analyzed using one of these two techniques.

Statistical Tests for Ordinal Data

If all of the data in the study are ordinal, using a **Spearman's rank correlation** would be appropriate. Spearman's correlation is similar to Pearson's correlation except that it uses ordinal, rather than interval level data. Spearman's correlation would be used to answer the question, "Is there a relationship between students' class rank in college and their class rank in medical school?"

Statistical Tests for Combined Ordinal and Nominal Data

The **Mann-Whitney *U* test** is a test to compare scores between two groups, similar to the student's *t*-test. When the variable the two groups are being compared on is ordinal or ranked, the Mann-Whitney *U* test is appropriate, where *U* designates the probability distribution.

The **Wilcoxon matched-pairs signed-ranks test** also compares two groups on rank-order data, but is used when the groups are matched like the matched-pairs *t*-test.

Practice Exam

Olle Jane Z. Sahler, MD, Julia B. Frank, MD, and Steven R. Daugherty, PhD

Questions

All the following questions about aspects of behavioral science are presented in the same formats used by the USMLE. The answers are accompanied by in-depth explanations. Although some of the topics covered here reinforce information in the text, many questions provide an opportunity to learn about additional topics not found in the text.

1. Among the following, the factor that most distinguishes gay and lesbians families from heterosexual families is
   A. gay or lesbian children
   B. increased conflict
   C. poorer emotional health
   D. poorer parenting skills
   E. societal prejudice

2. You have been asked to create a template for patient education to be used by all of the physicians in your managed care group practice. When planning for patient education, it is most important to remember that
   A. more disease information provided at the time of diagnosis leads to better adherence
   B. patients perceived as intelligent by the physician typically remember significantly more information
   C. patients' level of education is positively correlated with adherence
   D. patients' perception of the time spent giving information is positively associated with adherence
   E. patients' recall of instructions is improved by warnings about the consequences of non-adherence

3. Which of the following is true of stepfamilies?
   A. The prevalence has been decreasing
   B. They are becoming the most common family form
   C. They have fewer financial problems overall
   D. They have more pathology than any other family form
   E. They rarely end in divorce if there are stepchildren

4. You see a young college student who is suffering from depression and adjustment disorder. She has moved and her mother is struggling with her being so far away. She describes her family as very close and she and her mother "share everything." The family did not want her to go away to school but a large scholarship was impossible to turn down. She is struggling with not being an integral part of every family activity. This student's family is an example of which of the following family processes?
   A. Cohesion
   B. Enmeshment
   C. Parentification
   D. Scapegoating
   E. Splitting

5. A 35-year-old, chronically schizophrenic man is brought to the Emergency Department by his parents because of non-adherence to medication and an increase in symptoms. When interviewed by the social worker, the parents do not seem to understand his illness. His mother says she is very aggravated by his laziness, and his father says he just doesn't seem to be trying to do anything. Both sound angry as they talk about him. This pattern of family response has been called
   A. help seeking, help-rejecting
   B. high expressed emotion
   C. parentification of an adult child
   D. splitting
   E. triangulation

6. A 55-year-old man drinks 4 or 5 ounces of alcohol every night and more on the weekends. He brags of his "strong head for liquor." He denies any serious health or legal consequences related to drinking and says that he plans to teach his 15-year-old son to drink responsibly. "If he does like I do, he should be fine, don't you think, doc?" he asks. What advice should the doctor give to this man about educating his son in the use of alcohol?
   A. Avoiding daily drinking will prevent the son from developing an alcohol problem
   B. If he wants the boy to try alcohol, it should be at a meal with adults who do not condone drunkenness
   C. The boy will be fine if he drinks only beer or wine and avoids hard liquor until he is at least

18

D. The safe limit of alcohol use for an adolescent is 4 ounces in a 24-hour period

E. The son is at low risk for alcoholism because high tolerance is genetic

7. Case studies of physicians who seek care for problems in their intimate relationships suggest that distress is most commonly the result of

A. financial problems from the high cost of medical education

B. one partner being a physician and the other not

C. personality characteristics that affect communication or the capacity for intimacy

D. the particular specialty of the physician

E. the stress of the earlier phases of medical education (internship and residency)

8. The empathic way to present a patient or family with the option of agreeing to be treated under a "do not resuscitate" order is to

A. check in the chart for a previous advance directive, and avoid raising the issue if the patient's wishes are already known

B. emphasize that the patient will not be abandoned and that all treatment, including palliative care, will be provided

C. explain that "do not resuscitate" only means refusal of external chest massage, assisted respiration, or electrical defibrillation

D. explain that resuscitation does not generally improve or prolong the lives of patients with multisystem disease

E. let the patient and family talk together privately and then accept the decision they reach without question

9. Mr. G. has just been diagnosed with diabetes. His physician recommends changes in diet and once-a-day insulin injections, but is concerned that Mr. G. will not remember the instructions he has been given. In this, and similar situations, patient recall of physician instructions is maximized when the

A. most important information is given at the beginning of an interaction

B. patient is allowed to fill in the specific details to adapt the instructions to his/her own situation

C. patient is discouraged from interrupting by asking questions

D. physician provides extensive information

E. physician's instructions are all given completely in a single session

10. A 47-year-old, male, machine-tool operator drinks 2 six-packs of beer daily. He reports that he has recently become concerned that he might have an al-

cohol problem. He has not talked to anyone about it for fear that people will think that he is "being silly." According to the stages of change model he is most likely in which stage of change?

A. Action

B. Contemplation

C. Maintenance

D. Pre-contemplation

E. Preparation

11. Dr. J., a professor at UMC, is in the hospital after being diagnosed with colon cancer. During a recent visit by his physician, they only discussed non-medically related topics such as fishing and the trials and tribulations of watching one's children grow up. This description is an example of what type of awareness context?

A. Closed awareness

B. Delayed affectation

C. Mutual pretense

D. Open awareness

E. Suspicion awareness

12. A 35-year-old male patient calls the physician to be examined regarding "problems with my stomach." The patient reports nausea over the past week accompanied by some dizziness. During the physical examination, the patient reports substantial tenderness, but no difficulty with eating or defecation. The medical record shows that the patient has a history of a broad range of medical complaints for which no underlying cause can be determined. At this point the physician's best action would be to

A. ask the patient if the physician can speak to a family member

B. ask the patient to say more about his symptoms

C. gather a complete substance abuse history from the patient

D. tell the patient that he is fine and will feel better after a few days of rest

E. tell the patient that he may be a hypochondriac

13. Elisabeth Kübler-Ross has provided a much-used model for understanding patients' reactions to death and dying. When using this model, physicians should be aware that

A. Kübler-Ross adequately described the experience of dying for the average person

B. patients must reach the final stage of acceptance before death can occur

C. the stages exist as Kübler-Ross described them, but most patients do not experience them all

D. the stages of experiencing dying occur only in patients with a lingering death trajectory

E. while the emotional states described are real, they do not represent distinct sequential stages

14. Patient adherence with treatment is facilitated by the formation of a partnership between physician and patient. The notion of "self-monitoring" has been used to facilitate patient involvement in this relationship. Physicians who try to teach their patients the self-monitoring technique should be aware that

A. patients should monitor behavior (e.g., dietary intake) rather than outcome (e.g., weight loss)

B. recording behaviors daily or weekly is more effective than recording throughout the day

C. self-monitoring alone cannot increase adherence with treatment

D. self-monitoring does not improve patients' awareness of their adherence

E. self-monitoring works best when the patient is assertive

15. As attending physician, you have reviewed the histories obtained by first-year residents. This review reveals that many of the histories are incomplete. Among the items consistently absent are those regarding sexuality. Before discussing the results of this review with the first-year residents, you should realize that failure to obtain adequate sexual histories from patients is most often due to

A. the fact that most patients have no sexual issues

B. the patient's belief that sexual issues are private and should not be discussed

C. the patient's embarrassment about sexual topics

D. the patient's strong religious or moral qualms about sex that interfere with discussing the topic

E. the physician's discomfort with the subject of sex

16. A 33-year-old male married patient enjoys dressing in women's clothes. The patient states that this cross-dressing enhances sexual pleasure and that his wife cooperates with him by supporting this practice. This type of sexual behavior is most correctly described as

A. gender identity disorder

B. homosexuality

C. normal heterosexual behavior

D. transsexualism

E. transvestite fetishism

17. When passing the door of a patient on an oncology ward, a medical student overhears the patient asking his physician, "Why is this happening to me? I've always tried to be a good person." The student realizes that this statement indicates that the patient is most likely in which one of the following stages of coping with dying as described by Kübler-Ross?

A. Anger

B. Bargaining

C. Confusion

D. Denial

E. Depression

18. A young, heterosexual couple has been having sexual difficulties for about a year. The man complains of frequent impotence and woman has experienced anorgasmia. When approaching this problem, the physician should first evaluate for the presence of

A. anatomic structural disparity

B. autonomic nervous system abnormalities

C. endocrine disorders

D. performance anxiety

E. significant psychopathology in one or both of the partners

19. A 46-year-old, African American male confides to his physician that, although he used to enjoy the company of others, this holiday season he is reluctant to attend get-togethers. He states that he feels awkward and clumsy and that people are laughing at him behind his back. He is especially afraid that he will say the wrong thing, or spill his drink on someone. He seems agitated as he provides this account. Based on this patient's statements and presentation, the best preliminary diagnosis would be

A. agoraphobia

B. generalized anxiety disorder

C. histrionic personality disorder

D. narcissistic personality disorder

E. social phobia

20. Many families have a member who is considered the "health expert." This person often makes an initial health assessment and treatment plan and then decides whether a physician should be consulted. Although this role differs from family to family, this individual is most frequently the

A. best educated

B. oldest female

C. oldest female child

D. oldest male

E. oldest male child

21. Mr. S. reports that he consumes about 3 to 4 beers each evening to help him "settle down after a hard day of work." Using the CAGE questionnaire, you discover that: (1) he sometimes feels that he needs to reduce his drinking; (2) he feels bad some mornings about drinking the night before; (3) he becomes irritated when his wife "bugs him" about drinking every evening; and (4) he sometimes drinks in the morning. He says that he never "gets drunk." Based on this presentation, you should conclude that
   A. because only 10% of the population is alcoholic, he probably does not have an alcohol problem
   B. he is lying about never "getting drunk"
   C. he most likely has alcohol abuse or dependence
   D. he needs referral to an in-patient alcohol treatment center
   E. laboratory studies are needed to confirm the diagnosis of alcohol abuse or dependence

22. A 28-year-old woman is concerned because she is no longer interested in sex, either with her husband or anyone else. Questioning reveals that she never has an orgasm during intercourse with her husband. She reports no symptoms of acute or chronic illness. When taking this patient's history, which one of the following questions is most likely to help you to select a treatment approach?
   A. Are you satisfied with your sex life?
   B. Do you have an orgasm with manual or other clitoral stimulation?
   C. Does your husband have difficulty achieving or maintaining an erection?
   D. What do you think your problem is?
   E. What is the approximate frequency of your sexual activity?

23. A 50-year-old man with hypertension has responded well to the diuretic, hydrochlorothiazide (HCTZ). On his last visit to your clinic, his serum potassium was found to be low. You believe your patient has adhered to the regimen prescribed (low salt intake, moderate exercise three times a week, daily diuretic). Of the several possible options for correcting the low potassium, which of the following would be best in terms of maintaining good adherence?
   A. Change the HCTZ to a "potassium sparing" combination diuretic without changing the rest of the prescribed regimen
   B. Discontinue the low-salt diet until the serum potassium normalizes, then prescribe less intense sodium restriction
   C. Eliminate the diuretic until potassium levels return to normal

D. Have the patient consult with a dietitian to plan an intensive potassium-enriched diet in addition to maintaining sodium restriction
E. Supplement the diuretic with a daily potassium chloride tablet

24. You are caring for a husband and wife, both in their mid-40s, who have seen you previously separately and together. They both work outside the home and their two children are in high school. The wife recently saw you for a vaginal discharge. Cervical DNA probe test results for Chlamydia and gonorrhea have returned, but you have not yet talked with her about them. Her husband called and told your assistant he is calling on behalf of his wife and would like the results. Among the following, the best way of dealing with this is
   A. call the husband back and give him the results
   B. call the wife and tell her about her husband's inquiry
   C. e-mail the results to the wife, with copy to her husband
   D. tell the husband he should come in to discuss the results privately
   E. tell the husband you cannot share information without his wife's permission

25. Ms. Jones, a 52-year-old woman, presents to your office front desk shortly before lunch with a chief complaint of shortness of breath. She awoke this morning at her usual time of 7:00 a.m. with this symptom and it has persisted, requiring her to cancel a noon book club meeting she was chairing. She denies other symptoms and otherwise is in no acute distress. Her medical history is positive for endometriosis and chronic low back pain. You decide the patient should be evaluated without undue delay and ask your office nurse to
   A. give her 325 mg of aspirin and move her to an exam room
   B. move her to an exam room
   C. move her to an exam room and call EMS
   D. obtain an EKG and chest X-ray and move her to an exam room
   E. take vital signs and obtain an EKG and move her to an exam room

26. A 50-year-old male accountant develops diabetes mellitus that is not adequately controlled with diet and oral hypoglycemic treatment. The physician meets with him to discuss initiating insulin therapy. Saying that insulin is "poison," the patient declines the treatment. He, however, does not explain that his mother had to have her leg amputated one year after beginning insulin treat-

ment. When reflecting on this situation, which of the following is most correct?

A. A family system problem is interfering with the treatment plan

B. The patient and physician have differing belief systems about insulin

C. The patient's passivity makes the probability of adherence poor

D. The physician might gain acceptance of insulin by explaining treatment in more detail

E. The physician should tell the patient he is being irrational

27. A 10-year-old child is referred for assessment of difficulties in school. The child's developmental status would be best assessed by a focus on which of the following five domains?

A. Biological, environmental, physical, language, and physiologic

B. Gross motor, fine motor, neurosensory, behavioral, and visual

C. Math, reading, spelling, the creative arts, and handwriting

D. Physical, neurological maturational, cognitive, speech/language, and psychosocial

E. Sensory, gastrointestinal, physical, sexual, and psychological

28. A boy is observed bringing his hands to midline and is able to roll prone to supine. In response to voices, he begins to laugh and giggle. Medical record shows that the child's weight has doubled since birth. Assuming that the boy shows normal patterns of development, he is most likely what age?

A. 1 month
B. 3 months
C. 5 months
D. 7 months
E. 9 months

29. A girl is presented with a toy ball. After she plays with it for a moment, the ball is taken away and hidden. Even though it is completely out of sight, the child searches for the ball. Attainment of this degree of object permanence suggests that the child's age is closest to

A. 2 months
B. 4 months
C. 6 months
D. 8 months
E. 10 months

30. A young girl is tested for primitive reflexes such as the Moro, asymmetrical tonic neck, rooting, and palmar grasp. None is found to be present. The

earliest age range at which this finding is expected is

A. 1–2 months
B. 3–4 months
C. 5–6 months
D. 7–8 months
E. 9–10 months

31. During the first months of life, the child's experience of the world is focused on sensations and movement, and learning how action and experience correspond. The child has not yet attained the realization of object permanence. Attachment to the primary caretaker is the dominant social dynamic. The developmental psychologist, Piaget, refers to this stage of life as the

A. action versus inaction stage
B. exploratory stage
C. oral stage
D. sensorimotor stage
E. trust versus mistrust stage

32. The attribution of individual involvement is a critical factor in understanding the subjective etiology of disease. Personal responsibility for disease is *lowest* in which of the following types of belief in disease etiology?

A. Individual etiologies
B. Intellectual etiologies
C. Natural etiologies
D. Social etiologies
E. Supernatural etiologies

33. Mr. D. has been non-adherent with his treatment regime. His physician decides to make use of the goal-setting technique to increase his patient's adherence in the future. Published guidelines and clinical experience in the use of "goal setting" to increase patient adherence suggest that the technique will be most effective when

A. goals are defined by the physician to insure appropriate priorities

B. goals are graduated to maximize success experiences

C. goals are maintained consistently and may not be altered

D. goals are sufficiently broad to allow the patient leeway in meeting them

E. patients seek to "shoot for the moon" and achieve maximal results

34. Mr. J. has a documented history of alcohol abuse and symptoms consistent with alcoholism. Yet, he actively denies any drinking problem and distorts the amount, frequency, and consequences of his drinking. Using the stages of change

model, the clinician's next best action would be to

A. encourage his wife or significant other to convince the patient to stop drinking
B. express concern and suggest the patient think about his drinking
C. recommend an in-patient treatment program
D. schedule a return appointment but make no comment at this point
E. send the patient to a local AA meeting

35. You must tell your 55-year-old patient that he has metastatic prostate cancer. After you have made the patient feel as comfortable as possible and ensured that you will not be interrupted, you begin speaking with him. In this conversation, you learn that the patient knows very little about his condition. The best next step would be to

A. check that you are communicating on the same level
B. discover how much information he would like to have
C. discuss what support systems the patient has
D. establish physical contact by patting his hand
E. give him information in small non-"medspeak" chunks

36. A 75-year-old man presents with a 1-month history of difficulty sleeping, loss of interest in his usual activities, feeling worthless, difficulty concentrating, and thoughts of suicide. Three months ago he suffered a stroke from which he has recovered, except for some gait disturbance and problems using his left hand, which appear to be permanent. He has lost four pounds in the last 2 months. Based on this information, it is most reasonable to conclude that

A. a careful history and physical is indicated to detect a probable occult malignancy
B. he is feeling a sense of letdown from lack of full recovery and requires brief counseling
C. he should be enrolled in a "stroke survivors" group to boost his spirits
D. screening for a substance abuse disorder is indicated
E. he will likely require treatment with antidepressant medication

37. An 80-year-old woman from a local nursing home is brought to the Emergency Department unresponsive, with hypotension, tachycardia, tachypnea, and a temperature of 38.5 degrees. Initial laboratory and radiology results reveal a urinary tract infection (UTI) and a "questionable infiltrate in the right lower lung field." Your exam of the lung fields is inconclusive. You correctly decide to

A. give intravenous fluid resuscitation and await blood and urine cultures before giving antibiotics
B. give intravenous fluid resuscitation and treat both the UTI and possible pneumonia with appropriate Antibiotics
C. give intravenous fluid resuscitation and treat the UTI with an appropriate antibiotic
D. treat both the UTI and possible pneumonia with appropriate antibiotics and give oral fluids when the patient awakens
E. treat the UTI with an appropriate antibiotic and give oral fluids when the patient awakens

38. The hospital is considering building a new clinic in another part of the city. The administration has been asked to develop a description of the residents in the area to be served. Among the following, what information would be most helpful in determining health care needs?

A. A broad description such as "working poor"
B. Culture of the patient population
C. Detailed information about the primary and secondary groups
D. Socioeconomic status based on education and income
E. Statistics on race and household income

39. You inform a 40-year-old man that his 75-year-old father has developed liver metastases from his colon cancer that was resected 1 year ago. The man's face becomes bright red and he angrily replies, "The surgeon said it was all removed. I am going to sue the pants off that goon." Which of the following would be your best response at this point?

A. Ask, "What do you know about the typical course of colon cancer?"
B. Reply, "I'm sorry, but it's not the surgeon's fault that your father's cancer recurred."
C. Sit quietly for a few minutes and then terminate the interview.
D. State, "You are too angry at the surgeon for apparently misleading you."
E. State, "You must be very upset that your father is ill from his cancer again."

40. A 55-year-old man reports to his primary care physician that he has been suffering from periodic impotence with his wife. The physician should tell him that the most common cause of periodic impotence in middle-aged men is

A. abnormalities of the urinary tract
B. excess intake of alcohol
C. marital infidelity

D. onset of diabetes mellitus
E. physiological decline that accompanies aging

41. A terminally ill woman with heart disease says, "It's the doctor's fault that I got sick. She didn't take my blood pressure, and she never told me to watch my diet!" This behavior is most consistent with which of the following stages of coping with dying?
A. Anger
B. Denial
C. Depression
D. Fear
E. Guilt

42. Mrs. H. lost her husband of 50 years 6 months ago. Since that time she has stayed by herself, refused visitors, and cries frequently. Her daughter asks the physician how her mother "should be acting if she's all right." The physician should tell the daughter that normal coping with death often includes
A. feeling depressed for several months after the death
B. feelings of hopelessness lasting 2 or more years
C. profound guilt feelings lasting 6 months or more
D. sleep disturbances lasting 8 months after the death
E. threats of suicide during the initial weeks after the death

Items 43 and 44

During a routine physical exam, a middle-aged man reports recent stress in his marriage. He states that he and his wife rarely try to have sex, and the last time they tried, he was unable to maintain an erection. When questioned, he indicates that he commonly has morning erections. The medical record indicates no chronic illnesses and the patient is not currently taking any medications.

43. At this point the physician should
A. order a nocturnal penile tumescence study
B. recommend that his wife come in for a private session
C. request a joint visit with the patient and his wife
D. smile gently and tell him that this is bound to happen once in a while
E. suggest trying a different position during intercourse

44. At a follow-up visit 1 month later, the patient reports trying intercourse once more but without

success. At this point, the most appropriate intervention would be to
A. indicate that this is a normal change with aging and encourage him to accept it
B. recommend a penile implant
C. recommend attempting intercourse with a different partner, if his wife agrees
D. refer for joint sex therapy with use of sensate focus
E. suggest the use of the squeeze technique

45. Dr. Johnson told his office staff that the Chinese patients he treats have problems with English, believe in herbal medicine, and view women as inferior. Dr. Johnson's description of Chinese patients is an example of
A. bias
B. bigotry
C. intolerance
D. stereotyping
E. stigmatizing

46. When designing a program to assist "impaired" medical students, the organizers should remember that, compared to others in the population of the same age, medical students are most likely to abuse which one of the following drugs?
A. Alcohol
B. Barbiturates
C. Cocaine
D. Heroin
E. Tobacco

47. Part of being a competent physician depends not only on knowing the right thing to say in a given situation, but also knowing when not to say anything. In which of the following difficult situations is physician silence most appropriate?
A. A home visit is made to discuss changes in a cancer patient's pain medicine
B. A man is concerned about impotence
C. A recently diagnosed terminally ill patient is in the hospital
D. A woman is anxious about her inability to experience orgasm
E. Alcohol abuse is suspected in a patient being seen in the office

48. A 40-year-old patient whom you are seeing for an ear infection smokes a pack of cigarettes a day. After discussing her ear infection, you tell her that smoking greatly increases her risk for heart disease. She responds, "Yes, I'd really love to quit. I'm planning to do it sometime". You ask her when. She replies "Oh, once I lose some weight I think I'll try." This patient most likely would

be classified as being in which of the "stages of change?"

A. Contemplation
B. Maintenance
C. Pre-contemplation
D. Preparation
E. Procrastination

49. You are nearing the end of residency training and are looking at practice opportunities. You realize that there are numerous factors that will influence your decision regarding the practice you choose. Some are considered "intangible." One example of the intangible aspects to consider is the

A. accountant who conducts annual audits of the practice income
B. age and gender mix of the patients
C. daily rituals of the office staff and physicians
D. design and age of the practice building
E. framed mission statement hanging in the waiting room

50. The American Academy of Pediatrics and American Academy of Family Physicians convened a committee composed of primary care physicians and experts in the fields of otolaryngology, epidemiology, and infectious disease to develop a comprehensive review of the evidence-based literature related to uncomplicated acute otitis media. This committee was engaged in

A. force field analysis
B. formulation of policy
C. freezing
D. preparation for change
E. unfreezing

51. A faculty member is contemplating a career move to a new academic medical center. Based on the unique characteristics of organizations that are comprised of professional people, you would expect her to

A. accept that she has no latitude within the department to gravitate to those activities that she feels are most important
B. accept that she will need to sacrifice her own personal values and norms and give priority to organizational rules
C. anticipate that she will never find herself in conflict with the faculty she will be working with since they are all professionals
D. be able to create her own role within the department and negotiate for the resources she needs to accomplish that role
E. realize that power within the organization is relatively fixed and will not change while the university employs her

52. A new department is forming within an academic medical center. You have been asked to chair this new department and have been given the necessary resources to build a premier section for your specialty. From your medical school studies about organizations, you remember that the most important task in managing professional people is

A. dealing with reduced effectiveness
B. evaluating performance
C. hiring them
D. managing information
E. motivating them

53. Sally is just beginning to pull herself into an upright position by using the railings on her crib. Before she can learn to walk she, like any toddler, must first

A. develop leg muscles by crawling
B. develop sophisticated balance skills
C. master the mechanics of weight shifting
D. master object permanence
E. overcome separation anxiety

54. A 20 month-old-boy is playing while his mother watches. He moves a toy truck along the floor and then hands it to his mother. When communicating with this child, the physician should remember that at this age of development, a child's capacity for cognition is based on

A. formulation of internal mental symbols
B. movement and sensations
C. performance of actions to achieve outcomes
D. representation of reality through the use of words
E. what they see before them

55. The second year of life, sometimes called the "terrible twos", can be a trying time for parents and older siblings. The change in outlook on the world typical of this developmental stage is characterized by ability to

A. adhere to rule-based play
B. create plans
C. distinguish unique facial features
D. imagine alternatives
E. recognize adult standards

56. The parents of a 1-year-old child ask their physician about potential risks to their child's health. The physician should tell them that the most significant health risk to children during the second year of life is

A. environmental poisons
B. failure to thrive
C. hearing loss

D. infection

E. injury

57. You are talking with a 60-year-old man who has just been diagnosed with lung cancer. He has metastases to his lumbar spine causing back pain. He has no evidence of neurological problems. When you ask him if he would like to know the biopsy results, he replies that he trusts you to care for him and that he would rather not hear the results. Which of the following is your best response at this time?

A. "Even though you don't want to hear, we need to talk now so we can discuss treatment."

B. "I understand. There's really no reason why you have to know anyhow."

C. "I'll order some pain medication and come back tomorrow to see if you'd like to talk then."

D. "Is there anyone in your family I can talk to?"

E. "You must think I'm going to tell you bad news, and you don't want to hear it."

58. A monkey has learned that if he lifts his foot when a bell is sounded, he can avoid a painful electric shock. What biological mechanism most likely makes this simple learning paradigm possible?

A. Protein kinase delays the action potential of the neuron by blocking neurotransmitter release

B. Sequential stimulation of two adjacent neurons enhances the efficiency of their connecting synapse

C. The cerebellum reduces motor reactivity under the influence of serotonin activity

D. The hippocampus sends simultaneous sensory signals to relevant cortical storage areas

E. The orbito-medial frontal cortex matches sensory input with the desired behavior

59. Human behavior can be seen as a consequence of the interaction of heredity and learned behaviors. A key finding from research focused on this interplay tells us that

A. genetic and environmental influences interact across generations but not across individual developmental stages

B. genetic influences are easily distinguished from learned environmental adaptations

C. learned adaptive responses that contribute to survival are passed on to successive generations

D. learning influences individual development, but there is no evidence of an evolutionary effect

E. the capacity to learn, but not what was learned, is passed on genetically

60. Different types of learning have been identified and isolated in laboratory experiments. This allows research to be performed on the specific physiological substrates associated with particular types of learning. One type of learning has been called "implicit learning." This notion of implicit learning

A. involves the association of sensory stimuli with sequential motor system responses

B. is made possible by complex association mechanisms among diverse stimuli

C. occurs over a wide span of time

D. requires structures in the cortex for long-term information storage

E. requires the conscious participation of the individual

61. A 46-year-old homeless man appears at the free clinic complaining of GI distress and headache. He states that he has been living under the bridge of a local highway for the past 3 months. He has a spouse and two children, but has lost contact with them. When examining this individual, the physician should keep in mind that the most frequent health problems of the homeless are

A. HIV- and AIDS-related problems

B. mental illness and substance abuse

C. skin problems

D. upper respiratory infections

E. venereal diseases

62. A 45-year-old man is brought to the physician by his wife who complains, "he has always had his little quirks, but things are getting out of hand." She explains that her husband refuses to leave the house and has become increasingly terrified when forced to do so. Examination of the patient shows him to be in a highly anxious state characterized by sweating palms, shallow breathing, and a rapid pulse. He sits slouched over, avoids eye contact and scans the room around him as if waiting for something to happen. Based on these findings, the physician is most likely to diagnose

A. agoraphobia

B. delusional disorder

C. dysthymia

D. paranoid personality disorder

E. social phobia

63. A 19-year-old man is brought to the local emergency room in a delirious state. The patient is calm, but communication with him is difficult. He is non-responsive to questions regarding time and place. Further examination is disrupted when the patient begins to have seizures. This patient is most likely withdrawing from

A. amphetamines
B. benzodiazepines
C. hallucinogens
D. heroin
E. phencyclidine

64. Physicians who had treated many middle ear infections over decades of practice might disagree with the guidelines recommended by the committee and present evidence in opposition to the new guidelines. This is an example of
A. force field analysis
B. formulation of policy
C. freezing
D. preparation for change
E. unfreezing

Items 65 and 66

A 44-year-old woman is referred for evaluation by her employer because she has been increasingly difficult to deal with over the past week. When questioned by the physician, the woman is understandable but extremely talkative. In her conversation, she jumps from one topic to another. She reports that she recently embarked on a "great shopping spree" because she "deserves nothing but the best." After work she volunteers at four different community programs and says she is looking for additional activities to occupy her time. When asked how she finds the time for all of this, she reports that she needs only three hours of sleep per night.

65. Based on this information, the most likely diagnosis for this woman is
A. bipolar disorder
B. hypothyroidism
C. narcissistic personality disorder
D. obsessive-compulsive disorder
E. vascular dementia

66. Long-term treatment of this woman would most likely include
A. chlorpromazine
B. clonazepam
C. diazepam
D. fluoxetine
E. lithium carbonate

Items 67 and 68

A mother brings her 5-year-old daughter to the pediatrician complaining that the child has recently developed enuresis. The girl seems shy at first when talking to the physician, but soon begins to make eye contact and answer the physician's questions. The physician discovers that the child has recently begun to attend kindergarten and that her mother gave birth to a baby boy in the past month.

67. The girl's enuresis is most likely the result of what defense mechanism?
A. Projection
B. Reaction formation
C. Regression
D. Sublimation
E. Undoing

68. The first intervention the physician should try is to
A. advise the mother about helping the child cope with life transitions
B. observe and follow-up in anticipation of spontaneous recovery
C. prescribe a course of imipramine
D. suggest that the child change to a different kindergarten class
E. talk with the child about why enuresis is a bad thing

69. The physician asks Jennifer, a 2-year-old girl dressed in overalls and a baseball cap, whether she is a boy or a girl. The child seems confused by the question and looks at her mother while saying nothing. When given a set of toys to play with, the child selects a truck and proceeds to roll it around the room. This type of behavior suggests that the girl most likely
A. has no siblings at home
B. is at risk for developing a gender identity disorder later in life
C. is showing developmental age and gender appropriate behavior
D. will grow up to be relatively shy
E. will grow up to have a sexual preference for women

Items 70 and 71

A 25-year-old woman with a history of depression and substance abuse is referred for additional evaluation following a suicide attempt. During the interview the woman reports that the suicide attempt occurred in response to her boyfriend of 3 months breaking up with her. She describes herself as feeling "empty" and says that the ex-boyfriend "was everything to me." Without him, she says she is "not sure who I am or why I'm here." She begins crying, saying that, "Everyone always abandons me." When asked what she is going to do now, the patient becomes suddenly very angry and says, "You can't wait to get rid of me either."

70. Based on this initial interview, you suspect this patient may have a personality disorder in addition to depression and substance abuse. The most likely type is
    A. borderline
    B. histrionic
    C. narcissistic
    D. paranoid
    E. schizoid

71. The most effective primary treatment for the personality disorder described here would be
    A. a 6-month course of alprazolam
    B. behavior modification
    C. family therapy
    D. group psychotherapy
    E. individual cognitive behavioral therapy

72. Mr. Williams is in the emergency department with a complaint of trouble breathing. He is disheveled and malodorous. He has no permanent residence and typically sleeps under an overpass. A member of the team comments, "If people like this would just get a job and take care of themselves, they wouldn't be in this shape." This comment is an example of
    A. anchoring
    B. availability bias
    C. confirmation bias
    D. fundamental attribution error

73. Ms. Hunt comes from a family that has been poor for several generations. She recently left a relationship where she was being physically abused. She and her children now live in a temporary shelter. When her primary care physician asks her about returning to school or enrolling in a training program, she states, "I don't think that would help…nothing ever works out." This comment is most reflective of
    A. denial
    B. histrionic personality disorder
    C. learned helplessness
    D. obstinacy
    E. regression

74. A man is sitting in a corner by himself on the inpatient psychiatry unit. He suddenly bursts into loud laughter and then sits quietly giggling to himself as he picks at his fingernails. He is unkempt and malodorous. A nurse notices that the patient is sitting in his own feces and hurries over to clean the patient. As she approaches, the patient begins to wave his arms wildly, for no apparent reason. The most likely diagnosis is
    A. catatonic schizophrenia, excited type

B. disorganized schizophrenia
C. paranoid schizophrenia
D. residual schizophrenia
E. undifferentiated schizophrenia

75. A 55-year-old man who was diagnosed with schizophrenia at age 18 is asked to complete the Wisconsin Card Sort Test (WCST), a task that requires categorization and problem-solving abilities. Examination of the functioning of this patient's brain by means of a PET scan during the card-sorting task would most likely show that, when compared to non-schizophrenic individuals, the patient has decreased brain activity in the
    A. cerebellum
    B. frontal lobes
    C. occipital lobes
    D. parietal lobes
    E. temporal lobes

76. Culture affects almost all aspects of daily life, including medical care. When trying to gauge the impact of culture on day-to-day medical practice, the practitioner should remember that culture is
    A. a learned social phenomenon that has minimal impact on clinical encounters
    B. a learned social phenomenon that influences health, illness, and therapy
    C. a social phenomenon that may be important to the patient but should not affect physician choices
    D. genetically determined but changeable through genetic engineering
    E. genetically determined and therefore unchanging

77. An overview of U.S. census data over the past 50 years reveals some strong and continuing secular demographic trends. In particular, these data show that in the near future the population will have
    A. a decrease in the number of Hispanics throughout the 21st century
    B. a lower average age for the white population
    C. a steady increase in the size of ethnic minority populations
    D. less concern about culture as a factor in the delivery of health care
    E. zero population growth by the year 2020

78. Mrs. L., an 82-year-old African American woman, complains to her physician that she has "high blood." At times, Mrs. L. says she can feel her blood rising up to her head. She reports that when she drinks pickle juice and vinegar, she can feel her blood return to normal. Her physician tells her that she has hypertension and recommends a

low-salt diet. The African American illness of high blood is an example of a folk illness. When treating Mrs. L., the physician should remember that

A. as a folk illness, high blood had no defined etiology, pathophysiology, or treatment
B. high blood and hypertension are different names for the same thing
C. high blood and hypertension are examples of how interpretations of body symptoms are culturally influenced
D. physicians need to eradicate folk illness beliefs that are contrary to conventional medical beliefs
E. the physician needs to guide the patient away from her incorrect understanding of her condition

79. Yesterday, it seemed to be a simple matter to explain to a woman from Pakistan that the diarrhea which her child was experiencing needed to be treated with antibiotics and high fluid intake. Today, you learn that the child is not being given the medication as recommended, nor is the mother offering liquids as directed. At this point the most appropriate reaction on your part would be to

A. chastise the mother for endangering her child's well being by not following your directions
B. explore the possibility that the mother believes your recommendations will make the child worse
C. hospitalize the child whether or not the mother agrees
D. notify Child Protective Services that the child is not being well cared for
E. refer the mother to the nurse who is responsible for patient education

80. A patient reports that he has been taking buffered aspirin and doing strengthening exercises to alleviate back pain. The patient further reports that this approach worked for a good friend who was having a similar problem. This patient got his medical advice from which sector of healers?

A. Folk
B. Paraprofessional
C. Pharmaceutical
D. Popular
E. Professional

81. According to Kleinman's categorization, an example of a healer from the popular sector would be a

A. chiropractor
B. nurse midwife
C. parent

D. physician
E. psychic palm reader

82. The concept of explanatory models is useful in helping to understand differences among the perspectives of patients, family members, and healers. Over the years, clinical experience has shown that almost all explanatory models

A. do not change once they are formed
B. eventually come to be shared among patients, family members, and healers
C. include the five concepts of pathophysiology, natural history, preferred treatment, etiology, and ethnic identity
D. include the three concepts of etiology, treatment, and ethnic identity
E. shared between a patient and a provider lead to fewer conflicts

83. One of the core functions of physicians is to provide societal recognition of the sick role. In any given community, the function of the "sick role" is to

A. allow estimates of the prevalence of various diseases
B. force the individual to seek medical care
C. legitimize withdrawal from regular activities and requests for assistance
D. permit collection of epidemiological data on disease incidence
E. require hospitalization

84. Cultural background and ethnic identity are key elements in patients' medical decisions. Strong identification with a particular ethnic group is most likely to influence their

A. choice of healers
B. desire for good health
C. response to physiological effects of illness
D. type of health insurance
E. willingness to work

85. Mr. Schmidt has decided to seek complementary medical care for management of his Type I diabetes mellitus. He is a 34-year-old fifth generation European-American who regularly attends his local Episcopalian Church. He is a well-paid chemical engineer, who is married and has three children. For 24 years, he has followed physicians' recommendations regarding diet, exercise, weight control, and insulin injections with glucose monitoring. Despite his best efforts, his blood sugar and glycosylated hemoglobin levels have always been high. He now has multiple complications including decreasing eyesight, diminished kidney function, numbness in his legs, and a persistent sore on his

foot. During the past year, he has sought assistance from a local holistic health center. He is taking vitamins and Chinese herbal medicines; receiving acupuncture; and doing meditation. He continues to take insulin and monitor his blood sugar. All in all, he feels better than he has for years. Of all of the possible reasons why Mr. Schmidt decided to seek alternative therapies, which of the following reasons was probably *least* influential?

A. He agreed with the cultural and ideological underpinnings of Chinese medicine
B. He felt alienated from health care providers because of philosophical differences
C. He was dissatisfied with his physician's inattention to his personal struggles
D. He was disillusioned with the results of medical therapies
E. He was tired of the long waits and high costs associated with medical settings

86. A colleague asks your advice about improving his capacity to work with patients from different ethnic and cultural backgrounds. He lists different options he is considering. Of all the options he presents, you tell him that the one *least* likely to result in improved multicultural patient-centered care is

A. adapting our style of communication to fit patients' preferred styles
B. being aware of our personal biases and prejudices
C. being our genuine selves with the expectation that patients will understand our meanings
D. learning about ourselves as cultural beings
E. learning culturally appropriate patient-centered communication skills

87. Non-verbal gestures communicate different messages depending on ethnic background. Misconceptions about what is communicated can lead to difficulties in the patient-physician relationship. Among the following, which generality about how non-verbal gestures are interpreted is correct?

A. Arab patients: offering things with the right hand is revolting
B. Asians: looking away is experienced as disrespectful
C. Asians: speaking loudly is experienced as an expression of eagerness to be understood
D. Europeans: Making direct eye contact is experienced as invasive
E. Native Americans: pausing less than a few seconds for a reply to a question conveys lack of interest

88. You are an ophthalmologist. An elderly Chinese Vietnamese man is accompanied by his daughter-in-law to your office. In response to your open-ended questions, the daughter-in-law explains that her father-in-law's vision in his right eye has slowly become worse, making him almost blind because he lost the vision in his left eye after an injury about 20 years ago. Now his vision is so bad that he is a danger to himself and others. For example, he recently lit the gas stove while there was a newspaper nearby that caught fire. The family has tried traditional Chinese and Vietnamese treatments with no improvement and now the family wishes to obtain your opinion.

On your examination, you find there is a moderately dense cataract in the right eye and a dense corneal opacity in the left eye. You surmise that he might be afraid of surgery to repair the defects, so you take his hand, look caringly at him, lean forward, raise your voice a little so that he can hear you better, and say "Grandfather, you are going blind, but I can help you. We can operate on your eyes. We can use a plastic piece to replace your old lens on the right eye. And we can use part of another person's eye to replace part of your left eye that was damaged years ago. If you do not let us operate, however, you will go completely blind. If you sign this consent form, we can schedule the first operation next week." The daughter-in-law does not interpret for him, but says, "Thank you, doctor. I will tell my husband about your recommendations." Without looking at you, she leads her father-in-law away, but they never return. Looking back over this exchange, you decide that the *least* likely reason for this outcome is that you

A. called him grandfather
B. did not ask them about their reactions to the operations
C. did not ask who would make the decision and sign the consent form
D. looked directly at him for a prolonged period of time
E. said he would go blind if he did not have the operations

89. Ms. Sanchez, a 62-year-old Afro-Cuban woman, has to make some choices about her treatment for a breast mass. She arrived in the US 4 months ago after spending 3 years in a refugee camp on a military base. Through a U.S. government-sponsored program to promote refugee health, a physician discovered a lump in the patient's breast and performed a needle biopsy that revealed adenocarcinoma of the breast. In the last 2 months, the patient has missed several appointments with the surgeon to discuss various treatment approaches, including mastectomy, radiation therapy, and chemotherapy. Rather, she has sought assistance

from Cuban healers who have been treating her with herbal medicines and performing Santeria religious rituals. Her youngest son (who has been in the United States for 20 years and is a Christian) has taken her to the healers and has paid for her treatments.

Which of the following is the *least* likely reason for Ms. Sanchez to consult traditional Cuban healers rather than allopathic physicians?

A. Cultural factors, such as interpretation of signs and symptoms, and beliefs about disease
B. Economic factors, such as the cost of medical treatment
C. Historical factors, such as familiarity with the healer and the success or failure of treatments
D. Social factors, such as the patients' and healers' social classes, ethnic identities, and language abilities
E. Structural factors, such as distance to the healer and available transportation

90. A 4-year-old Cambodian child has a temperature of 39°C and linear bruises on the chest, back and upper arms. Her grandmother has brought her into the clinic because the child's parents are working. You do not have a Cambodian interpreter in the clinic and, instead, rely on the 8-year-old brother to help you communicate with the grandmother. What is the most likely cause of the bruises on this child?

A. Child abuse
B. Coagulopathy
C. Mongolian spots
D. Sepsis
E. Traditional health care practice

91. Recently you and other providers have been seeing a large number of patients from an immigrant community. These patients are presenting with a pattern of symptoms that does not fit any diagnosis with which you are familiar. Physical examination findings and all test results are normal. You and your colleagues should

A. ask the state health department to quarantine the entire community
B. assume that all patients from the community will present with the same syndrome
C. conclude that these individuals are trying to "work the system," perhaps to get pharmaceuticals to sell on the street
D. consider that the patients may be suffering from a culturally specific syndrome, perhaps related to the stress of immigration
E. tell the patients that they are not ill and should return home and resume all regular activities

92. One way of assessing families is to examine the family's structure or the way that it is organized. An outline of these structural components makes it easier to understand how family dynamics are likely to have an effect on the patient and the patient's care. Which of the following describes a structural element of a family?

A. Boundaries
B. Communication style
C. Family secret
D. Parentification
E. Scapegoating

93. Although various patterns of family systems exist, certain patterns are so common that they are given labels. Consider a patient whom a colleague tells you comes from a "disengaged" family system. Given this information, it is most reasonable to conclude that

A. boundaries around individuals within the system are closed
B. boundaries around the family system are closed
C. boundaries between the father and other family members are closed
D. emotional processes resonate quickly throughout the family system
E. interpersonal boundaries within the family system are diffuse

94. Sam and Ellen met several years ago in college and married recently. They seem somewhat apprehensive and ask their physician what they should expect in their interactions with their families during this early time in their marriage. The physician should tell them that most couples experience

A. being emotionally cut off from their families of origin
B. disengagement from parents
C. enmeshment with parents
D. the formation of a family subsystem with relatively closed boundaries around it
E. the formation of a family subsystem with relatively open boundaries around it

95. A task of adolescence is separation from parents. Some adolescents find this process easier than others do. Which of the following types of family system has the most difficulty adapting to the stage of adolescent separation?

A. Disengaged family
B. Enmeshed family
C. Extended family
D. Generational family
E. Overprotective family

96. Preventive intervention is critical for good health outcomes at any age. Of all of the areas that can be targeted for preventive education among adolescents, the one that would lead to the greatest reduction in the incidence of death to this age group is
   A. homicide
   B. motor vehicle accidents
   C. physical abuse
   D. sexually-transmitted disease
   E. suicide

97. A mother brings her 10-year-old boy to see the physician, complaining that he has been "walking in his sleep." She reports that he walks up and down the stairs two or three times, and then, after letting out a low moan, returns to bed and is once again quiet. She asks what his actions mean and, specifically, what he is dreaming about while he is climbing the stairs. The physician's best response would be to tell her that the
   A. best thing to do is wake him up and tell him to go back to bed
   B. boy is probably not dreaming while he is walking in his sleep
   C. boy is searching for something that he lost
   D. boy will stop walking in his sleep if he goes to bed later
   E. stairs are a symbol of the boy's drive to succeed in life

98. One way to think about families is in terms of constellations of interacting roles. Certain individuals assume or are given particular tasks or responsibilities. These responsibilities often reflect cultural expectations. In the traditional nuclear family, the father is usually assigned to what type of role?
   A. Competitive
   B. Functional
   C. Instrumental
   D. Socioemotional
   E. Symmetrical

99. A family may be a household, but not all households are families. A survey conducted in the mid-1990s showed that the majority of non-family households consisted of
   A. caretaker and patient
   B. non-married couples
   C. one-person households
   D. roommates
   E. same-sex couples

100. Family patterns and patterns of cohabitation change over time, affecting both the social position and the health status of people in the population. Based on U.S. government data, which of the following showed the largest increase among U.S. households during the last quarter of the 20th century?
   A. Households below the poverty level
   B. Households with three children
   C. Kinship households
   D. Married-couple households with children
   E. Single-parent housholds

101. A 15-year-old girl is blamed by her parents for the problems in the family. She is continually getting into trouble and acting out at school. What type of role is she most likely playing in her family system?
   A. Disengaged
   B. Emotionally cut off
   C. Enmeshed
   D. Parentified
   E. Scapegoated

102. A 12-year-old patient is exhibiting some depressive symptoms. She is responsible for taking care of the household and caring for her younger siblings after school until her parents return from work. What type of role is she most likely playing in her family system?
   A. Child-focused
   B. Enmeshed
   C. Instrumental
   D. Parentified
   E. Triangulated

103. A patient reports that there is emotional distance and many independent activities among members of the family. Even traumatic events involving family members evoke little response. What family dynamic best describes this family system?
   A. Disengaged
   B. Enmeshed
   C. Parentified
   D. Scapegoated
   E. Triangulated

104. Each time a family member has a problem it resonates quickly throughout the family system. There is little individual autonomy in the family, and much emotional intensity. When describing this family, the most appropriate term would be
   A. disengaged
   B. child-focused
   C. enmeshed
   D. parentified
   E. triangulated

105. An 18-year-old patient recently married as a way of leaving her parental home. Since her marriage,

she has had no contact with her parents. What label best describes the dynamic between this woman and her parents?

A. Emotionally cut off
B. Enmeshed
C. Parentified
D. Scapegoated
E. Triangulated

106. In the traditional nuclear family in the US, the wife usually is the main caretaker and nurturer in the family. What term best describes the functional role fulfilled by this traditional wife?

A. Child-focused
B. Enmeshed
C. Instrumental
D. Parentified
E. Socioemotional

107. An 8-year-old child has been bed-ridden for the past week with an unidentified infection. The parents are anxious about the state of the child's health. During times of illness such as these, this child is most likely to have difficulty coping with

A. dependency on others
B. limitation of activity
C. loss of affection from parents
D. removal from friends
E. unexplained nature of events.

108. A 27-year-old woman has been bed-ridden with the latest strain of influenza for the past 3 days. When visited by her family physician, she is most likely to complain about feelings of

A. anger
B. blame
C. guilt
D. helplessness
E. hopelessness

109. His physician has told Mr. P. that he has an elevated prostate-specific antigen (PSA) level but that before a definitive diagnosis can be made, the test must be repeated in a month. During this interval, Mr. P. becomes impatient. The most effective coping strategy for this and other medical problems requiring patience is

A. confronting the doctor
B. identifying the issues
C. practicing relaxation exercises
D. seeking information
E. venting frustration to others

110. Peter and Judy and their three children live in St. Louis. They receive food stamps and are considered of low socioeconomic status (SES). Jane has

hypertension and Peter has diabetes; both have frequent problems with respiratory infections. Which of the following statements about the relationship of their SES to their health status is TRUE?

A. Adverse health behaviors such as smoking and not exercising are more predictive than SES of health status
B. In "classless" societies such as the U.S. health status is fairly even across SES levels
C. Inability to afford health insurance results in adverse effects on health
D. SES affects health by limiting access to basics such as food, shelter, and clean water
E. The factor that is most predictive of experiencing adverse health is SES

111. Sam is 25-years-old, six feet tall, and lives in a low-income neighborhood. He often grabs a quick meal at one of the several fast-food restaurants or convenience stores he passes on the one-hour drive to and from his accounting job in the city, where he sometimes spends up to 10 hours a day. Six months ago, Sam's company implemented a workplace wellness program that includes healthy cafeteria meals and free access to a gym located in the office building, where Sam has been working out at lunchtime about twice a week. Sam was raised in a very traditional household (he still gathers with his family for a large dinner every Sunday), and both of his parents and two of his four brothers are obese. Over his past few yearly checkups, Sam's BMI has increased from 22.5 to 23.7 to 24.8. What can be said about Sam's risk of obesity?

A. His upbringing and family history of obesity will make it nearly impossible for Sam to avoid becoming obese himself.
B. It is normal and healthy for a man's BMI to increase steadily during his early 20s, and since he is still considered "normal weight" Sam should not be concerned.
C. The built environment surrounding Sam only promotes unhealthy choices and increases his risk of obesity.
D. The increase in Sam's BMI is not cause for concern because it is probably due to an increase in muscle mass from lifting weights at the company gym.
E. There are elements of his built and social environments that may both aid and constrain Sam's ability to maintain a healthy weight.

112. Hypnosis may be a helpful adjunct to treatment in all of the following conditions EXCEPT

A. alopecia due to chemotherapy

B. management of chronic pain

C. reducing the frequency and duration of flare ups of genital herpes

D. relief of irritable bowel symptoms

E. smoking cessation

113. While recovering from surgery to treat her breast cancer, a woman is encouraged to attend a support group for breast cancer survivors. She seems uneasy about attending. The physician should tell her that one of the main benefits of attending an illness-specific patient support group is that it may help to

A. do active problem solving

B. forget about the illness

C. laugh at adversity

D. learn to accept negative outcomes

E. see that others are worse off

114. Mr. H. has just been diagnosed with an inoperable cerebral tumor. Although his prognosis is poor, he continues to be cheerful and to talk amicably with all who visit him. When faced with a patient who appears cheerful in the face of a poor prognosis, the physician should

A. continue to remind the patient of his grave prognosis

B. gently point out to the patient that he is in denial

C. refuse to care for the patient until he accepts his prognosis

D. speak with his family about his condition

E. understand that the patient may need more time to adjust

115. Ms. G., a new patient, tells you that psychological feeling and physical health have nothing to do with each other. A patient, such as this, who believes that mind and body are separate would be *least* likely to respond to which of the following treatments for pain?

A. Analgesics

B. Antidepressants

C. Relaxation training

D. Surgery

E. Trigger point injections

116. Mr. R., a patient with hypertension, stops taking his medication. When questioned about this non-adherence, he is evasive and avoids eye contact with the physician. Which intervention is most likely to help him resume his treatment?

A. Changing to a drug covered by his insurance plan

B. Explaining the health hazards of elevated blood pressure

C. Explaining the side effects of the medications

D. Increasing his medication to three times a day rather than twice

E. Signing him up for a hypertension support group

117. A 45-year-old man makes an appointment to see his physician because he has a mild cold. Many patients who see a physician for this type of minor self-limited problem are really seeking

A. a particular diagnosis

B. a prescription

C. an excuse to avoid work

D. help with a psychological problem

E. reassurance

118. How and by whom health care decisions are made affects both diagnosis and adherence with recommended treatment. Although individual variations exist, in Asia, Mexico, and the Middle East, the dominant cultural model puts the burden of health decisions on the

A. community

B. family

C. patient

D. physician

E. religious leader

119. Some stressful life events are associated with a negative impact on health, while others are not. The impact a stressful event will have on a given person's health is most dependent on

A. the magnitude of the event

B. the number of people involved

C. the subjective experience of stress associated with the event

D. the type of change involved

E. whether the event is positive or negative

120. Decisions about end of life care are some of the most difficult that patients and their families have to make. When discussing options, the physician should tell them that, compared with death in a hospice, death in a hospital is likely to be more

A. conducive to family visits

B. dependent on technology

C. likely to focus on the timing of death

D. likely to respect religious practices

E. palliative in nature

121. Three weeks after the death of her husband, a distressed widow visits her primary care physician. She tells him that 2 days ago she was sure that she saw her husband alive, strolling along the opposite side of the street. "I called to him," she says, "but he didn't turn around." The physician should tell her that

A   a brief course of antidepressant medication is indicated
B. she is defending against her spouse's death
C. she needs to be hospitalized
D. she was having an hallucination
E. such experiences are common in grieving people

122. Coping with the death of a loved one is always difficult, but some deaths seem to be harder to deal with than others. The cause of death that seems to make grieving most difficult is death that involves
A. an automobile accident
B. cancer
C. heart attack
D. HIV/AIDS
E. suicide

123. Differentiating between normal grief and a psychiatric disorder is difficult because many of the defining diagnostic criteria are shared. Difficulty sleeping, anhedonia, appetite disturbance, and loss of energy are present in both grief and
A. anxiety
B. depression
C. panic disorder
D. personality disorder
E. psychosis

124. Examination of morbidity and mortality patterns of surviving spouses has shown that widows and widowers are at increased risk of death for how many months after the death of their spouse?
A. 6 months
B. 12 months
C. 18 months
D. 24 months
E. no set time period

125. A physician is conducting a history and physical examination on a 24-year-old single woman who is a new patient. When asked if she currently takes any non-prescription drugs, she confesses to using amyl nitrate about once a week. Her most likely reason for using this substance is to
A. calm down after work
B. ease her through a "bad trip"
C. enhance sexual experience
D. give her more energy
E. help her sleep

126. Mr. Jones is visiting his dentist who notices that his teeth are worn and ground down. When questioned, Mr. Jones reports that his wife has told him that he grinds his teeth in his sleep. "She says it really keeps her awake," he says. This teeth grinding most likely occurs during what stage of sleep?
A. Stage 1
B. Stage 2
C. Stage 3
D. Stage 4
E. REM Stage

127. During a well-child visit, a mother expresses concern over the weight of her 4-year-old daughter whose BMI has risen since last year from the 83rd to the 85th percentile for her age. The mother says that after last year's visit she was advised by a dietitian to limit the child's daily intake to about 1,200 calories per day, which she claims to have been doing ever since. She has also been keeping a journal of everything her daughter eats. She has brought the journal in for you to look at and you notice that, although the calorie intakes do appear to be within the recommendations, a substantial proportion of the child's diet consists of fast food meals, peanut butter and jelly sandwiches, and high-fat dairy products. Which of the following statements is NOT a potential explanation for why the child has continued to gain too much weight?
A. Even if the child is not exceeding the recommended daily calorie intake for her age, the high fat content of her diet may still cause her to gain weight excessively.
B. The child is consuming foods when she is at daycare or her grandmother's house that the mother is unaware of.
C. The dietitian's recommendation was incorrect. A 4-year-old child should not consume more than 900 calories per day.
D. The mother has been inaccurate in her estimations of portion sizes and her daughter has actually been consuming more than 1,200 calories daily.
E. The mother has not always read or had access to the proper nutrition facts labels for the foods her daughter has eaten and has often been inaccurate in estimating the number of calories in certain foods.

128. H.G. is a 21-year-old referred for psychological evaluation by the local court system. He was arrested for a series of burglaries. During his arrest, he severely injured one of the arresting police officers. When interviewed, he is very pleasant, even charming. He answers all questions while smiling and looking directly in the eye of the examiner. When questioned about the injury to the policeman, he continues to smile and expresses no remorse. Past history reveals that he was placed in juvenile detention for a year at age 14 after being

found guilty of vandalism and burglary. Based on this initial presentation, the physician makes a preliminary diagnosis of which of the following personality disorders?

A. Antisocial
B. Borderline
C. Histrionic
D. Paranoid
E. Schizotypal

129. A medical student is assigned to explain to a patient that he has a terminal condition. She researches the details and latest prognostic data about the patient's disease. In the morning, she makes a full and detailed presentation to the patient, citing the latest medical information including an in-depth explanation of the underlying biochemical mechanism of the illness. After the presentation, the patient confides to a nurse on the ward that he "really didn't get" most of what the student presented. The most likely defense mechanism being used by the student in this instance is

A. denial
B. intellectualization
C. isolation of affect
D. reaction formation
E. sublimation

130. Stressful life events can affect people's physical as well as psychological health. As measured by the Holmes and Rahe Stressful Life Events Scale, which of the following life events is associated with the greatest stress?

A. Death of a spouse
B. Divorce
C. Incarceration for more than 1 year
D. Loss of a job
E. Surviving an automobile accident

131. Neuronal development progresses through a series of defined stages as the child ages. Neuronal migration, which provides the substrate for brain development, is generally completed by

A. birth
B. 2 months of age
C. 4 months of age
D. 6 months of age
E. 12 months of age

132. Pathology can be viewed as the failure or disruption of normal processes. The failure of "guidance cues" in human development is most likely to result in a person who

A. demonstrates no sense of right and wrong
B. fails to adhere to treatment recommendations
C. is unable to draw shapes from memory

D. lacks neuronal adaptation to environmental stimuli
E. loses control over peripheral physical movements

133. A patient is having difficulty sleeping. His physician advises him to listen to a relaxation tape every evening for ½ hour prior to going to sleep. Eventually, the patient reports that he falls asleep almost at once as soon as he hears the voice on the tape, even without going through the relaxation routine. This phenomenon is most likely due to the operation of

A. biofeedback
B. classical conditioning
C. inhibition
D. intermittent reinforcement
E. modeling

134. An overweight middle aged woman of average height and in good general health comes to the physician requesting advice about diet and weight loss. She says that she has dieted repeatedly throughout her life, and now she cannot lose weight even if she eats only 1,400 calories/day. She is cold, constipated, and lethargic. She denies binging or purging, and she still has normal menstrual cycles. Her thyroid function tests are normal. The physician should

A. order a basal metabolic rate to investigate if she is hypometabolic
B. send her to Overeaters Anonymous for psychological support
C. suggest she try a very-low-calorie diet, or even a liquid fast, to restart the process of weight loss
D. suggest that people often underestimate dietary intake
E. try to motivate her to lose weight by emphasizing the health risks of obesity

135. Often, effective pharmacological treatments are identified before the mechanisms of action have been fully established. Recent research has shown that effective treatment of which one of the following conditions relies on the action of so called "second messengers?"

A. Bipolar disorder
B. General anxiety disorder
C. Huntington disease
D. Schizophrenia
E. Tourrette syndrome

136. A medication is prescribed for Mr. W. to help him cope with chronic generalized anxiety disorder (GAD). The general class of pharmacological

agents most commonly used for the treatment of this anxiety disorder is believed to be effective because it

A. decreases norepinepherine in the locus ceruleus
B. increases acetylcholine in the temporal cortex
C. increases GABA diffusely throughout the brain
D. reduces available dopamine in the medial forebrain bundle
E. reduces serotonin available post-synaptically

137. Animal models are often used to predict the action of new pharmacological agents in humans. A dog in a research laboratory is injected with a drug that imitates the effects of glutamate. Over the next hour, what behavior are you most likely observe from the dog?

A. Hiccups
B. Hypersomnolence
C. Manic-like hyperactivity
D. Seizures
E. Unusual quiescence

138. Evidence for the involvement of dopamine in the initiation of movement is most strongly found by monitoring the action of dopamine in which neuronal area?

A. Locus ceruleus
B. Mesolimbic-mesocortical tract
C. Nigrostriatal tract
D. Raphe nuclei
E. Tuberoinfundibular tract

139. One of the best indications of the level of serotonin activity in the brain can be found by monitoring 5-HIAA levels in

A. blood
B. spinal fluid
C. sweat
D. tears
E. urine

140. During rapid-eye-movement (REM) sleep, the words and images that provide the raw material for the mental representations called dreams originate in the

A. amygdala
B. basal ganglia
C. cerebellum
D. hippocampus
E. reticular activating system

141. Following an automobile accident, Mr. S. presents with monotone speech that is devoid of emotional inflection. He evidences no difficulty understand-

ing what is said to him. A CAT scan of the head is ordered. The results are most likely to show a lesion in

A. Broca's area on the left side
B. Broca's area on the right side
C. Exner's area on both the right and the left sides
D. Wernicke's area on the left side
E. Wernicke's area on the right side

142. Animal models provide a method of understanding the functional importance of the brain and neurological system. When observing the behavior of a rat that is receiving electrical stimulation of the orbital frontal cerebral region you are most likely to observe

A. excessive aggression
B. excessive fluid intake
C. hypersexuality
D. manic-like hyperactivity
E. refusal of food by a hungry animal

143. A professional stock trader spends his days monitoring the changing process of the financial markets and buying and selling according to his observations of market activity. An examination of his record of trading shows that sometimes he makes money and sometimes he loses money. The trader complains that he is preoccupied with trading stocks and can not stop following the markets even when he is on vacation. The mechanism that most likely underlies his excessive attention to the financial markets is

A. continuous operant reinforcement
B. fixed interval operant reinforcement
C. habituation
D. stimulus generalization
E. variable ratio operant reinforcement

144. Following a fall down the stairs, Mrs. F., a 77-year-old widow, is non-responsive to stimulation on the left side of her body. When asked to reproduce a presented figure, she is able to draw the right-hand side exactly, but neglects the left-hand side of the figure entirely. Based on this initial evaluation, further physiological examination of the patient is most likely to show a lesion in the

A. dominant parietal lobe
B. dominant temporal lobe
C. non-dominant parietal lobe
D. non-dominant temporal lobe
E. orbital medial frontal cortex

145. Myelination of the anterior and posterior commissures and the corpus callosum allows improved communication between the right and left hemi-

spheres. This process is most commonly completed during which Freudian stage of development?

A. Oral
B. Anal
C. Phallic
D. Latency
E. Genital

146. You are tracking the cardiac functioning of Mr. B. over a 24-hour period. Mr. B. is a 45-year-old office worker who currently does not engage in regular exercise. Assuming that Mr. B. evidences normal biological rhythms, you would expect to find the highest cardiac contraction rates

A. just after awaking in the morning
B. in the middle of the morning
C. in the afternoon
D. just before going to bed at night
E. during REM sleep

147. Although used interchangeably by many people in day-to-day life, the concepts of illness and disease refer to different aspects of a person's perception of health. In contrast to illness, "disease" refers to

A. chronic rather than acute medical problems
B. contracted health problems rather than inherited health characteristics
C. health from an epidemiological rather than a medical perspective
D. objective pathology rather than subjective experience
E. the impact of poor health on social functioning

148. The notion of the "sick role" encapsulates societal expectations for people with certain types of medical conditions. As generally applied, the concept of the sick role

A. applies only to those with long-term chronic conditions
B. defines the obligations of medical professionals to care for those who are ill
C. places responsibility for having the patient get well on the medical professional
D. relieves the individual from responsibility during an illness
E. specifies a set amount of time to be devoted to illness recovery

149. Mrs. White receives a letter from her HMO informing her that she had abnormal cells on the Pap smear taken during her last visit. The letter requests that she call and schedule a follow-up appointment, which she does. When she appears for a follow-up visit 2 weeks later, she talks about a pain in her back but does not mention or seem

to remember receiving the letter about her Pap smear. The defense mechanism that most likely accounts for Mrs. White's inability to remember the letter is

A. denial
B. intellectualization
C. rationalization
D. somatization
E. undoing

150. John, a patient with a long history of hypertension and cardiac problems, confides to his family physician that he is "feeling depressed" about the recent loss of his job. The physician's best response would be to

A. call John's wife to ask how he has been at home
B. explore the presence of depressive symptoms
C. refer John to a local psychiatrist for evaluation
D. tell John that his mood will pass in a couple of weeks
E. write John a prescription for an antidepressant

151. On the first day of kindergarten, the mother of a 5-year-old boy tells him that she will not leave right away when dropping him off at school. However, over the next few days, she finds that each day he insists that she stay a little longer and begins to cry when she starts to leave. Consequently, this morning she stayed with him for more than an hour. This change in the mother's behavior can be best explained as an example of the effects of

A. extinction
B. fading
C. negative reinforcement
D. positive reinforcement
E. secondary reinforcement

152. The mother of a 5-year-old child lingers for an hour after bringing her son to kindergarten. During this time the boy appears happy, but pays little attention to the teacher or the other children. Eventually the teacher convinces the mother to bring her son to the classroom, reassure him, and then leave. After several days of crying and being fearful after his mother leaves, the boy becomes calmer, stops crying, and displays less fear. This change in the boy's behavior is most likely the result of

A. extinction
B. intermittent reinforcement
C. maturation
D. shaping
E. sublimation

153. Paul, a second year medical student, is angry at his professor for being late to an appointment. When

the professor does appear, Paul tells him how angry he was with a physician he saw earlier in the day who made him wait for more than 30 minutes for no apparent reason. Paul is most likely using the defense mechanism of

A. conversion
B. displacement
C. projection
D. reaction formation
E. repression

154. Physical examination shows J.D. to have normal body strength, response to sensation, speech and comprehension. When engaged in conversation, he seems normal and communicates clearly. However, when asked to tie his shoelaces, he is unable to do so. This type of dysfunction is most commonly called

A. agnosia
B. anosognosia
C. aphasia
D. apraxia
E. aprosody

155. A 45-year-old man who exercises regularly and watches his diet admits to smoking a pack of cigarettes a day. He says that he has tried to quit repeatedly over the years. During his longest period of abstinence (three months) he gained 15 pounds. His father, an obese non-smoker, died of a heart attack at age 60. The patient believes that, for him, the risks of smoking are lower than the risks of obesity. The physician should

A. accept this assessment and focus on other aspects of the patients' life that may affect cardiovascular risk
B. confront the patient's rationalization of his addiction and suggest a 12-step program to help him quit.
C. examine his feelings about the early loss of his father as contributing to his smoking and suggest psychotherapy
D. explain that obesity has less of an impact on cardiovascular mortality than smoking, so he should quit again and accept the weight gain
E. if he did not use nicotine replacement or buproprion in his prior smoking cessation attempts, recommend these to reduce potential weight gain

156. When introduced to someone at a party, Sarah is able to converse in a normal manner. However, as the conversation progresses, it becomes evident that she is unable to recall any details from her remote past. She is able to remember the name of the person she had been talking to when questioned later in the evening. A deficiency of which of the following substances most likely accounts for this pattern of behaviors?

A. Copper
B. Niacin
C. Potassium
D. Thiamine
E. Zinc

157. A 45-year-old man is placed on a narcotic-based pain medication following abdominal surgery. This medication is prescribed on a time-contingent basis. He is told that he can only take one pill every 5 hours, regardless of how much pain he feels. This type of prescription is an example of a reinforcement schedule generally referred to as

A. continuous
B. fixed interval
C. fixed ratio
D. non-contingent
E. variable ratio

158. Which of the following is a top-down list of factors that could affect dietary intake based on the hierarchy of the social ecological model of health behavior?

A. Cost of fruits and vegetables at the local farmers' market, dieting practices of friends, number of fast-food restaurants in the neighborhood, personal preference for sweet and salty foods
B. Genetics, international trade agreements, lack of grocery stores in the community, traditional ethnic dietary practices
C. Local farming practices, social pressure to consume fast food, genetics, U.S. food imports
D. Parents' diets, personal dislike of most vegetables, number of grocery stores in the community, junk-food television advertisements
E. USDA subsidies to cattle farmers, quality of produce in local grocery stores, frequency of fast food consumption of co-workers, personal food preferences

159. J.F., a 43-year-old office worker, has smoked two packs of cigarettes a day for the past 25 years. He tells his physician that he eats a lot of "junk food" and gets little exercise. The behavior that is most likely to significantly reduce J.F.'s risk of heart disease is

A. modifying his diet to exclude high-fat foods
B. signing up for "Weight Watchers"
C. starting a rigorous weight-lifting program
D. stopping smoking
E. taking a cholesterol-lowering medication

160. H.Y., a 47-year-old woman, presents to her family physician feeling "a little out of sorts." In spite of feeling under the weather, she has made no changes in her daily routine as a legal secretary and mother. She only came to see the physician to have a rash evaluated so as not to expose her family and coworkers. Physical examination reveals a rash accompanied by a low-grade fever. A diagnosis of rubella is confirmed by tests. Based on this presentation, H.Y. has
A. disability, without sick role
B. disease, but not illness
C. illness, but not disease
D. infection, but not disease
E. sickness, but not disability

161. Calvin, a 2-year-old boy, is brought to see the pediatrician for evaluation of an earache. One week before, a nurse in the physician's office had given Calvin an immunization shot that elicited a great deal of crying. When you enter the examination room, Calvin is playing happily with his stuffed tiger and interacting calmly with his mother. As the nurse enters the room, however, he begins to cry and tries to leave. Calvin's reaction to the nurse is most likely the result of
A. classical conditioning
B. fading
C. negative reinforcement
D. positive reinforcement
E. shaping

162. A 3-year-old boy has recently begun to have major temper tantrums each morning when it is time to go to childcare. This causes considerable frustration for his mother who is then late for work. These temper tantrums are new. Previously, the boy had gone to childcare without incident. At her wit's end, the mother calls the pediatrician and asks for advice. The pediatrician recommends the use of a "sticker chart": the boy would get a sticker for each of three identified behaviors (eating breakfast, getting into the car, and walking into the childcare building). At the end of the day, the boy would be given a small treat if he has collected three stickers for that day. This strategy is an example of the use of
A. biofeedback
B. desensitization
C. flooding
D. shaping
E. token economy

163. You are observing an emotional outburst from a patient who is upset for an unknown reason. A CAT scan of this patient would show that, during this emotional behavior, the part of the brain that is likely to be the most active is the
A. cerebellum
B. limbic system
C. neocortex
D. pineal body
E. reticular activating system

164. A physician and his wife were invited to an early dinner party. However, office and hospital laboratory results had to be reviewed before the physician was able to leave work that night. As a result, the couple was unable to attend the dinner party that evening. The physician's behavior exemplifies the ethical principle of
A. beneficence
B. fidelity
C. honesty
D. justice
E. trust

165. A physician has practiced in a rural area of Minnesota for over 30 years. In general, his relationships with patients can be considered paternalistic, a style he learned from his father who was his partner until he died 20 years ago. One of the core characteristics of the paternalistic physician is
A. mutual exchange of information between physician and patient
B. patient passivity during encounters with physicians
C. respect for patient autonomy
D. sharing of medical decision making by physicians and patients
E. valuing patients' moral integrity

166. Mr. E., a 75-year-old, long-standing patient recently visited his physician for his annual check-up. As part of that routine evaluation, the physician discovered that Mr. E. was suffering from metastatic lung cancer. This was surprising because he was asymptomatic, except for mild fatigue. The physician is struggling with whether she should inform the patient of his condition now or wait until he begins to deteriorate. The best course of action would be to
A. encourage Mr. E. to obtain life insurance before she informs him
B. immediately inform him of his condition
C. tell his relatives, but not the patient
D. tell the patient that he has a "tumor", but it can be easily treated
E. wait until he becomes significantly symptomatic before informing him

167. In the US, an effective physician-patient relationship is central to delivery of comprehensive health

care services. Both patient satisfaction and positive care outcomes have been tied to maintaining a good relationship between physician and patient. One of the central characteristics of a good physician-patient relationship is

A. acknowledging differences in understanding of health-related issues
B. passive patient behavior when receiving medical services
C. patients' inability to make informed medical decisions
D. physician dominance in the relationship
E. the physician's superior moral integrity

168. A physician graduated from a combined medicine-pediatrics residency 5 years ago and began practice as the only physician in a rural county of her home state. In this role, she provides care to anyone who comes to her office, whether they are patients formally enrolled in her practice or not. Many of her patients are unable to pay their medical bills, but she continues to see them whenever they need her services. One of her regular patients, a community leader who always pays his bills on time, complained to her that he felt it was inappropriate for him to have to wait while she is caring for "deadbeats" who happened to show up at her office. The physician explained that because she is the only physician in the area, it is her obligation to ensure that medical services are available to all patients in the county. The physician's explanation is based on the ethical principle of

A. beneficence
B. fidelity
C. honesty
D. justice
E. non-maleficence

169. Informed consent is the basic underlying principle that governs medical decision making in the US. No medical decision should be made without it. This notion is best understood as the requirement that

A. all participating physicians concur before a medical procedure is performed
B. the patient has all necessary information before deciding to undergo medical treatment
C. the patient's family be advised before medical procedures are undertaken
D. the patient's primary care physician be informed before a sub-specialist performs a procedure
E. the physician be well-informed before consenting to perform a procedure

170. A first-year resident assumes the care of a woman who has had diabetes mellitus for many years. The patient was previously under the care of a recently retired faculty member noted for his authoritarian manner. She was notorious among office staff and clinic physicians for her lack of compliance with her physician's prescribed treatment regimens. When seeing the patient in the office for the first time, the resident noted that her diabetes was out of control despite multiple office visits, dietary counseling, large insulin doses, and a prescribed exercise regimen. To improve the patient's adherence to treatment recommendations, the first step the resident should take is to

A. explain the negative health consequences of non-compliance with recommendations
B. inform her that diabetes is incurable and improvement unlikely without good treatment
C. question the patient about her failure to follow treatment recommendations
D. show concern and ask what assistance she would like to help her manage the diabetes
E. tell the patient how she can best control her diet

171. A 52-year-old woman with metastatic breast carcinoma has been managed at her local community hospital since diagnosis. Her physicians have consulted with a renowned regional tertiary care center regarding all aspects of her care and have followed the consultants' recommendations meticulously. However, as the patient's condition gradually deteriorated, she requested transfer to the regional medical center. Although her treatment regimen was unchanged, shortly after arriving at the medical center the patient stated she "felt better" and was glad she was now under the care of "the famous specialists" at the center. The improvement in this patient's symptoms is likely due to

A. changes in nutritional supplements
B. natural history of the disease
C. nonspecific therapeutic effects
D. placebo effect
E. specific effects of treatment

172. Adherence to treatment refers to active participation by patients in choosing to remain faithful to recommended treatment plans. High levels of adherence are associated with better medical outcomes. Physicians should remember that patient adherence to treatment is most likely to *decline* when

A. patient and physician negotiate the treatment plan
B. patient and physician openly share opinions about the problem
C. the patient's knowledge about the disease increases

D. the physician controls medical decision making

E. the physician provides additional information about the condition

173. The presence of empathy is crucial in the development of the physician-patient relationship. Without empathy, communication is more difficult and patients may feel that the physician does not care about them. One of the core skills required for establishing empathy is
A. avoiding excessive emotional detachment
B. displaying appropriate nonverbal behavior
C. listening actively or reflectively
D. maintaining calm self-control
E. using open-ended questioning

174. Ms. K. is a 60-year-old woman with a history of diabetes and hypertension. Her son reports that, over the past month, she has become disoriented and confused: "One day she seems better, and then suddenly she seems worse." On the Mini-Mental Status Examination she is unable to correctly give the day of the week. Physical examination reveals muscle weakness on the left side of her body. Based on this preliminary examination, the most likely diagnosis for Ms. K. is
A. Alzheimer dementia
B. Creutzfelt-Jakob disease
C. Huntington disease
D. Pick disease
E. Vascular dementia

175. Before a physician can be empathetic with patients, he or she must first be clear what empathy means. Which of the following examples identifies an important behavioral manifestation of empathy?
A. Appearing relaxed and taking extra time
B. Minimizing nonverbal distractions
C. Remaining calm despite a patient's anxiety
D. Speaking in language that is similar to the patient's
E. Taking notes during a clinical interview

176. A family physician is counseling a patient concerning weight loss strategies to help relieve pressure and pain on arthritic knee joints. The patient becomes irate, stating that he feels criticized and put down. The physician reacts with amazement to what she sees as appropriate patient education. The patient's reaction is most likely the result of
A. a personality disorder
B. counter-transference by the physician
C. denial on the part of the patient

D. inadequate expression of empathy by the physician

E. transference by the patient

177. Unfortunately, increasing numbers of the disease states faced by physicians are iatrogenic in origin. Iatrogenesis is best defined as
A. a hypnotic suggestion made by the physician to increase patient compliance
B. a negative patient reaction to physician demeanor
C. a premorbid condition leading to Muchausen syndrome
D. malingering or presenting false information to the physician
E. the creation of additional problems or complications by the physician

178. Physician training requires basic socialization as well as the acquisition of basic medical knowledge. The acquisition of competence as part of this socialization process is best described as
A. being able to judge whether a patient is able to act in his/her best interests
B. combining technical expertise and effective human relations skills to be a "total" physician
C. having the human relations skills to perform well as a physician
D. having the mental capability to be responsible for one's behavior
E. having the technical expertise to perform well as a physician

179. A medical student was spending a month with a physician in private practice in rural North Carolina. The physician had been in solo practice for 20 years and was on call whenever he was in town. He had a loving and supportive relationship with his wife and family, all of whom agreed with and were committed to traditional principles of physician professional behavior. The doctor and his wife were planning on a quiet dinner to celebrate their 25th wedding anniversary when he was called to the hospital for a difficult and prolonged obstetrical delivery. The physician missed the dinner and the medical student was amazed that his wife did not become angry because their plans for the evening were upset. The medical student asked his wife why she was not angry about not having the anniversary celebration. Based on the information above, her most likely answer was
A. "He'll make it up to me next year"
B. "Patients come first when care is really needed"
C. "People would talk if he didn't go to take care of a patient"

D. "The kids are more fun to be with anyway"
E. "When you've been married this long, you know your husband's job comes first"

180. A 24-year-old, cohabitating woman has come to the emergency room four times in six months, seeking treatment for severe headaches. An MRI of the brain done at the second visit was normal. The headaches are preceded by visual distortions and accompanied by nausea. They tend to occur premenstrually or after a stressful week. On questioning, she has chronic pelvic pain but a work-up for endometriosis was negative a year ago. She also has cramping abdominal pain, bloating and gas that, at times, keep her from going to work. She does not have a primary care physician. The astute ER clinician suspects this patient
A. has a history of maltreatment or abuse by an intimate partner
B. has conversion disorder
C. has panic disorder
D. is malingering and has an undiagnosed opiate addiction
E. is suffering from hypochondriasis

181. A young physician was well known for allowing her patients sufficient opportunities to discuss all aspects of their medical care. She also respected their opinions and frequently negotiated management plans with them, deferring to their rights to determine what should be done for their bodies. The principle which best describes her behavior is
A. beneficence
B. justice
C. moral virtue
D. nonmaleficence
E. respect for autonomy

182. Expectations regarding the role of physicians in society are based on knowledge of traditional ethical principles and behaviors. Physician adherence to the majority of these principles and behaviors requires specific actions by the physician. Adherence to which of the following principles requires no action by the physician?
A. Beneficence
B. Justice
C. Moral virtue
D. Non-maleficence
E. Respect for autonomy

183. Miss M., a 93-year-old woman with invasive esophageal carcinoma, has been in a nursing home for 6 months because of progressive disease. She has a single sibling, a sister, who visits her periodically. Her course in the nursing home

has been marked by a 40% loss of body weight and, recently, several episodes of bleeding from her esophagus that required multiple transfusions. She is considered terminally ill with only a short time to live regardless of medical treatment. She has been mentally alert at all times, and competent to make decisions. She has decided to forgo additional transfusions and to die comfortably at the nursing home. In planning for this course of action, the most essential component of her care will be
A. her insurance coverage
B. her relationship with her physician
C. her relationship with the nursing home director
D. her sister's feelings about the decision
E. regulations regarding blood transfusions

184. Mrs. S. was an 80-year-old widow who lived in a retirement home. She was mentally competent and very wealthy. All financial support for living and medical expenses until the time of her death was secure in an unbreachable trust fund. A second trust fund for discretionary use was available as she chose. Unfortunately, she was notorious for poor financial decisions and had lost considerable amounts from the second trust since the death of her financier husband. Her children approached her physician and asked that their mother be declared mentally incompetent so they could control the second trust fund and prevent further losses. The physician refused their request on grounds it would violate a key expectation of his role as a physician. Had he consented to their wish, he would have violated the patient's expectation for physician behavior consistent with
A. beneficence
B. justice
C. moral virtues
D. maleficence
E. respect for autonomy

185. Research on the effects of the growing number of women entering medical practice has demonstrated a number of differences between the practice patterns of male and female doctors. This research has shown that
A. child-rearing is poorer than that of non-physician mothers
B. female physicians show greater confidence in their interpersonal skills
C. female surgeons are less aggressive about performing invasive interventions
D. female surgeons have lower technical skills than male surgeons
E. rates of pay for male and female physicians have equalized

186. Many life decisions, including career choice, can be the result of transference. An example of transference in career decision making would be choosing
    A. a career in health care after experiencing a significant childhood illness
    B. a helping profession when a family member has a history of substance abuse
    C. medicine based on a physician role model outside the family
    D. medicine because a parent is a physician
    E. medicine because of admiring a genial physician on television

187. When surveyed and asked to self-describe their personality, what proportion of physicians label themselves as "compulsive?"
    A. 20%
    B. 40%
    C. 60%
    D. 80%
    E. 95%

188. Dual-physician marriages are becoming increasingly common as more women enter the practice of medicine. These marriages face unique challenges. Surveys of two-physician marriages have found that
    A. female spouses consider family obligations when selecting practices
    B. males and females have similar earning potential
    C. marital partners choose practice sites regardless of spouse preference
    D. marital partners take equal length of time in training
    E. these marriages have a higher than average divorce rate

189. Diminished ability to carry out personal or professional responsibilities is referred to in the literature as "physician impairment." Which of the following examples would reflect physician impairment?
    A. Completed rehabilitation for cocaine dependence 6 months ago
    B. Compulsive gambling that only occurs on weekends
    C. Heated, public verbal exchange with the nursing staff
    D. HIV infection without current symptoms
    E. Status post stroke with residual impairment of gait

190. An emergency department physician wants to identify a psychological assessment tool that will help her screen emergency room patients for suicide risk. She has identified several assessment tools, but wants to investigate them further to determine if they will be useful for her particular purpose. Therefore, when investigating these tests she should pay special attention to information about their
    A. administration
    B. bias
    C. consistency
    D. reliability
    E. validity

191. When applying for a position as a bank teller, John was surprised when he was asked to complete the Minnesota Multiphasic Personality Inventory (MMPI). He had recently learned about the test in graduate school and knew it was very useful with certain patient populations. However, he had serious doubts about its usefulness in selecting employees. John's doubts about the MMPI's use for employee selection reflect concerns about
    A. bias
    B. convergence
    C. precision
    D. reliability
    E. validity

192. Universities and medical schools often use applicants' scores on tests such as the MCAT, GRE, and SAT as part of their admission decisions. These schools hope that these tests will help them determine which applicants will be successful in their programs. To be useful in this capacity, these tests must have strong
    A. criterion-related validity
    B. construct validity
    C. content validity
    D. face validity
    E. predictive validity

193. A clinician is interested in assessing the trait of obsessiveness. To obtain information about how much of this or any other trait or attribute a person possesses, the clinician should be most concerned with
    A. construct validity
    B. content validity
    C. criterion-related validity
    D. face validity
    E. predictive validity

194. Dr. Scott was considering giving the Benton Visual Retention Test to an 8-year-old patient who recently received a severe blow to the head in an accident. He tells you that this test has an interra-

ter reliability coefficient of .95. You should advise Dr. Scott to

A. abandon the test since its reliability is extremely low
B. consider this test since its reliability is very strong
C. continue to investigate the test since its reliability is moderate
D. give the test on two separate occasions to confirm the results
E. look for a test with a reliability coefficient over 1.00

195. A patient was referred for outpatient psychotherapy after a recent emergency room visit when he was given several psychological assessments. The therapist wants to re-administer the tests given in the emergency room to determine if there has been any significant change in the patient's condition. Since the therapist wants to be relatively certain that any changes in results reflect true changes in the patient's condition and not the change in environment, he needs to be most concerned about the tests'

A. adaptive capacity
B. bias
C. concurrent validity
D. content validity
E. reliability

196. Recent years have seen a lot of discussion in the popular press about intelligence and its assessment. After reading some of these accounts, one of your patients comes to you and, knowing that their child is about to be given an IQ test at school, asks you what the facts are. Which of the following statements about intelligence would you make, based on the current state of knowledge?

A. Intelligence tests are based on one agreed-upon definition of intelligence.
B. IQ and intelligence are the same thing.
C. Most differences in IQ scores are primarily due to environmental factors.
D. Race predicts what IQ score a particular individual will obtain.
E. Tests of intelligence generally attempt to measure ability not achievement.

197. The IQ score is norm referenced. This means that each individual's test score is compared to a normative range to derive the actual IQ. When looking at the distribution of IQ scores represented on the normal curve, approximately 68% of people score

A. >130
B. >100
C. 85–115

D. <100
E. <70

198. J.G. is a 19-year-old man referred for evaluation by his college Dean. The Dean acted after reports from students that J.G. was "impossible to live with" and was disrupting classes. At the initial interview, J.G. is dressed in mismatched clothing and seems anxious and suspicious of the physician. He giggles under his breath, and then laughs for no apparent reason. As the session progresses, J.G. confesses that he can hear what the physician is thinking. His speech is coherent, but characterized by odd choices of words that seem to hold some hidden private meaning for him. He reports no close friends other than his brother whom he sees once a month. Among the following types of personality disorder, which is the most likely diagnosis for this patient?

A. Antisocial personality disorder
B. Borderline personality disorder
C. Narcissistic personality disorder
D. Schizoid personality disorder
E. Schizotypal personality disorder

199. Daniel, a 6-year-old boy, is brought by his mother to see his pediatrician. She reports that during sleep, he sits up in bed and screams for about a minute, and then lies back down to sleep again. In the morning he seems to have no recollection of these episodes. The physician should advise the mother that Daniel is most likely experiencing

A. acute adjustment reaction
B. bruxism
C. hypnogogic hallucinations
D. night terrors
E. nightmares

200. A 55-year-old man with a history of hypertension is admitted to the hospital for removal of his gall bladder. He reports feeling anxious about his pending operation. His physician should keep in mind that the patient is most likely to recover sooner and request less pain medication if he

A. has complete information about the surgical procedure and recovery
B. has confidence in his surgeon's technical skill
C. is given post-operative pain medication on demand
D. is pleased with his nursing care
E. likes his surgeon personally

201. The Minnesota Multiphasic Personality Inventory (MMPI) is a sophisticated test with a built-in check to determine whether a person's responses are genuine or merely an attempt to "look good."

The validity scale on the MMPI that is used to assess the test taker's need to present himself or herself in a favorable or socially desirable light is the
A. F or Infrequency Scale
B. K or Correction Scale
C. L or Lie Scale
D. PY or Psychasthenia Scale
E. SE or Self-Esteem Scale

202. During an assessment, a patient is asked to look at a picture and make up a story about it. The patient tells a story about two lovers who are fighting, but then make up. The patient is most likely being psychologically assessed with the
A. Bender Visual Motor Gestalt Test
B. Benton Visual Retention Test
C. Minnesota Multiphasic Personality Inventory
D. Peabody Picture Vocabulary Test
E. Thematic Apperception Test

203. During assessment, a patient was administered the WAIS, MMPI, the Tactile Performance Test, the Speech Sounds Test, and the Categories Test. The patient is probably being evaluated for brain dysfunction with the
A. Bender Visual-Motor Gestalt Test
B. California Personality Inventory
C. Halstead-Reitan Neuropsychological Test Battery
D. Luria Nebraska Neuropsychological Battery
E. Thematic Apperception Test

204. A 10-year-old patient has been having academic difficulties at school. A psychologist suggests administration of a test that has confirmed validity in detecting brain damage, and also provides a non-verbal measure of personality. This test is frequently used to estimate intelligence and school readiness. The test most likely suggested by the psychologist is the
A. Bender Visual-Motor Gestalt Test
B. Draw-A-Person Test
C. Luria Nebraska Neuropsychological Battery
D. Rorschach Test
E. Wechsler Memory Scale

205. When individuals are forced to impose meaning on an ambiguous stimulus, it is assumed that responses will be reflections of their true feelings, thoughts, attitudes, desires, experiences, and needs. This assumption is an example of
A. reaction formation
B. subjective press
C. the Gestalt laws of perception
D. the law of effect
E. the projective hypothesis

206. A physician suspects that a patient may have been a victim of childhood sexual abuse and requests that certain psychological tests be administered to see if any indicators of abuse appear in the patient's results. However, when requesting the testing, the physician does not tell the patient or the psychologist administering the test that she wishes to screen for sexual abuse. She decided to do this to guard against
A. a placebo effect
B. bias
C. destroying the reliability of the test results
D. influencing the construct validity of the test
E. stigmatizing the patient

Items 207–209
Answer the following questions with reference to Table 1.

Table 1		Actual Disease		
		Yes	No	Totals
Screening Test	Positive	a	b	a + b
	Negative	c	d	c + d
	Totals	a + c	b + d	a + b + c + d

207. Which of the choices below best represents the false-positive error rate?
A. a/(a + b)
B. a/(a + c)
C. b/(a + b)
D. b/(b + d)
E. d/(b + d)

208. Which of the choices below best represents specificity?
A. a/(a + b)
B. a/(a + c)
C. b/(a + b)
D. b/(b + d)
E. d/(b + d)

209. Which of the choices below best represents positive predictive value?
A. a/(a + b)
B. a/(a + c)
C. b/(a + b)
D. b/(b + d)
E. d/(b + d)

210. You wish to determine the proportion of myocardial infarctions that are fatal within the first 24 hours after they occur. You decide to examine the records of all local emergency rooms and doctors' offices. Then, you will calculate the proportion of myocardial infarctions reported that resulted in death within 24 hours after the patient was seen initially. You briefly discuss your plan with a local biostatistician who immediately points out that your study is particularly subject to
    A. late-look bias
    B. lead-time bias
    C. measurement bias
    D. observer bias
    E. selection bias

211. An investigator is trying to determine whether medical screening programs using chest x-rays to detect lung cancer improve the survival time of the persons screened. She looks at the most recent year's data in the Connecticut Tumor Registry and discovers that the median survival time following the diagnosis of lung cancer is 6 months. She then performs a chest x-ray screening program in shopping centers and bowling alleys. She finds that in persons screened by this program, the median time from diagnosis to death is 9 months for the 95 cases of lung cancer discovered. The survival time difference is statistically significant. The investigator concludes that the screening program and subsequent treatment are adding an average of 3 months to the lives of lung cancer patients. You disagree on the basis of
    A. late-look bias
    B. lead-time bias
    C. measurement bias
    D. observer bias
    E. selection bias

212. A 16-year-old boy, who describes himself as gay, comes for a physical exam so he can play tennis at school. He seems subdued in the office, and the examiner asks how he is doing. He describes feeling socially isolated and says that he switched to tennis because he felt bullied and teased when he played team sports like basketball and soccer. His grades have dropped from A's and B's to B's and C's over the past year. He denies drinking or the use of street drugs, but he admits to feeling apathetic and sad. On questioning, he says that, at times, he feels life is not worth living, and he has had some suicidal thoughts, especially since he has come out to his parents. They seem unperturbed but a few close friends have turned away from him saying they "can't deal with it." As someone who defines himself as homosexual, is

he at higher or lower risk of suicide than heterosexual peers with this level of symptoms?
    A. Higher, due to self hatred for his sexual orientation ("internalized homophobia")
    B. Higher, due to the prejudice and discomfort he elicits in his peers
    C. Lower, as he is less likely to consider violent means of suicide than heterosexual peers
    D. Lower, because his openness suggests greater psychological maturity
    E. Lower, since, as a homosexual male, his suicide risk is closer to that of a female

213. Which of the following menu selections is the healthiest choice with regard to total calories, fat, and saturated fat?
    A. Chili's: Cobb salad – bed of lettuce topped with grilled chicken, applewood-smoked bacon, avocado, cheese, red bell peppers, egg, and avocado ranch dressing – with a cup of sweet corn soup
    B. Outback Steakhouse: Half a rack of baby back ribs – smoked, grilled and brushed with a tangy BBQ sauce served with Aussie fries
    C. Red Lobster: Walt's favorite – hand-breaded, butterflied shrimp, fried to a golden brown – and a side Caesar salad
    D. Subway: 12-inch sub – hearty Italian bread with black forest ham, Swiss cheese, and ranch dressing – and a bowl of vegetable beef soup
    E. Wendy's: Homestyle chicken fillet sandwich – specially seasoned, lightly breaded, and topped with mayonnaise – and a small order of fries

214. By definition, a woman is menopausal if she
    A. has frequent hot flashes, disturbed sleep, and irregular menses
    B. has not menstruated in the past three months
    C. has not menstruated in the past year
    D. has noted a significant change in the pattern of her menstrual function (i.e., scantier or heavier periods, worsening or milder premenstrual symptoms)
    E. is over 45, has unprotected sex, and has not conceived over the past year

215. A company concerned about productivity lost because of health problems instituted an intensive medical treatment and support program for the 10% of its workers with the most time lost due to illness during a certain year. The treated group had much better attendance and productivity the next year. You believe that the program actually had no effect. You explain that the outcome is

A. effect modification
B. excessive power
C. random error
D. the statistical regression effect
E. type II error

216. When there is public disclosure of financial records and quality standards, we refer to this kind of medical care as
A. acceptable
B. accountable
C. adequate
D. appropriate
E. available

217. When the care provided is compatible with the patient's belief system, we refer to this kind of medical care as
A. acceptable
B. accessible
C. adequate
D. appropriate
E. available

218. A radiologist agrees to charge a reduced fee to all patients who are referred to him by a local hospital. Although now only collecting 60% of his usual fee, the radiologist hopes to make up the shortfall by an increased volume of referrals. This payment mechanism is most indicative of a(n)
A. DRG payment model
B. group model HMO
C. IPA model HMO
D. PPO
E. staff model HMO

Items 219 and 220

The following unpublished data concern the relationship between preventive treatment with chicken soup and the frequency with which colds develop. Assume that the data are from a randomized, double blind trial of chicken soup versus placebo (e.g., gazpacho) over the course of 1 year.

Outcome	Treatment		
	Chicken Soup	Placebo	Total
No Colds	21	11	32
1 or More Colds	36	35	71
Total	57	46	103

219. To make the data more comprehensible, you decide to use percentages for your analysis. Which of the following sets of percentages is a correct and meaningful representation of the data above and provides the most useful basis for comparing the relative number of colds between the two main groups of the research design?
A. 63% and 76%
B. 52% and 57%
C. 65% and 51%
D. 10% and 14%
E. 5% and 95%

220. Which of the following would be the most appropriate significance test for these data?
A. Analysis of variance
B. Chi-square analysis
C. Paired t-test
D. Pearson correlation coefficient
E. Student's t-test

Items 221–226

A test for the detection of politically incorrect tendencies is devised. It is applied to a population of 200 adults in the US who insist they harbor no such tendencies. Before the test was administered, however, 20 of the 200 are found to actually harbor politically incorrect tendencies based on a "gold standard" set by a panel of experts. The new test detects 12 cases of political incorrectness, of which 8 are positive by the findings of the gold standard and 4 are negative.

221. Based on these data, the sensitivity of the new test is
A. 8%
B. 12%
C. 40%
D. 80%
E. 92%

222. The specificity of the new test is
A. 1%
B. 12%
C. 40%
D. 67%
E. 98%

223. The positive predictive value of the new test in this population is
A. 1%
B. 12%
C. 40%
D. 67%
E. 98%

224. The negative predictive value of the test is approximately
    A. 1%
    B. 12%
    C. 67%
    D. 94%
    E. 98%

Assume that the sensitivity and specifity of the new test remain unchanged but that the expert panel (i.e., the gold standard), after consulting with others, decides that instead of 20 cases of political incorrectness there are actually 150 cases.

225. The positive predictive value is now
    A. 1%
    B. 12%
    C. 67%
    D. 94%
    E. 98%

226. Given the revised prevalence of 150 cases of political incorrectness, the negative predictive value is approximately
    A. 1%
    B. 12%
    C. 35%
    D. 67%
    E. 98%

Items 227–230

You are the medical director of a company that manufactures plastic caps for the ends of shoelaces. You wish to screen the company's 1,000 workers for *capus plasticus pedo-reversilosus*, a condition that causes the worker to place caps for the laces of the right shoe on the laces of the left, and vice versa. The condition can be treated effectively with ice-water immersion and concomitant hypnosis, if it is detected early. From the literature on the subject, you determine that the sensitivity of the screening test is 94% and that the specificity is 90%. You estimate the prevalence of the condition to be 5%.

227. What percentage of positive screening test results will be false-positive results?
    A. 18%
    B. 23%
    C. 48%
    D. 67%
    E. 81%

228. What is the approximate positive predictive value of the screening test?

    A. 28%
    B. 33%
    C. 48%
    D. 67%
    E. 81%

229. How many cases of the disease will be missed if all 1,000 workers are screened?
    A. 3
    B. 16
    C. 18
    D. 47
    E. 95

230. Which of the following would be the most important information to know before deciding whether or not to implement the screening test?
    A. Cost of screening, follow-up, and treatment
    B. Disease incidence
    C. Genetic risk factors for the disease
    D. Prevalence of other diseases in the population
    E. Size of the population at risk

231. A screening test is applied to a population of 1,000 in which the prevalence of disease Y is 10%. The sensitivity of this test is 96%, and the specificity is 92%. The diagnostic work-up for each person found to have a true-positive result in the screening test would cost $50. A newer screening test has both a sensitivity and a specificity of 96% but costs $0.50 more per test than the older screening test. How much money would be saved or lost by choosing the newer test?
    A. $500 lost
    B. $500 saved
    C. $1,300 lost
    D. $1,300 saved
    E. $1,800 saved

Items 232–235

A friend of yours thinks that she may be pregnant. She purchased a product to test for pregnancy and found the following data provided in the product brochure.

True Status	Pregnancy Test Result		
	Positive	Negative	Total
Pregnant	253	24	277
Not Pregnant	8	93	101
Total	261	117	378

232. Turning to you for advice, your friend asks, "If the test says that I am pregnant, what is the probability that I really am pregnant?" Your answer is
    A. 67%
    B. 79%
    C. 85%
    D. 97%
    E. 100%

233. Your friend then asks, "If the test says that I am not pregnant, what is the probability that I really am not?" Your answer is
    A. 67%
    B. 79%
    C. 85%
    D. 97%
    E. 100%

234. Your friend is convinced that you actually know what you are talking about, so she asks, "If I really am pregnant, what is the probability that the test will discover that fact?" You confidently reply
    A. 57%
    B. 79%
    C. 88%
    D. 91%
    E. 97%

235. You caution your friend that the numbers that are provided in the product brochure might not apply to her because the
    A. false-positive error rate of the test is high
    B. prevalence in the population tested is unknown
    C. prevalence in the population tested may not match her prior probability
    D. test sensitivity is unknown
    E. test specificity is unknown

Items 236–238
A medical student is asked to assess the heart rate of a panel of 10 cardiac patients. The resting heart rates of these patients are 70, 68, 84, 76, 88, 66, 56, 60, 80, and 70 beats per minute.

236. Based on the measurements of this medical student, what is the modal heart rate for this set of data?
    A. 56
    B. 66
    C. 70
    D. 80
    E. 88

237. What is the median heart rate for this set of patients?
    A. 56
    B. 66
    C. 70
    D. 80
    E. 88

238. A trial of an antihypertensive agent is performed by administering the drug or a placebo, with a "washout period" in between, to each study subject. The treatments are administered in random order, and each subject serves as his or her own control. The trial is double blind. The appropriate significance test for the change in blood pressure with drug versus placebo is the
    A. ANOVA
    B. chi-square analysis
    C. paired t-test
    D. Pearson correlation co-efficient
    E. regression analysis

Items 239 and 240
Two different groups of investigators perform separate clinical trials of the same therapy. The trials have approximately the same sample size. In the first trial, the investigators find more successes in the treatment group and report a p-value of 0.04. Based on these results, the investigators recommend the therapy. In the second trial, the investigators find more successes in the treatment group but report a p-value of 0.08. Based on these results, the investigators do not recommend the therapy.

239. As a clinician reviewing these studies, it is most important to keep in mind that
    A. data that are not statistically significant may still be clinically important
    B. if the data achieve statistical significance, the studies will be clinically important
    C. statistical significance has not been achieved because alpha has been set too high
    D. statistical significance has not been achieved because beta has been set too low
    E. if the data do not achieve statistical significance, the studies cannot be clinically important

240. An appropriate means for reconciling the conflicting recommendations would be to
    A. analyze the data using multi-variant methods
    B. conduct a case-control study
    C. obtain expert opinion
    D. perform intention-to-treat analyses
    E. pool the data

241. A 17-year-old star on the high school football team is injured in an automobile accident. His injury is not life threatening, but will keep him bed-ridden for several months. When talking with this patient, the physician is likely to find that he is having the hardest time coping with
    A. dependency on others
    B. limitation of activity
    C. removal from friends
    D. the unexplained nature of events
    E. the pain of his injury

242. Both governmental programs and private insurance directives increasingly regulate relationships between physicians and patients. One such program, diagnosis-related groups (DRGs), is primarily used to
    A. assess the quality of subspecialty care in hospitals
    B. assign patients to appropriate hospital treatment
    C. provide support for patients following hospital discharge
    D. stipulate prospective payment to hospitals
    E. track epidemiological trends in the general population

243. A 15-year-old girl who was formerly a solid student with many friends and interests has become moody at home. She is irritable with her parents, and she constantly reacts to small frustrations with sobs and tears. She is often up late and then has trouble getting up in the morning. She seems to vary between lack of appetite and a tendency to eat lots of carbohydrates, especially chocolate. At times, she seems unusually animated around her friends, but she often refuses invitations to socialize, saying she is too tired, too fat, or that all her friends are "boring." Her grades have dropped over the past six months, and her mother overhears her say to a friend on the phone that she seriously wishes she were dead. This presentation is most consistent with
    A. attention-deficit/hyperactivity disorder
    B. body dysmorphic disorder
    C. borderline personality disorder
    D. major depression
    E. normal puberty

244. Which of the following activities is the best calorie-burning choice for a healthy new mother who is trying to lose her pregnancy weight and has only ½ hour each day to exercise at the local gym?
    A. Alternating between 5-minute intervals of walking briskly (~3½ mph) and running at a moderate pace (~10 min/mile) on the treadmill for 30 minutes
    B. Riding the stationary bike at a constant pace with moderate effort (~150 watts) for 30 minutes
    C. Swimming laps at a moderate pace for 30 minutes
    D. Using the rowing machine at a constant pace with moderate effort (~100 watts) for 30 minutes
    E. Any of the above

245. A 4-year-old girl is admitted to the hospital to have her tonsils removed. Her father, who had been the sole financial support for the family, was injured over a year ago in a work-related accident and has been unable to work since that time. The father is depressed about his disability and worried about how he will pay for his daughter's surgery. Under these circumstances, the daughter's procedure is most likely to be covered by
    A. Blue Cross
    B. Medicaid
    C. Medicare
    D. the local physician-hospital organization
    E. the physician's resource fund

246. The rising interest in preventive medicine in the US is in part a byproduct of broader changes in the health care delivery system. Health care providers being compensated under which type of payment system are most likely to be supportive of a new program aimed at the primary prevention of disease?
    A. HMO
    B. Indemnity insurance
    C. Medicaid
    D. Medicare
    E. PPO

Items 247 and 248

A study was conducted to examine the relationship between exposure to stressful life events and the risk of myocardial infarction. 30,000 subjects were recruited and each completed the Holmes and Rahe Stressful Life Events Scale, indicating which events they had experienced in the past 6 months. The resulting scores were used to divide the subjects into three equal groups: low events, medium events, and high events. All subjects were then followed over the subsequent year and the incidence of coronary events recorded. Results of the study are presented in the table below in terms of relative risks accompanied by the appropriate confidence intervals.

Relative Risk of Myocardial Infarction by Experience of Stressful Life Events

Group	N	Relative Risk	Confidence Intervals
Low	10,000	NA	
Medium	10,000	1.3	(0.74–1.56)
High	10,000	1.5	(1.10–1.73)

247. This type of study is best referred to as a
    A. case-control study
    B. clinical trial
    C. cohort study
    D. cross-over study
    E. cross-sectional study

248. Based on the results presented, the conclusion most supported by this study would is
    A. any increase in experience of stressful life events increases the risk of MI
    B. because no *p* values are given, no clear conclusions are possible
    C. no relationship can be demonstrated between stressful life events and subsequent MI
    D. only high levels of stressful life events are associated with increased risk for MI
    E. reducing exposure to stressful life events will reduce the number of MIs

249. A 15-year-old boy wants to try out for the wrestling team. In addition to weight-lifting, he has been secretly vomiting after each meal to drop to a lower weight category where he would be "stronger" than other wrestlers. At his pre-participation evaluation, he complains of feeling dizzy and tired, and serum electrolytes are obtained. Which of the following patterns of electrolyte disturbance is most likely in this situation?
    A. Chloride elevated; potassium elevated; carbon dioxide elevated
    B. Chloride elevated; potassium low; carbon dioxide elevated
    C. Chloride low; potassium elevated; carbon dioxide low
    D. Chloride low; potassium low; carbon dioxide elevated
    E. Chloride low; potassium low; carbon dioxide low

250. Data examining the current trends for AIDS-related deaths in one of the Midwestern states show a dramatic decrease in AIDS-related mortality, but little change in the incidence of AIDS.

Given this information, we should also expect to find
    A. a decrease in AIDS-related medical care
    B. a decrease in survival rate following diagnosis
    C. an increase in AIDS prevalence
    D. an increase in HIV infections among family members
    E. an increase in the number of people practicing safe sex

251. The concept of homeostasis helps to explain long-term physiological reactions to stressful events and how these reactions mediate strategies for coping with stress. In this context, the notion of homeostasis refers to
    A. average physical reaction time to unexpected stimuli
    B. balancing interpersonal with psychological needs
    C. the ability of the body to metabolize food and convert it to energy
    D. the capacity to balance the sex drive and the aggression drive
    E. the tendency for the body to maintain a particular state

252. Certain types of behaviors, such as the Type A pattern, are associated with increased chances of disability and disease. The manifest behavior and subsequent liability for disease of a person with a Type A behavior pattern is believed to be most closely linked to the fact that these people
    A. are exposed to more stressful environments
    B. are socially withdrawn when faced with stressful events
    C. have greater ability to withstand stress
    D. have greater competence in problem solving
    E. have more psychological need for control over situations

253. For the past three months, a 36-year-old man reports suffering from heart palpitations, sweating palms, vague apprehension, difficulty concentrating, and difficulty falling asleep. He reports that nothing makes him feel better except taking long walks along the lakefront by himself or singing a special song to himself. His relationships with others have deteriorated during this time period and he fears being fired from his job. Based on this presentation, the most likely diagnosis for this man would be
    A. agoraphobia
    B. generalized anxiety disorder
    C. panic disorder
    D. obsessive-compulsive disorder
    E. social phobia

254. A student is apprehensive about the upcoming anatomy exam. On exam day, she is observed sitting in the exam room opening and closing both fists while breathing deeply. She is probably trying to control her anxiety by means of
    A. biofeedback
    B. meditation
    C. progressive relaxation
    D. self-hypnosis
    E. the stress response

255. A 13-year-old female began pubertal development at 9 and had her first menstrual period at 10 years 6 months, and is at the 90th percentile for height. An older brother who teased her about gaining weight is now at college. Her mother and father are in the process of separating; her father is on a cholesterol-lowering diet. She is interested in going out for the school cross-country team and has started dieting to get in shape for the season. Which of the following is themost important risk factor for her to develop an eating disorder?
    A. Brother teasing her about her weight
    B. Dieting to get in shape for the cross-country team
    C. Early pubertal development
    D. Father being on a diet
    E. Parental separation and conflict

256. On a cold day in January, a 40-year-old, well nourished man arrives at the emergency room wearing running shorts, a tank top, and new, very expensive running shoes. He was picked up running along a controlled access highway. He says he has started training for a marathon and needed a long unbroken course to run on. His demeanor is haughty, alternating between amused condescension and irritable impatience. His speech is rapid and he is difficult to interrupt. As the examiner challenges his story, the details keep shifting. He is convinced he will win the marathon in the spring, even though this is his first training run. Since recently losing his job, he feels he will have more than adequate time to pursue his athletic goals. He is oriented to person, place and time. He can recall 3 of 3 objects at 0 and 5 minutes. He does serial sevens rapidly to 44 with three unnoticed errors. Digit span is 6 forward and 3 in reverse. He interprets the proverb, "Do not judge a man until you have walked a mile in his shoes" as meaning, "The way to win a race is to be sure you know what the other guy has on his feet." He responds to the question, "What would you do if you found a stamped letter lying in the street?" by saying, "I'd think it was my lucky day!" This description is most consistent with

    A. delusional disorder
    B. histrionic personality disorder
    C. mania
    D. masked depression
    E. narcissistic personality disorder

257. Thinking can be usefully separated into a number of different processes, each appropriate to different types of problems and situations. The situation in which a physician, while examining a set of patients, categorizes a number of symptoms as sharing some features in common, is best regarded as an example of
    A. concept formation
    B. convergent thinking
    C. hypothesis testing
    D. insightful thinking
    E. stimulus discrimination

258. A person's experience of reality is not simply absorbed from the environment, but constructed by means of mental representations. Language plays a key role in this process. Language shapes the individual's perception of reality by
    A. assigning meaning to sounds
    B. defining how experiences are described and what is remembered
    C. limiting what the individual senses
    D. modifying the meaning of words through vocal intonation
    E. restricting perception to only what can be put into words

259. Different people see the world differently. Even people with the exact same experiences may recall and respond to them differently. These individual differences in the manner in which experiences are perceived, processed, and assigned meaning are called
    A. cognitive styles
    B. defense mechanisms
    C. delusional thoughts
    D. schemas
    E. sensations

260. Defense mechanisms can be thought of as cognitive processes, as well as affective controls. The re-conceptualization of an event or memory in sufficiently abstract terms in order to distance it meaningfully and emotionally describes the defense mechanism of
    A. denial
    B. intellectualization
    C. projection
    D. repression
    E. sublimation

261. Intelligence is one of the variables most predictive of human development and behavior. Over the past several years, there has been considerable debate about what intelligence is and how it functions. Based on a growing body of work, we can now say with confidence that
    A. intelligence is determined by heredity and is uninfluenced by experience
    B. intelligence is generally defined in terms of verbal ability and problem-solving skills
    C. measures of intelligence are usually based on divergent thinking
    D. rapid processing of information is a universal characteristic of high intelligence
    E. there are significant differences in intelligence between races

262. Choose the answer that ranks the signs of thought disorder from least to most severe.
    A. Circumstantiality, loose associations, flight of ideas, tangentiality
    B. Circumstantiality, tangentiality, flight of ideas, loose associations
    C. Flight of ideas, circumstantiality, loose associations, tangentiality
    D. Loose associations, tangentiality, circumstantiality, flight of ideas
    E. Tangentiality, loose associations, cirumstantiality, flight of ideas

263. After hearing the description of a patient's illness, the physician repeats the essential symptoms to him and reflects back the patient's reaction to those symptoms. The physician receives confirmation from her patient that she, the doctor, understands the patient's description of his illness. In this example, the doctor has demonstrated
    A. accurate empathy
    B. clinical judgment
    C. concept formation
    D. divergent thinking
    E. paralinguistic communication

264. A woman decides she will give herself permission to buy a new dress after she loses 10 pounds. This procedure, in which the person plans rewarding consequences for attaining set goals, is best referred to as the technique of
    A. cognitive rehearsal
    B. cognitive restructuring
    C. problem solving
    D. self-control contracting
    E. skills training

265. A student is afraid that he will fail an upcoming examination. "I don't know what to do," he says, "I just keep telling myself that I'm so stupid and that there's nothing I can do." The student is encouraged to remind himself how much he studies and to remember that, "Hard work leads to good results." This technique, in which the student is encouraged to replace maladaptive cognitions with adaptive cognitions, is generally referred to as
    A. cognitive rehearsal
    B. cognitive restructuring
    C. problem solving
    D. self-control contracting
    E. skills training

266. A basketball player is trained to repeatedly visualize himself attempting and making a free throw in a game, with the fans yelling and the opposing players trying to distract him. The technique the athlete is using to visualize behaviors is an example of
    A. cognitive rehearsal
    B. cognitive restructuring
    C. problem solving
    D. self-control contracting
    E. skills training

267. Without the hippocampus, learning that is based on retention of long-term memories is impossible. What is the functional process by which the hippocampus and its associated structures of the limbic system facilitate this type of learning?
    A. They act as a trainer and guide the learning of motor skills in the brainstem
    B. They connect the various cortical storage sites to form combined memories
    C. They directly stimulate the release of neurotransmitter hormones from the adrenal gland
    D. They forward all incoming sensory information to the neocortex for permanent storage
    E. They promote synaptic depolarization to facilitate neuronal transmission

268. Dr. Hansen works in an office provided by the HMO that also refers all of her patients to her. Payments are made to the doctor, not based on how many patients she sees but on how many patients consider her to be their physician. Recently, the HMO began to offer performance-based bonus payments that substantially increased Dr. Hansen's income. Dr. Hansen is most likely working for what type of medical delivery system?
    A. Group model HMO
    B. IPA model HMO
    C. Network model HMO
    D. PPO care delivery system
    E. Staff model HMO

269. Major neural pathways of the hippocampus use an excitatory amino acid called glutamate as their neurotransmitter. Upon neuronal excitation, glutamate binds with two types of protein receptors, NMDA and non-NMDA, on the cell membrane of the post-synaptic neuron. How do NMDA and non-NMDA activation contribute to learning?
   A. Because stimuli activating NMDA receptors are weaker than those activating non-NMDA receptors, the NMDA response becomes conditioned to non-NMDA stimuli
   B. Combined NMDA and non-NMDA activation blocks depolarization of the synapse
   C. Combined NMDA and non-NMDA activation releases magnesium in the cell body, facilitating transmission at the synapse
   D. Convergence of NMDA and non-NMDA receptor activation slows, prolongs, and increases the efficiency of the synapse, facilitating complex sensory learning
   E. Glutamate activation neutralizes the antagonistic actions of NMDA and non-NMDA, permitting the neuron to fire

270. A white rat is placed in a cage that contains a lever and a shute through which food can be dispensed. The rat presses the lever and receives a food pellet. After receiving the food, the rat again presses the lever. This type of learning is most influenced by
   A. emotionally intense responses
   B. genetically programmed reflexes
   C. simultaneously occurring stimuli
   D. specific stimulus cues at critical periods
   E. the consequences of behavior

271. Reinforcement is the key event in operant conditioning. The effect of reinforcement is well known, but less is known about what makes something a reinforcer. For example, the Premack Principle tells us that
   A. a high frequency behavior or reward can be used as a reinforcer for a low frequency target behavior
   B. a low frequency behavior can be used to punish an undesired high frequency behavior
   C. a low frequency behavior, because of its higher value, can be used to reward a desired target behavior
   D. a moderate frequency behavior will have a more optimal effect than either a high or low frequency behavior
   E. if an individual seeks out and engages in an activity, it is because it is desirable and, therefore, a reinforcer

272. When a behavior, symptom, or learned association ceases to be reinforced, it tends to weaken or decrease in frequency. This phenomenon is best described as
   A. free operant behavior
   B. negative reinforcement
   C. positive reinforcement
   D. response extinction
   E. stimulus generalization

273. A 2-year-old girl is afraid of cats. To change this, she is put in a room with her favorite music playing while a friendly cat is gradually brought towards her. Finally, she is encouraged to pet the cat. This example is an illustration of which of the following principles of learning?
   A. Aversive conditioning
   B. Critical period learning
   C. Negative reinforcement
   D. Response extinction
   E. The Premack Principle

274. A man learns to control his blood pressure by means of trial-and-error practice while watching a gauge that gives him feedback about the fluctuations in his blood pressure. The effectiveness of this technique is based on the operant principle that
   A. a high frequency reinforcer will reward a low frequency target behavior
   B. behavior is controlled by selectively manipulating the consequences
   C. consequences are controlled by controlling the stimuli
   D. information about the consequences of behavior is reinforcing
   E. motor performance is more easily reinforced than other forms of responses

275. There are several distinct forms of learning. Which of the following answers best describes the developmental order of forms of learning from most genetically influenced to most environmentally influenced?
   A. Classical, operant, imprinting, reflex, one-trial, social
   B. Classical, reflex, imprinting, one-trial, social, operant
   C. Imprinting, reflex, one-trial, social, classical, operant
   D. Reflex, imprinting, one-trial, classical, operant, social
   E. Social, operant, classical, one-trial, imprinting, reflex

276. Social learning theory has expanded our understanding of how people learn and change their

behavior beyond simple, animal-based models. The operation of social learning is most easy to recognize because it is

A. dependent on the reinforcement value of relationships
B. distinct from classical and operant learning
C. the least dependent on evaluative feedback
D. the least influenced by environmental conditions
E. unrelated to the individual's survival

277. Because of its ability to mount a prolonged response to sustained and intense stressors, which of the following systems has the potential to have the most detrimental effects on the body under chronic stress conditions?

A. Autonomic nervous
B. Endocrine
C. Immune
D. Limbic
E. Musculoskeletal

278. A physiological state of arousal is induced. The emotional label (e.g., grief, anger, joy) that is given to this felt state of arousal is most likely to be dependent on

A. gender differences within the culture
B. sociocultural display rules
C. the context in which arousal occurs
D. the heredity of the individual
E. the intensity and quality of the arousal

279. You are observing the reactions of a husband and wife as they receive bad news regarding the health of their newborn child. Based on the type of gender differences in emotional reaction that have been documented cross-culturally, you would expect that, compared to a woman, a man will be more likely to

A. be less emotional
B. conceal his emotions
C. show happiness in public
D. show more anger when challenged
E. use different language to describe emotion

280. Theories improve our understanding of how the world works by providing models for the mechanisms of behavior. Which of the following theories of motivation is most closely associated with instinctual theory?

A. Arousal theory
B. Cognitive theory
C. Drive theory
D. Expectancy theory
E. Sociocultural theory

281. A 27-year-old woman reports that she often feels the urge to smoke after having sex or after eating. Which theory of motivation best helps to explain why she feels this impulse?

A. Arousal theory
B. Drive theory
C. Expectancy theory
D. Humanistic theory
E. Sociocultural theory

282. Many of the conflicts we feel in our day-to-day lives are explainable within the framework offered by behavioral psychology. For example, food that you find particularly tasty but that also may cause undesirable weight gain or cavities is an example of which type of conflict?

A. Approach-approach
B. Approach-avoidance
C. Avoidance-approach
D. Avoidance-avoidance
E. Oedipal

283. Patient adherence with medical prescriptions is influenced by a variety of factors, including the patient's motivation. The expectancy theory of motivation would most likely attribute a patient's adherence to medical treatment regimes to the patient's

A. belief system
B. cultural system
C. family history
D. homeostasis level
E. reinforcement experience

284. The notion that removing or avoiding an aversive stimulus can lead to behavioral change is most helpful in explaining

A. avoidance-avoidance conflict
B. cognitive dissonance
C. intrinsic motivation
D. secondary reinforcement
E. the opponent-process hypothesis

285. After he is discharged, Mr. G. reports that one of the nurses on the in-patient unit attempted to poison him. Although an investigation shows this allegation to be groundless, Mr. G. continues to insist that it is true. An examination of Mr. G. is most likely to find that he is experiencing

A. a delusional episode
B. an hallucination
C. an illusion
D. confabulation
E. sensory distortion

286. During the first month after the birth of his son, Harry awoke every night when the child cried. However, after the first month he no longer awoke, although his wife continued to do so. This change in behavior by Harry is most likely explained by the principle of
  A. accumulated fatigue
  B. adjustment reaction
  C. habituation
  D. just noticeable difference
  E. threshold detection

287. Changes in disease patterns over time are one source of information about their contributing causes. Over the past 10 years, demographic and epidemiological data regarding suicide worldwide have shown that suicide rates are
  A. generally constant over time
  B. higher for Hispanics who immigrated to the US than those in their country of origin
  C. lower for people in their teens and early twenties
  D. lowest among white men in the US
  E. lowest in industrialized nations

288. The overall suicide rate, per 100,000 general population in the US in 1998, including all age, gender and ethic groups, was
  A. 0.09
  B. 4.0
  C. 12
  D. 20
  E. 33

289. A 22-year-old man with schizophrenia is hearing voices telling him to kill himself. In the emergency room, a urine toxicology screen is positive for cocaine and you smell ethanol on his breath. Appropriate management would include
  A. confrontation regarding the severity of his substance abuse problem
  B. discharge to home, once sober, with follow-up in 1 week
  C. psychiatric hospitalization with one-to-one monitoring
  D. referral to Alcoholics Anonymous or Narcotics Anonymous
  E. referral to out-patient psychotherapy

290. As part of answering questions on a mental status examination, a patient with schizophrenia describes the voices he hears as coming from the plumbing. Commonly called lack of insight, this answer more precisely illustrates
  A. deficient short-term memory
  B. dissociation

C. disturbed source identification
D. impaired concentration
E. poor judgment

291. Rates of completed or successful suicides are substantially higher for the elderly than for the rest of the population. Clinical experience suggests that the elderly are more likely to complete suicide because they are
  A. less likely to communicate their intentions
  B. more experienced because they are older
  C. more likely to become clinically depressed
  D. more likely to choose overdose as the means
  E. more likely to live in poverty

292. A 70-year-old woman has been diagnosed with Alzheimer dementia. Because she had to leave school when she was 15 to support her family, she never graduated from high school. She has made her living for more than 50 years by cleaning office buildings. When questioned, she has little insight about her memory deficits. During the past year, she has been well cared for by her daughter while enrolled in a protocol for a new experimental treatment. Unfortunately, the results of the trial have been poor. Now her daughter is concerned that her mother might be suicidal. Which feature of this patient's history would be most likely to place her at risk for committing suicide?
  A. A family member is a caregiver
  B. Enrollment in an experimental drug protocol with poor results
  C. Lower socioeconomic status
  D. Minimal schooling
  E. No insight about the memory deficits

293. During combat, a young soldier sees a live grenade on the ground next to his friend. He immediately covers it with his body and is killed in the explosion. According to Durkheim's theory of suicide, which type of suicide does this example illustrate?
  A. Altruistic
  B. Anomic
  C. Egoistic
  D. Fatalistic
  E. Heroic

294. A 55-year-old man has just committed suicide. A complete post-mortem examination is most likely to show
  A. atrophy of the adrenal glands
  B. decreased corticotrophin-releasing hormone
  C. higher than normal concentrations of serotonin in the raphe nuclei
  D. hyposecretion of ACTH by the pituitary

E. low levels of 5-hydroindolacetic acid in cerebrospinal fluid

295. In an effort to control costs, a hospital reduces the nursing staff by 20%. The decision about whom to terminate is based on seniority and degree status within the nursing hierarchy. Initially, the hospital enjoyed considerable savings. However, over the next several months, the number of hospital admissions decreased by almost 30%. A subsequent analysis found that the bulk of nurses terminated came from the ranks of "admitting nurses" who were responsible for timely and efficient processing of new patients. As a result, there was an unintended reduction in patient flow that was compounded by less patient satisfaction. Because patients chose to go elsewhere for care, the hospital found itself in worse financial condition than before the decision to reduce the number of nurses. The notion of "unintended consequences" and the observation that changes in one part of the system will have consequences for other parts of the system is best captured within which of the following theoretical perspectives?
A. Conflict theory – adaptation
B. Formal – implicit theory
C. Goal attainment – structural functional analysis
D. Symbolic interaction – latent pattern maintenance
E. Utilitarianism – integration

296. While leading a tour for hospital executives from Third World countries, the tour guide is asked to explain why all of the patient rooms are either semi-private (two beds) or private. The guide gives a detailed explanation of sepsis, hospital infection rates, and clinical iatrogenesis, and, as an afterthought, mentions "patient preference" and the fact that insurance companies reimburse for both types of beds. No mention is made of the long-standing knowledge among the nursing staff that placing patients in private and semi-private rooms sharply reduces the number of patient requests for nursing assistance. Patient preference and reimbursement policies are examples of
A. approximate causes
B. implicit theory
C. latent functions
D. manifest functions
E. secondary explanations

297. A manufacturing company offers its 10,000 employees several types of insurance coverage. Each has somewhat different benefits with respect to levels of co-pay, access to specialists, prescription drug coverage, and a variety of other dimensions. The rationale is that employees will assess their own needs, maximize their benefits, and choose the desired plan accordingly. Which one of the following theoretical perspectives best captures this model of employee decision making held by the company?
A. Conflict theory – adaptation
B. Formal – implicit theory
C. Goal attainment – structural functional analysis
D. Symbolic interaction – latent pattern maintenance
E. Utilitarianism – integration

298. Of the following, which is the most appropriate medication for patients with bulimia nervosa?
A. Anti-psychotic medications
B. Appetite suppressants
C. Benzodiazapines
D. High-dose selective serotonin re-uptake inhibitors
E. Low-dose selective serotonin re-uptake inhibitors

299. Family-based therapy such as the "Maudsley method" has demonstrated effectiveness in the treatment of restrictive anorexia nervosa in early teenagers. Of the following, which describes a core feature of family-based therapy?
A. After weight restoration, parents must continue to monitor caloric intake to maintain recovery.
B. In early treatment, the focus is on behavior change and not underlying psychiatric pathology.
C. To begin recovery, it is essential to first determine what family issues caused the eating disorder.
D. To establish their authority, parents must make their child eat.
E. To support autonomy development, parents need to encourage their child to choose what to eat.

300. A 27-year-old woman comes to see her physician for a regular check-up. Examination reveals nothing out of the ordinary except for a general nervousness on the part of the patient. Finally, she reports that she is "beginning to feel old", and asks the physician what she should expect at her age. The physician should tell her that
A. brain cell development peaks by 30 years of age
B. her brain cells continue to grow in complexity until the late 40s

C. she has passed the time of peak intellectual achievement

D. she should cut back on athletic activity to avoid injury

E. the human body is in its peak physical condition from 20 to 30 of age

301. On the Mini Mental Status Examination, asking a person to name objects, repeat a sentence, and follow a verbal command all test for different types of
A. agnosia
B. amnesia
C. aphasia
D. apraxia
E. executive function

302. Different things motivate people. For some people, the notion of "achievement need" helps to explain the life choices that they make in their adult years. Achievement need can be best understood as
A. a desire to enhance cognitive development
B. an outgrowth of Type A behavior patterns
C. similar to innate cognitive ability
D. the core motive fostering the desire to have children
E. the desire for control over others

303. As people get older, their capacities change. Over the years, as a patient moves from adolescence to young adulthood, this transition will most likely be characterized by
A. a decline in task oriented behavior
B. decreased capacity to consider the consequences of impulsive action
C. decreased narcissistic tendencies and increased capacity for interpersonal relationships
D. increased difficulty with complex decision making
E. increased focus on maintaining an independent self-identity

304. Although during young adulthood many people marry, a number of people remain single at age 30. Studies examining the lives of these unmarried singles have shown that
A. approximately 20% of young adults choose long-term singlehood
B. more than half of non-married individuals are homosexual
C. most singlehood relationships survive for more than 5 years
D. singlehood has disadvantages for career opportunities

E. the proportions of sexually active single men and women are nearly equal

305. A well-educated, 75-year-old woman is brought by her family because of change in mental status. She has been treated in the past for depression, but has not been on medication for 5 years. She lives in an assisted living facility, where staff have noticed that she has rarely come to meals over the past 3 months. She seems sluggish and apathetic. On questioning, she describes feeling worthless and as though life has become meaningless. She formerly had many friends and enjoyed going on outings organized by the facility. When asked to answer questions on the mental status exam, she seems hesitant and self doubting, saying, "That's too hard," or "I am sure I won't be able to do that." She has to be prodded to finish tasks such as serial subtraction. Despite these findings, her final score is 28, well within the normal range for her age. This presentation suggests
A. delirium
B. dementia syndrome of depression
C. generalized anxiety disorder
D. senile dementia of the Alzheimer type
E. subcortical dementia

306. After several years of general clinical practice, you notice that, although individual variation exits, relationships of young adults with their parents share a number of common features. The most common relationship pattern you are likely to notice is that
A. establishing a collegial relationship with parents typically begins during young adulthood
B. most young adults resist financial help from their parents because they want to establish independence quickly
C. most young adults seek to pattern their "sense of self" after that of their parents
D. the process of raising questions about family or origin rarely begins before the age of 30
E. young adults maintain relationships with parents similar to those set in place during childhood

307. One way to gain insight into an ethnic group's system of beliefs and practices regarding health and disease is to develop an awareness of the underpinnings of those beliefs. Research suggests that health beliefs are most closely associated with cultural beliefs about the
A. natural world, such as ideas about germs, stars, and the sun
B. social world, such as ideas about family members' relationships

C. supernatural world, such as concepts of spirits, death, and afterlife

D. natural and supernatural worlds

E. natural, supernatural and social worlds

308. You have been asked by a local community agency to address a group of young adults about common developmental issues for people their age. As you prepare your remarks, you should remember that, as a group, the young adults you are addressing most likely

A. are striving to develop stable intergenerational relationships by seeking independence

B. are working at being part of the adult culture

C. generally disregard advice from older persons

D. have dreams and aspirations that are mostly developed from the wishes of the family of origin

E. occupy the majority of their time pursuing leisure activities and avoiding commitments

309. For most young adults, what event is most likely to be accompanied by a self-awareness of a transition into full-fledged adulthood?

A. Becoming a parent

B. Death of a parent

C. Getting married

D. Graduation from college

E. Starting a first job

310. Physical growth during puberty can be dramatic. Which of the following combinations of changes in height and weight is most commonly seen?

	Height	Weight
A.	+50%	+50%
B.	+25%	+50%
C.	+25%	+25%
D.	+10%	+25%
E.	+10%	+10%

311. During early adolescence, female children are generally taller than same-age male children. Among the following, which reason most likely accounts for this difference?

A. Boys expend more energy in physical activity and so require more time to grow.

B. Boys receive more familial attention than girls do.

C. Boys show compensating advances in mental capacity compared to girls this age.

D. Earlier height gain in girls reflects the body's adaptation to reproductive functioning.

E. Girls are better nourished at the onset of puberty.

312. In the US over the past century, the onset of puberty has been occurring earlier. Some children enter puberty as early as age 8 to 10. Current thinking suggests that the primary reason for this trend is an outgrowth of

A. changes in the average age at first marriage

B. decreases in chronic diseases of childhood

C. global warming

D. improved health and nutrition

E. social needs for earlier reproductive maturity and childbearing

313. A 54-year-old woman complains of pain in her lower back. During the subsequent history taking and physical examination, what variable will best tell the physician whether the patient's pain is acute or chronic?

A. Cause

B. Duration

C. Family history

D. Intensity

E. Site

314. Along with the gonads, the two other organ systems primarily involved in regulating puberty for adolescents are the

A. hypothalamus and the adrenal gland

B. hypothalamus and the pituitary gland

C. hypothalamus and the thyroid gland

D. pituitary gland and the adrenal gland

E. pituitary gland and the thyroid gland

315. An 11-year-old boy with diabetes is listening to his physician's explanation about appropriate care. The physician makes every effort to keep her explanation as simple as possible. The most important reason why children this age need simple explanations during a health care visit is that they

A. are at the stage of concrete operations

B. are highly distractible and do not listen well

C. do not trust authority figures, including physicians

D. have not achieved a high enough level of education

E. have not attained their full level of intelligence

316. Adolescence is a period of development about which many myths and much misinformation exists. A set of middle-aged parents asks what they should expect regarding their son as he moves through adolescence. You should tell them that research examining the actual events that accompany this period strongly suggests that, for most adolescents,

A. boys adjust to pubertal change more easily than girls

B. development is necessarily filled with turmoil

C. developmental struggles are relatively minor

D. developmental struggles are rare to non-existent

E. struggling with their transition to adulthood is psychologically traumatic

317. A 15-year-old girl comes to see her family physician for a checkup. At the end of her examination, she asks the doctor, with some embarrassment, if he would give her some advice on a problem that she is having. In counseling her, the physician should remember that this developmental period is typically characterized by
A. a strong focus on one-on-one intimate relationships
B. adjusting to the changes of puberty
C. desires to stand out among one's peers
D. goal formation related to career
E. intense concern about social and peer relationships

318. Research studies designed to test the effectiveness of newly developed oral medications typically have two groups of study subjects, those who receive the drug being studied and those who receive an inert pill which looks identical to the study drug. The use of these two groups in the study design is intended to eliminate which of the following factors that might contribute to the drug's efficacy?
A. Investigator bias
B. Natural course of the disease
C. Nonspecific treatment effects
D. Placebo effect
E. Specific treatment effects

319. The three leading causes of death for adolescents in the US during the 1990s were
A. accidents, suicide, and drug overdoses
B accidents, suicide, and homicide
C. cancer, accidents, and suicide
D. cancer, congenital heart disease, and accidents
E. suicide, accidents, and drug overdoses

320. When interventions are properly selected and performed by trained professionals, we refer to this kind of medical care as
A. acceptable
B. accessible
C. adequate
D. appropriate
E. available

321. S.G. is a 16-year-old who recently announced to her friends and family that she is gay. She was raised in a single-parent family and has a history of conflicts with her mother and her peers. During questioning, she reports that her mother keeps a handgun in the house "for protection." Given this history, the strongest risk factor for suicide for S.G. would be
A. being brought up by a single parent
B. being female
C. being lesbian
D. handgun in the household
E. family and peer relationship problems

322. The timing of puberty has a number of identifiable social, psychological, and behavioral consequences for adolescent boys. A survey of adolescents in the US has found that one of the more common behavioral correlates of late puberty in boys is
A. conduct disorders and delinquency
B. immature behavior and lower self-esteem
C. improved academic competitiveness
D. improved athletic competitiveness
E. improved musical abilities

323. The notion of a teenage subculture is a relatively new phenomenon. Historically, the transition between childhood and adulthood was seen as occurring directly, without this intermediate stage. The modern creation of a subculture is most likely due to
A. increased use of computer technology
B. increased use of illegal drugs
C. media influences such as MTV
D. pressure from adults to move into adult roles too quickly
E. society's moratorium on growing up

324. A 16-year-old girl is being evaluated for a possible eating disorder. She has lost 10 lbs in 3 months, but denies dieting or any intention of losing weight, "it just happened." Of the following combinations of symptoms, signs, and lab findings, which would raise suspicion about an underlying medical condition?
A. Amenorrhea, alopecia, low gonadotropins
B. Anorexia, carotenemia, neutropenia
C. Constipation, hypothermia, mildly elevated liver enzymes
D. Early satiety, bradycardia, low blood sugar
E. Fatigue, hyperpigmentation of the skin, hyperkalemia

325. Different behavior patterns characterize different developmental stages. Children in Piaget's preoperational stage of development are most likely to
A. be able to put together simple picture puzzles
B. be able to use symbols to represent reality

C. explore their environment by physical manipulation of objects

D. have sophisticated mental processes

E. need the presence of an event to think about it

326. A student is preparing to take a 3-hour multiple-choice exam. This will be a timed test. To do his best under this time pressure, the student should remember that
A. arousal is unrelated to performance
B. arousal levels that vary as the task proceeds are associated with optimal performance
C. high levels of arousal are best for optimal performance
D. low levels of arousal are best for optimal performance
E. moderate levels of arousal are best for optimal performance

327. Piaget used a number of simple tasks to demonstrate children's capacities at different stages of development. The so-called "three mountain" experiment is used to demonstrate the concept of
A. categorical reasoning
B. centering
C. egocentrism
D. object constancy
E. precausal reasoning

328. A child's natural tendency to see life in non-living objects and assign them human feelings and motive is usually called
A. animism
B. artificialism
C. autism
D. magical thinking
E. symbolization

329. Children develop both language and conceptual abilities before they enter school. For example, a 6-year-old child already has a vocabulary of about how many words?
A. 1,000
B. 5,000
C. 10,000
D. 25,000
E. 50,000

330. According to Erikson's theory of social development, the developmental choice faced by a 5-year-old boy is most likely that of choosing between
A. autonomy versus shame
B. identity versus role diffusion
C. industry versus inferiority
D. initiative versus guilt
E. trust versus mistrust

331. Two soldiers are hospitalized after a motor vehicle accident in which a third soldier was killed. Both are being treated for compound fractures of one leg and the opposite arm. The soldier who was driving the vehicle and feels responsible for the accident asks for pain medicine more often and wants higher doses than the soldier who was the passenger. This situation illustrates that the degree of pain people experience from particular conditions is strongly influenced by the
A. availability of narcotics
B. location and extent of tissue damage
C. meaning of the pain
D. prior level of fitness
E. time of day

332. Much of our sense of self is socially determined. The stable conceptualization of being either a male or a female despite superficial features such as dress or mannerism is most often referred to as
A. gender identity
B. parental identification
C. sex role schema
D. sex role stereotype
E. sexual orientation

333. Medicine and health care providers contribute to both increased longevity and better quality of life. Over the past century, life expectancy in the US has risen steadily. This increase in life expectancy at birth is largely due to
A. better nutrition with an emphasis on lower fat diets
B. higher levels of income and better health insurance
C. improved health and health care in older adults
D. reduced smoking among adults
E. reductions in infant mortality rates

334. Treatment of the elderly requires modification of general "rules of thumb" for therapeutic interventions. This is especially true when arriving at the correct dosing for medications. Lower medication doses are generally required for a comparable therapeutic effect in the elderly because of
A. age-related cardiovascular disease
B. drug interactions due to polypharmacy
C. lower tolerance of side effects
D. poorer absorption of oral medications
E. slower rate of metabolism

335. A 74-year-old woman presents with memory deficits and periodic loss of orientation to person, place, and time. Her family reports that deficits have appeared gradually over the past several

years. When approached by her son, she fails to recognize him and asks for an introduction. She is able to converse about events from the distant past, but cannot recall how or why she was brought to see the physician. Without any further information being given, the physician should assume that these symptoms are most likely the consequence of

A. Alzheimer disease
B. cerebral brain tumor
C. cerebrovascular accident
D. iatrogentic effect of medication
E. normal senile changes

336. A physician suspects that a newly referred 85-year-old woman patient may be in the early stages of dementia. The most direct way for the physician to identify dementia in its early stages is to
A. administer the Mini Mental Status Examination
B. administer the Wechsler Adult Intelligence Scale (WAIS)
C. ask a family member to describe the patient's recent behavior
D. do a CAT scan
E. observe the patient's behavior as she interacts with peers over a 2-day period

337. Assessment of Activities of Daily Living (ADL) in an elderly patient can be helpful in determining level of medical assistance needed. Included among the ADLs to be assessed are
A. ambulating, climbing stairs, and sitting
B. driving, using the phone, and watching TV
C. eating, bathing, and going to the toilet
D. shopping, cooking, and dressing
E. using the phone, driving, and cooking

338. A 64-year-old woman, who has been doing some reading about aging, comes to see her physician. Having just read Erikson and his stages of development, she decides that she is in the stage of *ego integrity vs. despair*. She asks the physician what this means. According to Erikson, the challenge of this stage of life is
A. adjusting to impending death and dying
B. balancing life's accomplishments and failures
C. coping with depression and loss
D. growing older with dignity
E. reviewing one's family life

339. Human development passes through a number of different stages across the lifespan. "Successful" development is most closely linked to
A. avoiding personal loss
B. economic status

C. educational attainment
D. maintaining good physical health
E. successful negotiation of transitions

340. During one day of working at a local health clinic, a physician encountered patients presenting with *empacho, mal de ojo, amok*, and a cold. All of these disorders are
A. conditions based on superstitious beliefs
B. culture-bound syndromes that describe a type of soul loss
C. ethnically recognized types of upper respiratory infections
D. illustrations of how people interpret bodily signs and symptoms in culturally specific ways
E. reflections of patients' lack of education

341. Puberty is marked by a number of predictable physical and social changes. The hormonal changes that are most closely linked to puberty are
A. marked by estrogen increases in girls only
B. occurring at about the same age for 90% of children
C. seen as early as age 7 with increases in adrenal steroids
D. seldom observed during the middle childhood years
E. unrelated to increased subcutaneous fat during middle childhood

342. The social and psychological changes that characterize middle childhood are made possible by accompanying physical changes. Among these changes is a pattern of neurological development characterized by a significant increase in the
A. circumference of the head
B. complexity of synaptic connections
C. mechanism of neuronal processing
D. number of neurons
E. number of neurotransmitters

343. Although behavioral changes are the dominant means of tracking development in middle childhood, a number of physiological correlates have also been identified. During the middle childhood years, changes in EEG activity are most often characterized by
A. a decrease in function-specific activity
B. a lack of stabilization between the hemispheres
C. a transition to primary delta activity
D. increases in alpha wave activity
E. the emergence of sleep-wake differences

344. An 8-year-old boy has recently been diagnosed with attention-deficit/hyperactivity disorder (ADHD).

During an examination of the child, the physician should check for what other behavioral traits that are often associated with ADHD?

A. Deficits in executive functions
B. Enhanced ability in visual-spatial tracking
C. Increased ability to process verbal directions
D. Increased susceptibility to childhood infectious diseases
E. Poor relationships with peers

345. Among the signs that a child has reached middle childhood (ages 6 to 12) are changes in the child's cognitive capacities. This cognitive development allows the child to

A. consider how another person will feel in the future
B. evaluate other people in terms of psychological attributes
C. form a self-generated philosophy of life
D. manipulate abstract concepts
E. predict behavior across differing social situations

346. A 10-year-old boy insists that the rules be followed when playing his favorite board game and lectures all participants about the importance of having rules. This insistence that all participants follow the rules is most likely because he wants to

A. avoid embarrassment
B. avoid punishment
C. be a replacement for his parents
D. be seen as good
E. give direction to others

347. You have been a family doctor in a small rural town for several years. A patient, Jasper Thomas, is a 68-year-old man who has Type II diabetes and hypertension. A reliable patient, Mr. Thomas arrives for his scheduled appointment and tells you he will not be able to be your patient because he is unable to pay his bills. As the two of you discuss the importance of continuing treatment, Mr. Thomas suggests to you that he could provide honey or other farm goods his wife could cook dinners for you, or he could work for you in exchange for your services. Several of your residency instructors occasionally bartered when their patients needed care so you are somewhat familiar with the idea. The appropriate way to deal with this issue is to

A. agree to this proposal, but because Mr. Thomas has so little money, ask only for two bottles of honey at each visit
B. explain to Mr. Thomas that because of his limited ability to do physical labor, he will only have to do 2 hours of light work, such as watering, to pay for each session

C. require Mr. Thomas to provide 8 hours of service at $20/hour, the local labor rate, to pay for each
session at your usual rate.
D. speak with your colleagues before making a decision, to establish what is most fair
E. tell Mr. Thomas you will get back in touch with him after you speak with your accountant.

348. You have been asked to arrange for play activities for a group of 8-year-old children. When making these arrangements, you should remember that children at this age will prefer

A. anyone of the same age who likes the same activities
B. playing in mixed-gender groups
C. simple fantasy games
D. structured games and sports
E. watching, rather than participating in sports

349. A 10-year-old boy was recently diagnosed with insulin-dependent diabetes mellitus. When counseling the child and his parents, the physician must remember that the child should be

A. encouraged to continue with school activities such as team sports and physical education
B. encouraged to explain to teachers and peers why his activities will be limited
C. exempted from family chores to attend to managing his illness
D. expected to be absent from school periodically as a consequence of his illness
E. expected to have difficulty relating to peers as he gets older

350. Physical changes during the middle years of adulthood set the stage for the later developmental stage of old age. Experience with adults in this age group has shown that

A. few people recognize changes in physical health before the age of 50
B. physical changes are most closely tied to chronological age and maturation
C. physical changes can be predicted from social and interpersonal factors
D. the age at which facial wrinkles occur and hair turns gray is fairly constant
E. the signs of aging appear in women earlier than they do in men

351. A chiropractor has applied to the local hospital for hospital privileges. Although the chiropractor is a long-time practitioner who has good referral relationships with several area physicians, there is considerable antagonism toward his applica-

tion from within the hospital's Board of Directors as well as the general physician staff. A number of physicians are concerned that allowing a non-physician privileges will lead to other requests from "fringe" practitioners. At the same time, the Chief of Staff is aware of the successful 1990 antitrust suit brought against the AMA by three chiropractors, and that the AMA's Code of Ethics no longer prohibits physicians from consulting with chiropractors or teaching in schools of chiropractic. The Chief's dilemma is best addressed within which of the following theoretical perspectives?

A. Conflict theory – adaptation
B. Formal – implicit theory
C. Goal attainment – structural functional analysis
D. Symbolic interaction – latent pattern maintenance
E. Utilitarianism – integration

352. A couple in their late 40s asks their physician what changes they should expect with respect to their sexual functioning as they age. Based on recent research examining changes in sexual functioning for men and women, the physician should tell them that

A. compared with women of color, Caucasian women begin menopause early
B. over age 60, sexual activity is inversely related to how many children they have
C. the female menstrual cycle begins to change during the 30s and 40s
D. The level of sexual desire for men is correlated with the level of sperm production
E. there is a "male climacteric" that corresponds to the female "menopause"

353. A 28-year-old man has not gone to a social or athletic event in three years. In the past, he had friends and enjoyed sports. He works from home in computer data entry. He is preoccupied with the asymmetry of his eyebrows and, over time, he has plucked out both eyebrows completely, trying to equalize them. He now consults a dermatologist about a hair transplant to repair the damage. This presentation is consistent with

A. body dysmorphic disorder
B. delusional disorder
C. factitious disorder
D. malingering
E. social phobia

354. At 10 p.m. you are checking your personal email. Your receive a message from a patient who you saw earlier that day indicating that she thinks she is experiencing a minor side effect from her new medication. The most appropriate course of action is to

A. answer the patient's email quickly so as not to harm the physician-patient relationship
B. establish that the email link is secure
C. offer to meet on Facebook to chat about the patient's concern in a conversational manner
D. because HIPAA prohibits emails between patients and physicians refuse to communicate with the patient
E. respond by email being precise and avoiding jargon because information communicated in this manner may be unclear

355. According to a report published by the University of Chicago on sexual behavior in the US,

A. marital status is an important predictor of sexual activity among older men, but not women
B. sexual activity for both genders is most frequent in the 20s and declines with age
C. sexual activity over a lifetime is positively correlated with socioeconomic status
D. there is little interest in or desire for sexual activity after the age of 60
E. women do not reach their sexual peak until their mid-50s

356. Although divorce patterns have fluctuated over the past 30 years, a number of age-related trends have been relatively stable. An examination of these age-related trends shows that

A. a couple marrying before age 21 has a lower risk of divorce than a couple marrying after 30
B. adults who divorce after age 50 are unlikely to remarry
C. adults who remarry later in life have less stable marriages than those who remarry as young adults
D. divorce is most common between the ages of 30 and 45
E. less than 10% of divorced adults remarry within 5 years after divorce

357. Although much of traditional research on human development has focused on children, increasing attention has been paid in recent years to patterns of development across the life cycle, including the so-called "middle-aged." Research into patterns of relationships between middle-aged persons and their older parents have shown that

A. although adult children ask their parents for financial support, they rarely ask for advice
B. feelings of dependency on parents have been resolved prior to this age

C. middle age is usually marked by increasing psychological distance from parents

D. most adult children and their parents have positive feelings about each other

E. relationships with siblings are more important than relationships with parents

358. Prematurity is a major risk factor for a number of developmental abnormalities. For the average woman of normal child bearing years who becomes pregnant, the chance of giving birth prematurely is closest to
A. < 1%
B. 5%
C. 10%
D. 15%
E. 20%

359. A girl is born prematurely at 28 weeks gestational age. Based on current clinical experience, the best estimate of this girl's chance of surviving until her first birthday is closest to
A. 25%
B. 33%
C. 50%
D. 75%
E. 90%

360. Low birth weight is associated with a number of physical and developmental problems. What is the approximate percent of infants weighing 1,000 grams or less at birth who survive and subsequently have major disability
A. 15%
B. 25%
C. 33%
D. 50%
E. 66%

361. Pregnant women who use substances, either legal or illegal, risk damaging the fetus in a variety of ways. Maternal use during pregnancy of which of the following substances is responsible for the greatest number of cases of mental retardation in the infant?
A. Alcohol
B. Cocaine
C. Lithium carbonate
D. Opiates
E. Tobacco

362. A 48-year-old man presents to his physician with complaints of clumsiness. Examination reveals a subtle, but apparent resting tremor accompanied by a "pill-rolling" gesture in his left hand. When walking, he moves slowly and shuffles his feet.

A preliminary diagnosis of Parkinson disease is made. Increased levels of which of the following neurotransmitters would best support this diagnosis?
A. Acetylcholine
B. Gammaamino-butyric acid
C. Norepinephrine
D. Prolactin
E. Serotonin

363. A student tells you that he seems to have an easier time cramming for an exam when he drinks coffee while he studies. This effect of coffee on learning ability is most closely linked to which of the following effects on brain activity?
A. Decreased blocker cyclic-AMP response element binding protein activity
B. Increased activity in the reticular activating system
C. Increased serotonin activity
D. Reduced glutamate activity
E. Reduced prolactin activity

364. A 35-year-old woman is concerned that she has been gaining weight over the past few months. She reports that her appetite has increased for unknown reasons. At the biochemical level, this woman is probably experiencing increased serotonin activity at which receptors?
A. 5-HT1
B. 5-HT2
C. 5-HT3
D. 5-HT4
E. All of the above

365. A patient admitted into the neurological ICU with a complete C5 transection is intubated, placed on a ventilator, and connected to electronic monitors. Every few hours, the staff rolls the patient over to prevent bedsores. However, nursing staff become concerned when they observe that the patient has not slept over the ensuing 2 days and seems to be increasingly agitated and distressed. Unable to communicate with the patient because of the intubation, the staff calls for a consultant who can read lips. The consultant discovers that the patient was forcing himself to stay wake because he thought the reason the nurses were turning him was: "If I fall asleep, I will die." It never occurred to the nursing staff that their actions might be so interpreted, and they quickly reassured the patient that this was not the case. The patient, now so informed, gratefully falls asleep. The difference in meanings held by the patient and nursing staff is best addressed within which of the following theoretical perspectives?

A. Conflict theory – adaptation
B. Formal – implicit theory
C. Goal attainment – structural functional analysis
D. Symbolic interaction – latent pattern maintenance
E. Utilitarianism – integration

366. A 50-year-old man with a history of schizophrenia reports to his physician that he has been feeling "uncomfortable" lately. When questioned more closely, the patient reports dry mouth, constipation, and infrequent urination; occasionally he has blurry vision and mild delirium. The physician suspects that these symptoms are a side effect of the medication the patient is currently taking. These symptoms most likely result from antagonism of which of the following receptors?
A. Dopamine
B. Histamine
C. Muscarinic
D. Norepinephrine
E. Prolactin

367. While flying to visit a relative for the holiday, you find yourself sitting next to a well-dressed woman in her late 20s. You make polite conversation with her at first, but then turn your attention to a book that you brought with you to read. Your reading is interrupted 15 minutes later when the woman begins to shake, hyperventilate, and sweat profusely. She is wild-eyed and her face is contorted in fear. Between great, gasping gulps of air she says that she is having a panic attack. At this point, what is the action you should take?
A. Ask her how frequently she has attacks
B. Give her a hard candy to suck on
C. Have her breathe into an airsickness bag
D. Hold her hand and tell her to calm down
E. Try to distract her by telling her a story

368. A first-time mother seeks advice from her physician as to how to care for her infant. She has been reading about sudden infant death syndrome (SIDS) and has been following the current medical recommendations for prevention. She asks if following these recommendations will alter her child's development in any way. The physician should advise her that her child will show
A. accelerated auditory discrimination
B. delays in developing a social smile
C. delays in learning to crawl
D. delays in speech acquisitionn
E. increased thumb-sucking behavior

369. A mother brings her 14-year-old daughter to the physician with concern that the girl "just doesn't seem to have much interest in anything." Examination shows the girl to be 5 feet 5 inches tall with a weight of 95 lbs. Enlargement of the parotid gland and halitosis is noted. Upon questioning, the girl confesses to binge and purge behavior, which she has kept carefully hidden from her parents. She reports feeling sad much of the time, and that she just does not fit in with others her own age. Continued physical examination of this girl is most likely to show which of the following additional signs?
A. A deep, red rash on the upper back
B. Elevated heart rate
C. Fine hair on the back and arms
D. Loss of tendon reflexes in the knees
E. Sensitivity to light

370. A 30-year-old woman seeks care for what she describes as "multiple chemical sensitivity." Since the age of 15, she has complained of headaches, body aches, fatigue, skin rashes, shortness of breath, unstable heart rate, and cramping abdominal pain. She also has painful menstrual periods and pelvic pain at mid cycle. Work-ups for endometriosis, asthma, and allergy have been negative, except for mild seasonal rhinitis that responds to intranasal steroids. She seems to derive a sense of self-worth from her interesting medical condition, having not been able to finish college, work consistently, or establish a close, intimate relationship. This presentation is most consistent with
A. avoidant personality disorder
B. malingering
C. obsessive-compulsive disorder
D. panic disorder
E. somatization disorder

371. Which of the following is required of health care providers?
A. Accepting Medicaid coverage
B. Accepting Medicare coverage
C. Certification
D. Charging the same rates to all patients seen, regardless of insurance status
E. Licensing

Answers

1. E. *societal prejudice.* Gay and lesbian families are gaining acceptance in our society but, at present, they continue to experience societal prejudice and non-acceptance manifested as an irrational fear of same-sex unions, a form of homophobia. Same sex couples can suffer social isolation that can increase the risk for substance abuse, depression, and even suicidality.

2. D. *patients' perception of the time their health care provider spent giving information is positively associated with adherence.* This supports the notion that one of the most potent forces in determining patient adherence is the relationship between the physician and the patient. In particular, in addition, if the exchange with the physician is positive, then the probability of adherence rises even further. Thus, although warnings are useful, the fear they induce can distract the patient from the details of the instructions. Too much information all at once can lead to information overload. Memory is dependent on attention and emotion as well as intelligence. Education is not related to adherence. In fact, highly educated patients may be equally as non-adherent as poorly educated ones, but for different reasons. For example, less educated persons may not understand; more educated persons may understand, but not believe or accept the information provided.

3. B. *they are becoming the most common family form.* Stepfamilies have greater complexity because roles, rules, relationships, and loyalities are often in flux. A clinician can assist by emphasizing the importance of family members being patient and flexible while the family acclimates to often dramatic change. At times, referral to a family therapist may be necessary to assist the family make the adjustments necessary for successful transition.

4. B. *Enmeshment.* Enmeshed families have few boundaries between family members. Emotions resonate quickly throughout the family so that emotional states are often shared. Enmeshment is an extreme form of cohesion. Parentification describes the situation where the child assumes or is given the authority and responsibility that should be vested in the parent. Scapegoating is using one person as the identified cause of all the family's frustrations or failures. Splitting

is seeing something or someone as all good or bad, usually in response to whether or not that person is fulfilling a need at the moment. People can be seen as good or bad multiple times a day.

5. B. *high expressed emotion.* This is a well-defined variable in family research. High expressed emotion may be understood as the family's failure to grant a patient the sick role, resorting instead to blaming and accusing to explain the patient's behaviors. High expressed emotion has been shown to predict relapse in schizophrenic patients living at home. It adversely affects the outcome of other chronic medical and psychiatric disorders such as depression and adjustment to chronic renal failure. Help seeking/help rejecting is a pattern of patient behavior related to personality disorder and neuroticism. Parentification is a term used to describe the inappropriate caretaking roles that children or adolescents sometimes assume in troubled families. It may adversely affect the child struggling to meet age inappropriate expectations, but has not been related to schizophrenia. Splitting is a maladaptive, psychological defense mechanism, not a quality of family interaction. Triangulation, a concept from structural family theory, involves two family members communicating through a third person, usually crossing generational boundaries. Triangulation is a conflict ridden situation with negative implications. In this case, the parents have a single view of their son.

6. B. *If he wants the boy to try alcohol, it should be at a meal with adults who do not condone drunkenness.* Intermittent but otherwise unrestricted alcohol use can lead to binge drinking, which is no safer than chronic daily drinking. High tolerance is a risk factor for alcoholism, not a protective one. The safe limits for an adult male are no more than 2–3 ounces of hard liquor or 8 ounces (two 4-ounce glasses) of wine in 24 hours, or an average of no more than 14 drinks per week. The limits for adolescents are unknown, but, in general, adolescents progress more quickly to addiction than adults do. Since low potency alcohol-containing beverages are served in higher quantities than stronger ones, it is still possible to develop alcoholism from wine or beer at any age. Note: The legal drinking age is 21 years.

7. C. *personality characteristics that affect commu-
        nication or the capacity for intimacy.* However,
        certain elements of physician identity (e.g., a
        desire to be in control, entitlement, inhibition
        of emotional expression, or expectations that
        the physician will be nurturing regardless of
        his/her own needs) may affect close relation-
        ships. Although medical education and practice
        can be stressful, it is possible for physicians in
        any specialty to have satisfying or troubled re-
        lationships. Stress about time is more often a
        symptom than a cause of relational problems
        and, in fact, physicians often overcommit
        themselves at work to avoid problems at home,
        even though they may perceive the demands
        as externally imposed. Financial problems are
        real but need not destroy close relationships.
        Couples in which both partners are doctors are
        not necessarily more or less stable than those in
        which one partner is a physician and the other
        is not.

8. B. *emphasize that the patient will not be aban-
        doned and that all treatment, including pallia-
        tive care, will be provided.* People may hear the
        request for a do not resuscitate (DNR) order
        as a statement that the case is hopeless and the
        staff have no real intention of caring for the
        patient. In fact, patients and families are often
        accepting of the possibility of death, as long
        as they know that care will be compassionate,
        attentive and appropriate. Advance directives
        must be revised at every stage of a patient's
        illness. A previous order either requesting or
        refusing resuscitation may not reflect the pa-
        tient's current priorities or status. The statement
        that resuscitation does not prolong or improve
        life is true, but does not address the concerns of
        patients and families about abandonment and
        neglect. Giving a technical definition of the or-
        der similarly avoids addressing the emotional
        aspects of the decision. Respect for privacy is
        important, but letting the family discuss the
        matter with no input from the health care pro-
        vider is a form of abandonment.

9. A. *most important information is given at the be-
        ginning of an interaction.* The first topic raised
        becomes the primary focus of attention and
        allows the patient time to consider the issues
        and to ask whatever questions he/she wishes.
        Giving extensive information or too many
        instructions all at once can overload the pa-
        tient. Without patient questions and feedback
        the physician does not know if information is
        understood. Allowing the patient to fill in his/

her own details may lead to drawing erroneous
conclusions.

10. B. *Contemplation.* The patient is contemplating
        whether he has a problem or not before de-
        ciding to act. He has moved beyond pre-con-
        templation but has not yet reached the level of
        preparing for action, taking specific action, or
        maintaining a plan of action.

11. C. *Mutual pretense.* Both patient and physician
        have tacitly agreed not to talk about the pa-
        tient's disease. There is no indication of any
        level of awareness in the exchange.

12. B. *ask the patient to say more about his symptoms*
        as a way to facilitate differential diagnosis and
        to increase rapport with the patient. The pre-
        sented symptoms are consistent with hypo-
        chondriasis, factitious disorder, malingering,
        or some as yet unidentified gastrointestinal
        problem. Telling the patient that he is a hypo-
        chondriac leaps to a diagnosis prematurely and
        is likely to anger him. Speaking with a family
        member is likely to leave the patient wonder-
        ing why corroboration from others is necessary.
        The presented history contains no special indi-
        cations for substance abuse. The patient is not
        "fine;" he is suffering. To simply send the pa-
        tient home trivializes his symptoms, and abets
        the patient if the complaint is due to malinger-
        ing.

13. E. *while the emotional states described are real,
        they do not represent distinct sequential stages.*
        A better way to think about these emotional
        states is as points along a continuous process;
        some points (e.g., anger) may be re-experi-
        enced several times. Different individuals as-
        semble the pieces of the experience of dying
        in different ways. There is no "average" ex-
        perience of death. Given enough time, most
        patients do finally accept death. Some, how-
        ever, never appear to allow themselves to do
        so. Culture, religious beliefs, life experience,
        and life satisfaction all play a part in a patient's
        reactions to death and dying. The pattern high-
        lighted by Kübler-Ross is a useful guide, but
        every individual's experience is different.

14. A. *patients should monitor behavior (e.g., dietary
        intake) rather than outcome (e.g., weight loss).*
        The rule is to monitor what is under patients'
        control rather than something that may be af-
        fected by factors beyond their control. Self-
        monitoring does improve awareness of adher-

ence and can, by itself, improve adherence. Paying close attention to behavior is most effective; therefore, recording throughout the day will increase awareness. Self-monitoring is dependent on awareness of one's behavior, not on any specific personality trait (e.g., assertiveness).

15. E. *the physician's discomfort with the subject of sex.* Often, physicians employ the psychological defense mechanism of projection to think that this discomfort resides only in the patient; but this is not the case. Physicians must not allow their own discomfort to interfere with discussing sexual issues. A number of important medical issues, including sexually-transmitted disease prevention, require such discussions.

16. E. *transvestite fetishism.* Fetishism requires the inclusion of some object in the experience as part of sexual arousal or gratification. When this fetish involves a man dressing in women's clothing, it is termed transvestite fetishism. Note that transvestites, in general, are predominately heterosexual; that is, their preferred sexual partner is usually of the opposite sex. Male transvestites see themselves as male and therefore are not transsexuals or subject to a gender identity disorder.

17. A. *Anger.* The patient is angry at what is perceived as an unfair consequence. Depression would manifest itself more as despair and a sense of hopelessness. Bargaining would be trying to strike a deal with some higher power. Denial is the refusal to accept the reality of the impending death. Confusion is not one of the traditional Kübler-Ross stages for dealing with death and dying.

18. D. *performance anxiety* is one of the more common reasons for impotence and anorgasmia. Although not a "disorder" as such, this anxiety should be explored before investigating for either physical or psychological pathology. A simple counseling session with each partner in this couple may save time and expense. At the very least, it will rule out performance anxiety and justify more detailed examinations.

19. E. *social phobia.* The recent onset, the fear of others making fun of him, and the conviction that he will do something shameful or stupid in public are all consistent with a diagnosis of social phobia. Personality disorders are lifelong, and so are ruled out by the recent onset. Agora-

phobia is a fear of being exposed, but in a more general sense than merely in social situations. Although social phobia is a type of anxiety disorder, it is distinguished by the stimulus that triggers the anxiety. Generalized anxiety disorder is ruled out by the clear link between social situations and the anxiety.

20. B. *oldest female.* Although family dynamic and cultural patterns differ, in most family systems the role of the non-physician health expert is generally someone who is older and female (think, "grandmother"). Age is perceived as giving the experience required for expertise and females are more often in the role of caretakers. Education is not a key qualification in this informal network.

21. C. *he most likely has alcohol abuse or dependence.* The CAGE questions ask the patient if he/she ever (1) tried to Cut down alcohol intake but did not succeed, (2) been Annoyed about criticism concerning drinking, (3) felt Guilty about drinking behavior, and (4) had to take an Eye-opener in the morning to relieve anxiety and shakiness. Mr. S. gave positive answers to all four of the CAGE questions and, thus, most likely has alcohol abuse or dependency. Although some recent research has suggested that the CAGE questions must be used thoughtfully when evaluating certain ethnic populations, a full set of positive answers suggests that an alcohol problem exists. The positive predictive value of the CAGE questions is high enough that even though the prevalence of alcoholism is only 10%, the patient has a greater than 50% chance of having a problem. Not all alcoholics get drunk; many so-called "functional alcoholics" show few outward signs of a problem. Inpatient treatment is not indicated for patients who are able to function (e.g., hold a job), although counseling or attending AA meetings would be a reasonable course of action. It is likely that Mr. S. is in a state of denial, and may reject any suggestion that he has a problem. Alcohol problems are typically diagnosed by behavior, not by laboratory testing.

22. B. *Do you have an orgasm with manual or other clitoral stimulation?* This question helps to determine whether the woman is anorgasmic, or whether some other issue might be the root of her concern. A "yes" answer suggests that changes in sexual technique might make sexual intercourse more appealing. Asking about satisfaction and frequency misses the point; the

patient has already expressed dissatisfaction and her concern about infrequency is her initial presentation. If her husband were impotent, it is unlikely that she would complain about her own lack of interest. Asking her what the problem is labels her feelings as a problem. A more targeted question will yield more specific and useful information.

23. A. *Change the HCTZ to a "potassium sparing" combination diuretic without changing the rest of the prescribed regimen.* Although the answer may seem to hinge on pharmacological considerations, the real issue is maintaining the patient's routine so as to foster continued compliance with treatment. The patient is already adherent. Having the patient learn a new routine may reduce compliance and, by extension, lower the probability that the disease will be adequately managed.

24. E. *tell the husband you cannot share the information without his wife's permission.* Confidentiality of information shared between a patient and physician is essential for a trusting professional relationship. Past, present, and future information created or received in the course of providing treatment, obtaining payment for services, or performing research should be considered confidential and only available to the patient or his/her designee and only with the patient's permission. Also, it is the patient's right to know, upon request, with whom protected health information has been shared and under what circumstances it will be shared in the future. In establishing a confidentiality agreement with patients, it is important for the physician to explain that confidentiality will be diligently maintained except in circumstances where information revealed to the physician indicates pending danger to the patient or others in society. In these situations, it is the physician's duty to act in the patient's best interests and in the interests of others who may be in danger or at risk.

25. B. *move her to an exam room.* When patients come to a physician for medical care, they may have one or several problems that need to be addressed. The initial and most important step in the clinical decision-making process is defining their problem(s). This is an evolutionary process, beginning with a careful and complete history and a physical examination. The patient will describe his or her problem to the physician or nurse, who will then use open

and close-ended questions to clarify the history. A physical exam will enable the physician to establish a preliminary problem list and differential diagnosis. In this care, the patient's presenting problem was "shortness of breath" that had been present for almost five hours and preceded a potentially stressful situation (chairing a meeting). Careful questioning will likely reveal the patient has had this symptom previously in stressful situations, but not with exertion or physical activity. In this setting, normal vital signs and physical findings by the physician would indicate the patient's problem is related to anxiety; additional workup is unnecessary. However, if this is the first episode and a strong link with anxiety cannot be established, the physician needs to lengthen the differential diagnosis to include other conditions such as acute coronary syndrome or pulmonary embolism. If these diagnoses are being seriously considered, immediate transfer of the patient for workup (e.g., EKG, CBC, cardiac enzymes, chest x-ray) and treatment in an emergency department setting would be appropriate.

26. B. *The patient and physician have differing belief systems about insulin.* The physician sees insulin as a good treatment while the patient sees it as a danger. The key issue here is that this difference in belief systems makes any communication about treatment options difficult. There is no evidence for family intervention here; although the family might share the patient's beliefs, the issue is not one of family dynamics. Nor would a detailed explanation of insulin treatment be effective if the patient rejects the idea in the first place. Beliefs that differ from those of the physician are not a sign of irrationality, just of different life experiences. Adherence would be poor, not based on passivity, but on the patient's active rejection of the treatment option offered.

27. D. *Physical, neurological maturational, cognitive, speech/language, and psychosocial* development comprise the cluster of domains usually assessed. Development is not a single dimension, but proceeds along several parallel dimensions. In certain circumstances, any of the domains listed might be appropriate for evaluation. However, answer D provides a checklist of the classic five.

28. C. *5 months.* The physical behavior, level of responsiveness to external stimuli, and appearance of the ability to laugh combined with

the child's weight gain all indicate a child of approximately this age. Recognizing what is normal behavior at each stage of development is critical for advising parents and detecting developmentally linked pathology.

29. D. *8 months.* The realization that objects out of sight continue to exist is a critical developmental milestone. On average, children gain this capacity shortly after 6 months of age. Note that we must infer this sense of object constancy from the child's searching behavior, as it is not yet possible to communicate with the child and receive verbal answers.

30. C. *5–6 months.* Each of these reflexes, present at birth, are lost as the child matures. The Moro and rooting reflexes disappear at about 3 to 4 months of age, tonic neck at about 4 to 6 months of age, and palmar grasp at about 5 to 6 months of age. Thus, 5–6 months of age is the earliest age at which these reflexes would be expected to have disappeared. Note that persistence of the Babinski and placing reflexes is expected until about 1 year of age.

31. D. *sensorimotor stage.* This stage is the beginning of cognitive development. It is during this stage that the rudiments of assimilation and accommodation are first apparent. Schemas at this stage are combinations of movements and sensations, not objects with lives of their own. Freud called this same developmental period the oral stage. Erikson termed this age trust vs. mistrust.

32. C. *Natural etiologies.* Individual, social, and supernatural etiologies all involve some degree of personal responsibility, such as ignoring behavioral risk factors, causing conflict in social relationships, or offending or provoking the supernatural, respectively. Intellectual etiology is not one of the usual categories of etiology used to describe illness causation.

33. B. *goals are graduated to maximize success experiences.* No one likes failure. Success in reaching a goal can, by itself, be reinforcing. Making goals incremental makes each step more attainable and helps to keep the patient motivated and on track. Goals that are too broad are ambiguous. Goals set by the provider without patient input may ignore difficulties of which the physician is unaware and typically do not have the level of "buy in" from the patient needed for success. "Shooting for the moon" may feel

great if the moon is actually hit, but the chances of failure are too great, and the goal just looks unattainable (and, therefore, non-motivating) to the patient. Goals must be flexible so they can be altered as circumstances change.

34. B. *express concern and suggest the patient think about his drinking.* The patient has not yet accepted the fact that there is a problem. Encouraging immediate corrective action (AA, in-patient treatment) is premature. Rather, the expression of concern helps to communicate the physician's perception that a problem exists. Failure to mention the problem and simply scheduling a follow-up visit will not assist the patient in realizing that a problem exists.

35. B. *discover how much information he would like to have.* Although patients have the right to know everything that you do about their medical condition, they also need to have some control over the level of detail with which facts are presented. For example, at what level of detail should the physician explain the physiology of the condition? Discussing support systems before giving any information about the disease would be premature. Prior to communicating about the patient's condition and gauging his reaction, physical contact may be misunderstood. Before you decide how to talk to the patient (e.g., in small chunks or laying all of the information out at once), ask the patient what he thinks would be most helpful. Every patient is different.

36. E. *he will likely require treatment with antidepressant medication.* The patient's symptoms, difficulty sleeping, loss of interest in his usual activities, feelings of worthlessness, difficulty concentrating, thoughts of suicide and weight loss, converge to support a diagnosis of depression, occult malignancy, or substance abuse. His depression is unlikely to be successfully relieved by merely trying to boost his spirits through brief counseling or peer support. Depression is a condition that usually responds well to adequate pharmacological intervention, especially when it is coupled with psychotherapy. To fail to treat this patient's depression is to fail to relieve his suffering.

37. B. *give intravenous fluid resuscitation and treat both the UTI and possible pneumonia with appropriate antibiotics.* This patient has signs of shock (hypotension, tachycardia, and tachypnea) and so requires fluids and other blood pressure supports as a first step in treatment.

Shock is non-specific and has many causes. The presence of fever could indicate infection as the specific underlying cause. Physicians construct the differential diagnosis after careful consideration of information gained from the history and physical examination. The information is assessed in light of current knowledge of disease pathophysiology and prevalence in populations matching the demographic and medical characteristics of the patient well-being examined. Then, a list of possible diagnosis is developed based on the likelihood of the patient having particular illnesses and conditions. The list is revised as additional information becomes available, such as laboratory and radiologic studies, until the correct diagnosis becomes obvious. Establishing a comprehensive differential diagnosis is extremely important because, until a specific disease is confirmed, the physician must target tests and medical treatments toward conditions in the differential diagnosis that are of greatest threat to the patient. Failure to include the eventual "correct diagnosis" in the differential diagnosis list will lead to misdirected testing and ineffective treatment, thereby jeopardizing the patient's recovery. In this case, the differential diagnosis for an 80-year-old patient presenting with low blood pressure, tachycardia, tachypnea, and fever includes infections at one or more possible sites, including the urinary tract, lungs, abdomen, and CNS. Until the exact site(s) of infection are determined, the patient must be treated with antibiotics that cover infections at the most likely sites.

38. A. *Broader descriptions such as "working poor"* or "disadvantaged" are useful most often if there is an accepted definition of these terms. Working poor (unable to meet basic needs despite having a job) is more useful than SES based on education and income for the purposes of describing health care needs. There are jobs that pay high salaries that do not require many years of education and low paying jobs that require advanced education. Part-time employees and retired workers further complicate the description of the population of potential patients. The area to be served by a new clinic would likely have more than one culture or could be predominately one race or ethnic group with several levels of assimilation.

39. E. State *"you must be very upset that your father is ill from his cancer again."* This statement focuses the conversation on the patient's reactions to his father's illness, not his reaction to

the surgeon. Reflecting the patient's emotional state indicates that you have heard it, while reframing it in terms of his father. Sitting quietly leaves the patient wondering what you, the physician, are thinking. Defending the surgeon makes you seem to be siding with him so that you now become the target of the patient's anger. Talking about his anger with the surgeon leads the patient away from the real source of his negative affect, namely, the return of his father's illness.

40. E. *physiological decline that accompanies aging.* The incidence of impotence in men rises with age. However, many men continue to be sexually active all their lives. Men who continue to be sexually active retain capacity. Men who attempt sexual relations only sporadically may find that they have more difficulty with sexual functioning. The main point is to realize that, although impotence may be the result of a pathological condition, a simpler explanation is most likely.

41. A. *Anger,* the second of the five stages or emotional states of coping with death and dying as described by Kübler-Ross. Note that the patient blames someone else for her condition. Denial is a refusal to accept the reality of the impending death. Guilt, not one of Kübler-Ross's stages, is more likely to be felt by friends and relatives of the dying person, or anyone who feels that they should have done more. Depression means despair, a realization that the death is unavoidable, but not yet accepted. Not telling a patient what is happening is likely to produce fear. However, patients need to be told bad news in a way that they can tolerate. Coming to grips with news of impending death takes time. Kübler-Ross's five stages are: denial, anger, bargaining, depression, and acceptance.

42. A. *feeling depressed for several months after the death.* This depressive reaction is called grief and is considered normal for months to about 1 year following the loss of a loved one. Patients need to know that grief is normal and takes time to resolve. Normal grief is self-limiting and most authorities agree that pharmacotherapy is rarely necessary. The other four symptoms listed as options, however, suggest complicated or prolonged grief. Some therapeutic intervention is likely to be required.

43. C. *request a joint visit with the patient and his wife.* It is unclear whether the stress in the

marriage is contributing to the lack of sexual activity, or whether the lack of sexual activity is contributing to the sense of stress within the marriage. A joint visit with both the patient and his wife will help to clarify this issue and provide additional information about the sexual expectations of both partners. Because the patient has erections in the morning, a nocturnal penile tumescence study is not necessary. The low level of sexual frequency and the report of impotence are unlikely to be resolved by a change in sexual position. Saying that this is bound to happen, does not address the patient's concern, and may miss some underlying issue that needs to be resolved. A joint visit will allow the physician to observe how the couple interacts together, something that is not possible by just interviewing the spouse separately.

44. D. *refer for joint sex therapy with use of sensate focus.* Penile implant seems unnecessary given erection in the morning. The squeeze technique is used to treat premature ejaculation, which is not the problem presented by this patient. Other partners are less likely to help the couple function sexually together than they are to cause them to abandon their relationship. This level of dysfunction is not a normal part of aging. A middle-aged man should be able to continue to perform sexually for as long as he wishes to do so.

45. D. *stereotyping.* Dr. Johnson has stereotyped or generally applied a set of characteristics to a group of people. He has made generalizations based on some observations but failed to consider individual differences. Except for Native Americans, all individuals are immigrants or descended from immigrants to the US. He has also not considered the degree of assimilation of particular persons into the majority culture. He has not placed a lower value on Chinese patients as in stigmatizing. Bias would indicate that Dr. Johnson is inclined to behave in a positive or negative manner toward Chinese patients. Bigotry and intolerance indicate rejection and prejudice. Thus, Dr. Johnson has generalized a few characteristics to a group of people, but he has not imposed action as in bias, intolerance, bigotry, or stigma.

46. A. *Alcohol* is the most abused drug for all ages and all occupational groups. Surveys of medical student populations suggest that medical students are more likely to abuse alcohol than are their peers in other educational programs.

Less than 20% of medical students smoke, and anonymous surveys show that even fewer use the other drugs listed as options. Most physicians who abuse other drugs also abuse alcohol. In considering use rather than abuse, it appears that caffeine is the drug used most often by medical students.

47. C. *A recently diagnosed terminally ill patient is in the hospital.* Silence in this setting allows patients time to collect their thoughts and to ask whatever questions they may have. Just being present can help to assuage the fears of abandonment felt by some terminally ill patients. Substance abuse always requires a response when identified; silence only allows the problem to get worse. During a home visit with a clear goal, silence does not attend to the task at hand. Silence, in the face of questions about sexual inadequacy, may be misinterpreted by the patient as embarrassment on the part of the physician.

48. C. *Pre-contemplation.* She is not yet thinking about change, but she is thinking about thinking about it. This may seem like just putting it off, a type of procrastination, but procrastination is not recognized as a formal part of the stages of change model. To be in the stage of contemplation, she would be actively thinking about change. For preparation she would be making arrangements to facilitate change. For maintenance, she would be acting to keep changes in place once they have begun.

49. C. *daily rituals of the office staff and physicians* are important components of day-to-day practice. Because they are not things or people, they are considered intangible. These social norms and mores are real and influence workplace atmosphere. Buildings and framed mission statements are solid physical things. The types of patients in the practice and the accountant who audits the practice are identifiable, concrete individuals.

50. E. *preparation for change.* If the committee concluded that current practice should change they would formulate practice guideline recommendations. The unfreezing stage would begin.

51. D. *be able to create her own role within the department and negotiate for the resources she needs to accomplish that role.* Professionals seek autonomy and the latitude to define their own goals and the methods for accomplishing

those goals. Professionals generally seek careers and settings consistent with their sense of self and personally held values. Controls over professional behavior arise from internalized standards of conduct reinforced by the review of professional peers. Professionals can differ about acceptable standards of conduct, or the best way to achieve the collective goals of the profession.

52. C. *hiring them.* Because professionals expect to be able to define their own goals and the methods for achieving them, hiring decisions are critical. Whether or not a person gains entrée into an organization is the core control mechanism for managing professional conduct. Exclusion is the ultimate professional sanction. Professionals are expected to be self-motivated, to aspire to effectiveness, to gather the information they need, and to evaluate their performance by comparing themselves to their peers.

53. C. *master the mechanics of weight shifting.* Crawling is not a necessary preparation for walking. In fact, not all children learn to crawl. Object permanence is a milestone in cognitive development, not a prerequisite for the physical milestone of walking. Balance is important and continues to develop as children mature, but compared to the balance skills required to stand on tiptoes or bend to pick up an object, walking requires very unsophisticated mastery of balance. Separation anxiety is generally a stage of socioemotional growth resolved by age 2; it is unrelated to walking.

54. A. *formulation of internal mental symbols is a hallmark of toddlerhood.* At this time, transition objects begin to appear. Having mastered object permanence, the child is no longer bound to full reliance on just what is before him. Although some language is present, it is not yet the organizing framework for mental representations. Instead, the child's representations are based on his experiences and relationships, not on concepts given to him linguistically by others.

55. B. *the ability to create plans allows the child to plan how to gratify impulses.* This is what makes the two's so terrible. Not only are children this age impulsive, but they also can negotiate around simple impediments meant to protect and contain them. The ability to imagine alternatives does not become manifest until the child is 5 or 6 years old. Children can

distinguish facial features from early infancy. Although 2-year-olds have some idea of the standards of good and bad conduct, these standards are not internalized; instead, a child of this age seeks simply to not get caught. Rule-based play is characteristic of middle childhood.

56. E. *injury,* as confirmed annually by epidemiological data. After age 1, injuries of all types are the number one cause of death among children. Automobile accidents account for a substantial proportion of these deaths, although fire-related death is also a prominent cause of mortality. Patterns of injury-related morbidity parallel those for mortality.

57. C. *"I'll order some pain medication and come back tomorrow to see if you'd like to talk then."* The patient needs to feel some control in this situation. Although the patient has the right to know everything, he also has the right to say he does not want to hear. Note that this does not mean that the physician will not tell the patient anything, only that the patient will be given time to prepare to receive the information. Going to a family member jeopardizes confidentially unless the patient requests this route of communication.

58. B. *Sequential stimulation of two adjacent neurons enhances the efficiency of their connecting synapse.* Protein kinase, the hippocampus, the orbitomedial frontal cortex, and even the cerebellum are all associated with higher order learning and memory functions.

59. C. *learned adaptive responses that contribute to survival are passed on to successive generations.* Better learning leads to better evolutionary survival. What is learned in one generation seems to be more easily learned in the next, suggesting that the learning is passed on. Genetic and environmental influences interact in complex ways that are difficult to separate. The interaction between genetics and environment changes as the individual moves through various developmental stages. This interaction is highlighted by the notion of so-called "critical periods" of development (e.g., brain growth spurt).

60. A. *involves the association of sensory stimuli with sequential motor system responses.* Implicit learning is felt by some to be the most primitive type of learning, and to form the foundation

for all other learning. Implicit learning can occur below the level of the person's awareness. Implicit learning is comprised only of simple experienced associations, not higher level cognitive processes, and therefore does not require higher-order cortical functioning. Finally, implicit learning occurs over a short span of time after the experience of a sensation, which is then followed by motor functioning.

61. B. *mental illness and substance abuse.* By some estimates, as many as 50% of all the homeless suffer from mental illnesses or substance abuse problems, including alcoholism. These problems may be the cause of the homelessness, or a result of coping with difficult conditions. Note that as a group, homeless individuals are more likely to suffer from all of the options listed, but are most likely to suffer from mental health issues.

62. A. *agoraphobia.* The patient displays anxiety, which the history suggests is related primarily to leaving the safe confines of his home. Patients with social phobia are more likely to fear being shamed or doing something to embarrass themselves in public. Dysthymia is depressive symptoms lasting more than 2 years. The patient lacks the global mistrust of paranoid personality disorder and the clear, identifiable delusion of delusional disorder.

63. B. *benzodiazepines.* Abrupt withdrawal can produce delirium and seizures. Withdrawal from amphetamines produces fatigue and hunger and withdrawal from heroin results in flu-like symptoms including nausea and cramps. Hallucinogens and phencyclidine have no specific withdrawal effects.

64. A. *force field analysis*, the term used by social psychologists in the change process for the presentation of views for or against change.

65. A. *bipolar disorder.* This patient matches the DSM-IV criteria for bipolar disorder, manic phase. The distinguishing features are grandiosity, talkativeness, flight of ideas, distractibility, excessive involvement in activities, and decreased need for sleep for at least 1 week. A person with obsessive-compulsive disorder would manifest ritualistic behavior. Narcissistic personality disorder is characterized by a life-long pervasive pattern of seeing self as grandiose and the center of the universe. *Hyper*thyroidism is possible, but not *hypo*thyroid-

ism which would be associated with decreased activity, sluggishness, and an increased need for sleep. The patient does not display characteristics of dementia and her age makes vascular dementia, in particular, unlikely.

66. E. *lithium carbonate*, the treatment of choice for long-term control of bipolar disorder. Note that lithium must be taken consistently and at close-to-toxic levels to be efficacious. Fluoxetine is one of the selective serotonin reuptake inhibitors (SSRI), a common treatment for depression and obsessive-compulsive disorder. Chlorpromazine is an antipsychotic. Clonazepam and diazepam are anti-anxiety medications.

67. C. *Regression,* returning to an earlier level of functioning. The girl has lost the capacity to control her bladder as she returns to the wished-for infant state. Regression is common in children when siblings are born into the household. Reaction formation suggests a reversal, doing the opposite of what one really feels. Projection refers to experiencing one's own thoughts or emotions as coming from others in the external world. Undoing is a ritual reversal which "fixes" or repairs what is wrong in the sense that obsessive-compulsive hand washing fixes the feeling of being dirty. Sublimation is diverting unacceptable drives into personally and socially acceptable channels.

68. A. *advise the mother about helping the child cope with life transitions.* The regression response should abate as the girl learns other means of coping, such as feeling like a participant in her sibling's care, and receives positive reinforcement for attending school. Changing kindergarten classes is unlikely to resolve the issue. The source of the problem is separation from home, not problems with the school environment. A child at this age should not be enuretic; simply waiting does not address the problem. Imipramine would be a proper pharmacological choice, but should not be given without an exploration of the child's life circumstances. The child already knows that enuresis is "bad" and is probably embarrassed by it. Merely talking to a child about what is an unconscious response is unlikely to be effective.

69. C. *is showing developmental age and gender appropriate behavior.* The clothing is her parent's, not her, choice. She would not be expected to be able to identify herself by gender until about age 3. The truck does not have any gender-spe-

cific meaning for her, but is merely an object that can be moved in a fun way. This behavior does not suggest either a gender identity problem or a tendency towards homosexuality. Her social behavior gives no clues as to her level of shyness later in life, or the presence or absence of siblings at home.

70. A. *borderline* best matches the following DSM-IV criteria: unstable mood and self-image, self-detrimental impulsivity, unstable but intense interpersonal relationships, difficulty being alone, self-mutilation and suicidal gestures. Paranoid features a life-long pattern of pervasive mistrust of everyone and everything. Histrionic is preoccupied with being the center of attention. Narcissistic presents self as grand and omnipotent. Schizoid individuals just want to be left alone.

71. E. *individual cognitive behavioral therapy*. A number of practitioners have reported significant improvement in people with borderline personality disorder when treatment is a combination of social skills training and cognitive reframing of emotional reactions. Group therapy is more appropriate for posttraumatic stress disorder, substance abuse recovery, and providing coping support. Alprazolam is an anti-anxiety medication often used to treat panic disorders. Family therapy might be a useful adjunct to individual therapy, but should not be the primary approach. Behavior modification is used to treat a wide range of disorders from autism to phobias but does not appear to be as effective as cognitive behavioral therapy.

72. D. *fundamental attribution error* is a cognitive disposition that involves minimizing the role of external factors and ascribing the cause of an individual's behavior or situation to his or her character or personality. Availability bias is the tendency to use easily recalled information in forming judgments. Anchoring is the tendency to focus on a preliminary conclusion and cease exploration of alternatives. Confirmation bias is the tendency to seek information to confirm a hypothesis, rather than seeking information to refute it. Stigmatization is assigning negative perceptions to a person on perceived differences from the general population. All are cognitive dispositions that can lead to medical errors.

73. E. *learned* helplessness is an acquired response to adversity wherein individuals develop the belief

that they do not have control over their experiences and are powerless to change them. Denial is a defense mechanism that involves a failure to acknowledge or accept information or an experience. Histrionic personality disorder is a Cluster B personality disorder characterized by excessive emotionality and excessive needs for attention. Obstinancy is the trait of being stubborn or perversely adhering to an opinion in spite of reason. Regression is a defense mechanism where individuals revert to developmentally earlier styles of managing stress.

74. B. *disorganized schizophrenia* matches DSM -IV criteria. This type of schizophrenia is accompanied by the most bizarre behavior, the most regression in capacities, and the most pronounced thought disorders. In paranoid schizophrenia, there is less loss of faculties and less pronounced symptoms. In addition, delusions of grandeur or persecution are common. Catatonia is manifested by either excessive excitement, or pronounced decrease in movements, often with bizarre posturing. Undifferentiated is the classification used when the patient is schizophrenic, but does not fit any of the other classifications. Residual refers to situations where, although manifesting schizophrenic symptoms in the past, the patient is now symptom free, except for a few negative symptoms.

75. B. *frontal lobes*. Reduction in frontal lobe metabolism during the WCST is standard for schizophrenic people. The temporal lobes are involved in the production of schizophrenic symptoms, but are not the primary locus of the dysfunction for those who have schizophrenia. Parietal lobe dysfunctions center on agraphia, acalculia, and constructional apraxias. The occipital lobes are intimately involved with processing visual input. The cerebellum is involved in movement and certain types of memory.

76. B. *a learned social phenomenon that influences health, illness, and therapy*. Culture is learned, not genetically determined. Furthermore, culture has a significant impact on ALL clinical encounters and should be taken into consideration by physicians when therapeutic options are being identified and evaluated.

77. C. *a steady increase in the size of ethnic minority populations*. The average age of the white population is increasing rather than decreasing. The population is projected to grow over the next century, although at a slower rate than in

the past. Expected demographic changes include an increase in all minority populations to the point that whites will comprise less than 50% of the total population in the 21st century. The U.S. population is becoming increasingly ethnically diverse, and ethnic minority populations are increasing in size. Thus, culture will remain a highly significant factor in the delivery of health care.

78. C. *high blood and hypertension are examples of how interpretations of body symptoms are culturally influenced.* Folk illness or culture-bound syndromes are ailments that are explained by coherent, although generally non-European, concepts about etiology, pathophysiology, and treatment. When they are expressions of mental or social distress, they also have symbolic meanings. Folk illnesses and culture-bound syndromes are not a separate category of disease, but are examples of how all signs and symptoms are culturally interpreted. Biomedical concepts and folk illness concepts may be consistent or contradictory. In the case presented, two cultural systems have interpreted signs and symptoms differently, as hypertension and high blood. Regardless of how a conventionally trained physician views an illness, labeling other people's beliefs as superstitious is degrading. Working with patients' views of their own bodies is the most respectful, empowering, and productive approach to developing a treatment plan that is likely to be successful.

79. B. *explore the possibility that the woman believes that your recommendations will make the child worse.* Chastising the mother, notifying Child Protective Services, and hospitalizing the child are incorrect strategies because they do not take into consideration the possibility that the real problem is a failure to communicate across cultures. All of these approaches are likely to alienate the mother and make it less likely that she will ever be receptive to negotiating therapeutic plans for her child or any other family member. Referring the mother for education may be appropriate at some time, but as an initial step, it is incorrect because it simply passes off the patient to someone else. Referrals allow the physician to conveniently extricate him-/herself from a difficult situation, but the problem is not identified and addressed.

80. D. *Popular sector.* Folk sector refers to secular or sacred healers who have authority throughout

a community. The professional sector refers to health care providers who are licensed and sanctioned by the government. The paraprofessional and pharmaceutical healers are not part of the usual categorization of healers according to the commonly cited Kleinman model.

81. C. *parent.* Kleinman's three sectors of healers are popular or lay; folk; and professional. The popular sector includes everyday people whose authority is acquired through experience, such as parents, neighbors, and community members. The folk sector includes sacred and secular healers whose authority is derived by inheritance, apprenticeship, religious position, or divine choice, such as ministers, astrologers, psychics, and lay midwives. The professional sector includes people whose authority is achieved by schooling and by licensure, both of which are determined by the profession's organizations and sanctioned by the government; medical doctors, homeopaths, chiropractors and nurse midwives are examples.

82. E. *shared between a patient and a provider lead to fewer conflicts.* Kleinman devised the notion of explanatory models (EMs) to describe people's ideas about a sickness event. EMs have five components: etiology of the condition, timing and mode of onset of symptoms, pathophysiological processes, natural history, and appropriate treatments; ethnic identity is not one of the five components. EMs change over time as more information is gathered and as the disease unfolds. Different people hold different EMs about the same sickness event, but Kleinman predicts that the more agreement there is between a provider's and a patient's EMs, the fewer conflicts there will be between them about diagnosis and management.

83. C. *legitimize withdrawal from regular activities and requests for assistance.* "Sick role" is a social notion and refers to the fact that others must agree that a person is sick before he or she is eligible for special treatment. The other options are incorrect because they refer only to medical or epidemiological illness.

84. A. *choice of healers.* This choice includes the ethnic background of the provider, how that provider is viewed within the patient's particular ethnic community, and how the provider understands and responds to the patient's belief system. Desire for good health and physiological

response appear to be applicable across ethnic groups. Type of health insurance and willingness to work are not typically culturally linked.

85. A. *He agreed with the cultural and ideological underpinnings of Chinese medicine.* Given his ethnicity, gender, religion, socioeconomic class, and language, he probably felt little social and cultural dissonance between himself and medical care providers. But he may have felt dissatisfied with his level of personal care, disillusioned with results, and tired of long waits and high costs; and he may have found that he disagreed with the philosophical beliefs behind the approaches to illness that are typical of conventional medical institutions. He may or may not have learned about or accepted the cultural and ideological underpinnings for the alternative approaches he was using. In fact, most people participate in complementary medicine regimens without knowing their derivation and without forsaking allopathic approaches.

86. C. *being our genuine selves with the expectation that patients will understand our meanings.* Effective education and skill development require that we learn about ourselves as cultural beings, which includes being aware of our personal biases and prejudices. It is vital to learn about patients as cultural beings, learn patient-centered communication skills, and be aware of potential abuses of power. Effective communication often requires giving up our preferred "genuine" selves in exchange for adapting our approach to fit patients' preferred styles.

87. E. *Native Americans: pausing less than a few seconds for a reply to a question conveys lack of interest.* Teaching that looking at someone in the eye communicates sincere interest probably has its roots in European culture. Other cultural groups, such as Asians, feel that direct eye contact is invasive and disrespectful; instead, intermittent eye-to-eye contact with periods of looking away communicates respect. Speaking loudly to Asians can be experienced as an expression of anger. For Arab patients, giving things with the left hand is revolting because the left hand is symbolically dirty, while the right hand is symbolically clean.

88. A. *called him grandfather.* You did do some things well, such as calling him by a family title respectful of his position (grandfather). Other things you did well were speaking in lay

people's terms and asking open-ended questions about their perceptions of the problem early in the interaction. The remainder of your comments, however, could have caused problems. The non-verbal cues that were meant to improve communication could have the opposite effect. Direct eye contact can feel rude, as though you were staring. This is especially true among Asians who typically make only brief intermittent eye contact. Saying he will go blind unless he does as you suggest can sound as if you are placing a curse on him. Also, you did not ask how he would feel about receiving an organ transplant. To some individuals, regardless of culture, the idea of having the body part of someone else implanted in themselves is frightening and emotionally disturbing. At this point you also have no information about any religious or other prohibitions that might influence the patient's willingness to undertake such a procedure. Finally, rather than the patient, it is the family, particularly sons, who need to hear the information and who will make the decision. The son would probably want to sign the consent form as well.

89. B. *Economic factors, such as cost of medical treatment.* Economic factors are probably least significant because the patient is eligible for government refugee assistance funds. Structural factors may play a role, as she may not know how to drive and may be confused by the public transportation system, but her family has apparently helped her overcome these factors when she visits the Cuban healers. Cultural and social factors are probably playing the largest roles. The patient's interpretation of her breast lump, her experience of her bodily symptoms, her concept of the word "cancer," and her experiences with cancer and cancer treatments in Cuba are potential major factors. In addition, her spiritual beliefs about the cause of the problem, her ethnic identity and newly-arrived refugee status, her acceptance or rejection of a "sick role," and her social network's assessment of her condition and recommendations for treatment may also be influencing her to choose traditional Cuban healing treatments over surgery, radiation, and chemotherapy.

90. E. *Traditional health care practice.* Traditional healing practices may take on forms that are unfamiliar to medical practitioners. Linear bruises on the back, chest, or extremities are most likely the result of the Southeast Asian practice of "coining". For illnesses caused by

bad wind, or built-up pressure, rubbing the body with a mentholated cream followed by rubbing a silver coin vigorously over the area is believed to release the pressure, thus relieving the illness. Coining has been confused with child abuse, and parents have been reported to child protective services by physicians who are uninformed of the practice. Mongolian spots are congenital hyperpigmented areas, most often seen on the lower back or buttocks. The hyperpigmentation fades with age but may never disappear completely. Sepsis can present as petechiae which can progress to purpura, ecchymoses, and frank hemorrhage. Petechiae are usually distributed widely over the entire body.

91. D. *consider that the patients may be suffering from a culturally specific syndrome, perhaps related to the stress of immigration.* Telling symptomatic patients that they are not sick gives no consideration to the possibility that cultural and psychological factors may be a significant part of the problem. Making assumptions about working the system or that this may be a type of malingering represents negative stereotyping of the community. Quarantine is a drastic measure that is not warranted at this point.

92. A. *Boundaries.* The family structure consists of such arrangements or organizational characteristics as boundaries, triangles, and subsystems. Communication style, parentification, scapegoating, and family secret are components of family process or patterns of interaction, not structure.

93. A. *boundaries around individuals within the system are closed.* Disengaged families have more boundaries between individuals than normally interactive families. Thus, other family members are less likely to be aware of and influenced by individual stresses or joys. The boundaries around the entire family system, however, vary and would not necessarily be closed. The term disengaged is more correctly applied to all the members rather than just the father. Answers D and E are descriptive of enmeshed families.

94. D. *The formation of a subsystem with relatively closed boundaries around it* is most common during the first months of a marriage. An open boundary around their relationship makes it difficult to establish their own identity as a couple. Most young married couples keep some connection with their parents and do not completely cut off or disengage from them unless there has been a major rift, such as around the choice of spouse. Enmeshment with parents would intrude on the couple's time together and their identity as a unit, and is developmentally inappropriate in young adulthood.

95. B. *Enmeshed family.* Enmeshed families are most likely to have difficulty with individuals separating and establishing their own identity. Disengaged families usually have less difficulty with independence. Generational and overprotective families may have some difficulty with separation, but not to the extent of an enmeshed family. Extended family refers to membership in a group rather than to how people in that group rely on each other.

96. B. *motor vehicle accidents* account for approximately 50% of adolescent deaths. Successful educational interventions would include not driving while under the influence of alcohol or drugs, driving at safe speeds, and wearing a seat belt. Adolescents' sense of personal invulnerability ("It can't happen to me") makes them especially prone to recklessness and "death defying" behavior. This attitude also makes them vulnerable to sexually-transmitted diseases, homicide, suicide, and various forms of abuse, but the incidence of mortality associated with these problems pales in comparison with motor vehicle accidents.

97. B. *boy is probably not dreaming while he is walking in his sleep.* Sleep walking (somnambulism) occurs in delta (Stage 4) sleep. Most dreams occur in REM sleep, a different stage of the sleep cycle. Assigning meaning to the somnambulism is strictly speculative, although it is likely that talking with the boy will reveal that he has some anxiety when he is awake. If awakened while sleep walking, the boy will be groggy and have a difficult time waking up (deep delta sleep). There is no evidence that changing the time of going to sleep affects somnambulism.

98. C. *Instrumental.* In some approaches to family sociology, men are traditionally seen as performing more goal-directed task-oriented roles while women perform more socioemotional care-taking roles. In more recent times, familial roles have been in flux with a move toward more symmetry between gender roles. In some couple relationships, this change has been accompanied by increasing competitive-

ness between fathers and mothers who share bread-winning and child-rearing duties.

99. C. *one-person households.* Approximately 80% of the non-family households in the mid 1990s were persons living alone. Therefore, none of the other arrangements listed as options approach this percentage. It is important to note that some of the selections presented would be considered "family" by many professionals who work with families, but not as defined by the U.S. census.

100. E. *Single-parent households* comprised about 30% of all parent-child living arrangements in the mid-1990s compared to less than 15% in 1970. Families below the poverty level actually declined slightly in number over that same time period. The size of households dropped from 3.14 in 1970 to 2.67 in 1994. Kinship households decreased from 80% of total households to around 70% in 1994. The number of married-couple households with children decreased as well. Note that single-parent families headed by women are more likely to be below the poverty line, and that 25% of children in the US live in poverty.

101. E. *Scapegoated.* When a person is scapegoated (identified as being the sole source of a problem), they help to dissipate the tension or stress in the family, usually by directing it outside the family. In the case presented, the girl and her difficulties at school become the focus of parental attention and frustration so that they do not have to deal with root problems such as a dysfunctional marital relationship. The term scapegoat is biblical in origin and refers to the archaic practice of symbolically placing the sins of a community on the head of a goat that was then driven into the wilderness.

102. D. *Parentified.* When a child is parentified, he or she is placed in the position of assuming parental authority over household decisions, especially those that include supervising and disciplining siblings. Typically, the oldest child, especially the oldest daughter, is given this role. Resentment from the other children in the family can lead to emotional isolation. Inability to spend time with peers because of home responsibilities can lead to social isolation. Depression is a common outcome.

103. A. *Disengaged.* The strength of disengaged families lies in fostering independence and auton-

omy. This is at the expense, however, of not teaching members how to work well together and nurture each other.

104. C. *enmeshed.* Enmeshed families are characterized by an unusually strong emotional connectedness. Because of this connectedness, family members have difficulty making autonomous choices and acting independently when necessary and appropriate. Exiting from the family, even briefly to attend kindergarten, for example, can produce exaggerated separation anxiety.

105. A. *Emotionally cut off.* Emotional cut off is more likely to create pseudo-independence rather than true independence. The need to completely abandon a relationship in order to exert autonomy suggests that the patient has learned an "all or none" approach (i.e., complete absorption vs. no contact) to interacting with others.

106. E. *Socioemotional.* In most cultures, women have been trained to take primary responsibility for raising and socializing children (i.e., teaching them how to behave acceptably within their community and larger society) and providing them with the emotional tools (e.g., good self-esteem) to become contributing members of their socioeconomic and political group.

107. E. *unexplained nature of events.* Young children view illness and associated noxious treatments as punishment. Many studies have shown that when they are provided with simple explanations about why they are sick and why certain therapies are necessary, they become less anxious and more cooperative, even when painful procedures (venipuncture, intramuscular injections) must be performed. Children who are sick fear separation from parents but usually do not fear loss of affection. Disappointments about limitation of activity and removal from friends can be overcome by providing alternative distractions. People of any age usually enjoy the dependency on others allowed by being ill, if it is short term.

108. D. *helplessness.* Helplessness ("I'm such a wreck I just can't do anything for anybody, including myself") is often the most difficult emotion for a patient to tolerate. It is easier to actively experience anger ("I'm so mad that I have to be sick during the holidays!"), guilt ("I should have gotten a flu shot"), or blame someone ("My sister gave this to me when she visited

last week") than to feel there is nothing one can do. Hopelessness would be an unusual reaction to a short-term, self-limited illness.

109. C. *practicing relaxation exercises.* Relaxation is the most effective coping style for a problem requiring patience. The other styles are more likely to create or increase frustration and anxiety for the patient, the physician, and others, none of whom can change the circumstances. Some patients use waiting time to seek information. In the absence of diagnosis, this behavior can lead to erroneous conclusions and unnecessary worries.

110. E. *The factor that is most predictive of experiencing adverse health is* SES, probably due to the stress of limited personal control over live circumstances. Low income families in the US are unlikely to lack basics such as food and clean water. In the US, as in other countries, there is a powerful social gradient in health status such that those with the lowest income have the most morbidity and mortality. Research from the Whitehall studies confirmed that access to health care did not eliminate the adverse effects of low SES on health and that, while problematic health behaviors are more common in those of low SES, these predict a smaller proportion of health problems than does SES.

111. E. *There are elements of his built and social environments that may both aid and constrain Sam's ability to maintain a healthy weight.* Living in a low-income neighborhood, high availability of cheap unhealthy food, long work hours and job stress, and cultural norms that encourage the consumption of certain foods – often in excess – can all contribute to Sam's adoption of obesity-promoting behaviors. On the other hand, spending up to 10 hours a day in a work environment that is supportive of healthy lifestyle choices may influence Sam toward behaviors that will help him maintain a healthy weight. This illustrates a concept called *risk regulation.* Although poor dietary intake and lack of physical activity are the actual *risk factors* for obesity, risk regulators are those factors that either present opportunities for or impose constraints on those behaviors. Since Sam is six feet tall, the increase is his BMI over three years indicates that he has gained about 8 lbs each year, which is not necessarily normal or healthy and the weight gain is likely to continue into overweight (if not obesity) if he does not change something about his lifestyle. Since

the company gym opened only 6 months ago, the increase in BMI cannot be a result of Sam's lunchtime workouts. Additionally, the company's workplace wellness program indicates that not all parts of Sam's built environment promote unhealthy behaviors. Despite his family history and having grown up in an environment that encouraged overconsumption, Sam is not necessarily destined to become obese.

112. A. *alopecia due to chemotherapy.* Hypnosis, a form of therapeutic communication in which patients learn to focus their attention on one area and reduce their focus on others, has a long history of usefulness in medicine. The systems most susceptible to psychological factors such as imagery, focus, and suggestion are the autonomic nervous system, the endocrine system, and the immune system. The autonomic nervous system influences muscle tone, vital signs, and gastrointestinal function, making hypnosis helpful in irritable bowel syndrome and chronic pain, especially headaches and pain involving muscle spasm. Effects on the immune system may account for the impact of hypnosis on the course of herpes outbreaks. Smoking cessation is improved by reduction in anxiety, refocusing away from discomfort and imagining a positive outcome. Hypnosis may reduce pain, nausea, and anxiety in patients receiving chemotherapy, but it does not affect hair loss.

113. A. *do active problem solving.* In discussion, the group shares methods that aid in coping and can offer each member suggestions about how to handle particular issues. Group members are unlikely to forget their illness, which is the major topic they are there to discuss. The group works together to maintain optimism, not to simply accept the worst. There is small comfort in learning that others are worse off, because the patient may get there eventually. The group aids the patient in confronting the problems of the disease realistically, and setting aside the façade of bravery which often seems to be necessary in the presence of others who do not have the disease.

114. E. *understand that the patient may need more time to adjust.* Denial may represent an important coping mechanism for the patient at this early stage of knowing about his diagnosis and prognosis. Stripping away the patient's coping mechanism at this moment can accentuate the patient's discomfort. Lastly, it will only alien-

ate the patient to force him to "see the truth" until he is ready to do so.

115. C. *Relaxation training.* A patient who feels that the mind and body are separate is more likely to accept any kind of physical treatment (surgery, injections or pills, even antidepressants, if they are explained as affecting the body) than an obviously mind-oriented therapy such as relaxation training.

116. A. *Changing to a drug covered by his insurance plan.* Barriers to non-adherence include cost, side effects, and a complicated medical regimen. Exploring whether cost is an issue and changing to a drug covered by insurance would decrease the burden to the patient and would immediately make the treatment more attractive to anyone, regardless of financial status. Explaining the health hazards of elevated blood pressure and the side effects of the medication would be a good idea but will not, in themselves, change the patient's behavior. Increasing the number of pills he has to take each day complicates the regimen and will make him even less likely to take his medication.

117. E. *reassurance.* Many patients (sometimes called "the worried well") see a physician seeking reassurance. Their needs can often be met with periodic, scheduled office visits to give them a chance to discuss their health concerns without having to manufacture an illness. If this does not seem to solve the problem as expected, it would be appropriate to probe for deeper psychological problems, which the patient may be reluctant to disclose or feel are outside the purview of "medical treatment." While some patients are seeking prescriptions and work excuses, this is less common than needing simple reassurance about their health status. Many patients with minor complaints are not particularly interested in a precise diagnosis for their problem.

118. B. *family.* In these family-centered cultures, the family is the primary decision-making body; lesser roles are played by the patient, the physician, and the community. In certain circumstances, a religious leader may be consulted but the family makes the decision. Physicians should be aware that decisions to seek care, who will be consulted, and adherence with treatment recommendations will be the result of collective, extended family discussions requiring more time and repeated explanations to achieve consensus.

119. C. *The subjective experience of stress associated with the event* is the major determinant of the degree of impact a stressor will have. The magnitude of the event will be experienced differently from person to person. Whether the event is positive or negative, how many people are involved (and so may have an opinion about how to handle the event, adding to the stress), and the type of change that accompanies the event all need to be taken into account, but their effects are dependent on the subjective interpretation of the person.

120. B. *dependent on technology.* A hospital death is more likely to involve "high technology," whereas a hospice death strives to involve friends and family, emphasizes pain control and palliation, and focuses on the process of death as a natural occurrence rather than as something to be fought and avoided. Religious practices should be equally respected in both settings.

121. E. *such experiences are common in grieving people.* People who are grieving often report the belief that they have seen the dead person or that they have heard the dead person speak to them. These experiences are usually comforting to the bereaved person. These events are neither hallucinations nor episodes of psychosis requiring hospitalization or further formal psychological intervention. Persons who are undergoing normal grief are not depressed and do not need to be medicated.

122. E. *suicide.* Suicide is the most difficult death to grieve because of the anger survivors feel toward the person who committed suicide for causing such pain. In addition, survivors can feel overwhelming guilt for not recognizing the depth of the person's despair or otherwise stopping the suicide. The other types of deaths do not involve the same feelings of abandonment or responsibility in the bereaved.

123. B. *depression.* Grief is actually the prototype for depression, and the typical signs and symptoms of grief resemble those of a major depressive episode. While some of these symptoms exist in the other options provided, they are most characteristic of depression.

124. A. *6 months.* The risk of death for the survivor after the death of a spouse is significantly increased within the first 6 months. Deaths due to cardiac problems are especially likely. Suicide is also prominent among older spouses who

were married for many years. The suicide may take the form of inanition, or a lack of desire to continue living, manifested by not eating or not taking essential medications. Such a death may not be recognized as suicide.

125. C. *enhance sexual experience.* The hypoxia that accompanies using amyl nitrate ("poppers") is reported to increase the intensity of sexual experience. The mechanism appears to be the same as in autoerotic-asphyxiation, which is frequently achieved by masturbating while hanging.

126. B. *Stage 2.* Teeth grinding, or bruxism, occurs during Stage 2, the most common type of sleep. Bruxism is associated with waking time anxiety, which may not be recognized by the patient. When this anxiety is identified and resolved, the bruxism usually abates. Most other sleep disorders (somnambulism, night terrors, enuresis) are associated with Stage 4 sleep. The pathology of narcolepsy is linked to the mechanisms that produce REM sleep.

127. C. *The dietitian's recommendation was incorrect. A 4-year-old child should not consume more than 900 calories per day.* This statement is false. According to the recommendations of the American Academy of Pediatrics, which are consistent with the USDA's Dietary Guidelines for Americans, the estimated daily intake necessary for a 4-year-old female is 1,200 calories. This estimate is based on a child who is sedentary; up to an additional 400 calories may be necessary for a child who is physically active. The remaining choices (A, B, D, and E) are all, in fact, potential explanations for this child's excessive weight gain. Although there is conflicting evidence, several research studies have shown a positive relationship between fat intake (total fat and percentage of calories from fat) and BMI and body fat percentage among children, independent of total calorie intake (choice A). Error in parental reporting of children's intake is an inherent limitation of the study of children's diets. It is also possible for the child actually to be consuming more calories than the mother is aware of (choice B). It is entirely possible, and even highly likely, that the mother's journal of her child's diet contains inaccuracies, either due to incorrectly recording portion sizes (choice D), lacking access to the proper nutrition facts of foods (choice E), or a number of other reasons.

128. A. *Antisocial* personality disorder. Although all of the formal criteria are not met by the information presented, the criminal background and lack of regret combined with the man's charming manner are suggestive of antisocial personality disorder (Cluster B). A borderline person is characterized by unstable affect and relationships. A person with paranoid personality disorder approaches the world and everyone in it with mistrust. Someone who is histrionic tends to be flamboyant. People with schizotypal personality disorder are strange or eccentric and often avoided by others because of these eccentricities.

129. B. *intellectualization.* To deal with the personal distress and anxiety she feels, the student strips away the affect of this emotionally charged encounter and replaces it with academic content that is not emotionally relevant to the patient. Using different terms, the student substitutes cognition for affect and empathy. Simply removing the expression of affect would be isolation. Reaction formation entails acting the opposite of actual, but unconscious, feeling and desires. Sublimation refers to achieving gratification of an unacceptable impulse by acting in a socially acceptable manner. Denial refers to refusing to accept some clear feature of external reality.

130. A. *Death of a spouse.* The Holmes and Rahe Scale lists events that are related to life changes. Those events that are most disruptive to important personal relationships seem to have the most negative effects on health. Although more true for men than women, one's spouse is often the primary source of social support and comfort. Of the life changes listed, this loss seems to be the hardest to bear, especially for men. Divorce is likely to produce high levels of anger, which can, under some circumstances, be mobilizing. Although surviving an automobile accident can be a very stressful event, it does not disrupt social support to the degree that death of a spouse does. Incarceration and loss of a job affect social status. Such stresses are typically easier to handle than the loss of a relationship.

131. A. *birth.* Although neuronal migration is virtually complete in the full-term newborn, the formation of dendrites and axons continues into childhood as the brain adapts to the environment. The number of dendrites peaks around puberty; after that, synaptic connections that are not used regularly disappear through dendritic pruning.

New connections can be made until the time of death. Thus, contrary to the popular saying, you *can* teach an old dog new tricks!

132. D. *lacks neuronal adaptation to environmental stimuli.* Guidance cues are substances that provide a mechanism by which neuronal connections are made in response to sensory experience.

133. B. *classical conditioning.* The voice on the tape is similar to the bell used by Pavlov to induce salivation in a dog. The voice has become so closely associated with relaxation and sleep that it produces the reaction by itself without the need for the full relaxation routine. Inhibition is the mechanism by which an undesirable behavior is stopped from occurring. Intermittent reinforcement refers to providing a positive or negative consequence irregularly rather than each time the target behavior occurs. Modeling is demonstrating a behavior. Biofeedback is a self-regulation intervention typically relying on graphical representation of a physiological parameter that is linked to a particular behavior.

134. A. *order a basal metabolic rate to investigate if she is hypometabolic.* Persistent dieting may induce hypothalamic changes that down regulate the entire HPA axis. In such cases, both TSH (a pituitary hormone) and the thyroid hormones remain relatively balanced, and peripheral measurements of these hormones will be normal, but the patient is still hypometabolic. The test for this involves feeding the patient a standard carbohydrate load and measuring exhaled CO_2. Patients who are hypometabolic have symptoms resembling hypothyroidism. Paradoxically, increased intake may stimulate metabolism and allow for further weight loss. Patients do sometimes have trouble honestly estimating their intake of food (as they do with alcohol). Rather than confront the patient, however gently, it would be better to have her keep a detailed food record for a few days. In reviewing it with her, she may recognize the problem herself, rather than experiencing the humiliation of having it pointed out to her. Very-low-calorie diets are indicated primarily for people who are obese and need to lose weight quickly for medical reasons. Such diets must include behavioral and psychological support for patients to help them maintain their losses over time. Overeaters Anonymous is a useful support group, but is targeted mainly to people who either binge or describe themselves as emotional overeaters. The patient is already motivated to lose weight and discussing health risks is likely to merely increase her sense of frustration and helplessness.

135. A. *Bipolar disorder.* Treatment with lithium or other similar medications blocks inositol-1-phosphate. Schizophrenia, Tourette syndrome, and Huntington disease are influenced by dopamine, a first, or primary, messenger. General anxiety disorder is related to GABA.

136. C. *increases GABA diffusely throughout the brain.* GABA is an inhibitory transmitter. GABA and its precursor, glutamate, are found in about 70% of all brain synapses. Benzodiazepines bind to GABA chloride receptors, making more GABA available post synaptically. The increased availability of GABA reduces synaptic firing and reduces the felt sensation labeled as anxiety. Increases in norepinephrine are associated with a reduction in depressive symptoms. Excess dopamine is, among other things, associated with schizophrenia. Certain anti-anxiety medications, such as buspirone, reduce anxiety by raising serotonin levels. Acetylcholine levels are most closely associated with dementia, memory, and REM sleep.

137. D. *Seizures.* Excess glutamate has long been associated with seizures. Manic activity is associated with high levels of norepinepherine and serotonin. Quiescence is the result of benzodiazepines, barbiturates, or other agents that increase GABA; excessive amounts of these agents can lead to hypersomnolence. Severe hiccups are sometimes treated with neuroleptic medications to suppress spasms of the diaphragm, which produce the hiccups.

138. C. *Nigrostriatal tract.* Although three pathways are critical for dopamine activity (the mesolimbic-mesocortical, tuberoinfundibular, and nigrostriatal), control over movement is governed by the nigrostriatal tract. Action on the mesolimbic-mesocortical tract accounts for the anti-psychotic properties of neuroleptic medications. The tuberoinfundibular tract provides a neurosecretory pathway associated with activity in the anterior lobe of the pituitary gland. The locus ceruleus is typically associated with norepinepherine and depression. The raphe nuclei are the source of serotonin activity.

139. B. *spinal fluid.* Spinal fluid is a direct source of information about the central nervous system and

so gives the best indication of serotonin levels in the brain.

140. D. *hippocampus.* The memories and images of REM sleep appear to originate in the hippocampus. Electrical activity in the hippocampus during REM sleep mirrors electrical activity in the cortex during the waking hours. The pons, lying above the cerebellum, is also active during REM sleep and seems to be critical for its initiation. The reticular activating system plays a critical role in sleeping and waking, but is not directly implicated in REM sleep. The amygdala is concerned with emotions, not image-based memory. The basal ganglia coordinate sensorimotor activity.

141. B. *Broca's area on the right side* is involved in the production of expressive speech. Lesion of Broca's area on the left side would lead to idiosyncratic, non-grammatical speech. Wernicke's area lesions are associated with so called "fluent aphasias." There is no impairment in speech production, but the patient has difficulty comprehending what is said to him. A lesion in Exner's area is associated with agraphia or difficulty writing.

142. E. *refusal of food by a hungry animal.* This region of the brain plays a critical role in regulating all drives, including that of eating. Hypersexuality results from removal of the amygdala (the Klüver-Bucy syndrome). Excessive aggression may result from a variety of abnormalities including excessive norepinepherine and lesions of the temporal lobes. Excessive fluid intake suggests diabetes insipidus, which is caused by impaired functioning of antiduretic hormone due to injury of the neurohypophyseal system. Manic-like hyperactivity is most likely to result form intoxication with amphetamines or cocaine, which affect dopamine along the nucleus accumbens pathway.

143. E. *variable ratio operant reinforcement.* Variable ratio reinforcement makes both learning and extinction more difficult. Although there has been no recent payoff, the patient believes that the next response (trade) may be the one that pays off. Because the patient does not know when the payoff is coming, the urge to trade again is overwhelming and irresistible. Note that for ratio schedules, the payoff is contingent not just on the passage of time, but on the quantity of the patient's actions. Variable ratio (random) operant reinforcement is the mecha-

nism by which individuals become addicted to gambling. Winning occurs frequently enough to keep the person interested and hopeful. The randomness of winning makes it possible to believe that next time will be "the" time. Habituation refers to a developing insensitivity to repeated stimuli, such as when a person no longer attends to police sirens after living in the city for a while.

144. C. *non-dominant parietal lobe.* The constellation of clinical findings associated with a lesion in the non-dominant parietal lobe includes neglect of the left side and constructional apraxia. The patient typically denies any problem. Lesions of the orbito-medial frontal cortex result in withdrawal, fearfulness, and explosive moods. Lesions of the dominant parietal lobe are accompanied by Gerstmann's syndrome (agraphia, acalculia, finger agnosia, and right-left disorientation). Temporal lobe lesions are characterized by general psychotic behavior if the lesion is on the dominant side, and dysphoria, irritability, and loss of visual or musical ability if on the non-dominant side.

145. C. *Phallic* is the third Freudian psychosexual developmental stage corresponding roughly to 4 to 6 years of chronological age. The myelination process is completed by about age 5.

146. C. *in the afternoon.* The combination of normal activity levels and internal biochemistry make this the time of highest contraction rates. Although heart rate would be greater during REM sleep compared with other stages of sleep, the heart works hardest when a person is awake.

147. D. *objective pathology rather than subjective experience.* Illness is the subjective label, or a self-description. Disease is a physiological fact. Illness can exist without disease (e.g., PMS) and disease can exist without illness (e.g., hypertension).

148. D. *relieves the individual from responsibility during an illness.* The sick role incorporates two rights and two obligations. The two rights are to be excused from normal responsibilities and to not be blamed for the illness. Note that although patients may have certainly contributed to their condition (e.g., smokers with lung cancer), they are treated, not blamed for their condition. The two duties are to get well and to seek help to get well. Note that the sick role is about social relationships to other

people and is distinct from the notions of illness (subjective label) and disease (objective pathology).

149. A. *denial.* She does not address the Pap smear information at all, as if this particular feature of reality does not exist for her. Intellectualization would be replacing affective reaction by excessive cognition (such as excessive information seeking). Rationalization implies justification, or saying why an unacceptable action or thought is acceptable in this case. Undoing suggests ritualistic action to reverse or repair something that is not acceptable. Somatization is having physical symptoms that have a psychological but not organic etiology.

150. B. *explore the presence of depressive symptoms.* Depression commonly accompanies long-term cardiac conditions and must be identified and managed along with any other health problems. Some studies have suggested that as many as one in five cardiac patients suffers from some identifiable form of depression. The added psychological burden of losing a job, especially if the loss is associated with the illness or due to downsizing, situations over which the patient has no control, magnifies the possibility that the patient presented is depressed. Referral to a psychiatrist is premature and may not be necessary. If a single physician can manage both the cardiac problems and depression, this places less burden on the patient and reduces the chance of missing negative synergies in the drugs that are prescribed. Giving medications, involving family members or telling the patient not to worry before exploring the full extent of the symptoms are never good ideas. Always complete the evaluation before recommending an intervention.

151. C. *negative reinforcement.* By lingering, the mother avoids the negative consequence of her son's crying and displeasure. Thus, she increases lingering to avoid the onset of the negative stimulus. Extinction signifies a reduction in an identified response. Positive reinforcement would mean that the mother get some benefit or pleasure which continues the behavior. Fading is gradual removal of the stimulus to below the level of the person's awareness while the behavior continues. A secondary reinforcer is something that, by itself, is not desired, but it changes behavior because of what can be done with it (e.g., a token economy).

152. A. *extinction.* The child's crying behavior stops or is extinguished. Intermittent reinforcement occurs when some, but not every, response is reinforced. Sublimation is a Freudian defense mechanism in which unacceptable impulses are satisfied by channeling them into socially acceptable avenues. Shaping is the process of shifting reinforcements to gradually eliminate all but the desired responses. Maturation suggests that behavior change results simply from a natural developmental process.

153. B. *displacement.* The student experiences his anger as directed at an unnamed physician, not the professor who just made him wait. The student is still angry, but the object receiving the anger has shifted. Reaction formation refers to overt action that is the opposite of what a person unconsciously thinks or feels. Conversion is a type of somatization in which physical symptoms have a psychological etiology. Repression is pushing experience out of consciousness so that it is non-recoverable. Projection is when a person perceives his or her own thoughts and feeling as existing in the outside world.

154. D. *apraxia.* Loss of ability to do simple, specific coordinated movements, such as tying shoelaces or drinking from a straw. Aphasias are difficulties with comprehension or the production of language. Aprosody is the loss of the normal variations in stress, pitch, and rhythm of speech that convey emotional expression in human communication. Agnosia is the loss of the ability to recognize the import of sensory stimuli (e.g., tactile agnosia is the inability to recognize objects by touch). Anosognosia is unawareness or denial of a neurological deficit despite the presence of a clear disability (e.g., hemiplegia).

155. E. *if he did not use nicotine replacement or buproprion in his prior smoking cessation attempts, recommend these to reduce potential weight gain.* Weight gain from smoking cessation is real, but not a valid reason not to quit. Increased exercise or the use of buproprion or nicotine replacement may reduce the amount of weight gain. No matter what the patient's genetic risk, smoking is the most serious, modifiable cardiovascular risk factor that he has. Obesity itself is not clearly a risk factor. If the patient's father was obese and had heart disease, the problem may have been related to hyperlipidemia, which can be modified by diet and drugs. The doctor's psychodynamic specu-

lation may be valid, but addressing it in formal mental health treatment is not likely to be necessary or sufficient to induce habit change. Although the patient is rationalizing his addiction, support for smoking cessation is generally not built around 12-step programs. These target the social, interpersonal, and spiritual consequences of addictions that have adverse effects on relationships. Nicotine addiction is more pro-social, and group support, for which there is limited evidence of efficacy, primarily involves education, behavioral techniques, and encouragement.

156. D. *Thiamine.* Clinically manifested as Korsakoff's syndrome, the memory gaps associated with thiamine (vitamin B_1) deficiency are generally filled by confabulation. Korsakoff's syndrome is a result of long-term alcohol abuse and is only treatable if detected early, prior to neuronal damage. Wilson's disease is an autosomal-recessive disorder, characterized by a deficiency in copper metabolism. Niacin deficiency results in pellagra, which is manifested as dermatitis, inflammation of mucous membranes, diarrhea, and psychic disturbances. Deficiencies in potassium are manifested as electrolyte imbalances that can lead to muscle cramping and cardiac conduction abnormalities. Zinc deficiency produces anemia, short stature, hypogonadism, impaired wound healing, and geophagia.

157. B. *fixed interval.* The medication is taken on a preset, unchanging time schedule. Note that if the patient feels more pain, he cannot obtain more medication. A continuous schedule would be one where the patient takes medication whenever he feels in pain. Fixed and variable ratio schedules provide relief depending on how many times a behavior is done (e.g., pain is reported). Non-contingent suggests that reinforcement is not linked to behavior (e.g., feelings of pain) at all.

158. E. *USDA subsidies to cattle farmers, quality of produce in local grocery stores, frequency of fast food consumption of co-workers, personal food preferences.* USDA farm subsidies are an example of a factor at the outermost level of the social ecological model (society) that could affect dietary intake. Crops that are subsidized by the government may be cheaper and represent a larger portion of the U.S. food supply than do crops that do not receive subsidies. The abundance of such foods and their rela-

tively low cost, in turn, can make them more likely to be consumed by any given individual and by the population as a whole. The quality of produce in local grocery stores (which may be influenced by the aforementioned society-level factor of subsidies) is a community-level variable that can affect dietary intake. At the interpersonal level, the behaviors (including fast-food consumption) of one's co-workers and other acquaintances often influence (either consciously or not) an individual's dietary choices. A personal taste or distaste for certain foods is an individual-level variable affecting dietary intake.

159. D. *stopping smoking.* Risk for heart attack returns to the level of people who have never smoked after 2 years of abstinence. Stopping smoking is difficult. The success rate of a single attempt to quit is below 10% without physician help and about 20% with help. Weight lifting may improve muscle tone, but will not provide the benefits of a cardiovascular workout. Losing weight and modifying diet are almost always good ideas, but the impact of stopping smoking will be more dramatic. Cholesterol-lowering medication is useful but must be combined with diet to be effective.

160. B. *disease, but not illness.* H.Y. has an objective physical health problem without the subjective self-label of illness. Sickness refers to the social role assumed by patients who are relieved of duties and responsibilities. She is performing all her tasks and so is not disabled.

161. A. *classical conditioning.* The child first cried when given the shot by the nurse. Now he cries when he sees the nurse, without any shot being involved. Thus, he has the same distress response, but it has become generalized to a new stimulus. Shaping, fading, negative reinforcement, and positive reinforcement all refer to operant conditioning.

162. E. *token economy.* This is an example of secondary reinforcement. The boy receives stickers that have no intrinsic value, but are reinforcing because of what they signify. Biofeedback requires trial-and-error practice to modify an internal physiological state by learning to change some proxy external stimulus (e.g. using a heart monitor to learn to control heart rate). Desensitization and flooding are treatments for phobias. Shaping involves reinforcing successively better approximations of desired be-

haviors (e.g., a child's putting away some toys, then most toys, then all toys).

163. B. *limbic system:* hippocampus, hypothalamus, anterior thalamus, cingulate gyrus, and amygdala. The limbic system constitutes the circuit through which the emotional response reverberates. The neocortex is a control mechanism and handles most higher-level thought processes. The cerebellum is important for learning skills and for some memory functions. The reticular activating system helps control sleeping and waking. The pineal body is the site of melatonin synthesis.

164. B. *fidelity.* Fidelity refers to the ethical principle of faithfulness to one's duties and obligations as a physician. Justice in medicine is the fair administration of medical services, while beneficence is acting in the best interests of patients. Although the principle of beneficence might apply to the physician's behavior in this example, it does not apply as well as the principle of fidelity. The principle of medical honesty refers to truthfulness in physicians' dealings with patients. Trust is not an ethical principle.

165. B. *patient passivity during encounters with physicians.* Characteristics of a paternalistic physician role in physician-patient relationships include physician dominance, patients serving as passive recipients of medical information and services, and physician assumption that patients adhere to the physician's decisions about medical management. In contrast, the other choices offered are characteristics of a contractual, patient-centered relationship between physicians and patients.

166. B. *immediately inform him of his condition.* Studies have shown that terminally ill patients prefer to be told of their condition without delay. However, physicians may shy away from this discussion because it makes them feel uncomfortable. Being informed allows patients to make plans that can considerably benefit both patients and their survivors. Physician fears of patient decompensation and agony being precipitated by such knowledge have been unfounded. Mr. E. is the person responsible for telling relatives about his disease and only if he wants them to know. To encourage Mr. E. to buy life insurance before telling him about his disease is blatantly dishonest, toward both Mr. E. and the insurance company.

167. A. *acknowledging differences in understanding of health-related issues.* The preferred physician-patient relationship includes respect for the roles of physician and patient as provider of medical expertise and autonomous recipient of services, respectively. This relationship values mutual exchange of information, active involvement of patients in all aspects of their care, collaborative decision making, and respecting differences in background and understanding of health-related issues. The other options provided are concepts and beliefs consistent with traditional (but increasingly outdated) paternalistic physician-patient relationships.

168. D. *justice.* Justice refers to the fair administration of medical services and most closely applies to the case presentation. In contrast, fidelity is faithfulness to one's duties and obligations as a physician; beneficence is acting in the best interests of patients; non-maleficence is not harming patients; and honesty is truthfulness in dealing with patients.

169. B. *the patient has all necessary information before deciding to undergo medical treatment.* Informed consent focuses on the right of the patient to decide about a plan of care, after being provided with all relevant information. Informed consent does not allow the physician to withhold any information and does not pertain to providing all information to one or more family members, unless the patient is incompetent to make decisions and has appointed a health care proxy.

170. D. *show concern and ask what assistance she would like to help her manage the diabetes.* The patient has a long history of diabetes mellitus and poor adherence to treatment recommendations. Although the patient may benefit from additional dietary counseling and information about the health consequences of poorly controlled diabetes, she has likely received this information during previous visits. Rather than confront the patient about her reasons for not adhering to the treatment plan or ensuring that she understands that the diabetes is her problem, the best first step is to demonstrate concern about her and that her opinions regarding her treatment are valued. An authoritarian physician-patient relationship has not produced the desired results in the care of this patient and a patient-centered approach should be emphasized in her future medical management.

171. C. *nonspecific therapeutic effects.* The patient's treatment regimen at the medical center was identical to the regimen at her local hospital. Therefore, symptom changes due to nutritional supplements, placebo effects, and specific effects of treatment are unlikely. Although symptom severity may fluctuate because of the natural history of the disease, significant fluctuations at this stage of metastatic breast cancer are not typical. The probable cause for improvement in the patient's symptoms is the nonspecific therapeutic effect associated with being treated at an impressive and renowned tertiary medical center. It is likely that this improvement is being mediated through a greater sense of hope, increased confidence in her health caregivers, and a diminished sense of anxiety.

172. D. *the physician controls medical decision making.* Physician behaviors that decrease patients' involvement in their medical care and the decision-making process also decrease adherence to treatment. The other options provided are associated with *increased* patient adherence to treatment regimens.

173. C. *listening actively or reflectively.* While the other options provided represent components of empathy, it is the reflection of feeling as well as content that serves as the necessary and sufficient core element of empathy.

174. E. *Vascular dementia.* The age, history of hypertension and diabetes, relatively rapid onset, and lateralizing neurological signs are all suggestive of vascular dementia. Alzheimer dementia has a more insidious onset and lateralizing signs are not an associated feature. Huntington is an autosomal dominant disorder that appears prior to age 40. Pick disease is a rare dementia; clinical findings are similar to those of Alzheimer dementia. Creutzfelt-Jacob disease is a rapidly progressive dementia that is fatal within two years.

175. D. *Speaking in language that is similar to the patient's* will facilitate relationship building. Asking questions and conveying responses at the patient's language level increases understanding and also allows the patient to discuss the illness without being overwhelmed with jargon or other confusing medical terminology. Empathy is best defined as understanding another person's thoughts and feelings. One of the most concrete ways to promote under-

standing is to use words that both parties understand.

176. E. *transference by the patient.* Transference is bringing into current life the experiences, beliefs, and perceptions of previous relationships. If the patient had experienced previous relationships that were hallmarked by criticism, then subsequent relationships (including the medical encounter) may be perceived in a similar fashion. While the behavior of people with personality disorders may be hard to understand, it is most appropriate to consider situational explanations before labeling a patient with a diagnosis that implies long-term pathology.

177. E. *the creation of additional problems or complications by the physician.* Iatrogenic effect is frequently applied to the negative consequences of drug therapy (e.g., superinfection following antibiotic therapy), but the broader concept applies to any adverse condition resulting from action by the physician (e.g., wound dehiscense following surgery). Iatrogenesis may also be present in elements of the medical interview such as the absence of empathic responses leading the patient to feel undervalued and, thus, impairing self-esteem.

178. B. *combining technical expertise and effective human relations skills to be a "total" physician.* Medicine is both an art and a science. The art of medicine is concerned with understanding human nature, how people perceive events, and what motivates people's behavior. The science of medicine is understanding physiological functioning, how to diagnose disease, and the pathophysiology of a variety of conditions in order to make judgments about appropriate treatment. Applying the art of medicine to the science of medicine permits the physician to interpret signs and symptoms in a given individual and negotiate a treatment plan that is most likely to be successful.

179. B. *"Patients come first when care is really needed."* This physician's family has supported traditional principles of physician obligation in patients for 20 years. A key belief inherent in that obligation is that patients' needs must be placed ahead of physicians' needs in situations where medical services are necessary. While a spouse is an adult partner who can choose such a lifestyle and make a commitment to such principled behavior, a physician's children may feel

hostage to disappointment, such as lack of contact with the physician parent or feeling unable to rely on parent support or presence. Obligations as a physician and obligations as a parent typically conflict rather than overlap, making it essential that the physician be explicit about the motivation behind what may otherwise be felt as confusing and rejecting behavior.

180. A. *has a history of maltreatment or abuse by an intimate partner.* Epidemiological investigation has shown that a history of victimization is associated with both chronic pelvic pain and irritable bowel syndrome. Her headaches are classic migraines. Though the association of migraines with victimization is less clear, the fact that she does not have regular medical care despite having a recurrent, chronic illness is also a clue that she has been recently victimized in a relationship. The common thread is the effect of severe stress on various monoamine neurotransmitter systems, which control pain thresholds and autonomic nervous system activity. ER physicians often dismiss such patients as drug seeking, since their pain does not correlate with end organ damage or clear tissue injury. The diagnosis of malingering implies that she is only feigning symptoms, although in this case she has symptoms with a known pathophysiology, in a classic pattern, and with typical comorbidities. Malingering and drug seeking should not be the first hypothesis the clinician adopts. Hypochondriasis describes a conviction of severe illness in the face of contradictory evidence. The vignette does not describe the patient as magnifying her symptoms or being overly concerned about their implications. Conversion disorder describes patients with symptoms that do not have recognized pathophysiology and are associated with an identifiable psychological conflict, again possible but not likely here. Although panic disorder patients are intensely concerned about somatic symptoms, this patient's symptoms are not those of panic attacks, which by definition have acute onset and subside quickly. Pain is generally not a panic symptom.

181. E. *respect for autonomy.* The principles of nonmaleficence (not intentionally harming patients), beneficence (improving patients' welfare) and justice (assuring fair distribution of health care services) do not directly apply to the behavior described. Moral virtue refers to behaviors that conform to generally accepted moral standards.

182. D. *Nonmaleficence* refers to not intentionally harming one's patients. Adherence to the other principles and behaviors requires specific action by the physician: justice, assuring fair distribution of health care services; respect for autonomy, encouraging patient involvement and self-rule in medical management decisions; beneficence, improving patients' welfare; and moral virtue, behaving according to moral standards.

183. B. *her relationship with her physician.* The patient's relationship with her physician will allow thoughtful discussion of all treatment options and decisions regarding her end-of-life care. Her physician will know her as a patient and person, aware not only of her medical history but also her philosophy of life and death. Given her competence (ability to make appropriate decisions regarding her medical management) and terminal medical condition, decisions regarding her care should not be unduly influenced by input from her sister, her insurance company, regulatory bodies, or the nursing home administration.

184. C. *moral virtues.* To consent to the children's wishes, the physician would have been blatantly dishonest. Since the first trust fund provided life-long living and medical care for the patient independent from the management of the second trust fund, the principles of nonmaleficence, beneficence, justice, and patient autonomy are not involved in the physician's decision.

185. B. *female physicians show greater confidence in their interpersonal skills.* However, significant stress factors continue to exist for females versus males. Lower pay or salaries, less confidence in business aspects of practice, and the demands of balancing family and child-rearing duties are examples often cited as unique stresses for female physicians. The old misconception that female surgeons would be likely to perform fewer operations has been repeatedly disproved.

186. B. *a helping profession when a family member has a history of substance abuse.* Transference refers to responses based on our own emotional needs from familial or developmental experiences. While choices A, C, and D may reflect important childhood issues, the emotional transference of familial substance abuse is likely unconscious and thus more accurately

reflects this process. Wanting to be like a physician on television is a conscious choice, an imitation, not the unconscious attachment that transference implies.

187. D. *80%.* Compulsivity is a common trait in many physicians. It must be seen for both its positive as well as harmful qualities.

188. A. *female spouses consider family obligations when selecting practices.* While divorce rates in dual-physician marriages are lower than the general population, women physicians often place a higher priority on family and childbearing responsibilities. As such, interrupted training time, lower salaries, and part-time employment occur more frequently for female than male physicians.

189. B. *Compulsive gambling that only occurs on weekends.* While HIV infection reflects a controversial subject, physicians can practice in limited roles with HIV. Stroke recovery does not necessarily represent impairment depending on the location of the stroke. Physicians show a high level of successful drug rehabilitation. However, compulsive gambling represents an unaddressed addiction that often becomes progressive.

190. E. *validity* means that the test assesses what it is supposed to assess. In this case, that a test to identify suicidal people actually assesses suicidality. To have validity (accuracy), a test must first have reliability (precision or consistency), but having reliability tells us nothing about validity. Bias reflects a tendency of the test or tester to produce skewed results. Administration refers to how the test will be given.

191. E. *validity.* Does the test assess qualities that are important to being a bank teller? Does it separate success from failure or help to predict who will be successful in this particular job? Reliability and precision refer to consistency, that is, does the test give the same result every time (test-retest reliability)? Bias is a deviation from truth and suggests a flaw in the test itself, or in its administration. Convergence is a type of validity, but not the type of interest here. For convergence, different tests that purport to assess the same thing would give the same result.

192. E. *predictive validity,* or that the validating criterion (success in school) will exist in the future. Content validity means that the items on the test seem related to the subject matter being assessed. Criterion-related validity means that the test matches some existing criterion, as when a person diagnosed as depressed tests as depressed on a depression inventory. Construct validity requires that the test's assessment be consistent with some underlying theoretical perspective. Face validity means that, on first impression, the items on the test seem to be about the subject being assessed.

193. A. *construct validity.* Does the test match the abstract theoretical notion represented by the trait of obsessiveness? Predictive validity refers to a match between the test results and validating criteria that will exist in the future. Content validity means that the items on the test seem related to the subject matter being assessed. Criterion-related validity means that the test matches some existing criterion, as when a person diagnosed as depressed tests as depressed on a depression inventory. Face validity means that, on first impression, the items on the test seem to be about the subject being assessed.

194. B. *consider this test since its reliability is very strong.* A number close to 1.00 is very good reliability. A number over 1.00 is not mathematically possible.

195. E. *reliability.* How likely is the test to give the same results on a consistent basis so that any change in results represents real change and not just random fluctuation? Adaptive capacity has nothing to do with evaluating how useful a test may be. Concurrent validity means that other, external criteria confirm the results of the test. Bias is deviation from truth and reflects an inability of the test to give an accurate representation of reality.

196. E. *Tests of intelligence generally attempt to measure ability not achievement.* IQ tests measure capacity (how much is the child able to learn), not achievement (how much did the child actually learn). A number of different definitions of intelligence exist, and a number of different types of intelligence have been proposed (e.g., emotional intelligence). IQ is a derived measurement; intelligence is the inference from that measurement. A number of researchers have demonstrated some racial bias in IQ tests leading to the development of "culture-free" tests. A good test administrator should take these biases into account. Most differences in IQ scores are primarily due to heredity.

197. C. *85–115.* The IQ has a mean of 100 and standard deviation of 15. In a normal distribution, 68% of the scores will be within one standard deviation of the mean (plus and minus), 50% of the scores will be over 100 and 50% will be under 100. About 2.5% of the population will have scores under 70 or over 130. A score of 70 is the IQ criterion cutoff for mental retardation. However, social capacities, as well as IQ, are used for a diagnosis of mental retardation.

198. E. *Schizotypal personality disorder,* by DSM-IV-TR criteria. J.G. evidences odd thinking, a belief in telepathy, suspiciousness, social anxiety, inappropriate affect, lack of close friends, and odd speech patterns. A narcissist sees the world and self in grand terms. The schizoid has no friends, but likes it that way and just wants to be left alone. Borderline people are in constant chaos with unstable mood, self-image, and relationships. Antisocial personality disorder is the diagnosis applied to a person lacking a conscience.

199. D. *night terrors.* Night terrors are a Stage 4 (deep) sleep disorder that have the classical presentation described here. Night terrors tend to run in families and can be a precursor to temporal lobe epilepsy. In contrast, nightmares are called dream anxiety disorders. These are essentially bad dreams that occur in REM sleep. Hypnogogic hallucinations occur while falling asleep and are one of the symptoms of narcolepsy. Bruxism is teeth grinding and occurs in Stage 2 sleep. Acute adjustment reaction is a time-limited form of posttraumatic stress disorder.

200. A. *has complete information about the surgical procedure and recovery.* Knowing what is going to happen reduces stress and allows for faster recovery with less reported pain. Good relationships with hospital medical personnel are the best predictor of satisfaction with hospital stay, but have not been shown to shorten recovery time. Giving pain medication on demand tends to lessen the patient's fear of pain, but does little to reduce the need for the medication.

201. C. *L or Lie Scale.* The Lie Scale reflects the tendency to answer in ways that are socially desirable but rarely practiced. The Infrequency Scale measures the tendency to give statistically rare responses, and serves as a check on random responding. The Correction Scale allows mathematical adjustment of MMPI scores to increase true positives. The Psychasthenia Scale assesses liability to anxiety. A Self-Esteem Scale is not part of the MMPI.

202. E. *Thematic Apperception Test* or TAT. For the TAT, patients are presented with a number of ambiguous pictures and asked to create a story about what is happening in the pictures. Stories are scored for unconscious themes such as the need for power, need for intimacy, or need for achievement. The MMPI is a multidimensional, norm referenced test that provides a profile of the patient's personality. The other choices are tests that seek to diagnose neurological or developmental impairment.

203. C. *The Halstead-Reitan Neuropsychological Test Battery* is a wide-ranging battery of standardized instruments seeking to generate a complete picture of the patient's neurological functioning. The Luria-Nebraska Neuropsychological Battery provides a similar assessment, but makes use of different standardized tests. The Thematic Apperception Test is a way of assessing the patient's unconscious needs and preoccupations. The California Personality Inventory provides a profile of the patient in a manner similar to the MMPI. The Bender Visual Motor Gestalt Test looks at cortical functioning related to mental representation, retention, and reproduction of presented figures.

204. A. *Bender Visual-Motor Gestalt Test* looks at cortical functioning related to mental representation, retention, and reproduction of presented figures. The Wechsler Memory Scale examines short-term memory and might be used to assess a patient with suspected Alzheimer dementia. The Rorschach and the Draw-A-Person tests are projective tests intended to assess a patient's unconscious content and preoccupations. The Luria Nebraska Neuropsychological Battery includes a wide-ranging group of standardized instruments seeking to generate a complete picture of the patient's neurological functioning.

205. E. *the projective hypothesis* assumes that responses to ambiguous stimuli reveal information about the person responding. Subjective press is the perceived field of stimuli directing behavior. The Gestalt laws of perception focus on the role of context and mental set in governing what is perceived. Reaction formation is a Freudian defense mechanism in which real but unconscious feelings are hidden by acting in an opposite manner (e.g., love is manifested as hate).

206. B. *bias.* If the tester knows the hypothesized outcome, she may unwittingly act to confirm it. Stigma is a problem with most psychiatric diagnoses. Patients feel and can be treated with a level of shame not associated with illnesses considered strictly "physical." Construct validity refers to the degree to which the test matches a given theoretical concept. This is not the issue here. Reliability is the extent to which the test results are reproducible or consistent. A placebo effect is found when the patient shows improvement even though the intervention lacks any known therapeutic benefit.

207. D. b/(b + d). In a 2 × 2 table, specificity is d/(b + d), or the number of true-negative test results. Specificity is the ability of a test to exclude a disease when it is truly absent. Test results for those who do not have a disease can be either negative (i.e., true-negative results) or positive (i.e., false-positive results). The formula (1 − specificity) is the number of negative cases remaining after the true-negative cases have been subtracted (i.e., the false-positive results). This is shown as 1 − [d/(b + d)] = b/(b + d) or the false-positive error rate.

208. E. d/(b + d). Specificity is the probability that the test correctly identified a healthy person. This is the proportion of all disease free people (b + d) who are categorized as disease free by the test (Cell d), or d/ (b + d).

209. A. a/(a + b). The positive predictive value is the probability of disease in a patient with a positive test result. This is the proportion of all patients with positive test results (a + b) who truly have the condition (Cell a), or a/(a + b).

210. A. *late-look bias.* Late-look bias is a tendency to detect only those cases of a serious disease that were mild enough to be identified prior to death. Many cases of massive myocardial infarction result in death before a patient can reach the doctor's office or emergency department. Consequently, your study might underestimate the probability of early death following an infarction. Other errors, such as classification error (i.e., the result of inconsistency in the diagnosis of myocardial infarction), could create bias in your findings as well. Selection bias is a problem when subjects are recruited for study participation or assigned to treatment in a non-random manner. Neither of these conditions is operative here. Observer bias or measurement bias occur when there is distorted interpretation of the outcome in study groups. In this case, the outcome is death, which is not usually subject to interpretive error. Lead-time bias is the detection of a disease by screening earlier in its natural history than it would have otherwise been detected, resulting in a measured increase in survival time after diagnosis when there is actually no change in real survival time.

211. B. *lead-time bias.* Screening for lung cancer with chest x-rays has proved to be generally ineffective, not because cases are never found, but because when they are, the natural history of the disease is not changed from what it would have been if the disease were found and treated after symptoms developed. Lead-time bias is the prolongation of survival time after diagnosis, not because death comes later, but because diagnosis comes earlier (i.e., when the patient is asymptomatic).

212. B. *Higher, due to the prejudice and discomfort he elicits in his peers.* Homosexual men have higher rates of suicidal behavior, especially in adolescence, compared to heterosexual peers. This appears to be related to the stigma and discrimination that they face, either due to the admission of their sexual orientation or to the effeminate behavior some homosexuals demonstrate, or both. Such discrimination disrupts the supportive peer relationships that are crucial to the well-being and self-esteem of teenagers. Although achieving the capacity for intimacy is thought to be a somewhat later developmental imperative, opportunities to imagine and experiment with sexual relations are also crucial to adolescent self-esteem and identity development. Homosexuality makes this developmental task more complex if there is little peer support. Additionally, the boy may have few opportunities to meet appropriate partners and a dearth of positive role models. Homosexuality is not clearly associated with cognitive maturity and, in fact, awareness of sexual orientation often predates adolescence. Non-violence and female patterns of suicidal behavior are not particularly associated with homosexuality in men. Internalized homophobia is not necessarily a feature of homosexuality. When homophobia is found, it is typically related to the degree of non-acceptance and discrimination that the person has experienced in his social environment growing up.

213. D. *Subway: 12-inch sub – hearty Italian bread with black forest ham, Swiss cheese, and ranch*

dressing – and a bowl of vegetable beef soup. Despite the traditionally fattier meats (ham and beef) and the sandwich being topped with cheese and creamy dressing, this fast-food meal is actually the healthiest dinner selection of the five choices listed, totaling 755 calories, 18 grams of total fat, and 5 grams of saturated fat. This meal provides only slightly more than a third of the calories of a standard 2,000 calorie adult diet, only about ¼ of the recommended total fat intake of no more than 30% of total calories from fat, and less than ¼ of the saturated fat recommendation of less than 10% of total daily calories. The other selections weigh in as follows: (A) Chili's Cobb salad and sweet corn soup: 1,500 calories, 76 grams of fat, 36 grams of saturated fat (75% of an adult's daily calories in one meal!); (B) Outback ribs and fries: 1,190 calories, 76 grams of fat, 33 grams of saturated fat (more than half of day's calories and about 1½ times the saturated fat recommendation for an adult!); (C) Red Lobster shrimp and Caesar: 820 calories, 51 grams of fat, 7 grams of saturated fat (the total calories in this dish are better than most and the saturated fat is OK, but the total fat is more than three quarters of the daily adult recommendation); (E) Wendy's chicken fillet and small fries: 790 calories, 33 grams of fat, 6.5 grams of saturated fat (though not nearly as hefty in calories, this single meal contains about half of the maximum recommended daily calories from fat for an adult). The take-home messages: fast-food is not always bad, salads are not always good, and some of our favorite restaurant meals are loaded with much more than the flavor that makes them so enticing.

214. C. *has not menstruated in the past year.* Current research separates the perimenopause from menopause, which is diagnosed when the woman has not had a period for the past year. Hot flashes, disturbed sleep and irregular menses are common symptoms of perimenopause, a period of declining ovarian function that may last for years before cessation of menses. Perimenopausal women are less able to conceive than younger women, but women who do not wish to become pregnant should use contraception until they are fully menopausal, as pregnancy is still possible up to that point.

215. D. *the statistical regression effect.* When subjects with the most extreme values for any measure are observed over time, the values tend to become less extreme. This is the statistical regression effect, or "regression to the mean." This would be the most likely reason that moderation of extreme absenteeism is seen even though the treatment program has had no effect.

216. B. *accountable.* Accountability of care is the disclosure of standards of care to the public and an acceptance of responsibility by providers for the judgment of the public.

217. A. *acceptable.* Care may be accessible and available, but will not be utilized if it is unacceptable to patients. Acceptability requires that patients and providers communicate in the same language, that care is delivered with compassion, and that cultural beliefs and practices of patients are respected. If the quantity of available care is commensurate with need but the care is unacceptable to patients in the community, the care provided cannot be considered adequate.

218. D. *PPO (preferred provider organization).* A PPO is formed when an insurer establishes a network of contracts with independent practitioners. Practitioners agree to give discounts to patients of the insurer in exchange for increased volume of referrals. DRG (diagnosis-related groups) is a federal prospective payment system that limits the amount the government will pay to treat specific diseases. All HMOs (health maintenance organizations) are prepaid group practices. In the situation presented, payment is fee-for-service at a discount or PPO.

219. A. *63% and 76%.* When data from a table are expressed as percentages, the percentage of the dependent variable is usually shown as a function of the independent variable. For this table, the assignment to either chicken soup or gazpacho is the independent variable and the frequency of colds is the dependent variable. To express the frequency of colds as a function of treatment assignment, the percentage of subjects in each group developing (or not developing) colds should be shown. The percentage of subjects in the chicken soup group developing one or more colds is 63% and in the gazpacho group is 76%. The only other meaningful fact that could be learned from the data is the percentage in each group that did not develop colds (37% and 24%, respectively). However, this was not among the choices provided.

220. B. *Chi-square analysis.* The chi-square analysis is the appropriate significance test for the

comparison of two dichotomous data sets (all nominal data). The dichotomous outcome here is having a cold or not having a cold. The two groups are chicken soup or gazpacho. The *t*-tests are used for comparing means and require two groups of continuous, not dichotomous, data. The Pearson correlation coefficient is used to assess the strength of association between two continuous variables. The analysis of variance acts like a *t*-test, but compares more than two groups. The chi-square value for this table is 1.987 at 1 degree of freedom and is not statistically significant at a *p*-level of .05.

221. C. *40%.* Sensitivity is the proportion of positive cases that also have a positive test result. We have been told that there are 20 cases. Of these 20, 8 had positive test results with the new test. The sensitivity is 8/20, or 40%. The sensitivity can also be calculated by setting up the following 2 × 2 table:

Test Status	True Status		
	Positive	Negative	Total
Positive	8 (a)	4 (b)	12
Negative	12 (c)	176 (d)	188
Total	20	180	200

The cells in the table contain the data we have been given. We know that there are 20 cases of political incorrectness, so the total for the first column in the table, the positive column, must be 20. Cell a shows the positive cases detected by the test; we know that there are 8 of these. If Cell a is 8 and column 1 adds to 20, Cell c must be 12. We know that there are 12 positive test results, representing the total in row 1 of the table. If Cell a is 8 and the row 1 total is 12, Cell b must be 4. The total for the table must be 200. Cells a, b, and c add up to 24, so Cell d must be 176. The sensitivity is a/(a + c) or 8/(8 + 12), which is 40%.

222. E. *98%.* The specificity of a test is the proportion of negative cases that it identifies as negative cases. In the case presented, there are 180 negative cases in the population, according to the available gold standard. The test identifies 4 of these as positive and the remainder, or 176, as negative. The proportion of negative cases correctly identified as such by the test is 176/180, or approximately 98%. This can be verified

from the table provided in the explanation above. Given that the specificity is d/(b + d), this becomes 176/(4 + 176), or 98%.

223. D. *67%.* The positive predictive value is the probability that the condition is present given a positive test result. This is the proportion of all positive results (cell a plus cell b) that are true-positive results (cell a). The formula for the positive predictive value is therefore a/(a + b). In this case, the calculation is 8/(8 + 4), or about 67%. Recall that the predictive value, which is calculated as a percentage of subjects with a particular test result, includes subjects with and without the condition and is therefore dependent on the prevalence. Neither sensitivity nor specificity is dependent on prevalence.

224. D. *94%.* The negative predictive value is the probability that a disease is absent given a negative test result. This is the proportion of all negative test results (Cells c and d) that are truly negative (Cell d). The negative predictive value is therefore d/(c + d), which here is 176/(12+176). This is 93.6%, or approximately 94%. The negative predictive value is much higher than the positive predictive value in this instance because there are few cases of the condition in the population (i.e., the prevalence is low). The probability that anyone in the population has the condition is only 20 out of 200 or 10%. Therefore, the probability that a negative test result is correct is fairly high because of the specificity of the test and the low prevalence of the condition being studied.

225. E. *98%.* The positive predictive value is profoundly influenced by the prevalence, even when the operating characteristics of the test remain unchanged. The sensitivity of the new test is 40%, and the specificity is 98%; these values have not changed. We have now been told that there are 150 actual cases in the study population. Cell a in a new 2 × 2 table shows the number of true-positive results, or the sensitivity multiplied by the prevalence. This is 0.40 × 150, or 60. The total for column 1, the positive cases, must be 150, so Cell c is 90. The number of non-cases is equal to the total population, or 200, minus the 150 cases, or 50. The number of true-negative cases is equal to the specificity, or 0.98, multiplied by the number of non-cases, or 50. This is 49, and this number is placed in Cell d. Cells b and d must add up to 50, so cell b is 1. The table is as follows:

Test Status	True Status		
	Positive	Negative	Total
Positive	60 (a)	1 (b)	61
Negative	90 (c)	49 (d)	139
Total	150	50	200

The positive predictive value is a/(a + b), or 60/(60 + 1), which is slightly greater than 98%.

226. C. *35%.* The negative predictive value is d/(c + d). This is 49/(90 + 49), or approximately 35%. The negative predictive value has fallen as the prevalence has risen. The probability that disease is absent, given a negative test result, declines as the overall probability of disease being absent declines.

227. D. *67%.* The easiest approach to this question is to construct a 2 × 2 table based on an arbitrary sample size. The prevalence is 5%. If the sample size is 1,000, then 50 workers will have the disease. The sensitivity of the test is 94%. Of the 50 workers, 94%, or 47, will be detected by the test. This is Cell a. Cells a and c must add up to the prevalence of 50, so Cell c is 3. Of the 1,000 workers, 950 are disease-free. Since the test specificity is 90%, the test will correctly identify 90%, or 855, of these workers. This is Cell d. Cells b and d must add up to 950, so Cell b is 95. The table is drawn up as follows:

Test Status	Disease Status		
	Positive	Negative	Total
Positive	47 (a)	95 (b)	142
Negative	3 (c)	855 (d)	858
Total	50	950	1000

The percentage of positive test results (Cells a and b) that are false-positive results (Cell b) is b/(a + b), or 95/(47 + 95). This is approximately 67%. The high percentage of false-positive results obtained despite the fairly good specificity of the test is the result of low prevalence.

228. B. *33%.* The positive predictive value is a/(a + b). Based on the table shown, this is 47/(47 + 95), or approximately 33%. Note that the false-positive

error rate (the probability that disease is absent when the test result is positive) and the positive predictive value (the probability that disease is present when the test result is positive) add up to 100%, or 1.

229. A. *3.* The prevalence of the disease is given as 5% of the population, and we are told that the population is 1,000 workers. Therefore, we can expect 5% of 1,000, or 50 persons, to have the disease. Of these 50 cases, 94%, or 47 cases, will be detected by our test. This is what sensitivity tells us. Therefore, the positive cases not detected, or the remaining 3 cases, are the false-negative cases. The number of false-negative cases is (1 – sensitivity) multiplied by the prevalence. In this example, that is [(1 – 94%) × 50] or (6% × 50), which is the 3 cases in Cell c of the table.

230. A. *Cost of screening, follow-up, and treatment.* We have already been told that the disease in question can be treated and we know the operating characteristics of our screening test. If the screening test is prohibitively expensive, we cannot implement it successfully. We need to consider the cost of follow-up testing because 67% of our positive test results will be false-positive results, and all of these subjects will need additional testing to demonstrate whether they do not, in fact, have the disease. Lastly, the cost of treatment for the true-positive cases must not be prohibitive or it will not be possible to provide therapy. The prevalence of other diseases in the population is not critical information, although if other diseases are considered more important and more prevalent, they might be a higher company priority. Disease incidence would be an important consideration in deciding how often to repeat the screening test after the initial round of testing. Once the prevalent cases have been detected, only incident cases remain to be found at subsequent screenings. The size of the population might influence the overall cost of screening, but of greater concern is the cost effectiveness of the program for the company (i.e., whether the company profits by treating the disease and improving the work force.) If the company profits, the size of the population will not be a limiting factor, and if the company loses, the program will not be cost effective in even a small population. Lastly, identifying a genetic risk factor is usually important only in an effort to prevent disease or to determine which persons are at increased risk for a disease, not in a

program designed to screen for an established disease.

231. D. *$1,300 saved.* Regardless of which test is used, the entire population, or 1,000 people, will be screened. We do not know the cost of the original test, but we know that the new test costs $0.50 more per application. Therefore, screening the population of 1,000 will cost ($0.50 × 1,000), or $500 more with the new test than the old; however, the specificity of the new test (i.e., 96%) is higher than the specificity of the old test (i.e., 92%). We know that the prevalence of disease Y is 10%, so 90% of the population, or 900 people, are disease-free. The original test will correctly identify 92%, or 828, of these 900 subjects, and there will be 72 false-positive results. Each person whose test result is falsely positive will need the diagnostic work-up that costs $50 per person. The newer test will correctly identify 96%, or 864, of the 900 subjects who are disease-free, and there will be 36 false-positive results. Thus, there are 36 fewer false-positive tests with the new test than with the old test. The number of true-positive results remains unchanged because the sensitivity of the new test is the same as that of the old test (i.e., 96%). All of the subjects that test positive will require the $50 work-up, and there will be 36 fewer of these with the new test. The savings resulting from not having to do the work-ups for 36 people is (36 × $50), or $1,800. When the $500 in additional costs associated with the new test is subtracted from $1,800, there is a net savings of $1,300 if the new test is used.

232. D. *97%.* The positive predictive value is equal to the true-positive results divided by all the positive test results. This table is shown with the true disease status in rows rather than columns. The positive predictive value is therefore 253/(253 + 8), or 253/261, which is approximately 97%.

233. B. *79%.* This question is asking for the negative predictive value, or the proportion of all negative test results (24 + 93) that are truly negative (93). In this case, 93/(24 + 93) yields a result of approximately 79%.

234. D. *91%.* The probability that a test will detect a condition when it is actually present is the sensitivity. This is equal to the true-positive test results (253) divided by the true-positive cases (253 + 24), or 253/277, which is approximately 91%.

235. C. *prevalence in the population tested may not match her prior probability.* The predictive value, both positive and negative, is dependent on the prevalence. In the case of an individual, the prevalence is not applicable, but the probability of the condition in the individual, or the prior probability, is analogous to the prevalence. Both indicate the probability of the condition before testing and influence the probability after testing. The data in the product brochure are derived from a population in which the prevalence of pregnancy is 277 out of 378 women or about 73% of the population. If your friend is unlikely to be pregnant, perhaps because of consistent use of effective contraceptives, her prior probability of pregnancy may be much lower than 73%. If this were true, the estimates of positive and negative predictive value calculated above would not be applicable. All data should be assessed on the basis of both internal validity (i.e., correctness) and external validity (i.e., generalizability to people other than the study participants.) The data reported in the pregnancy test brochure are most likely correct, but whether or not they pertain to your friend is uncertain.

236. C. *70.* The mode is the most frequently occurring score. There are two 70s and only one of every other number.

237. C. *70.* The median is the middle number. Note that you must rank order the scores from highest to lowest first. If there is an even number of subjects, add the two middle numbers together and divide by two.

238. C. *paired t-test.* This is a before-after trial, so the data are paired. There are two groups (active treatment group and control group), so the independent variable is dichotomous. The outcome variable is blood pressure measurements, which are continuous data. The appropriate test for this situation is the paired *t*-test.

239. A. *data that are not statistically significant may be still clinically important.* When statistical significance is not achieved, the implication is that there is more than a 5% probability (if alpha is set at .05) that the outcome difference is due to chance. However, a *p*-value of .08 still indicates a 92% probability that the outcome difference is not due to chance. In other words, failure to reject the null hypothesis does not mean that the null hypothesis is true. If a therapy is desperately needed and looks promising on the basis

of trials that fail to show statistical significance, there are circumstances under which judicious use of the therapy would be appropriate. But a note of caution is warranted: with large samples, statistical significance may be achieved for outcomes that are not important clinically.

240. E. *pool the data.* The two studies show similar results, one with and one without statistical significance. If the studies were sufficiently similar, a quantitative meta-analysis would be appropriate. Pooling data effectively increases the sample size, providing greater power to detect a significant outcome difference. An alternative would be to recruit more subjects, but this approach is obviously more expensive. When sample sizes are small, power is reduced, and type II (false-negative) error increases.

241. B. *limitation of activity.* In general, athletes are able to tolerate pain, removal from friends, and even short-term dependency better than inactivity. He is old enough to understand the cause-and-effect relationship between his accident and his injury.

242. D. *stipulate prospective payment to hospitals.* DRGs represent categories of diagnosis for which a standard hospital stay and resultant cost of care is anticipated. Hospitals are paid by insurers, such as Medicare, on the basis of the diagnostic group rather than the actual care delivered. Efficient care results in a profit for the hospital. Complications result in hospital costs exceeding the DRG reimbursement and a potential financial loss for the hospital.

243. D. *major depression.* When depressed, children and adolescents are often more irritable than sad. Very brief upswings of mood are common, even when the child/adolescent is predominantly down. This vignette describes sleep disorder, changes in appetite, self loathing and lack of usual interests, along with suicidal ideation. Her social isolation and falling grades are signs that her problems are affecting general functioning, making depression the most appropriate diagnosis. Attention-deficit/hyperactivity disorder typically shows up earlier in life, although the diagnosis may be missed if the child is able to compensate in school. In any case, ADHD is not associated with changes in sleep, appetite, and energy. Puberty can contribute to mood lability and intensification of moods but normal puberty is not associated with deteriorating general adjustment and suicidal ideation.

In girls, the risk of major depression rises with puberty, and the hormonal changes of adolescence may be part of the pathophysiology of depression. However, it is a mistake to dismiss mood symptoms as "just hormones" when there are potentially serious consequences. Borderline personality disorder, by definition, is not diagnosed until after age 18. Some instability is expected during this stage of development, in which identity is being forged. Dissatisfaction with body image is common in both normal and ill adolescents, but body dysmorphic disorder implies that the person is completely preoccupied with some physical characteristic. In addition, concern specifically about weight is excluded from the criteria for this disorder.

244. E. *Any of the above.* People often ask, "What is the best exercise/activity for weight loss?" The answer is that there is no answer. Just about any physical activity can aid in weight loss, provided that an individual burns more calories that he or she is consuming. The amount of calories burned by a particular regimen is a product not only of the particular mode of activity, but also the intensity and duration of that activity. The four activities, intensities, and durations listed actually all burn the dame number of calories (about 210 calories in a 150-pound woman). When it comes to providing physical activity guidance for weight loss, the best activity is the one (or more) that an individual is willing and able to do.

245. C. *Medicare.* She is the dependent of someone who is disabled and, therefore, qualifies for Medicare. Medicaid provides payments for people who meet criteria of need as set by individual states. Blue Cross is an example of a large, private indemnity insurance company. A physician-hospital organization is a cooperative managed care arrangement in which physicians and hospitals share patients and financial risks. Most physicians do not have a special resource fund.

246. A. *HMO.* Only prepaid health care, such as HMOs, benefit from keeping patients healthy. Prepay means the provider already has the money and benefits if the patient does not get sick and require the use of health care services. If patients stay healthy, the provider makes more money. Under fee-for-service systems, as in the other choices offered in this question, the provider only makes money when the patient accesses care.

247. C. *cohort study.* A cohort study is a type of prospective observational study. In this case, the groups were first identified and then followed forward in time. A cross-sectional study examines associations between events at a single point in time. A case-control study is generally retrospective. A clinical trial is an intervention study to test the relative effectiveness of a new treatment or procedure. A cross-over study exchanges the treatment and placebo groups at some predetermined point in the study. This means that everyone in the study will be in the treatment group for at least part of the study.

248. D. *only high levels of stressful life events are associated with increased risk for MI.* Answer this question by using the confidence intervals provided. The basic rule is that only those relative risk confidence intervals with do not include the number 1 (1.0) can be considered statistically significant comparisons indicating that different levels of risk exist for the two compared groups. Using this rule, only the HIGH group is significantly different from the baseline (LOW) group because only this confidence interval does not include 1.0.

249. D. *Chloride low; Potassium low; Carbon dioxide elevated.* Vomiting leads to the loss of stomach acid consisting of both H^+ and Cl^- The loss of H^+ results in an elevated serum carbon dioxide level. In an attempt to decrease the elevated blood pH toward a more normal level, H^+ shifts from the intracellular to the intravascular space. However, to maintain electrical neutrality, a cation needs to move into a cell as H^+ is lost from it. The cation that shifts into cells is K^+, causing the serum level to fall. Thus, the loss of H^+ and Cl^- from the stomach, combined with the shifting of K^+ into the cells causes abnormal serum electrolytes characterized by hypochloremic, hypokalemic metabolic alkalosis. This does not occur with infrequent vomiting, but vomiting three times a day over time will likely lead to these changes.

250. C. *an increase in AIDS prevalence.* The conceptual formula is (prevalence = incidence × duration). Therefore, if mortality declines, then duration increases. This, in turn, leads to an increase in prevalence. No data are presented for infection rates among family members, changes in medical care, the number of people practicing safe sex, or the survival rate after diagnosis.

251. E. *the tendency for the body to maintain a particular state.* Homeostasis is an optimal state where demands on the body are balanced by appropriate responses in terms of resources. Note that homeostasis is a dynamic state that changes over time with development and maturation. The central issue is a biological balance of the organism with the environment, not psychology versus physiology. Balancing sex and aggression drives is a core dynamic in Freudian psychology.

252. E. *have more psychological need for control over situations.* Type A or cardiovascular disease-prone behavior patterns feature greater anger, sense of time urgency, and need for control. The response to stress, not the exposure to stress, defines Type A. There is no relationship between Type A and problem solving or social withdrawal.

253. B. *generalized anxiety disorder.* The diagnosis requires that symptoms such as those described be present at least one month. Anxiety is a normal emotional response. The diagnosis of generalized anxiety disorder is made when the emotional state endures or rises to the level of dysfunction. Agoraphobia is fear of situations from which escape is difficult or help unavailable in the event of panic-like symptoms. Obsessive-compulsive disorder features obsessions (ideas that will not go away) or compulsions (actions a person feels compelled to perform). Social phobia is a fear of appearing inept or shameful in public, either in general, or limited to public speaking. The diagnosis of panic disorder requires three panic attacks within a 3-week period. No panic attacks are described by this patient.

254. C. *progressive relaxation.* The student is practicing a behavioral strategy to reduce physiological arousal and allow for better concentration on the exam. Self-hypnosis is a technique for altering mental state and can include making suggestions to oneself about what to think, feel, or do in a given situation. Meditation is a systematic method of fixing attentional focus on a neutral stimulus that permits the control of physiological responses. A stress response would entail the manifestation of reactions to stress. Biofeedback allows the altering of internal physiological states by modifying an external stimulus that serves as a proxy to that internal state. For example, slowing the rhythm on a cardiac monitor to reduce the actual heart rate.

255. B. *Dieting to get in shape for the cross-country team.* Early pubertal development can lead to a female feeling as if she "does not fit in" or "stands out". However, there is no consistent pattern of pubertal development associated with developing an eating disorder. Likewise, although teasing about weight is now considered a form of bullying, even when it is done in jest, it most likely is only important in the context of an individual who is already highly vulnerable to develop an eating disorder (i.e., the "last straw"). Parental separation can have both positive and negative effects; patients often note that the decrease in parental fighting actually reduces their stress level. Although dieting in the family can be a trigger, maternal influence is generally stronger through paternal influence and her father being on a diet to treat hypercholesterolemia is less likely to precipitate an eating disorder. Dieting to get in shape for cross-country running is the greatest risk factor for this girl. In susceptible individuals, not only does dieting often lead to increasingly more restrictive intake, but since cross-country running is dominated by very thin athletes, there will be constant reminders of a thin ideal. A competitive individual may focus on being the thinnest runner, if she can't be the fastest.

256. C. *mania.* Mania in this case is illustrated by poor judgment, unrealistic self appraisal, irritability, and pressured speech. The patient's recent loss is a soft clue that he is having a mood episode, since mania may be triggered by events that could just as well induce depression. His intact memory with poor concentration and his personalized and idiosyncratic interpretation of proverbs and judgment questions are also typical of mania. Delusional disorder is also associated with unrealistic thinking, but connotes a long-standing pattern of false belief, without disorganization of thought or impaired concentration. Manic patients often seem narcissistic (self absorbed, manipulative, and grandiose), but narcissistic personality disorder does not imply an acute change in mental status, signs of cognitive impairment, or grossly poor judgment. In any case, personality disorders cannot be diagnosed based on a person's immediate state; by definition, they begin early in life and are evident across many situations. The patient's scanty clothing and labile mood could be considered histrionic (seductive and emotionally exaggerated), but these traits can also be seen in the context of acute mania. Finally, masked depression is not a well accepted term. When used, it connotes someone who denies feeling depressed and who may primarily complain of somatic symptoms. On systematic questioning, however, the person with masked depression will have depressive ideation (hopelessness, worthlessness, helplessness, suicidal thoughts) and neurovegetative signs (anhedonia, sleep problems, apathy, changes in weight or appetite, bodily anxiety).

257. A. *concept formation.* The physician is developing a classification scheme. This type of thinking is also called inductive reasoning. Insight suggests some sudden realization about a situation or relationship. Stimulus discrimination entails noting the difference between two or more experiences. Hypothesis testing involves seeking evidence that is consistent with, or that contradicts, a given proposition. Convergent thinking is the result of different reasoning processes that yield the same result.

258. B. *defining how experiences are described and what is remembered.* Reality is created as linguistic labels are assigned. The words we use to describe a situation help to give the context, and therefore the meaning, to events. Recent research suggests that humans are hardwired for language and that children can discriminate linguistic from nonlinguistic patterns from an early age. Sensation and perception are not limited by language, although recollection of them may be. Sound can have an associational meaning that precedes language. The meaning of words is altered by the way they are pronounced or the intonation that accompanies them (prosody), but reality is linked to the linguistic labels, not to the particular form of their expression.

259. A. *cognitive styles.* Cognitive style denotes individual differences in taking in and coping with life experiences. Note that the emphasis here is on coping by the assignment of meaning. Cognitive styles, like computer programs, process incoming information in idiosyncratic ways depending on each person's past experience. Sensations are the result of physiological perception. Defense mechanisms are Freudian concepts in which people cope with uncomfortable emotional states by means of unconscious mental processes. Schemas are the mental patterns or templates against which a person compares experiences and then categorizes them and assigns meaning to them. Delusions are false beliefs not shared by others of the same culture.

260. B. *intellectualization* cloaks an experience in abstract academic terms and removes it from the immediacy of emotional experience. That is, emotions are replaced by thoughts. Sublimation provides satisfaction by channeling unacceptable impulses into socially acceptable outlets. In repression, an event and any reactions to it are forgotten and generally not retrievable. Denial is the refusal to accept some clear feature of external reality. Projection entails seeing one's own thoughts or feelings as part of the external world.

261. B. *intelligence is generally defined in terms of verbal ability and problem-solving skills.* Most IQ tests assess intelligence by assessing these capacities. In some cultures, a slower, more reflective approach is seen as a sign of higher intelligence. Cross-cultural testing finds little to no differences in intelligence among races, if the tests are unbiased. Racial differences that appear within the US disappear when people are tested in their countries of origin. Although as much as 70% of intelligence may be derived from heredity, the role of environment is critical to determining a person's ultimate functional capacity. Most measures of intelligence require convergent thinking (i.e., looking for preset solutions to the problems presented).

262. B. *Cirumstantiality, tangentiality, flight of ideas, loose associations.* Circumstantiality may be non pathological, especially in people who are anxious or trying to communicate by giving extra details. Tangentiality implies that the person is having trouble following a train of thought or suppressing associations, and unaware that he or she is not logical and goal directed. Flight of ideas is a more severe form of tangentiality, when the connections between ideas may be discernible, but off the point, pressured, and idiosyncratic. As thought disorder becomes more severe, the logical connections between ideas are lost and people connect things by superficial rather than semantic qualities (e.g., by the sound of a word rather than the sense, clanging). With loose associations, the connections are random or arbitrary.

263. A. *accurate empathy* is the ability to understand the patient on the patient's terms and to have the patient confirm that understanding with the physician. Clinical judgment refers to decisions about diagnostic procedures and recommendations for treatment. Concept formation refers to gathering information to identify the common elements of a class of disorders. Divergent thinking is looking for creative, new, "out of the box" solutions to problems. Paralinguistic communication refers to the non-verbal cues that punctuate and give context to verbal communications.

264. D. *self-control contracting.* The patient contracts with herself that when a goal is reached, she gets a reward. Cognitive restructuring refers to relabeling or reframing the situation. Cognitive rehearsal is the process of visualizing action before actually attempting it. Problem solving refers to any cognitive routine to arrive at an acceptable solution to a presented dilemma. Skills training involves working with a person as an individual or in a group to help them learn and practice particular behaviors. Often this might be used to help people learn basic social skills such as greeting and conversing with others.

265. B. *cognitive restructuring.* The student is being urged to change the assumptions he has made about the outcome of future behaviors. Positive cognitions are more likely than negative cognitions to lead to productive behaviors. The mechanism behind this observation is unknown but may relate to feeling more relaxed, under control, and optimistic, three emotional states that enhance performance. Cognitive rehearsal is the process of visualizing action before actually attempting it. Problem solving refers to a cognitive routine to arrive at an acceptable solution to a presented dilemma. Skills training involves working as an individual or in a group to learn and practice particular behaviors. The target skill may be technical (learning how to do a certain job) or social (learning how to share). In self-control contracting, a person contracts with him or herself that, when a goal is reached, a reward will be received.

266. A. *cognitive rehearsal* is the process of visualizing action before actually attempting it. Like an actor, the player visualizes the task he must accomplish before attempting it. Cognitive restructuring involves changing the assumptions that are behind future behaviors. Problem solving refers to a cognitive routine to arrive at an acceptable solution to a presented dilemma. Skills training involves learning and practicing particular behaviors with the aid of an instructor or model. In self-control contracting, a person contracts with him or herself that, when a goal is reached, a reward will be received.

267. B. *They connect the various cortical storage sites to form combined memories.* Memories, themselves, are encoded all over the cortex. The hippocampus serves as an index or locator permitting them to be retrieved. The cerebellum serves as a trainer and guide for the learning of motor skills. The thalamus forwards incoming sensory input to the cortex.

268. A. *Group model HMO.* The physician works in facilities run by the HMO and is paid on the basis of capitation and profit-sharing arrangements. In a staff model HMO, physicians are employees paid a salary. In a network model HMO and the IPA model, physicians own the facilities in which they practice. A PPO is a fee-for-service system in which physicians agree to charge less in exchange for increased volume of patients.

269. D. *Convergence of NMDA and non-NMDA receptor activation slows, prolongs, and increases the efficiency of the synapse facilitating complex sensory learning.* This convergence signals that the stimuli are important and provides inducement for the structural changes required for long-term memory. Stimulation of the non-NMDA receptors triggers the depolarization that releases magnesium blockade of NMDA receptors. This results in a combined NMDA and non-NMDA receptor activation and produces a prolonged synaptic response.

270. E. *the consequences of behavior.* In this operant conditioning paradigm, what happens after the behavior is the key event. Anything that makes the behavior more likely to be repeated is called a positive reinforcer. Any stimulus event that makes the behavior less likely is called punishment. If stimuli occur spontaneously and are unconnected to behavior, they will have no effect, or can result in the unintentional conditioning of "superstitious" behavior. Genetics provides the substrate for behavior, but it is the appearance of stimuli in the environment that makes conditioning happen. The level of drive can determine the intensity of responses, but not the learning of the actual response set.

271. A. *a high frequency behavior or reward can be used as a reinforcer for a low frequency target behavior.* A behavior that occurs frequently has high value and can, therefore, be used to reinforce other behaviors that are less common. The valance of low frequency behaviors is variable (i.e., they can be aversive or merely

neglected) and so do not predictably influence behavior. Moderate levels of arousal are associated with optimum performance, but moderate frequency behaviors do not optimize learning. Individuals do seem to engage in behavior that they find desirable, but this is not a statement regarding the Premack Principle.

272. D. *response extinction.* When reinforcement stops entirely, the behavior tends to stop, although it may unexpectedly reappear in the future as spontaneous recovery. Note that if the reinforcer is not stopped completely, an intermittent reinforcement schedule is initiated, which will make the behavior even harder to stop in the future. Positive reinforcement is anything that, when applied, increases the chance of the behavior happening again. Stimulus generalization occurs when a similar, but not identical, stimulus elicits the same response. Negative reinforcement is anything that, when removed, makes a given behavior more likely in the future. Free operant behaviors are not associated with any clear conditioning regimen.

273. D. *Response extinction.* This is an example of systematic desensitization. Note that the fear is not attacked directly. Instead, the feared object is gradually introduced while another response (relaxation) is in place. While the new response (feeling relaxed) is in place, the old response (becoming fearful) can not occur and extinction results. A critical period (e.g., imprinting) is a time in a developmental sequence when specific (e.g., environmental) stimuli have especially great impact on subsequent learning and development. The Premack Principle holds that high frequency behaviors can be used as reinforcers for low frequency target behaviors. Negative reinforcement is anything that, when removed, makes a given behavior more likely to occur in the future. Aversive conditioning is the use of noxious stimuli to inhibit an already learned response.

274. D. *information about the consequences of behavior is reinforcing.* The vignette describes an example of biofeedback in which an internal physiological state is altered by using externally provided cues. In this instance, it is the information provided by the gauge, not the actual physiological change, high frequency behavior, or motor performance, that is reinforcing.

275. D. *Reflex, imprinting, one-trial, classical, operant, social.* The sequence moves from lower level CNS to higher level cortical functioning.

276. A. *dependent on the reinforcement value of relationships.* Social learning involves our sense of and the value we place on other people and our relationships with them. The principles of classical and operant conditioning still apply. Social learning is a key part of individual survival and depends on the feedback of environmental cues like any type of learning. In this case, however, how we regard, and are regarded by, other people is the primary reward or motivation for behaviors.

277. B. *Endocrine.* Neurological responses to stress are electrochemical and instantaneous. In contrast, endocrine responses involve the release of endocrines into the blood stream. This produces a slower but more prolonged response due to reliance on the circulatory system for transportation of the active agents to the target organ.

278. C. *the context in which arousal occurs.* The context, and the individual's past experience with that context, will define the meaning and the labeling of the emotion. Whether arousal is felt as joy or anger depends on the cues available to us in the behaviors of others and our own cognitive attributions.

279. D. *show more anger when challenged.* Although emotional expressions can be different in different cultures, cross-cultural studies show that greater anger when challenged seems to be almost universal for males. The other options are more culture specific.

280. C. *Drive theory.* Drive theory concerns the motivational influences of survival instincts such as the need for, among others, food, water, air, and sex. Arousal theory focuses on the need of the organism to maintain an optimal, but idiosyncratic, level of activation. Expectancy theory frames motivation in terms of conditioned, expected associations. Cognitive theory focuses on the labeling of behavior and the mapping of activity within a perceived environment. Sociocultural theory points out that the impetus for many behaviors can be linked to the specific social and cultural milieu in which they occur.

281. C. *Expectancy theory.* The woman has come to expect (learned) that something (smoking) and gratification are associated. Drive theory focuses on the motivational influences of survival instincts such as the need for food, water, air, or sex. Arousal theory focuses on the need for the organism to maintain an optimal, but idiosyncratic, level of activation. Humanistic theory focuses on the desire for self-actualization and self-expression. Sociocultural theory points out that the impetus for many behaviors can be linked to the specific social and cultural milieu in which they occur.

282. B. *Approach-avoidance.* The taste of the food reinforces approach behavior, while the probability of unwanted weight gain serves as a negative reinforcer for avoidance behavior. In the conflict presented, the approach reinforcer (good taste), is more immediate and so may influence behavior more strongly. The long-term negative reinforcer (that it will make you fat in the unspecified future) is not only deferred to some later time but also is less certain to occur than the pleasure of the taste right now. The notion of an Oedipal conflict comes from Freudian, not behavioral, psychology.

283. E. *reinforcement experience.* Past experience with reinforcement determines what consequences are expected for present behaviors. The past is the best, although not always accurate, predictor of the future. Belief system refers to the patient's personal, culturally derived sense of how the world works. Family history is often a key indicator of susceptibility to particular diseases, but not of patient adherence. Cultural systems are the source for belief systems about how the world and disease states work. Homeostasis is a seeking of equilibrium both within the organism and between the organism and the environment.

284. E. *the opponent-process hypothesis* explains how a behavior that begins as a habit to achieve pleasure (positive reinforcement) needs to be sustained in order to avoid the pain of withdrawal (negative reinforcement). This hypothesis underlies substance abuse and addiction behaviors. Avoidance-avoidance conflicts occur when one has to choose between the lesser of two evils. Cognitive dissonance occurs when a person performs a behavior contrary to an existing attitude and changes attitude to match the manifest behavior. Intrinsic motivation occurs when the very fact of doing the behavior is reinforcing in its own right. Secondary reinforcement refers to a stimulus that is not directly reinforcing, but that can be exchanged for something that is reinforcing (e.g., token economy).

285. A. *a delusional episode.* Delusion refers to a false belief that is not shared by others in the same culture. If we all believe that sacrificing a vir-

gin will stop the volcano from erupting, that is a shared belief and therefore an aspect of culture. If I think this by myself with no support from others, we call it a delusion. An illusion is a misperception of an existing stimulus. An hallucination is a perception of a stimulus (e.g., seeing or hearing something) when such a stimulus does not exist. Sensory distortions, like illusions, involve misperceiving something. Gaps in memory can be filled in with fictitious content called confabulations.

286. C. *habituation* occurs when a stimulus loses its novelty and no longer evokes the same level of response. Threshold detection is the lowest level at which a stimulus can be perceived. Just noticeable difference is the smallest difference that can exist between two stimuli that allows them to be distinguished. Accumulated fatigue is the result of sleep deprivation over time and is a common problem among new parents. We do not have enough information about the parents' general activity level, however, to make this diagnosis. Adjustment reaction suggests difficulty coping with a new or stressful situation. The wife may be less likely to habituate because, for her, the child's cry is a cue for action. She is likely to become more, not less, attuned to it over time.

287. B. *higher for Hispanics who immigrated to the US than those in their country of origin.* Suicide rates tend to be higher in industrialized countries as a result of the *anomie* (a sense of normlessness or being unsure what rules govern behavior) referred to by Durkheim. Suicide rates are highest among white males. In fact, two of every three successful suicides are committed by white males. Suicide rates shift over time. The rate for the elderly is in a long-term downward trend, while that for adolescents is on the rise. Currently, the suicide rate for people in their teens and twenties is similar to that of the population average, about 12 per 100,000. This makes suicide one of the leading causes of death among teenagers because their overall death rate is low.

288. C. *12* per 100,000 according to data from the Centers for Disease Control and Prevention, an agency of the U.S. Government. The rate for the elderly is roughly twice as high as that of the general population, although much lower than it was 50 years ago. The rate for adolescents has risen over the past 30 years so that it is now at about the level of the general population.

289. C. *psychiatric hospitalization with one-to-one monitoring.* Because 50% of all schizophrenic patients attempt suicide and 10% are successful, precautions should be taken. The concomitant substance abuse raises the risk. Danger of suicide is the clearest reason to hospitalize a person for psychiatric reasons. Discharge, even with referral to a self-help program or out-patient therapy, gives the patient the opportunity to carry out the commands of the voices he hears. The immediate threat to life should be addressed before any treatment of the substance abuse problem is initiated.

290. C. *disturbed source identification.* Studies of memory and false memory have shown that the ability to correctly identify the source of a perception or belief may be manipulated or defective. For example, if a person watches an event and then hears a description with different details, the person may think that s/he witnessed something that never happened, not recognizing that the false memory came from the description. Schizophrenic hallucinations often seem to the person to be coming from outside, rather than from within the brain; another type of source misidentification. Not knowing whether one dreamed an experience or actually lived it is another common example of this phenomenon. Short-term memory is measured by giving the person unrelated objects to remember and asking him or her to say them after a period of distraction or delay. Dissociation is a state of trance in which some percepts are not registered or registered in a distorted fashion, and often not remembered accurately. Impaired concentration is measured by history and performance on serial sevens and digit span tests. Poor judgment is inferred from history and from the person's responses to conventional hypothetical situations.

291. A. *less likely to communicate their intentions.* Because they are less likely to give warning, preventive intervention is more difficult. The elderly, like the rest of the population, are most likely to use firearms as the method of choice for completed suicide. Being older does not connote more practical experience with suicide. The elderly have a lower incidence of clinical depression than other age groups in the population. Over the last three decades of the 20th century, government programs for the elderly and general prosperity in the country meant that the elderly were not more likely to live in poverty than people in other age groups.

292. B. *Enrollment in an experimental drug protocol with poor results.* Anything that might increase a sense of hopelessness increases the risk for suicide. If anything, her level of schooling and her lifetime job suggest that she is at less at risk for suicide. Suicide rates are higher among individuals with higher socioeconomic status (defined as a combination of education plus occupation). Having a family member as a caregiver means reduced isolation and, so, reduced suicide risk.

293. A. *Altruistic.* The soldier sacrificed himself to save a friend. Egoistic suicide is associated with a personal agenda, such as revenge on a loved one. The term anomic suicide stems from the term *anomie* which connotes a sense of normlessness and lack of social rules. Anomic suicides occur in situations of social upheaval and chaos, when normative rules are unclear. Fatalistic and heroic suicide are not part of Durkheim's typology.

294. E. *low levels of 5-hydroindolacetic acid in cerebrospinal fluid.* Decreased corticotrophin-releasing hormone suggests a lower level of physiological arousal and, therefore, less energy to carry out suicidal ideation. Higher levels of ACTH are associated with stress responses, but not suicide. Suicidal individuals have lower, not higher, levels of serotonin. No association has been uncovered between suicide and adrenal functioning.

295. C. *Goal attainment – structural functional analysis.* The tension in the scenario presented is between two goals of the hospital: (1) to take care of patients and (2) to be profitable. More nursing staff provide the chance for better patient care, but at an economic cost. In a rush to control cost, the important functions of the admitting nurses in serving as a patient's first contact with the hospital and as the conduit for initiating the management plan accurately and quickly were overlooked. This led to unintended (and negative) consequences. Structural-functional analysis would examine both the manifest and latent functions of various individuals and groups within the organization. This analysis should uncover that the admitting nurses, although of junior status in the hospital hierarchy, fulfill a key function that allows the hospital to meet its intended goal of good patient care. When analyzing an organization, it is critical to assess both the intended and unintended consequences of organizational decisions.

296. D. *manifest functions.* Here, behavior is explained on the basis of readily apparent and often discussed "facts," suggesting that the reason for the use of private rooms is to better serve the patients. The question implies that the real reason may be the staff's needs, not the patient's, which would be a latent function. The explanation given is not intended to identify cause as much as to offer justification. Secondary explanations refer to alternative, but tangential, reasons for the presented events. Implicit theory is the internal subjective explanation from which we work that gives meaning to our world.

297. E. *Utilitarianism–integration.* Integration and consensus are achieved by allowing choices in hopes of maximizing satisfaction for the greatest number of people. Structural functional analysis examines how organizational and situational components work to allow the attainment of specific ends. Conflict theory examines the social structures and processes that emerge as the result of competition for dominance and other scarce resources. Symbolic interaction focuses on the meaning of actions and the context that gives meaning to those actions. Implicit theory refers to the subjective theory of action that organizes and gives meaning to the world in which a person moves.

298. D. *High-dose selective serotonin re-uptake inhibitors (SSRIs).* The only SSRI with FDA-approval for the treatment of both major depressive disorder and bulimia nervosa is fluoxetine. However, patients can benefit from SSRIs (reduce binge eating and purging) even if they are not depressed. Patients may respond to normal doses of SSRIs initially, but often require doses that are two to four times normal. Although some anti-psychotic medications have demonstrated effectiveness, they are not considered the standard of care for bulimia nervosa unless there are extenuating circumstances. Appetite suppressants are not effective in the treatment of bulimia nervosa and, depending on the category of drug, may be addictive. Likewise, although benzodiazepines and other anxiolytics may help reduce anxiety, they do not help with the underlying behaviors and also are highly addictive.

299. B. *In early treatment, the focus is on behavior change and not underlying psychiatric pathology* The Maudsley method and other family-based approaches focus on empowering the parents and the affected individual to take con-

trol of the eating disorder, and are intentionally "agnostic" in searching for causality. Thus, there is no need for parents to establish their authority because they already have authority, but it is being usurped by the eating disorder; there is no value in "making" the patient eat. Parents provide a structured, nurturing, limit-setting meal time experience (not without conflict) so that healthy weight is reestablished. Searches for the cause(s) of the eating disorder are not only useless, but tend to focus on blame, fault, and guilt, which are all dis-empowering. At one time, treatment focused on the underlying psychopathology in the individual and the family with the assumption that once these were resolved, weight restoration would occur on its own. However, when parents allow their child to chose what or how to eat, the eating disorder, not the patient, tends to make such decisions, perpetuating the dysfunctional eating behaviors. The poor nutritional and metabolic state resulting from an eating disorder also impairs effective mental health treatment. The evidence is now clear that the first order of business in treatment is focus on behavior change (by both the patient and the family) and not underlying psychiatric pathology. As physical health recovery proceeds and the patient demonstrates the ability to maintain normal weight (although often with continuing disordered eating thinking patterns), parents take a less active role. Parents do not need to monitor their child's caloric intake, but they do need to continue to provide supportive, nurturing parenting while aware of the possibility of relapse and paying attention to the return of eating disorder behaviors.

300. E. *the human body is in its peak physical condition from 20 to 30 years of age.* Patients often rely on their physician to tell them what is "normal" at every phase of life. "Feeling old" may be a sign of daily stress or perhaps the beginning signs of mild depression. The patient should be encouraged to elaborate on what she means by "feeling old." Athletic activity should be encouraged to foster cardiovascular fitness, maintain bone density, and promote better mental health. Brain cell development peaks in utero, while complexity is highest during the teenage years. Peak intellectual achievement may occur very late in life, but is most common in the 40s.

301. C. *aphasia.* The most common type of aphasia (nominative, dysfluent or Broca's aphasia), results from lesions in Broca's area and compromises the ability to produce speech, although comprehension is intact. Receptive, fluent, or Wernicke's aphasia implies lesions of Wernicke's area and describes problems of comprehension, with speech that may be fluent but syntactically and semantically imprecise. Conduction aphasia results from lesions of the tract connecting the two brain areas. Such lesions damage the ability to repeat what one has heard, despite intact comprehension and speech production. Thus, these three aspects of the Mini Mental Status Examination all relate to the concept of aphasia. Apraxia is the loss of a previously acquired ability such as tying one's shoes, putting on a shirt, drawing, or copying a drawing. Agnosia is the inability to recognize objects or parts of one's own body. Amnesia is loss of memory. Disturbance of executive function encompasses such things as problems doing things in sequence, suppressing impulses, or directing attention at will. The Mini Mental Status Examination is a well standardized, bedside test that systematically assesses each domain, to aid in the recognition of both focal and diffuse brain pathology. The MMSE is especially helpful in dementia, a global brain state that may affect most or all of these abilities, depending on which areas are most affected.

302. A. *a desire to enhance cognitive development.* The need refers to the desire or impulse for cognitive growth and activity. Ability offers the potential for cognitive activity, but not the drive. The desire for dominance and control over others is separate from internal cognitive enhancement. The desire to have children does not spring from cognitive need. Type A behavior patterns are hard driving and competitive, but distinct from the desire for cognitive engagement and development.

303. C. *decreased narcissistic tendencies and increased capacity for interpersonal relationships.* The focus on the creation of an independent identity fades with maturation into young adulthood. Sense of self emerges from the reality of relationships and less from the idealization of self. Task-oriented behaviors continue as career goals are identified, and are supported by increased experience with complex decision making. With experience, perspective increases and with it the capacity to manage and control impulsive behavior.

304. E. *the proportions of sexually active single men and women are nearly equal.* It is not true that,

overall, there are more single women than there are single men. Less than 20% of young adults choose long-term singlehood. Most singlehood relationships last less than 3 years. Singlehood has career advantages in terms of the hours that can be spent working and can offer an increased sense of psychological autonomy. Overall, only 6% of males and 3% of females are homosexual. Many of these individuals are married, and half of them have children. It is no more true to say that most single people are homosexual than to say that married people cannot be homosexual.

305. B. *dementia syndrome of depression.* The Mini Mental Status Exam (MMSE) s particularly helpful for differentiating dementia of the Alzheimer type from depression with reversible cognitive impairment or "pseudodementia", which is quite common in older depressed people. The cognitive problems of depression are mostly those of processing speed, effortful concentration, and motivation to perform. Depressive ideation makes people overestimate their impairments. Demented patients, by contrast, may be unaware of their deficits. They tend to have problems that stem from different areas of brain cortex (marked deterioration of short-term memory, aphasias, apraxia, disorientation, and disturbance of executive functioning). Scores below 24 on the MMSE are a reliable indicator of dementia, if the patient has made a good effort. The maximum MMSE score is 30. Scores between 24 and 30 require careful assessment to distinguish early dementia from other forms of cognitive impairment. In this case, subacute onset, past personal history of depression and depressive ideation help corroborate the depression diagnosis. Subcortical dementia differs pathologically and clinically from Alzheimer dementia. In later stages, both seem similar, but early in the course of illness, parietal lobe and hippocampal functions are more disturbed in Alzheimer dementia, leading to amnesia, psychosis, aphasia, and apraxia. In contrast, subcortical pathology preferentially disrupts the basal ganglia and frontal lobes, affecting motor activity, mood, executive functioning, social behavior, and judgment. Although patients with any form of dementia may seem apathetic, self doubt and feelings of futility are associated more specifically with depression. Delirium connotes an acute change in mental status due to some metabolic, toxic, or circulatory condition that does not permanently damage brain tissue but disrupts the function of the reticular activating system. Delirious patients may score very low on any form of mental status evaluation due to their fluctuating level of consciousness and global brain dysfunction, but a three-month course of illness is not consistent with delirium. Generalized anxiety disorder is associated with agitation, worry, bodily anxiety, and dread, and, by definition, lasts at least six months.

306. A. *establishing a collegial relationship with parents typically begins during young adulthood.* Only as a young adult can the child begin to see the parent as a mutual participant in the adult world. Many young adults describe their sense of self by contrasting it with their parents. Financial assistance from parents to help pay for adult children's education, a first home, or having children is usually gratefully accepted. The process of questioning family origins and making commitments often begins in adolescence. Adult relationships are different from those between parents and their young children. Although old patterns can linger, the young adult's capacity for independence and self-determination alters the balance of dominance in the relationship.

307. E. *natural, supernatural, and social worlds.* An ethnic group's cultural ideas about the natural, supernatural, and social worlds influence its system of maintaining health and treating disease. The natural realm includes ideas about the connections between people and the earth's elements of soil, water, air, plants, and animals. The social realm encompasses ideas about individuals and the appropriate interaction between people of different ages, genders, lineages, and ethnic groups. The supernatural realm includes religious beliefs about birth, death, afterlife, reincarnation, spirits, and interactions between the spiritual world and the human world. To fully understand any ethnic group's perspective about health and disease, we must put it into context with other aspects of that culture, such as beliefs about what a person is, the kinship system, and the meaning of suffering, life, and death.

308. B. *are working at being part of the adult culture.* Most young adults want to be a part of the adult world. Their dreams and aspirations flow from their life experience and the culture outside the immediate family. Seeking independence can make stable intergenerational relationships difficult. Young adulthood is a time for making commitments to intimate relationships and to

career. Advice from older persons is sought and valued.

309. A. *Becoming a parent.* All of the options listed may give individuals pause to reflect on their identity and place in life, but nothing conveys the enduring meaning of becoming an adult as much as the advent of a child. Parenthood represents a psychological, social, and financial break from the past.

310. B. *25% increase in height and 50% increase in weight.* Weight increases more than height as physical development progresses. The period just before puberty is when the greatest growth spurt in height occurs.

311. D. *Earlier height gain in girls reflects the body's adaptation to reproductive functioning.* There is no evidence that the eating habits or nutrition of boys and girls differ appreciably. Most growth occurs during delta sleep and is unaffected by waking time or activity level. Nor is growth related to the attention that is paid to the child. Although boys and girls show slight differences on standardized tests (boys do better on mathematics and visual-spatial problems while girls do better on verbal tasks), this is more likely related to cultural mores and social roles than to height differences.

312. D. *improved health and nutrition.* Childhood diseases, in general, have little impact on the timing of puberty. Although many things have been cited as consequences of global warming, changes in the timing of puberty is not one of them. Given higher infant survival rates, later age at first marriage, and longer life expectancy, the social demand would be for later puberty, not earlier.

313. B. *Duration.* Chronic pain is generally defined as having duration beyond reasonable expectancy for the particular injury. Lasting more than 6 months is a typical threshold for the diagnosis of chronic pain. Intensity refers to the patient's level of discomfort. Family history will reveal any predisposing factors. The site and cause of the pain are useful in planning management and in establishing the probable level of residual disability.

314. B. *hypothalamus and the pituitary gland.* The hypothalamus regulates the endocrine balance that is central for pubescent development. It also regulates eating, body temperature, and the sleep-wake cycle. Efferent pathways from the hypothalamus control the pituitary gland by both neural projection and a vascular link. The adrenal gland is composed of two parts. The medulla produces epinephrine and is responsible for the fight-or-flight response. The cortex produces both cortisol and aldosterone that are responsible for mobilizing nutrients, regulating the response to inflammation, and regulating salt and fluid levels. ACTH secreted by the pituitary gland regulates cortisol production. Thyroid hormone helps maintain the functioning of neuronal structures. Abnormalities in thyroid production have been linked with anxiety, depression, and bipolar disorder.

315. A. *are at the stage of concrete operations,* according to Piaget's theory of cognitive development. During this stage, children can abstract from their experiences, but have trouble reaching beyond those experiences to general abstractions such as hypothetical situations. This capacity is gained only with the transition to formal operations. Capacity for understanding in the situation presented is linked to development, not educational level. The measured IQ is remarkably stable from about age 5 onward. Although an infant may be distractible, a boy at this age should be able to pay attention long enough to hear what the physician has to say. In general, adolescents do trust those who care for them. Rebellion is manifested as symbolic struggles for identity, not rejection of everything related to the parents or other adults.

316. C. *developmental struggles are relatively minor.* Progression to adulthood follows a reasonably continuous pattern. The stresses and strains of adolescence make for good drama, but do not reflect the experience of most teenagers. Most adolescents derive their core values from those of their parents. Adjustment difficulties during adolescence are about the same for both boys and girls.

317. E. *intense concern about social and peer relationships.* Adjustment to the physical changes of puberty occurs at earlier ages (11–13 years). Although intimate relationships are become increasingly important during middle adolescence (14–17 years), peer relationships still predominate. This is the first age at which career preference is likely to be carried to action, but career preference is unlikely to be the girl's main preoccupation. The desire for conformity

is likely to be stronger than the desire for recognition.

318. D. *Placebo effect.* The placebo effect is a change in the patient's illness attributable to the symbolic import of a treatment. Patients in such studies are unaware if they are receiving the drug being studied or the inert pill. Assuming all other treatments are identical, the placebo effect should be the same (contribute equally to the findings in both groups) and, therefore be eliminated as a differentiating factor. Specific treatment effect refers to the therapeutic effect (e.g., antimicrobial action) of the new drug being studied and is usually what the study is intended to measure. Non-specific treatment effects are effects due to factors unrelated to the drug being studied, such as how clinic staff treat the patients. Natural course of the disease refers to fluctuations in disease severity, which occur irrespective of treatment. Investigator bias refers to how preconceived ideas of research outcomes held by the investigators affect study results.

319. B. *accidents, suicide, and homicide.* These data are from the Centers for Disease Control and Prevention. This list reflects a pattern of risk-taking behavior. Risk-taking behavior reflects the lack of understanding of long-term consequences, feelings of invulnerability, impulsivity, and poor judgment seen in many adolescents.

320. D. *appropriate.* Care is appropriate when the "right thing is done in the right way by the right person for the right reason." These are criteria for professional competency and comprehensiveness. Appropriateness is therefore defined by professional standards of care.

321. E. *family and peer relationship problems.* Although there have been a few published studies linking homosexuality in male adolescents with suicide attempts, no such association has been found for girls. Having a handgun in the house offers a means but not the motive. Children raised in single-parent families do have higher suicide rates, but these reflect dysfunctional relationships. Boys, not girls, have higher rates of successful suicide. Girls are more likely to attempt suicide and survive.

322. B. *immature behavior and lower self-esteem.* Boys who develop later are treated as if they are younger, and may feel deficient when they compare themselves to their peers. Athletic ability is more likely in those who experience early puberty due to the boost in muscle development provided by testosterone. No relationship has been found between timing of puberty and academic ability, delinquency, or musical ability.

323. E. *society's moratorium on growing up.* Pressure to grow into adult roles quickly would leave little social space for the subculture. MTV reflects the subculture, but did not create it. Drug use can be a part of adolescent exploration, but is not the force that created the subculture. The existence of the teenage subculture predates the age of computers.

324. E. *Fatigue, hyperpigmentation of the skin, hyperkalemia.* Although fatigue is common in restrictive anorexia nervosa as weight loss occurs and metabolism decreases, the skin does not become hyperpigmented. Hyperkalemia is associated with starvation in third-world countries with significant protein-calorie malnutrition, but the diet of most patients with eating disorders has enough high-quality protein to preclude kwashiorkor, which also takes at least several months to develop and generally is associated with chronic malnutrition. The triad of fatigue, hyperpigmentation, and hyperkalemia suggests adrenal insufficiency (Addison disease). Insufficiency of adrenal mineralocorticoids leads to hyperkalemia and the resulting chronically elevated ACTH secreted to stimulate adrenal activity also stimulates melanin production, leading to darkening of the skin, often most noticeable in skin creases that do not tan. Early satiety is associated with gastric atony, bradycardia is a sign of hypometabolism, and hypoglycemia is associated with low caloric intake as seen in anorexia nervosa. Likewise, constipation and hypothermia are characteristic consequences of low caloric intake. Although not often measured as part of routine screening, mild elevations of liver enzymes can be seen with low weight due to poor caloric intake. True anorexia occurs later in the course of the illness, but orange/yellowish discoloration of the skin is commonly seen. A high intake of carotene-containing vegetables and the relatively low thyroid activity ("sick euthyroid syndrome") associated with malnutrition and weight loss accounts for this as thyroid hormone is needed to metabolize carotene. Neutropenia is also associated with weight loss. Hypogonadotropic amenorrhea is a classic element of anorexia nervosa. Alopecia also

occurs with starvation, but may be worse after weight restoration as new hairs enter the growing phase, resting hairs fall out.

325. B. *be able to use symbols to represent reality.* The preoperational stage lasts from about 2 to 6 years of age. During this stage, the child leaves behind preoccupation with sensations and motion and represents the world to him or herself as composed of constant objects. Exploring the environment, manipulating objects, and needing to have an object present to trigger thought are more closely linked to the sensorimotor stage (ages birth to 2). Sophisticated, but inflexible, thought processes are the hallmarks of concrete operations (ages 6 to 12).

326. E. *moderate levels of arousal are best for optimal performance.* The Yerkes-Dodson Law states that excessively high arousal (high anxiety) impedes performance, while low arousal (apathy) fails to provide the necessary motivation to do well.

327. C. *egocentrism,* that is, the inability to see the world from another's point of view. In this classic demonstration, children are presented with a diarama of mountains and asked to describe what a person standing on the other side of the mountains would see. In early developmental stages, children can only respond in terms of what they see and cannot imagine the perspective of the other person. Precausal reasoning sees events or objects that share similar properties as connected. Object permanence or constancy, the capacity to realize that objects out of sight continue to exist, is demonstrated by asking the child to find an object that has been covered. Attaining object constancy is an indication that the child has attained Piaget's preoperational stage.

328. A. *animism.* The child's tendency to understand all objects as living things is actually reinforced by fairy tales and other stories that attribute action and motives to non-human things. Magical thinking is believing that thought equals action, and that the child's desires actually cause events to occur. Autism is a psychiatric condition manifested as an inability to relate to other people, a preference for sameness in the environment, and lack of language development.

329. C. *10,000.* Most of these words are descriptive of things in the child's environment or are used to denote events in the child's life. Children at this age are, however, still mastering some of the finer points of grammar such as tenses.

330. D. *initiative versus guilt.* Trust versus mistrust is most important for the first 2 years of life, as children learn whether or not they can depend on their caretakers. Autonomy versus shame is the time of toilet training, generally encountered between ages 2 and 4. Industry versus inferiority corresponds with the Freudian latency period, ages 6 to 12. During this period children strive to display their competencies to themselves and others. Adolescence, ages 12 to 18, is the time when issues of identity are predominant.

331. C. *meaning of the pain.* A classic study done during World War II showed that soldiers with similar degrees of injury expressed different levels of pain, as measured objectively by how much narcotic they required for relief, depending on the meaning of their injuries. Those for whom the injury meant they would be sent home were in measurably less pain than those who expected to return to combat. Like any other subjective, conscious experience, pain is influenced by how much attention is paid to it, which, in turn, is a factor of what the pain means. The person's general state of morale (hopeful, cheerful, empowered vs. depressed, hopeless, helpless) also influences subjective pain, as shown by the efficacy of treatment for depression in helping people recover from painful states. Every other option presented (degree of tissue injury, availability of narcotics, general fitness, and time of day) may influence pain but was matched between soldier groups. In research terms, these are controlled conditions that highlight the effect of the variable of interest.

332. A. *gender identity* refers to the psychological sense of self. Gender identity is more strongly determined by culture and parental assignment than by the physical genitalia with which the child was born. People with a mismatch between physical gender and psychological identity are termed transsexual. Sex role stereotypes reflect inflexible notions of what constitutes appropriate behaviors for males and females. Sexual orientation refers to the gender of a person's preferred sexual partner, either homosexual or heterosexual. Sex role schemas are mental templates or categories that help provide an understanding of the differences in male and female behaviors.

Parental identification refers to the child's focus on and attachment to parental figures, and is one of the major contributors to gender identity.

333. E. *reductions in infant mortality rates.* Life expectancy at birth is defined as median survival time. Therefore, anything that results in loss of life at a young age has a disproportionate impact on life expectancy. All of the other options are associated with better health and reduced mortality, but occur too late in life to have the degree of impact on life expectancy that infant mortality has.

334. E. *slower rate of metabolism.* All of the other options presented are also naturally operative in any given individual. However, lower metabolic rate and decreased clearance due to poorer liver and kidney function are issues for all elderly. Thus, among the options given, slower metabolic rate is the most important determinant of drug dosages.

335. A. *Alzheimer disease* accounts for 65% of all dementias in the elderly. The patient's age and presentation argues against "normal senility." Loss of memory and failing to recognize family members is not a normal part of the aging process. The gradual onset tends to rule out tumor or stroke. The patient is not reported to be taking other medications, nor is the pattern of cognitive change described consistent with any particular medicine regimen.

336. A. *administer a Mini Mental Status Examination,* which will give specific information about deficit areas. A CAT scan is likely to be normal at this stage. Family members' recollections and a 2-day observation lack structure and systematic data gathering. The WAIS is a test for assessing intelligence, not dementia.

337. C. *eating, bathing, and going to the toilet.* The other activities are frequently performed on a daily basis, but are not included in formal ADL listings and assessment. Ambulating and stair climbing are key components of the SF-36, a frequently used survey to assess the overall health status of people in the general population.

338. B. *balancing life's accomplishments and failures.* Maintaining ego integrity requires that one make reasonable decisions based on a fair appraisal of external life circumstances. The patient presented here has quite a bit of life to look back on. The issue now is does she feel a sense of accomplishment and purpose in this life that will carry herself forward in the coming years? Or does it seem to her that she has wasted life, and has more regrets than successes? Note that in the face of despair at this stage, Erikson's recommended therapeutic intervention is "regression in the service of the ego." This means mentally returning to a previous developmental stage and revisiting previous life-defining decisions. Once these earlier decisions are reviewed, the person can then move forward developmentally with a firmer ego foundation.

339. E. *successful negotiation of transitions.* This implies anticipating the need for change and making adjustments in activities and expectations to accommodate these changes. Accepting change means accepting new roles in both work and personal life, and learning to play these roles well. It is impossible to move through life without experiencing some loss. Coping with these losses and arranging a new life pattern in the face of them is the key to successful development across the lifespan.

340. D. *illustrations of how people interpret bodily signs and symptoms in culturally specific ways.* Entities that are recognized by certain ethnic groups but not others have been studied as folk illnesses or culture-bound syndromes. These entities are physical ailments. Each has a specified etiology, pathophysiology, and treatment. In some situations, they may also be expressions of mental or social distress, which have specific symbolic meanings. These folk illnesses and culture-bound syndromes are not separate categories of diseases but are examples of how all signs and symptoms are culturally interpreted. The use of culturally derived categories is not a sign of ignorance or lack of education.

341. C. *seen as early as age 7 with increases in adrenal steroids.* Increases in adrenal steroids during middle childhood are the biochemical markers for the beginning of the process of puberty. The increase in these adrenal steroids precedes the hormonal changes in estrogen, testosterone, and progesterone seen in both girls and boys during adolescent development.

342. B. *complexity of synaptic connections.* More complex connections provide the neural substrate for increasingly sophisticated behavior and thought patterns. It is not the size of the brain as

registered by head circumference that matters most, but the evolving interconnections within the brain that set the stage for development. It is the interconnections among the neurons, not their shear numbers, that allow for more complex social behavior. The mechanism of neuronal processing does not change nor do new neurotransmittors appear.

343. E. *the emergence of sleep-wake differences.* Sleep patterns, such as length of sleep cycle and differentiation among sleep stages, mature to adult-like patterns between 10 and 13 years of age. Hemispheric differentiation is established during infancy and is a central organizing principle for brain functioning. Function specific activity increases as certain areas of the brain become more adept at specialized tasks. Delta wave activity occurs in the deepest stages of sleep and is never primary in waking brain function. The amount of delta activity actually declines with age; as a result, the deepest stages of sleep do not occur in the elderly. Alpha wave activity suggests a disengagement from external stimuli and is most easily fostered by closing the eyes. As children explore and become more involved in their world, alpha wave activity is likely to decrease.

344. A. *Deficits in executive functions* such as reasoning and decision making. Although ADHD children can be disruptive to teachers in the classroom, they are not more likely to have poor relationships with their peers. Some clinical experience suggests that they may concentrate more on peer relationships to compensate for poorer academic performance. Deficits in attentional mechanisms make processing verbal directions more difficult, not easier. Persons with ADHD show no essential difference on visual discrimination tasks, although they may have difficulty adhering to the instructions of the testing situation. They may show deficits in visual-spatial tracking tasks. ADHD does not make children more susceptible to childhood infectious diseases.

345. B. *evaluate other people in terms of psychological attributes.* Children become less egocentric and are able to see the world from others' point of view as they mature. They are also able to classify these perceived differences and characterize people as having different "personalities." Manipulation of abstract concepts, anticipating the future, predicting in hypothetical situations, and having a personal philosophy are all char-

acteristic of Piaget's stage of formal operations, which generally occurs after age 12.

346. D. *be seen as good.* At his stage of development, being good means following the rules. Knowing and following the rules is likely to garner approval of supervising adults, but also allows the child to generate self-approval by internalizing these standards. The issue here is not avoiding either embarrassment or punishment from others, but achieving a positively valued sense of self. The directions given by the child are the result of trying to adhere to the rules and not the result of a desire to dominate others. The child seeks rules, not to replace the parents, but to please them by being a "good boy."

347. E. *tell Mr. Thomas you will get back in touch with him after you speak with your accountant.* The decision to barter your services raises a host of legal and financial questions that vary from state to state. Major issues to consider relate to IRS and CMS regulations, fair value of goods and services, and the changed legal and interpersonal nature of the physician-patient relationship when the physician becomes an "employer" of the patient. While bartering is becoming a more frequent occurrence, the relationship, malpractice, and regulatory issues require careful consideration. Understanding the financial, contractual, and legal ramifications of entering into this type of arrangement is critical.

348. D. *structured games and sports.* Between 6 and 12 years of age, play becomes truly interactive. To allow this interaction, children need structures and rules to govern their increasingly elaborate play. Competency is key. Children want to participate and show what they can do. To be relegated to the sidelines as one just watching is often taken as a sign of social shame. Same-gender play is generally preferred by both sexes. This is not a time for fantasy, but a time for doing in reality, a time for demonstrating that the child can make things happen. Children at this age also have preferred playmates and develop semi-exclusive play groups. Children do not seek to play with just anyone, but crave the company of their "friends."

349. A. *encouraged to continue with school activities such as team sports and physical education.* The child has a medical condition, but one that, with proper attention, need not limit his quality of life. To encourage the child's withdrawal

from normal activities risks stigmatizing him and reducing his chances of developing and maintaining supportive peer friendships. There is absolutely no reason for the child to take on the sick role and seek to be exempted from regular activities. To label the child as "unfit" risks harming him more than the disease will by itself. With proper management, the child can live a full, happy life without an increase in school absences or exemption from family chores.

350. C. *physical changes can be predicted from social and interpersonal factors.* People who have and enjoy social relationships early in life show less physical decline later in life. The exact reasons for this finding are unclear. It may be that generally healthy people have more interpersonal relationships, or that these relationships actually support physiological functioning over time, or that the presence of social relationships serves to buffer stressful life events, and so reduce physiological strain. Most individuals report signs of aging beginning in their 40s. However, different people manifest signs of aging at different times. Wrinkles and physical decline occur across a wide variety of ages. Women do not age sooner than men. In fact, life expectancy for women is, on average, 15 years longer than that for men.

351. A. *Conflict theory – adaptation.* The hallmark of this situation is conflict about change. The question is whether or not the system will adapt to the new request, or will seek to maintain its current routine. Resolution will likely depend on the power of external influences and the perception of possible gains within the hospital organization.

352. C. *the female menstrual cycle begins to change during the 30s and 40s,* the beginning of the process that culminates in menopause. Men continue to produce sperm, although in declining quantity, throughout their lives. Sexual desire in males is neither the cause nor consequence of sperm production. Recent research has found no differences in the age of onset of menopause in different ethnic or racial groups. The number of children a couple has is not related to sexual activity in the elderly.

353. A. *body dysmorphic disorder.* Body dysmorphic disorder connotes undue preoccupation with some trivial or imagined physical defect. By definition, preoccupation with weight specifically is

excluded. Everyone evaluates personal appearance differently from how others perceive it. In body dysmorphic disorder, the person's distorted image of a body part must cause distress and impair function. Social phobia may be associated with similar avoidance of social situations, but the root is fear of ridicule, humiliation, or rejection. Factitious disorder describes someone who induces illness in order to obtain the benefits of the sick role to gratify unconscious needs for attention, sympathy, and relief from responsibility. Malingering involves feigning illness for conscious secondary gain, such as receiving opiates, escaping military duty, receiving compensation, or avoiding prison. Civilian malingerers may have antisocial personality traits. Delusional disorder typically involves more complex and pervasive false beliefs than preoccupation with a single physical trait. Delusions usually relate to interpersonal factors rather than physical ones, and the condition is typically associated with the seeking of medical care.

354. B. e*stablish that the email link is secure.* The Health Insurance Portability and Accountability Act (HIPAA) requires that all protected health information (PHI) sent via email be secure. Home systems may not be secure. While timeliness, keeping emails brief, and transmitting the minimum information necessary are important components of physician-patient correspondence, they are not as important as the physician's responsibility to first ensure that PHI is protected. At the conclusion of the exchange, all correspondence should be placed in the patient's medical record.

355. B. *sexual activity for both genders is most frequent in the 20s and declines with age.* However, this does not mean that sexual activity is confined to these ages. Sexual desire and arousal are experienced by many elderly people. The best predictor of whether an elderly person is having sexual relations is the availability of a partner, making marital status a good predictor for both genders. The University of Chicago study found that married people have more sex than single people. Although the sexual peak can differ for different women, most women report a peak in their 30s. The relationship between sexual activity and socioeconomic status (SES) is not linear. More sexual activity seems to occur in lower and very high SES groups.

356. D. *divorce is most common between the ages of 30 and 45.* Couples who marry young are at higher

risk for divorce. More than 50% of adults re-marry within 5 years after becoming divorced. Divorced people of any age tend to remarry, producing so-called "serial monogamy." Some-one who is divorced once is more likely to get divorced again.

357. D. *most adult children and their parents have positive feelings about each other.* Older parents continue to be sources of help and advice for their adult children, and children of the elderly constitute their major support system during times of illness or other personal crises. Once they have their own children, adults tend to look at their parents differently, with a new understanding of the problems and dilemmas of parenthood. Feelings of dependency on parents continue throughout the lifespan, although the behaviors which express this dependency change over time. Child-parent, not sibling, relationships tend to hold the extended family together and provide a shared identity among family members even into middle age.

358. C. *10%.* One in ten children in the US is born prematurely. The risk for prematurity is higher in African American mothers, teenage mothers, mothers from lower socioeconomic groups, and mothers who smoke.

359. E. *90%.* Some of the most dramatic advances in medicine at the end of the 20th century have been in the area of neonatal intensive care. Low birth weight infants who would have faced certain death in the 1960s and 1970s now routinely survive.

360. B. *25%.* Although survival rates for premature infants have improved dramatically over the past few decades, the child who survives is at higher risk of disabilities than a full-term infant. Long-term respiratory difficulties are common, as are a host of dysfunctions due to hypoxia.

361. A. *Alcohol.* Fetal alcohol syndrome is the leading prenatal cause of mental retardation. Convincing women who are pregnant, or are likely to become pregnant, to avoid alcohol consumption is the simplest known method for reducing the risk for retardation. Opiate (e.g., heroin, methadone) usage is associated with diffuse neurodevelopmental deficits, but not with mental retardation in particular. Women who smoke have a harder time becoming pregnant in the first place, and if they continue smoking after the child is born, increase the child's risk

for asthma and sudden infant death syndrome (SIDS). Children of mothers who use cocaine may evidence withdrawal reactions following birth. Lithium carbonate, used to treat bipolar disorder, can cause Epstein's anomaly, a cardiac malformation of the tricuspid valve.

362. D. *Prolactin.* Parkinson disease is characterized by reduced levels of dopamine in the substantia nigra. A number of treatments, including L-dopa, are available. Dopamine is a prolactin-inhibiting factor. Thus, prolactin levels can serve as a rough indicator of overall dopamine levels in the brain. Acetylcholine is more closely associated with Alzheimer dementia. Norepinephrine is linked to mood disorders. Serotonin is implicated in a wide variety of disorders including mood disorders, anxiety, and schizophrenia. Lower levels of GABA are associated with anxiety disorders.

363. A. *Decreased blocker cyclic-AMP response element binding protein activity.* Rolipram in coffee inhibits blocker CREB that allows cramming. Serotonin activity is linked to long-term memories, but it is the pulsed application of serotonin, not the absolute amount, that fosters long-term memory. Glutamate in the hippocampus does allow for formation of long-term memories, but coffee does not act directly on glutamate. Prolactin is linked to sexual activity, not memory. The reticular activating system is important in regulating the sleep-wake cycle and general motivation, but not directly in memory acquisition or retention.

364. B. *5-HT2* activity works to modify appetite by means of phosphoinositide, a secondary messenger. Stimulation of the 5-HT1 receptors causes contraction of the gastrointestional system and inhibits central nervous system activity. The action of the 5-HT3 receptors is not clear at this time. Stimulation of the 5-HT4 receptors increases adenylate cyclase activity. The answer of "all of the above" is incorrect because the action on appetite is specific to the 5-HT2 receptor.

365. D. *Symbolic interaction – latent pattern maintenance.* Communication is possible when actions have a common meaning within a shared frame of reference. In this case, the assumptions about the meaning of the action (rolling the patient over) were different. The nurses rolled the patient over to prevent bedsores, but the action prevented the patient from sleeping

and communicated to the patient that sleeping would be fatal. Structural functional analysis examines how organizational and situational components work to allow the attainment of specific ends. Conflict theory examines the social structures and processes that emerge as the result of competition for dominance and other scarce resources. Integration maps the process by which the diverse components of a system are able to function together as a whole. Implicit theory refers to the subjective theory of action that organizes and gives meaning to the world in which a person moves.

366. C. *Muscarinic.* The vignette presents a patient with symptoms of anticholinergic intoxication, a result of antagonism of the muscarinic receptors. Antagonism of histamine receptors is linked to central nervous system effects. Antagonism of the dopamine receptors produces anti-psychotic effects. Antagonism of norepinephrine receptors produces an anti-depressant effect. Antagonism of the prolactin receptors results in disruptions of sexual functioning.

367. C. *Have her breathe into an airsickness bag* as the most readily available way to control her hyperventilation and reduce the "air hunger" that is causing her gasping for breath. A panic attack is an overwhelming event that cannot be controlled by simply trying to calm a person down or telling a story. Her acute symptoms must be addressed before trying to gather information about the frequency of attacks. Giving the woman a hard candy is unlikely to have an effect on the panic attack and might actually put her at risk for choking.

368. C. *delays in learning to crawl.* Infants who sleep on their stomach have a risk of SIDS two to three times that of infants who sleep on their back. Educating parents to place their infants to sleep on their back has been key to reducing the incidence of SIDS. However, children who spend more time on their back have less practice lifting and balancing themselves and, therefore, show delays in learning to crawl, which normally occurs at about 7 to 9 months. Speech and social smile are not delayed by placing infants on their back, because this position allows for a broader visual field and may even facilitate these developmental tasks. Auditory discrimination has no known relationship to sleeping position. Thumb-sucking behavior occurs with relatively equal frequency whether the child is placed on the stomach or on the back.

369. C. *Fine hair on the back and arms,* or lanugo. The girl presented in the vignette most likely is suffering from anorexia nervosa. She is 20% below normal body weight for her height and within the usual age range for onset. Another classic sign is amenorrhea. Note that binge and purge behavior, a classic sign of bulimia, also occurs in about 50% of all anorexics. Sadness suggests the possibility of depression, a common accompaniment to anorexia nervosa. Anorexia is not consistently linked to rashes, loss of tendon reflexes, heart rate, or light sensitivity. However, in the severest forms of the illness, idiosyncratic medical complications, such as bradycardia, may appear.

370. E. *somatization disorder.* Somatization is a term that generally connotes the expression of distress in physical rather than psychological terms. Somatization disorder describes a long-standing pattern of unexplained or excessively distressing physical symptoms in four domains: neurological, sexual, gastrointestinal, and pain. If a person develops fewer than the required criterion symptoms or if the symptoms start after age 18, then the diagnosis would be Somatoform Disorder, NOS. While somatization disorder, rigorously defined, is a reliable diagnosis, it does not take into account our developing understanding of the neurophysiology of subjective distress. A proposed diagnosis that more closely relates to the phenomenon is "multiple unexplained physical symptoms" or MUPS. This diagnosis is not in the current DSM. How we experience our bodies is highly influenced by the balance between central norepinephrine, histamine, interleukins, acetylcholine, dopamine, and endogenous opiates, which are, in turn, regulated by serotonin, hypothalamic, and pituitary hormones, and other neurological factors. The thresholds and stability of these neurological processes are, in turn, affected (sensitized or desensitized) by prior experience and elements of the current environment. Attributing somatic distress entirely to psychological processes is especially easy to do when a patient is convinced of an unproven cause for the distress. Patients are "accused" of somaticizing when, in fact, they and their physicians lack a common language and a common framework for understanding the way in which they experience bodily sensations. There are many reasons people avoid social situations and cannot fill normal social expectations. Avoidant personality is only diagnosed if the patient expresses a desire for relationships but avoids

them for fear of consequences such as rejection, humiliation, or exploitation. Malingering is often invoked to explain why a distressed person with no objective signs of disease seeks attention, but it cannot be diagnosed without evidence the person is not actually in distress (or has purposefully inflicted distress) and is seeking secondary gain. Obsessive-compulsive disorder involves intrusive thoughts about contamination, danger, being harmed or doing harm to others associated with compulsions to try to control these thoughts. Panic disorder does present with multiple somatic complaints, but these come in acute bursts and follow a typical pattern related to peripheral autonomic arousal (pounding heart, air hunger, dizziness, restlessness) and are associated with overestimation of how dangerous the symptoms are.

371. E. *Licensing* is required in order to be granted legal permission to deliver clinical care. Certification recognizes achievement of a higher standard of competency by a professional organization, but is not required for practice. Practitioners can choose to participate in whichever insurance plans they like (or none at all). This includes both Medicaid and Medicare. Health care practitioners can also charge fees as they see fit, and may, for example, set up different payment systems for patients paying out-of-pocket.

Contributors

Bennett, Forrest C., MD
(Selected Theories of Development; The Fetus, Newborn, and Infant; Toddlerhood and the Preschool Years)
Professor of Pediatrics
Department of Pediatrics
University of Washington School of Medicine
Seattle, WA

Borkan, Jeffrey M., MD, PhD
(Culture and Ethnicity)
Professor and Chair,
Department of Family Medicine
Brown Medical School
Memorial Hospital of Rhode Island
Pawtucket, RI

Borson, Soo, MD
(Geriatric Health and Successful Aging)
Professor and Director of the Memory Disorders
Clinic
Department of Psychiatry and Behavioral
Sciences
University of Washington School of Medicine
Seattle, WA

Botelho, Richard, BMedSci, BMBS
(Motivating Health Behavior)
Professor of Family Medicine (ret)
University of Rochester School of Medicine
Rochester, NY

Calderón, José L., MD
(Health Literacy)
Associate Professor
Medical Sciences Institute
Charles Drew University of Medicine and Science
Los Angeles, CA

Carr, John E., PhD
(Co-Editor; *Cognition and Social Interaction; Emotion and Learning; Evolving Models of Health Care; Predisposition; Principles of Psychotherapy; Stress, Adaptation and Stress Disorders; The Medical Encounter and Clinical Decision Making*)
Professor emeritus

Departments of Psychiatry & Behavioral Sciences
and Psychology
University of Washington School of Medicine
Seattle, WA

Castellani, Brian, PhD
(Theories of Social Relations)
Associate Professor, Department of Sociology
Kent State University
Ashtabula, OH

Catalanotti, Jillian S., MD, MPH
(The U.S. Health Care System)
Assistant Professor of Medicine
Assistant Professor of Health Policy
The George Washington University
Washington, DC

Chapman, Alexander L., PhD, RPsych
(Suicide)
Associate Professor of Psychology and
Associate Chair (Graduate), Psychology
Department
Simon Fraser University
Burnaby, BC, Canada

Cook, Stephen R., MD, MPH
(Obesity)
Assistant Professor of Pediatrics
Center for Community Health
Golisano Children's Hospital
University of Rochester Medical Center
Rochester, NY

Culhane-Pera, Kathleen A., MD, MA
(Culture and Ethnicity)
Adjunct Professor of Family Medicine
Brown Medical School
West Side Community Health Services
St. Paul, MN

Dansie, Elizabeth J., PhD
(Biostatistics)
Acting Instructor and Research Fellow
University of Washington
Seattle, WA

Daugherty, Steven R., PhD
(Epidemiology; Biostatistics; Review Examination)
Director of Education and Testing
Kaplan Medical
Adjunct Professor
Department of Psychology
Rush University Medical Center
Chicago, IL

Davis, Barbara J., PhD
(Nutrition, Metabolism, and Feeding Disorders)
Associate Professor of Neurobiology and
Anatomy
University of Rochester School of Medixcine
Rochester, NY

Doerr, Hans O., PhD
(Selected Theories of Development)
Professor emeritus, Department of Psychiatry &
Behavioral Sciences
University of Washington School of Medicine
Seattle, WA

Eklund, Nancy, MD
(Sexuality and Sexual Disorders)
Volunteer Faculty, Family Medicine
Miller School of Medicine
University of Miami
Miami, FL
and
Founder and Medical Director
Miami Center for Holistic Healing
Miami, FL

Evans, Kristin A., MS
(Obesity)
Doctoral Fellow
Department of Community and Preventive Medicine
University of Rochester Medical Center
Rochester, NY

Farrow, James A. H., MD
(The Adult Years)
Professor, of Pediatrics and Medicine
Executive Director, Student Health Services
Tulane University
New Orleans, LA

Frank, Julia B., MD
(Associate Editor; *Adjustment Disorders,
Bereavement, and Demoralization; Anxiety
Disorders and Dissociative Disorders; Delirium*

*and Secondary Syndromes; Dementia; Evolving
Models of Health Care; Introduction to
Psychopathology; Major Mood Disorders; The
Nervous System; Personality and Impulse Control
Disorders; Pharmacological Interventions
for Psychiatric Disorders; Principles of
Psychotherapy; Somatization and Somatoform
Disorders; The Psychiatric Evaluation; Review
Examination*)
Associate Professor and Director of Medical
Student Education in Psychiatry
George Washington University School of
Medicine and Health Sciences
Washington, DC

Gómez, Maria Fernanda, MD
(Substance Abuse)
Associate Professor of Clinical Psychiatry and
Behavioral Sciences
Associate Director, Psychosomatic Medicine
Albert Einstein College of Medicine of Yeshiva
University
Montefiore Medical Center
Bronx, NY

Hafferty, Frederic W., PhD
(Theories of Social Relations)
Professor of Medical Education
Mayo Clinic
Rochester, MN

Haldeman, Douglas C., PhD
*(Health Care Issues Facing Gay, Lesbian,
Bisexual, and Transgender Individuals)*
Independent Practice
Seattle, WA

Hosokawa, Michael C., EdD
*(Health Care in Minority and Majority
Populations; Social Behavior and Groups)*
Professor, Department of Family and Community
Medicine
Director of Graduate Studies and Faculty
Development
Department of Family and Community Medicine
University of Missouri School of Medicine
Columbia, MO

Houghtalen, Rory P., MD
*(Anxiety Disorders and Dissociative Disorders;
Major Mood Disorders;Schizophrenia and Other
Psychotic Disorders)*

Medical Director, Education and Mental
Ambulatory Services
Unity Health System
Clinical Associate Professor of Psychiatry
University of Rochester School of Medicine
Rochester, NY

Jean-Louis, Girardin, PhD
(Chronobiology and Sleep Disorders)
Associate Professor, Department of Medicine
SUNY Downstate Medical Center
Brooklyn, NY

Kodish, Ian M., MD, PhD
(The Nervous System)
Acting Assistant Professor
Center for Child Health, Behavior, and
Development
University of Washington School of Medicine
Seattle, WA

Kreipe, Richard E., MD
(Eating Disorders)
Professor of Pediatrics
Medical Director, Western New York
Comprehensive Care Center for Eating Disorders
Golisano Children's Hospital
University of Rochester School of Medicine
Rochester, NY

Larsen, Lars C., MD
*(The Medical Encounter and Clinical Decision
Making; The Physician-Patient Relationship)*
Professor of Family Medicine and Vice Chair for
Academic Affairs
Department of Family Medicine
Brody School of Medicine and East Carolina
University
Greenville, NC

Layden, Brianne K., BA
(Suicide)
Graduate Student
Psychology Department
Simon Fraser University
Burnaby, BC, Canada

Lenahan, Patricia M., LCSW, LMFT, BCETS
(Geriatric Health and Successful Aging)
Adjunct Lecturer
University of Southern California School of
Social Work

University of California Irvine
Santa Ana, CA

Lillrank, Sonja M., MD, PhD
(Schizophrenia and Other Psychotic Disorders)
Clinical Assistant Professor of Psychiatry and
Behavioral Sciences
George Washington University School of Medicine
and Health Sciences
Washington, DC

Maiuro, Roland D., PhD
(Interpersonal Violence)
Senior Research Scientist
Moss Rehabilitation Research Institute
Albert Einstein Health Care Network
Seattle, WA

Martell, Christopher R., PhD
*(Health Care Issues Facing Gay, Lesbian,
Bisexual, and Transgender Individuals)*
Clinical Associate Professor
Department of Psychiatry & Behavioral Sciences
University of Washington School of Medicine
Seattle, WA

McBride, J. LeBron, PhD, MPH
(The Family)
Director of Behavioral Medicine
Floyd Medical Center
Associate Clinical Professor
Mercer University School of Medicine
Macon, GA

McCauley, Elizabeth, PhD
(The School Years)
Professor, Psychiatry & Behavioral Sciences
University of Washington School of Medicine
Seattle Children's Hospital
Seattle, WA

McClafferty, Hilary H., MD
(Complementary and Integrative Medicine)
Clinical Assistant Professor of Medicine
Assistant Fellowship Director
Arizona Center for Integrative Medicine
University of Arizona Health Sciences Center
Tuscon, AZ

McGinnis, Charlotte, MA
(Suicide)
Simon Fraser University
Burnaby, BC, Canada

McGowen, K. Ramsey, PhD
(Poverty and Homelessness)
Professor and Director of Medical Student
Education in Psychiatry
Department of Psychiatry and Behavioral
Sciences
East Tenessee State University
Johnson City, TN

Myers, Emily F., MD
*(Selected Theories of Development; The Fetus,
Newborn, and Infant;Toddlerhood and the
Preschool Years)*
Fellow in Neurodevelopmental-Behavioral
Pediatrics
University of Washington School of Medicine
Seattle Children's Hospital
Seattle, WA

Nunes, João V., MD
(Associate Editor; *Chronobiology and Sleep
Disorders; Disorders of Infancy, Childhood, and
Adolescence; Evolving Models of Health Care;
The Nervous System; Predisposition; Substance
Abuse*)
Associate Medical Professor, Physiology and
Pharmacology
Chairman, Department of Behavioral Medicine
Sophie Davis School of Biomedical Education
The City College of New York
New York, NY

Pantalone, David, PhD
*(Health Care Issues Facing Gay, Lesbian,
Bisexual, and Transgender Individuals)*
Assistant Professor of Psychology, Suffolk
University
Behavioral Scientist, The Fenway Institute
Boston, MA

Pleak, Richard R., MD
*(Disorders of Infancy, Childhood, and
Adolescence)*
Associate Professor of Clinical Psychiatry &
Behavioral Sciences,
Director of Education & Training, Child &
Adolescent Psychiatry
Hofstra North Shore-LIJ Medical Center
Albert Einstein College of Medicine
Glen Oaks, NY

Posner, Michael I., PhD
(Brain Networks in Health and Illness)
Professor emeritus of Psychology
Department of Psychology
University of Oregon
Eugene, OR

Quill, Timothy E., MD
(Palliative Care)
Professor of Medicine, Psychiatry, and Medical
Humanities
University of Rochester School of Medicine
Rochester, NY

Ragnauth, Andre K., PhD
(Substance Abuse)
Assistant Medical Professor
Department of Physiology, Pharmacology, and
Neuroscience
Sophie Davis School of Biomedical Education
The City College of New York
New York, NY

Rothbart, Mary K., PhD
(Brain Networks in Health and Illness)
Adjunct Professor of Psychology in Psychiatry
Weill Medical College of Cornell University
New York, NY
Professor of Psychology
University of Oregon
Eugene, OR

Russo, Dennis C., PhD
*(The Medical Encounter and Clinical Decision
Making; The Physician-Patient Relationship)*
Clinical Professor of Family Medicine and
Psychology
Head, Behavioral Medicine
Department of Family Medicine
Brody School of Medicine and East Carolina
University
Greenville, NC

Sahler, Olle Jane Z., MD
(Co-Editor; *Complementary and Integrative
Medicine; Evolving Models of Health Care;
Review Examination*)
Professor of Pediatrics, Psychiatry, Medical
Humanities, and Oncology
University of Rochester School of Medicine
Rochester, NY

Medical Consultant, Integrated Complementary Medicine Program
ThompsonHealth, Inc.
Canandaigua, NY

Samenow, Charles P., MD, MPH
(Sexuality and Sexual Disorders; Physician Health, Impairment, and Misconduct)
Assistant Professor, Department of Psychiatry and Behavioral Sciences
George Washington University School of Medicine
Washington, DC

Seitz, Frank C., PhD
(The Medical Encounter and Clinical Decision Making)
Professor, Department of Psychiatry & Behavioral Sciences
University of Washington School of Medicine
Seattle, WA

Shah, Mindy S., MD
(Palliative Care)
Clinical Instructor in Medicine
University of Rochester School of Medicine
Co-Director, Division of Palliative Care
Unity Hospital
Rochester, NY

Simeone, Rachel E.
(Eating Disorders)
Undergraduate Student
University of Rochester
Rochester, NY

Smith, Sandra A., PhD, MPH
(Health Literacy)
Director, Center for Health Literacy Promotion
Clinical Faculty, Department of Heath Services
School of Public Health & Community Medicine
University of Washington
Seattle, WA

Spike, Jeffrey P., PhD
(Ethical and Legal Issues in Patient Care)
Professor, McGovern Center for Humanities and Ethics
Director, Campus-Wide Ethics Program
UT Health (formerly, The University of Texas Academic Health Science Center at Houston)
Houston, TX

Starr, Taylor B., DO, MPH
(Eating Disorders)
Instructor and Fellow in Adolescent Medicine
University of Rochester School of Medicine
Rochester, NY

Sugg, Nancy K., MD, MPH
(Interpersonal Violence)
Associate Professor of Medicine
University of Washington School of Medicine
Seattle, WA

Swenson, Amanda, MD, MSPH
(Health Care in Minority and Majority Populations)
Assistant Professor of Clinical Family Medicine
Department of Family and Community Medicine
University of Missouri School of Medicine
Columbia, MO

Viola, Joseph C., PhD
(Personality and Impulse Control Disorders)
Assistant Professor of Clinical Psychology
Professional Psychology Program
George Washington University
Washington, DC

Vitaliano, Peter P., PhD, MS
(Epidemiology; Stress, Adaptation, and Stress Disorders)
Professor of Psychiatry & Behavioral Sciences, and Psychology
University of Washington School of Medicine
Seattle, WA

Von Gizycki, Hans J., PhD
(Chronobiology and Sleep Disorders)
Assistant Professor
SUNY Downstate Medical Center
Brooklyn, NY

Walters, Kristy N., MA
(Suicide)
Graduate Student
Psychology Department
Simon Fraser University
Burnaby, BC, Canada

Zemenides, Peter D., MD
(Delirium and Secondary Syndromes)
Resident in Psychiatry

George Washington University School of
Medicine and Health Sciences
Washington, DC

Zigler, Rachel E., MD
(Nutrition, Metabolism and Feeding Disorders)
University of Rochester School of Medicine
Rochester, NY

Zizi, Ferdinand, MBA
(Chronobiology and Sleep Disorders)
Clinical Instructor, Department of Health Sciences
SUNY Downstate Medical Center
Brooklyn, NY

Subject Index

A

abuse
- elder 184, 215
- emotional 213
- intimate partner 214
- physical 212
- psychological/emotional 212
- sexual 213
- sibling 213
- social/environmental 212
access to care 159
accommodation 85
accreditation 244
acculturation 150, 156
accurate empathy 287
acetylcholine 336
action potential 25
acupressure 257
acupuncture 257
acute stress disorder 366
acute stress response 53
adherence 290
adjustment disorders 348
adolescence 107
adoption studies 17
adrenocorticotropic hormone 72
advance directives 276, 278
advanced sleep phase syndrome 48
affect 323
affective disorder 373
affiliation 77
African American 155
Alaska Native 155
alcoholism 118
alertness 74
allopathic medicine 7
allostasis 52
allostasis overload 52
allow natural death (AND) 279
altered mental status 359
Alzheimer disease (AD) 118, 181, 352
amygdala 27, 54
analysis of variance (ANOVA) 422

anorexia nervosa 41, 199
anterior-lateral pathway 27
anticipatory anxiety 58
anticipatory grief 272
antidepressants 335
antipsychotics 335, 363
- atypical 336
- typical 336
antisocial personality disorder 402
anxiety 118, 183
- separation 96
- stranger 96
anxiety disorders 365
anxiolytics 335
Apgar score 94
aphasia 325
apoptosis 57
appraisal 60
apraxia 325
arborization 22
Asperger disorder 400
assimilation 85
assisted living facility 126
association area
- multimodal sensory 29
- somatosensory unimodal 29
attachment 77, 96, 349
attention 74
attention-deficit/hyperactivity disorder 401
attention network 33
auditory hallucinations 382
autism spectrum disorder 399, 400
autonomic nervous system 26, 55, 344, 365
autonomy 100, 102, 125
avoidant personality disorder 366

B

Ballard Neonatal Examination 95
basal ganglia 28, 336
behavior
- reflexive 68
behavioral therapy 330

behavior modification 66
beneficence 274
benzodiazepines 369
bereavement 273, 349
beta-adrenergic blocking agents 369
bias 135, 136
binge eating disorder 199
biofeedback 71
biologic set points 40
biomedical model 7
biomedicine 7, 151
biopsychosocial model 8, 261, 320
biostatistics 416
biphasic protest-despair response 77
bipolar disorders 339, 373, 374
bisexual 167
body image 107, 175
body mass index 193
bonding 18, 68, 96
borderline personality disorder 332
boundaries 122
brain death 277
brain networks 24
brainstem 26
Brazelton Neonatal Behavioral Assessment Scale 95
brief psychotic disorder 386
Broca's speech area 28
bulimia nervosa 199
burnout 309

C

capacity for decision making 275
caregiver burnout 129
case-control study 413
causes of death 157
central nervous system 26
central sleep apnea syndrome 49
central tendency 416
cerebellum 27
cerebral cortex 27
cerebral hemisphere 27
certification 244

chemical structure 335
Cheyne-Stokes respiration 50
childhood disintegrative disorder
    401
childhood-onset fluency disorder
    399
child maltreatment 213
chiropractic 257
chronic motor or vocal tic disorder
    403
chronobiology 44
circadian oscillator 47
circadian rhythm 44
circadian rhythm disorders 47
client-centered therapy 331
climacteric 115
clinical equipoise 281
Cluster A 389
Cluster B 389
Cluster C 389
Code of Hammurabi 6
cognitions 331
cognitive behavioral therapy (CBT)
    72, 331, 346, 368, 378
cognitive development
– adolescence 108
– infancy 96
– late life 118
– middle age 115
– middle childhood 105
– preschool 101
– toddler 99
– young adult 112
cognitive distortions 368
cognitive function 31
cognitive restructuring 71
cognitive style 76
cognitive therapy 331
cohesion 122
cohort study 412
coma 277
comfort care 279
communication 74, 79
compensation 86
complementary and alternative
    medicine 254
concept formation 74, 75
concrete operational stage 105
conditioning
– aversive 70
– classical 69

– operant 69
conditioning therapy 70
conduct disorder 402
confidence interval 417
conflict theory 142
connectivity 32
consciousness 74
conservation 86, 105
contingency management 70
continuity of care 244
contraception 110, 163
conversion 346
coping skills 60
corpus callosum 28, 29
cortex
– orbito-frontal 28
– prefrontal 28
– premotor 28
– primary motor 28
– primary somatosensory 29
– ventromedial prefrontal 28
countertransference 287
critical periods 18, 24, 68
cross-fostering studies 17
cross-sectional study 413
cultural competence 146
cultural humility 146
cultural mapping 80
cultural sensitivity 135
culture 134
culture-bound syndromes 147
custodial care 126

D

data
– objective 294
– subjective 294
default mode network 33
defense mechanisms 76
delayed sleep phase syndrome 48
delirium 271, 325, 359
delivering bad news 265
delusional disorders 386
delusions 324, 382
dementia 118, 352
demoralization 350
denial 77
Department of Health and Human
    Services 243

depression 59, 110, 118, 183
depressive episodes 339
despair 119
development
– coordination disorder 399
– disorders 396
– milestones 396
– trajectories 109
Diagnostic and Statistical Manual
    of Mental Disorders 317
dialectical behavior therapy 332,
    372, 392
diathesis 19
diathesis-stress model 228
diencephalon 26
dieting 201
diffusion 25
disease 5
disinhibited social engagement
    disorder 405
disorder of written expression 398
dissociation 369
dissociative identity disorder 371
divorce 127
DNA code 15
DNA methylation 15
doctrine of double effect 279
do-not-intubate (DNI) 267
do-not-resuscitate (DNR) 267, 278
dopamine 41
dopamine receptors 336
dopaminergics 335
dorsal column-medial leminiscal
    pathway 27
dorsal prefrontal association area
    28
dual acting antidepressants 369
dyscalculia 398
dyslexia 397
dyspareunia 169
dysthymic disorder 374

E

ego 87
egocentrism 100
ego integrity 119
ejaculation, rapid 169
electroacupuncture 257
Emancipated Minor Doctrine 276
emancipated minors 129

Emergency Medical Treatment and Active Labor Act 249
emotional regulation 109
empathy 78
empty nest 116, 125
encopresis 403
endogenous reward system 69
energy homeostasis 40
Engel, George 8, 320
entrainment 44
enuresis 404
enzymatic degradation 25
epidemiology 416
epigenetic factors 15
equianalgesic dose 270
erectile dysfunction 167
Erikson, Erik 87, 105
error (statistical)
– Type I 419
– Type II 419
estradiol 107
ethnic identity 150
ethnomedicine 7
euchromatin 16
euthanasia
– involuntary 280
– voluntary 280
evolution 22
exchange theory 143
executive function 325
executive functions 9, 24
executive loop 28
explanatory model 5, 149, 289
exposure
– imaginal 71
– interoceptive 71
– in vivo 72
exposure therapy 71
expressive language 99, 398
expressive language disorder 398

F

family 121
– blended 122
– extended 121
– life cycle 123
– nuclear 121
– of origin 122
– of procreation 122
– risk studies 17

– same-sex 122
– therapy 129
Federally Qualified Health Center 249
first-degree relatives 17
Fisher's exact test 421
folk healers 149
folk illnesses 147
follicle-stimulating hormone (FSH) 107
Folstein Mini Mental State Examination (MMSE) 325
forebrain 26
formal operations 108, 112
FoxP2 gene 79
Freud, Sigmund 87, 320
frontal eye field 28
frontal lobe 28, 217
full-term infant 92
functional brain network 32
futility 278

G

Galen 7
Gamblers Anonymous 394
game theory 143
Gaussian curve 416
gender 102, 167
gender dysphoria 167
gender identity 97, 101
gene-environment interaction 10, 58
gene expression 15
gene oscillation 44
gene promoter region 15
General Adaptation Syndrome (GAS) 52
generalized anxiety disorder 367
generalized other 141
generativity 116
genetic-environmental-developmental interaction) 34
genetic influence 33
genetic vulnerability 200
genogram 123
genotype 15
Gesell, Arnold 88
Gestalt therapy 330
ghrelin 42
glial cells 24

glutamate 68, 339
gonadotropin-releasing hormone (GnRH) 107
Good Samaritan Law 275
grief 272, 349
– anticipatory 349
– complicated 272, 349
groups
– primary 133
– secondary 133
growth spurt 107
gut hormone 40

H

hallucinations 325
harm reduction 6, 340
harm reduction programs 210
health 5
health care proxy 277
health care system 243
Health Insurance Portability and Accountability Act (HIPAA) 287
health literacy 237
health maintenance organizations 245
helplessness
– learned 59
hemispheric dominance 29
heritability 17
hierarchy of resort 150
hindbrain 26
hippocampus 27, 54
Hippocrates 7
Hippocratic Oath 285
Hispanic 155
histone modification 15
Holmes and Rahe 60
home hospice 264
homelessness 223
homeostasis 7, 10, 52, 140, 141, 373
homosexuality 167
hormonal changes 104
hospice 264
hospice care 188, 279
hypersexuality 169
hypnosis 346, 369, 372
hypnotic agents 363
hypoactive sexual desire 167

hypomania 339, 373
hypothalamus 26, 39, 217
hypothalamus-pituitary-adrenal (HPA) axis 26, 54, 365
hypothesis formation 86

I

id 87
identity formation 109
illicit drugs 110
illness 5
illusions 324
impairment 308
implicit theory 140
imprinting 18, 68
impulse control disorders 392
incentive modification 66
incest 171, 213
incidence 409
infant mortality 157
informed assent 286
informed consent 274, 275, 286
infradian rhythm 44
insomnia 50
integrated sciences model 10, 225, 319
integrative medicine 255
intellectual disability 396
intellectualization 77
intelligence 74, 75
intermittent explosive disorder 392
internal capsule 26
International Statistical Classification of Diseases and Related Health Problems 317
interpersonal psychotherapy (IPT) 331, 378
interpersonal violence 177
intersex 178
intimacy 113
intimate relationship 109
isolation 113

J

jet lag 47
joint attention 100
justice 274

K

kleptomania 393
Kohlberg, Lawrence 89
Kraepelin, Emil 320

L

language 74, 96
language development
– infancy 96
– preschool 101
– toddler 99
language impairment 398
Latchkey children 126
Law of Effect 69
LEARN 153
learned helplessness 216
learning
– explicit 67
– implicit 67
– one-trial 68
– social 69, 78
learning disability 398
legal custody 128
lemniscal system 27
leptin 40, 42
licensing 244
life events 60
life expectancy 157
lifestyle 6
limbic lobe 28
limbic loop 28
limbic system 26, 68, 323
linkage mapping 17
literacy 235
living will 277, 278
locus of control 20
long-term care 187
long-term memory 99
long-term potentiation (LTP) effect 68
loss 118
luteinizing hormone (LH) 107

M

macrocephaly 92
major depressive disorder 374
major depressive episode 373
malpractice 274

managed care plans 245
mania 336, 339, 373
Mann-Whitney U test 423
massage therapy 260
masturbation 110
matched-pairs *t*-test 423
maternal-fetal infections 93
mathematics disorder 398
Mature Minor Doctrine 276
McNemar's test 421
median forebrain bundle 70
Medicaid 246, 248
Medicare 246, 247
medicine
– psychosomatic 8
membrane ion channel 25
memory 74, 105
– declarative 75
– sensory 74
– working 74
menarche 109
menopause 115
mental retardation 396
Mental Status Examination 295, 323
metabolic syndrome 56
Meyer, Adolf 320
microcephaly 92
midbrain 26
middle childhood 104
mid-life crisis 116, 126
mind-body medicine 261
Mini Mental Status Exam 182
minority/majority populations 155
mirror neuron 29, 79
monoamine oxidase inhibitors 369
mood 323
mood disorder 373
– due to a general medical condition 374
mood stabilizers 335
moral development 106
– adolescence 108
– middle childhood 106
– young adults 112
morality 102
– conventional 89
– postconventional 89
– preconventional 89
motivational interviewing 72
motor development

– infancy 95
– preschool 101
– toddler 98
motor loop 28
multigenic disorders 18

N

narcolepsy 48
National Center for Complementary and Alternative Medicine 255
Native American 155
naturopathic physicians 260
neglect 213
network efficiency 32
networking 137
network intervention 209
neuroendocrine network 45
neurogenesis 76
neuronal plasticity 10
neurons 24
neurotransmitters 25
nightmare 50
night terrors 50
nigrostriatal pathway 336
NMDA receptors 68
nonmaleficence 274
non-NMDA receptors 68
non-REM sleep 46
norepinephrine 41
normal distribution 416
not elsewhere classified 392
null hypothesis 419
nursing home 126

O

obesity 193
object permanence 85, 96, 99
obsessions 324
obsessive compulsive disorder 367
obstructive sleep apnea syndrome 49
occipital lobe 29
odds ratio 413, 418
oppositional defiant disorder 402
outcome expectancy 305
ovulation 107

P

palliative care 264, 279, 349
palliative sedation 271
panic 365
panic disorder 365
parallel processing 23
paraphilia 169
parietal lobe 29
participatory decision making 290
pathological gambling 393
patient autonomy 274
Patient Protection and Affordable Care Act 250
Patient's Bill of Rights 286
Patient Self-Determination Act 286
Pearson correlation 421
pedigree studies 17
peer friendships 109
peer groups 105
perception 74, 76
personal identity 109
personality 19
pervasive developmental disorders 399
phenotype 15
phobia
– simple 366
– social 366
phonological disorder (articulation disorder) 399
physical growth
– adolescence 107
– infancy 95
– middle childhood 104
– toddler 98
physician-assisted death 271
physician-assisted suicide 183, 279, 286
Piaget, Jean 85
placebo 336
plasticity
– experience-dependent 24
– experience-expectant 24
– neuronal 22
play 99
post-exposure prophylaxis 165
post-structuralism 142
posttraumatic stress disorder 183, 366

posttraumatic stress disorder (PTSD) 216
poverty 220
predictive value
– negative 412
– positive 412
predisposition 323
preferred provider organizations 245
prefrontal cortex 54, 336
pregnancy
– unplanned 165
preoperational 100
preterm birth 94
prevalence 409
– period 409
– point 409
prevention
– primary 6
– secondary 6
principle of association 67
proband 17
problem-solving therapy 72
projection 77
protected health information 287
psychiatric evaluation 322
psychoanalysis 320, 330
psychodynamic psychotherapy 330, 372
psychoeducation 378
psychogenic megacolon 404
psychological defenses 330
psychological test batteries 325
psychopathology 317
psychosis 381
psychosocial moratorium 109
psychosomatic disorders 346
psychotherapy 320
pubertal development 107
p-value
– computed 419
– criterion 419
pyromania 393

Q

quality of life 278
quetiapine 336

R

racism 160
rape 170
– date 214
– marital 214
– statutory 170
rapid-eye-movement (REM) sleep 46
rapport 292
rational emotive therapy 331
rational pharmacology 335
rational suicide 183
reactive attachment disorder 405
reading disorder 397
reappraisal
– positive 20
receptive language 99
receptive language disorder 398
receptors 25
reference group 133
regional specialization 23
regression 77, 108
regression analysis 421
reinforcement
– negative 69
relative risk 418
relaxation 71, 346
reliability 414
– test-retest 414
repeated measures ANOVA 423
repression 77
reproductive system 113
resilience 20, 349
respite care 126, 188
response latency 336, 379
reticular system 27
Rett disorder 401
reuptake 25
risk 409
– attributable 413
– relative 413
risk factors 412
Rogers, Carl 331
rumination 324

S

scaling (statistical)
– interval 420
– nominal/categorical 420
– ordinal 420
– ratio 421
schema 331
schizoaffective disorder 386
schizophreniform disorder 386
screening test 409
secondary syndromes 363
second messenger systems 25
sedative hypnotics 335
selection
– natural 66
selective mutism 404
selective serotonin reuptake inhibitors 335
self-efficacy 305
Selye 52
sensate focus therapy 169
sensitivity 410
separation anxiety disorder 404
septal nucleus 27
seriation 86, 105
serotonin 41, 67, 200
sex 167
sex role development
– adolescence 109
– late life 119
– middle age 115
– middle childhood 106
– young adult 113
sexual
– abuse 212
sexual aversion 167
sexual behavior 173
sexual functioning 109
sexual harassment 171, 311
sexual health 162
sexual identity 113, 167, 173
sexual intercourse 110
sexually transmitted disease 110
sexually transmitted infection (STI) 165
sexual orientation 110, 113, 160, 167, 173
sexual pain disorders 169
sexual play 102
sexual response 162
sexual trauma 169
shift work 47
sickness 5
sick role 5, 149
singlehood 113

sleep architecture 46
sleep-disordered breathing 49
sleep disturbances 181
sleep hygiene 46, 339, 346
sleep patterns 46, 108
slow-wave sleep (SWS) 46
smoking cessation programs 210
social behavior 139
social class 134
social cognition 105
social conscience 102
social dissonance 150
social-emotional development
– adolescence 109
– infancy 96
– late life 119
– middle age 116
– middle childhood 105
– preschool 102
– toddler 100
– young adult 113
social learning theory 89
social processes 77
social referencing 100
social relations 139
social structure 134, 139
social support 60
social systems 134, 140
society 134
socioeconomic status 134
somatization 343, 344
somatoform disorders 346
Spearman's rank correlation 423
specificity 412
speech sound disorder 399
sructural/functionalism 141
SSRIs 335, 369
stages of change model 303
stagnation 116
standard deviation 417
standard error 417
standard score distribution 418
State Children's Health Insurance Program (SCHIP) 248
statistics
– descriptive 417
– inferential 417
stereotype 135
stereotypic movement disorder 403
stigma 135, 174
stimulants 335

stimulus generalization 69
stress 7, 10, 160, 216, 223, 346
stress response 11, 52
student's *t*-test 422
stuttering 399
substance related disorders 206
substance use 184
substituted judgment 269
successful aging 187
suicide 110, 118, 183, 227, 310
suicide risk assessment 230
superego 87
surrogacy 128
symbolic interactionism 143
sympatho-adrenomedullary (SAM)
   axis 54
sympathy 78
synapses 23
synaptic pruning 24
synaptic transmission 67
system dynamics 140

T

temperament 18, 97
temporal lobe 29, 217
testosterone 107
thalamus 26
therapeutic alliance 333
therapeutic index 339
thinking 74
third party payment system 245
thought disorder 382
tobacco 110
token economy 71
Tourette disorder 402
traditional Chinese medicine 257
traditional naturopaths 260
training 34
trait 15
transcription 15
transference 287, 330
transgender 167, 178
transient tic disorder 403
transitivity 86
transivity 105
transsexual 167
transsexualism 178
trauma syndrome 216
tricare 248

trichotillomania 394
type A personality response style
   20

U

ultradian rhythm 44
utilitarianism/rational choice theory
   143

V

vaginismus 169
validity 414
 – construct 414
 – content 414
 – convergent 414
 – criterion-related 414
 – divergent 414
 – face 414
 – predictive 415
variability 416
vegetative state 277
Veterans Affairs 249
violence 110
 – domestic 212
 – family 212
 – intimate partner 212
 – stranger-to-stranger 216
virtual reality 72
vulnerabilities 60

W

Wernike's area 28
Wilcoxon matched-pairs signed-
   ranks test 423
World Health Organization 5

Y

Yerkes-Dodson Law 53

Z

zeitgeber 44